THE
HISTORY
ENCYCLOPEDIA

THE
HISTORY
ENCYCLOPEDIA

Follow the development of human civilization from prehistory to
the modern world, with over 1500 photographs and artworks

Simon Adams • Philip Brooks • John Farndon • Will Fowler • Brian Ward

LORENZ BOOKS

CONTENTS

PREHISTORIC PEOPLES.....14

ANCIENT CIVILIZATIONS.....72

WORLD RELIGIONS.....130

EXPLORATION AND DISCOVERY.....188

SCIENCE AND TECHNOLOGY.....246

THE STORY OF MEDICINE.....304

ANCIENT WEAPONS.....362

MODERN WEAPONS AND WARFARE.....420

Reaching for the Future

Human beings have rarely been prepared to accept life as it is. Throughout history, we have sought to investigate our world and to understand it. The world today is the point we have reached in a process of civilization that began in prehistoric times. The study of history allows us to discover how we got here. It is a look deep into ourselves and what made us. By looking at how human beings have developed since earliest times, what drove us and the achievements we made, we can begin to understand the complex process that created the modern world.

Prehistoric Peoples

The story of history begins with the emergence of the first people, our ancient ancestors. They had to learn skills to enable them to survive. By trial and error, they learned which plants and fruits were good to eat, and how to make weapons so that they could hunt animals.

Gradually, groups of families joined together. There was safety in numbers, and large groups were less likely to suffer attacks from wild animals or other tribes. People also began to learn that there were advantages to cooperation. They could share the new skills that they mastered, for example how to use fire. Working together made it possible to hunt for larger game, such as elephants. Later, people began to specialize in making weapons and other tools, or in looking after the children of the clan or tribe. In return for these jobs, they would receive a share of the food gathered or hunted by other members of the group.

Cooperation and experience led slowly to a more comfortable life. Humans were free to embark on their first artistic efforts and spiritual searches. Roaming tribes of hunter-gatherers later learned that they could plant seeds to ensure reliable crops of vegetable foods. They could also raise herd animals for a readily available source of meat. This led to the first permanent villages, which grew up on the banks of rivers, where there was a constant supply of fresh water and also fish to catch. Light, easy-to-work soil was also important, because the tools for the first farmers were very basic.

As the early villages expanded and became towns, society developed further. The towns grew into cities and some people specialized in trades. Potters, tool and weapon makers, brick makers, spinners, weavers and priests could now rely on their trades to earn sufficient food and housing. They did not need to hunt or farm. These were the beginnings of civilization, which began in different parts of the world at different times.

RELIGION
Most ancient religions involved the worship of many different gods, but often one particular god was in charge of all the others. For the Romans, Jupiter was the chief of the gods.

HUNTERS' TROPHY
Hunting took a lot of effort, so people made sure they used every last bit of the animal. The flesh provided meat and the bones were carved to make simple tools. This woman is cleaning an animal skin. It might be used to make clothes or a rug.

Ancient Civilizations

The development of villages into towns and then into cities, the process of civilization, gathered momentum. Town leaders started to take nearby regions under their own control. Civilization started at different times in various parts of the world. However, in areas that could not support intensive farming, such as the Great Plains of North America and the dry regions of the Middle East, Far East and Africa, cities never gained a real foothold.

Geography and climate dictated the nature of the civilizations that emerged. In North Africa and the Middle East, for instance, great rivers such as the Nile in Egypt and the Tigris and Euphrates in Mesopotamia allowed the development of large and increasingly complex civilizations. In other regions, agriculture and transport were limited by mountains, deserts and other barriers. There, different types of civilizations emerged, such as the Greek city-states, or the unique empires of Central and South America.

THE COMING OF WEALTH
With civilization came trade and wealth. This palace was built by an Etruscan nobleman in the last millennium B.C. The Etruscans were western Europe's first wealthy civilization. They had trading links with the Phoenicians and Greeks.

The main definition of a civilization is the building of cities, but there are other characteristics too. Most ancient cultures developed their own system of writing, for example cuneiform in Mesopotamia, hieroglyphics in ancient Egypt and the first Chinese characters. The first writings recorded grain stores after a harvest and kept track of trade transactions. The first traders swapped goods, but then systems of money evolved, from the use of cowrie shells as currency to the minting of metal coins.

Trade brought wealth, and this enabled civilizations to expand. Cities conquered neighboring cities and gradually built up into huge empires. Grand buildings were erected, including palaces for leaders, and mighty temples in which to worship the gods.

FEATS OF ENGINEERING
The Romans of Italy were champion builders in the ancient world. Many of the aqueducts, bridges, roads and buildings they constructed all over their vast empire can still be seen to this day.

World Religions

Since earliest times, humans had tried to investigate all aspects of the human condition and to make sense of the world. Religion emerged as early people thought about the nature of the world and their position within it. Aspects that could not readily be understood were said to be the actions of superior beings, such as spirits or gods. This led to the development of belief systems and religions. The rituals associated with

these became more complex as civilizations developed. Temples were built where people could honor their gods and communicate with them by means of prayer.

Early religions were based on the idea that there were many spirits or gods, who had varying degrees of interest in humankind. Many of the gods worshiped by different cultures had similar characteristics. However, between 2000 B.C. and 1 B.C., religions emerged around the Middle East that were based on belief in a single god. These are known as monotheistic belief systems, as *mono* means "single" and *theistic* means "related to God." The

MANY GODS
The goddess Lakshmi is one of many gods worshiped by Hindus. In Asia, belief in religions based on multiple gods is very popular.

first was Judaism. Christianity (based on the teachings of Jesus of Nazareth) and Islam (based on the teachings of Muhammad) are the world's other main monotheistic religions. In China, Buddhism, which is more a spiritual way of life than a true religion, developed as people started to follow the teachings of the Buddha (the enlightened one).

Belief in a single god has been the most successful type of religion in the Arab and Western worlds. However, Hinduism and other religions based on multiple gods are still very strong, especially in Asia.

HOLY TEACHER
Many of today's major religions developed from the teachings of a single founder. Guru Nanak founded the Sikh religion in the 1400s. He was born a Hindu but did not agree with the ritual and religious wars of the time.

Exploration and Discovery

Religion and other aspects of human culture spread as people set out to explore their world. The great civilizations of the ancient world, such as the Egyptians, Phoenicians, Greeks and Romans, were all skilled boat-builders. They set sail around the Mediterranean to create new trade links and to conquer new territories.

STEAMSHIPS
For centuries ships had to rely on strong oarsmen or on the wind in their sails. In calm weather, a ship could be becalmed for days. Then, in the 1800s, the first steamships were built and sea transportation became much more reliable.

Later, races such as the Vikings probed through and around Europe as well as west toward North America, while the Chinese explored eastern Asia and the Polynesians roamed through much of the Pacific.

From the 1400s, exploration became a major force in expanding countries. The Europeans set sail in search of sea routes to the Far East, where they could trade for silks and spices. The major maritime explorers were the Portuguese, Spanish, English, French and Dutch. Within 100 years explorers had created maps of most of the world. For this reason, the period from the 1400s to the 1700s is known as the Age of Exploration.

After this time there were still gaps to be filled, and explorers probed into the land areas of North and South America, Africa, Asia and Australia. The trader, the soldier and the priest followed the explorer, and by about 1850, most of the world had been mapped. This was not the end of the exploration story, though. Trade links were established, but there was much left to discover, for the advancement of science. Exploration of inaccessible areas has continued right up to the present, particularly in the snowy polar regions, the deepest parts of the ocean, the most remote rainforests and, of course, into space.

MAORI CANOES
The Maoris of New Zealand were skilled seamen. They traveled in fleets of intricately carved canoes that were able to carry up to 100 warriors.

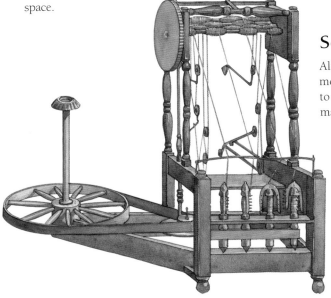

THE INDUSTRIAL AGE
The invention of the steam engine revolutionized machine technology. The first factories were built and the industrial age began. This machine for spinning cotton was adapted to run on steam power in 1771.

Science and Technology

Although science and technology seem very modern ideas, human beings have been striving to understand how things work and inventing machines to help them make their lives easier ever since they first walked the Earth.

However, most of the foundations of modern science were laid by Greek thinkers, such as Archimedes, and by the engineers of the Roman Empire.

During the Middle Ages, alchemy emerged, which was the "science" of trying to turn base metals into gold. This practice paved the way for the development of modern chemistry during the 1600s.

The 1700s are often known as the Age of Enlightenment. Men and women thinkers refused just to accept what had been handed down as fact. They demanded rigorous proof before they would accept any information as truth.

This approach was the real forerunner of scientific method. It allowed the creation of the instruments and thought processes that enabled scientists to look ever deeper into our world. This also led to a desire to look beyond the Earth and examine the workings of the universe in order to see how humans fit into the bigger picture.

The Story of Medicine

One of the most exciting aspects of science is the research into treating human illnesses and ailments. At its very earliest stages, medicine was a matter of herbal remedies found by trial and experiment. Medicine was not regarded as something to do with the body alone. It also involved a spiritual, magical or religious element. From this point of view, illness is a sign that the body is out of balance or that a person has fallen foul of the spirits or gods. Treatment involves philosophical or religious aspects as well as physical ones.

From around 500 B.C., Greek thinkers and doctors came to the idea that illness resulted from natural causes, and that cures depended on healthy living and the use of drugs. The Chinese and Indians had already developed their own systems of medicine. Further advances came around A.D. 1000–1500, largely from physicians living in the Islamic world. These men relearned the discoveries of the Greeks and then built on it to analyze disease and create medicines. The growing Islamic interest in alchemy led to the creation of purer chemicals and better drugs, but it wasn't until the 1500s that medicine began to develop in the West.

During the Renaissance, the study of anatomy helped medical pioneers to understand how the body functions. Then, from around 1850, medical developments really started to accelerate. One reason for this was an acceptance of scientific method after the Industrial Revolution. More and more scientific breakthroughs were made. Doctors and researchers gained increased understanding of the human body and were able to make more sense of the biological and chemical principles that make it work.

THE HUMORS
Many Greek and Roman doctors believed that disease was caused by an imbalance between the four "humors" (elements or qualities) in the body. Using heat was one way to draw the excess humors out.

LADY WITH THE LAMP
Florence Nightingale pioneered hygienic nursing techniques during her time as a nurse in the Crimean War. Grateful soldiers nicknamed her the Lady with the Lamp for her care and kindness to them.

SPECIALIZED WEAPONRY
The knife or dagger was one of the earliest and simplest weapons of all. However, even dagger design became highly specialized. The notched blade of this 17th-century dagger was designed to disarm an opponent during a sword fight.

Ancient Weapons

A less welcome part of human history has been the growth of warfare. As early people banded together to form tribes and clans and build villages, they also acquired valuable possessions such as food stocks and animals. For the first time, weapons were needed, not just for hunting, but for self-defense and attack against other humans. Later, rulers of the first civilizations often wanted to take over a neighboring state. This might give them control of a vital river, rich farmland, or raw materials. Many societies gave warriors a place of special honor.

Warfare spurred the development of technical skills such as metalworking. Soldiers saw the advantage of bronze weapons over copper ones, and then the advantage of iron over bronze. As civilizations grew larger, so did their armies and this called for increased numbers of better weapons.

The development of weapons did not end when the ancient civilizations fell. The centuries after the end of the Roman Empire are sometimes known as the Dark Ages. Many parts of the world lost some features of civilization, but warfare continued, for example in the raids of the Vikings. Then, in the Middle Ages, people began to relearn ancient skills, such as building in stone. New types of weaponry appeared, including steel-bladed swords, cannons and gunpowder. At the same time, new methods of warfare emerged, such as the use of soldiers on horseback.

FIGHTING AXES
A Native American swings his tomahawk, ready to throw it at an enemy. Hand axes, such as the tomahawk, were used as weapons from the earliest times. They could be used to hack enemies in hand-to-hand combat and could also be thrown.

Modern Weapons and Warfare

The modern age of weaponry really began in the period after the Industrial Revolution. Radical new materials and manufacturing capabilities allowed the creation of weapons that could be mass-produced. The rapid developments in physics and chemistry that accompanied industrial advancement also allowed designers to understand more clearly how weapons worked. They could improve the speed and power of ammunition, for example, by making explosive-filled shells rather than iron cannon balls. New explosives were also developed to replace gunpowder. These and other advances helped make weapons longer-ranged, more accurate and more devastating in their effect.

BOMBS FROM THE SKY
These B-17 bombers were flown during World War II. The ability to drop missiles accurately from the air changed the nature of warfare forever. It increased the number of civilian casualties.

By 1901, the machine gun had been invented, the submarine was on the verge of becoming a practical weapon, and powered, heavier-than-air craft were about to take to the air. These processes accelerated in World War I, which saw the introduction of the tank and of chemical weapons.

During World War II, existing weapons were refined and tanks and aircraft carriers came to the forefront. New technologies included radar and jet propulsion. Most decisively of all, the first atomic weapons were used. Military technology has continued to develop with great speed ever since and, as in every other area of human activity and civilization, including science and medicine, warfare has been transformed by the computer revolution.

SMG
Submachine guns, or SMGs, were first used during World War I. Both world wars forced rapid advances in weapon technology.

PREHISTORIC PEOPLES

BY PHILIP BROOKS

From the moment when apelike hominids first walked on two legs, the story of humans began. This section looks at how prehistoric people survived, how they mastered hunting, fire and metalworking, and how they made the first art.

First Steps

▲ HOMINIDS
The first human-apes appeared about four million years ago in Africa. They came down from the trees where they lived and began to walk on the ground on two legs. Scientists call them australopithecines.

▼ KEY DATES
How humans and human society developed in different parts of the world.

IN THIS SECTION WE WILL LOOK BACK to the very beginnings of the human story. It starts at a time when people lived in caves and sheltered under cliffs, when the only tools were made of stone, when everyone had to hunt or forage for their own food, when clothes had to be made from animal skins. There were no cities, no large buildings, none of the comforts of modern life, and no one had worked out how to write. The term "prehistory" means the time before people were able to write their history down. Writing developed at different times in different parts of the world, so the date when the prehistoric period ended varies from one place to another. In Mesopotamia in Southwest Asia, for example, writing came around 3000B.C. In western Europe, by contrast, widespread use of written scripts coincided with the Roman conquerors around 3,000 years later.

Prehistoric life can sound grim. Life was hard, travel must have been difficult, and many people died young without the benefits of effective medicine. Yet the period sees the beginnings of the very things that make humanity what it is today. Technology was simple, but it made possible amazing monuments such as Stonehenge. Artists had only basic materials, yet they produced masterpieces on cave walls. People cared for

▼ CAVE ART
It seems that humans have always felt the urge for artistic self-expression. During the Ice Age, people lived in caves. Wall paintings from that time show people's skill in making their homes colorful and attractive.

	2–1 MILLION YEARS AGO	1 M.Y.A.–400,000 B.C.	400,000–30,000 B.C.	30,000–12,000 B.C.
AFRICA	Early hominids, the first human-apes, are alive in eastern Africa.	*Homo erectus,* a type of early human, use stone hand axes as a multi-purpose tool.	*Homo sapiens,* humans, appear in various places south of the Sahara.	
MIDDLE EAST & ASIA	*Homo erectus* is established in both Java and China, and has probably mastered the use of fire.		Neanderthals and "modern" humans are living side by side in Mesopotamia.	Rock painting
EUROPE		First known settlement of *Homo erectus* in Europe.	Neanderthals and "modern" humans are present, and may breed, but Neanderthals die out.	Europe freezes in the Ice Age. Artists make great cave paintings in France and Spain.
AMERICAS				The first settlement of North America begins as men and women cross the Bering land bridge from Siberia.

Skull of *Homo habilis*

Saber-toothed cat

M.Y.A.: Million years ago

▲ MAMMOTH
SHELTER
*Homes were built from
whatever materials
were available. Remains
of mammoth bones
suggest they were used
to build massive shelters
almost 10 feet high.*

▶ FISH CARVING
*After the Ice Age, food
supplies were
much better.
Fish carvings
found in
Europe
suggest that
fish had
become part of
the staple diet.*

their sick, using medicines
made from plants, and
some illnesses were
cured this way.
    Prehistoric Peoples
looks at prehistoric life all
over the world. It begins with
the origins of the human race in Africa and how people spread out
around the world. It tells how people developed simple tools,
survival skills such as hunting and food gathering, and the ability to
make clothes and simple shelters. Gradually, human activities such
as art, religion, and ceremonies developed, signs that social groups
were becoming more complex.

Next, *Prehistoric Peoples* shows the enormous progress made by
early peoples, starting with the invention of pottery and the
beginnings of farming, which helped men and women control their
food supply. Trade then enabled more people to travel and new
ideas to spread around the world. The next "revolution" was
when people learned how to use metals, by working copper,
making bronze, and smelting iron. Finally came the
invention of writing, the development of large cities and
societies, and the end of the prehistoric period. Throughout
this period, people overcame tremendous obstacles, such as
the huge climate changes of an Ice Age.

▼ WATCHTOWER
*Eventually people
began building
permanent settlements.
The walled city of
Jericho dates from
about 7000 B.C. and is
one of the earliest cities
discovered so far. It had
watchtowers like this
one, which were more
than 30 feet high.*

12,000–9000 B.C.	9000–6000 B.C.	6000–4000 B.C.	4000–2000 B.C.	2000 B.C.–A.D. 1
Japanese pot	*Auroch, an early bull*	The climate of what is now the Sahara Desert is very wet. Cattle herding is common in many parts of the region.	*Cuneiform writing from Mesopotamia*	
The dog is domesticated in the Middle East. The first pottery is produced in Japan.	Farming is established in the Fertile Crescent.	Trading towns such as Çatal Hüyük, Turkey, begin to develop.	Potter's wheel invented; bronze-working begins; writing develops. Cities built in Mesopotamia.	
The great ice sheets begin to thaw as temperatures increase. Sea levels rise.	*Clovis points*	Farming spreads to eastern Europe, probably from Turkey.	Stone circles and other megalithic monuments become common in western Europe.	First ironworking transforms tools and weapons.
People in Chile build houses from wood and skins—the first evidence of shelters in the Americas.	The Clovis culture: on the Great Plains people hunt using stone-pointed spears.	*Cotton plant*	The farmers of Mexico domesticate the maize plant. Other crops spread through North America.	The Olmec people of Mexico build the region's first large cities.

Finding the Evidence

▲ BURIAL URN
Some prehistoric peoples cremated their dead by burning the bodies on a funeral pyre. The ashes, and sometimes the bones, of the dead person might then be buried in a pottery urn like this one.

INDING EVIDENCE ABOUT prehistory is like doing a gigantic jigsaw puzzle with most of the pieces missing. Often very little is now left of the prehistoric peoples who lived thousands of years ago. Archaeologists study every scrap of evidence they can find for clues as to how ancient peoples lived. Sometimes all that remain are a few bits of broken pottery, the foundations of some houses, or the occasional tool or weapon. Archaeologists have to learn what they can from fragments such as these.

Even when there is a big site—a stone circle, for example, or the remains of an ancient town—there are often more questions than answers. What were stone circles used for? Who ruled the first towns? How did people find out how to make bronze? Why did the cave artists paint their pictures? Questions like these still baffle archaeologists. The experts can suggest answers, but there are no certainties.

Graves can often give archaeologists some of the most fascinating clues about prehistory. They can be almost like time capsules. In many periods, it was the custom to bury a person with some of their possessions. Archaeologists call these items grave goods. These objects can tell us a great deal about the dead person's lifestyle, job, and wealth. They can also reveal something about the beliefs of the time. This is because grave goods were usually intended for use in the next world. Such finds suggest that people in prehistoric times believed in life after death. Some of the best evidence, though, comes from the bodies

◄ CHAMBERED TOMB
This type of tomb, common in prehistoric Europe, often contains several burials. These reveal a lot about ancient society. For example, the grave of a ruler or chief was usually treated differently than the others. It might be more carefully constructed or contain richer goods.

DEATH AND BURIAL
Archaeologists rarely know what they will find when they excavate a grave. There may be only a skeleton, or there may be lavish grave goods also. Whatever they find, it will probably be very fragile if it has been in the ground for thousands of years.

▶ GRAVE GOODS
Items in graves often reveal evidence about the spread of technology. For example, these grave goods from a cemetery at Varna in Bulgaria show that their owners had discovered how to work metal.

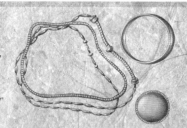

◄ TOLLUND MAN
Bodies buried in swamps and bogs are protected from the air. Skin, hair, and even clothing can be preserved for hundreds of years. Tollund Man was found buried in a bog in Denmark, and dates from about 251 B.C.

▲ PASSAGE-GRAVE BURIAL MOUND
Many passage graves, from around 3,000 B.C., have been found in northern Europe. A passage leads to the tomb at the mound's center.

themselves. By looking at a skeleton, for example, a trained observer can tell roughly how old the person was at their time of death and whether that person was male or female. It is also possible to measure how tall the dead person was and to determine quite a lot about build, physical development and strength. Often, archaeologists can find out about a person's diet by studying the teeth and doing chemical analyses of the bones. Sometimes they can even say why a person died, as some illnesses, such as arthritis, can be detected from the bones.

Studying the features and contents of an ancient grave can provide enough evidence to work out the approximate date when the person was buried. Factors such as the condition of the bones, the way the person was buried, and the type of grave goods that are found with the skeleton, can help to date the burial. How deep the body lies in the ground is also a clue. The deeper it is buried, the older it is likely to be. Archaeologists working in a vertical trench, for example, can often see layers of objects in historical order, from the oldest to the most recent, almost like a timeline.

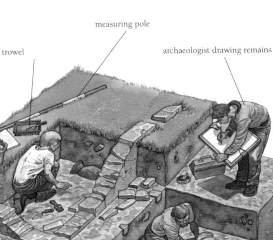

measuring pole

trowel

archaeologist drawing remains

ancient skeleton

grave goods

foundations of settlement

▶ ARCHAEOLOGICAL DIG
Archaeologists excavate an ancient site. They are working at several different levels. The skeleton is on an earlier level than the remains of the settlement above it. The archaeologists dig with care, using light tools, such as trowels and brushes, to avoid causing damage. Most importantly of all, they record in detail everything that they find.

▼ EXCAVATING GRAVES
Archaeologists have to be very careful when excavating dead bodies. This is not just because they are delicate. These are remains of real people, and they should be treated with respect. At this grave at Les Eyzies in France, archaeologists have worked slowly to remove the bones, which are at least 10,000 years old.

Dates and Dating

Prehistoric people lived thousands or even millions of years ago. However, because these people left no written records, archaeologists have to rely on other evidence to work out the dates of the remains they find. They have many ways of doing this, from studying the site of the find to using chemical analysis. Even so, nearly all the dates can only be approximate. The older the remains are, the less precise the dates are likely to be.

The abbreviations used with dates in this book are:

- M.Y.A. indicates "Million Years Ago." It is used for very ancient dates, a million or more years ago.

- B.C. indicates the number of years "Before Christ." Jesus lived 2,000 years ago, so you can work out a "number of years old" by adding 2,000 to a B.C. date.

The Toolmakers

▲ PEBBLE TOOL
Early hominids chipped away the sides of pebbles to make simple, sharp-edged tools.

ROBABLY THE BIGGEST prehistoric mystery of all is how the human race began. Many scientists think that modern humans evolved, millions of years ago, from creatures that looked somewhat like apes. They hoped to find a missing link, part-ape and part-human, between modern humans and our animal ancestors. No one has found this missing link. But paleontologists (people who study fossils, the preserved remains of animals and plants) have discovered the remains of a group of creatures called early hominids. These are animals that share many features with humans. Hominids looked somewhat ape-like and had smaller brains than modern humans, but they walked on two legs and could make simple stone tools. Our ancestors were probably like ancient hominids.

No one has ever found a complete

skeleton of an early hominid. Often all that remains is a fragment of bone or a single tooth. Scientists have tried to find out all about the hominids from such meager evidence. However, they often disagree about which species of hominid a particular find belongs to, and how the various species relate to each other.

The earliest hominids, who lived in Africa between four million and 800,000 years ago, are called the australopithecines (southern apes). They stood and walked upright, but were shorter than modern humans, standing between 3 and 5 feet tall. Their bodies had a similar shape to humans', but their flat-nosed faces looked ape-like. Their brains were much smaller than human brains, but larger than those of today's chimpanzees and gorillas.

Australopithecines probably spent most of their time on the ground. Like modern gorillas

◀ AUSTRALOPITHECUS ROBUSTUS
Stocky and ape-like, this hominid probably spent much of its time living in trees, but it came down to the ground from time to time to search for food. Like the modern chimpanzee, it probably ate plants most of the time.

HOMO HABILIS

Since Louis Leakey discovered the first specimen of *Homo habilis* in 1964, many similar remains have been found in Africa—especially in the fossil-rich beds of Kenya and Tanzania. Although it is not certain whether these creatures are direct human ancestors, they are definitely our close relatives.

▼ PREDATOR
Early hominids had to guard against fearsome meat-eaters like this saber-toothed cat. Sometimes the best escape from dangerous animals such as this was to take to the trees.

▲ A LARGER SKULL— A LARGER BRAIN
Homo habilis had a much larger brain than the australopithecines, the southern apes. This was one reason why its discoverers decided that it should be included in the genus *Homo*, just like modern humans.

▼ A FIRM GRIP
Homo habilis had a hand that could grip objects firmly. This, together with its brain size, meant that the creature could make simple stone tools and may have been able to build basic shelters from tree branches and leaves.

pebble tool

simple brushwood shelter

and chimpanzees, they climbed trees to hide from enemies or to shelter from the rain. Remains of their teeth suggest that they ate mainly plants, plus a little meat. They probably also used the first simple tools.

In 1964, paleontologist Louis Leakey announced the discovery of the fossilized remains of a previously unknown hominid. It had a larger brain than the southern apes, so Leakey decided to place it in the genus *Homo*, the same as our own species. The fossil was 1.7 million years old, which makes it our oldest close relative. Stone tools were found near the remains, so Leakey named the fossil *Homo habilis* (handy man).

Like people today, the *Homo habilis* people probably ate quite a lot of meat, but no one knows whether they hunted animals for food or ate the remains left by other animals. Archaeologists have found remains of stone tools next to animal bones, such as simple choppers and hammers made from pebbles. They were probably semi-nomadic, staying in an area for a little while before moving on to a new area for food. When they moved, they left their tools behind.

Hominid uses its upright stance to gather berries.

▶ "LUCY"
The most complete set of bones found belonged to a hominid that lived just over three million years ago. Archaeologists nicknamed it "Lucy." The bones show that it was a slim, possibly female, creature just over 3 feet tall. It weighed about 60 pounds and could walk upright. The slim build and upright stance suggest a more human-like creature than the other australopithecines.

▲ *ROBUSTUS* SKULL
The robust australopithecines had heavy skulls with massive jaws and strong ridges of bone across the brows. There were also flanges (areas of bone sticking out from the cheeks) on either side.

▲ *AFRICANUS* SKULL
Although Australopithecus africanus *had a more lightly built skull than* Australopithecus robustus, *it still had a heavy jawbone. No one is certain exactly how these two species were related.*

▲ OLDUVAI GORGE
One of the most important hominid sites is Olduvai Gorge, on the Serengeti Plains in East Africa. Fossils of several hominids, including *Homo habilis*, have been found there, which makes this one of the great hunting grounds in the search for human origins. The gorge contains fossilized remains ranging from 100,000 to around 2 million years old, the older fossils embedded in the deepest rocks. Scatters of tools, from crude pebbles to stone axes, lie near the bones of their makers.

Key Dates

- 3.6M.Y.A. Southern apes are present in Laetoli, northern Tanzania.

- 3 to 3.75M.Y.A. Southern apes present in Hadar, northern Ethiopia. The most famous example is known to modern archaeologists as "Lucy," a member of the species *Australopithecus afarensis*.

- 1.8M.Y.A. Lake Turkana, Kenya, is home to various hominids, including australopithecines and creatures with larger skulls.

- 1.75M.Y.A. *Robustus* australopithecines live at Olduvai Gorge, northern Tanzania.

- 1.75M.Y.A. The toolmaker *Homo habilis*, the oldest known member of our genus, lives at Olduvai Gorge.

The Coming of Fire

AROUND 1.6 MILLION YEARS AGO, A GROUP OF hominids mastered a completely new skill. They learned how to use fire, which must have brought about a huge change in their lives. Suddenly, they were able to cook food instead of eating raw meat and plants. They could keep their drafty caves and rock shelters warm in winter. The heat and flames could even be used as weapons against enemies. Fire probably gave them a safer and more comfortable life than the earlier hominids had enjoyed.

The hominids who mastered fire were about 5 feet tall. They had bigger brains and longer limbs than previous hominids, more like those of modern humans. Scientists called them *Homo erectus* (upright man). The *Homo*

◀ FIRE STICK
One way early people made fire was to put dry grass on a stick called a hearth. Then they rubbed another stick against the hearth to make a spark and set the grass alight.

FOOD AND RESOURCES

With their larger brains, *Homo erectus* people were probably better at hunting and finding new types of food than previous hominids. Their travels across Africa may have been to search for new sources of food. Besides hunting animals and gathering plants, they probably killed injured animals or scavenged meat left by other predators.

▲ HACKBERRIES
Gathering nuts and fruit, such as these hackberries, provided a large part of the diet of *Homo erectus*. They had to learn by trial and error which berries were good to eat and which were poisonous.

◀ WOOLLY RHINO
The *Homo erectus* people tried eating whatever meat they killed. They may have eaten large creatures like this woolly rhinoceros, hunting them in groups and sharing the meat.

▲ EAST TURKANA
Close to the mountains and lakes of Kenya, the site of East Turkana was one of the first homes of *Homo erectus* around 1.5 million years ago.

erectus people were more advanced in other ways. They made better tools than the earlier hominids and developed a hand ax, a pointed flint tool with two sharp cutting edges. Hand axes were useful for cutting meat, so the *Homo erectus* people could butcher animals more efficiently. As a result, they may have had more incentive to develop their technology—for example, creating smaller tools such as cutting blades.

Homo erectus people probably had more advanced social skills than earlier hominids. They may even have developed a simple language, which would have enabled them to talk to and cooperate with each other. This meant that they could perform tasks as a group, such as hunting large animals. They may have used fire in their hunting. Some archaeologists think that they lit bush fires to drive large animals into an ambush, where the creatures could be killed by a hunting group.

Fire also enabled them to survive in colder climates. This encouraged *Homo erectus* people

to travel more widely than earlier hominids. Like *Homo habilis*, they were probably always on the move, making temporary camps as bases for hunting and gathering. Some of these homes may have been seasonal, occupied during the spring or summer when fruit, nuts, and leaves were plentiful. But *Homo erectus* people also traveled beyond their native Africa, and they were probably the first hominids to settle in Asia and Europe.

◀ **HOMO ERECTUS**
Cave-dwelling Homo erectus *people prepare to cook a meal in front of their cave. One member of the group makes stone tools, perhaps to cut up the dead animal; another tends the fire; and two children help an adult dismember the carcass before it is cooked on the hot fire.*

▲ **ERECTUS** SKULL
The skull of Homo erectus *was wider and larger than that of* Homo habilis, *giving room for a larger brain. Because the jawbone of* Homo erectus *jutted forward, this species still had a face that looked more like an ape's than a modern human's.*

◀ **EARLY HOMINID SITES, EAST AFRICA**
Most of the early remains of *Homo habilis* and *Homo erectus* have come from a cluster of sites in Kenya and Tanzania in East Africa. The structure of the rocks there has helped preserve these fossils. For example, at Olduvai Gorge, hominid bones and tools were left by the shores of a lake, later to be covered by mud and volcanic lava and preserved. Still later, geological faults caused the rocks to move, making the fossils visible.

Key Dates

- 1.6 M.Y.A. The Pleistocene period begins. Animals such as horses, cattle, and elephants appear.

- 1.6 M.Y.A. The earliest *Homo erectus* ever found comes from East Turkana, Kenya.

- 1.6 M.Y.A. *Homo erectus* camp at Chesowanya in the Kenya Rift Valley. This shows possible evidence of the use of fire.

- 1 M.Y.A. *Homo erectus* living in Olduvai Gorge.

- 500,000 years ago *Homo erectus* reaches northern Africa. Sites with evidence of *Homo erectus* have been found in Morocco and Algeria.

The Spread of Hominids

A ROUND A MILLION years ago, the world's wildlife was on the move. Many tropical animals started to travel northward and eastward. Gradually, they moved away from the sweltering jungles toward cooler parts of the globe. Food was often difficult to find for the early hominids, so the *Homo erectus* people followed the tropical animals to places with more moderate climates. In doing so, they traveled great distances, from modern Africa as far as present-day Java, China, Italy, and Greece.

▲ A PLACE TO SHELTER
At Terra Amata, southern France, there is evidence that hominids made a camp with simple shelters. These small huts were made out of tree branches, weighted down with stones.

In Europe and Asia, *Homo erectus* people set up camps to which they returned year after year. One of the most famous of all is a series of caves at Zhoukoudien, China. Hominids stayed here for thousands of years (from about 600,000 to about 230,000 years ago), and archaeologists have found the remains of more than 40 *Homo erectus* people at the site. In the caves the archaeologists found a variety of tools, including choppers, scrapers, awls, points, and cutters, most of which were made from quartz. The more recent in date the tools, the smaller and more finely worked they are. There is also evidence of fire in the Zhoukoudien caves. Similar remains have been found in *Homo erectus* sites in Europe and Southeast Asia. They reveal a people who gathered leaves and berries but were also cunning enough to hunt large mammals. The people moved around from one season to the next. If they could not find caves, they built simple shelters from branches and stones. They probably wrapped animal skins around themselves to keep warm in the winter.

One mystery is that many surviving *Homo erectus* skulls have had their bases removed. Some scientists think that this was done so that survivors could take out the brain. Perhaps these people were the first cannibals? There may be other reasons, such as to make containers to carry water.

Another puzzle is how *Homo erectus* died out. There are no *erectus* remains later than about 200,000 years ago. It is not known whether they perished because other hominids killed them, because their food supplies ran out, or because of ill health.

ANCIENT CULTURE

The *Homo erectus* people were able to produce a wider variety of tools, weapons, and other items than the earlier hominids, although the only objects to survive in large numbers are their stone tools. They were skilled flintworkers, creating implements with razor-sharp edges for butchering meat, cutting plant food, and scraping hides. They were probably also woodworkers, using wood to build simple shelters and make weapons such as spears and clubs.

▶ PAINT
Stones marked with red ocher, a natural earth pigment, have been found at Becov in Bohemia, Europe. These finds date to 250,000 years ago and suggest that people may have decorated their bodies or items that they made. They may have mixed the ocher with fat to make a form of paint.

◀ HAND AX
The double-edged stone tool was *Homo erectus*' most common and useful implement. It fitted comfortably into the hand and was easy to carry around. The two sharp edges could be used for cutting or chopping.

◀ UPRIGHT MAN
Homo erectus people looked much like modern humans, except for their ape-like faces. But they were not as tall as most people today.

▼ ON THE HUNT
A group of Homo erectus *people have worked together to trap three elephants in a swamp. They are now about to move in on one of the animals, to attack it with wooden spears and clubs.*

swampy ground

wooden spear

wooden club

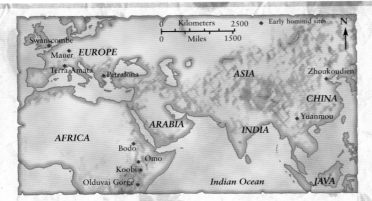

▲ *HOMO ERECTUS* SITES
This successful hominid spread from Africa to both Asia and Europe. In addition to sites in China, there are also many places in Europe with early hominid remains. In the case of most of the European sites, experts are uncertain whether the occupants were *Homo erectus* or an early form of our own species.

Map labels:
Swanscombe
Mauer EUROPE
Terra Amata Petralona
AFRICA
Bodo
Omo
Koobi
Olduvai Gorge
ARABIA
ASIA
CHINA
Zhoukoudien
Yuanmou
INDIA
Indian Ocean
JAVA

0 Kilometers 2500
0 Miles 1500
♦ Early hominid sites N

Key Dates

- 1 M.Y.A. *Homo erectus* people are established in Olduvai Gorge.

- 1 M.Y.A. *Homo erectus* invents the hand ax.

- 900,000 B.C. *Homo erectus* is present in central Java. The hominids' long-distance movements show them adapting to different environments.

- 700,000 B.C. *Homo erectus* reaches Ubeidiya, by the Jordan and Yarmuk rivers, Israel.

- 500,000 B.C. *Homo erectus* settles in Europe.

- 400,000–230,000 B.C. *Homo erectus* living at Zhoukoudien Cave, near Beijing, China.

Neanderthals

▲ CAVE WOMAN
Neanderthals like this female may have been the first hominids to care for the sick and disabled. This prolonged the lives of individuals who would otherwise have met painful early deaths.

A TYPICAL CAVE MAN IS usually portrayed as a stocky creature with heavy bones, a thick ridge across the brows, and a blank expression on his face. As far as we can tell, the Neanderthals, who lived in Europe and the Middle East 70,000 to 35,000 years ago, did look somewhat like this. They are our closest relatives among the hominids and were intelligent, with brains a similar size to our own. In fact, the Neanderthals were so similar to modern humans that some scientists place them in our own species, giving them a subspecies (*Homo sapiens neanderthalensis*). Others give them a species of their own (*Homo neanderthalensis*).

The Neanderthal people used their intelligence to develop tools and technology. Although their tools were still made of stone, they now had specialized items such as chisels and borers. They made these tools by chipping small flakes off carefully selected cores, or lumps, of flint. To chip off a flake of the right size and sharpness, a Neanderthal flintworker needed skill, patience, and a very great deal of practice.

Some of the most fascinating evidence about the Neanderthals comes from their burial sites. Several of these have been discovered, from the Dordogne, France, to the Zagros Mountains in Iran. They reveal the bodies placed carefully in their graves. Items such as animal horns or bones were deliberately placed around them, probably as part of a burial ritual. Sites like these have led modern archaeologists to believe that the Neanderthals were the first hominids to develop burial ceremonies. The burial sites also provided a great deal of evidence that enabled scientists to work out what these people looked like, from

Neanderthal   Modern human

◀ SKELETONS
Stockily built and with a large head, Neanderthals were strong hominids with brains about as big as our own. Modern humans were taller and more upright.

NEANDERTHAL LIFE
During much of the Neanderthals' lifetime, Europe and Asia were in the grip of an ice age. The Neanderthals had to adapt to the cold, making clothes from skins and finding whatever shelter they could. This necessity, together with their large brains, made them inventive and adaptable.

chopper

scraper

borer

◀ NEANDERTHAL TOOLS
The Neanderthals developed different tools for scraping, cutting, butchering, and boring holes in hides. These flint-working skills have been perfected over many generations.

◀ POLLEN GRAINS
By examining prehistoric pollen under a microscope, scientists have found that trees such as alder, birch, oak, and elm grew in areas in which the Neanderthals lived.

▲ NEANDERTHAL GRAVE
Skeletons from this grave at La Chapelle-aux-Saints in France, were found to be deformed and stooping. This could mean the people suffered from arthritis.

flower offerings

bone offerings

animal horns

◀ BURIAL
A group of Neanderthals buries one of their dead. As mourners look on, two members of the group make offerings of pollen and flowers, which are placed carefully on and around the deceased's body. Animal horns are positioned to mark the grave. Rituals like this are the earliest known ceremonies.

their stocky build to the size of their heads and brains.

Some of the skeletons showed signs of bone diseases, such as arthritis, that must have developed over many years. Any individual who developed such a disease would not have been able to hunt and gather food. Other members of their family group must have fed them and looked after them. So besides being intelligent, the Neanderthals may have been the first carers, helping relatives who were not able to fend for

themselves. The Neanderthals died out around 35,000 years ago, but it is not certain why. They may have perished through disease or have been killed by Cro-Magnons, *Homo sapiens* who lived at the same time. New evidence is now being found to suggest that Neanderthals interbred with Cro-Magnon people.

▲ NEANDERTHAL SITES
The homeland of the Neanderthals stretched from France and Germany to Mesopotamia in the east. The eastern and western populations were separated during ice ages, but both groups produced similar tools and buried their dead in a similar way.

Key Dates

- 120,000 B.C. Neanderthals living from Europe to Mesopotamia.

- 100,000–40,000 B.C. Neanderthals develop stone tools for several different purposes.

- 100,000 B.C. Neanderthals and *Homo sapiens* both living at Qafzeh, Israel.

- 50,000 B.C. Remains of a burial site of this date found at Shanidar Cave, northern Iraq.

- 40,000 B.C. Skull of this date found at Monte Circeo, Italy, had been smashed to remove the brain.

- 35,000 B.C. Neanderthals die out.

Wise Man

▲ FIRE
The discovery of fire by Homo erectus *was an enormous technological advance that* Homo sapiens *would have inherited.*

BY THE TIME OF THE Neanderthals, members of our own species, *Homo sapiens*, or "wise man," were also living in many parts of the world. In some places, Neanderthals and humans lived close together, which suggests that Neanderthals could not have been our direct ancestors. If they lived together, we could not have evolved from both species. If this is correct, who were they?

Homo sapiens may have evolved from *Homo erectus*, or from another similar hominid that has not yet been discovered. Hominid bones, found in sites all over the world, seem to share features of *Homo erectus* and *Homo sapiens*. Although similar in size to ourselves, these hominids have bone ridges above the eyes and flattened skulls rather than dome-like heads. They date mostly from around 150,000 to 120,000 years ago and are classified by archaeologists as archaic *Homo sapiens*.

Some remains of *Homo sapiens* date from not long after these "archaic" bones.

◄ HUMAN FORM
The first members of Homo sapiens *were similar in appearance to modern people, except that they were generally somehat shorter. Their upright build made them well adapted to walking on two legs.*

▶ COUNTING STICK
Lengths of bone with small notches cut into them have been found at some Homo sapiens *sites. These may have been counting devices or an early form of writing. They may have been used to record a person's share of food.*

◄ EARLY HUMAN SKULL
Early humans had broad skulls that contained large brains. Their faces were flat, so they did not have the ape-like appearance of hominids like Homo habilis *or the Neanderthals.*

THE EARLY HUNTERS
The search for food was the most important part of life for early *Homo sapiens*. Some groups hunted herds of antelopes on the grasslands. Others went into the hills after wild sheep and goats or to the coast in search of seals and seafood.

◄ SEALS
For northern people who lived near the sea, animals such as seals were a valuable quarry. The animals provided a supply of meat, skins, bones (for tool-making), and blubber.

▲ BONE CARVING
Among the hominids, humans are the only artists. Early hunters liked to carve the creatures they chased, and animal bone was an ideal material—soft enough to carve but hard enough to last.

▲ SKULL, QAFZEH, ISRAEL
This is one of several skulls that have puzzled archaeologists. Experts are not sure if it is a Neanderthal or a human. The latest tests suggest that the two species lived together and bred, so specimens like this may have had a parent from each species.

Some experts think humans evolved in one area of Africa and then spread gradually across the world. This idea, which archaeologists refer to as the "Out of Africa" theory, is backed up by research based on DNA. This is the chemical in *Homo sapiens* bodies containing genes.

Other scientists believe that modern humans evolved separately in different parts of the world. For example, the population in Southeast Asia could have descended from *Homo erectus* people on Java. Europeans could have evolved from hominids from the Middle East that had interbred with Neanderthals.

By 100,000 to 90,000 years ago, modern humans had evolved in southern and eastern Africa. From here they traveled northward, crossing the Sahara and reaching the Middle East. For thousands of years the Sahara was wetter than it is today, and it was covered with grasslands cropped by grazing mammals. Hominids could cross this green Sahara with ease. By 75,000 years ago there were modern humans in eastern Asia. Later still, they would reach and settle in Europe.

As our ancestors spread across the globe, they settled in many different environments, from the warm African grasslands to the cold forests of northern Europe. They used their skills to adapt to each new place, using local materials to make clothes and huts, finding out about plants and animals, and learning how to fish. These early people were very advanced compared to many species.

▶ PREPARING SKINS
A hunted animal was not just a source of meat. The skins of larger creatures were removed, scraped clean, and trimmed. Then they were made into clothes, coverings for shelters, and simple bags and containers.

◀ EARLY HUMAN SITES
By 35,000 years ago, early humans had spread across most of Africa. They developed different lifestyles and tools to cope with the different conditions and materials that they found. The people of northern Africa, for example, produced quite finely worked flint scrapers and hand axes, similar to those made by the Neanderthals in Europe. In the south, however, many of the tools were much less finely chipped stone points and scrapers, but they were still sharp and effective.

Map labels:
- Mugharet el-'Aliya
- Jebel Irhoud
- Nazlet Khatir
- *Sahara Desert*
- **AFRICA**
- Singa
- Dire Dawa
- Omo
- L. Victoria
- ◆ *Homo sapiens* sites, Africa
- L. Tanganyika
- *Indian Ocean*
- L. Nyasa
- *Atlantic Ocean*
- *Kalahari Desert*
- Pietersburg
- Florisbad
- Klasies River Mouth
- N
- 0   Kilometers   2500
- 0   Miles   1500

Key Dates

- 150,000–120,000 B.C. Archaic *Homo sapiens*, the most ancient form of our own species, appears.

- 100,000 B.C. Modern humans begin to evolve in Africa.

- 100,000–70,000 B.C. African sites south of the Sahara show signs of modern human occupation. *Homo erectus* is still alive but is slowly replaced by *Homo sapiens*.

- 100,000–40,000 B.C. The Sahara is cooler than today. Hominids cross it to reach northern Africa.

- 75,000 B.C. Ice sheets in the northern hemisphere begin to get larger.

The First Europeans

▲ BISON CAVE PAINTING
When they discovered how to make colors out of earth and minerals, people began to paint pictures like this bison.

LIFE WAS HARD FOR THE first humans who lived in Europe. The climate was colder than it is today. Food could be difficult to find, and dangerous animals lurked in the forests. People survived by adapting and by becoming skilled at making things, such as tools and shelters. Slowly, over many thousands of years, they perfected the essential skills for survival.

The early Europeans are often called Cro-Magnons, after a site in the Dordogne, France. Cro-Magnon people kept themselves warm by making clothes from animal skins. They sheltered in caves when they could, but natural shelter was not always easy to find. They learned how to make simple homes, using whatever materials they could find. Tree branches provided a framework; this was covered with turf or animal skins to keep out the wind and rain. Another solution was to make a

framework from the massive bones of woolly mammoths they had killed.

The Cro-Magnons were skilled toolmakers. Their best and sharpest tools were made from flint, which they could work into small points for spearheads and knives. They also used materials such as bone and deer antler to make tools. Small pieces of bone could be carved to make pointed needles, and antlers could be adapted to make tools such as hammers.

Wood was another useful material. Small flakes of flint could be wedged into a twig to make a knife with a handle. The shafts of spears were also made of wood. It is likely that wood was used in many other ways too, such as making simple containers, but all evidence of this has perished with time.

The greatest achievement of the early European people was in their art. It ranged from sculpture to cave painting and tells us a great deal about everyday life. Pictures of

◀ KALEMBA ROCK SHELTER
About 35,000 years ago, hunter-gatherers used this natural shelter at Kalemba in Zambia. Like other similar shelters all over Africa, it provided a good resting place for people out hunting animals or searching for plants to eat.

GROWING SKILLS

The remains and tools of early *Homo sapiens* seem primitive, but early humans were in fact very intelligent. They were using their abilities to adapt to all sorts of different environments. Human language must also have been developing during this period, but unfortunately no record of it exists.

◀ BEZOAR GOAT
This species of goat was a popular quarry for hunters in the rocky, mountainous regions of the Middle East. Groups of hunters would drive a herd into a canyon. Then they could kill as many as they needed and share out the meat among a large number of people.

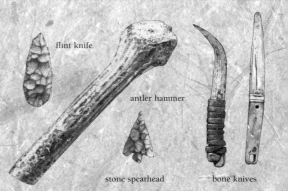

flint knife

antler hammer

stone spearhead

bone knives

▲ TOOLS
People learned to use several different materials to make tools. If no good stone was available, people used bone and antler for knives and points, as well as for tools like hammers.

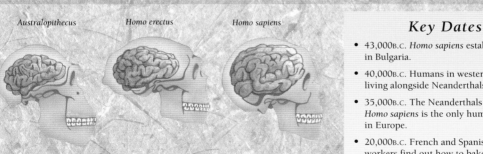

◀ HUNTERS' CAMP
Early hunters traveled quite long distances looking for food but returned to regular camps at places where there was shelter and a water supply. A campsite could be used by members of the same tribe or group for thousands of years.

animals show the creatures they hunted, from wild oxen and deer to woolly mammoths and rhinoceroses. It is also possible to make out the skin clothing they wore. Female figurines suggest that the people worshiped a mother goddess or goddess of fertility. People who were intelligent enough to produce the art and tools of the early Europeans probably also had quite an advanced society. Although they lived in family-based bands, it is quite likely that these small groups may have come together at certain times. They probably joined together to hunt or for religious ceremonies celebrating important times of the year.

Australopithecus   *Homo erectus*   *Homo sapiens*

▲ THE GROWING BRAIN
Studies of early *Homo sapiens* show that their brains were similar in size to those of modern humans and much bigger than those of the earlier hominids. The australopithecines, which were the size of modern chimpanzees, had brains with an average cubic capacity just over half that of *Homo erectus*. Even the brain of *Homo erectus* was little over half the total volume of *Homo sapiens*' brain. Human inventiveness, creativity, language, and social skills are all the result of our bigger brains.

Key Dates

- 43,000 B.C. *Homo sapiens* established in Bulgaria.
- 40,000 B.C. Humans in western Europe living alongside Neanderthals.
- 35,000 B.C. The Neanderthals die out. *Homo sapiens* is the only human form in Europe.
- 20,000 B.C. French and Spanish flint-workers find out how to bake flints so they can be pressure flaked to make very fine shapes.
- 16,000–12,000 B.C. Human settlement in Russia and Siberia. Mammoth-bone huts built at Mezhrich.
- 6000 B.C. Europeans develop microliths, tools made of tiny fragments of flint.

The Ice Age

▲ CARVING
This head is carved from a piece of mammoth tusk, a favorite material for sculpture during the Ice Age.

THE EARTH'S WEATHER IS ALWAYS changing. For the last two million years, the temperature of the planet has seesawed up and down. This has produced a series of warm periods with cold ice ages in between. The last of these ice ages reached its peak about 18,000 B.C. The time around this peak (30,000 to 12,000 B.C.) is so important in human history that it is always known as the Ice Age.

Humans had spread over much of the world by the beginning of the most recent Ice Age. All that time, the ice sheets had pushed down from the north, covering huge areas of the globe. Places such as Scandinavia, Siberia, and northern Britain became unfit for humans.

During this period, much of northern Europe was covered with sparse tundra. Large parts of Spain, Greece, and the Balkans were in forests. The area north of the Black Sea in Russia was a vast grassland. These varied habitats were a challenge to early people, and they had to adapt to different conditions. Big-game hunters moved across the Russian plains. Hunter-fishers lived on the tundra and at the edge of the ice sheets. Hunters and food gatherers took shelter in the forests. People had to devise different tools, hunting techniques and social skills to suit these varied lifestyles.

Ice Age tools are more varied than those of previous peoples. People in the Ice Age still used stone for their knives and choppers. But they used more bone and

◀ MAMMOTH
This large Ice Age mammal ranged widely across Europe, Asia, and North America. It died out around 10,000 years ago.

ICE AGE LIFE

The Ice Age made life difficult in many places. The cold was not just uncomfortable, it meant that some food plants could not survive. In addition, many areas had few or no trees, so that people had no wood to make shelters. These difficulties forced people to find new ways of life. They had to experiment with new foods (such as fish) and new materials (such as bones and antlers).

▼ MAKING FIRE
In a cold, damp climate, fire became even more important as a source of warmth. Making fire by rubbing sticks together to create a spark may have spread across Europe during the Ice Age.

◀ REINDEER
There are many surviving tools, harpoons, and carvings made from antler. This shows that reindeer-like animals were hunted across Europe during the Ice Age. Reindeer provided tasty, nutritious meat, as well as hides, bone, and antler.

▲ HARPOON POINTS
Ice Age hunters used harpoons for killing animals such as seals and for fishing in the rivers for salmon. The points took a long time to carve from deer antler and were prized possessions.

▶ MAMMOTH HUNTING
Large, fierce, and with two powerful tusks, woolly mammoths were an awesome sight for the people of the Ice Age. But these dangerous creatures were such a good source of meat, skins, bones, and ivory that the people risked injury or even death hunting and trapping them.

antler than before. They discovered how to use antler to make strong handles for stone blades and ax heads. They carved bone to make needles, which were essential to sew together hides and furs for warm clothes.

People still hunted large mammals such as the woolly mammoth. They also learned how to track and hunt animals that live in herds, such as reindeer. This gave them a rich source of hides, meat, and antlers.

Because resources were scarce, Ice Age people probably became the first traders, swapping food and materials. Flints and furs, for example, could be traded for food in times of shortage. People traveled more, they met other groups, and they probably found out about new sources of food. Contact with other tribes was an aid to survival. When different groups met, it became necessary to have a leader to act as spokesman. This was also a time when personal adornment first became important. A bone pendant or bright body paint could mark out the leader of a group.

▲ ICE AGE WORLD
Lower sea levels made the world's continents larger during the Ice Age, and some landmasses that are now separate were joined together. But the ice sheets in Europe, Asia, and the Americas made vast areas of this land unfit for human life.

Key Dates

- 32,000–28,000 B.C. Aurignacian culture in western Europe produces flint scrapers and sharpened blades.

- 30,000–12,000 B.C. Main period of last Ice Age.

- 24,000 B.C. Hunter-gatherers in Europe build permanent dwellings.

- 20,000 B.C. Hunters in western Europe develop spears and spear-throwers. Hunters in Poland use mammoth-tusk boomerangs.

- 18,000 B.C. Peak of Ice Age.

- 18,000–12,500 B.C. People settled near Kebara Cave, Israel, make grinding stones. This suggests they were gathering and processing grains.

Images of the Ice Age

▲ MAMMOTH CARVING
Ice Age art was not always realistic, and carvers often made striking, stylized shapes. In the case of this mammoth, the shape of the animal reflects the shape of the bone from which it is carved.

THE PREHISTORIC CAVE paintings of Europe show a wide variety of creatures. These include groups of wild horses, herds of reindeer and wild oxen, wild cats, birds, and mammoths. The animals are shown in action, galloping and running across the cave walls as if they are being chased by human hunters. They are dramatic action pictures, yet they were produced in dark, damp conditions in chilly caves. Ice Age artists also made sculptures and modeled figures from clay. They engraved cave walls and carved antlers and mammoth tusks into models of animals.

The paintings and sculptures are often hidden so deep in underground caverns that many of them were not rediscovered until the 1900s. It is not known why the paintings were hidden away like this. In fact, no one really knows why the pictures were produced at all. Most experts agree that there was probably some religious reason for the

paintings. They may have been used in magic ceremonies designed to help hunters or to promote fertility. Sometimes there are several different outlines in the same place, one drawn over another. This makes some cave paintings and engravings very difficult to see. Experts have spent many hours redrawing them in

▲ PAINTING TECHNIQUES
Artists used brushes or pads of animal hair when painting on cave walls. They sometimes put on the paint with their fingers or created a bold outline by drawing with charcoal.

ICE AGE ART

Because we do not know why Ice Age artists made their pictures and sculptures, it is difficult to decide what their work means. It does show how important animals and the natural world were to them. The cave paintings show the kind of animals these people ate and hunted and also which creatures they thought were the most powerful. These images, and the small carvings of the time, also provide some clues about Ice Age beliefs.

◀ ANTLER SPEAR-THROWER

A spear-thrower helped a hunter hurl his spear faster and farther than he otherwise could by acting as an extension of his arm. This made it easier to kill swift creatures such as deer. Hunters prized their spear-throwers, which were usually made of antler. This material lent itself to carving, and spear-throwers are often beautifully decorated. Swift-running animals like the horse shown here were favorite subjects.

◀ VENUS FIGURINE

Carvings of female figures, with their hips and bellies enlarged, have often been found at Ice Age sites. Archaeologists think they are fertility goddesses, and so have named them "Venus" figures, after the Roman goddess of love.

▶ IVORY HEAD

This female head from France, carved in ivory, shows a goddess. Goddess figures have been found in most areas of Europe, from France to Russia, so goddesses were probably the most important deities in Ice Age religion.

▲ CAVE PAINTING, LASCAUX
The caves at Lascaux, France, contain perhaps the most brilliant of all the known prehistoric paintings. Discovered in 1940, they show a variety of animals, including reindeer and horses. These finely drawn, brightly colored paintings began to show signs of damage in the 1960s because the atmosphere in the caves was affected by so many visitors. The caves were closed to the public, who now visit a replica called Lascaux II.

their notebooks to try to make the outlines clearer. For the prehistoric artist, the act of making the image seems to have been more important than the finished result. Perhaps the actual process of painting or engraving was part of a religious ceremony.

Ice Age painters used chalk to make white, charcoal for black, ocher (a kind of earth) for yellow, and iron oxide for red. Sometimes artists used minerals that they could heat to make other colors. The pigments were mixed with water and applied with fur pads, animal-hair brushes, or just with the artist's fingers.

Another technique involved spitting the paint out of the mouth or a reed to make a simple spray effect. The artists used oil lamps to light the caves and sometimes built crude wooden frameworks to gain extra height while working. With these simple techniques, Ice Age artists produced images that were surprisingly complex for such a simple society.

◀ ANTELOPE
This painting from a cave at Font de Gaume, France, shows the skill of the ancient artists. They caught the outline of the creature's head and horns, and cleverly shaded the animal's hide to create a sense of its bulk.

▶ MAKING PAINT
Artists found their colors in the earth and rocks. They mixed soils and minerals that they found with a medium such as water or animal fat. This produced a type of spreadable paint. They could also draw directly onto the rock surface with pieces of charcoal (burnt wood) or chalk.

iron oxide

brushstrokes   chalk   charcoal

◀ LAMP
Many cave paintings are hidden in dark, underground caverns. The artists needed light to see what they were doing, so they used fires, flaming torches, or stone lamps like this one. The animal fat was burned in the lamps, to give a bright, but rather smelly, flame. Several hundred Ice Age lamps have been found by archaeologists.

Key Dates

- 30,000B.C. Earliest European cave art.

- 30,000B.C. European musicians make flutes from lengths of animal bone.

- 23,000B.C. First cave paintings made in the Dordogne, France.

- 23,000B.C. Venus figurines made in France and central Europe.

- 18,000–8000B.C. Main period of cave painting in caves at Lascaux, France, and Altamira, Spain.

- 16,000B.C. Antler and bone carving reaches its peak. Finely engraved and carved spear points and spear-throwers made.

- 11,000B.C. Cave painting ends.

The First Australians

▲ ENGRAVINGS
These patterns were cut into rocks at Panaramitee, Australia, thousands of years ago. They may be the world's oldest rock engravings.

D URING THE ICE AGE, the sea level was much lower than it is today. The channels separating Australia from islands such as Timor in Indonesia were far narrower. As a result, groups of islanders took to the sea in bamboo rafts or simple boats in search of fish and shellfish. Some time before 32,000 years ago some Indonesians found themselves on the coast of what is now Australia. No one knows whether they had deliberately looked for new land were blown off-course on one of their fishing trips. They moved inland and became the first humans to inhabit the Australian continent.

The remains of early settlement in Australia are quite

▶ DUGOUT CANOE
Early sailors, like the people who first crossed from Southeast Asia to Australia, may have hollowed out and smoothed wooden logs to make simple dugout canoes.

patchy. The people were spread over a wide area and must have covered vast distances both by sea and on foot. Stone tools, hearths, shell debris, fish bones, and other remnants point to a scattered population between 32,000 and 24,000 years ago. Important sites include Devil's Lair Cave near Perth, Western Australia, a rock shelter near the Cleland Hills in Northern Territory, and Koonalda Cave in South Australia.

At Devil's Lair, archaeologists found several items that were probably used in religious ceremonies. There were some stone plaques and a pit with human teeth that had been removed by sharp blows. At Koonalda Cave, the inhabitants engraved lines on the rock walls. Native Australians carried on making rock engravings into the 1900s. The finds dating from prehistoric times show how far back a rich native Australian culture goes.

Many early Australian sites were occupied for thousands of years. This can also make exact

A SCATTERED PEOPLE
The first Australians traveled vast distances across their country to find food and good campsites. When they settled, they spread out thinly across the country. Sites in the south, which were well away from their original landing places, seem to have been most popular. The settlement process probably took place very slowly, spreading across the country over thousands of years.

◀ NECKLACE
People wore necklaces made of shells and animal teeth. Jewelry like this may have been a sign that the wearer was an important person. Such necklaces have been found in Asia as well as Australia. This indicates that the two regions were linked by a common people.

◀ HAND STENCILS
Stencils like this were probably made by spitting paint around and over the artist's hand. This type of art has been practiced in Australia since at least 22,000 B.C. The images, which are on the walls of rock shelters in southern and eastern Australia, show the importance of art to the island continent's earliest people.

dating of the art and artifacts difficult for archaeologists. One rock shelter, at Puritjarra, was used for nearly 7,000 years.

People had reached the island of Tasmania at the southeast tip of Australia by 32,000 years ago. They remained there even when the final Ice Age was at its coldest, when much of the island was covered by tundra and grassland. They lived in caves and rock shelters and survived by hunting the local animals, mainly the kangaroo and the wallaby. The new Tasmanians developed their own style of art. They painted hand stencils on cave walls and made tools

from a natural form of glass that they discovered in a crater formed by a meteorite from space.

The native people of Australia developed a lifestyle long ago that has lasted in some places to the present day. Over the millennia they adapted as their environment changed, from the chill Ice Age to the hot, dry climate of today.

▼ MAKING TOOLS
Early Australians became expert stoneworkers. They could chip away stones to make tools that were the right shape for the job and grind the edges of tools such as axes to make them sharp. Some of their tools were traded over long distances.

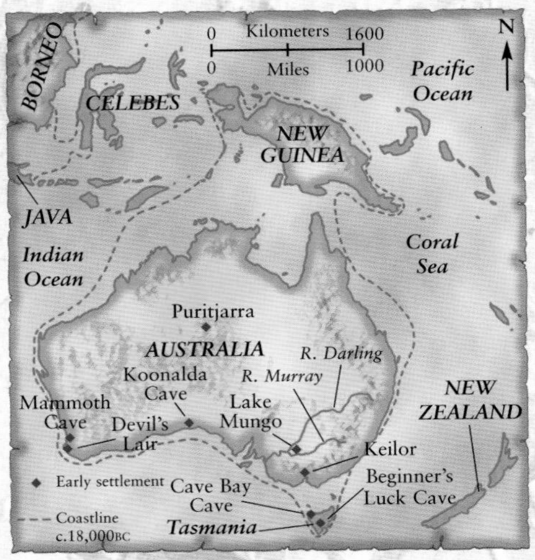

◀ EXPLORERS' MAP
Because the sea level was lower, larger pieces of land were above water, so the first people to travel to Australia had a shorter sea journey than travelers would have to make today. They probably crossed from places such as Java or the Celebes, sailing from island to island until they reached the northwestern coast of Australia. Even for such short trips, they needed to be good sailors and navigators. They probably built up their sailing skills over many years fishing off the Southeast Asian coasts.

Map labels: BORNEO, CELEBES, JAVA, NEW GUINEA, Pacific Ocean, Indian Ocean, Coral Sea, Puritjarra, AUSTRALIA, R. Darling, R. Murray, Koonalda Cave, Lake Mungo, NEW ZEALAND, Mammoth Cave, Devil's Lair, Keilor, Early settlement, Cave Bay Cave, Beginner's Luck Cave, Coastline c.18,000BC, Tasmania. Scale: Kilometers 1600 / Miles 1000. N.

Key Dates

- 30,000B.C. Human settlement of Australia probably begins.

- 29,000B.C. People are living in Tasmania, which is linked to the Australian mainland by a land bridge.

- 25,000B.C. Puritjarra Rock Shelter, near the Cleland Hills, Northern Territory, is occupied.

- 24,000B.C. Signs of human occupation near Lake Mungo, New South Wales.

- 22,000B.C. Traces of human settlement at Koonalda Cave, on the Nullaboor Plain, South Australia.

- 10,000B.C. The population of native Australians is about 300,000 people.

Early Americans

THE FIRST AMERICANS probably came from the extreme north tip of Asia, which is now Siberia. In the Ice Age the two continents were connected by a land bridge. The first peoples to cross this narrow neck of land found themselves in North America's bleakest, coldest spot. There would have been little vegetation. Most of their food came from hunting and fishing. They were well prepared for this, because the climate in Siberia was similar to that in North America. Many moved south in search of better weather and more plentiful food.

Archaeologists disagree about exactly when the first Americans arrived. The earliest firm evidence of

▲ THE JOURNEY FROM SIBERIA
It was a long, hard journey from Siberia across the land bridge to North America. We do not know what made people start this journey, but perhaps the harsh Ice Age conditions made them want to look for a place where food, warmth, and comfort were easier to find.

humans dates to between 15,000 and 12,000 years ago. However, in the same period, there is more widespread evidence for a hunting people who lived in western North America. Archaeologists call them the

THE GREAT MIGRATION

How do we know that the first Americans came from Siberia? One clue lies in the way the early Americans made tools and weapons. Many chipped tiny flint blades from bigger lumps of stone. They jammed these flints into grooves along the edge of a piece of bone to make a spearhead. Spearheads with this design have been found in both Siberia and North America.

▼ MAMMOTH TUSKS
These fossilized tusks are among many mammoth remains preserved at the Hot Springs mammoth site, South Dakota. They show that the first American hunters were catching the same quarry as their ancestors in Asia.

▲ CLOVIS POINTS
North American mammoth hunters fitted these finely worked sharp stone points to their spears. They made these points out of several different types of stone.

▲ WEAVING
A few fragments of twine have survived at Guitarrero Cave, Peru, to show that people could weave 10,000 years ago. These pieces may have been part of a bag or similar container.

Clovis people. They left behind finely worked flint spearheads, now called Clovis points after the town in New Mexico where the tools were found. These have been found at several places near the bones of large mammals such as mammoth and buffalo. Clovis people probably hunted solitary animals, driving them into swamps where they could be killed.

As the ice melted, the mammoths became extinct, although no one really knows why. The Clovis people vanished as a variety of new environments, from vast woodlands to arid deserts, developed in North America. People learned to adapt to each environment, evolving into distinct societies, whose lifestyles changed little until recent centuries.

In South America there is also evidence for human settlement by 12,000 years ago. At Monte Verde, Chile, the cremated remains of humans have been found in a cave. This site also contains remains of two rows of huts with wooden frames that supported a covering of animal skins. The huts had clay-lined pits for cooking, and there were larger, communal hearths outside.

It is just possible that human life began in South America much earlier than the

▶ MONTE VERDE
The huts at Monte Verde, Chile, made of wood covered with skins, provide the earliest evidence in America for manmade shelters. The remains were preserved in peaty soil, along with items such as a wooden bowl and digging sticks.

◀ SPEARHEAD
Spears, with notched bone spearheads bound tightly to wooden shafts with animal sinews, were used by early American hunters.

huts at Monte Verde. At Pedra Furada Rock Shelter, Brazil, there are areas of painted rock which some scientists date to around 32,000 years ago. Not all authorities agree with this dating, or with similar dates for some of the stone tools found at Monte Verde. If the early dates are correct, it is likely that settlement also began much earlier in North America but that the people left no surviving remains.

◀ NEW ARRIVALS
The first North Americans worked their way between the two main ice sheets. The Bering Land Bridge was created between Siberia and Alaska because the sea level was some 330 feet lower than it is today. Some people may also have come along the west coast on boats or rafts, stopping every so often along the edge of the Cordilleran Ice Sheet. When they finally reached beyond the ice, they found a vast empty land. Some people quickly moved east and west, while others pushed on further south.

Key Dates

- 13,000B.C. Hunters from Siberia cross the Bering Land Bridge.

- 12,500B.C. Humans at Meadowcroft Rock Shelter, Pittsburgh, Pennsylvania—the earliest known settlement in North America.

- 11,000B.C. People living at Monte Verde in southern Chile.

- 9000B.C. Clovis people hunting on the Great Plains.

- 8000B.C. Human settlers are accompanied by dogs.

- 7500B.C. The people of the Sloan site, Arkansas, bury their dead. This cemetery is the earliest discovered in North America.

The Thaw Begins

▲ FISH CARVING
Stone carvings of fishes, like this one, were found at Lepenski Vir on the river Danube. They may have portrayed a fish god.

AT THE END OF THE ICE AGE there was a great change in the world's climate. In much of Europe, Asia, and North America, the ice melted, making the sea level rise and causing floods in flat areas near the sea. The land bridge between Siberia and Alaska disappeared, cutting off North America from Asia. Britain, which had been joined to Europe, was now cut off by the North Sea. Large areas of land were lost around the coasts of Denmark and Sweden.

The change must have been terrifying at first. Many people fled the floods to settle in new areas. Their way of life changed. At the same time, the warmer weather transformed the landscape. In many places, ice and tundra were

▶ THATCHED TENTS
The Middle Stone Age settlement of Lepenski Vir was home to around 100 hunting and fishing people. They lived in tent-like houses made of wooden poles which were probably covered with thatch.

replaced by thick woods of birch and mixed forests in northern Europe, and deciduous woods in the south. People soon realized that these changes gave them new types of food. Among the woods lived animals such as wild pig and deer. Near the coast there were seals, waterfowl, and, in many places, shellfish. Food was more plentiful because the climate was warmer.

People developed new methods of hunting and fishing. These new techniques were more efficient than previous methods, so they did not have to move around so much to hunt for food. They set up special camps where food of a certain type was plentiful, or where they could mine flint to make their tools and weapons.

Most settlements in this period were by rivers or near the sea, where the people could usually rely on a good food supply. Rivers and coastal waters were the highways of the Stone Age. Rivers provided a way of traveling through the dense forests. People paddled along in their dugout canoes, perhaps exchanging valuable goods, such as furs or flint tools, with other travelers they met along the way.

LIFE DURING THE THAW

As the ice melted, some people moved inland, but for many the sea was too useful to leave behind. Such shellfish as oysters and whelks supplied tasty, nourishing food, so many people returned to the coast for at least part of the year.

scrapers, blades, and points from Star Carr

▲ FOREST FRUITS
The trees and shrubs of the new woodlands and forest edges yielded fruits such as blackberries to feed European gatherers.

▲ WILD BOAR
This woodland animal thrived in Europe after the thaw. It became a favorite target for many European hunters.

▲ TOOLS FROM STAR CARR
Hunter-gatherers camped regularly at Star Carr, near a lake in Yorkshire, England, at the end of the final Ice Age. They left behind many stone tools, such as scrapers, which they must have used to prepare animal skins, and smaller sharp cutting blades for butchering meat.

The new lifestyle meant that the people who lived in Europe after the Ice Age were on the whole better fed and more comfortable than their ancestors. They were more settled, so they had time to develop more advanced toolmaking skills. This made them more successful still. As a result, many more of their children began to survive to become adults. The total number of people began to rise, and the population began to spread, finding better places to settle and new sources of food.

▼ PINCEVANT

These round tents, held up with wooden poles, were the summer homes of people at Pincevant, France, at the end of the final Ice Age. All that was left to show modern archaeologists that tents had been pitched there were the rings of stones that had held the edges in place, together with hearths and some animal bones.

◀ SPREADING FORESTS

As the ice melted, forests spread slowly across Europe, covering the area in broadleaved trees. The spread of the forests began in the south, working its way north over a period of about 6,000 years toward Poland and Scandinavia, where mixed conifer and broadleaved forests grew. This new pattern of forests and woodland provided large areas of Europe with their typical landscape, one that survived for thousands of years. It still survives in some parts of Germany, central Europe, and Scandinavia.

Spread of broadleaved forest
- up to 11,000 B.C.
- 11,000–8,500 B.C.
- 8,500–7,500 B.C.
- 7,500–5,000 B.C.

Scandinavia

N

Atlantic Ocean

EUROPE

Mediterranean Sea

AFRICA

0 Kilometers 800
0 Miles 500

Key Dates

- 13,000 B.C. The ice thaws, sea levels rise, and lowland areas flood.

- 11,000 B.C. The dog is domesticated in the Middle East.

- 8000 B.C. Temperatures reach roughly their present levels in Europe.

- 8000 B.C. The Mesolithic period, or Middle Stone Age, begins in Europe.

- 7500 B.C. Red deer hunters settle at Star Carr, Yorkshire, England.

- 6500 B.C. Britain is cut off from Europe.

- 5500 B.C. Denmark is cut off from the rest of Scandinavia.

- 5000 B.C. Deciduous forests cover much of Europe.

A Better Food Supply

▲ MATTOCK HEAD
Deer antler was a good material to make a heavy tool such as a mattock. This was used by gatherers for loosening soil and cutting away plant roots for food.

MANY THINGS CHANGED IN North America at the end of the Ice Age. People were suddenly much freer to go where they wanted in search of food and raw materials. They found a range of different regions, from the grassy Great Plains to the drier areas of the southwest, all of which could be settled. At first they moved south, following the mammals and hunting them with their stone-pointed spears. They also spread out east and west across the continent, finding more and better sources of flint for tools and weapons. Archaeologists have traced many of the stone tools to where they were first made. Some of them were carried hundreds, or even thousands, of miles, which shows how far the hunters journeyed.

It took several thousand years for the climate and vegetation to settle down into the pattern that still exists today. As this happened, species such as mammoths became extinct, and people turned to smaller animals for food. The hunters also developed lighter, more accurate spears, which enables them to bring down game without having to ambush it first. On the grasslands there were still large creatures, such as buffalo. These provided hunters with a number of different products, such as meat to eat and hides to make leather and bones for tools. From around 9000 B.C., the people of the plains began to develop a lifestyle that would continue, with very little change, for many thousands of years.

The people of Asia, like the Europeans, took advantage of a better, more reliable food supply. They were healthier, and their population began to increase. However, they still relied on many of their old techniques for survival and shelter. In some places, people started to settle down and build permanent huts. Elsewhere, hunters still built temporary shelters from branches or mammoth bones and hides.

As the ice thawed in Africa and the Middle East, many areas

◀ ANTLER HEADDRESS
Archaeologists found this unusual antler headdress at the British Stone Age site of Star Carr, Yorkshire. It may have been used in a religious ceremony or as a disguise when hunting deer.

HUNTERS' WEAPONS
By the late Ice Age, weapons had improved. Although spearheads and harpoon points were still made of stone, antler, and bone, they were carefully carved so they worked well whenever they were used. When food was scarce, a hunter could not afford to lose his quarry because a blunt spear allowed an animal to escape.

▶ ANTLER POINTS
Hunters used deer antler to make deadly harpoon points. By carving away notches along one edge, then sharpening one or both ends, they made a barbed point. The advantage of this was that when a weapon was thrown at an animal it went in easily, but would not slip out as the creature ran away. Barbed points are still used by Arctic hunters.

◀ REPAIRING SPEARS
Stone spearheads such as North American Clovis points are virtually everlasting. But wooden spear shafts often break or split, so hunters had to fit their points to new ones. They fixed the points by splitting the shaft, jamming in the head, and binding animal sinew around the joint.

▾ HOME OF SKIN AND BONE
Like the people of the Ukraine, Siberian hunters built homes out of large animal bones and tusks, covered with skins and reinforced with timber if they could find it. Stones weighted down the skins on the ground. The people may have learned how to build these tents in the Ukraine before traveling eastward to their new homes.

that had been desert were covered with vegetation. Plants began to flourish in the Nile Valley and the eastern Mediterranean. This was a land of wild grasses, and people began to gather their seeds, grind them into flour, and make bread to eat. One group of people who we know did this were the Natufians, a people who lived near the Wadi en-Natuf, in what is now Israel.

These cereal gatherers were learning a lot of vital information about the various kinds of grain. For example, which provided the tastiest seeds, when best to harvest them, and the most effective tools to use. Later, they would put this knowledge to good use, changing to a settled way of life and becoming some of the world's first farmers.

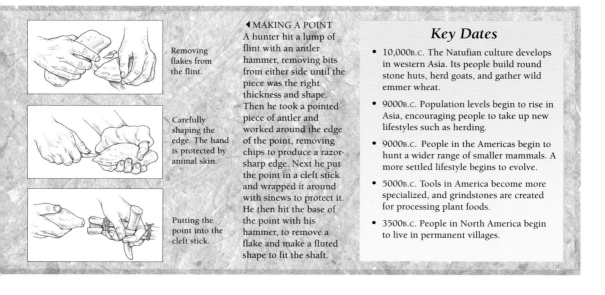

Removing flakes from the flint.

Carefully shaping the edge. The hand is protected by animal skin.

Putting the point into the cleft stick.

◀ MAKING A POINT
A hunter hit a lump of flint with an antler hammer, removing bits from either side until the piece was the right thickness and shape. Then he took a pointed piece of antler and worked around the edge of the point, removing chips to produce a razor-sharp edge. Next he put the point in a cleft stick and wrapped it around with sinews to protect it. He then hit the base of the point with his hammer, to remove a flake and make a fluted shape to fit the shaft.

Key Dates

- 10,000B.C. The Natufian culture develops in western Asia. Its people build round stone huts, herd goats, and gather wild emmer wheat.

- 9000B.C. Population levels begin to rise in Asia, encouraging people to take up new lifestyles such as herding.

- 9000B.C. People in the Americas begin to hunt a wider range of smaller mammals. A more settled lifestyle begins to evolve.

- 5000B.C. Tools in America become more specialized, and grindstones are created for processing plant foods.

- 3500B.C. People in North America begin to live in permanent villages.

Rock Paintings

▲ SAN HUNTERS
This modern rock painting by the San people, or bushmen, from the Kalahari Desert shows hunters chasing their quarry. It is one of many recent rock paintings done in a style similar to that used in prehistoric times.

UNLIKE CAVE PAINTINGS, which were hidden deep underground, rock paintings were made on rocks and cliff faces out in the open air. Some of these drawings are engraved into the rock with a sharp stone tool. Others are painted with natural pigments in a similar way to that used for the cave paintings of the final Ice Age. Rock art occurs all over the world, from Africa to Australia. The drawings are usually easier to find than the cave paintings of western Europe, and in some places they are quite common. Some rock drawings date from 8000 B.C., but others were made as recently as the 1800s. The more recent pictures are often similar in style to the ancient images. This makes them difficult to date, but it also shows how the art and lifestyles of many peoples

altered little until the early 1900s. Rock art can tell us a great deal about the people who created it—especially the creatures they hunted and farmed, because animals appear in these paintings more than any other subject.

Some of the most interesting and best preserved rock art is found in Africa. In the Saharan region, the types of animals in the pictures show how different the area was compared with the desert of today. After the final Ice Age, when the Sahara was covered in grasslands and dotted with oases

◀ HAND PAINTING
One method used by rock artists was to take some paint into the mouth and spit it onto the rock to produce a stencil of the hand.

THE VARIETY OF ROCK ART

The most common subjects in rock art are animals, people, and patterns. Although the subjects are similar, the style of the pictures can vary greatly around the world. Some, like the paintings of the Sahara, are very realistic. Others, like the human figures of South America, are more like symbols than pictures of real people.

▶ GAZELLES
Artists from the Tassili Massif in the Sahara drew these gazelles. They were painted over 6,000 years ago. This was before the beginning of farming, when Saharan artists were still drawing the animals they hunted for food.

▲ BISON
The people of Bhimbetka, India, made rock drawings of animals for thousands of years. Bison, antelope, and deer, as well as people, were favorite subjects, and some, like this example, were filled in with delicate abstract patterns.

▲ HUMAN FIGURE
This rock engraving of a stylized person comes from Venezuela. No one knows what the circles and curves around it are, but they may be symbols of the Moon or Sun.

or shallow lakes, the area was home to wild oxen and gazelles. The local people hunted these animals and drew them on the walls of their shelters. After about 6000B.C., they began to draw domestic cattle, which shows that the change from hunting to farming near the oases happened around this time.

Other African paintings, such as those of the San people of what is now the Kalahari Desert, show hunters chasing their quarry. They are also shown fishing from their boats and gathering food. Pictures like these are almost certainly more than just decorations on shelter walls. The hunting pictures were probably produced as part of a ceremony performed before the hunt. The people hoped that drawing a successful hunt would make their own hunt turn out well. In a similar way, a picture of a group of men dancing around an antelope was probably intended to transfer some of the real animal's strength to the men of the tribe.

Paintings with a religious or ceremonial purpose are even more common in Australia. Stories of how the world was created have always been important to the native Australians. Each tribe has its own ancestor, usually an animal that is linked with some special part of the landscape. One Australian myth, which tells how the world was made, describes the way in which the rainbow serpent, who came from the sea, slithered onto the shore and created the landscape as he snaked his way inland. Rainbow serpents first begin to appear in rock paintings made by native Australians some 6,000 years ago.

▲ SPIRIT BEINGS
Australian rock painting represents spirits that were believed to be the ancestors of a particular tribe. They formed the center of the tribe's religious beliefs. The ancestors of different groups took different forms. Some were said to be animals; others were features of the landscape. They were all regarded with the deepest reverence by their people, as they are today.

◄ HUNTERS
Many rock drawings were made by hunting peoples, like these figures by the San people of the Kalahari Desert. The painted hunters seem to be moving with great agility, almost like dancers.

► LEAF
Depictions of plants are rarer in rock art than animals or people. They do occur occasionally, as in this Australian example from a site in the Northern Territory. Plant pictures may be linked to religion or the ancestors, or may have been done simply to create a decorative effect.

Key Dates

- 25,000B.C. Early inhabitants of Australia may be developing rock art.

- 20,000B.C. Rock artists may already be active in some parts of Africa.

- 11,000B.C. Rock art in central India shows hunters and prey.

- 8500B.C. The earliest rock paintings found in Saharan Africa portray wild animals.

- 8000B.C. The main period of cave painting ends in Europe. Rock art on cliffs and in shallower caves becomes common.

- 6000B.C. Saharan rock artists depict cattle, reflecting the change to the herding of livestock.

The First Farmers

▲ WHEAT
Finding a staple crop that provides basic energy needs is an important step in farming. Wheat is one of the most common. Others are millet, rice and maize.

HUNTERS AND GATHERERS were highly skilled at finding food. However, their success was dependent on the weather, local conditions and luck. If the weather turned bad or the local supplies ran out, people faced starvation. Around 11,000 years ago, a group of people in the Middle East changed this. They began to produce their own food by farming. It was one of the most important developments in the history of humankind.

Farming gave people control over their food supply. They did not have to wander through the countryside looking for food any longer. They could settle in one place, and as a result they began to build stronger, more comfortable houses than before. Farming also offered a more reliable supply of food, although in years when the harvest was bad, people had to return to gathering for a while.

The first farmers lived at the eastern end of the Mediterranean (now Israel, Palestine, and Syria) and in an upland region north of the river Tigris in what now forms parts of Iran and Iraq. This region has more rain than the surrounding plains, and grasses such as wheat and barley grow there naturally. Because of its climate and its shape on the map, the area is now known as the Fertile Crescent.

The people of the Fertile Crescent had gathered wheat seeds for thousands of years. They knew which types grew most vigorously and produced the best grain. By about 9000B.C., they realized that they could plant these grasses and harvest them. At around the same time, they started to herd the wild sheep and goats. These animals provided milk and wool as well as meat. During the next 3,000 years, people also began to keep livestock, pigs, and cattle.

In good years, farming gave the people of the Fertile Crescent more food than they

◄ STONE TOWER
Jericho's tallest building was a stone tower. No one knows why the tower was built. It could have been a watchtower, or it might have had some religious purpose.

THE FARMERS' WORLD

Although farming created a lot of hard work, the people of the first agricultural villages did not spend all their time in the fields. In many places, they developed quite complex religious beliefs and ceremonies. They produced new styles of art, including sculptures modeled from plaster and pottery decorated with striking abstract designs of lines and rectangles. They also started to make larger baskets and clay containers for storing surplus grain.

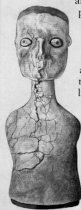

◄ FIGURE SCULPTURE
The world's earliest large-scale human sculptures were produced in Ain Ghazal, Jordan. They were moulded in lime plaster over a skeleton of straw bundles. The eyes were outlined with dark paint. No one knows why they were made.

▶ SPOUTED BOWL
From the early farming site at Khirokitia, Cyprus, came this decorated pottery bowl. It was buried in the grave of an eight-year-old child, and was obviously a favorite object, as it had been repaired before the burial.

◄ PLASTERED SKULL
Around 6000B.C., the religious ceremonies of Jericho involved the use of human skulls. The skulls were covered with plaster, which was molded to copy the person's ears, nose, mouth and other facial features. Cowrie shells were placed in the eye sockets, and teeth were added.

could eat. They stored the surplus in grain bins or baskets and traded it for materials, for tools, or for items such as pots and furniture.

Gradually, the farmers and craftworkers became rich. They built more and bigger houses clustered together. These groups of houses developed into small towns. The houses were made of mud bricks, providing warmth in winter while staying cool in summer. One of the first of these towns was Jericho, built near a spring north of the Dead Sea. The land around the town was good both for growing crops and for grazing herds and flocks of animals, and soon Jericho became a very prosperous town. It was not long before other towns were built in this area.

As farming spread farther afield, it was not very long before other regions began to produce their food in a similar way, and the pattern of human life had changed forever.

◀ EARLY FARMER
To begin with, farming was difficult, backbreaking work—even more so than the toil of hunting and gathering. There were only stone and wooden hand tools to work the soil. Seed had to be scattered by hand, and harvesting had to be done in the hot sun with a simple stone sickle.

◀ FARMING IN THE FERTILE CRESCENT
To begin with, farming was most successful where there were light soils. These could be easily worked with basic hand tools. There also had to be plants growing wild that were suitable for cultivating. From its beginnings near the Persian Gulf, the river Euphrates and the eastern Mediterranean, farming spread gradually outward. Egypt to the south and Turkey and Greece to the northwest were places where farming arrived early.

Key Dates

- 10,000 B.C. Cereal gathering begins in Palestine.
- 9000 B.C. Farming begins in the Fertile Crescent.
- 9000 B.C. The people of Syria and nearby regions sow wheat.
- 9000 B.C. Jericho develops as a small settlement around a spring.
- 8000 B.C. Animal herding is well established in the Zagros Mountains.
- 7000 B.C. Cereal farming is widespread from Turkey to the Fertile Crescent, in the Zagros Mountains, and in parts of Pakistan.

Plants and Animals

▲ DATE PALM
Early farmers in the Fertile Crescent used the date palm for its fruit, wood, leaves, and fibers.

THE FIRST FARMERS DID NOT simply take wild grasses and plant them in rows in their fields. They had to work hard to turn the wild species they found into true cereal crops. To begin with, they had to choose the plants that were the most suitable for food. In Europe and Asia, farmers chose grasses such as wheat and barley. Farmers in eastern Asia grew millet. Tropical African growers cultivated yams. The first farmers in North America selected corn, while those in South America chose potatoes and another root vegetable, manioc.

Farmers watched for the individual plants that were strongest or biggest. American corn farmers, for example, collected the seed from plants yielding the biggest cobs, and sowed these, to produce a crop with larger cobs next year.

Farmers in the Fertile Crescent had a different problem with their wheat. One species that grew well was wild einkorn wheat. But its seeds tended to break off and fall to the ground when they ripened, which made them difficult to harvest. Eventually the farmers noticed that a few plants had seeds that did not fall so quickly, so they bred their crops from these. Soon they

▼ CATTLE ROCK PAINTING
When the people of the Sahara began to farm, their artists started to paint pictures of cattle. This example shows a herd of cattle, of the type that were kept more than 4,000 years ago. The painting also includes some of the people who herded them. It comes from a site in the Tassili mountains, in the central Sahara.

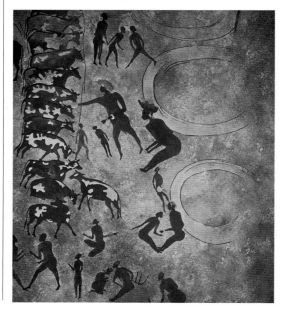

ON EARLY FARMS

Early farms looked quite unlike modern ones. The animals and plants were different, and the farmer and his family usually shared their house with the animals. There were no machines, just simple tools and a lot of hard work. The whole family helped, especially at busy times such as harvest. Even young children lent a hand, which was good training for when they would be farmers themselves.

wild einkorn

domestic einkorn

◀ WILD AND DOMESTIC WHEAT
The main difference between wild and domestic einkorn wheat is the seeds. In the domestic variety these are much larger. The plant's stalk is also stronger, which stops the seeds from falling off before the harvest.

▶ WILD AND DOMESTIC CORN
Modern domestic corn has a larger seed cob than the ancient wild variety. Early farmers probably bred corn cobs that were larger than the wild varieties but not as big as today's giant cobs.

wild corn

domestic corn

◀ WILD AND DOMESTIC CATTLE
The wild auroch was the ancestor of early farm cattle. Bones found by archaeologists show that early domesticated cattle were smaller than the wild ones. But early farmers probably tried different sizes to see which suited them best.

auroch

cattle

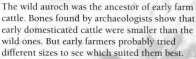

◄ A FARMING VILLAGE
The first farming villages in Turkey were small clusters of mud-brick houses, where people and animals lived close together for safety. In the hot, dry summers, the village streets were baked hard and dusty, but in the winter they became a mass of puddles and sticky mud. These farmers kept goats and cattle descended from the wild aurochs.

had developed a new species, domesticated einkorn wheat, with seeds that broke away only during threshing.

Early farmers bred their animals in a similar way, selecting the beasts with the features they wanted and breeding from them. But the changes to the animal species were less dramatic than with the crops. The pigs farmed in the Fertile Crescent, for example, were much smaller and more like wild boars than modern domestic pigs. Cattle, too, were smaller than modern cows, and sheep and goats looked like the wild species.

Most early domestic animals were smaller than their wild cousins. This is probably because farmers bred good-tempered, docile creatures that were less aggressive and easier to handle than wild animals. Instead of choosing large specimens, farmers would have selected animals that produced the best-tasting meat or the highest yield of milk. Gradually, the farmers built up knowledge and experience, and they must have discovered that the smaller animals often had the features they wanted.

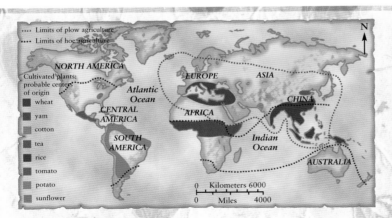

▲ PLANT DOMESTICATION
Farmers in different parts of the world grew different types of crops. In each area, one or two crops became the most commonly grown. They were varieties that were easy to grow in that particular area and provided a good basic crop.

Key Dates

- 9000B.C. Sheep domesticated in northern Mesopotamia.

- 8000B.C. First domesticated cereals grown around Jericho.

- 7000 B.C. Sheep and goats kept in the eastern Mediterranean.

- 7000B.C. Barley grown in the Fertile Crescent. Emmer wheat in Palestine. Einkorn wheat in Turkey and Mesopotamia.

- 7000B.C. Pigs are domesticated in southern Turkey.

- 6000B.C. Cattle kept by farmers in north Africa and the eastern Mediterranean.

The Coming of Trade

▲ DAGGER
This dagger, with its long flint blade and its snake-shaped handle, was probably made for decorative effect rather than for use in battle.

FARMING MADE SOME PEOPLE well-fed, rich, and successful. They could trade the extra food they produced in exchange for luxury goods. Soon, this became a way of life for many farmers, and trading towns began to appear in the Fertile Crescent and in Anatolia (Turkey). Most of these early towns disappeared long ago. As one set of mud-brick buildings fell into disrepair, they were knocked down. People built new houses on top of the old foundations. This happened many times over hundreds of years, and the town's ground level gradually rose as each group of houses was replaced. When a town was finally abandoned, the ruins, with their buildup of floor levels, was left in the form of a mound. In Syria and Palestine this type of ancient mound is called a tell. In Turkey it is known as a hüyük.

One of the most famous of these early town mounds is Çatal Hüyük in central Turkey. When archaeologists began to dig this mound, they found that it concealed an ancient town, occupied by a trading people who lived there between 7000 and

▶ BUILDING WORK
Clay was the main material for building in early trading towns of the Middle East. It could be molded into brick shapes while wet and left to dry in the sun. Surfaces were plastered to give a weatherproof finish outside and a smooth surface for decoration within.

6000B.C. The countryside around the town was rich farming land. Charred remains from the town have shown that the people grew wheat, barley, lentils, and other vegetables, as well as eating such fruit as apples and wild nuts such as almonds.

The people of Çatal Hüyük probably traded in food products and raw materials for making tools. A favorite material was obsidian, a black glass formed naturally in volcanoes. Archaeologists have found a range of different tools and weapons made of flint and obsidian on the site.

The houses of Çatal Hüyük were built of mud brick. They were square or rectangular and built close together. One amazing feature of the town was that it had no streets. People entered their houses from the flat

MYSTERIES OF A TURKISH TOWN

There are still many mysteries surrounding the town of Çatal Hüyük in central Turkey, in spite of all the work of the archaeologists. No one knows for sure the meaning of the wall paintings in many of the rooms that have been excavated. The bulls, birds, leopards, and human figures were probably gods. However, it is not clear what the gods stood for, or how they were worshiped.

▲ BULL PAINTING
This mural is from a shrine at Çatal Hüyük. It shows a group of people baiting a gigantic bull. Bulls had religious significance because they were associated with a male god.

▶ CLAY SEALS
Oval-shaped stamps with abstract patterns may have been used as seals. Each person would have had a seal with a different design and used it to mark his or her property, as proof of ownership.

▶ BIRD WALL-PAINTING
These birds are probably vultures. People in some cultures left their dead out of doors until vultures had picked away the flesh.

roofs, stepping down wooden ladders to the floor below. Defending such places was easy.

Many houses contained at least one room set aside for religious ceremonies. These rooms, or shrines, are decorated with bulls' heads made of plaster and fitted with real bulls' horns. They also have wall paintings of animals and figures. Many of the figures are female, and archaeologists have also found more than 50 small statues of pregnant women, suggesting that the people worshiped a mother goddess.

In addition, the shrines contain platforms that may have been used as altars in some form of religious ceremony. When residents of Çatal Hüyük died, their bodies were left in the open air, where the flesh was removed by the vultures. Then their relatives brought the bones back into the town and buried them beneath these platforms.

Ladder gives access to roof.

Flat roof provides work space and route to neighboring houses.

Decorated room used as religious shrine.

Roof made of layers of timber, reeds, and mud.

◄ TOWN HOUSES
Houses at Çatal Hüyük were made mainly from mud brick. This material was even used for fixtures such as benches and hearths. The houses were packed closely together with only a few courtyards between them. This made the town compact and helped to make it easier to defend, with few corners where enemies or wild beasts could lurk.

◄ EXCAVATING A SITE
The most common way for archaeologists to dig is to make a trench, a rectangular hole across the site. They can find remains from different periods because these lie in bands like a layer cake, revealing small areas across a broad time span. When there are many remains of buildings and other structures, such as at Çatal Hüyük, archaeologists will sometimes excavate to a shallow depth, over a broader area to cover more of the site.

Key Dates

- 8000 B.C. Trade begins to develops in the Fertile Crescent and Anatolia.

- 7000 B.C. Çatal Hüyük becomes important as a town and trading center.

- 7000 B.C. Jericho expands; religious rituals include decorating skulls with plaster and shells.

- 6800 B.C. Pottery is widely used in the eastern Mediterranean.

- 6500 B.C. More elaborate burials at settlements such as Çatal Hüyük and Jericho show that some people were more important than others.

- 5000 B.C. Trade links established between Turkey and the eastern Mediterranean.

Pots and Potters

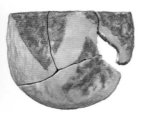

▲ PAINTED POTTERY
The earliest pottery was plain, but potters soon learned how to paint their wares to make them more attractive. This pot is from an early farming community in Europe.

WE TAKE POTTERY, SUCH as cups, bowls, mugs, and plates, for granted. Before pottery was invented, our earliest ancestors used hollowed-out stone containers and woven baskets. The first pottery was probably made around 10,500 B.C. Pots are made from clay, which was dug from the ground, so they are cheap. They could be made in a variety of shapes and sizes, and held liquids as well as dry foods. Once people had discovered how to make pots, they never stopped finding new uses for them.

Pottery was probably discovered by accident. Early peoples baked bread and other foods in ovens which they made from earth. They piled up a mound of clay and made a hollow center in which they lit a fire. Inside, it became very hot. Eventually someone must have noticed that the sides of the clay oven had hardened with the heat.

It was probably some time before anyone had the idea of using this hardened clay to make containers. The earliest pots so far discovered

come from Japan. From Japan, knowledge of pottery may have spread to China, where slightly more recent vessels have been found. However, in the rest of Asia, Europe, and Africa, pottery is much more recent. It is possible that it may have been discovered independently, as it was in America.

The first pots were made by the coiling process. The potter made a long, thin sausage of clay and looped it in a circle, spiraling upward to make the sides of the pot. Another ancient technique was to form pots by using a stone mold which was removed when the potter achieved the right shape. Much later, some time after 3000 B.C., the potter's wheel was invented. This device is still used by potters all over

◀ TERRACOTTA FIGURE
Pottery can be molded into all sorts of shapes, not only containers. People soon realized that they could use it to make small, portable statues. These were common among early farming communities, and archaeologists have excavated shrines with large numbers of these figures.

POTS AND POTTERS

In hunter-gatherer societies, people generally collected food as they needed it. Farming produced a glut of food at harvest time. People now needed containers to store this food, so pottery and farming flourished at the same time. The earliest pottery is unglazed. This means that it absorbs moisture, so that it is best used for dry goods such as grain and other solid foods.

◀ UNGLAZED POTS
Simple unglazed storage jars are still made in many parts of the world. These jars, elegantly shaped and decorated with patterns made by the potters' fingertips, come from Ghana. Pots like this are sometimes given a colorful glaze.

▲ ROUND-BASED POT
This is one of the oldest pots so far discovered by archaeologists. It comes from Nasunahara, Japan, and dates to around 10,500 B.C. The pot has a beaded pattern in bands around the rim.

▶ JOMON POT, JAPAN
Jomon or cord-marked pottery was produced in Japan around 10,000 B.C. The clay was coiled into shape, and the pots had pointed bases. They were probably hardened by heating on an open fire, rather than by firing in an enclosed kiln like later pots. This pot, used as a storage jar, stands about 9 inches high.

the world. The finished pots were fired and hardened in a kiln, which was similar to an ancient oven.

One advantage of pottery is that it is extremely long-lasting, and pots have survived to provide evidence for archaeologists. Each region and period has its own style of pottery. The color of the clay, the thickness of the pot, the style of decoration all vary from place to place and time to time. An archaeologist can often tell, even from a fragment of pottery, when and where it was made. They can therefore give a date to the sites where they find pots. Pots of foreign origin also provide clues as to trade and links between various countries.

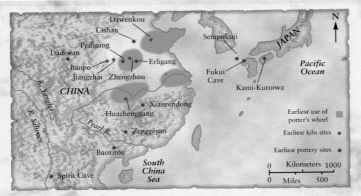

▲ POTTERS AT WORK
The potter in the foreground is making a pot by coiling clay. She has prepared long, sausage-shaped pieces of clay and wound them around to build up the shape of the vessel. When she is happy with the overall shape, she will moisten her fingers and rub the surface of the pot to make it smooth. She may then make handles and stick them to the sides.

▲ EARLY POTTERY SITES
Archaeologists have discovered many remains of both early pottery and kilns in China and Japan. These areas continued to be at the forefront of developments in pottery until the 1800s. Kilns, glazing, and, much later, waterproof porcelain, were all discovered and first used in the Far East.

Key Dates

- 10,500 B.C. First Japanese pottery.
- 7000 B.C. Unbaked, sun-dried clay vessels made in Syria and Turkey.
- 7000 B.C. Hunter-fishers of southern Sahara are the first potters in Africa.
- 6500 B.C. First European pottery.
- 6000 B.C. Fishing communities in southern China make pottery.
- 3500 B.C. The tournette, a simple device for turning a pot, appears in Mesopotamia and Egypt.
- 3000 B.C. Potter's wheel invented in the Middle East.
- 1500 B.C. Glazed pottery which is resistant to water made in China.

European Settlements

FARMING SEEMS TO HAVE spread to Europe from the east, from around 7000B.C. It reached Europe from Turkey and then spread westward toward the Atlantic coast.

Then, as now, the European climate and landscape varied greatly. In the Balkans, where farming in Europe started, it was dry, and the land was suitable for sheep and goats, as well as for cereal growing. In northern Europe, early farmers led a very different life. The weather was colder, the soil heavier, and much of the ground was covered with forest. This was not good country for sheep and goats, so pig-rearing and cattle-herding were more popular. People could grow cereal crops, but the heavier soil was harder to cultivate than in the south. Gradually, over many centuries, the northerners developed strains of cereals that could grow in the heavy soil.

The woods of the north had many benefits. They were good foraging-grounds for pigs, and also provided a variety of food plants for people. They also sheltered animals, such as deer and wild boar, that could be hunted for both food and skins. The northern Europeans continued to hunt and gather to add variety to the food they produced on their farms.

The plentiful timber was also useful for building. The farmers of central and northern Europe cut down trees to make a stout framework for the walls and roofs

▲ FARMING SETTLEMENT
A small farming village in western Britain consisted of a few round thatched houses clustered together. Next to the houses were fields for animals and crops. A trackway gave access to the fields and connected this village with its neighbors.

CRAFTS OF THE FARMERS

With the settled way of life that came with farming, people began to develop their craft skills. Among the most important were building and pottery. These early farmers were skilled woodworkers. They made fences, tools, and containers.

face pot, Hungary

Bandkeramik pot, Germany

▲ RAISED PATHWAY
People sometimes built farming villages in marshy land. They made wooden walkways raised on posts so that they could cross the swamps safely.

▲ DECORATED POTS
Potters decorated pots by drawing patterns or simplified faces in the damp clay. Another design was made up of lines and dots in a style known by the German name *Bandkeramik*, meaning "banded pottery."

▲ SEATED FIGURE
This pottery statuette from a farming site in Hungary shows a man holding a sickle. He may be a grain god, or just an ordinary farmer.

of their homes. They used split logs to make the walls and plastered them over with daub, a mixture of mud and straw, to fill the gaps. This helped to keep out drafts. The roofs, which had a steep pitch to throw off snow and rain, were thatched. Some of these houses were up to 150 feet in length and are known as longhouses. They were Europe's first sizable, permanent dwellings. Besides a large room for the family, they usually also contained a storeroom

for crops and an area for cattle. Sometimes humans and animals shared the same room. It was cramped and smelly, but people put up with this to make sure their animals were safe.

Farming villages became established in many river valleys. People used the rivers to travel between neighboring villages to trade. As they traveled, they also exchanged ideas about new discoveries and inventions. As a result, pottery techniques and styles improved and spread, and new ideas about crop and animal cultivation were shared. The people of Europe were developing skills that would stay in use for thousands of years.

◀ EUROPEAN FARMERS
At Langweiler, Germany, farmers build a longhouse for their family and animals. They have constructed the walls and are now thatching the roof. To do this they have gathered reeds from a nearby river. Reeds make a longer-lasting thatch than grass or straw.

▲ FARMING REACHES EUROPE
From the Middle East and Turkey, farming spread gradually west along coasts and river valleys. The three main areas of farming in Europe were the Balkans, the Mediterranean coast, and north and west Europe, to which farming came last.

Map labels:
- Early European farming settlements
- Coastline of the time
- Spread of farming
- 0 Kilometers 1000 N
- 0 Miles 500
- North Atlantic Ocean
- Elsloo
- Langweiler
- Cuiry-les-Chaudardes
- Arene Candide
- EUROPE
- Bylany
- Starcevo
- Tirpesti
- Smilcic
- Karanovo
- Black Sea
- Coveta de l'Or
- Mediterranean Sea
- Nea Nikomedeia

Key Dates

- 7000B.C. Farming reaches eastern Europe, probably from Turkey.

- 6200B.C. Farming begins in Sicily and southern Italy.

- 5400B.C. Farming spreads across northern Europe, from Hungary, through Germany, to the Netherlands.

- 5000B.C. Farming communities such as Langweiler are thriving.

- 5000B.C. Farming has spread across southern Europe and has reached the south of France.

- 4000B.C. Farming established in most of Europe.

Asian Communities

▲ HARPOON HEADS, CHINA
Items like these bone harpoon points from the farming site at Banpo, China, show that hunting and river fishing were still key sources of food.

GOOD SOIL AND USEFUL LOCAL crops encouraged Asian people to begin farming. This is how agriculture began in eastern Asia, in places such as the highlands of northwest and central India and areas around the banks of the Yellow River in China. Both regions had good natural resources and a climate suitable for farming. Archaeologists have found the remains of several early farming villages in both places.

Central India had grassy uplands suitable for cattle grazing and river banks with rich soil for crops. Farming began early here, around 7000B.C. Barley was a popular crop, and farmers herded cattle, goats, and sheep on the hills. In some places, people gathered together to build villages. One of the first was called Mehrgarh, a cluster of houses by the river Bolan in northwest India. The houses were square or rectangular, and built of mud bricks plastered with mud. The flat roofs were made of reed thatch supported on long wooden poles. Inside, there were several rooms. Thick walls and small windows kept

▲ RICE FARMER
When the people had worked out how to cultivate the waterlogged fields of southern China and Southeast Asia, rice became the staple crop of these areas.

the houses warm in winter and cool in summer. The style remained much the same for the next 1,000 years.

Communities like Mehrgarh grew. People built storehouses for grain to ensure a reserve when supplies became short. Some members of the community grew rich, perhaps by trading. Their graves contain favorite possessions, such as beads of shell or limestone.

Meanwhile, agriculture was developing in China. Here, millet was the favored crop, and the pig was the

SUCCESSFUL FARMERS

Successful farmers could grow more food than they needed and could therefore trade with their neighbors. They began to own luxury items such as jewelry and finer, decorated pots. When archaeologists excavate items like these, they know that they must have belonged to a very wealthy person.

◄ WATER JAR
An amphora jar, from Banpo, China, has a narrow neck, which means that it was designed to hold liquid. A rope was threaded between the two loop handles so that it could be carried easily, and rested on a stand or embedded upright in the soil.

◄ POTTERY LID
This decorative lid, with a knob in the shape of a human face, was found at Banshan, a farming village in northwest China. It is around 8 inches across and is an example of the kind of items owned by people who were rich or had high social rank.

▶ YANGSHAO POTTERY
Later Chinese farmers, around 3000B.C., produced several different styles of pottery. One type, called Yangshao, is finely painted, like these two decorated bowls.

first creature to be domesticated. Farmers also grew vegetables, such as cabbages, and harvested fruit, such as plums. Later, they began to grow rice, which became the staple in most of eastern Asia. Rice was especially successful in southern China, where the ground was wetter.

Chinese farmers quickly learned that their soils needed a rest after a season of cultivation. They developed a method of farming that switched from one field to another. This allowed the land to have a fallow period, in which the land was not plowed or sown. They found that by leaving a long fallow period between periods of growing, the land could be restored. Much later, around 1100B.C., they began to alternate crops of millet and soy beans. The bean plants brought goodness back to the soil, so that it was less important to have a fallow period.

Techniques of farming spread steadily across China. Wet farming techniques needed for rice were passed from south to north, along with strains of rice that grew more successfully in the north. China also had contact with Korea and Japan. These two areas had successful hunting and fishing communities. Agriculture did not become established there until much later.

straw thatch

plastered wall

supporting pole

central hearth

▲ FARMER'S HUT, BANPO
Chinese archaeologists found the remains of a cluster of houses belonging to the early farming community of Banpo in northern China, dating from about 6000B.C. The buildings were oblong or round. They were built with a stout wooden framework filled in with a basketweave of thin branches. This was plastered over to make a smooth, weather-resistant wall. Thatch covered the roofs, but there was a central hole to let smoke escape from the fire in the floor below.

wooden poles support reed thatch

▲ MUD-BRICK HOUSE
One of India's oldest farming villages is Mehrgarh, by the river Bolan in northwest India. The houses are mostly square, have several rooms, and are made of plastered mud bricks.

▼ BURIAL
The dead at Mehrgarh in northwest India were buried in free areas in the village itself. The bodies were positioned on their sides, their knees bent. Grave goods were placed with them. Rich people's graves contained items such as stone and shell beads.

Key Dates

- 7000B.C. Barley growing begins in India.

- 6000B.C. Indian farmers build storehouses for their surplus food.

- 6000B.C. Millet is the main crop of farmers in northern China.

- 5500B.C. Date palms are cultivated in Mesopotamia.

- 5500B.C. Indian farmers produce their own strains of wheat.

- 5000B.C. Farmers of the Yangtze Delta area cultivate rice.

- 3500B.C. Trade networks link the regions of China.

- 3000B.C. Millet grown in Korea.

The Americas

▲ DEER FIGURE
People of southwestern North America made figures like this split-twig deer. These figures date to a period after 3500 B.C. and are often found near hunters' weapons and equipment.

Whether they were fishing or harpooning seals in the far north, hunting buffalo on the Great Plains, or gathering food in the south, the people of the Americas followed the food supply. Because crops grew in the least extreme weather conditions, they also had to move with the seasons. They became used to a restless life.

In Central America, environmental changes were often fast and unpredictable. Torrential rain was followed by baking sun. The people here longed for more control over their food supply, and they turned to agriculture before the rest of the Americas. However, they still needed good weather for their crops, which is perhaps why so many of them worshiped gods of rain and sun. The farmers hoped that worshiping these deities would bring them the most favorable conditions throughout the agricultural year.

One of the earliest crops in Central America was corn (maize), a plant that has been important in American farming ever since. It was developed from a

▲ HUT AND HUNTER
In eastern North America, hunters often built short-term shelters, like this hut. They made a framework of thin wooden poles, joined together at the top. This they covered with grass. Huts like this could catch fire easily, so the hearth was outside.

local wild grass called teosinte. Farmers tried different varieties, choosing the plants that grew best in local conditions. This proved a successful approach, and maize farming spread quite quickly.

Farther north, in what is now the southwestern United States, the first farmers experimented with various types of gourd and with plants such as sunflower and sumpweed. As the farmers of Central America began to trade more widely, they took their

AMERICAN FARMERS

The Americas contain a variety of different climates and environments, all with their own native plant species. For the early farmers, the challenge was to choose the best plants for their own region. Often this was simply a question of selecting from local species that were known to do well. But sometimes an imported crop, such as cotton in southern North America, was a success.

◄ POTATOES
Between 3000–2500 B.C., farmers in the hills of the Andes were growing the potato. For thousands of years, this useful root crop was grown only in South America, and many varieties of potato are still found only in the Andes.

▲ STONE WEIGHTS
Hunters in Kentucky attached these stone weights to the handles of their spear-throwers. This made their spears travel much farther and faster. As a result, when a spear hit an animal it was much more powerful.

◄ CLAY FIGURINE
Mysterious statuettes like this one have been found in numerous North American settlements. They have little in the way of modeling or facial features, so it is impossible to tell whether they represent male or female figures. They are made of clay and decorated with lines and dots. The clay was not fired, though; it simply became hard with age. No one knows what these figures were for.

domesticated maize, beans, and squash with them, and these joined the local plants to become staple crops in the north. For many people in the southwest, the plants were a welcome addition to foraged foods.

In South America people tried to cultivate a variety of crops, including gourds, squashes, manioc, potatoes, and various types of bean. In each area, they selected the best plants for local conditions and tried different growing methods over thousands of years. The region where farming caught on most quickly was Peru. In the Andes Mountains, hunter-gatherers began to grow crops such as gourds and beans to add to their existing

▼ RIVER TRANSPORTATION
Simple wooden canoes provided transportation along North America's rivers. There were various ways of making these. They could be "dug-outs," made by hollowing out a log. Another design was made of thin tree bark attached to a wooden frame.

diet. They carried on using this mixed form of food supply for many thousands of years.

In the coastal areas, rivers had created narrow valleys as they flowed off the mountains to the sea. In the rich soil found in these valleys, people began to grow squashes and peppers, to which they later added maize. They also developed methods of irrigation to bring water from the rivers to their fields.

Animal farming was at first less popular in the Americas than in other parts of the world. There were few native species that were easy to farm. But in the Andes Mountains one species, the llama, was valued for its wool and milk, as well as being used as a beast of burden. The people of the Americas developed a variety of crops and farming techniques, but in many places wild foods were still widely available, and many groups carried on their lifestyle of hunting and gathering.

▼ SUNFLOWERS
This giant member of the daisy family is found mainly in North America. Farmers prized it for its seeds, which can be eaten. Later they learned how to extract the oil from the seeds, using it for cooking. Some species also have edible roots.

▶ COTTON
This valuable crop was first cultivated in two separate areas, Peru and Ecuador in South America and Mexico in North America. From Mexico, traders took it farther north, where farmers in the Southwest later began to grow the plant.

Key Dates

- 8500 B.C. Agriculture established in Peru. Crops grown include squash, beans, and grasses.

- 7000 B.C. In Central America people gather avocado, chillies, squash, and beans. These are plants farmers will begin to cultivate in the next 2,000 years.

- 6300 B.C. Farmers in Peru grow various root crops, such as oca and ulluco.

- 5400 B.C. The use of llamas for wool, milk and transportation is found in the Andes.

- 5000 B.C. Mexican farmers grow maize.

- 5000 B.C. Domesticated plants of Central America, such as the bottle gourd, begin to spread to North America.

Hunting and Gathering

▲ GIRAFFE
Artists painted both farm animals and the hunters' favorite quarry on the walls of rock shelters in the Sahara Desert. The giraffe was one of the creatures that people living in Africa both herded and hunted during prehistoric times.

FARMING WAS NOT FOR everyone. Hunting and gathering can provide a steady, reliable source of food as long as there are not too many people living in a small area. Africa is one part of the world where some peoples made the change to farming while others continued to hunt and gather for much longer.

After the final Ice Age, the Sahara was a much damper, greener environment than it is today. It became the scene for some of Africa's earliest experiments in farming. Rock paintings show how the people began to herd cattle, together with other local species such as giraffe.

When the Sahara dried out and gradually turned to desert, most agricultural activity was pushed to the south, between the Sahara and the Equator. This was where the climate allowed farmers to develop crops such as yam and

sorghum, a cereal crop that was suited to warm places. This area became the heartland of African farming.

Still farther south, people carried on hunting and gathering. They ate a number of local plants, especially various palms and a shrub called bauhinia. In addition, they found out how to use other plants for more specialized purposes. A good example was the bottle gourd, which was suitable for making into containers.

The African hunter-gatherers also improved their tools. To make knives, they used tiny blades of sharp flint, which they glued into wooden handles using natural tree resin. They also carved hooks from bone for fishing. Such uses of the materials around them show how highly adapted they were to their environment.

Australia was another place where the traditional lifestyle of hunting and gathering continued. To begin with,

◀ ZULU HUNTER
Today, some African peoples still get some of their food by hunting, but now their spears are tipped with metal rather than the stone of earlier times.

USEFUL SPECIES

The early hunter-gatherers of Africa and Australia had a vast knowledge of plants. When they came across a new species they would try it out. This was a dangerous process, as many plants were poisonous. They gradually discovered plants that were good to eat and others that worked as medicines. Modern scientists are still investigating the plant medicines used by the world's hunter-gatherer peoples.

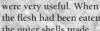

◀ GOURD
Some species of gourd were very useful. When the flesh had been eaten, the outer shells made excellent containers. People made bowls with the larger fruit, while using smaller ones to make items such as dippers and cups.

◀ ALMONDS
Nuts, such as almonds, that are native to North Africa and the Middle East, are a nutritious food. Gatherers made a point of going to the forest when they were in season. Nuts are easy to store and contain plenty of energy-building protein, useful to hunter-gatherers when meat is in short supply.

▶ JUNIPER BERRIES
Gatherers soon knew everything about the plants in their area. They discovered that some plants, though not good to eat, had other useful properties. Berries such as juniper, which grows all over the northern hemisphere, were valued for their perfume and their use in medicine.

people stayed near the coast, living on fish, eels, and, especially, shellfish. Remains of the shells, left in dumps that archaeologists call middens, have been found along both the north and southeast coasts. As time went on, the native Australians explored the river valleys, moving gradually inland. People discovered that cereal plants such as millet made good food. They developed hunting skills that enabled them to survive when they moved even farther inland toward Australia's hot and dry interior.

The early Australians traveled for miles, exchanging tools and shell jewelry, and creating the beautiful rock art, which can still be found all over the country. As they did this, they were also developing a complex series of myths about their ancestry that reflected their hunting and gathering lifestyle. Most important of all are the stories of Dreamtime, the period when the earth and the spirits of people were created. These myths held, and still hold, great religious significance for native Australians, and they reveal a people of profound beliefs.

▲ HUNTER-GATHERERS
This group of hunter-gatherers have found an area rich in food and have made a camp with a brushwood shelter that they will occupy for weeks or even months. While two men butcher the antelope they have killed, another group of people returns from gathering vegetables and wood for the fire on which they will cook the meat.

▶ ENGRAVED PEARL SHELL
In societies that did not use metals, all sorts of items were adapted for use as jewelry. This ornament, engraved with abstract designs, was made by native Australians from a piece of pearl shell.

◀ BARK PAINTING
A hunter throws his spear at a crane in this bark painting from Australia's Northern Territory. This style of painting is known as "x-ray," because the designs on the crane depict the bird's insides.

Key Dates

- 10,000B.C. Obsidian, a type of volcanic glass, used to make tools in the Rift Valley area of eastern Africa.

- 9000B.C. People move into the Sahara region; increased rainfall allows grasslands to grow along the edges of what is now desert.

- 7000B.C. African communities in the Sahara begin making pottery.

- 6000B.C. People start herding cattle in some parts of the Sahara region.

- 4000B.C. Sahara reaches its wettest, most temperate conditions, with Lake Chad at its largest.

- 3500B.C. Ostrich eggshell beads become popular as necklaces in eastern Africa.

The First Metalworkers

▲ GOLD BULL
The settlement of Varna, on the Black Sea, was one of Europe's first metal-working sites. Hundreds of gold ornaments, bracelets and beads have been discovered there.

As they created art on surfaces in caves, ancient peoples must have seen gold. They would also have seen copper, as it has a greenish tinge in the rock. Deposits of metal in rock are rare and difficult to extract. It was a long time before anyone worked out how to remove the material and then to work it into something useful. Eventually, someone found a place where there was enough metal to remove and found that it could be hammered into shape. Metal was beaten into ornamental objects such as beads, which were soon highly valued.

When craftworkers started to make pottery, they built kilns that could reach temperatures as high as 1,470°F. Before long, they found that heating certain rocks, or ores, in the kiln melted the metal they contained, so that it could be poured off and collected. They had discovered the process called smelting. This made it possible to extract much larger amounts of metal from the ore. People could make all kinds of items, such as jewelry and tools, out of copper instead

▲ BRONZE AGE SETTLEMENT
Most of the people of Bronze Age Europe lived in small villages with thatched houses, like those built by the first farmers. An area would be set aside for metalworking away from the houses, so that there was less risk of fire.

THE MAGIC OF METAL

The first metals must have seemed like magic. By heating the ore, the metalworker could make metal appear, apparently out of nowhere. It would first be seen in hot, liquid form, then it would miraculously set when it cooled. Copper and gold glittered beautifully in the light, so people found these metals very attractive.

▼ LONG-HORNED OXEN
Small, precious objects, such as pieces of jewelry, were among the first items to be made of metal, because they did not use too much of it. Early metalworkers could produce work of great skill, as these copper oxen found in Poland show.

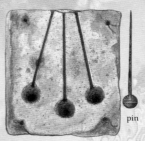

mold

pin

◀ MOLD AND PIN
A Bronze Age mold and matching pin show how the process of casting could be used to produce a number of items at speed—in this case three pins at the same time. The small holes at each corner would have matched with bumps in the other half of the mold, to ensure a perfect fit.

▶ COPPER AND TIN
The first important alloy was bronze, a mix of copper and tin. Tin is not common, so bronze developed slowly where there were good tin deposits—China, the Middle East, and parts of France, Germany, and Britain.

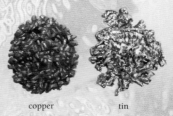

copper

tin

▶ CASTING

Metal items, such as tools and weapons, could be made by casting. The metalworker prepared a stone mold in two parts that fitted together exactly. When the halves were joined and secured with twine, the hollow inside the mold had the shape of the object to be cast. Hot molten metal was poured into the mold through a hole in the top. When the metal had cooled and set, the metalworker took the mold apart to reveal the object. The same mold could be used again and again.

of other materials. There was still a problem, however. Metals such as gold and copper were easy to work, but they were soft. They made good jewelry, but poor tools. The solution was to combine one metal with another to make an alloy that was hard-wearing. The best alloy discovered in the ancient world was bronze. This was made by mixing copper with a little tin. It was tough, quite easy to work, had a pleasant, gold-colored appearance, and could be sharpened.

Bronze became a popular material for jewelry, tools, and weapons. Sometimes, once a metalworker had smelted some copper and mixed in some tin, he would let the molten metal set into a bar and then hammer it into shape. Liquid metal can also be cast in a mold to produce all sorts of complex shapes. Casting was popular because it was easy to produce many identical items using the same mould. However, since hammering hardened the metal, this method was still used to make objects such as weapons, which had to be very strong.

Metal technology probably began in the Middle East around 3000B.C., and spread to other parts of the world during the next 2,000 years. The development of bronzeworking is so important that historians sometimes call this period the Bronze Age. Bronze did not reach all parts of the world. There was no Bronze Age in Australia, South America, or many parts of Africa. In such places, although people may have used gold or copper occasionally, they mostly made do with the stone technology they had developed. They had to wait until the coming of iron before they could take full advantage of metals.

▲ THE SPREAD OF COPPER IN EUROPE

In Europe, copper working began in two main centers, Iberia (southern Spain) and the Balkans, where plenty of the metal was available. From these centers, archaeologists have mapped and dated discoveries of bronze objects. This gives a rough idea of how knowledge of the craft spread across the European continent.

Key Dates

- 9000B.C. Copper used in some parts of Asia for tools and weapons.

- 6000B.C. Smelting and casting are developed in the Middle East and southeastern Europe.

- 4000B.C. Knowledge of metalworking begins spreading to Europe, Asia, and North Africa.

- 3000B.C. Bronze technology develops in the Middle East.

- 3000–1000B.C. Better trade routes enable bronzeworking techniques to spread across much of Europe.

- 2000B.C. Bronzeworking develops in China.

- 2000B.C. Bronze is used widely in Asia for everyday tools and weapons.

Megaliths

▲ NIGHT SKY
People have always looked to the sky in their religion. Most stone circles and rows of standing stones are arranged to line up with the Sun, Moon, or stars.

Towering standing stones, massive stone circles, and vast rows of stones are the most awesome of all prehistoric remains. Some of them are so huge that no one knows how Bronze Age people ever managed to build them. Because they are so big, they are known as megaliths, a term that comes from two Greek words meaning huge stones.

Another mystery is exactly what these vast monuments were for. Archaeologists think they may have been used for religious ceremonies. The stones are often lined up with yearly movements of the Sun and stars, so the ceremonies were almost certainly linked to the calendar and the seasons. They may have been fertility ceremonies, relating the crop-growing season to the annual movements of the stars.

There are two famous groups of megaliths in Europe, one on England's Salisbury Plain, the other in Brittany, France. Many of the British monuments are stone circles the most famous are at Stonehenge and Avebury. The main monument in Brittany is a series of rows, or alignments, of stones near the village of Carnac. In both cases there are many other prehistoric monuments nearby, such as smaller circles and alignments, earthworks, burial mounds, and single standing stones. Together these structures make up

▲ BUILDING STONEHENGE
Stonehenge in Wiltshire, England, the greatest of all the stone circles, was built with the simplest technology. The builders probably used sleds or rollers to move the stones, each weighing about 40 tons, about 15 miles to the site, before heaving them into place with a combination of ropes and levers.

THE CHANGING MONUMENTS

The megalithic monuments of Europe have stood for thousands of years, but they have not always looked the same. Archaeologists have found many holes in the ground where additional stones and wooden posts once stood, making these sites even more complex than they are today. The monuments were also altered throughout prehistory, with the removal of some stones and the addition of others.

◄ DOLMEN
Groups of stones like this are called dolmens. They started out covered with earth as the chambers of prehistoric burial mounds. When the mound was moved or eroded away, the roof and its supports were left.

▲ CALLANISH STONE CIRCLE
This is quite a small circle of 13 tall, thin stones. It is in the Hebrides islands, off Scotland, and is at the focal point of lines of standing stones. The stones, some of which are 15 feet high, were quarried only a short distance away from the site. Archaeologists have calculated that each of the stones could have been dragged along by about 20 people.

▶ FESTIVAL AT AVEBURY
Another British stone circle, at Avebury in Wiltshire, may been the scene of an annual harvest or farming festival like the one shown here. The form of the ritual is unknown, but there were probably processions, offerings, and observations of the stars or Moon.

entire regions that would have been known as holy places, landscapes devoted to religion.

The builders of the megalithic monuments had to move and lift huge stones, dig long ditches, and pile up enormous mounds of earth. Yet the people of the Bronze Age had no complex machinery, only rollers, levers, ropes, and simple hand tools. It must have taken the labor of hundreds of people over many years to move the stones. Clearly, a great deal of organization was needed, and probably a ruler with enough power to keep everyone at work on the task. Planning was also important, so that the builders could work out the precise positions for the stones. These vast temples suggest that Bronze Age societies were far more advanced than you would expect, considering the simple tools they had.

◀ MEGALITHIC SITES
Britain, Ireland and northern France are the main areas where megalithic monuments can be found. This probably shows that the people of these three areas were in regular contact, traveling across the English Channel and Irish Sea, when the megaliths were erected. They must have had similar religious beliefs and ceremonies, although we now know very little about these. There were once many more megaliths, but in the 1700s and 1800s farmers cleared away large numbers of these monuments from their fields.

Key Dates

- 4000B.C. Ditched enclosures common in many parts of Europe.

- 4000B.C. Long barrows and megalithic tombs become common for high-status burials in Europe.

- 3200B.C. People in Europe begin to build stone circles.

- 3000B.C. In Europe, much land is cleared for agriculture.

- 2100B.C. Stones added to a site originally made up of ditches and earth banks make Stonehenge Britain's biggest megalithic site.

- 1500B.C. The age of stone circles and standing stones comes to an end.

Lake Villages

▲ POTTERY
The lake village people used lots of pottery vessels. Some were narrow-necked, like this jug, which was made for carrying water.

THE SHORES OF ALPINE LAKES in Europe are made up of bogs and marshland. They are difficult to cross and very hard to build on. Yet archaeologists have discovered the remains of several hundred Bronze Age villages in the European Alps. The small settlements, with their simple wooden houses, were in the middle of swamps by the shores of lakes such as Constance and Neuchâtel, on the borders of modern Switzerland, France, and Germany. Why did people put up with damp, boggy conditions?

The lakes themselves were rich in fish, which could be dried or smoked, to preserve them for times when food was less plentiful. Some way beyond the lake shores was grassland, which provided grazing for animals. The foothills of the Alps were thickly forested, offering a good supply of wood for building and fuel. Most important of all, the swampy conditions made it very easy to defend the villages against enemies.

Many villages sprang up by the lakes. People cut down trees from the alpine foothills to build their houses. Roofs were thatched with reeds from the lakesides. Each house was raised above the marsh with stout wooden poles rammed deep into the earth. Wood was also used to make pathways across the swamp and to build strong fences around each village. Most villages

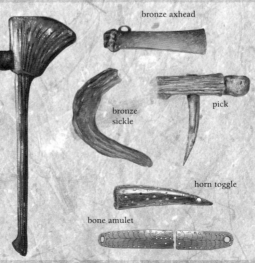

TOOLS FOR THE JOB

In prehistoric times, most of the lakeside region of Europe was wooded right down to the lake shores. So, before they could start building homes, the villagers had to clear away some of the trees and prepare logs for building. For this, they needed heavy stone axes with long wooden handles. Once they were settled, they could use lighter metal tools for everyday work in the fields and around the village.

▶ AX HANDLE
Waterlogged soil near the Swiss lakes has preserved ancient wooden objects, such as this ax handle. This gives us knowledge of craft skills that we lack for most prehistoric peoples.

bronze axhead

bronze sickle

pick

horn toggle

bone amulet

◀ TOOL KIT
After about 2000 B.C., the alpine lake people started to use bronze to make many of their tools. Axes for chopping and sickles for harvesting were two typical metal items. There were also picks with bone or antler handles.

◀ BONE AND HORN
Many items were made of these materials. Animal horn was a good material to make toggles to fasten coats and tunics. Bone could be carved into all sorts of shapes, including fastenings and pierced objects which may have been sacred charms.

were quite small, with up to 20 houses. Eventually, after 30 or 40 years, the wet ground made the poles supporting the houses rot. Either they were replaced or the people moved on to another site.

Trapped deep beneath the water, however, an amazing amount of evidence of these villages has been preserved. Archaeologists have brought to the surface some of the timbers from the houses and pathways, as well as bronze implements. In some cases even remains of the people's food and clothing have survived, preserved in the cold water.

Some of the settlements had at least one large house. This was probably the home of the village chief. Archaeologists have found decorated bronze weapons and jewelry in these houses, showing that these chiefs were rich and powerful.

▼ ON THE LAKESHORE

This view of a prehistoric lake village shows how close the inhabitants were to the resources they needed to live—reeds and fish in the lake itself, timber from the forests, and fertile fields nearby. For communities like this, easy access to these resources made it worthwhile to build in such a difficult, marshy area.

▼ LAKESIDE VILLAGE

Sites near lakes have always proved popular in places such as Austria, Switzerland, and their neighboring countries. Places such as Zurich, Neuchâtel, Lausanne, and Konstanz are all built by large lakes. Many of these modern towns and cities are built on the sites of prehistoric lake villages. The picture shows a lakeside village in the Austrian Alps. Today, many people like to visit lakeside sites because of the stunning scenery.

▲ REEDS

For thatched roofs, by far the best material is reed. It is strong and long-lasting and grows in abundance along the edges of lakes.

Key Dates

- 3000B.C. Trading villages well established on the shores of the Black Sea; the inhabitants work copper and gold and trade along the local rivers.

- 3000B.C. People settle along the shores of lakes in Europe's alpine region.

- 2000B.C. Substantial wooden villages are built by the settlers in alpine areas. The people purposely select sites that are easy to defend and learn how to fortify their villages with boundary fences.

- 1600B.C. The heyday of the lake villages comes to an end.

The Iron Age

BRONZE WAS A USEFUL METAL, but it was not as hard as stone. Neither was it always easy to find the copper and tin needed to make it. Many people carried on using flint tools and weapons. Then, in around 1300B.C., some metalworkers in the Middle East discovered iron.

Iron is a common metal in many parts of the world. It is easy to smelt, provided that the temperature in the furnace is high enough. It can be sharpened easily and can be strengthened by hammering. When metalworkers first began to smelt iron, they did not realize it was a common material. Because it was new and unusual, it was used for weapons carried by high-ranking men such as chiefs. Soon, however, they saw how common and useful iron was and began to make iron tools and weapons in large numbers.

Ironworking gradually spread throughout the Middle East and into southern Europe. Iron weapons helped empire-building peoples,

▲ IRON DAGGER
Forged from iron and carried in a bronze sheath, this British dagger probably belonged to an important person such as a chief. It dates from the time when European society was led by warriors.

such as the Hittites of Turkey, to conquer new territory. They helped the Greeks, who were building colonies around the Mediterranean, in much the same way. In India, where the people had found little copper, iron

▼ IRON AGE SETTLEMENT
When the people of Iron Age Europe built a fort, they defended it by building deep ditches. The earth from the ditches was thrown up to make massive banks, giving extra protection. Forts like this covered a huge area, with enough space for people, houses, and animals.

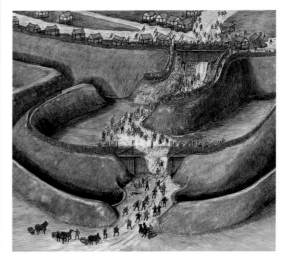

REMAINS FROM THE IRON AGE

Many of the most impressive remains from the Iron Age are actually made of bronze. Iron tools and weapons were made in large numbers, but most have rusted away. Bronze objects, on the other hand, are longer lasting, even if buried in the ground. As a result, many bronze items, buried in the graves of high-ranking chieftains, have survived.

◀ ▼ BROOCHES
Iron Age people fastened their clothes with brooches, which were usually made of bronze and could be very ornate. The fibula style had a long pin that worked like a modern safety pin.

▶ LA TÈNE HORN
The curving, swirling lines of the decoration on the end of this horn are typical of the Celtic La Tène style, which developed during the late Iron Age in Europe. It is one of four horns made of bronze found in an Irish lake.

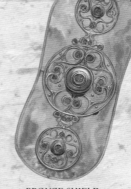

▲ BRONZE SHIELD
A shield, found in Battersea, London, was decorated by hammering the metal to make raised patterns. Colored glass and stones were added.

fibula brooch

spectacle brooch

detail of trumpet end

made metal technology widely available for the very first time.

In Europe, iron transformed people's lives. It enabled the Celtic people, who lived in western Europe, to become warlike and powerful. They built large hill forts, protected by earthworks and fences, and fought off attackers with iron weapons. A whole village could fit into one hill fort, and these forts became bases for warrior chiefs.

The first phase of the European Iron Age is known as the Halstatt period, after a site in Austria where a number of iron swords were found. Halstatt chiefs grew rich, both from trading and from forcing neighbors to pay them tribute. Some chiefs even owned goods imported from as far away as Greece and Italy.

After about the 5th century B.C., the Celts began to produce metalwork beautifully decorated in a free, swirling style. This style is called La Tène, after the Swiss lakeside site where archaeologists have found many iron and bronze items.

By the time the Romans were building up their empire in Europe, the Celts were powerful enough to fight the Romans' armies and halt them for a while. The Celtic chiefs issued their own coinage, built strong forts, and traded with Rome in times of peace. For several centuries, these men of iron were Europe's strongest and most feared leaders.

▲ IRONWORKERS
In order to produce workable iron, the ore (the rock containing the metal) had to be heated to a high temperature. Early ironworkers made kilns of earth to contain the fire so that it could build up enough heat.

▲ IRON AGE SITES
Although Europe has perhaps the most famous of all Iron Age cultures, people in many other parts of the world discovered how to work iron. Eastern Asia and Africa were two areas that had notable Iron Age societies.

Key Dates

- 1300 B.C. Middle Eastern people discover iron and make iron tools and weapons.

- 1000 B.C. Ironworking established in central Europe.

- 800 B.C. Beginning of Halstatt period.

- 600 B.C. Iron discovered in China; hotter furnaces enable the Chinese to cast iron, something impossible in the west until much later.

- 500 B.C. Ironworking begins in Africa.

- 500 B.C. Ironworking well established in most of Europe.

- 450–100 B.C. Fine metalwork of the La Tène period made in Europe.

The Birth of Civilization

▲ PAINTED POT
Pottery from the Mesopotamian cities is often of a very high quality: thin, well shaped, and with elegant decoration.

WHILE MANY OF THE EVENTS described in this book were happening, another development, more earth-shattering than all the rest, was beginning at different points on the globe. Small towns were growing into cities. Their inhabitants were putting up large temples and palaces, inventing written languages, and creating complex societies in which there were many different jobs for people to do. There were farmers, craftworkers, priests, governors, and kings. This new city-based way of life is what we now call civilization.

The place where civilization first began was Mesopotamia, the land between the Tigris and Euphrates rivers in what is now Iraq. This was part of the Fertile Crescent, where farming had started. It was the reliable food supply produced by farming that made the developments that followed possible.

As the farmers became more experienced, they worked out how to irrigate their fields so that they could bring water to the drier areas. This made the food supply more constant. The farmers could also increase

◀ WOMAN AND BABY
This figure of a mother holding a baby is made of clay. It dates from the 'Ubaid period, which lasted from 5500 to 4000 B.C. At this time, towns were growing into cities, craftworkers were becoming more and more skilled, and local leaders were gaining in power.

the size of their fields by cultivating previously difficult areas.

At the same time, the people of Mesopotamia began to build large, comfortable mud brick houses. They created beautiful painted pottery, fine clay sculptures, intricate copper implements, and elegant jewelry with turquoise beads. People from other areas wanted these items, so the Mesopotamians traded with their neighbors, carrying their cargo by boat down the rivers and along the Persian Gulf. Gradually, the traders of Mesopotamia became rich, and their towns grew into cities. With cities came more power and more complex government. The priests, who were among the most powerful people, built bigger temples, another mark of civilization. Then came writing. At first, this was only a few simple symbols to show who

ARTS OF CIVILIZATION

One of the features of civilization was that society became more complex. In other words, it was divided into more social classes, with more powerful leaders and more difference between rich and poor. The rich people demanded better, more luxurious goods, from pots to jewelry, and in Mesopotamia this led to the growth of arts and crafts. Pottery, metalworking, building, and sculpture are all crafts that developed quickly at this time.

◀ POTTERY FRAGMENTS
Ancient rubbish heaps are treasure troves for archaeologists. Many pieces of broken pottery have been unearthed from the 'Ubaid period, from 5500 B.C. to 4000 B.C. They often have striking painted decoration.

◀ NECKLACES
Mesopotamian necklaces could have thousands of beads in several separate strings. The large one, found at a farming site called Choga Mami, has around 2,200 beads, crudely shaped from clay.

◀ WRITING
The scribes of Mesopotamia wrote by making marks in clay tablets with a wedge-shaped reed. This writing is called cuneiform, from a Greek word meaning wedge.

▶ HEAD FROM STATUETTE
Terracotta heads like these show the style of sculpture in Mesopotamia, with some features, such as the eyes, enlarged.

owned what. Later people developed more complicated writing systems that enabled people to record stories and religious texts.

The development of writing marks the end of prehistoric society. This happened at different times in different parts of the world. During the lifetimes of some of the prehistoric peoples, civilization was already present in Mesopotamia and other parts of the globe. Civilization came early to the Middle East, Egypt, the Indus Valley in India, and parts of China. Elsewhere, in Europe, North and South America and much of Africa, societies based on cities came much later.

In western Europe, for example, it was only with the arrival of the Romans that cities and writing appeared. The Romans took over the area they called Gaul (modern France) in the 1st century B.C., some 3,000 years after the first cities were built in Mesopotamia. Today, people in some parts of the world lead successful traditional lifestyles, adapted to their environment, just like their prehistoric ancestors. But even they are affected by the decisions of governments and businesses based in the world's cities.

▼ 'UBAID HOUSE
Houses, like this one in modern Iraq, became larger and more complex in the 'Ubaid Period. They were still made of mud bricks, but had a large central hall, many smaller rooms, a staircase, and drainage into open gullies outside.

roof of plaster covering rushes on wooden poles

mud-brick staircase

main central room

smoothly plastered floor

open drain

▲ MARSH ARABS
These Marsh Arabs live in southeastern Iraq. They herd water buffalo and build houses out of reeds. This traditional lifestyle of the Marsh Arabs existed alongside the growing cities of Mesopotamia.

▼ ZIGGURAT
A Sumerian ziggurat consisted of a stepped platform made of sun-dried mud bricks. Only priests were allowed to climb to the top. An early example of a ziggurat is the White Temple of Uruk, made of whitewashed bricks, which dates back to the late 3000s B.C.

Key Dates

- 3500 B.C. The first cities are built in Mesopotamia. Among the most important are Uruk and Ur on the banks of the Euphrates River.

- 3200 B.C. Civilization spreads to Egypt.

- 3100 B.C. Writing is developed in and around the city of Uruk; people write on clay tablets.

- 2500 B.C. The first cities are built in the Indus Valley, Pakistan.

- 2300 B.C. Several of the Mesopotamian cities unite as a single kingdom under Sargon of Agade.

- 1800 B.C. Civilization develops separately in northern China.

ANCIENT CIVILIZATIONS

BY PHILIP BROOKS

Evidence of the first civilizations can be found in many forms, from tomb treasures in Egypt to amazing temples in Mexico. This section goes back in time to discover the amazing cultures of the ancient world.

The Dawn of Civilization

W HAT IS A CIVILIZATION? The term comes from the Latin word, *civis*, which means "citizen of a city". So a civilization is a group of people living together in a large town or city, who have developed a culture — a way of life with its own special flavor. There are several key ingredients in a civilized culture. An early civilization may not have all of them, but it will certainly have some. They include writing, a system of government, organized religion and the ability to construct buildings and monuments on a grand scale. *Ancient Civilizations* describes some ancient cultures that developed along these lines.

Most of the features of civilization began to develop thousands of years ago during the Stone Age. But it took a long time for people to bring all these ideas together and to build cities on a large scale. This happened at different times in different parts of the world, as is shown on the Timeline below.

No one knows why civilizations occurred in some parts of the world much earlier than others. But cities can only grow when the food supply is reliable enough to supply the town-dwellers, who have no way of growing their own food. People had to develop

▲ BUILDINGS
The magnificent royal palace of Persepolis was built in ancient Persia's greatest city to reflect power and wealth.

▼ TIMELINE
The civilizations of the ancient world cover a vast time span of about 4500 years: from the first cities of Sumer to the later kingdoms based in Africa.

▲ RELIGION
This stone carving from the Indus Valley civilization may have been a god or a king. As far as we know, all ancient civilizations had some form of organized religion.

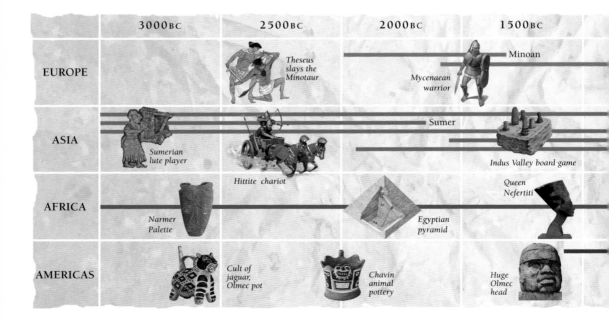

	3000 BC	2500 BC	2000 BC	1500 BC
EUROPE		Theseus slays the Minotaur	Mycenaean warrior	Minoan
ASIA	Sumerian lute player	Hittite chariot	Sumer	Indus Valley board game
AFRICA	Narmer Palette		Egyptian pyramid	Queen Nefertiti
AMERICAS	Cult of jaguar, Olmec pot	Chavin animal pottery		Huge Olmec head

efficient farming, and ways of storing and trading food, before they could build large cities. Trade in food also provided a network for trading the products of city workshops — items made of pottery, metal, and wood which city people sold.

Many ancient civilizations built up large empires, either by conquering their neighbors in battle or by building up trade networks which allowed them to dominate the surrounding peoples. This meant that many ancient cultures became rich, and their power spread over a large area of the globe. The Roman empire and the empire of Alexander the Great are two examples.

Civilizations such as these have left large amounts of evidence behind them. Archaeologists — people who study the remains of cultures — are still digging up artefacts made by craft workers thousands of years ago. Complex funeral customs, as in ancient Egypt, can tell us a great deal about the civilization. Together with ancient documents and the remains of ancient cities, these things provide a fascinating glimpse of how life was lived thousands of years ago.

▲ WRITING
The marks on this ancient bone are the earliest examples of Chinese script. Writing is a key feature of a civilization.

▶ TRADE
The Romans traded in ships such as this. As civilizations developed and produced a surplus of goods, they set up trading links with others.

▲ FARMING
A civilization can only develop when its food supply is secure and the growing of crops is not left to chance. Evidence shows that rice was cultivated in China around 5000BC. Rice farming arrived in Japan in about 200BC.

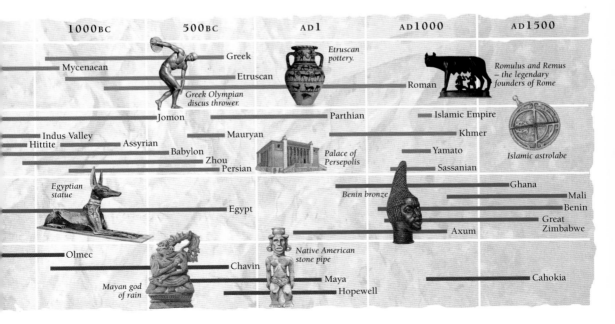

| 1000BC | 500BC | AD1 | AD1000 | AD1500 |

Greek
Mycenaean
Greek Olympian discus thrower.
Etruscan
Etruscan pottery.
Roman
Romulus and Remus – the legendary founders of Rome

Jomon
Parthian
Islamic Empire
Khmer
Islamic astrolabe

Indus Valley
Hittite
Assyrian
Mauryan
Babylon
Zhou
Persian
Palace of Persepolis
Yamato
Sassanian

Ghana
Mali
Benin

Egyptian statue
Benin bronze
Egypt
Axum
Great Zimbabwe

Olmec
Chavin
Native American stone pipe
Mayan god of rain
Maya
Hopewell
Cahokia

The Sumerians

HOME TO THOUSANDS of people and bustling with activity, the world's first cities were built in Mesopotamia, the land between the Tigris and Euphrates rivers in what is now Iraq. The narrow streets and whitewashed mud-brick houses of cities such as Uruk and Ur were home to craftworkers who made pottery and metalwork that were traded as far afield as Arabia and India. People from the region made the world's first wheeled carts and chariots, and invented the world's first known writing system, called "cuneiform" script. For these reasons, Mesopotamia became known as "the cradle of civilization".

One group of people to settle in Mesopotamia were the Sumerians. They arrived in Sumer, the southern part of the area, in about 5000BC. The climate was hot and dry but farmers learned to use water from the rivers to irrigate their fields and grow plentiful crops of wheat, barley, dates and vegetables.

The Sumerians' first city was Uruk, which they built by the River Euphrates. By 3500BC, some 10,000 people lived there. The winding streets of the city surrounded its biggest building, the temple of Anu, the greatest of the Sumerians' many gods. Here the priests worshipped Anu in the hope that he would bring good weather and rich harvests. The people, who knew that they would starve if the harvests were poor, brought generous offerings to the temple. This made the priests some of the richest, most powerful people in the city.

Soon, other cities were founded all over Mesopotamia. They were similar to Uruk, with large temples, called ziggurats, and mud-brick houses. Each city was independent, with its own ruler, priests and merchants. As the cities grew rich from their trade, they competed with each other for power over the whole region.

The Sumerian cities remained independent until about 2350BC. Then the Akkadians, from an area north of Sumer, conquered the area and made it part of their large Mesopotamian empire.

▶ PLOW
Sumerian farmers developed the ox-drawn plow in about 4000BC. It was much more efficient than a hand-held plow and meant that they could grow a great deal more food.

◀ LUTE PLAYER
Musicians playing lutes, pipes and tambourines, provided entertainment while people banqueted, drank beer, and watched celebrations. The people of Ur enjoyed music at home and at great festivals such as New Year.

FERTILE LAND
Separate city states made up the Sumerian civilization but there were similarities between them. Each used the Tigris and Euphrates for trade and transportation and all had mud-brick buildings. Also, they relied on fertile farmland to produce food. The region was so fertile, it is often called the Fertile Crescent.

▶ GRAVE GOODS
Gold items, such as jewelry, were placed in the tombs of the early kings and queens of Ur. Servants followed their king or queen to the grave. After a royal death, the servants walked into the huge tomb, drank poison, and lay down to die next to the body of their royal master or mistress.

▲ STANDARD OF UR
Pictures made from shells and precious stones show a row of Sumerian farmers herding cattle and sheep. Below them, workers carry heavy loads. These pictures, known as the Standard of Ur, may once have decorated a Sumerian musical instrument.

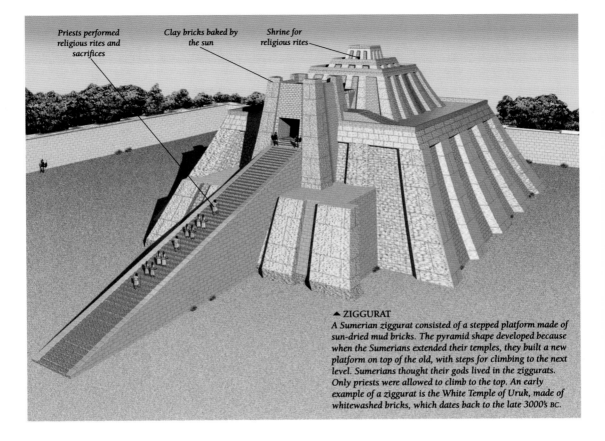

Priests performed religious rites and sacrifices

Clay bricks baked by the sun

Shrine for religious rites

▲ ZIGGURAT
A Sumerian ziggurat consisted of a stepped platform made of sun-dried mud bricks. The pyramid shape developed because when the Sumerians extended their temples, they built a new platform on top of the old, with steps for climbing to the next level. Sumerians thought their gods lived in the ziggurats. Only priests were allowed to climb to the top. An early example of a ziggurat is the White Temple of Uruk, made of whitewashed bricks, which dates back to the late 3000's BC.

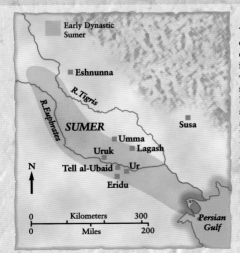

◀ SUMER
The Sumerian civilization consisted of independent, walled city states such as Ur, Lagash, Umma and Uruk. It arose in the area known as Mesopotamia, or "the land between two rivers", which covered much of what is now present-day Iraq.

Key Dates

- 5000BC The Sumerians, a farming people, settle in southern Mesopotamia.

- 4000BC Ox-drawn plow introduced.

- 3100BC Uruk becomes one of the world's first cities. Sumerians develop the potter's wheel and wheeled transport.

- 2900BC Earliest known writing.

- 2500BC Ur becomes a major city.

- 2350BC King Sargon from Akkad conquers the area of Sumer.

- 2100BC Ur is the most important Mesopotamian city, under King Ur-Nammu.

- 1700BC Ur declines, and the city of Babylon gains in strength.

Ancient Babylon

AROUND 1900BC, the Amorites, a people from Syria, moved into Mesopotamia, the land between the Tigris and Euphrates rivers. They farmed barley, herded sheep and goats and were skilled in all sorts of crafts, from metal working to perfumery and from leather making to beekeeping.

The Amorites made their capital at the city of Babylon, by the Euphrates. During the late 1700s BC, their king Hammurabi conquered the whole of southern Mesopotamia, which became known as Babylonia. The conquered land contained peoples of many different cultures and laws, so Hammurabi decided to unify the laws. They were inscribed on a stone stela, or tablet, for all to see.

Under Hammurabi, Babylon became a great center of science and learning. Babylonian scholars developed a numbering system, based on groups of 60, which is how we get our 60-minute hour and 360-degree circle. The scientists of Babylon were also renowned astronomers, recording the movements of the moon and stars across the night sky.

Many neighboring rulers were jealous of Babylon's power and the wealth the Babylonians earned from trade and the city was attacked many times. Hittites, from the area that is now Turkey, raided Babylon, then Kassites, from mountains to the east, invaded and took over the city. They turned Babylon into an important religious center, with a large temple to the supreme god, Marduk.

▲ CLAY LION
A clay lion which stood guard outside one of the Babylonian temples. Its intricate detail shows that the Babylonians were skilled sculptors. The lion was a popular symbol of royal power.

▶ ISHTAR GATE
The Ishtar Gate, decorated with spectacular blue stone, straddled the Processional Way which led into the city of Babylon. Three walls ringed the city, each so thick that two chariots could drive side by side along the top.

SCIENCE AND LAW
Babylon was a sophisticated city and a center for science, literature and learning. Scholars studied mathematics and astronomy, the science of the stars. Their ideas continue to influence us today.

◀ THE LAWS OF HAMMURABI
Hammurabi's laws were carved into a stela of black basalt rock. They include laws about money, property, the family and the rights of slaves. According to the law, a wrongdoer had to be punished in a way that suited the crime. The phrase "an eye for an eye and a tooth for a tooth" originates from Hammurabi's laws.

▲ MAP OF THE WORLD
A stone map showing the known land masses surrounded by a ring of ocean. The map was made by Babylonian scholars more than 3000 years ago. They labeled it with wedge-shaped cuneiform writing.

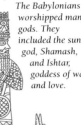

◀ HANGING GARDENS
King Nebuchadnezzar built fabulous hanging, or terraced, gardens for his wife Amytis to remind her of the green hill country of her home in Media. One of the ancient world's great wonders, no one today really knows what the gardens looked like.

▼ DRAGON OF MARDUK
The dragon symbolized Marduk, supreme god of the Babylonians. The Babylonians worshipped many gods. They included the sun god, Shamash, and Ishtar, goddess of war and love.

In around 900BC, the Chaldeans, horsemen from the Gulf coast, invaded Babylon. Their greatest king, Nebuchadnezzar II, rebuilt the city more magnificently than before. He gave it massive mud-brick walls, strong gates and a seven-story ziggurat. He also built a palace for himself and the Hanging Gardens, which was one of the Seven Wonders of the ancient world.

Babylon became the largest city in western Asia. Trade along the rivers, and via the caravan routes leading eastward to Iran, also made it wealthy once more. Its magnificence survived until it was again invaded, this time by the Persians.

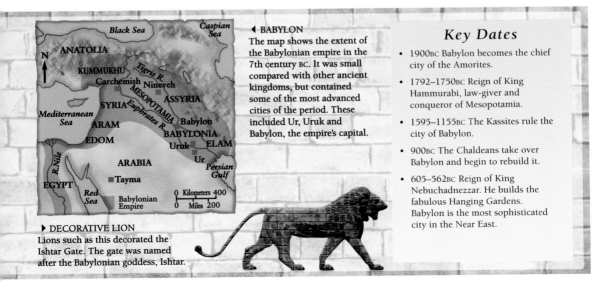

◀ BABYLON
The map shows the extent of the Babylonian empire in the 7th century BC. It was small compared with other ancient kingdoms, but contained some of the most advanced cities of the period. These included Ur, Uruk and Babylon, the empire's capital.

▶ DECORATIVE LION
Lions such as this decorated the Ishtar Gate. The gate was named after the Babylonian goddess, Ishtar.

Key Dates

- 1900BC Babylon becomes the chief city of the Amorites.

- 1792–1750BC Reign of King Hammurabi, law-giver and conqueror of Mesopotamia.

- 1595–1155BC The Kassites rule the city of Babylon.

- 900BC The Chaldeans take over Babylon and begin to rebuild it.

- 605–562BC Reign of King Nebuchadnezzar. He builds the fabulous Hanging Gardens. Babylon is the most sophisticated city in the Near East.

The Hittites

FROM THE COLD, mountainous region of central Anatolia (modern Turkey) came the Hittites, powerful peoples who flourished between about 1600 and 1200BC. A warlike group, they battled constantly with their neighbors for control over Mediterranean trade.

The Hittites had to master a harsh homeland, finding lands to farm wheat and barley and raise sheep and cattle. They built a huge stronghold at Hattusas, in the center of their kingdom. From here, they recruited and trained a powerful army. They were among the first to use horses in warfare and developed the chariot as one of the most feared weapons of battle.

They attacked the Mitanni, from northern Mesopotamia, and took over Syria. Their charioteers even threatened the power of the great Egyptian empire. The Hittites also used peaceful means to increase their power. They made treaties with the Egyptian pharaohs, which have been found in clay tablets in the massive royal archives at Hattusas. These show that the Hittites sometimes bought off their rivals with gold.

The Hittites had a strong land army but found it hard to defend their coasts. Invaders from the sea, known as the "Sea Peoples", attacked them constantly. This, together with bad harvests and pressure from Egypt, led to their downfall in around 1200BC.

▲ PRISONER
Egyptian mosaic tile, dating from c.1170BC, shows a Hittite prisoner.

◀ SOLDIER OR GOD?
No one knows for sure whether this armed man is a soldier or a Hittite god. He seems to be flexing his muscles. Placed at the gate of the city, he would have put fear into the hearts of any attacker.

▼ LION GATE
Fearsome-looking lions decorated the stone gateways of Hattusas, the Hittite capital and one of the strongest cities of its time. Set among cliffs and mountains, the city was well protected from enemies.

ARMIES
Both the Hittites and Assyrians had powerful armies but the Assyrian army was the most feared and efficient of its time. Consisting of foot soldiers and heavily armed cavalry, Assyrian armies were huge, several thousand strong. Many of the soldiers were captured people from lands that the Assyrians had conquered.

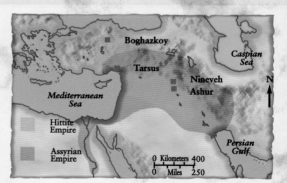

◀ CHARIOTEERS
Much of the Hittite military success came from their skill as charioteers. Their chariots, which could hold up to three people, one to drive the horses, and two to fight, were feared by all.

▲ HITTITES AND ASSYRIANS
The Hittites controlled much of modern Turkey and parts of northern Mesopotamia and Syria. Their real center of power was around Hattusas and the cities of Alaca and Alisar. The Assyrian empire stretched from the Mediterranean to the Persian Gulf.

The Assyrians

▲ WINGED
SPHINX
*Massive carved
stone sphinxes
guarded city gates
and palaces.
Winged beasts,
they had bull or
lion bodies and
human heads with
long beards, like
those worn by
Assyrian kings.
The Assyrians
believed the
monsters gave
heavenly
protection and
warded off evil
wrongdoers.*

THEY WERE THE MOST FEARED people of the ancient world. The armies of the Assyrians attacked swiftly, ransacking villages, battering down city walls, and killing anyone in the way. They carried away precious metals, timber, building stone — anything they could use. They took prisoners to work as slaves on building projects in their cities along the upper Tigris river — building luxurious palaces, towering temples, and massive city walls.

The Assyrians seemed unstoppable. They conquered an empire that stretched from the Nile Delta to the ancient cities of Babylon and Ur. They built beautiful cities, such as Nineveh, Nimrud and Khorsabad, which were among the most magnificent the world had ever seen. Their royal palaces were decorated with stone reliefs that portrayed the success and glory of their kings. The reliefs survive today and show us much about the Assyrian kings and their lives — their war triumphs, use of chariots and battering rams, victory celebrations, conquered people bringing them lavish tribute, and hunting scenes.

The main strength of the Assyrians was their army but as Assyria grew in size, the soldiers could not defend the whole empire at once. One conquered city could not defeat the Assyrians but when the people of Babylonia and Media joined forces they could win, and the vast Assyrian empire quickly crumbled.

▼ THE ROYAL HUNT
*Assyrian kings enjoyed hunting,
particularly for lions, wildest of
all creatures. They wanted their
people to think their strength was
god-like and often had themselves
portrayed performing feats of
incredible strength and bravery.*

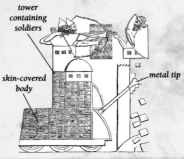

▲ COURT LIFE
A stone relief shows musicians with harps and flutes playing at the palace of Assurbanipal in Nineveh. Reliefs such as this tell us much about court life.

▼ BATTERING RAMS
Assyrian soldiers used a fearsome fighting machine, part battering ram, part tower, to attack and break through the walls of enemy cities. While the metal-tipped battering ram was driven against the walls, soldiers on the tower used picks to break them down.

tower
containing
soldiers

skin-covered
body

metal tip

Key Dates

- c.2000BC Hittite farmers settle in Turkey.
- 1550BC Hattusas becomes Hittite capital.
- 1380–1346BC Hittites flourish.
- 1250BC Assyrians and Sea People attack Hittite empire.
- 1200BC Hittite empire declines.
- 883–859BC Nineveh built.
- 744–727BC Assyria reaches greatest power.
- 721–705BC King Sargon builds Assyrian capital, Khorsabad.
- 664BC Assyrians conquer Egypt.
- 612BC Nineveh destroyed.
- 609BC Babylonians defeat Assyrian army.

The Persian Empire

▲ PERSIAN SOLDIER
Mosaics of Persian soldiers decorated the palace of Susa. They were the keepers of law and order. An elite force of 10,000 warriors were called "immortals" because when one died, he was replaced immediately.

THEY BEGAN AS A SMALL nation from the region near Babylon. Suddenly, in around 549BC, the Persians seemed to be everywhere. Led by Cyrus the Great (r. 559–530BC), the Persian army pushed west and east, conquering a vast area that stretched from modern Turkey to the borders of India. Cyrus, and the emperors that followed him, gained enormous wealth from their conquests. They built cities with huge palaces, drank from gold and silver vessels, and surrounded themselves with luxury.

The Persian Empire was vast and mountainous and contained many different peoples, who often rebelled against Persian control. To keep order, the Persian rulers had a very effective army. Known as "the immortals", these 10,000 specially trained men were feared wherever they went and moved quickly to put down rebellions.

The emperors did not only rely on brute force. They also organized the empire so it could be controlled easily. They divided it into 20 provinces, each governed by a satrap, an official who ruled on behalf of the emperor. Each province raised taxes and tributes. The satraps were extremely powerful in their own right, so the emperor sent spies, known as "the king's ears", to each province to listen out for treachery and to check that the satraps were sending all the taxes to the emperor, not keeping some for themselves. The Persians also built a network of roads to link the corners of their empire. Spies, tax collectors and traders could travel easily around the countryside.

▲ TRIBUTES
Once a year representatives from the provinces came to the royal palace at Persepolis. Everyone brought gifts for the emperor — gold from India, horses from Assyria, two-humped camels from Bactria.

KING OF KINGS
Cyrus the Great belonged to the Achaemenid dynasty. He, and the Persian emperors who followed him, gave themselves the title King of Kings. They lived in great splendor and had absolute power. Below them, and their nobles, most of the population were farmers, craftworkers, serfs and slaves.

▶ SILVER GOAT
A silver ornament in the shape of a goat from the royal city of Persepolis. The Persians loved animals and used many different creatures to decorate all sorts of objects.

▲ DARIUS THE GREAT
Emperor Darius I ruled the Persian Empire from 522 to 486BC. He was head of the army and a wise ruler. He also founded Persepolis. During his reign, the empire reached its greatest extent.

▼ PERSIAN NOBLES
A Persian nobleman stands between two soldiers. Nobles were wealthy and educated. Darius appointed his satraps, or provincial governors, from noble-born families.

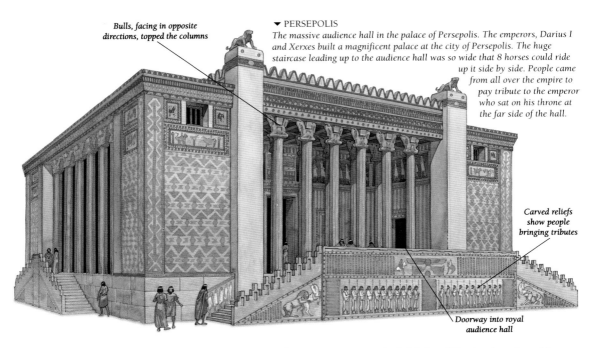

Bulls, facing in opposite
directions, topped the columns

▼ PERSEPOLIS
The massive audience hall in the palace of Persepolis. The emperors, Darius I
and Xerxes built a magnificent palace at the city of Persepolis. The huge
staircase leading up to the audience hall was so wide that 8 horses could ride
up it side by side. People came
from all over the empire to
pay tribute to the emperor
who sat on his throne at
the far side of the hall.

Carved reliefs
show people
bringing tributes

Doorway into royal
audience hall

The Persians' wealth grew and the emperors brought skilled workers from all over the empire to build cities and palaces. Stone masons came from Greece, brickmakers from Babylon and goldsmiths from Egypt. The Persians also imported raw materials such as cedar wood from the Lebanon and ivory from Ethiopia.

Some people did fight off Persian invasions. The Scythians, fearless horsemen from the north, held back Persia's army, and the Greeks fought off two invasion attempts. The Greeks hated the Persians and eventually Alexander the Great, the famous conqueror from the Greek world, destroyed the Persian empire in 333BC.

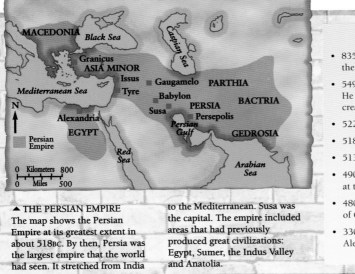

▲ THE PERSIAN EMPIRE
The map shows the Persian Empire at its greatest extent in about 518BC. By then, Persia was the largest empire that the world had seen. It stretched from India to the Mediterranean. Susa was the capital. The empire included areas that had previously produced great civilizations: Egypt, Sumer, the Indus Valley and Anatolia.

Key Dates

- 835BC The Medes, from Media, southwest of the Caspian Sea, rule much of Iran.

- 549BC Cyrus becomes leader of the Persians. He conquers Media, Ionia and Lydia, so creating the first Persian empire.

- 522–486BC Reign of Darius I.

- 518BC Darius conquers parts of Egypt.

- 513BC Darius takes over the Indus Valley area.

- 490BC Persians invade Greece but are defeated at the Battle of Marathon.

- 480BC Xerxes leads another attempted invasion of Greece.

- 330BC Persia becomes part of the empire of Alexander the Great.

Parthians and Sassanians

ONQUERED BY THE GREAT Macedonian leader, Alexander the Great, the Persian empire ceased to exist. But after Alexander's death in 332BC, Persian leaders began again to take control of their native land. Once more they created a large empire, uniting diverse people, from sheepherders in Iran to Mesopotamian farmers, under all-powerful emperors, whom they called the King of Kings.

Alexander, and the Achaemenid emperors before him, had shown the Persians that they needed a strong army to create a great empire. But the new Persian leaders, under two dynasties, the Parthians (240BC–AD226) and the more successful Sassanians (AD226–646), who replaced them, went further. They rebuilt society as a system of rigid social classes: nobles, priests, warriors, high and low officials, and peasants.

◀ PARTHIAN SHOT
Parthian cavalry pretended to retreat, then, unexpectedly, fired arrows backwards with deadly accuracy.

Everyone knew their place. People's whole lives, from the type of job they did to their choice of marriage partner, from how much tax they paid to the type of food they ate, all depended on the class to which they belonged.

This rigid class system kept the country united. At the top of the social tree, and sovereign ruler, was the emperor, the King of Kings himself. The people were reminded of his greatness, because the Sassanian emperors put their own images on everything they created. Their palaces and cites were decorated with stone reliefs and sculptures showing them in battle or enjoying sports such as hunting and horseback riding.

▶ ROCK RELIEFS

Sassanian rulers recorded their achievements in stunning reliefs carved on the cliff faces of their native province of Fars. These show subjects such as Persian knights and Sassanian troops.

ZOROASTRIANISM
The Persians adopted Zoroastrianism as their religion. Zoroaster, or Zarathustra as he was also called, lived in about 1000BC. He taught that life was a fight between good and evil. Zoroastrians believed that the source of good in the world was the Wise Lord, a god of light and truth called Ahura Mazda. A sacred fire burned in every Persian temple as a symbol of his light and eternal goodness.

▶ AHURA MAZDA
The chief god of the Persians was Ahura Mazda, source of all goodness. A winged figure, he was the symbol of Zoroastrianism. Priests tended his sacred fire. They were called Magi, from which comes the word "magic".

▲ SACRED BULL
In ancient Persia, the bull was a symbol of power. The Persians also believed it was the first animal to be created and that, after the first bull was killed, all the other animals of the world were born from its soul.

▶ PARTHIAN AND SASSANIAN EMPIRES
The map shows the Parthian and Sassanian empires. They were not as vast as the first Persian empire but these later empires were still large. Parthian lands stretched from the farming area of Mesopotamia, north of the Persian Gulf, to the homelands of herders and nomads in central Iran. The domains of the later Sassanians stretched still further east to the Indus River.

◀ CTESIPHON
The capital city, Ctesiphon, stood on the Tigris River, near to present-day Baghdad in Iraq. It grew dramatically in size during the Sassanian period, possibly containing several hundred thousand people. The Sassanians divided the city into two large suburbs. One part was for captives from the Roman empire, and the other was for the emperor and his family. The royal family lived in this large stone-built palace with its great vaulted central hall.

▲ STUCCO PANEL
Part of a decorative border from a Sassanian house. The upper classes loved luxury and their homes were decorated with ornate plasterwork, called stucco. This plasterwork was decorated with guinea fowl.

One of the most important classes was the priests. They were the leaders of the Zoroastrian religion. This faith had been developed in about 1000BC but the Sassanians made it the state religion, although contemporary eastern religions and other cults exerted an influence.

Under these later Persians, trade, industry and the arts flourished. They made developments in farming and improved irrigation systems. The local population rose but farmers worked the land too hard. Crops failed and the region became poor once more. Eventually, the Muslim Arabs invaded, finally ending the later Persian empires.

Key Dates

- c. 240BC–AD226 Parthian dynasty rules lands in Persia.

- AD109 Silk trade links China and Parthia.

- AD224 Ardashir, son of high priest Sasan destroys Parthian power. He founds Persian Sassanian dynasty.

- AD226–642 Sassanian dynasty rules Persia.

- AD531–578 Reign of Khusrau Anushirvan. He reforms tax system and improves irrigation in Mesopotamia.

- AD614–628 Reign of Khusrau Parviz, conqueror of Egypt and Syria, the last of the great Sassanian kings.

- AD637 Muslim Arabs invade and destroy Sassanian Empire.

Islamic Empire

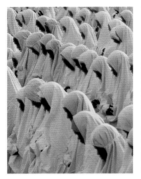

▲ MUSLIM WOMEN
Traditionally, Muslim women cover their heads out of doors and wear clothes that cover them completely.

IN THE 7TH CENTURY AD, a new faith appeared that has become one of the world's greatest religions. It emerged in the Arabian peninsula, where the Arab people lived by farming and trading. They had worshipped many gods but in about AD610, the prophet Mohammed, a merchant from Mecca, announced that a new religion had been revealed to him. It was based on belief in a single god, Allah, and he called it Islam, meaning "submission to God's will".

Mohammed and his followers, who are called Muslims, spread the new faith throughout Arabia and beyond. Soon it became the basis of a new and growing empire, which brought learning, art and science to peoples as far afield as Morocco and Persia.

The early Muslims sent out missionaries to convert people. They were followed by Arab merchants, who traveled across the desert with processions of camels, known as caravans, trading in

◀ DOME OF THE ROCK
The Dome of the Rock in Jerusalem is the oldest surviving mosque, or place of Muslim worship. It was built at a place where Mohammed was said to have stopped on his journey to heaven.

luxuries such as precious stones, metals and incense.

Next followed armies, led by the caliph, ruler of the Islamic world. Within 30 years of Mohammed's death, they had conquered a huge area, stretching from Tunisia in the west to Persia in the east. Later, Islamic armies pushed even farther afield, conquering Spain and reaching the borders of India.

Islam was based on the Koran, the Muslim sacred book. Muslims were expected to learn how to read Arabic so that they could read the Koran. This meant that the Islamic empire became highly educated. Schools were attached to every mosque and universities were founded in major cities such as Baghdad. Muslim scholars also collected information from all the conquered countries. Soon the Islamic

SCHOLARSHIP
Baghdad was a center of culture and learning and Muslim scientists were famous worldwide. Arab scholars studied the stars, mathematics, medicine, engineering, history, geography and philosophy. Islam tolerated other religions so Christian and Jewish scholars were also welcome.

▲ ASTROLABE
Islamic scientists developed the astrolabe. A flat disc with a rod that could be pointed to the sun or stars, it helped Arab sailors find their way.

◀ CALLIGRAPHY
The art of calligraphy, or beautiful handwriting, was one of the many arts that flourished in the Islamic world.

▼ HOUSE OF LEARNING
Islamic scholars study in a mosque, a Muslim place of worship. Arabic textbooks, particularly in medicine, were used in Europe for centuries.

▲ BAGHDAD
Through the centuries, Baghdad has survived repeated damage by wars, floods and fire. Today it is home to millions of Muslims.

▶ SPREADING ISLAM
Arabian merchants blazed new trails across the deserts to spread the new faith. They crossed western Asia and northern Africa.

empire contained the world's finest scientists, doctors and most able writers. The arts also flourished and houses and mosques were decorated with beautiful tiles and stonework.

Religious faith, learning and a powerful army made the Islamic empire successful and long lasting. It survived until the 13th century.

▲ ISLAMIC EMPIRE
The Islamic empire reached its height in AD750, as shown in the map. In some areas, such as Spain, Muslim rule lasted for hundreds of years. In other areas, such as North Africa and much of western Asia, large Muslim communities continue to exist to this day and Muslims can now be found all over the world.

Key Dates

- AD632 Death of Mohammed.

- AD634 The first caliph, Abu Bakr, conquers Arabia.

- AD635–642 Muslims conquer Syria, Egypt, and Persia.

- AD661 The beginning of the Omayyad dynasty.

- AD698 Muslim soldiers capture Carthage.

- AD711 Muslims begin to invade Spain. The empire expands to include northeastern India.

- AD750 Abbasid dynasty founded.

- AD762 Baghdad becomes the Abbasid capital.

Indus Valley Civilization

IN AROUND 2500BC, a mysterious civilization grew up on the plain of the Indus River, in what is now Pakistan. Archeologists have so far been unable to read their writing, find out what their religion was, or work out why their civilization collapsed. But we do know that the Indus Valley people were very successful. They farmed the fertile soil by the Indus and used clay from the river banks to make bricks. With these they built several huge cities.

Most of what we know about the Indus Valley Civilization comes from the remains of their great cities Mohenjo-Daro and Harappa. They built them on the flood plain of the river. Because the river flooded regularly, they constructed massive mud-brick platforms to raise the buildings above the level of the flood waters.

▲ GODDESS
Small clay figures showing a woman with a decorative head-dress, have been found at Mohenjo-Daro. These were most likely representations of a fertility or mother-goddess.

Each city was divided into two areas. One was where the people lived. Flat-roofed, mud-brick houses were arranged in neat rows along straight streets and alleyways. Most houses had a courtyard, a well for water, and even built-in toilets with drains to take the waste to sewers beneath the streets.

The other half of each city was a walled area containing the larger buildings — a public bath, a great hall, and a massive granary, or grain store, the size of an Olympic swimming pool. Priests and worshippers may have used the baths for ritual washing before religious ceremonies. Near the granaries were large threshing floors where farmers brought their grain to be threshed before selling it to the people of the city.

The Indus civilization continued for about 800 years but then began to decline. Houses fell into ruin and many people left. No one knows for certain why this happened. Bad floods and a rising population may have forced farmers to grow too much food, exhausting the land and causing poor harvests and famine.

◀ GOD-KING
A stone bust showing a man dressed in a patterned shawl. The quality of the carving and the thoughtful expression may mean that the man was an Indus god or perhaps a king.

DAILY LIFE
From the evidence, it seems that Indus Valley cities were full of life and activity. Archeologists have found weights and measuring sticks, which suggests that they were trade centers. Merchants and traders probably thronged the streets, which also contained skilled craftworkers. Farmers too brought their crops into the cities to sell.

◀ CLAY SEALS
Stone seals, such as this, probably belonged to merchants who used them to "sign" documents and property. Seals featured an animal, such as bull, antelope, water buffalo, or tiger, each of which was found in the region.

▶ CART MODEL
Small clay models, such as this one, pulled by a pair of bullocks, prove that the Indus people used the wheel. They would have used full-size carts to carry grain and other produce.

▲ GAME PLAYING
Archeologists have found board games and toy animals showing that Indus people enjoyed playing games.

▼ MOHENJO-DARO
The streets of Mohenjo-Daro ran straight and crossed at right-angles, just like the streets of a modern American city. The city seems to have been carefully planned, which was unusual at the time.

Houses with bathrooms and toilets

Straight streets organized on a grid pattern

Houses of mud bricks, baked in a kiln

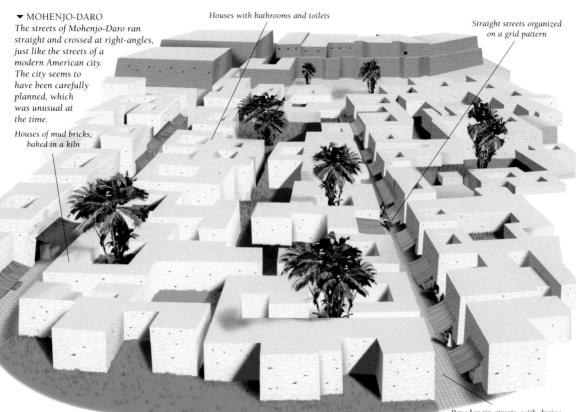

Paved main streets, with drains running underneath

▶ INDUS VALLEY
The map shows the extent of the Indus Valley Civilization. It was centered on its great cities, such as Mohenjo-Daro and Harappa, but many people lived in the country in small towns and villages, making their living on the land. They became rich growing corn to trade in the cities, adding to their diet by hunting wild animals. They were also probably the first people to grow cotton as fabric for clothes.

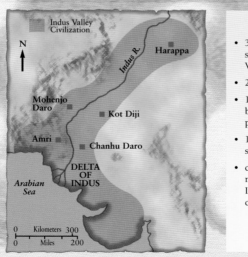

Indus Valley Civilization

N

Indus R.

Harappa

Mohenjo Daro

Kot Diji

Amri

Chanhu Daro

DELTA OF INDUS

Arabian Sea

0 Kilometers 300
0 Miles 200

Key Dates

- 3500BC Groups of farmers settle in scattered communities in the Indus Valley.

- 2500BC First Indus cities built.

- 1800BC Decline of Indus Cities begins. Population falls and cities are poorly maintained.

- 1000BC Much of population has shifted to Ganges Valley.

- c.1500BC Aryan peoples from the northwest invade Indus Valley. Invasions may have been a cause of cities' destruction.

Mauryan India

ORE THAN ONE thousand years after the decline of the Indus Valley Civilization, a new and glorious empire emerged in the Indian subcontinent. It was known as the Mauryan empire, after the Mauryan dynasty, or ruling family. Between 322BC and 185BC, the Mauryan emperors brought peace and Buddhism into war-torn India and united that vast area for the first time.

India's huge subcontinent has always been home to a huge variety of peoples with different languages, beliefs and customs. By the 6th century BC, there were 16 separate states in northern India alone. Most were centered on mud-brick cities along the Ganges River. The Ganges cities were often at war with each other, competing for fertile land. In the 4th century BC, one kingdom in the northwest, Magadha, emerged

▲ BATTLE OF KALINGA
A noble Indian warrior. In 261BC, Asoka conquered the kingdom of Kalinga. Hundreds of thousands of people were killed. The cruelty of the battle changed Asoka for ever.

as a major power and began to defeat its neighbors. Its leader was Chandragupta Maurya, a nobleman and warrior.

Chandragupta drove out Greek invaders and built an empire that included the whole of northern India from the Hindu Kush to Bengal. His son continued the expansion but it was under his grandson, Asoka, that the Mauryan empire reached its greatest glory.

Asoka began with further conquests, including the kingdom of Kalinga, but he was shocked by the destruction of war. He decided to become a Buddhist and determined that others should follow his new faith of peace and non-violence.

Asoka sent out missionaries and ordered messages about his beliefs to be put up all over his empire. Buddhist texts and sayings were carved on pillars and specially smoothed cliff faces. They explained his belief that everyone is responsible for the welfare of others. They also instructed people to tolerate the beliefs of others and always to avoid violence.

Inspired by his new faith, Asoka built hospitals and introduced new laws. A network of roads was built that connected towns throughout the empire. Farming improved and trade expanded. The Mauryan empire brought peace and prosperity to many parts of India. However, it needed Asoka's leadership to hold it together. After his death, the empire fell apart when Brihadnatha, the last Mauryan emperor, was killed.

RELIGION
Two of the world's great religions — Hinduism and Buddhism — came from India. Hinduism dates back some 4000 years. Asoka introduced Buddhism. By the end of the Mauryan period it was the most widespread faith in northern India. Asoka also sent Buddhist teachers to neighboring countries, such as Burma, to spread the faith.

◀ COLUMN
Asoka's columns were usually topped with one or more lions. Sayings on the column written in local script told people to avoid violence, eat vegetarian food and respect the beliefs of others. They also reminded everyone of how Asoka's rule helped ordinary people, by building roads, rest houses and wells.

◀ BUDDHA
The founder of Buddhism was Siddhartha Gautama, an Indian prince who was born in 563BC.

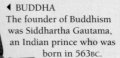

▲ RAMAYANA
An Indian miniature shows a scene from one of India's great epic poems, the *Ramayana*. Its hero, Rama, was identified with the Hindu god, Vishnu.

◀ HOLY RIVER
Indians have bathed in the River Ganges for centuries although the temples may not have been there during the time of the Mauryans. To Hindus, the Ganges is sacred. It is believed that bathing in its waters washes away sins.

▲ STUPA
The Mauryans built Buddhist shrines, called stupas, in the form of dome-shaped massive mounds, sometimes known as "temple mountains". Asoka built many stupas. One of the oldest to survive is at Sanchi, in central India.

◀ MAURYAN EMPIRE
The map shows the Mauryan Empire at the time of Asoka. His grandfather, Chandragupta, took control of much of northern India, and also made conquests in Pakistan and Afghanistan. Chandragupta's son, Bindusara, conquered large areas of central and southern India, although the southern tip remained unconquered.

Map labels: HIMALAYAS, Indus R., R. Ganges, Sarnata, Pataliputra, MAURYAN, Bharhut, Ujjain, Tamluk, EMPIRE, Arabian Sea, DECCAN PLATEAU, Tosali, KALINGA, Mauryan Road, N, Bay of Bengal, Suvarnagiri, Mauryan Empire, 0 Kilometers 500, 0 Miles 300

Key Dates

- 327–325BC The Macedonian leader, Alexander the Great, conquers the Indus Valley and the Punjab.

- 322BC Chandragupta Maurya takes over the Punjab and founds Mauryan empire.

- 303BC Chandragupta conquers the Indus Valley and part of Afghanistan.

- 301BC Bindusara, Chandragupta's son, comes to the throne and extends the Mauryan empire.

- 269–232BC Reign of Asoka. Buddhism becomes state religion and Mauryan empire flourishes.

- 184BC The death of Brihadnatha, the last Mauryan emperor.

Ancient Egypt

FIVE THOUSAND YEARS AGO, a great civilization — that of Egypt — emerged in northern Africa. Ruled by powerful pharaohs, ancient Egypt dominated the region for three thousand years and was one of the most successful of the ancient civilizations.

The Egyptian civilization began with Narmer. In about 3100BC, he unified two kingdoms — Upper and Lower Egypt — and became the first king or pharaoh. The pharaoh was the most powerful and important person in the kingdom and was believed to have the same status as a god. Under Narmer, and the pharaohs who followed, Egypt prospered. To help them wield their power, the pharaohs trained a civil service of scribes or writers. The scribes recorded and collected taxes and carried out the day-to-day running of the kingdom, which was divided into a number of districts. Merchants traveled to neighboring areas such as Palestine, Syria and Nubia, and the Egyptian army followed, occupying some of these areas for a while.

▲ THE NARMER PALETTE *The slate shows Narmer. He was also called Menes, meaning "the founder".*

The land of ancient Egypt was dry and inhospitable and the Egyptians relied on the great River Nile for survival. It was the life blood of the region and provided everything — fertilizer for the land, water for farming and irrigation, and a highway for Egyptian boats, called "feluccas", which were some of the world's earliest sailing craft.

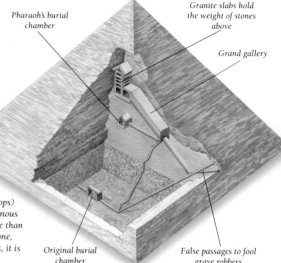

Pharaoh's burial chamber

Granite slabs hold the weight of stones above

Grand gallery

▶ GREAT PYRAMID
The pyramid of Khufu (Cheops) at Giza, the largest, most famous pyramid of all. Made of more than two million blocks of limestone, some of which weigh 15 tons, it is 160 yards tall.

Original burial chamber

False passages to fool grave robbers

AFTERLIFE
The Egyptians believed in life after death. They also believed that their pharaohs were gods, who would continue living after their bodies had died. For this reason they built the pyramids to safeguard their bodies.

▶ THE SPHINX
Half pharaoh, half lion, the great Sphinx at Giza symbolized royal power. Some 20 yards high and 60 yards long, it was carved out of limestone rock in about 2620BC.

▲ THE GREAT PYRAMIDS
The pyramid of Chephren, pictured above, dates from 2560BC. The top of the original flat casing still survives. Many pyramids had steps on the outside. Literally tens of thousands of workers labored to build the great pyramids.

Once a year the Nile flooded, its rich silt nourishing the land on either side. All the land watered by the river was needed for cultivation, but during the floods, no one could work the land. This was when all the able-bodied men of the kingdom went to labor on large-scale building projects, such as cities and temples to the many gods of Egypt. They also built the great pyramids, the tombs and last resting places of the pharaohs and some of the biggest stone structures ever built. The desert lands were where these burial tombs were built.

Body wrapped in bandages

Decorated mummy case

◀ MUMMIFICATION
When a pharaoh died, his body was preserved. The inner organs were removed and the body was treated with a chemical and then wrapped in linen bandages. The "mummy" was then put in a decorated coffin and left in the pyramid tomb.

▶ CLOTHING
Egyptian clothes were usually made of linen, woven from flax. The richer the person, the finer the cloth.

◀ BRICK MAKING
Tomb paintings tell us much about Egyptian daily life. Here Egyptian crafts-people make building bricks using soft clay from the Nile, combined with straw.

▲ HIEROGLYPHICS
The Egyptians invented a form of picture writing, now known as hieroglyphics. There were more than 700 different picture signs, each one corresponding to one sound or word.

▼ PAPYRUS
The Egyptians invented a kind of paper, called papyrus. They made it from the stems of papyrus reeds that grew beside the Nile. The English word "paper" comes from the word papyrus.

Ancient Egypt

▲ RAMESES II
This huge statue of Rameses II, who reigned from 1304 to 1237BC, stands in front of the great temple of Abu Simbel. It was one of many monuments that he had built to remind Egyptians of his power.

PHARAOHS RULED ancient Egypt for the whole of its long 3000-year history. The later pharaohs, from the period known as the New Kingdom, were the most powerful. They extended the empire, and sent ambassadors all over western Asia. They built huge temples and erected colossal statues of themselves. For about 500 years, New Kingdom Egypt was the world's most magnificent civilization.

The Egyptians believed their pharaohs were gods. To them the pharaoh was both Horus, the falcon-headed sky god, and Amun-Re, the sun god. This god-like status gave the pharaohs absolute power. They appointed the priests, as well as all civil servants and chief ministers. They also controlled the army, which grew large with recruits from conquered regions all the way from Sudan to Syria.

Everywhere they went ordinary Egyptians were reminded of the pharaoh's power. In front of the temples were massive stone statues of the king in the guise of the sun god. Carved inscriptions told anyone who could read of the pharaoh's godly rank. People also read of the pharaohs' victories in Palestine and Nubia and of their peace treaties with the Hittites of Turkey.

▶ TUTANKHAMUN
Pharaoh Tutankhamun was only 18 when he died. However, he is the most famous pharaoh because when archeologists found his tomb in the 1920s, its contents, including his golden death mask, were still complete.

◀ TOMB TREASURES
Most ancient Egyptian tombs were robbed hundreds of years ago but when it was opened up, Tutankhamun's tomb contained everything that had been buried with him, including food, furniture, jewelry and his glittering gold coffin.

EGYPTIAN WOMEN
Women of all classes in ancient Egypt had many rights, compared to women later in history. They ran the household and controlled their own property. They followed skilled professions; such as midwifery, served as priestesses, and could hold important positions at court.

◀ NEFERTITI
The wife of the New Kingdom pharaoh Akhenaten was Queen Nefertiti. She ruled with her husband, assisted in religious ceremonies, and had a strong political influence.

▲ HUNTING
Egyptians enjoyed hunting. The pharaoh and nobles hunted in the desert, where they caught antelopes, gazelles and wild oxen. They also hunted geese and other waterfowl on the banks of the Nile.

The most famous of the Egyptian pharaohs came from the New Kingdom. They included Rameses II and Seti I, who were renowned military leaders, Akhenaten, who briefly abolished all the gods except for the sun god, the boy-king Tutankhamun, and Hatshepsut, a powerful queen who ruled with all the might of her male relatives.

After the glory of the New Kingdom, Egypt survived numerous invasions and changes of pharaoh. The last ruler of an independent ancient Egypt was Queen Cleopatra VII, famous for her love for the Roman leader Mark Antony. Much Egyptian culture, from its gods to its funeral customs, survived, but after Cleopatra's death in 30BC, Egypt became part of the huge Roman empire.

◀ ANCIENT
EGYPT
The map shows the extent of ancient Egypt. Lower Egypt was in the north. The kingdom of Upper Egypt was in the south. Farther south still was Nubia, a source of precious materials such as gold and ivory, which the Egyptians later conquered.

Key Dates

- 3100–2686BC Upper and Lower Egypt are united.

- 2686–2181BC Old Kingdom. The pharaohs build up their power and are buried in pyramids.

- 2182–2040BC The pharaohs' power breaks down and two rulers govern Egypt from separate capital cities, Heracleopolis and Thebes.

- 2040–1786BC Middle Kingdom.

- 1786–1567BC Invasion forces sent to Egypt from Syria and Palestine.

- 1570–1085BC New Kingdom. Egyptian pharaohs rule once more and the civilization flourishes.

- 1083–333BC The empire collapses. Egypt divides into separate states.

- 333–323BC Egypt becomes part of Alexander the Great's empire.

African Civilizations

Africa is a huge and ancient continent. Its northern region produced the great Egyptian civilization. But further south, below the Sahara desert that divides the continent, other civilizations and kingdoms also appeared. Many were skilled metalworking cultures that produced tools, beautiful jewelry and sculpture. They sent merchants on long trading journeys. Some merchants crossed the vast Sahara desert with their camels, braving heat and drought to reach the ports of the Red Sea coast and the trading posts of North Africa.

African civilizations were scattered far and wide across the continent. But there were several main centers. Ghana, Benin, Mali and Songhai were small kingdoms that flourished, at different times, in West Africa. The people were Bantu-speakers, descendants of the Bantus, farmers and herders who originated in West Africa about 4000 years ago. They opened up trade links with the Muslim rulers of North Africa, sending ivory, ebony, gold, copper and slaves northwards and bringing back manufactured goods such as pottery and glassware. They learned how to work iron, perhaps from people in North African cities such as Carthage. As demand for their goods increased, their kingdoms flourished.

There were also numerous trading kingdoms in East Africa. The most famous was on the Zimbabwe plateau. Here the Shona people had fertile land and rich sources of copper and gold. Their merchants traveled to the east coast of Africa, where they traded with ships coming from

▲ BENIN BRONZES
Craft workers from Benin, in what is now Nigeria, made beautiful cast bronze figures — such as this head of a royal woman.

▶ AXUM
The Ethiopian kingdom of Axum traded with India and the Islamic world. Its rulers built a palace at Takaji Mariam and many stone obelisks, some over 30 yards high. Most people lived in small thatched huts.

EARLIEST CIVILIZATIONS

South of Egypt, the first civilization to emerge in Africa was the kingdom of Kush, which flourished on the Nile from about 500BC to AD350. Its capital was Meroe, an important iron-working center. From about 500BC, metal working spread south to other parts of Africa.

◀ GOLD
Skilled gold workers from the ancient kingdom of Kush made this gold papyrus holder in about 590BC. Much later, African gold workers, especially from Ghana and Mali, became famous all over the world.

▲ ROCK PAINTINGS
Sub-Saharan Africa is rich in rock paintings. This one was painted in the West African kingdom of Mali, which flourished between AD1200–1500.

Stone tower, probably used for religious ceremonies

Thatched buildings

Stone walls, over 30 feet high

◀ GREAT ZIMBABWE
The great oval stone enclosure at Great Zimbabwe was the center of the Shona empire. Its stone walls still stand today and contain the remains of several buildings, possibly the ruler's home.

▼ LALIBELA
Some areas of Africa converted to Islam but Axum became Christian in the 4th century. By the 1200s, local masons had carved entire churches, such as this one, from rocky outcrops at Lalibela, southeast of Axum.

India, the Islamic empire and even China. Further north were still more trading and metalworking kingdoms in what are now Zambia and Ethiopia.

The people of the African kingdoms led lives that were well adapted to their environment. They sought out good land for crops and cattle, and found good sources of metal ore. Their kingdoms lasted a long time and many remained prosperous until the Europeans colonized Africa in the 19th century.

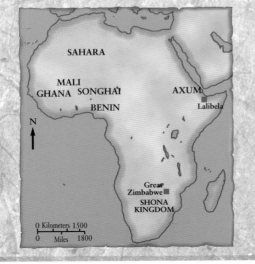

▶ AFRICAN CIVILIZATIONS
The peoples of Africa settled along fertile river valleys and in areas where there were sources of metals such as iron and gold. Soon even the inhospitable Sahara Desert had its settlements, oases and stopping-places for merchants. The Sahara also provided salt, one of the most valuable substances in the ancient world.

SAHARA

MALI
GHANA SONGHAI
BENIN

AXUM
Lalibela

N

Great Zimbabwe
SHONA KINGDOM

0 Kilometers 1500
0 Miles 1800

Key Dates

- AD320–650 Kingdom of Axum, East Africa.

- AD700–1200 Kingdom of Ghana, West Africa.

- AD1100–1897 Kingdom of Benin, West Africa.

- AD1200–1500 Kingdom of Mali, West Africa.

- AD1270–1450 Great Zimbabwe is capital of Shona kingdom.

- AD1350–600 Kingdom of Songhai, West Africa.

Minoan Crete

▲ FISHERMAN
A young Minoan fisherman holds fish caught from the Mediterranean Sea. The Minoans were seafarers. Fishing was the basis of their economy.

JUST OVER 100 YEARS AGO, British archeologist Arthur Evans made an extraordinary discovery. He unearthed the ruins of an ancient and beautifully decorated palace at Knossos, on the Mediterranean island of Crete. The palace was enormous. It had hundreds of rooms, courtyards and winding staircases. It reminded Evans of the ancient Greek story of the labyrinth, a maze-like structure built by the legendary Cretan king Minos. He did not know who had built the palace, so he called its builders Minoans, after the mythical king.

Remains in the palace gave many clues so today we know much more about the Minoans. They may originally have come from mainland Greece. They traveled to Crete where, for nearly 1000 years, they created a rich and wonderful culture that reached its height between 2000 and 1700BC. Seas teeming with fish and a rich fertile soil meant that the Minoans had a prosperous and comfortable lifestyle.

The Minoans built many palaces on Crete but Knossos was the largest. The building contained shrines, religious symbols and statues of goddesses. There were several large and lavishly decorated rooms, probably royal throne rooms. Some smaller rooms were full of tall jars, called pithoi, which would have held oil, wine and other produce. Possibly a priest-ruler lived at Knossos, which may also have been a center for food and trade.

Walls in the Cretan palaces were covered in beautiful paintings, many of which have survived. Some show natural scenes and others show the Minoans themselves, working, enjoying themselves and taking part in religious ceremonies.

◀ SNAKE GODDESS
A pottery goddess from Knossos wears typical Minoan clothing — an open bodice and pleated skirt. Her snakes may symbolize fertility.

◀ WALL PAINTING
The palace at Knossos contained about 1300 rooms. Many were decorated with wall paintings like this one showing a beautiful Minoan woman with long braided hair.

BULLS AND MINOTAURS

According to Greek myth, Crete was ruled by King Minos. He was the son of Europa, granddaughter of the sea god Poseidon and Zeus, ruler of the gods. Poseidon sent Minos a magnificent white bull for sacrifice. Bulls were sacred to the Minoans and their images appear throughout Knossos.

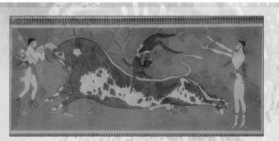

◀ SLAYING THE MINOTAUR
Theseus, the Greek hero, slays the Minotaur, a monster who was half man, half bull. According to Greek myth, Minos kept the Minotaur in a labyrinth or maze. Every year, young men and women were sacrificed to him.

▲ BULL LEAPING
A wall painting shows young Minoan men and women leaping over the backs of bulls. This daring feat was probably part of a religious ceremony that took place in the courtyard at Knossos.

▼ STORAGE JAR
Hundreds of these earthenware storage jars, or pithoi, have been found at Knossos, many as tall as a grown man.

◄ DAILY LIFE
Minoan towns were full of bustle and life. Most were near the coast. Houses were brightly painted and usually two or three stories high. Olive trees grew on the island and olives were used for oil and cooking.

The Minoans were seafarers. They traded with many countries, importing copper from Turkey, ivory and gold from Egypt and lapis lazuli from Afghanistan.

Suddenly, this flourishing culture suffered a disaster. Palace walls collapsed and there were great fires.

Possibly this was due to a massive earthquake or a volcanic eruption on the nearby island of Thera. The Minoans rebuilt their palaces but in 1450BC disaster struck again. Myceneans invaded from mainland Greece and the Minoan civilization was overrun.

Key Dates

- c.6000BC Mainland Greeks arrive in Crete.

- 2000BC Minoans build palace at Knossos.

- 2000–1700BC Minoans build palaces at Phaistos, Mallia and Zakros. Minoan culture flourishes.

- 1900BC Cretans use potter's wheel.

- 1450BC Minoan civilization collapses with eruption on Thera and the arrival of invaders from Greece.

◄ MINOAN CIVILIZATION
Crete is the largest Greek island and the birthplace of the Minoan culture, one of the first European civilizations. The map shows the extent of this glorious civilization. Apart from the Palace of Minos in Knossos, the Minoans also built fabulous palaces in Mallia, Phaistos and Zakros and established trading posts throughout the Mediterranean.

Map labels:

Sea of Crete

WHITE MTS   C R E T E   Knossos   Mallia   Gournia

DICTAEAN MTS   Zakros

Hagia Triada

Phaistos

Mediterranean Sea

N

Kilometers   100
Miles   60
0   0

Mycenae

IN ABOUT 1600BC a warlike group came to power in mainland Greece. They were the Mycenaeans, called after one of their largest strongholds at Mycenae in the northeastern Peloponnese. The Mycenaeans created the first Greek civilization. They lived in massive hilltop citadels or fortified settlements, made stunning gold objects and produced soldiers who were famed for their bravery.

The Mycenaeans probably consisted of several different groups of people, each with their own ruler. Each group was based in its own citadel. Mycenae was the largest but there were others at Tiryns and Gla. The people all spoke an early form of Greek and their massive fortifications were built with such huge stones that people later thought that giants must have hauled the stones into place. From their native Greek mainland, the Mycenaeans voyaged far into the Aegean and

▲ MASK OF "AGAMEMNON"
This beautiful gold mask would have belonged to a Mycenaean king. When the king was buried, the mask was placed over his face. Archeologists once thought the mask was a portrait of Agamemnon, a hero of the Trojan War.

Mediterranean Seas. Their merchants traveled west to Sicily and east to the Turkish coast, where they set up a trading post called Miletus. They also visited many of the Greek islands, trading with local people or setting up colonies. Their greatest conquest was the large island of Crete, where they defeated the Minoans. This conquest gave them access to many new trade routes that Minoan merchants had used.

The ruins left by the Mycenaeans look very bleak today, with their bare stone walls on windswept hillsides. But the kings and nobles did themselves proud, building small but luxurious palaces inside their citadels. Each citadel also contained houses for the king's soldiers, officials, priests, scribes and craftworkers. Farmers settled in the hill country and surrounding plains. They supplied the king and his people with food and sheltered in the citadel during times of war.

The Mycenaean civilization continued until about 1200BC when a great fire destroyed the citadel of Mycenae. Although the Mycenaeans hung on for another 100 years, their power began to decline.

THE TROJAN WAR
Ancient Greek myths tell of a great war between Greece and Troy. Paris, Prince of Troy, fell in love and ran away with Helen, Queen of Sparta and wife of King Menelaus. King Menelaus, his brother Agamemnon and a huge army beseiged Troy for 10 years, finally capturing the city. Historians believe the legend is based on a real battle involving the Mycenaeans.

▲ WARRIOR
Mycenaean warriors wore finely decorated helmets and highly elaborate armor. They were very important in Mycenaean society.

▶ THE TROJAN HORSE
The Greeks tricked the Trojans with a huge wooden horse. They pretended to leave Troy, leaving the horse behind. The Trojans pulled the horse into the city. Hidden inside were Greeks. Late at night, they came out of the horse and captured Troy.

◀ **MYCENAE**
The Mycenaeans built their huge citadels on the tops of hills, near the coast. Farmlands stretched back on to the inland plains. Huge walls surrounded the citadels. Some said the walls had been built by Cyclops, the legendary one-eyed giant. Within Mycenae was a palace and many other buildings. A town lay outside the fortification.

▲ **SEA CREATURES**
The Mycenaeans often decorated objects with sea creatures such as dolphins, or the octopus on this stemmed drinking cup. They valued the sea, which they traveled for trade and conquest.

◀ **MYCENAEANS**
The map shows the main areas of Mycenaean influence and their extensive trading routes. They lived on sites near the coast. Many of their major citadels were on the Peloponnese, the large peninsula that makes up the southern part of the mainland. There were also major settlements at Athens and around Lake Kopais. From these strongholds, the Mycenaeans traveled to most of the islands in the Aegean Sea.

Key Dates

- 1600BC Mycenaean civilization begins to develop in groups on Greek mainland.

- 1450BC The Mycenaeans invade and conquer the Minoans of Crete.

- 1200BC Decline of Mycenaean civilization.

- 800BC Homer's epic poems, the *Iliad* and the *Odyssey*, record some of the traditions of the Mycenaeans.

The Etruscans

▲ ETRUSCAN POT
Etruscan pottery was often beautifully decorated with abstract designs or pictures of animals. Many skilled craftworkers lived and worked in the cities.

ONE OF THE LEAST-known early peoples, the Etruscans lived between the Arno and Tiber rivers in western Italy. From the 8th to the 1st centuries BC, they built a series of cities and grew wealthy by mining copper, tin and iron. We do not know where the Etruscans came from originally, and they remain a mysterious people. They could write, but none of their literature has survived, and many of their cities lie beneath modern Italian towns.

The Etruscans' strength came from living near the coast. They established iron mines by the sea, at Populonia and the nearby island of Elba, and used these as the basis for trade. Skilled seafarers, the Etruscans crossed the Mediterranean to trade with the Phoenician settlers at Carthage, North Africa. They constructed harbors for their ships but built their cities slightly inland to safeguard against pirate attacks.

They also traded with Greece but the Greeks began to set up rival trading colonies in southern Italy. By the

▲ CHARIOT-RACE MURALS
Etruscans may have been the first people to introduce chariot racing, as shown in this tomb painting from Chiusi. Later, it became a popular Roman pastime.

6th century BC, the Etruscans and Greeks were at war. The Gauls, ancient people of western Europe, were also making raids. Etruscan leaders realized that their best protection was to join forces, and 12 of their cities came together in a league to encourage trade and defend each other from attack.

The Etruscans were also skilled artists. Their art was stongly influenced by the Greeks. The most spectacular Etruscan remains are tombs. Rich families built large

MUSIC AND DANCE
Archeologists in the 19th century discovered thousands of Etruscan wall paintings and bronze statues. Many of these show that music and dance were an important part of Etruscan culture.

◀ FLUTE PLAYER
Musical instruments, such as these pipes, may have played a part in religious ceremonies, and in entertainment for the noble families.

▶ LYRE PLAYER
Etruscan musicians probably played the lyre, a sort of small harp, to accompany poetry, songs and dancing.

▲ ROOF DECORATION
This brightly painted head dates from the 6th century BC. Made of clay and fired in a kiln, it decorated the roof of a building in the Etruscan town of Veii.

Terracotta tiles

Colonnades
provided shade in
the summer

Buildings were organized
around an open area

▶ ETRUSCAN PALACE
*Some leading Etruscan
families became rich
and powerful through the
iron trade. As cities grew
and prospered, these
noblemen ruled over
their people from
luxurious palaces like
this one near Siena.*

Rammed earth walls

tombs with several rooms, decorated
with portraits of the owners' families.
These are some of the best preserved paintings to
survive from the ancient world. There were also many
fine sculptors in the northern Etruscan cities. They
worked in bronze, producing figurines, statues, and
items such as engraved mirrors and decorative panels
for furniture and chariots.

The Romans — the Etruscans' final enemies —
prized this artwork highly. When Rome and her allies
conquered Etruscan cities in the 3rd century BC, they
took away thousands of bronze statues.

◀ TRADE
*The Etruscans traded with
Phoenicia and Greece,
becoming the first wealthy
civilization in western Europe.
With profits from the iron
trade, they could enjoy luxuries
such as this gold vase.*

◀ ETRUSCANS
The map shows the
extent of Etruscan
influence and how
this grew. Etruria,
the land of the
Etruscans, stretched
from the River Arno
to the Tiber. The
major Etruscan
cities, such as
Caere, Chiusi, and
Tarquinia, were
independent states
with their own
rulers. Rome,
originally a small
town on the edge of
Etruria, became a
city in the time of
the Etruscans.

Original Etruscan Territory
Etruscan Expansion
Greek Colonies

Cortona
Telamon
Vulci
Tarquinii
Caere
CORSICA
ITALY
Adriatic Sea
SARDINIA
Tyrrhenian Sea
SICILY
Mediterranean Sea

0 Kilometers 250
0 Miles 150

Key Dates

- 800BC Etruscans set up cities.
- 540BC The Etruscans trade with the Phoenician city of Carthage, and forge an alliance with the Carthaginians.
- 524 and 474BC The Etruscans and Greeks battle over trade in Italy. The Greeks, with colonies in southern Italy, are victorious.
- 413BC The Etruscan league of cities makes an alliance with the Greeks.
- 273BC Romans conquer Caere.
- 265BC Romans destroy Volsinii.

Classical Greece

▲ ZEUS
The Greeks worshipped many gods and goddesses. Zeus, above, was supreme. Greeks thought the gods lived on Mount Olympus, Greece's highest mountain.

THE WAY OUR countries are governed, the books we read, the plays we watch, even many of our sports, all have their origins in the classical Greek civilization, which flourished some 2500 years ago. The Greeks did not have a huge empire. For much of their history their civilization consisted of several separate city-states. But their art, science, philosophy and ways of life have had an enormous influence on our lives.

The Greek countryside is rocky and mountainous. Early Greeks lived near the coast or in fertile plains between the mountains. Gradually, these early settlements became city-states. The Greeks were good sailors and boat-builders and their civilization began to flourish when they sailed to Italy and the eastern Mediterranean to trade with their neighbors. They also set up colonies in these areas and around the coast of the Aegean Sea.

As their wealth increased the Greeks built fine cities. The largest and richest was Athens. The citizens of Athens enjoyed much leisure time and Athens

◀ PARTHENON
The largest temple on the Acropolis, the Parthenon was built in 432BC. The pillars were marble and its beautiful frieze showed a procession in honor of the goddess Athene.

became the center of Greek culture. Greek dramatists such as Sophocles wrote some of the finest plays in western theater. Their musicians created fine music and architects designed elegant buildings and temples. The Greeks also started the Olympic Games.

Greek education was famous throughout the ancient world. Philosophers, or thinkers, came to Athens to discuss everything from the nature of love to how a country should be governed. The Athenians developed a new form of government, in which people had a say in who ruled them. They called it democracy, or government by the people. Not everyone was actually allowed to vote but their system was the ancestor of modern democratic government.

Athens remained strong for several centuries until the Romans began to take over the Mediterranean world. War with another Greek city state, Sparta, also weakened Athens. In 404BC Sparta defeated Athens.

ENTERTAINMENT
The ancient Greeks believed in enjoying themselves. They enjoyed music and art and went to theater regularly. Sport too was very important and had religious significance. The first ever Olympic Games were held in 776BC, in honor of the god Zeus. Like today, they were held every four years.

◀ ATHLETE
A Greek discus thrower. The Olympic Games were only for men. Women were not even allowed to watch. They held their own games, in honor of Hera, goddess of women.

Actors wore these masks – the one on the left for comedy, that on the right for tragedy.

▲ AMPHITHEATER
Greek theaters were large, open-air arenas with rows of stone seats. There were regular drama festivals where playwrights such as Aristophanes, Euripides and Sophocles competed for the award of best play.

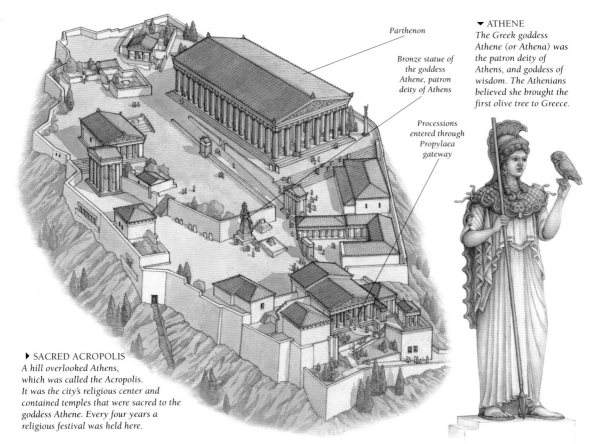

Parthenon

Bronze statue of
the goddess
Athene, patron
deity of Athens

Processions
entered through
Propylaea
gateway

▼ ATHENE
The Greek goddess
Athene (or Athena) was
the patron deity of
Athens, and goddess of
wisdom. The Athenians
believed she brought the
first olive tree to Greece.

▶ SACRED ACROPOLIS
A hill overlooked Athens,
which was called the Acropolis.
It was the city's religious center and
contained temples that were sacred to the
goddess Athene. Every four years a
religious festival was held here.

◀ ANCIENT GREECE
The Greeks spread out
from their homeland in
the Peloponnese, setting
up colonies in southern
Italy, Sicily, the Aegean,
and the coasts of the
Black Sea.

▼ ELGIN MARBLES
These marble sculptures,
known as the Elgin
Marbles, were taken from
the Parthenon to England
in 1815 by Lord Elgin.
They remain in the
British Museum.

ITALY

MACEDONIA

THESSALY

ATTICA

Aegean
Sea

Ionian
Sea

Smyrna

Eretria
Athens

Corinth

Sparta

Miletus

SICILY

Lindos

N

Mediterranean Sea

0   Kilometers   400
0   Miles   250

CRETE

Classical Greece

THE HEART OF A GREEK CITY was the agora, or market place. This was a central square surrounded by the city's main public buildings – temples, law courts, market halls and shops. Everyone came to the agora to do their shopping, meet friends, listen to scholars, or just gossip. The city council also met in the agora.

Beyond the agora lay streets of private houses. They were usually arranged around a courtyard with overhanging roofs and small windows to keep out the summer sun and winter cold. In the summer, much of the life of the house took place here.

Men and women were not equal in ancient Greece. Women did not have the vote and were allowed little in the way of money or private property. Most women aimed to marry and give birth to a son. Men enjoyed much more freedom. There was even a room in most Greek houses, called the andron, which was used only by the men of the household.

Boys and girls were also treated differently. In the cities, boys went to school from age 7 to 12. They learned reading, writing, music and poetry, as well as sports such as wrestling. Most girls stayed at home with their mothers, where they learned skills such as spinning, weaving and cooking, so that they would be able to run homes of their own.

Life was rather different in Sparta. From early childhood, boys were taught skills to prepare them for fighting and life in the army. All men had to do military service. Girls too were trained for a hard, outdoor life.

When a Greek person died, people believed that he or she would go to Hades, the underworld. The Greeks imagined this as a dark, underground world, surrounded by a river, the Styx. People were buried with a coin, to pay Charon, the ferryman who would row them across the River Styx into the next world.

◄ WOMEN
Greek women wore folded material called chitons, fastened at the shoulder. Few houses had water so, balancing jars on their head, women collected water from the local well or fountain.

◄ VENUS DE MILO
This beautiful statue of Aphrodite is known as the Venus de Milo. Although carved after the time of classical Greece, it still demonstrates the ancient Greek ideal of the perfect body.

LEARNING AND PHILOSOPHY

The Greeks were educated people and valued learning. Western philosophy, which means "love of wisdom" began in ancient Greece. Greek philosophers studied astronomy, science and asked deep questions about the meaning of life.

◄ SOCRATES
The most famous of all the ancient Greek philosophers was Socrates (469–399BC). During discussions, he asked continuous questions, sometimes pretending not to know the answers in an attempt to trip up his opponents.

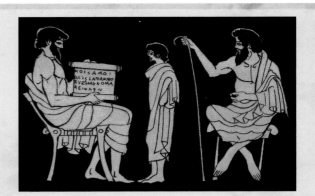

▲ GOING TO SCHOOL
Boys from rich families were taken to school by a slave called a paidogogos. The tutor used papyrus rolls to teach the child, but the boy would practice writing on a wax tablet, using a pointed tool called a stylus.

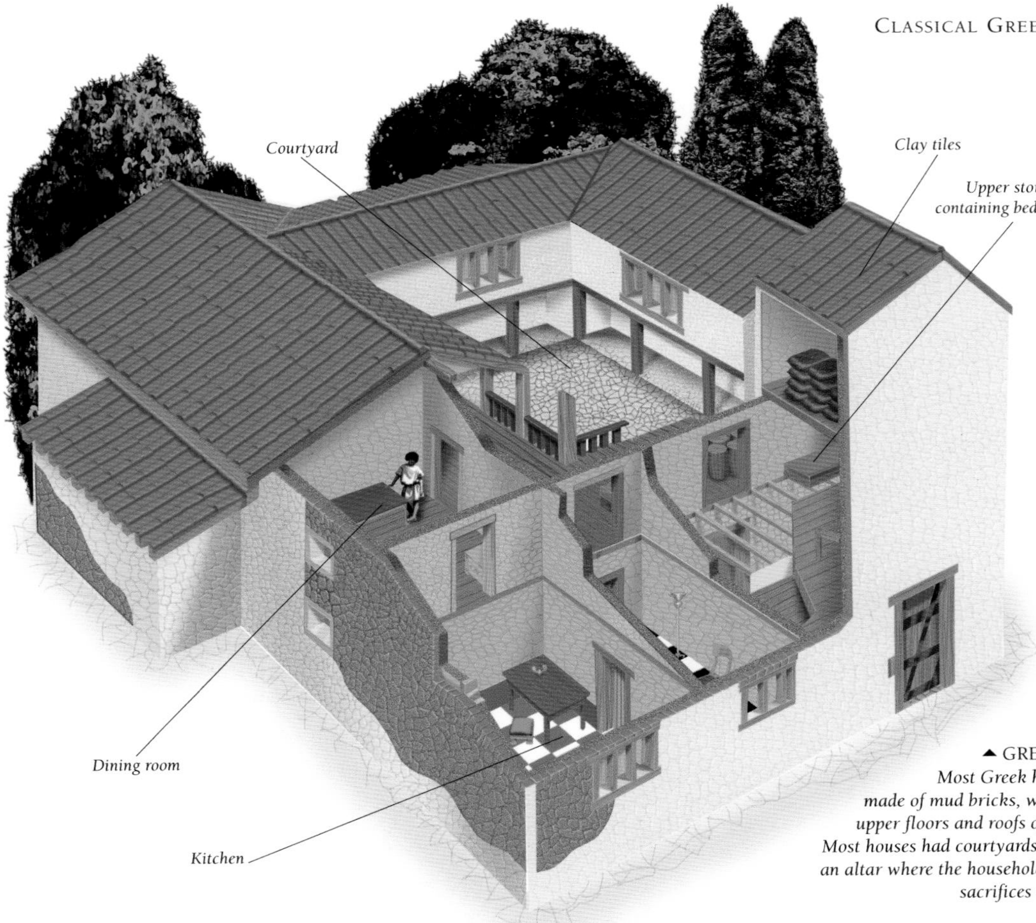

Courtyard

Clay tiles

*Upper story
containing bedrooms*

Dining room

Kitchen

▲ GREEK VILLA
*Most Greek houses were
made of mud bricks, with wooden
upper floors and roofs of clay tiles.
Most houses had courtyards containing
an altar where the householders offered
sacrifices to the gods.*

▶ SPARTA
Spartan footsoldiers
were heavily armed.
When attacked, they
formed a solid line
or phalanx, spears
pointing outwards.
Sparta was far
inland. Its people
had to be tough to
live in their remote
mountain region.

◀ COINS
The Greeks used silver coins. Slaves
toiled in mines near Athens, digging
out silver by hand. Some coins were
decorated with an owl, symbol of the
goddess Athene.

Key Dates

- 900BC The Greeks begin to trade in
  the Mediterranean.
- 776BC First recorded Olympic Games.
- 700BC Greek city states develop.
- 490BC Persia attacks Athens but is
  defeated at the Battle of Marathon.
- 480BC The second Persian war also
  leads to defeat for Persia.
- 443–429BC Athens flourishes under
  its greatest leader, Pericles.
- 431BC The Peloponnesian Wars
  begin between Athens and Sparta.
- 404BC The Spartans defeat the
  Athenians.

Hellenistic Age

▲ COIN
The head of Alexander the Great (356–323BC), wearing the horns of an Egyptian god appears on this coin. His exploits gained him almost legendary status.

I
N 336BC, A YOUNG MAN called Alexander became ruler of the small kingdom of Macedonia, north of Greece. Within just a few years, he and his well trained army had conquered one of the greatest empires of the ancient world. They swept across Asia Minor and marched down the eastern Mediterranean coast to take over Phoenicia (modern Syria) and Judea (modern Palestine). Then they moved on to Egypt, where Alexander was accepted as a child of the Sun God. From there, Alexander and his men went north once more, to take Persia, then the world's greatest empire. Soon Persia too was in Alexander's hands, together with the area of the Indus Valley, on the borders of India. Alexander was preparing to conquer Arabia when he died of a fever, aged only 33.

Alexander was one of the most brilliant generals and powerful leaders the world has known. He was highly educated — his teacher was the Greek philosopher Aristotle — but also a skilled horseman and had boundless energy. After conquering Persia, he would

▲ ALEXANDRIAN LIBRARY
The city of Alexandria contained a fabulous library where many of the works of the great Greek writers were preserved on papyrus rolls. The library burned down in AD391.

have continued into India but his men were exhausted.

By the time he died, Alexander had traveled 20,000 miles on his epic journey of conquest. Everywhere he went, he took with him the Greek culture and way of life, so spreading it over a huge area. He founded cities, often called Alexandria after him, and left behind

◀ BUCEPHALUS
Alexander had a favorite horse, Bucephalus. Legend says the horse was wild and only responded to Alexander.

ALEXANDER
When Philip II of Macedonia was killed, Alexander took over a kingdom that was the strongest in Greece. Philip was about to attack Persia when he died. Alexander inherited his ambition.

▶ ALEXANDRIA
The Castle of Qaitbay stands in the present-day city of Alexandria in Egypt. Alexander founded this city in 332BC. He founded others, many of which were named after him.

▲ DELPHIC ORACLE
The Greeks often consulted an oracle for advice before undertaking a momentous event. The most famous was the oracle at Delphi. Philip II and Alexander consulted her.

◄ BATTLE OF ISSUS
At the Battle of Issus, in 333BC, Alexander with a much smaller force defeated the much larger Persian army under Darius III. It was a tremendous victory, opening Syria and Egypt to Alexander's advance.

▼ TIARA
As the Macedonian army swept across Persia, they took what booty they could carry with them. They especially prized Persian metalwork, such as this gold tiara and other items made from gold and silver worn by Persian nobles.

workers who filled them with classical buildings — temples, theaters, houses, all in the Greek style. For 300 years, this Greek style remained fashionable all over western Asia. Historians now call this period the Hellenistic Age, after Hellas, the Greeks' own name for their country.

Alexander's vast empire did not survive his death. His generals carved it up between them. Ptolemy, ancestor of Queen Cleopatra, ruled Egypt; Antigonous took over Greece and much of Turkey; Seleucus,

founder of the Seleucid dynasty of Persian kings, controlled the area from Turkey to the Indus. Only cities named Alexandria remained to remind people of the great general from Macedonia.

◄ ALEXANDER'S WORLD
The map shows the extent of Alexander's empire and the major routes he took. From its heartland in Greece and the Aegean coast of Turkey, Alexander's empire spread east to the River Indus. The Macedonians founded several Alexandrias in Persia, as well as the more famous one in Egypt.

Key Dates

- 356BC Alexander born in Macedonia.

- 336BC Alexander becomes ruler of Macedonia and puts down uprisings in Greece.

- 333BC Alexander defeats the Persians at the Battle of Issus.

- 332BC Macedonians conquer Egypt. Alexander is accepted as pharaoh.

- 331BC Alexander wins the Battle of Gaugamela, the final defeat of the Persians.

- 326BC Alexander and his army reach the Indus River.

- 323BC Alexander dies of a fever. His empire breaks up.

Ancient Rome

▲ ROMULUS AND REMUS
According to legend, two brothers – Romulus and Remus – founded Rome. Abandoned as babies, they were left to die but a she-wolf suckled them and they survived.

TWO THOUSAND YEARS ago a small Italian town grew to become the most important city in the whole of the western world. The name of the town was Rome. Built on seven hills near the River Tiber, Rome was already powerful by the 3rd century BC. It had a well-organized government, a fearsome army and had taken over the whole of Italy. Over the next 200 years, Rome expanded its influence to become the center of a great empire. By AD117, the Roman Empire stretched from Britain to North Africa, and from Spain to Palestine.

At the heart of this great empire was the city of Rome itself. At the center of the city was the forum, a market square surrounded by large public buildings, such as temples, baths and stadiums. The Romans took much from the ancient Greek culture. Many of their public buildings looked similar to Greek ones, with classical pillars and marble sculptures.

Beyond the forum were streets of dwelling places. City land was expensive. Poorer Romans could not afford houses so they rented apartments arranged in multi-story blocks, like modern apartment buildings. On the ground floor of each block were stores full of goods and craftworkers. Between the stores was an entrance way, leading to the apartments above. Some had larger, more expensive, rooms. Others, further up the building, were smaller and cheaper. Few had their own water supply or proper kitchen.

In the countryside too, many ordinary Romans lived in poverty, working the land to supply food for the cities. Here, land was cheaper and more plentiful so the wealthiest Romans built themselves large, graceful villas, or country houses. These often had their own baths and an underfloor heating system.

◀ HUNTING
In the countryside, Romans hunted wild boar with dogs. Hunting provided enjoyment and also gave the Romans a more varied diet.

SOCIETY
Roman society was divided into classes, or social groups. At the top were generals, governors, magistrates and other important officials. Further down were bankers and merchants. Below were craftworkers and shopkeepers. Bottom of the social pile were slaves. Romans were either citizens, free people with rights, or non-citizens.

▼ SHIPS
The Romans used ships for war and trade. Slaves labored to drive them forward by means of banks of oars on either side.

▲ AT THE BATHS
Roman cities had large public bath complexes. There were different rooms with baths of different temperatures, and bathers went from one to the other, finishing up with a cold plunge and an invigorating massage. People went to the baths not only to get clean but also to meet friends and socialize.

◀ STREET SCENE

Some of the best preserved ancient Roman houses are in Ostia, the port of the city of Rome. Sand blowing in from the coast covered the houses, protecting mosaic floors and walls. The town was full of apartment buildings with stores and bars beneath.

Poorer people lived in smaller, upper apartments

Craftworkers made and sold wares in workshops on the ground floor

An entranceway led past stores to a stairway going up to the apartments

Lower apartments had larger rooms and were more expensive

▲ CLOTHING

Most Romans dressed simply and according to class. Outside, Roman citizens only wore a toga, a large piece of white woolen cloth, wound round the body. Roman women wore long linen or woolen tunics.

◀ SHOE

Romans wore leather shoes or sandals, which laced part way up the leg.

▼ NEPTUNE

The Romans worshipped the same gods as the ancient Greeks but gave them different names. The Greek Poseidon, king of the sea, became the Roman Neptune, shown here.

Key Dates

- 753BC According to legend, Rome is founded by Romulus and Remus.

- 509BC Rome becomes a republic.

- 146BC Rome defeats Carthage.

- 58–50BC Julius Caesar conquers Gaul.

- 44BC Julius Caesar is assassinated.

- 27BC Augustus becomes first of the Roman emperors.

- AD117 Emperor Trajan conquers Dacia (Romania). Empire is at its largest extent.

- AD324 Christianity becomes the official religion of the empire.

- AD410 Invading Goths conquer and destroy the city of Rome.

Ancient Rome

As ROME'S INFLUENCE grew, so its government changed. The city had once been ruled by kings but in 509BC, it became a republic, governed by elected consuls. A senate advised the consuls. Under the consuls, Rome's power grew until, by the 2nd century BC, only Carthage, the powerful North African trading empire, could stand up to its might. In 146BC the Romans destroyed Carthage. Rome continued to be a republic until 27BC when, after a civil war, Augustus became the first Roman emperor. For the next 500 years, a series of emperors ruled an empire that was the largest in the western world.

There were many reasons for Rome's success. The empire had a strong, well-organized army. The Romans also gained rich spoils whenever the army conquered a new territory. In this way, Rome had access to a wide range of raw materials, including iron from central Europe and gold and silver from Spain. As the Romans conquered new territories, they introduced their own system of government, language and laws into the conquered regions.

◀ AQUEDUCT
The Romans built many aqueducts to bring in water from the rivers in the countryside to the city. Rome had many aqueducts and was the only ancient city with a reliable water supply. Roman aqueducts still stand today in cities as far apart as Nîmes, France and Istanbul, Turkey.

The empire also included many talented engineers, who built bridges and aqueducts as well as the first large domes. The Romans developed concrete. They also built a huge network of long, straight roads across the empire, linking all parts of the empire to Rome. Many of these routes are still used today.

By AD220, the power of Rome appeared complete. The Romans seemed to be able to build anything and their army seemed to be able to conquer any country. But in the end, the empire became too large. Peoples from the lands on the fringes of the empire in central Europe began to rebel, and it was difficult for the army to move quickly and crush their revolts. Rome's vast empire began to fall apart. In AD395, the empire divided into two and within a few years the last Roman emperor was overthrown.

ROMAN ARMY
Without their powerful army, the Romans would have had no empire. The Roman army conquered new territories and defended frontiers. It also worked on huge engineering projects such as bridges and roads.

◀ LEGIONARY
The best-trained soldiers in the Roman army were the 150,000 legionaries. They were highly disciplined,and wore metal armor.

▶ JULIUS CAESAR
Caesar was a consul who ruled Rome as dictator. He conquered Gaul (France) and invaded Britain. His enemies assassinated him in 44BC.

▲ TRAJAN'S COLUMN
Roman legions attack Dacians in this detail from Trajan's Column in Rome. Made of marble, the column was built to the orders of Emperor Trajan, who led a campaign against the Dacians in AD117.

▶ COLOSSEUM
The Roman emperors staged great "games" to win the favor of the Roman people. The Colosseum in Rome, shown here, was the most famous arena. Opened in AD80, it could hold up to 50,000 spectators who crowded in to see gladiators fight.

▼ GLADIATOR
Specially trained, gladiators fought each other to the death or were forced into combat with wild beasts from all over the empire. Slaves and prisoners of war were used as gladiators.

Underground cells contained gladiators and cages for wild animals

The floor of the arena could be flooded with water for mock sea-battles with miniature ships

Massive arches and vaults held up the weighty structure

◀ ROMAN EMPIRE
At its largest extent, in around AD117, Rome's empire stretched right across Europe into western Asia. Hadrian's wall, northern England, was the northern frontier. Egypt was the empire's southernmost point. In AD395, the empire, which was too large, divided. The eastern empire became known as the Byzantine Empire.

Roman Empire

N

BRITISH ISLES
North Sea
GERMANY
Atlantic Ocean
GAUL
Black Sea
DALMATIA
ITALY
CORSICA
Rome
GREECE
ANATOLIA
Antiochia
IBERIA
SARDINIA
Athens
CYPRUS
Jerusalem
Carthage
Mediterranean Sea
NORTH AFRICA
EGYPT
Red Sea

0   Kilometers   500
0   Miles   300

Early Dynastic China

CIVILIZATION IN CHINA grew up quite separately from the rest of the world. In many ways, Chinese civilization was far in advance of Europe and western Asia, whose people did not know what was happening in China. The Chinese invented many things, including metal working and writing, without any contact with other peoples. This made the Chinese way of life quite distinctive.

Periods of Chinese history are named after dynasties or ruling families. One of the earliest was the Shang dynasty, which began in about 1650BC. Many of the key features of Chinese daily life evolved at this time, such as farming and ancestor worship. The Shang Chinese also became skilled at working in bronze and jade.

They developed a form of writing, which later became the written characters still used in China today.

China is a vast country and the Shang dynasty controlled only northern China. The ruling priest-kings were supremely powerful. To the Chinese, they were god-like figures, who could communicate with their ancestors in heaven.

The Shang built many capital cities, possibly

▲ RITUAL VESSEL
This bronze container was used for religious offerings. An ancestor spirit, in the form of a tiger, stands protectively over a man. Other beasts, probably also spirits, cover the tiger's skin.

▶ BRONZE CASTING
Shang Chinese pour molten bronze into a mold. The Chinese had developed bronze casting by about 1650BC and used bronze for making dishes and other items. The king appointed special officials to run the industry.

BELIEFS
The ancient Chinese believed spirits controlled everything. They also worshipped their dead ancestors. One teacher who influenced Chinese beliefs was Confucius. Another was Lao-tze (b. 604BC), founder of Taoism (The Way). This teaches the need to be in harmony with earth, nature and the cosmos.

▶ ORACLE BONE
When a priest wanted to ask ancestor spirits a question, he wrote the question on a piece of bone. He put the bone into the fire until it cracked, then "read" the marks. They were the first form of Chinese writing.

◀ CONFUCIUS
One of the greatest of the Chinese philosophers was Confucius (551-479BC). He taught his followers to help and respect others, to value the family and to respect elders.

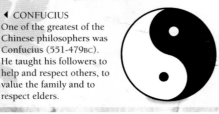

◀ YIN AND YANG
Yin and yang symbol. Traditional Chinese beliefs are based on the idea that everything and everyone contains yin — darkness — and yang — lightness. Health and well-being occur when they are balanced.

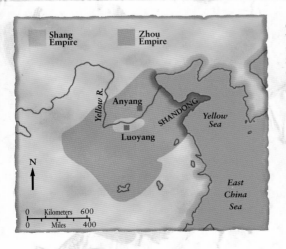

Houses on strong wooden stilts

Oxen drew hand plows

Rice grew in flooded fields

moving them because of floods from China's great rivers. They built the first at Erlitou, then founded the cities of Zhengzhou and Anyang. Archeologists have found remains of wooden houses, a palace, storerooms and streets at Anyang. They also found a king's grave. It contained pottery, bronze and jade items, and nearly 4000 cowrie shells, which the Shang used for money. Also in the tomb were the remains of 47 other people, probably servants sacrificed when their ruler died.

In the 11th century BC, the Zhou dynasty, from north of Anyang, took over from the Shang. The Zhou rulers introduced coins into China and Zhou craftworkers discovered how to work iron. They also invented the crossbow. The Zhou ruled for around 800 years, letting local lords look after their own areas. But the lords began to fight each other. The Zhou dynasty ended and China entered what is known as the Warring States period.

◄ FARMING
For thousands of years the Chinese have farmed the fertile land around the Yellow River, which often floods. The Shang Chinese grew millet, wheat and rice. They also domesticated cattle, pigs, dogs and sheep.

◄ EARLY DYNASTIC CHINA
The map shows the territories of the Shang and Zhou dynasties. The Shang homeland was by the Yellow River, where its waters left the mountains to flow down on to a broad fertile plain. Here they built their main cities — Anyang was a Shang capital. The Zhou came from farther north but also occupied the plain. They made Luoyang their capital city.

Shang Empire

Zhou Empire

Yellow R.

Anyang

SHANDONG

Yellow Sea

Luoyang

N

East China Sea

| 0 | Kilometers | 600 |
| 0 | Miles | 400 |

Key Dates

- 1650–1027 BC Shang dynasty. China's first great Bronze Age civilization develops.

- 1027–256 BC Zhou dynasty. The kingdom is divided into many states and the king rules through local lords.

- 481–221 BC Warring States period. Local noblemen clash in large-scale battles. China becomes weaker.

- 221 BC The first Qin emperor unifies China.

Qin China

▲ LUCKY DRAGON
The dragon was a Qin symbol of good luck. When he came to the throne, Qin Shih Huangdi made the creature his own symbol. Ever since, the emperor, the dragon, and the idea of good fortune have been linked closely in China.

BY THE THIRD century BC, war had torn China apart. Seven different states fought each other. For years, no state was strong enough to win a decisive victory and take control of China. Then, in 221BC, the armies of Qin defeated their enemies and brought the seven states together under their leader, Zheng. He took the title Qin Shi Huangdi, the First Sovereign Emperor of Qin.

The First Emperor ruled for only 11 years. But the changes he made lasted much longer and helped later dynasties, such as the Han and Yūan, to rule effectively. His empire was so large, and contained people of so many different backgrounds, that Zheng had to be ruthless to keep China united. Troops executed anyone who disagreed with his policies. They also burned books by writers who disagreed with the emperor.

Another way of making this huge country easier to govern was to create national systems that all

▲ TERRACOTTA ARMY
The First Emperor's tomb contained 7500 life-size terracotta models of the emperor's army, from foot soldiers and crossbowmen to charioteers and officers. Each was based on a real-life soldier. Automatic crossbows were placed by the entrance to fire if anyone tried to rob the tomb.

people could use. The First Emperor ordered that everyone in China should use the same systems of weights, measurements and writing. He also began a program of building roads and canals, so his officials and merchants could travel easily around the country.

The Xiongnu, a nomadic people from the north of China, were always threatening to invade. So the emperor built the Great Wall to keep out the invaders. He ordered his builders to join up many existing walls along China's northern frontier. Working on the wall

INVENTIONS
The ancient Chinese were very inventive. By 150BC, they had mastered silk-making, invented the wheelbarrow and learned how to make paper.

◀ FIRST EMPEROR
Qin Shi Huangdi's streak of cruelty earned him the title "The Tiger of Qin". He dealt strictly with the rulers of the old warring states. Those not killed in battle were stripped of their power and status.

◀ COINS
Chinese people had used money, in the form of miniature metal knives and spades, long before the Qin period. But the First Emperor introduced round coins, with holes cut in the middle so people could carry them easily by threading them on to a string.

▶ WHEELBARROW
The Han Chinese invented the wheelbarrow more than 1000 years before people in the West.

▲ GREAT WALL
Today the Great Wall winds more than 1,800 miles across northern China. It is the longest structure ever created by humans.

The main wall was about 30 feet high

Watchtowers were about 35 feet high

Watchtowers with loopholes for firing crossbows

was hazardous. For much of its length, the wall ran through mountains. It was exhausting work carrying stone and moving earth to create ramparts. Many workers died. Other people suffered because they had to pay high taxes for the wall.

Qin Shi Huangdi worked hard to keep his empire together. After his death, war caused the empire to break up for a while.

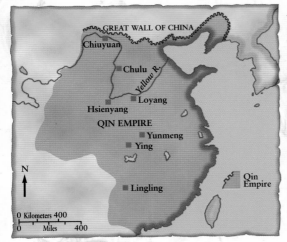

Chinese peasants and soldiers labored to build the Great Wall

◀ BUILDING THE GREAT WALL
The Great Wall was built as a solid obstacle against invasions. It was also a communications network. Officers signaled to each other using bonfires, and messengers could ride along the top of the wall.

◀ QIN EMPIRE
The map shows the extent of the Qin Empire. From the heartlands along the banks of the Yellow River, the empire of the Qin stretched north to the fort at Juyan, south to Panyu (near modern Canton), and west into the province of Sichuan. Qin is pronounced chin, the origin of the name China.

Map labels: GREAT WALL OF CHINA; Chiuyuan; Chulu; Yellow R.; Loyang; Hsienyang; QIN EMPIRE; Yunmeng; Ying; Lingling; Qin Empire; N; 0 Kilometers 400; 0 Miles 400

Key Dates

- 246BC Zheng becomes ruler of the kingdom of Qin.

- 230-222BC A series of victories brings the armies of Qin control of most of the warring states.

- 221BC Qin defeats the last of the warring states. Zheng becomes the First Emperor.

- 213BC The First Emperor orders books by authors opposing his rule to be burned.

- 210BC Qin Shi Huangdi dies.

- 209–208BC A peasant rebellion reduces the power of the Qin government.

- 207BC Qin empire breaks up.

Han China

▲ BRONZE HORSE
This beautiful bronze horse was made nearly 2000 years ago by skilled Chinese craftworkers.

THE PERIOD OF THE Chinese Han dynasty was a time of exciting change. Technology and industry improved, farming became more efficient, and Chinese merchants traded along routes that stretched right across the huge continent of Asia. These developments were so wide-reaching that even today, many Chinese people think of the Han period as the true beginning of China.

The Han emperors took over the government of the Qin dynasty. They organized China into a series of local provinces, each with its own commander. The Qin dynasty had ruled by force but the Han emperors found more peaceful ways of wielding their power. When Han ironworkers discovered how to increase the temperature of their furnaces, they were able to make a much wider range of better quality products. The emperors saw the value of this and put all the iron foundries under state ownership. This gave them control of all the tools and weapons that were produced.

The emperors also tried to control trade, especially the rich trade in silk, which Chinese merchants carried along the overland routes across central Asia. Neighboring areas were only allowed to trade with China if they paid regular tribute to the emperor.

▲ MEASURING EARTHQUAKES
This wonderful object was used to detect earthquakes. The slightest tremor loosened a trigger in a dragon's jaw. The jaw opened, releasing a ball into a frog's mouth below.

CIVIL SERVICE
The first Han emperor, Gaozu (r. 206–195BC) was not highly educated, but he knew he needed well qualified officials to run his empire. He started the civil service with a small group of scholars, who recruited more and more officials.

◄ EXAMINATIONS
Emperor Wu Di (r.140–87BC) thought of the first civil service exams. He founded a special university where candidates could study the writings of Confucius, which they had to learn by heart in order to pass their exams.

▶ GOOD MARKS
The circles on this 19th-century Chinese exam paper indicate where the tutor thought the student's calligraphy was particularly good.

The Han emperors also set up a civil service to administer the empire. They created a huge number of officials, who got their jobs by taking an examination. Candidates had to answer questions on the teachings of the philosopher Confucius. This civil service, with its system of examinations, lasted some 2000 years — much longer than the Han dynasty itself.

The most important of all the changes that took place under the Han emperors were in technology. Paper and fine porcelain, or china, were both Han inventions. Scientists of the Han period even made the world's first seismograph for predicting earthquakes. They also invented a water clock, the wheelbarrow and the stern-post rudder, for better steering of boats at sea. At the same time, merchants brought many new materials into China, from wool and furs to glass and pearls. Peaceful and wealthy, Han China was probably the most advanced civilization of its time.

▶ PRECIOUS SILK
The Chinese used silk for kimonos, wall hangings and, before the Han invented paper and ink, even as a writing material. Silk making began in China some 4000 years ago. The Chinese kept the details of its production secret and earned a huge income from trading in the luxurious fabric.

▼ THE JADE PRINCESS
This body of a Han princess, wrapped in jade, dates back from the 1st century BC. The Chinese believed jade was magical. They thought it would preserve anything wrapped in it for ever.

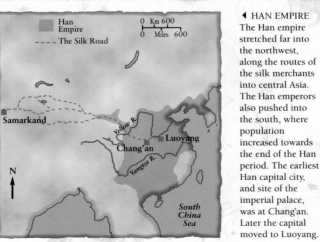

◀ HAN EMPIRE
The Han empire stretched far into the northwest, along the routes of the silk merchants into central Asia. The Han emperors also pushed into the south, where population increased towards the end of the Han period. The earliest Han capital city, and site of the imperial palace, was at Chang'an. Later the capital moved to Luoyang.

Han Empire
- - - - The Silk Road

0 Km 600
0 Miles 600

Samarkand

Yellow R.

Luoyang

Chang'an

Yangtze R.

N

South China Sea

Key Dates

- 207BC Gaozu overthrows the Qin dynasty. The Han dynasty rules from the city of Chang'an.

- 140–87BC The reign of Han Wu Di. He defeats the northern nomads. The Han empire reaches its largest extent.

- 124BC Competitive examinations for the civil service begin.

- 119BC Iron industry nationalized.

- AD25 Later Han period begins. The emperor moves the capital to Luoyang.

- AD105 An official called Cai Lun develops the paper-making process.

- AD220 Power struggles weaken the court and the Han empire collapses.

Early Japan

OR THOUSANDS OF YEARS after the last Ice Age, the people of Japan survived by hunting and gathering. Archeologists call these early people the Jomon. They used tools made of stone and bone and by about 10,500BC, had produced some of the world's first pottery, even though they did not use the potter's wheel.

▲ POTTERY FIGURINE
Jomon potters showed their skill making figurines like this.

During the 3rd century BC, a new people arrived in Japan, probably from the mainland of Asia. Known as the Yayoi, they were the first people in Japan to grow rice in irrigated fields. They also brought metal working to Japan as well as domesticated animals, woven cloth and the potter's wheel, and established a new, settled agricultural society.

The Yayoi people began farming rice on the southern Japanese island of Kyushu. Soon their farming way of life had spread to much of Japan's main island, Honshu. Yayoi farmers used stone tools, such as reaping knives, and made hoes and spades out of wood. Bronze was used mainly for weapons and finely decorated

◀ FARMING RICE
Early Japanese cultivated rice in wet paddy fields. Rice farming probably came to Japan from Korea between 500 and 300BC.

IMPORTED SKILLS
Settlers who came from mainland Asia brought important skills to early Japan. These were bronze and iron casting, useful for making effective tools. They also brought the potter's wheel, so the Japanese could make earthenware objects like jugs and pots, and they introduced land irrigation for growing rice.

◀ BRONZE BELL
Bells like this, covered with decorative patterns and simple pictures of humans and animals, were made in both the Yayoi and Yamato periods. Unlike western bells, they did not have clappers, so must have been rung by beating.

▲ FISHING
Japanese fishermen pursue a whale through high seas in this typically stylized image. Early people in northeastern Japan relied on fish for much of their diet. Whale was an important food source.

▼ TOMB HORSE
When a Yamato emperor died, the people surrounded his burial site with thousands of pottery objects, such as this horse. They were meant to protect the tomb and its contents.

◀ SHINTO
A Shinto temple in Nikko, Japan. Shinto is the traditional religion of Japan. It dates back to very early Japan and was based on a love of nature and belief in spirits, called kami.

items such as bells and mirrors. From this evidence, archeologists believe that only rich or high-status Japanese, such as chiefs, priests and warriors, used metal items. Their owners may have used many of these bronze items, including bells, in ceremonies to celebrate the passing of the seasons or rituals performed during rice planting and harvesting.

By the 3rd century AD, some of the warrior-chiefs had gained power over large areas of Japan. These powerful families became the leaders of the next

Japanese culture, the Yamato. They claimed to be descended from the sun goddess and their power soon stretched across the whole of Japan. They led their soldiers on horseback, and copied the government of the Chinese emperors, with large courts and ranks of officials. The Yamato built hill-top settlements to defend themselves and huge burial tombs, surrounded by moats, were also used for self-defence. These tombs, filled with armor, jewelry and weapons, indicate the great power and wealth of the Yamato emperors.

◀ EARLY JAPAN
The Yayoi rice farmers spread northwards from southern Japan. They are named after the section of modern Tokyo where remains of their culture were found. The later Yamato culture began on the Yamato plain in southeastern Honshu. The greatest number of Yamato remains, especially palaces and tombs, is still to be found in this area.

Key Dates

- 8000BC Jomon culture of hunter-gatherers dominates Japan.

- 200BC The Yayoi people begin to introduce rice farming.

- AD250 Rise of the Yamato culture.

- AD350 The Yamato emperor rules the whole of Japan.

- AD538 The first Buddhists to settle in Japan arrive from Korea.

- AD604 After a period of weakness, Prince Shotoku Taishi strengthens imperial power and introduces new forms of government based on Chinese models.

- AD710 The Yamato period ends and the state capital moves to the city of Nara.

The Khmers

▲ GLAZED JAR
This Vietnamese jar was made around the 11th century AD. It has a finely-cracked cream glaze, decorated with brown leaf sprays.

DEEP IN THE JUNGLES of Cambodia stand the remains of some of the largest temples and palaces ever constructed. They are reminders of the great civilization of the Khmers, who flourished between the 9th and 15th centuries AD, and were ruled by kings so powerful that their people believed them to be gods.

The Khmers lived in a difficult, inhospitable part of the world. Dense tropical forests covered much of their country and every year the monsoons flooded their rivers, making it difficult to grow crops. But they began to clear the forests and adapted to the rains, growing rice in the flooded plains on either side of the great Mekong River.

As time went on, the Khmers learned how to dig canals and reservoirs, to drain away and store the flood water. Then they could water their fields during the rest of the year, when there was little rain.

While their farmers were busy in the fields, the

▲ ANGKOR WAT
The greatest of all the Khmer temples was Angkor Wat. Started by King Suryavarman II in 1113, it covers a vast area. It contains several courtyards lined with shrines and topped with huge towers. The picture shows a detail from the Elephant's Terrace.

Khmers were opening up trade routes through Siam (Thailand) into India. As a result of these links, Khmer artists and architects copied Indian styles, and the Khmers began to adopt the Hindu religion.

RELIGIOUS TEMPLE

The Khmer kingdom lasted for 500 years. Angkor Wat was its most fabulous achievement. The Khmers were Hindus, who believed in gods such as Vishnu, Shiva and Brahma. Their images appear in reliefs all over the temple. Also at Angkor Wat were statues of Nagas, mythical seven-headed snakes. The Khmers believed they were kindly water spirits.

▶ ANGKOR STATUE
The sculptors who worked at Angkor Wat created fabulous work. This intricate stone carving forms part of a massive gateway to the temple. It has survived for hundreds of years in the Cambodian jungles.

▲ ASPARAS
Carved in relief on the walls and in the courtyard of Angkor Wat, these dancing women were known as *asparas*. Covered in jewels and wearing towering headdresses, they entertained kings.

◀ CUTTING TREES
The Khmers had to clear large areas of tropical forest for farming and to build their temples. They used elephants to move and carry heavy trees. They also used elephants in warfare.

The godly status of the Khmer kings gave them enormous power and made most people eager to work for them. From the 12th century onwards, the kings began enormous building projects — temples covering many acres, surrounded by huge lakes and long canals. Thousands of laborers, toiling in groups of 25 or more, hauled massive blocks of stone through the forest to the building sites to create towering temples. They also built hospitals, reservoirs and roads.

The Khmer kingdom lasted until the 15th century, although the people had to fight off several invasion attempts by neighbors jealous of their wealth. Finally, in 1431, an invading army from Siam proved too strong for the Khmers, who fled to a small area in the south of the country.

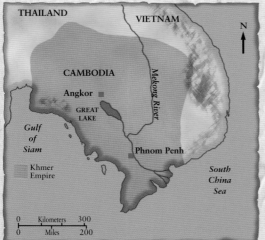

◀ KHMERS
The kingdom of the Khmers occupied much of modern Cambodia, plus the southern part of Vietnam. Around one million people lived in and around the capital, Angkor. The rest of the population occupied the floodplains of rivers such as the Mekong.

Key Dates

- AD802 The Khmer empire is founded under King Jayavarman II (r.802–850).

- AD881 King Yasovarman I builds the earliest surviving Khmer temple.

- AD1113 Work starts on building Angkor Wat.

- AD1177 The Cham sail up the Mekong River and attack Angkor Wat.

- AD1200 King Jayavarman VII builds a new temple, Angkor Thom.

- AD1431 Siamese invaders destroy Angkor; the Khmer empire collapses.

North American Civilizations

THE EARLY CIVILIZATIONS of North America are famous for their burial mounds, remains of which still exist today. These huge structures contain thousands of tons of earth. Large numbers of people must have labored for months or even years to build them. The most famous of the North American civilizations were the Hopewell people, who were based in the Ohio River valley, and the mound builders of the Mississippi area.

Hopewell mounds were gathered together in groups. At Hopewell itself, 38 mounds form a complex of 45 hectares. Most are round or rectangular mounds. They contain several bodies. The Hopewell people left offerings and belongings in the graves with their dead. These included tools, beads, jewelry and ornaments.

Some of the graves were made from raw materials that came from far away because the Hopewells traded over long distances. They imported sea shells from Florida, obsidian (a naturally occurring form of glass) from the Rockies, and flint from Illinois. In return they made goods such as pipes, pottery figurines and copper ornaments as far as southeastern Canada.

After about AD400, the Hopewell trading network began to break down, and the civilization went into decline. No one knows why this happened. Perhaps the population was too large for the local food supply. The climate became colder which may also have cut down the food supply.

But by this time another mound-building group were living in the Mississippi area. They mainly lived in small settlements but created a large city, of perhaps 30,000 people, at Cahokia. This city consisted mainly

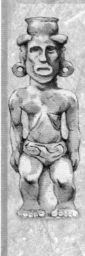

CROPS
The most important crop for the early North American civilizations was maize. Together with beans and squash, it may have come into North America from Mexico. Most early North Americans relied on agriculture, which enabled them to create more permanent settlements.

◀ STONE PIPE
Native Americans may have used this carved stone pipe, dated about 100BC, to smoke various plants, including tobacco. Archeologists found the pipe in Ohio.

▼ HOMES
Houses made from a framework of wooden poles, covered with thatch, provided homes for early Native Americans in the river valleys of southeastern North America.

▲ MASK
The Kwakiutl, Native Americans from the northwest Pacific coast, carved this elaborate mask. Unlike the Ohio peoples, they relied mainly on fishing for their food.

of wood and thatch houses on the fertile river flood plain. In the central area were more than 100 earth mounds. The largest was the vast Monk's Mound, which was more than 90 feet high and topped by a wood and thatch temple. Cahokia was probably the home of local chiefs, whose period of greatest power lasted some 200 years, from 1050 to 1250AD.

Egg-shaped mound

Serpent's mouth

▼ HOPEWELL BURIAL
This is a cross-section through the Great Serpent mound. When a person died, the family usually cremated the body inside a sacred enclosure. After the cremation, they built up an earth mound to cover the enclosure. Later, other people were sometimes buried in the mound.

◀ GREAT SERPENT MOUND
The 420 yard-long earth mound in Ohio is in the form of a snake. Its jaws are open, and it is swallowing an egg, which is, in fact, an oval burial mound. The snake is probably the symbol of a god or an ancestor of the Hopewell people.

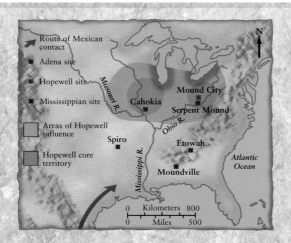

Route of Mexican contact
Adena site
Hopewell site
Mississippian site
Areas of Hopewell influence
Hopewell core territory

N

Missouri R.
Mound City
Cahokia
Serpent Mound
Ohio R.
Spiro
Etowah
Mississippi R.
Atlantic Ocean
Moundville

0 — Kilometers — 800
0 — Miles — 500

◀ NORTH AMERICA
The Hopewell people had their main centers in Ohio and Illinois. The Mississippi people came from the area where the Mississippi and Missouri rivers joined. But the influence of both peoples spread much farther. Archeologists have found their goods all over eastern North America, from Florida in the South to Canada in the North.

Key Dates

- 200BC Beginnings of Hopewell civilization.

- AD400 Hopewell civilization declines.

- AD400–800 Maize growing spreads across southeastern North America.

- AD900 Rise of the Mississippi civilization.

- AD1050–1250 Cahokia is a major center of Mississippi civilization.

- AD1250 Power shifts to Moundville, west-central Alabama.

People of the Andes

▲ STAFF GOD
This 12 foot-high image, part human, part jaguar, stood in the Castillo, the main temple at Chavín de Huantar.

IT SEEMS AN UNLIKELY PLACE to settle. The high Andes mountains make travel, building and farming difficult. But in the 12th century BC, a group of people started to build cities and ritual centers in these harsh conditions. We know these people as the Chavín, after their city at Chavín de Huantar. During their most prosperous period, their settlements spread for many miles along the coastal plain.

At Chavín, near the Mosna River, they built a large temple complex with a maze of corridors and rooms. Here they hid the images of their gods, who were often beings that combined human and animal features — jaguars, eagles, and snakes. Archeologists think that people came to the temple to ask the gods about the future, and that priests inside the hidden rooms replied by blowing conch-shell trumpets.

The Chavín were powerful for around 500 years, after which several local cultures sprang up in the region. The Huari people took over much of the Chavín's territory and a civilization of sun-worshippers emerged at Tiahuanaco, Bolivia.

▲ GATEWAY OF THE SUN
The Gateway of the Sun stood at the entrance to the temple at Tiahuanaco, near Lake Titicaca, Bolivia. It was carved out of one enormous piece of stone.

TIAHUANACO

The Tiahuanaco civilization emerged near Lake Titicaca, where they built an extraordinary city and temple complex. On the shores of the lake, the Tiahuanaco people drained large areas of marsh to make farmland to feed the city's population. With the Huari, they controlled the Andes region.

◀ ANIMAL POT
Tiahuanaco's potters were some of the most skilled in South America. They made many of their pots in animal shapes.

▲ TEMPLE WALL
The main buildings at Tiahuanaco included a huge temple whose walls were decorated with stone heads. Tiahuanaco was probably also a bustling city as well as an important ceremonial site.

◀ JAGUAR CULT
Fearsome deities appear in all early Central American civilizations. The jaguar was especially sacred.

The Olmec

THEY WERE KNOWN AS THE PEOPLE of the jaguar. The Olmec came from a small area by the Bay of Campeche in central Mexico. Like the Chavín of South America they worshipped gods that were half-human and half-animal. A jaguar figure seems to have been their most favored, and most feared, deity.

The Olmec were the ancestors of the later Mexican civilizations, such as the Maya and Toltec. Like them, the Olmec cleared the tropical forest to farm maize, squash, beans and tomatoes. Like them too, they built their temples on tall pyramids, expressed

◀ JAGUAR SPIRIT
The image of the jaguar spirit appeared on all sorts of Olmec objects, such as this pot.

◀ COLOSSAL HEAD
Archeologists have found huge heads, such as this, at many Olmec sites. About 4.5 feet tall and carved from a single piece of rock, they were probably portraits of Olmec rulers. Olmec sculptors also used precious materials such as jade to carve human heads.

their beliefs in stone carvings, and were a strong warlike people.

But the Olmec did not use warfare to build a large empire. They probably used their army to protect the extensive trade links they set up in central America. This trade brought them a plentiful supply of raw materials, especially rocks such as basalt, jade and obsidian. Olmec sculptors used these materials to produce massive carved heads and decorative reliefs showing their gods.

N ↑

La Venta
CENTRAL AMERICA

Olmec Culture

Chavín Culture

Pacific Ocean

SOUTH AMERICA

Chavín de Huantar

| 0 | Kilometres | 1600 |
| 0 | Miles | 1000 |

◀ ANDEAN CIVILIZATIONS
The map shows the Andean civilizations of the Chavín and their principal city, Chavín de Huantar. It also shows the site of the Olmecs, whose civilization emerged in Mexico. The religious center of Olmec culture, and its chief city, was La Venta.

▼ BIG-HEADED BABY
The features of Olmec figures like this pottery baby, with its elongated head and slanting eyes, have been a puzzle to archeologists. It was probably a religious offering left in a temple.

Key Dates

- 1200–900BC The Olmecs rule north-central Mexico.

- 850–200BC The civilization of Chavín de Huantar is at its peak.

- 200BC Many small, independent cultures develop in the valleys of the Andes.

- AD500–1000 Civilizations of Huari and Tiahuanaco.

The Maya

▲ CHAC
One of the most important of the many Maya gods was Chac, the god of rain.

DURING THE 19TH century, archeologists in Mexico were amazed when they stumbled across tall, stone-built, pyramid-shaped temples and broad plazas. They belonged to the Maya, an ancient Mexican people. The Maya created wonderful cities and were scholars. They invented their own system of writing and were skilled in mathematics and astronomy. But they were also a violent people. Their cities were continuously at war with each other. They took prisoners, who were later sacrificed to their gods.

The Maya lived in Mexico before 2000BC. But their cities became large and powerful much later, after AD300, in what historians call the "Classic" phase of their civilization. They developed efficient farming, producing maize, squash, beans and root vegetables to feed their rising population of city-dwellers.

By the Classic period, some Maya cities were huge, holding up to 50,000 people. The people lived in mud-brick houses around the outer edges of the cities. Most of the houses had only one or two rooms, and little in the way of furniture — just thin reed mats to sit on and slightly thicker mats for mattresses.

The chief Maya cities included Palenque, Copan, Tikal and Chichen Itza. In the heart of each of the cities was a complex of pyramid-shaped temples. The Maya continually rebuilt these temple-pyramids, adding more earth and stone to make them larger and taller.

The Maya survived for hundreds of years, but eventually constant civil war ate away at their wealth and power. Chichen Itza declined around 1200 and by the 16th century AD, when the Spanish conquered Mexico, only a few small Maya towns were left.

▲ TIKAL
Tikal was one of the largest cities of the Mayan civilization. Its ruins lie in the tropical rain forest of what is now northern Guatemala.

CRAFTS AND SKILLS
The Maya were skilled craftworkers. They produced fine pottery, carved stone reliefs and jade ornaments. They used razor-sharp flints for stone carving. Some flints were highly decorative and therefore buried as offerings to their gods.

◀ COSTUME
A Maya warrior wears a distinctive headpiece and carries a wooden spear. The Maya wove cloth from plant fibers such as cotton, and used plants to produce colorful dyes.

▼ CODEX
The Maya developed a series of picture symbols for writing, called glyphs. They carved these on stone tablets and also wrote them in books, called codices, made of paper, cloth or animal skins. They were the first Americans to develop picture writing.

▲ CALENDAR
Astronomers and mathematicians, the Maya also invented calendars. One was a solar calendar, like ours, based on 365 days in the year. The other had a year of 200 days and was used for religious ceremonies.

▲ WALL OF SKULLS
These carvings come from a 200 foot-long wall at Chichen Itza. The wall once supported a fence on which heads of sacrificial victims were displayed, skewered on poles.

▲ WARRIOR
The people of Chichen Itza had an army of warriors who were feared all over the Yucatan peninsula. Their prisoners of war were often sacrificed to the gods.

▼ MAYA CITY
The center of a Maya city contained tall pyramid-shaped temples. Staircases led up each face of the pyramid to a shrine. Special courts were included in the temple complex, including a ball court for playing games.

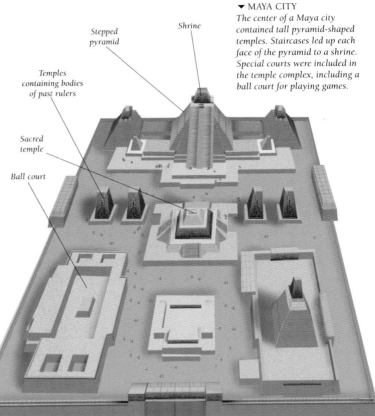

Stepped pyramid

Shrine

Temples containing bodies of past rulers

Sacred temple

Ball court

◀ THE MAYA
The Maya came from the Yucatan, the large peninsula that sticks out from the eastern coast of Mexico. They built most of their cities here and in the area to the southeast, now part of Guatemala and Honduras.

Key Dates

- 300BC–AD300 Many of the Maya cities are founded.

- AD300–800 "Classic" phase of Maya civilization flourishes.

- AD900 Most Maya cities are in decline.

- AD900–1200 Cities in the northern Yucatan flourish under the warlike Toltecs, from Tula.

WORLD
RELIGIONS

By Simon Adams

*Throughout history, human beings have sought
to make sense of their world through
spirituality, faith and a system of values.
This section explores all aspects of religion,
from shamanism to a belief in one god.*

Faith and Spirituality

▲ OHM SYMBOL
Every religion has its own symbol. This identifies the religion and its believers. Hindus use the Ohm symbol. Jews have the menorah (candlestick), Christians have the cross, and Muslims use the hilal (crescent moon and star).

▼ KEY DATES
The panel below charts the history of religion, from the earliest religion of the ancient Egyptians to the new religions founded during the 1900s.

THROUGHOUT HUMAN HISTORY, people have asked questions about life and their place in the world. They have wondered why evil and suffering exist, how the world came into existence, and how it might end. Above all, they have asked if there is a god who guides and directs the world or whether events just roll on forever without purpose or end.

There is no definite answer to these questions, but people have tried to make sense of their lives through religion. The first religions, such as Hinduism, were pantheistic—that is, they involved the worship of many gods. With Judaism, a new type of religion, known as monotheism (the worship of a single god), began. Christianity and Islam are also monotheistic religions.

At first sight the teachings of the various religions appear to be very different. In fact, they can be placed into two main groups. The first group includes Hinduism and Buddhism. These religions state that the world is a spiritual place and that it is possible to escape the endless circle of birth, death, and rebirth and reach a totally spiritual life. The second group includes Christianity and Islam. These religions say that the world is essentially good but that humans make it bad. They urge people to behave well in order to change the world and make it a better place.

All the various religions use similar techniques to put across their messages. They tell stories and myths to explain complicated subjects in a way that is easy to understand. They use symbols that identify the faith and its believers, and they use rituals, such as

▲ THE GOSPELS
All religions have their own holy book or books. These contain the words of God or the gods, as told to his earthly prophets (messengers). Jews have the Torah, Christians have the Bible, Sikhs have the Guru Granth Sahib, and Muslims have the Qur'an. Many religions also have books of religious laws, such as the Jewish Talmud.

B.C.

c.3100 Kingdom of Egypt founded. The ancient Egyptians worship many gods.

c.3000 *I Ching* compiled.

c.2166 Birth of Abraham, founder of the Jewish nation.

c.2000 Celtic tribes practice a very local religion with their own group of gods.

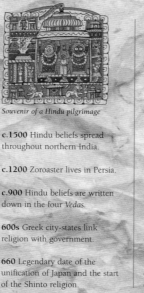

Souvenir of a Hindu pilgrimage

c.1500 Hindu beliefs spread throughout northern India.

c.1200 Zoroaster lives in Persia.

c.900 Hindu beliefs are written down in the four *Vedas*.

600s Greek city-states link religion with government.

660 Legendary date of the unification of Japan and the start of the Shinto religion.

Tutankhamun's death mask

c.500s Mahavira founds Jainism.

c.500s Life of Lao-Tzu, legendary founder of Taoism.

551–479 Life of Confucius.

539–331 Zoroastrianism is the official religion of the Persian Empire.

Zoroastrian cup for Jashan ceremony

c.500 Jewish *Talmud* (laws) are written down.

c.500 The *Mahabharata*, a Hindu epic, is written.

The Buddha

485–405 Life of the Buddha.

c.250 Buddhism spreads to Sri Lanka and to Southeast Asia.

c.200 The *Ramayana*, the final Hindu epic, is written.

146 Greece comes under Roman rule. Many Greek gods are taken over and renamed by the Romans.

c.6 B.C.–A.D. 30 Life of Jesus Christ, founder of Christianity.

Christian baptism. Finally, religions develop societies that bind believers together. These techniques help worshipers to understand their faith and apply it in their daily lives.

Examining the development of the world's religions is one way to chart the history of humankind. Holy scriptures are the oldest written records we have. Not all the information contained in them need be read as historical fact. However, the latest archaeological discoveries are proving that many stories in the religious texts are based on true events.

At the start of the third millennium A.D., the majority of the world's population follow a religion. There are also people, known as agnostics, who are not convinced that there is a god, but do not rule out the possibility. Atheists are people who do not believe in the existence of any god at all. Some people worship nature, while others, known as humanists, believe in the supremacy of human beings and their ability to make sensible decisions for themselves.

◀ A PHYSICAL GOD
Many religions see a human as a form, or manifestation, of their god on earth. Egyptians thought this way about their pharaoh, and some Chinese religions thought that the Emperor (left) was also a god.

▲ WORLD PICTURE
This is a mandala, a Buddhist representation of the world through pictures and diagrams. Buddhists believe that it is possible to overcome suffering in the world if people follow guidelines to help them live a good life.

A.D.

c.30 The first Christian churches are founded.

100s Mahayana Buddhism emerges and gradually spreads to China.

313 Christianity is tolerated throughout Roman Empire. Many Romans convert to Christianity.

Jesus Christ

570–632 Life of Muhammad, the founder of Islam.

600s Islam spreads throughout Middle East and North Africa.

Muslim shahadah (statement of faith)

600s Buddhism spreads to Tibet and Japan.

680 Decisive split between the Sunni and Shi'ah Muslims.

800s Vikings spread their Norse religion throughout northern Europe.

1054 Christianity splits into Roman Catholic and Orthodox Churches.

1469–1539 Life of Guru Nanak, the first Sikh guru.

1517 Roman Catholic Church splits as the Reformation gives rise to Protestant churches.

1699 Guru Gobind Singh forms the *Khalsa* (Sikh community).

1830 Joseph Smith translates the *Book of Mormon*.

Modern Rastafarians

1863 The Baha'i religion is founded.

1870s The Jehovah's Witnesses are formed.

1930–74 Emperor Haile Selassie is Black Messiah to Rastafarians.

Israeli flag

1939–45 More than six million Jews are killed during World War II.

1954 L Ron Hubbard founds the Church of Scientology.

1954 Sun Myung Moon founds the Unification Church, or Moonies.

Ancient Egypt

THE ANCIENT EGYPTIANS lived in the rich and fertile valley of the river Nile, which flowed from Central Africa, in the south, to the Mediterranean Sea, in the north. From around 3100 B.C. they built a great civilization along the river banks which lasted for almost 3,000 years. Ancient Egypt was governed by 31 dynasties (families) of kings, who were known as pharaohs. Pharaohs were believed to be gods on Earth.

Throughout their long history, the Egyptians worshiped many gods, each responsible for a different aspect of daily life. Their main god was Ra, the sun god. He was reborn every morning at dawn and traveled across the sky during the day. In the form of the Sun, Ra brought life to Egypt. He made the plants grow and the animals strong. The ancient Egyptians

▲ THE GREAT PYRAMIDS AT GIZA
Some pharaohs were buried in vast tombs called pyramids. About 100,000 people, many of them slaves, toiled for 20 years to build the Great Pyramid at Giza for Pharaoh Khufu. The shape might have been a symbol of the Sun's rays, or a stairway to heaven.

▶ FLOODS OF TEARS
Osiris was the god of farming. After he was killed by his jealous brother, Seth, Osiris became god of the underworld and the afterlife. Egyptians believed that the yearly flooding of the Nile marked the anniversary of Osiris's death when his queen, Isis, wept for him.

AFTER DEATH
The Egyptians believed that a dead person's spirit would always need a home to return to. That is why they took such trouble to embalm (preserve) dead bodies as mummies. The body was treated with special salt so that it would not rot. Then it was wrapped in linen bandages.

◀ MUMMY MASK
Tutankhamun was a pharaoh who died 3,500 years ago. In 1922 his tomb was discovered. The wrapped-up mummy was wearing a solid-gold death mask. The mummy had been placed in a nest of three ornate wooden coffins, inside a stone box called a sarcophagus.

▶ ANUBIS
The god Anubis led the dead person to the underworld. He was also the god responsible for embalming. Anubis was always shown with the head of a jackal, a type of wild dog. Since real jackals often lived in cemeteries, the animal had come to be associated with death.

called their pharaohs the Sons of Ra. Pharaohs were said to be immortal, which meant that they would never really die. They were buried in vast pyramids and, later, elaborate underground tombs. Special objects and treasures were buried with them, to ensure that they traveled safely to the afterlife.

The Egyptians believed that everything in life was controlled by the gods. They worshiped them in order to keep them happy and gain their protection. People tried to lead good lives so that after death they could enter the next world, which they called the Field of Reeds. They thought this was something like a perfect version of Egypt itself. To get there, first they had to pass through the dangerous *Duat* (underworld). Then they were judged by Osiris, god of the afterlife. If they had lived a good life and passed the test, they would

▲ IN THE BALANCE
In order to get into the heavenly kingdom after death, an Egyptian had to pass a test in a place known as the Hall of Two Truths. The person's heart was weighed to see if it was heavy with sin. If their heart was lighter than the Feather of Truth, the dead person had passed the test and was then presented to Osiris, god of the afterlife. If their heart was heavier, a monster called Ammit ate the heart, and the person died forever.

live forever in the Field of Reeds.

The Egyptians placed detailed handbooks in their coffins to help them in this quest. These instruction manuals contained spells for the dead person to recite at each stage of the journey through the *Duat*. The most famous of these manuals is the *Book of the Dead*.

◀ CANOPIC JAR
The liver, lungs, intestines, and stomach were removed from the body before it was mummified. The organs were dried out, wrapped in linen, and stored in containers called canopic jars.

▶ CAT MUMMY
The Egyptians considered cats to be sacred. Some people even took their dead pet cat to the city of Bubastis, where the cat god Bastet was worshiped. There it would be embalmed and buried in a cat-shaped coffin in the cat cemetery.

▲ EYE OF HORUS
Lucky charms called amulets were wrapped in among a mummy's bandages. The eye amulet stood for the eye of the god Horus, son of Osiris and Isis. Horus lost his eye in a fight with his evil uncle Seth, but it was magically restored. The eye amulet symbolized the victory of good over evil, so everything behind it was protected from evil.

Key Dates

- c.3100B.C. The Egyptian kingdom is founded.
- c.2630B.C. Building of first pyramid with stepped sides.
- c.2528B.C. Great Pyramid built.
- c.2150B.C. Last pyramids built.
- 1504–1070B.C. Nearly all pharaohs, from Thutmose I to Ramses XI (and including the boy-king Tutankhamun), are buried in the Valley of the Kings.
- 332B.C. Egypt is conquered by the Greek ruler Alexander the Great.
- 30B.C. Egypt becomes part of the Roman Empire.

The Classical World

THE CIVILIZATION of the ancient Greeks began around 1575B.C. in Mycenae (southern Greece). The Greeks had no word for religion, yet religion affected every aspect of daily life. People believed that 12 major gods lived on Mount Olympus, the highest mountain in Greece. The god Zeus was their ruler. The gods rewarded good people, and they intervened regularly in human affairs.

The Iliad, said to be written by the poet Homer around 800B.C., tells the story of the historic siege of Troy by the Greeks. This event from real history is explained and presented as a squabble between the gods. In *The Iliad*, the gods used the Greeks and Trojans to fight on their behalf.

In addition to the pantheon (collection) of 12 main gods, the Greeks believed in the existence of thousands of others. Some gods had more than one role. Athena was the goddess of wisdom and a war goddess, as well as the sacred spirit of the olive tree. She was also the patron (protector) of the city of Athens. Aphrodite was the goddess of love and beauty and also the sacred spirit of the myrtle tree.

The Greeks built temples where they could worship their gods. These were erected in the highest part of a city, which was known as the acropolis. People also built shrines in their homes where they could worship

▲ EARTH AND SKY GOD
Zeus was the king of the gods. As ruler of the sky, he brought rain and storms. As ruler of the land, he took charge of morals and justice.

▶ THE DELPHIC ORACLE
Greeks used to visit the Temple of Apollo in Delphi to consult the oracle. This was the voice of the god Apollo, heard through a young priestess, the Pythia.

ROMAN GODS AND BELIEFS

The city of Rome was founded in 753B.C. The Roman Empire grew to one of the largest in the world. When they conquered Greece in 146B.C., they added the Greek gods to their own. Often, they changed the gods' names into Latin. By the A.D.300s, however, many Romans had become Christians, and the old gods were neglected.

◀ PAN'S PIPES
Pan was originally the Greek god of the countryside, later associated with the Roman god Faunus. He was usually shown as half-man, half-goat. Pan had many lovers, one of whom, Syrinx, escaped him by turning herself into a reed bed. From these reeds, Pan made a set of musical pipes.

◀ MITHRAIC TEMPLE
The Romans adopted the gods of many peoples they had conquered. Mithras was a Persian god of light and truth. There were Mithraic cults across the Roman Empire.

▶ NIKE
The Greek goddess Nike was known as Victoria to the ancient Romans. She was the goddess of victory. She had a devout following among soldiers in the Roman army.

their favorite gods. This might be a shrine to Hestia, goddess of the hearth (fireplace) and family life. Some gods were worshiped in secret by members of mystery cults. Believers went through a special initiation (joining) ceremony. Once they were in, they took part in elaborate rituals. The two most famous cults were those of Demeter, the goddess of farming and harvests, and Dionysus, the god of wine. Throughout the year, the Greeks celebrated their gods at numerous festivals and ceremonies. In Athens, 120 days of the year were dedicated to festivals.

Stories about the gods and their activities had explained the workings of the world. However, Greek philosophers worked out more everyday explanations. The most famous were Socrates (469–399B.C.), Plato (c.427–347B.C.), and Aristotle (384–322B.C.). As their philosophical ideas took hold, religion became less important to the Greeks, and their gods became part of myth and legend.

▲ POSEIDON
Poseidon was god of earthquakes and the sea. He was associated with horses and was said to be the father of Pegasus, the winged horse. Greeks believed that Poseidon was the brother of Zeus and Hades. He was often shown carrying a three-pronged spear, called a trident.

▶ KINGDOMS OF THE GODS
Zeus ruled the land and sky, and Poseidon looked after the sea. Their brother, Hades, was god of the underworld. He ruled there with his wife, Persephone.

▼ JUPITER
The main god of the Romans was Jupiter. Like Zeus, he held supreme power over all the other gods and showed his power through thunderstorms and lightning.

▶ APOLLO
The Greek, and later Roman, god Apollo was associated with light, healing, music, poetry, and education.

Greco-Roman gods

These Greek gods were adopted, or adapted, by the Romans. Their Roman names are in parentheses.

- Aphrodite (Venus), goddess of love
- Apollo (Apollo), god of healing
- Ares (Mars), god of war
- Artemis (Diana), goddess of hunting
- Demeter (Ceres), goddess of grain
- Dionysus (Bacchus), god of wine
- Hades (Pluto), god of the underworld
- Hephaistos (Hephaestus), god of fire
- Hera (Juno), wife of Zeus (Jupiter)
- Hermes (Mercury), messenger god
- Persephone (Proserpina), goddess of death, queen to Hades (Pluto)
- Poseidon (Neptune), god of earthquakes and the sea
- Zeus (Jupiter), supreme god

Northern Europe

THE VIKINGS OF SCANDINAVIA lived in a cold and inhospitable world of long winters and short summers. They had to fight for their survival. Between the A.D.800s and 1000s they sailed overseas in search of new lands to conquer and settle. They soon earned a reputation as a warlike people.

Norse, or Scandinavian, religion reflected this harsh way of life. Its origins trace back to the earliest Northern European gods of the Bronze Age. The Vikings believed that the universe was made up of nine different worlds. These were connected by the world tree, Yggdrasil, which was often represented as a giant ash. This tree was thought to contain all the people yet to be born. The world inhabited by people was known as Midgard. The home of the gods was Asgard. The chief Norse god, Odin, lived here, along with all the other gods. He was god of both war and wisdom and had many supernatural powers.

◀ IN DEATH
Vikings were buried with the weapons and treasures that they would need for the next life. Viking chiefs were buried or put out to sea in their boats. Some were laid beneath burial mounds. Even the poorest person was buried with a sword or a brooch.

▶ VIKINGS AND CELTS
Vikings and Celts traveled far in search of new lands to settle. They took their religious beliefs with them. The Celts spread out from the Danube valley across Europe. Viking settlements ranged from North America in the far west to Russia in the east.

Viking homelands
Celtic homelands
NORTH SEA
GREAT BRITAIN
York
Dublin
London
ATLANTIC OCEAN
Paris
R. Rhine
R. Elbe
RUSSIA
Kiev
CASPIAN SEA
SPAIN
FRANCE
Seville
Rome
R. Danube
BLACK SEA
Constantinople
MEDITERRANEAN SEA
N

0 Kilometers 1000
0 Miles 600

THE CELTS

The Celts spread from their German homeland across the whole of western Europe from around 2000B.C. As the Roman Empire expanded, however, the Celts were pushed to the edges of Europe, to Ireland, Scotland, Wales, and Brittany. Different, local religions developed, each with its own group of gods. There were common themes, however. The Celts all believed in warrior-heroes with supernatural powers, and they all believed in the sacred Earth Mother. She was the goddess of fertility who brought them life.

▶ MISTLETOE
The druids were the high priests of Celtic religion. They performed the sacred rituals and often used mistletoe in their ceremonies. The plant is still important as part of Christmas festivities.

◀ HARVEST FESTIVAL
From around 2,000 years ago the Celts wove stalks of wheat into human "dollies" or other shapes. These objects were made to give thanks for a successful harvest.

▲ THE LINDISFARNE GOSPEL
The natural world was central to Celtic religion. Celtic influence can be seen in early Christian manuscripts, which were illuminated (illustrated) with pictures of animals and plants.

◄ FREYA
The goddess of love, Freya, was married to Odin, but he left her. Freya wept tears of gold and searched the skies for him in a cat-driven chariot.

▼ RIDE OF THE VALKYRIES
Odin was served by a band of female warriors called the Valkyries. After a battle, Odin and the Valkyries searched the battlefield for dead heroes, whom they carried to Valhalla (Viking heaven).

Vikings believed that the human world, Midgard, was constantly threatened by forces of darkness and evil, such as the frost giants, who covered the world with snow and ice. Thor, the god of thunder, tried to keep these giants away with his hammer. Many Vikings wore a hammer around their necks, or painted a hammer on their door, as protection against evil spirits.

The Vikings held many different beliefs about what happened after death. A sick person who died went to a serpent-filled kingdom ruled by Hel, a witchlike figure. Warriors who died in battle went to Valhalla. This was a huge communal hall, like a perfect version of a Viking longhouse. There were feasting and mock battles there.

By A.D.1000, many Vikings had become Christians. This is reflected in the late Viking belief that the world would end in one final battle, called the Ragnarok. The gods and forces of evil would destroy themselves in this battle. A new world would be born, occupied by two people, Lif and Lifthrasir. Like Adam and Eve, they would worship one supreme god who lived in heaven.

◄ CELTIC CROSS
In around A.D.435, a Christian Briton, who later became St Patrick, went to Ireland to convert the Celts. He was successful, and Celtic art merged with Christian symbols, such as the cross.

▼ LINDISFARNE MONASTERY, ENGLAND
After the conversion of Ireland, Celtic-Christian missionaries took their religion back to England, and to Scotland. Celtic Christianity stressed the importance of missionary work, regular prayer, and a modest lifestyle. In monasteries such as Lindisfarne, monks spent their time in prayer and study. They also educated the local people and converted them.

Key Dates

- c.2000B.C. Celtic peoples spread throughout western Europe.

- A.D.100 The Romans push the Celts to the edges of western Europe.

- c.A.D.435 St. Patrick converts Celts in Ireland to Christianity.

- A.D.600s Celtic missionaries convert England and Scotland to Christianity.

- A.D.793 Vikings begin to raid Christian monasteries in Britain.

- A.D.800s Many Viking raids across northern and western Europe.

- 1000s Vikings begin to convert to Christianity.

Tribal Religions

THE ANCIENT RELIGIONS of Egypt, Greece, and Rome disappeared with the fall of the civilizations that fostered them. The same is true of the religions practiced by the civilizations of the Americas, such as, the Mayans, Incas, and Aztecs. Other religions, such as those followed by the Vikings and Celts, merged with other beliefs. However, some ancient religions survive to this day, even if they are restricted to one very small area. These are the religions practiced by the tribal peoples of Africa, the Americas, Australasia, and Asia.

Although these religions vary widely from place to place and people to people, they share much in common. For tribal peoples, the spiritual world plays a very important role in daily life.

The Maasai of East Africa worship a single god, who brings them life from the Sun and makes sure the crops grow. Most tribal peoples, however, believe that there are many gods and spirits. Some spirits are evil, and good spirits must be summoned up to overcome them. The Kalabari of eastern Nigeria, for example, make ancestral screens on which they place pictures of their ancestors. Through these, they communicate with the spirit world and try to control the effect that spirits have on their lives. Elsewhere in Africa, local gods protect the oases and waterholes and help to heal the sick.

In all tribal religions, ritual plays an important part in a person's life. Birth, becoming an adult, marriage, and death are all celebrated with elaborate ceremonies. Often the

▲ KUBA MASK
Many African peoples, such as the Kuba tribe of Zaire, make sacred masks. These represent the different spirits they call upon at ceremonies to celebrate birth, marriage, or death.

▶ TOTEM POLE
The Native Americans of the Pacific northwest coast carve elaborate totem poles out of tree trunks. Each pole provides a full history of a family. It records the family's earthly history and its relationship with the spirit world. A spirit might take the form of an animal, such as a bear, wolf, or eagle.

ABORIGINAL RELIGION
The Aborigines of Australia trace their history back to a time called Dreamtime. This was the time of creation, when ancestral beings shaped the land and made all living things. These beings were half-human and half-animal. Aborigines consider these beings to be their ancestors and also believe that they live on forever as spirits.

◀ HOLY WATER
Aborigines believe that the land is sacred. Mountains, water holes, and other natural features are all places where the spirit world and the natural world combine.

▼ TELLING TALES
Stories of the Dreamtime have been passed down through the generations. One way has been through detailed bark paintings.

◀ ULURU
The ancestral beings created every aspect of the landscape, including Uluru (Ayers Rock). The rock has many sacred caves. It is a special place for all Aborigines.

◀ YANOMAMO SHAMAN
*Shamans are healers who contact
the spirit world in order to seek divine
help. They are common in Siberia and Arctic
North America, as well as among the many tribes
of South America. These include the Yanomamo
peoples, who live in the Amazon rainforest, in Brazil.*

people wear masks and beautiful costumes. In West
Africa, the Mende people hold a masked dance, or
masquerade, for young girls when they come of age.
This unites all the young women and prepares them for
marriage and motherhood. The Dogon of West Africa
hold elaborate dances and chant in a secret language
when someone dies.

Most common is the worship of ancestors and
respect for elderly people in the tribe. This is common
in tribes across the world, from the Native Americans to
the people of Papua New Guinea. Stories of ancestors'
exploits are passed down through the generations.
Myths and legends explain how the world was formed
and how good and evil came to exist side by side.

▼ BODY PAINT
Aborigines paint their bodies for
special ceremonies. Each line of
body paint may represent a different
Dreamtime ancestor.

▲ GUM TREE
The Aborigines
include the natural world in their
ceremonies. Carved trees have been
found, especially in New South Wales.
These were a central part of Aboriginal
coming-of-age and funeral rituals.

Key Dates

- c.40,000B.C. Aborigines from
  Southeast Asia settle in Australia.

- c.30,000B.C. First settlements by
  Amazon River, South America.

- c.1000B.C. Polynesians sail from
  Southeast Asia and settle in the
  Pacific Islands.

- c.500B.C. African societies expand
  south of the Sahara Desert.

- A.D.400 Polynesians reach
  Hawaii and Easter Island.

- 1000 Polynesian Maoris reach
  New Zealand.

- 1000–1600 Giant statues are
  erected on Easter Island.

Zoroastrianism

THE PROPHET ZOROASTER, OR ZARATHUSTRA, as he is also called, was born in northeast Persia (modern-day Iran) around 1200B.C. Not much is known about his life, except that he became a priest and was married with several children. His teachings soon became influential. When Cyrus the Great became king of Persia in 539B.C., Zoroastrianism became the official religion of his vast empire. In later years, Persian armies spread the religion as far afield as Greece, Egypt, and northern India.

For more than 1,000 years, until the arrival of Islam in the A.D.600s, Zoroastrianism remained a major religion throughout the Middle East. Today it is confined to small pockets in Iran, India—where followers are known as Parsis (Persians)— and East Africa. Zoroastrianism is also practiced in a few cities in Europe and North America, but it has fewer than 130,000 believers worldwide.

▲ THE PROPHET
Zoroaster lived in Persia about 1200B.C., more than 600 years before the Buddha and 1,200 years before Christ. This makes him the earliest prophet of any world religion.

▶ COMING OF AGE
Young Zoroastrians are welcomed into the faith when they are seven at a special ceremony called the Navjote. *The child is given two sacred objects, a white tunic and a length of cord. The cord, called the* kusti, *has 72 strands of thread. The way the strands join together to work as one has made the* kusti *a symbol of fellowship.*

THE THANKSGIVING CEREMONY

The Zoroastrian ceremony of Jashan (thanksgiving) is to ensure the harmony and well-being of both the spiritual and physical worlds. Zoroastrians offer thanks for their physical lives and ask for blessings from the spiritual world. The Amesha Spentas (spirit guardians of the seven good creations) and the spirits of good people who have died are all invited down to join the ceremony.

◀ AT THE CEREMONY
Jashan is presided over by a *zaotor*, the officiating priest, and a *raspi*, his assistant. Other priests may also be present.

▲ SEVEN GOOD CREATIONS
Everything at Jashan represents one of the seven good creations. A metal cup or tray represents the sky. Fruit represents plants and milk represents cattle. Wine represents humans. Burning sandalwood and frankincense represent the earth. Water and fire represent themselves. Seven flowerbuds represent the Amesha Spentas.

Zoroaster believed that the Supreme God, whom he called Ahura Mazda, had taught him through a series of visions. He learned that there are seven good creations—sky, water, earth, plants, cattle, humans, and fire. Each of these is guarded by a spirit. The seven spirit guardians are known as the Amesha Spentas.

Zoroaster wrote his teachings down in 17 *gathas* (hymns) as part of the Zoroastrian sacred scripture, the *Avesta*. The *gathas* are very difficult to read and can be interpreted in many different ways.

According to Zoroaster, the world is a good place, although it contains evil. People can follow Ahura Mazda and live a good life, or they can choose to follow Angra Mainyu, the force of evil. These opposing forces are in constant conflict, but it is everyone's duty to follow good. If they do, they will be rewarded in the afterlife with happiness. If they follow evil, they will find only sorrow.

Zoroaster's teachings have been very influential, even if not many people practice his religion today. Its central ideas of the battle between good and evil and a final day of judgment had a large impact on Judaism, Christianity, and Islam.

◄ GUARDIAN SPIRIT
Zoroastrians believe that everyone is looked over by a fravashi, *or guardian spirit. These spirits represent the good in people and help those that ask. The* fravashi *symbol can also represent a person's spiritual self or Ahura Mazda.*

▼ THE TOWER OF SILENCE
Zoroastrians believe that dead bodies provide a home for Angra Mainyu, the force of evil. Bodies cannot be buried in land or sea, nor can they be cremated, since earth, water, and fire are all good creations. For this reason, they are left on top of a specially built tower, the Dakhma *(Tower of Silence), as a meal for the vultures.*

▲ HOLY SMOKE
Fire is important to Zoroastrians. For them, it is the living symbol of Ahura Mazda. They worship in fire temples and offer prayers to the sacred fire.

▲ ASH SPOT
Before entering a fire temple, Zoroastrians remove their shoes. Once inside, they place a pinch of ash from the sacred fire on their forehead. Then they pray to the fire.

Key Dates

- c.1200 B.C. Birth of Zoroaster.

- 539–331 B.C. Zoroastrianism is the official religion of the Persian Empire.

- 331 B.C. Alexander the Great destroys the Persian Empire and the manuscript of the *Avesta*.

- 129 B.C. Zoroastrianism is again the official religion in Persia.

- c.A.D.400 The *Avesta* is rewritten.

- A.D.637 Islam becomes the main religion in Persia.

- A.D.716 Zoroastrians settle in Gujarat, India. These are the ancestors of modern-day Parsis.

Hinduism

THE WORD "HINDU" comes from the Persian word *sindhu*, which means "river." It refers to the religion of the people who lived by the river Indus around 2500 B.C. This ancient civilization was centered around the cities of Mohenjo-Daro and Harappa (in modern-day Pakistan). Over the centuries, the religion spread across northern India to the valley of the Ganges River.

In the 900s B.C., the Hindu scriptures were written down. Two thousand years later Indian rulers took Hinduism to Sri Lanka and Southeast Asia. Today, it is practiced around the world. There are more than 800 million Hindus, 700 million of whom live in India.

Hinduism does not have one central belief. It has evolved slowly over time, drawing in ideas from other religions. There are many different types of Hinduism and many different ways to be a Hindu.

Most Hindus believe that they have four aims in life. The first, *dharma*, is to live a good life by being kind to others and telling the truth. The second, *artha*, is to be wealthy and prosperous in life. *Kama* is to enjoy pleasure, and *mosksha* is to be freed from the world and its desires.

Hindus also believe that they pass through four stages in life. These are being a student, then a householder, then a thinker, and finally an ascetic (someone who is rid of all worldly pleasures). Not everyone achieves these four aims and stages, but if they do, they will be reincarnated (reborn) into a better life. For Hindus, this eternal cycle of life, death, and then rebirth into a new life is very important.

◀ BRIDE AND GROOM
A Hindu marriage ceremony contains many religious rituals. At the end of the ceremony, the couple take seven steps, making a vow at each one. The steps represent food, strength, prosperity, well-being, children, happiness, and harmony.

HINDU WORSHIP
Worship is an important part of Hindu religion. Hindus worship in temples, at shrines, and in their own homes. Most people pray alone, rather than in large groups. Sunrise and sunset are the most popular times of day. Worship can involve singing, prayer, and offering up gifts to the gods.

▶ HINDU TEMPLE
Temples have tall, ornate towers and four gateways which represent the four directions of the universe. Hindus visit the temple throughout the day to worship at its main icon (holy image).

◀ SITE OF LIGHT
Varanasi, on the banks of the Ganges, is the most important pilgrimage city in India. Varanasi is known as the City of Light, because it was here that the god Shiva's light reached up to the heavens.

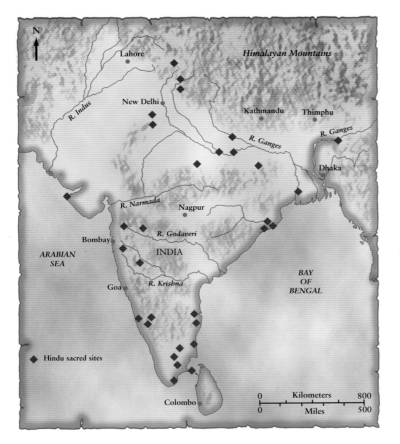

◀ THE BIRTH OF HINDUISM

Hinduism began in the Indus valley in present-day Pakistan. It spread throughout northern India, along the valley of the Ganges. In the early A.D. *700s, Arab conquerors brought Islam to the valley of the Indus River. Over the next seven centuries, Islam spread slowly across northern India, and sometimes there was conflict between Hindus and Muslims.*

▼ HINDU PRIESTS

A brahmin (priest) looks after the temple and acts as a go-between between the worshiper and a god. Wandering priests or holy men are known as sadhus. These men lead an ascetic way of life. This means they give up worldly pleasures and wander from place to place begging for food.

▼ PILGRIMAGE

Going on a pilgrimage is an important part of Hindu worship. Places of pilgrimage include large cities, such as Varanasi and sacred rivers, such as the Ganges. Holy mountains, temples, and small, local shrines are visited by pilgrims, too.

▲ MEMENTO

To remind them of their pilgrimage, Hindu pilgrims often bring back small mementoes from the shrine they have visited.

Key Dates

- c.1500 B.C. Hindu beliefs spread throughout northern India.
- c.900 B.C. Hindu beliefs are written down in the four *Vedas*.
- c.500 B.C. The *Mahabharata* is written down by Vyasa, a wise man.
- c.300 B.C. The *Ramayana* is written down by Valmiki, a poet.
- A.D.850–1200 Chola dynasty of northern India takes Hinduism to Sri Lanka and Southeast Asia.
- 1900s Hinduism spreads throughout world, as Indians settle in Europe, Africa, and the Americas.

Hindu Gods and Goddesses

HINDUS BELIEVE IN ONE SUPREME, ultimate god, Brahman, an unseen but all-powerful force who can appear in numerous forms. Some of these forms are worshiped by all Hindus, while others are worshiped only in one place or by a few people. The most important gods are those who created the world and its life and who are powerful enough to destroy it. There are gods of fire and war and many lesser gods that represent the forces of the natural world, such as the Sun and the wind.

Brahman brought the entire universe into existence. However, he is impersonal and takes no recognized appearance for his worshipers. Hindus therefore think of him in a variety of different appearances and worship him that way. The most important way in which Brahman makes himself known is through the Trimurti, a holy trio of three great gods. These are Brahma, Vishnu, and Shiva. According to Hindu belief Brahma created the world, Vishnu preserves life, and Shiva both destroys life and then recreates it.

Brahma is not worshiped like other gods, because after he created the world he had finished his work. However, when the world ends and needs to be recreated, he will return to create the world all over again. At that time he will be worshiped again.

Vishnu is known as the one who takes many different forms. He is very important because he preserves human life, the life of the world, and the life of the universe itself. As a result, his different images are found in many temples and shrines.

▲ DANCE OF DESTRUCTION
Shiva is the destroyer and recreator of life. He is sometimes called the lord of the dance. He ends the dance of life so that a new dance can begin.

▼ BRAHMA
Brahma is the god of creation. After he created the first woman, he fell in love with her, but she hid herself from him. So Brahma grew three more heads so that he could see her from every angle.

GODS IN MANY FORMS

Hindus worship many minor gods. Some, such as Surya, the sun god, Indra, the god of war, and Vayu, the wind god, are described in the Hindu scriptures. Others are specific to particular places. Hindus believe every part of Brahma's creation is divine and worship some animals, including Naga the snake god.

◀ THE ELEPHANT GOD
Ganesh is the remover of obstacles and also the lord of learning. His parents were Shiva and Parvati. One day Ganesh was protecting Parvati, but his father did not recognize him and beheaded him. When he realized his mistake, Shiva replaced Ganesh's head with one from the first creature he saw, which was an elephant.

▲ LUCKY LAKSHMI
Lakshmi is one of the many friendly forms of the mother goddess. She is the goddess of fortune and brings wealth and good luck to her followers.

▼ MAHADEVI AS DURGA
Mahadevi is the Hindu mother goddess. She appears in many forms, both fearsome and gentle. In one form she is the wife of Shiva. As Durga, she is a fierce, demon-fighting warrior.

The third god of the trio is Shiva. Like Vishnu, he has many different forms and he has over a thousand names, such as Maheshvara, the lord of knowledge, and Mahakala, the lord of time. He is often shown with three faces. Two of the faces have opposite characteristics, such as male and female, or peace and war. The third face is always calm, to reconcile (bring together) the two opposites.

Kurma, the turtle

Matsya, the fish

Varaha, the boar

Narasimha, half-man, half-goat

Vamana, the dwarf

Rama

Krishna

Krishna with his mistress, Radha

Parasurama

Buddha

Kalki

▶ RESTORING HARMONY
Vishnu is the god who preserves life, maintaining the balance between good and evil in the universe. If evil seems about to take control, Vishnu comes down to Earth to restore the balance. On Earth Vishnu takes the form of one of his ten incarnations, or avatars, the most important being Krishna. Nine of these avatars have visited the Earth already. The final one will arrive when the Earth is nearing the end of its current life. This tenth incarnation of Vishnu will destroy the world, then recreate it.

▲ MONKEY GOD
The epic poem the *Ramayana* tells how the monkey god, Hanuman, helped Rama to defeat the demon king Ravana. Hanuman is worshiped as the god of strength and heroism.

▼ KARTTIKEYA
The boy god Karttikeya has many different names, and there are many different stories about who his parents were. He was born to defeat evil and is often shown with a peacock, which is the national bird of India.

Ten Avatars of Vishnu

1. Matsya the fish, who saved the lawgiver Manu during the Flood.
2. Kurma the turtle, who held the Earth on his back after the Flood.
3. Varaha the boar, who raised the land out of the water with his tusks.
4. Narasimha, who destroyed the demon king Hiranyakasipu.
5. Vamana the dwarf, who tricked Hiranyakasipu's evil nephew, Bali.
6. Parasurama, who defeated an army of warriors with his ax.
7. Rama, who killed King Ravana.
8. Krishna, who told the *Bhagavad Gita* to Arjuna, his chariot driver.
9. Buddha, who founded Buddhism.
10. Kalki, who will appear at the end of the world on a white horse.

Hindu Scriptures

▲ A YOGI
Yogis are holy men who practice yoga, which means union of the individual soul with the universe. Yogis have played an important part in bringing Hindu teachings and scriptures to a wide audience in Europe and the Americas.

THE HINDU RELIGIOUS BOOKS were written down in Sanskrit (the ancient language of India) over the course of more than 1,000 years. Hindus have many different types of scripture, which fall into three groups.

The first group, the four *Vedas*, were originally passed down by word of mouth from generation to generation. *Veda* means "knowledge." The *Rig Veda* was the first to be written down, in about 1200 B.C. It contains religious hymns. Next came the *Sama Veda*, which consists of chants for Hindus to sing as part of their worship, and the *Yajur Veda*, which contains words to be spoken by Hindu priests. The last one was written in about 900 B.C. This is the *Atharva Veda*, which is full of magic spells and incantations. Hindus believe that the words of the *Vedas* are divine, so not a single word of them can be changed.

From around 700 B.C., Hindus began to wonder about the meaning of life and other philosophical questions. Over the next 400 years, this gave rise to the second major group of religious books. The *Upanishads* (sittings near a teacher) answer such questions as where we come from and why we are here. They explore the key concepts of Hinduism, such as reincarnation. They describe ordinary life as a cycle of birth, suffering, death, and rebirth, and urge people to seek *moksha* (freedom from cycle of death and rebirth). The *Aranyakas* (forest books) deal with the meaning of rituals. The *Puranas* (ancient myths) contain stories of creation and the

▲ THE VEDAS
The four Vedas *are the oldest Hindu scriptures of all. The oldest and best known, the* Rig Veda, *contains holy songs about the ancient gods of fire, earth, air, and water. These were written to be accompanied by traditional Indian instruments, such as the sitar, the shenai (a reed instrument), and the tabla (a type of drum).*

FESTIVALS AND CELEBRATIONS
The Hindu year is filled with many festivals celebrating the gods and natural events, such as the end of winter or the rice harvest. Some are national festivals celebrated by Hindus all over the world. Others are celebrated only in particular parts of India.

◀ THE FESTIVAL OF LIGHTS
The five-day festival of Diwali celebrates the return of the god Rama from exile. Diwali is held in October or November. Candles are lit in every house so as to welcome Lakshmi, goddess of wealth.

▲ SPRING CELEBRATIONS
Holi, celebrated in March, marks the start of spring and the Hindu New Year. Holi is a fun festival. People of all castes (classes) join in by throwing colored powders over each other.

▼ EFFIGIES FOR BURNING
Dusserah lasts nine days and is a celebration of good winning over evil. In southern India people burn effigies (models) of demons to symbolize Rama's victory over the evil king, Ravana.

lives of the gods. As in the *Vedas*, the words in the *Upanishads* are holy and cannot be changed.

The final group of religious books are two epic poems. The first of these appeared in about 500 B.C. The *Mahabharata* is the longest poem in the world, with more than 200,000 lines. It includes myths and philosophical discussions. At the heart of the book is the *Bhagavad Gita* (Song of the Lord), which is a conversation between Krishna, one of the avatars of Vishnu, and his chariot driver, Arjuna. The second epic, the *Ramayana*, was written down in about 300 B.C. It tells the story of Rama, another avatar of Vishnu, and how he rescued his wife, Sita, who had been kidnapped by the demon king, Ravana, king of Lanka.

▲ AN ILLUSTRATION FROM THE MAHABHARATA
Much of the Mahabharata *concerns a long war between two families, the Kauravas and the Pandavas. Along the way there are many tales that explain aspects of history. One tells how the river Ganges came to be. Another describes the Great Flood.*

▲ SITA IN RAVANA'S PALACE
The Ramayana *(Rama's Progress) was a popular folk story long before it was written down. In it, the evil king Ravana captures Rama's wife, Sita. He carries her off to his palace in Lanka (modern-day Sri Lanka). It was years before Rama rescued her.*

▼ GANESH CHATURTHI
In September the birthday of Ganesh is celebrated all over India. Huge images of the elephant-headed god are paraded through the streets. Ganesh often holds sweets in his hand, as he was very fond of them.

▶ HINDU HOLY MAN
Every 12 years, religious fairs or festivals are held in four different cities in India. Millions of people come to these events to bathe in the sacred rivers, listen to the teachings of the various *gurus* (teachers), and join in the many processions. Among those who make the pilgrimage to these events are *sadhus* (holy men).

Hindu Festivals

- February—Pongal-Sankranti (festival for the rice harvest)
- March—Holi (spring festival)
- March—Shivaratri (birthday of the god Shiva)
- May—Rathyatra (festival for Vishnu as lord of the universe)
- August—Janmashtami (birthday of Krishna, avatar of Vishnu)
- September—Ganesh Chaturthi (birthday of the god Ganesh)
- September/October—Dusserah
- October/November—Diwali (the festival of lights)

Jainism

▲ PALM OF PEACE
The open palm is the official symbol of Jainism. It represents peace. Sometimes the word Ahimsa *(nonviolence) is written on the palm.*

THE JAIN RELIGION began in the valley of the Ganges River, India, in around 500B.C. It slowly spread through northern India and today has 4.5 million followers in India, mainly in the business community. It also flourishes among Indians elsewhere in the world, such as in the United States.

Jainism was founded by a rich man, Mahavira. At the age of 29 he renounced (gave up) his wealth and became an ascetic, giving up worldy goods and begging for his food. He wanted to break the endless cycle of birth, life, death, and rebirth, by finding enlightenment, or spiritual peace. After 12 years of fasting and meditation, he achieved *kevala* (perfect knowledge). He then assembled a group of 12 followers and spent the next 30 years as a preacher until he starved to death at Pava, a village not far from his birthplace. Today Pava is one of the holiest sites of the Jain religion.

Jains take their name from *jina*. A *jina* is someone who has reached enlightenment. Jains believe that time is endless and is divided into a series of upward or downward movements that can last millions of years. In each of these movements, 24 *jinas* appear. Mahavira was the most recent. The *jinas* come to guide others towards enlightenment. They are also called *tirthankaras*.

Jains study the teachings of the *tirthankaras* and also take five vows to help them achieve spiritual peace. The vows are *ahimsa* (not to harm any living thing), *satya* (to speak the truth), *asteya* (not to steal), *brahmacharya* (to abstain from sexual activity), and *aparigraha* (not to become attached to people, places, or possessions).

▼ RESPECT FOR LIFE
Monks and nuns often wear masks to avoid breathing in and killing insects. They also carry a brush to sweep insects out of the way so that they do not tread on them.

JAIN BELIEFS

Jains do not believe in a god, and they do not pray to gods to help them in their lives. Instead, they study the works of the *tirthankaras* and practice meditation and self-discipline. They believe this is their only hope of release from the world and achieving spiritual liberation. Many Jains have jobs and live in the material world. Some Jains become monks or nuns to keep their mind uncluttered as they search for enlightenment.

◄ LORD BAHUBALI
Bahubali defeated his half-brother in battle but did not kill him. Instead, he became a holy man. Jains consider him to be the first *tirthankara* of the present age. Every 12 years, pilgrims go to the Indian town of Sravanabegola to worship at his giant statue and anoint it with colored water.

▲ PARSHVANATHA, 23RD TIRTHANKARA
The word "tirthankara" means "builder of the ford." Jains believe that they help people across samsara (the river of rebirth) to spiritual freedom. This page shows the 23rd Tirthankara.

Although there are not many Jains in the world today, their belief in nonviolence has had a major effect on modern politics. The Indian leader Mahatma Gandhi, who led his country to independence from Britain in 1947, was profoundly influenced by the idea of nonviolence, although he was not a Jain himself. Gandhi used it as a political weapon. Through his example, non-violent protest has become common in modern times, especially in the U.S., where Martin Luther King and the Civil Rights movement achieved change peacefully in the 1960s.

▼ PLACE OF WORSHIP
A Jain temple is elaborately constructed, with many courtyards, balconies, domes, and spires. At its center is a shrine that contains a sacred image of one of the tirthankaras. Worshipers meditate quietly or chant a mantra *(prayer).*

▼ PICTURING THE UNIVERSE
The Jains see the universe, or *loka*, as divided into three main sections. At the bottom are eight hells, and at the top are many heavens. In between is the *Madhya Loka* (middle world), which contains rings of continents and oceans. In the center of these rings is the *Jambudvipa*, where Jains live.

▶ HEAVEN ON EARTH
Jain temples are meant to be earthly replicas of the *samasavarana* (the heavenly halls where the *tirthankaras* live). That is why Jain temples are so beautiful.

Key Dates

- c. 800 B.C. Parsva, the next-to-last *tirthankara*, lives in India.

- c. 500 B.C. Mahavira, the last *tirthankara*, founds Jainism, which spreads throughout northern India.

- c. A.D. 300 Jainism splits into two groups, the Digambaras and Shvetambaras. They have different ideas about the status of women and how detached from daily life a Jain should be.

- A.D. 981 Giant statue of Bahubali is built at Sravanabegola.

- 1900s The idea of nonviolence influences political protests.

Buddhism

An eight-spoked wheel is the symbol for the Noble Eightfold Path. These eight different states of mind sum up the Buddha's teaching on how to find enlightenment.

BUDDHISM WAS founded by Siddhartha Gautama, who became known as the Buddha (enlightened one). The Buddha was born in northern India in 485B.C. By the time of his death in 405B.C., his teachings had spread across India, eventually reaching Southeast Asia, Korea, and Japan. Today, there are more than 330 million Buddhists around the world, mainly in eastern Asia but also in Europe and North America.

The Buddha taught that it was possible to overcome suffering in the world and become enlightened by following the Eightfold Path. The steps along this path are right knowledge, right attitude, right speech, right actions, right livelihood, right effort, right state of mind, and right concentration. Buddhists must make sure that each of these aspects of their life is *samma* (right). The Eightfold Path involves a great deal of discipline, so Buddhists often find a teacher to help

them. Once they have understood the path, they try to practice it. This takes them toward enlightenment. Ultimately, they aim for *nirvana* (a state of supreme happiness and bliss).

Nirvana is difficult to achieve, for Buddhists believe that we constantly travel through an endless cycle of life, death, and rebirth, either as humans or in other

forms. All these lives are subject to *karma* (the law of cause and effect). This means that every action has a result, either good or bad. If we do bad things, we increase our negative *karma* and keep being reborn into new lives. If we do good things, we gain positive *karma*.

Buddhists try to get rid of negative *karma* by

◀ BUDDHA'S FOOTPRINT
The Buddha did not want his followers to make him into a god, so at first there were no statues of him. He was shown only through symbols, such as his footprint.

THE SPREAD OF BUDDHISM

Buddhism began in northern India in around 500B.C. and then spread to Sri Lanka and Southeast Asia and into Tibet, China, and Japan. The early forms of Buddhism are known as Theravada (teaching of the elders). In the first century A.D., a new branch of Buddhism called Mahayana (great vehicle) developed.

▶ BUDDHISM DIVIDED
Theravada Buddhism is strongest in Sri Lanka and Southeast Asia. Mahayana Buddhism is practiced in Tibet, Mongolia, China, Korea, Japan, and Vietnam.

Samarkand Dunhuang Xian (Ch'ang An) KOREA JAPAN
Kashgar CHINA Kyongju Kyoto
Kabul TIBET *Himalayan Mts.*
Kandahar NEPAL Lhasa R. Yangtze PACIFIC OCEAN
Peshawar BHUTAN Guangzhou (Canton)
Sanchi BURMA Prome
ARABIAN SEA Ellora Thaion Dong Duong
INDIA Angkor Wat
Amaravati THAILAND

Birthplace of Buddhism ■
Route of Buddhist expansion

Anuradhapura

INDIAN OCEAN SUMATRA BORNEO

0 Kilometers 1500
0 Miles 1000

Palembang

N

▼ HUMAN FAILINGS
At the center of the Wheel of Life are three animals. They symbolize the weaknesses that human beings must overcome. The pig represents greed. The rooster stands for delusion (holding false beliefs). The last creature, the snake, symbolizes hatred.

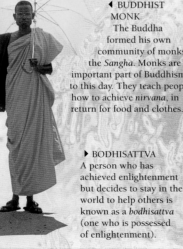

following the Eightfold Path, doing good deeds and meditating. They believe that if they succeed, they will be released from the law of *karma* and stop *samsara* (wandering from life to life). They will be free from suffering and achieve the peace of *nirvana*.

The Buddha preached that life is always changing and that people should not look for happiness in material things, such as wealth and possessions. Instead, they should get rid of fear, passion, greed, ignorance, selfishness, and all the other vices that keep them attached to the world. In this way, they become enlightened and can achieve *nirvana*.

▲ THE WHEEL OF LIFE
Buddhists believe that when a person dies, they are reborn into one of six realms (regions) of existence. The gods, the fighting gods, the hungry ghosts, hell, beasts, and humans each have their own realm, shown on this thangka, *or religious drawing.*

◀ BUDDHIST MONK
The Buddha formed his own community of monks, the *Sangha*. Monks are an important part of Buddhism to this day. They teach people how to achieve *nirvana*, in return for food and clothes.

▶ BODHISATTVA
A person who has achieved enlightenment but decides to stay in the world to help others is known as a *bodhisattva* (one who is possessed of enlightenment).

Key Dates

- 485–405B.C. Life of the Buddha.

- 250B.C. Buddhism spreads to Sri Lanka and Southeast Asia.

- A.D.100s Mahayana Buddhism emerges.

- A.D.100s Buddhism spreads to China and Central Asia.

- A.D.300s Buddhism reaches Korea.

- A.D.600s Buddhism reaches Tibet and Japan.

- A.D.868 The sacred Buddhist text, the *Diamond Sutra*, is printed.

- 1000s Buddhism dies out in India as Muslim armies invade.

The Life of the Buddha

▲ LOTUS FLOWER
The water lily, or lotus flower, often symbolizes Buddhism. The flower stands for enlightenment, because it grows out of slimy mud, which symbolizes suffering.

PRINCE SIDDHARTHA Gautama was born into a royal family in northeastern India in 485 B.C. His father sheltered him from the suffering in the world, but while he was out of the palace one day Gautama came face to face with a sick man, then an old man, and finally a dead man. He was only 29, but Gautama understood that sickness, old age, and death would come to him eventually, too. He decided to follow a holy way of life in order to come to terms with the meaning of life. He left behind his wife and family and lived a poor life without any luxuries at all. He meditated every day and fasted (did not eat). Gautama suffered a great deal. His hair fell out, and he grew thin and weak. After six

years, Gautama decided that his extreme lifestyle was not the best way to find peace. He decided to find a middle way, somewhere between an ascetic, monk-like existence and a life in the everyday world.

One evening, Gautama was sitting in the shade of a bodhi tree (tree of enlightenment) in Bodh Gaya, a village in northeastern India. After meditating here for a long time, he achieved the state of perfect peace, or *nirvana*. From this moment on, he became known as the Buddha (enlightened one). Today the sacred Mahabodhi temple stands on the site of Buddha's enlightenment.

During his deep meditation the Buddha came to understand the Four Noble Truths. These are the central Buddhist teachings. By understanding these truths, and following the Eightfold Path of right living,

◀ GOLDEN BUDDHA
From around 200 B.C., people began to build statues of the Buddha. He is usually shown sitting cross-legged, with each foot resting on the opposite thigh. This is called the lotus position. It is used in yoga to help concentrate the mind.

BUDDHIST TEMPLES

When the Buddha died, his remains were divided, and *stupas* (Buddhist burial mounds) were built over them. These soon became places of pilgrimage and were often decorated with elaborate carvings and encrusted with stone. Shrines and temples to the Buddha or *bodhisattvas* are found throughout the Buddhist world.

▶ KATHESIMBHU
Buddhists make pilgrimages to this stupa in Nepal to see relics of the Buddha.

◀ BOROBUDUR
The Buddhist temple at Borobudur on the Indonesian island of Java has a central stupa at the top. It is reached by climbing past eight terraces, shaped as squares and circles. These represent a Buddhist's journey from hell, through earthly life, and up to heavenly worlds at the summit.

a person can rise above suffering and achieve the state of *nirvana*.

The Buddha gathered together a group of five disciples (followers) and took up a life as a holy teacher. For the next 45 years he traveled around northern India, teaching his message and begging for food. His first sermon was at Sarnath, near Varanasi in northeast India. He preached in a deer park, which is why some images of the Buddha show him with deer at his feet.

When the Buddha died, his last words to his followers were, "Do not cry. Have I not told you that it is in the nature of all things, however dear they may be to us, that we must part with them and leave them." He meant that Buddhists must not be too attached to anything, as this will only bring sorrow and suffering and will hinder them on their quest for *nirvana*.

◀ DEATH OF THE BUDDHA
When the Buddha died at the age of 80, he became known as the Tathagata (Thus-gone). Having achieved nirvana when he died, the Buddha was not reborn into life again like other people. Buddhists believe he moved beyond life to a blissful state where he neither existed nor did not exist.

▶ TEMPLE
At the center of a Buddhist temple is a shrine that houses images of the Buddha and other holy men. Leading off from it are rooms for meditation and teaching.

▼ MONASTERY
Buddhists as young as eight years old enter monasteries, where they study to become monks. Monasteries usually have classrooms, libraries, rooms for meditation, and shrines.

▼ TRAVELING TEMPLE
In Thailand, tiny temples containing a statue of the Buddha are carried to remote parts. This gives villagers a place to worship.

The Four Noble Truths

The Buddha revealed these Four Truths in his first sermon at Sarnath. They form the basis of all his other teachings. To understand them you must concentrate and be peaceful.

1. Suffering exists in the world, and so all existence is *dukka* (full of suffering and dissatisfaction).

2. Suffering exists because of *tamba* (the yearning for satisfaction).

3. The only way to overcome suffering is to achieve *nirvana*.

4. *Nirvana* can be reached by following the Eightfold Path.

Types of Buddhism

As BUDDHISM SPREAD from India throughout the rest of Eastern Asia, it changed. It adapted to local cultures and adopted elements from other religions. Early Buddhism emphasized the importance of meditation. It stressed that people are on their own in the world and can reach *nirvana* only through their own efforts. This strand of Buddhism is known as Theravada (the teaching of the elders). The other strand of Buddhism is known as Mahayana (great vehicle). Followers of Mahayana believe that people are not alone and that they must work together to achieve *nirvana*. Help also comes from the Buddha, other *buddhas* (enlightened ones), and

▲ PRAYER WHEEL
Tibetan Buddhists often carry a prayer wheel with a mantra (chant) inside on a strip of paper. Each turn of the wheel counts as a single prayer.

▶ WORLD PICTURE
A mandala is a representation of the world through pictures and diagrams. It can be a vast temple, or a picture printed on paper or silk. Tantric Buddhists chant mantras over mandalas as they are made. They believe that they give off powerful energy.

BUDDHISM ABROAD
Buddhism varies from country to country, but two aspects of the religion are common to Buddhists everywhere. Monks are important, especially to Tibetan Buddhists. Meditation is practiced by all Buddhists, but especially by the Zen Buddhists of Japan. When they meditate, Buddhists rid their minds of all thoughts and find inner stillness. In this state, they can concentrate on gaining enlightenment.

◀ THE DALAI LAMA
The leader of Tibet is the Dalai Lama. The present Dalai Lama left Tibet in 1959, eight years after China first occupied his country. From his exile in India, he has campaigned peacefully for China to restore Tibet's independence.

▲ HEADDRESS
Some Tibetan *lamas* wear headdresses for religious services. This one shows the five *buddhas* of meditation.

◀ SPIRITUAL HOME
The Potala stands high on a hilltop in Lhasa, the Tibetan capital. It is the traditional palace of the Dalai Lama, though the present Dalai Lama is in exile. It also serves as a temple and monastery and houses the tombs of previous Dalai Lamas.

bodhisattvas. *Bodhisattvas* are people who have already reached *nirvana* but have chosen to stay in the world to help others achieve it, too. Both Theravada and Mahayana Buddhists believe that the Buddha himself was only one in a long line of enlightened people and that many other *buddhas* exist also.

Mahayana Buddhism differs from country to country. In China, Buddhism was practiced alongside the ancient Chinese religions of Confucianism and Taoism. Many *bodhisattvas* acquired Chinese names. In Tibet, the use of ritual, symbolism, meditation, and magic became important. Tantric Buddhism, as it is known, uses mantras or sacred chants written in *tantras* (secret books) to help people attain *nirvana*. Spiritual teachers, known as *lamas*, educate people in Buddhism. *Lamas* are also said to guide a dying person's spirit between death and rebirth.

In Japan, Zen Buddhism adapted the Chinese practice of meditation. Zen meditation requires the person to sit cross-legged in the lotus position. As they meditate, they think about a *koan* (riddle), such as "What is the sound of one hand clapping?" The purpose behind such riddles is to make people focus on the meanings behind words. In this way, they escape their conventional ways of thinking and free their minds to reach *nirvana*. Zen meditation can take place in a garden, a teahouse, or even through practicing ancient arts, such as flower arranging or archery.

▶ THE BOOK OF BUDDHISM
This picture of the Buddha preaching is based on an illustration in the Diamond Sutra. This sacred Buddhist scroll is over 5 yards long and contains one of the Buddha's sermons. It is the world's oldest printed book.

◀ JAPANESE TEAHOUSE
Teahouses are beautiful places to meditate. The *sado* (tea ceremony) was perfected in the 1500s by Sen Rikyu. He stressed the importance of *wabi* (simplicity) and *sabi* (peacefulness).

▼ ZEN GARDEN
Zen Buddhists create peaceful gardens as places for meditation. Instead of colorful flowers, there are rocks, sand, and grass. Raking the sand into patterns can be a form of meditation in itself.

The Buddhist Year

- In India, Buddhist New Year is celebrated in March or April. In Tibet, it is celebrated in February.

- The birth of Buddha, known as Vesakha in Theravada Buddhism, is celebrated in May.

- In Tibet, Buddha's enlightenment is celebrated in May.

- Buddha's Asalha (first sermon) is celebrated by Theravada Buddhists in July.

- Kattika is a Theravada festival to celebrate missionaries who spread the Buddha's teachings. It is held in late November.

Sikhism

THE SIKH RELIGION was founded by Guru Nanak. He was born in 1469 in the Punjab province of what is now Pakistan and northwestern India. The Sikh holy book, the *Guru Granth Sahib*, was gathered together by the end of the 1500s. Despite persecution by Hindu and Muslim rulers of India, Sikhism slowly gained strength. Today there are more than 20 million Sikhs, mainly in the Punjab but also wherever Punjabis have settled in the world, notably Britain, East Africa, Malaysia, and North America. The word *sikh* is Punjabi for "learner." Sikhs see themselves as learning their faith from one true teacher, Sat Guru (the Sikh god). *Gurus* (teachers) reveal God's teachings. The Sikhs recognize 12 *gurus* in total. They are God, ten leaders of the faith, and the Guru

Granth Sahib, the holy book.

The first *guru* was Nanak. He lived during a period of great conflict between Hindus and Muslims in India. Some Hindus were seeking a god above any religious conflict, and Nanak joined them in their search. "There is no Hindu or Muslim, so whose path shall I follow?" he wondered. Nanak came to believe that there was one God, who created everything, and that everything depended on him. Nanak also believed that God does not appear on Earth but makes himself known through teachers, or *gurus*.

Sikh beliefs are summed up in the words of the *Mool Mantra*, the first hymn written by Guru Nanak.

◀ GURU NANAK
The founder of the Sikh religion was born in the Punjab in 1469. Born a Hindu, Nanak did not agree with the religious wars at the time. He also felt that too much ritual made God distant to us.

THE SIKH HOMELAND
Sikhs were often under attack from Muslim, Hindu, and Afghan armies, so in 1799 they established their own kingdom in the Punjab. This lasted until British forces occupied it in 1849. When the British left in 1947, the Punjab was split between India and Pakistan. Since the 1980s, some Sikhs have campaigned for the Punjab to become an independent Sikh state. This would be called Khalistan (the land of the *Khalsa*).

N

Himalayan Mountains

• Tawalpindi

Lahore •   Amritsar
PAKISTAN   Kartarpur
                               Anandpur •
                  Beas

• Ravi

Ganganagar

                        INDIA

▬ Punjab

Delhi •

0 ___ Kilometers ___ 150
0 ___ Miles ___ 100

▲ GURU RAM DAS
Ram Das became the fourth *guru* in 1574. He founded the city of Amritsar. His followers dug out the Harimandir Sahib, the vast holy lake that surrounds the Golden Temple.

▶ THE GOLDEN TEMPLE
Guru Nanak saw that it was easy for worship to become a meaningless ritual. He said that God can always be found within oneself. However, as long as Sikhs understand that buildings are not holy in themselves, they can build temples at important holy sites. The Golden Temple at Amritsar, Punjab, is the holiest Sikh shrine. It was built in 1601 and contains the Guru Granth Sahib, the holy book of the Sikhs.

"There is only God. Truth is his name. He is the creator. He is without fear. He is without hate. He is timeless and without form. He is beyond death, the enlightened one. He can be known only by the Guru's grace." Sikhs meditate so that they can understand the *gurus'* teachings.

Nanak ensured that after his death another *guru* would take over and continue his work. Nanak died in 1539. Nine more *gurus* carried Sikhism forward until the death of Guru Gobind Singh in 1708. Guru Gobind Singh chose the Sikh holy scripture, not a person, to be his successor. That is why the scripture is called the *Guru Granth Sahib* and is considered to be the 11th guru. The holy book and its teachings guide the Sikh community to this day.

▼ GURU ARJAN
Arjan became the fifth *guru* in 1581. He collected all the hymns of previous *gurus* with his own contributions and combined them into the *Guru Granth Sahib*, the Sikh holy book. He died in 1606.

▲ GURU HAR KRISHAN
Har Krishan was only five when he became the eighth *guru* in 1661. He died of smallpox three years later. He is the only *guru* to be shown without a beard, because he was too young to grow one.

▼ GURU GOBIND SINGH
Gobind Singh, the tenth *guru*, is the second-most-important *guru* after Guru Nanak. He established the *Khalsa* (community of Sikhs) and resisted the Hindu and Muslim rulers of India.

Key Dates

- 1469–1539 Life of Guru Nanak, the first *guru*.
- 1577 Guru Ram Das founds the city of Amritsar.
- 1604 The *Guru Granth Sahib* is installed in the Golden Temple.
- 1699 Guru Gobind Singh forms the *Khalsa* (Sikh community).
- 1799 Maharajah Ranjit Singh founds an independent Sikh kingdom in the Punjab.
- 1849 The Punjab becomes part of British India.
- 1947 The Punjab is split between India and Pakistan.

Sikh Teachings

IN 1699 THE LAST of the ten *gurus*, Guru Gobind Singh, called the Sikhs together at the *mela* (fair) in Anandpur. He called for a volunteer who was willing to die for his faith. One man stepped forward and went into a tent with the *guru*, who came out soon afterward with a bloody sword. Four more men then volunteered, and they also followed the guru into the tent. Then the *guru* opened the tent and revealed that all the five men were still alive.

This event marks the start of the *Khalsa* (Sikh community), whose members pledge to uphold the Sikh religion and defend all those in need, perhaps even to lose their lives for their faith. In order to make all Sikhs equal, Guru Gobind Singh gave all men the name Singh (lion) and all women the name Kaur (princess).

▲ THE CHAURI
The chauri, or whisk, is a symbol of authority. Just as a whisk was waved over a guru to keep the flies away in the Punjab, so the chauri is waved over the holy book to show respect for it.

▶ THE GURU GRANTH SAHIB
The Sikh holy book is a collection of teachings by Guru Nanak and other gurus. The book starts with verses written by Nanak, which are recited every day by Sikhs in their morning prayers.

FESTIVALS
All Sikh festivals are times of meditation and thought. Sikhs hold two types of festival. *Gurpurbs* remember the birth or martyrdom of one of the ten gurus. Sikhs prepare for a *gurpurb* by reading the whole of the *Guru Granth Sahib*, which takes about 48 hours. *Melas* are fairs. They are times of strenuous activity, with sports events, mock battles, and firework displays.

▼ SIKH WEDDINGS
When Sikhs marry, the bride and groom's families are joined together also. Verses from the *Guru Granth Sahib* are read out, and the couple walk around the holy book after each verse as part of their wedding vows.

▼ GOBIND SINGH'S BIRTHDAY
At the festival to celebrate Guru Gobind Singh's birthday, Sikhs read the *Guru Granth Sahib*, pray, meditate, and sing together. People wear traditional costume.

kara

kirpan

kangha

◀ THE FIVE Ks ▶

When the Khalsa was founded in 1699, Guru Gobind Singh asked Sikhs to wear five symbols to show their allegiance to the Sikh community. These are known as the Five Ks, because their names all begin with the letter "k." They are kirpan *(a curved dagger),* kangha *(a comb),* kara *(a steel bangle),* kachh *(short pants worn as underwear), and* kesh *(uncut hair). Sikh boys and men wear a turban to keep their* kesh *tidy. However, the turban itself is not one of the Five Ks.*

Sikhs become members of the *Khalsa* in an initiation ceremony known as an *amrit sanskar*, which is often performed at the Vaisakhi festival, held in April to commemorate the founding of the *Khalsa*. The ceremony is private and takes place in the local *gurdwara* (Sikh temple). Many Sikhs wait until they are adults before joining the *Khalsa*, although boys as young as 14 do join. Women can join, but it is rare for them to do so. All candidates must be approved by existing members of the *Khalsa*.

At the ceremony, five members of the *Khalsa* each hand over one of the Five Ks to the new recruit. These are symbolic objects that all Sikhs must have. In return,

the young Sikh pledges to defend the faith, serve other people, pray every morning and evening, and not smoke or drink alcohol. He is then given a sweet drink called *amrit* and says, "The *Khalsa* is of God and the victory is to God." After a few prayers, the new recruit is admitted to the *Khalsa*.

Sikh religious and community life revolves around the *gurdwara*. Its name means "the door of the *guru*." This is where the *Guru Granth Sahib* is kept, and where Sikhs gather to sing, meditate, and study. There is no holy day of the week reserved for worship, as in many of the other religions. Services can take place at any time.

▼ HOLY LITTER
The *Guru Granth Sahib* takes pride of place in any festival procession. It is carried on a litter by five Sikh elders, dressed in yellow and white. The litter is decorated with garlands.

▲ ANANDPUR FAIR
At the time of the Hindu festival of Holi, Sikhs gather for a *mela* (fair) to remember the life of Guru Gobind Singh. They hold athletic and horse-riding events and compete in the martial arts. The greatest of these *melas* is the Hola Mohalla in Anandpur, Punjab.

Sikh Festivals

- December/January—Guru Gobind Singh's birthday.
- February—Hola Mohalla, in memory of Guru Gobind Singh.
- April—Formation of the *Khalsa*.
- May—Martyrdom of Guru Arjan (1606).
- August—Celebration of the *Guru Granth Sahib* (1606).
- October—The Hindu festival of Diwali marks Guru Hargobind's release from prison in 1619.
- October—Guru Nanak's birthday.
- November—Martyrdom of Guru Tegh Bahadur (1675).

Religion in China

▲ THE I CHING
The I Ching *is based on the ancient art of divination, telling the future. Special disks might be thrown. The way they landed was then interpreted.*

CHINA DOES NOT have a single religion. Instead Chinese religion is made up of four separate religions and philosophies (ways of thinking). The main three are Confucianism, Buddhism, and Taoism. Together, they are known as the *San-chiao* (the three ways). The fourth is the popular folk religion practiced throughout the country. The Chinese practice all these religions in their daily lives, picking out those parts that seem most helpful or useful at the time. Few people follow just one.

The first way, Confucianism, is based on the practice of divination (foretelling the future). This is explained in five books, all compiled long before the birth of Confucius. The books are the *I Ching* (*Book of Changes*), the *Shih Ching* (*Book of Poetry*), the *Shu Ching* (*Book of History*), the *Li Chin* (*Book of Rites*), and the *Ch'un-ch'iu* (*Spring and Autumn Annals*). Confucius's own teachings are contained in the *Four Books of Confucianism*. Together these books produce a code of good behavior for people to follow, rather than a formal religion for them to worship. Followers of Confucius can believe in any god or none.

▲ GOOD WORK
Confucius expected farmers to work hard and produce food for their family and country. Many Chinese festivals celebrate farmers' closeness to the land and their success in getting the harvest in.

Confucius tried to balance the opposing forces of *yin* (darkness) and *yang* (light) in the universe. He stressed the need for order and respect on Earth so that there will be a harmonious balance between heaven, Earth, and human beings. To achieve this, people have to learn from the past to see how they should behave today. Confucius ignored existing religious beliefs and stressed instead the importance of serving other people. He said

CONFUCIANISM

Confucius was a philosopher and teacher who lived at a time of great disturbance in China. He wanted to bring order and peace to his country and taught that people should respect their ancestors and parents and work hard. *Li* (good conduct) was very important. Confucius taught that if everyone did their duty to the emperor and behaved well, the country would be strong and at peace.

◀ RELIGIOUS RULER
Confucius's Chinese name, K'ung Fu-tzu, means "master king." His parents gave him this name because, when he was born, it was foretold that he would be a king without a crown.

▲ CHINESE TEMPLE
Confucius did not found a religion, but throughout China, shrines and temples were erected in his honor. Confucianism became the state religion.

▼ LOOKING
FORWARD
*Children are very
important in Chinese
life. They represent the
future of the family. In
the Chinese language,
the character for "good"
(hao) shows a mother
and child, representing
harmony and fertility.*

▶ CONSULTING
THE I CHING
*The I Ching consists of 64
hexagrams (six lines) made up of
broken (yin) or unbroken (yang)
lines. Users draw stalks from a
container, and throw them to the
ground. Then, they consult the I
Ching, compare the way that their
sticks have fallen to what is in the
book and see what they foretell.*

that people should not do anything to other people that
they would not like others to do to them. Above all, he
taught that it was pointless to worship a god, or honor
your ancestors, if you did not serve other people first.
The second and fourth ways, Taoism and folk religions,
are described on the next page. The third way,
Buddhism, has already been described. Together, all
four ways showed people how to live their lives as
good citizens and therefore keep a balance between
yin and *yang* in their lives.

▲ EMPEROR TEAON-KWANG
The Chinese believed that the very first Chinese
emperors were gods and that their successors had a
mandate (approval) from heaven. Emperors were
worshiped and treated with great respect.

▼ BELL
Once, when Confucius
heard a bell ringing, he
decided to give up worldly
comforts and live on rice
and water for three months
as he meditated. To this
day, the Chinese believe
that bells calm the mind
and help clear thinking.

Key Dates

- c.3000B.C. The *I Ching* is written
  down by Wen Wang.

- 500sB.C. Life of Lao-Tzu.

- 551B.C. Confucius is born.

- c.495–485B.C. Confucius travels
  to neighboring states in the hope
  of realizing his ideals.

- 479B.C. Confucius dies.

- 221B.C. China is united for the
  first time under Emperor Qin
  Shi Huangdi.

- 202B.C.–A.D.220 Under the Han
  dynasty, Confucianism becomes
  the official religion of China.

- A.D.100s Buddhism reaches China.

Taoism

▲ YIN AND YANG
Yin and yang depend on each other and intertwine. The force of yin *represents darkness, water, and the female aspect of things. Its opposite,* yang, *represents light, activity, air, and maleness.*

THE SECOND WAY of Chinese religion, alongside Confucianism and Buddhism, is Taoism. *Tao* means way, or path, and Taoists believe that there is a life force running through the natural world like a path. Taoists follow this path because it is the natural way, and they do not struggle against it. The path is sometimes called the watercourse way, because, like a river, the path flows in one direction. Like water, it is both powerful and life-giving. Taoists go with the flow of life. Taoist belief is summed up in the saying "Tao never acts, yet there is nothing that is not done."

The legendary founder of Taoism, Lao-tzu, lived at about the same time as Confucius, but little is known about him. He is supposed to be the author of the *Tao Te Ching,* one of the two major works of Taoism. The other is the *Chuang Tzu.*

From these books, two kinds of Taoism have developed—popular and philosophical. The popular form is concerned with religion and includes many gods, goddesses, and spirits. Believers seek their help against the many demons that live in the world. They also use ritual and magic to capture the *Te* (power) that brings enlightenment and, they hope, immortality.

Philosophical Taoism is much more mystical and peaceful than religious Taoism. Followers gain an understanding of the Tao by meditation and control of their bodies. They attempt to live in harmony with the Tao. They believe that the body, mind, and environment are closely linked and affect each other.

◀ LAO-TZU
The legendary founder of Taoism lived in China in about 500B.C. He was probably a scholar. One day he traveled on his ox to a border post, where he was asked to write down his teachings. He did, and the book he wrote is known as the Tao Te Ching. *After writing it, Lao-Tzu disappeared and was never heard of again.*

THE FOURTH WAY—CHINESE FOLK RELIGION

Popular religion in China is very festive, with everybody joining in parades and events. It is concerned with caring for dead ancestors and achieving a balance between the forces of *yin* and *yang.* The art of Feng Shui helps in this. Feng Shui is the practice of placing objects, buildings, and even people in the best place to catch the currents of *ch'i* as they circulate.

▼ CHINESE DRAGON
People dressed as dragons, lions, and other animals parade through the streets to celebrate Chinese New Year. The dragon brings happiness and good luck and represents the generous spirit of New Year.

▼ FORTUNE COOKIE
People give each other special cookies called fortune cookies at New Year. Inside them are pieces of paper with a motto.

This belief is shown in the practice of a form of martial art called t'ai chi. Taoists believe that the body has invisible meridians (channels) that run through it carrying blood and *ch'i* (vital energy). The meridian lines feed the vital organs, such as the heart, and ensure a balance between *yin* and *yang*. If this balance is lost, or the flow of *ch'i* is disrupted, acupuncture needles can be used to rebalance the body and ease the flow of *ch'i*.

Taoism never became a major religion in China, although it gained ground during the 1st century A.D. It remained popular until 1949 when the Chinese Communists took power. Communists believe that any religion stops people from working to help themselves, fooling them into just doing what they're told. It is for this reason that the new Chinese government destroyed many of the Taoist temples.

▲ RELIGIOUS TAOISM
Taoists believe in three star gods (shown here from the top left). These are the gods of long life, wealth, and happiness. Taoists also recognize eight immortals (people who will never die), five of whom are shown here. The immortals show living people how to become immortal themselves.

▼ MARTIAL ART
T'ai chi is a form of exercise that focuses the mind and the body. People who practice it draw on the strength of the Earth and the ch'i of the heavens.

▼ BURNING MONEY
At a Chinese funeral, mourners burn fake money. The bills are meant as a bribe to the gods of the underworld so they will let the dead person through to heaven.

▼ A HOUSEHOLD SHRINE
Most houses have a shrine dedicated to a god. Popular gods include Fu Hsing, who brings happiness, and Tsai Shen, who brings wealth. Despite Communist disapproval of gods and religion, some homes place a picture of the first Communist leader, Chairman Mao, in pride of place at their shrine.

Chinese New Year

The major festival in China is New Year, which falls between January 21 and February 19. Each New Year is associated with one of twelve animals.

- 2000 is the Year of the Dragon.
- 2001 is the Year of the Snake.
- 2002 is the Year of the Horse.
- 2003 is the Year of the Goat.
- 2004 is the Year of the Monkey.
- 2005 is the Year of the Rooster.
- 2006 is the Year of the Dog.
- 2007 is the Year of the Pig.
- 2008 is the Year of the Rat.
- 2009 is the Year of the Ox.
- 2010 is the Year of the Tiger.
- 2011 is the Year of the Rabbit.
- 2012 is the Year of the Dragon.

Shinto

▲ TORII GATE
Every Shinto shrine is entered through a gate called a torii. The torii separates the shrine from the ordinary world outside. It can be some distance from the shrine itself.

THE ANCIENT RELIGION of Japan is called Shinto (way of the gods). The name was first given to the religion in the A.D.600s. It comes from the Chinese words *shen* (divine being) and *tao* (way). The religion itself, however, is much older, and dates back to Japanese prehistory, perhaps 1,000 years or more before. No one knows who founded Shinto, because it is so old.

The mysterious origins of Shinto are recorded in two books, the *Kojiki* and *Nihongi*, which were compiled at the beginning of the A.D.700s. Both books were influenced by Chinese thinking, brought to Japan by Buddhist and Confucian teachers.

Over the years, Shinto became the main religion of Japan, but the Japanese do not follow a single religion. Shinto is practiced alongside Confucianism, Taoism, Buddhism, and, more recently, Christianity. The Japanese take elements from each as they need them.

In many ways, Shinto is not really a religion. It is better described as a collection of attitudes and values about life and society which all Japanese people share. It emphasized the divinity of the emperor and the need to obey the government. There is no formal doctrine (set of beliefs) and no single book or collection that contains the main ideas of Shinto. However, all followers of Shinto believe in the forces of nature, which make themselves felt in *kami* (gods). *Kamis* live in every living thing. The Japanese

◀ TOSHO-GU SHRINE
Shrines are built to honor the kami *or past emperors. Tosho-gu Shrine in Ueno Park, Tokyo, was built in 1651 to commemorate the shogun (ruler) Tokugawa Ieyasu. The shrine's entrance is lined with lanterns. People go to shrines to escape the noise and pressure of everyday life. Sometimes they hang up little prayers that they have written.*

JAPANESE RELIGION
Shinto is the main religion in Japan, but it is quite common to see Buddhist priests at a Shinto shrine, and sometimes temples to Buddha have been built within Shinto shrines. Elements of Confucianism and Taoism are also common in Japanese religion.

▶ HIROHITO
The Japanese believe their first emperor, Jimmu, was descended from Amaterasu, the sun goddess. In 1946 Emperor Hirohito said that he was human and renounced his divinity.

◀ MOUNT FUJI
Almost every mountain in Japan has its own god. Sengen-Sama is the goddess of Mount Fuji, the most famous and distinctive mountain in the country. Every year pilgrims climb the mountain at dawn to watch the sun rise.

worship about eight million different *kami* at national and local shrines. The Japanese consult the *kami* at the shrines, asking them for advice or support, and then they follow their instructions. Festivals and rituals play an important part in Shinto.

During the 1800s, Japan began to update its government and economy with ideas imported from Europe. Japanese citizens were given the freedom to worship as they pleased. However, Shinto remained important because it expressed beliefs that are still held by the Japanese people.

▶ THE SUN GODDESS
Amaterasu was the sun goddess, who retired into a cave. The world was plunged into darkness and wicked gods created chaos. The good gods enticed Amaterasu out of the cave by making her curious about what was going on without her. Light and peace were then returned to the world.

▲ PORTABLE SHRINE
At a Shinto festival the kami *(god) leaves the shrine and is carried through the streets in a* mikoshi *(portable shrine), to bless everyone in the community. As they process through the streets, the shrine-bearers shake the* mikoshi *to awaken the* kami.

▲ A REQUEST
Japanese people often buy little plaques called *emas*, which they hang up at the temple or shrine. *Emas* are a request for help from the *kami*. This one asks for luck in love. Others request good health or success in an exam or job interview.

▼ CHILDREN'S DAY
Carp kites are flown to mark Children's Day each May. The carp is a fish that has a long struggle upstream. This represents the difficult journey through life.

Key Dates

- 660 B.C. According to legend, Japan was unified under the first emperor, Jimmu.

- A.D. 600s Chinese Buddhism and Confucianism reach Japan.

- A.D. 645 Reforms of the emperor decide that he is the Son of Heaven and a descendant of the sun goddess, Amaterasu.

- A.D. 700s The key Shinto texts, the *Kojiki* and *Nihongi*, are compiled.

- 1945 Shinto loses its status as Japan's official state religion.

- 1946 Emperor Hirohito renounces his divinity.

Judaism

JUDAISM IS THE RELIGION of the Jewish people. Jews trace their origins back to Abraham (the Father of Many Nations), who lived in Mesopotamia (modern-day Iraq) more than 4,000 years ago. They believe that God revealed himself to Abraham and promised to make him the father of a great nation. Abraham and his family settled in Canaan (modern-day Israel), and this became the center of Judaism. As Jews chose or were forced to settle elsewhere, the religion gradually spread. Today there are more than 13 million Jews worldwide, many of them in Israel and the United States, and in Russia, Ukraine, and other countries of the former USSR.

Judaism was the first great faith to believe that there is only one God. An important statement, called the *Shema* (in the *Tenakh*, the Jewish holy book), says, "Hear, O Israel: the Lord our God, the Lord is One."

Jews believe that God is the creator of the world and that he chose their ancestors, the Israelites, to be his special people. He led the Israelites out of slavery in Egypt and brought them to Canaan, the Promised Land. God's holy name is the Hebrew (Jewish) word *Yhwh*, usually written as

▲ JEWISH LIGHTS
The menorah, a type of multi-branched candlestick, is a symbol of Judaism. A seven-branched menorah stood in King Solomon's temple in Jerusalem.

▼ THE FERTILE CRESCENT
Most of the events in the Hebrew Bible took place in the region known as the Fertile Crescent. This is a huge arc of fertile land, stretching from the Tigris and Euphrates rivers in Mesopotamia (modern-day Iraq) and through the Jewish homeland of Israel to Egypt.

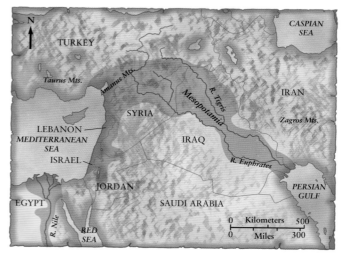

MODERN JEWISH GROUPS

Different customs have evolved in the various Jewish communities around the world. The two main groups are the Orthodox (traditional) Jews and the Reform Jews. Orthodox Jews stick to the traditional way of doing things. They hold their services in Hebrew, follow the ancient food laws, and separate men and women in the synagogue, the Jewish place of worship. Reform Jews reject traditional customs that seem old-fashioned to them. They hold their services in the local language, rather than Hebrew. They modify or discard the food laws, and they allow women to become rabbis.

▶ ETHIOPIAN JEWS
The Falasha are Jews who live in Ethiopia, east Africa. Their ancestors converted to Judaism more than 2,000 years ago. In the 1980s, about 45,000 Falasha emigrated to Israel to escape the war and drought in Ethiopia.

◀ THE TALMUD
Study of the scriptures is an important part of Jewish education. The main books are the Hebrew Bible, or *Tenakh* and the *Talmud*, a book of Jewish laws written in Babylon around 500 B.C.

Yahweh. Yahweh means "I am" or "I am who I am."

Jews believe that God communicates with people through prophets. The greatest prophet was Moses, to whom God revealed the *Torah*, the first five books of the Bible. The *Torah* contains God's sacred laws, the best-known of which are the Ten Commandments. Keeping these laws is central to the Jewish way of life.

Jews believe that in the future God will send a Messiah (anointed one), who will right all wrongs, reward good people, and punish evil. His arrival will mark the end of history and the beginning of God's kingdom on Earth. Some Jews believe that when this happens the dead will be resurrected (brought back to eternal life). Other Jews believe that when they die their souls will go on living.

▲ THE GREAT FLOOD
According to the Bible, God sent a flood to destroy everything and rid the world of sin. Noah and his family were the only people to survive. Noah built an ark (huge boat), in which he saved his family and the animals.

▶ MODERN ISRAEL
Six million Jews were killed in the Holocaust, in World War II. After the war, Jews stepped up their campaign to have their own country, where they could live and worship without threat of persecution. In 1948 the state of Israel was created as a Jewish homeland. Since then, thousands of Jews from all over the world have emigrated to Israel.

▲ RELIGIOUS TEACHER
Rabbis are the spiritual leaders for the Jewish community. They conduct services and teach children about Judaism.

▼ HASIDIC JEWS AT THE WESTERN WALL
Hasidism is a strict form of Judaism that originated in southeast Poland in the 1700s. It was founded by a Jewish scholar named Dov Baer. Hasidic Jews have many special customs. The men wear black suits and hats, and have side curls and beards. *Tzaddiqim* (Hasidic leaders) established new communities after World War II, when many Hasidic Jews were killed. These include the Lubavich sect in New York City.

Key Dates

- c.2166 B.C. Birth of Abraham, the founder of the Jewish nation.

- c.586–537 B.C. Judaism spreads beyond Canaan, when hundreds of Jews are forced into slavery in Babylon.

- c.500 B.C. The *Talmud* is written.

- A.D.70 The Jewish population spreads throughout the Roman Empire. This is known as the Diaspora (dispersal).

- 1939–45 During World War II, six million Jews are killed by the Nazis; this is called the Holocaust.

- 1948 The state of Israel is founded.

The Chosen People

▲ STAR OF DAVID
The Israeli flag features the six-pointed Star of David, which is a symbol of Judaism. In Hebrew, it is known as the Shield of David because King David had this star on his shield.

THE JEWS BELIEVE that they are God's chosen people. According to the Bible, the story of God's special relationship with the Jews started with Abraham. God asked him and his family to leave his home in Mesopotamia and travel to Canaan (modern-day Israel). In return for Abraham's faith and obedience, God promised that he would become the founder of a great nation and that his descendants would inherit the land of Canaan. This agreement between God and Abraham is known as the covenant.

Many years later, God made another covenant with his people. Abraham's descendants, the Israelites, were living in slavery in Egypt. God chose Moses to be their leader and to take them out of Egypt to the Promised Land (Canaan). This is known as the Exodus. At Mount Sinai, God gave Moses Ten Commandments and promised to protect his chosen people if they kept these laws.

The journey to the Promised Land took a long time. The Bible says that the Israelites spent 40 years wandering in the wilderness and that Moses died before they entered Canaan. Under his successor, Joshua, and later leaders, the Israelites gradually captured the land from its existing inhabitants.

The Israelites settled in Canaan, but over the years they stopped obeying God's laws. For this reason God allowed them to be threatened by the Philistines and other enemies. God renewed his covenant with the

▼ THE PROPHET EZEKIEL
Throughout Jewish history, God has spoken through prophets or wise men. Ezekiel was a priest who was deported to Babylon in 586B.C. He told his fellow-exiles to keep their faith in God.

PLACES OF WORSHIP

Jews usually meet to worship at a synagogue. Prayers are held there in the morning, afternoon, and evening each day, but many Jews attend only on Saturday, the Jewish Sabbath, or holy day. Worship is often led by the rabbi. It includes prayers and *Tenakh* readings.

▶ TEMPLE REMAINS
The Western Wall is all that is left of the temple in Jerusalem. It is a sacred place, where Jewish people go to pray. Some write prayers on pieces of paper, which they tuck between the blocks of stone in the wall.

◀ THE TEMPLE IN JERUSALEM
In Jerusalem, King Solomon built the first temple, which became the center of Jewish worship. His temple was destroyed by the Babylonians in 587B.C., but later temples were built on the same site, the last by King Herod. This was destroyed by the Romans in A.D.70. The Western Wall is all that remains of it.

Israelites through David. He promised to make David a great king and to protect his people if they obeyed his laws. God told David to build a magnificent temple in Jerusalem as a sign of this covenant. The temple was eventually built by David's son, Solomon.

Hundreds of years later, in 586B.C., Canaan was seized by the Babylonians, who took many Jews away to Babylon as slaves. In the Bible, the *Psalms* (songs) tell how the Jews missed their homeland during this period, but how they believed that God would return them to the Promised Land. Eventually Babylon was defeated by the Persians, and the Jews returned home.

Jews today look back on their history. As they did in the past, they strongly believe that if they obey God, he will continue to look after them.

◀ KING SOLOMON
For much of their history, the Jews were ruled by a series of kings. King Solomon, the son of David, was famous for his wisdom. He built the first temple in Jerusalem.

▲ DAVID AND GOLIATH
As a shepherd boy, David killed the giant Goliath with just a stone and a sling. He later became the king of Israel. David established Jerusalem as the capital city of his kingdom.

▼ HOUSE OF WORSHIP
A synagogue is a place where Jews meet to pray and to study the *Tenakh*. All synagogues are built facing in the direction of Jerusalem. There is usually a cupboard in the end wall, known as the Ark of the Covenant, which contains the *Torah* scrolls. In Orthodox synagogues, men and women sit in separate areas.

▲ INCENSE BURNER
Incense is sometimes burned in synagogues. The smoke symbolizes people's prayers, rising up to God.

Key Dates

- c.2166B.C. Birth of Abraham.

- c.1700B.C. The Israelites move to Egypt to escape a famine.

- c.1446B.C. Moses leads the Israelites out of Egypt.

- c.1406B.C. The Israelites enter Canaan (the Promised Land).

- c.960B.C. Solomon completes the temple in Jerusalem.

- c.930B.C. The kingdom divides into Judah and Israel.

- c.586B.C. The Babylonians destroy the temple and enslave many Jews.

- c.537–445B.C. The Jews return to Judah and rebuild the temple.

Jewish Scriptures

THE HEBREW BIBLE IS the sacred book of the Jewish people. It also forms the first part of the Christian Bible, in which it is known as the Old Testament. It tells the story of the Jewish people and their special relationship with

God. The events it describes took place over a period of more than 2,000 years.

The Hebrew Bible is not one single book, but a collection of books written over many centuries by many different authors. It contains books of law, history, poetry, and prophecy. The Jews group the books of their Bible into three main sections: the *Torah* (law), the *Nevi'im* (prophets), and the *Ketuvim* (writings).

The most important part of the Hebrew Bible is the first five books, known as the *Torah*, or law. It contains the Ten Commandments and other laws given by God to Moses. The *Torah* also tells the story of the Jewish people from the time of their founder, Abraham, to the time of Moses. One of the most important themes of the *Torah*

▲ SPICE BOX
At the end of the Sabbath some Jews breathe in spices from a spice box to keep the sweet smell of the Sabbath with them all week.

◄ THE SHOFAR
The shofar is a trumpet made from a ram's horn. In ancient times, the Israelites used it to rally their warriors in battle and to summon people to worship. The shofar is still blown in synagogues at Yom Kippur (the Jewish fast) and Rosh Hashanah (Jewish New Year).

RITES AND RITUALS

Each week Jews keep their holy day, the Sabbath, the day of rest as ordered by God in the Ten Commandments. This starts with a family meal on Friday evening and lasts until sunset on Saturday. Throughout the year, Jews celebrate a number of festivals. Some of them commemorate specific events in Jewish history, such as the Exodus from Egypt. Other festivals are connected to the seasons and the events of the farming year.

▼ THE HAGADAH
At Pesach (Passover), Jewish families share a special meal, called the *seder*. During the meal they read from a part of the *Talmud* called the *Hagadah*. It tells how the Israelites escaped from Egypt.

▼ SUKKOT
At the autumn festival of Sukkot (the festival of booths) Jews remember the 40 years that they spent in the wilderness. They make booths (tents) out of leaves and branches to symbolize the ones that they used in the desert.

◀ TORAH COVERS
Each synagogue has a copy of the Torah, written on a long scroll. Jews believe that the Torah is too sacred to touch, so the reader uses a pointer to keep their place in the text. The Torah is often stored in a decorated, protective cover. Popular images on Torah covers include the lion, which represents the tribe of Judah, and the menorah.

▼ KOSHER FOOD
The Torah contains laws about food, which forbid Jews to eat certain types of meat, such as pork or rabbit, or to eat the blood of animals. Another law states that they cannot eat meat and milk in the same meal. Many Jews buy their food, especially meat, from special shops where it has been prepared according to the food laws. Food prepared in this way is called kosher.

is God's covenant (agreement), made first with Abraham and his descendants and then again with Moses. This covenant showed the Jews that they were God's chosen people.

After the *Torah* is the section of the Bible known as the *Nebi'im*. This is made up of eight books, believed to have been written by Jewish prophets, including Samuel, Isaiah, and Ezekiel. The *Nevi'im* continues the history of the Jews, from their conquest of the Promised Land up to the fall of the Jewish kings. In their books, the prophets explained the meaning of these events and warned the Jews about the dangers of disobeying God.

The remaining 11 books of the Hebrew Bible are called the *Ketuvim*. This section contains books of wisdom, poetry, prophecy, and history. Among them is the *Book of Psalms*. This is a collection of hymns and prayers, many of which were written by King David.

▲ COMING OF AGE
Bar Mitzvah is the ceremony at which a boy becomes an adult member of the Jewish community. It happens when he is 13 years old and takes place in the synagogue. As part of the ceremony, the boy reads aloud from the *Torah*. Some Jews have a similar service to mark girls' entry into adulthood. This is called Bat Mitzvah.

▼ DECEMBER FESTIVAL
Hanukkah celebrates how the Jews reclaimed the temple from the Greek rulers in 164 B.C. The temple's lamp had only enough oil for one day, but burned for eight days. On each of the eight days of the festival, Jewish families light one more candle on a *menorah*. They do this using the ninth candle, or *shamash*, in the center of the candlestick.

The Jewish Year

- February/March—Purim (celebrating how Esther saved the Jews from the Persians)

- March/April—Pesach or Passover (commemorating the Exodus, when the angel of death killed every first-born Egyptian, but passed over the Israelites)

- May/June—havuot (marking the giving of the law to Moses)

- September/October—Rosh Hashanah (Jewish New Year)

- September/October—Yom Kippur (the Day of Atonement)

- September/October—Sukkot

- December—Hanukkah

Christianity

THE FOUNDER OF CHRISTIANITY was Jesus Christ, a Jewish teacher and healer who lived in what is now Israel during the first century A.D. His followers grew steadily in number. In the A.D.300s the Roman emperor, Constantine, decreed that Christianity should be tolerated throughout his empire. An important figure around that time was Augustine, who was bishop of Hippo (in modern-day Algeria, Africa) from A.D.396 until A.D.430. Augustine developed Christian thought in his *Confessions*, mixing them with Greek ideas. His interpretation of Christianity spread throughout Europe.

From the 1500s, as Europeans explored other continents, they took Christianity with them. Today Christians live on every continent of the globe. They total almost two billion, which makes Christianity the world's biggest religion.

Christians believe in one God. They believe that Jesus Christ was the Messiah promised in the Old Testament. The Christian God has three parts, known as the Holy Trinity. The Trinity consists of God the Father, God the Son (Jesus), and God the Holy Spirit.

Christians believe that God came to Earth in the form of a man, Jesus. He showed

▲ THE CROSS
Jesus was crucified (put to death on a cross), but Christians believe he rose from the dead. This has made the cross a symbol of Jesus's sacrifice. Christians see it as a symbol of victory and hope, too.

▲ THE VIRGIN MARY
The Bible says that Jesus's mother, Mary, was a virgin. The power of the Holy Spirit made her pregnant, so that Jesus could be born as a human being.

THE CHRISTIAN CHURCH

The first Christian Church was the Catholic (universal) Church, with the Pope at its head. In the A.D.1000s there was disagreement about the use of icons (holy pictures). This led to a split between the Catholic Church in Rome and the Orthodox Church, based in Constantinople. This is called the Great Schism (split). The Protestant churches were founded in the 1500s. This period is called the Reformation.

▲ MARTIN LUTHER
Luther was a German monk. He felt the Catholic Church abused its position of power. In protest, he founded the first Protestant church in the 1520s.

▶ JOHN CALVIN
Calvin set up a Protestant church in Switzerland. Like Luther, he tried to get rid of church traditions and simply follow the teachings of the Bible.

▼ ORTHODOX ICONS
Orthodox churches are usually full of beautiful icons. These are religious pictures or statues of Jesus, Mary, or the saints.

◀ ST. PETER'S BASILICA
The Pope lives in the Vatican, a tiny country within the city of Rome. The Pope's church is St. Peter's, begun in 1506 by Pope Julius II.

people how to confess the things they had done wrong in the past and have a fresh start with God. During his lifetime Jesus gathered a large body of followers. This alarmed the Romans, who occupied what is now Israel, and also the Jewish religious authorities, who feared that Jesus was damaging their own power base. Jesus was put on trial and sentenced to death by crucifixion. According to Christian belief, when Jesus died, he paid the price for everyone's sins. The Bible says that, three days after his death, Jesus rose from the dead. Christians believe that when they die, they can look forward to eternal life in heaven.

Jesus said in the Bible that he is still with all Christians in spirit, and that he will come back at the end of the world to judge all people. Those who have faith in him will be saved and go to heaven. Those who have not will be banished to hell.

Jesus promised his disciples (followers) that after he was gone he would send a helper for them, the Holy Spirit. Christians believe this Spirit is still active in the world today.

▶ THE ASCENSION
Jesus appeared to his followers on many occasions in the 40 days following his resurrection, when he came back to life. Then one day he was taken up into heaven before his disciples' eyes. This event is known as the Ascension.

◀ EUROPE IN THE 1500S
During the Reformation, northern Europe became mostly Protestant, while southern Europe remained mostly Catholic. Most Orthodox Christians live in Russia and parts of eastern Europe, such as Greece and the Balkans.

Key Dates

- C.A.D.30 Birth of the Christian Church. Jesus's disciples start to preach the Christian message.

- A.D.313 Emperor Constantine grants tolerance of Christianity. It eventually becomes the official religion of the Roman Empire.

- 1054 The Orthodox Church breaks away in the Great Schism.

- 1517 Martin Luther publicly criticizes the Catholic Church and starts the Reformation. Protestant churches are founded.

- 2000 Christians celebrate the millennium, 2,000 years after the traditional birth date of Jesus.

The Life of Jesus

JESUS CHRIST WAS BORN IN about 6 or 7 B.C. in Judah (modern-day Israel), which was then a province of the Roman Empire. His mother was Mary, a young Jewish woman from Nazareth.

According to the Bible, the Angel Gabriel appeared to Mary and told her that she would have a child who would be God's son and the savior of the world.

We know very little about Jesus's childhood, except that he lived in Nazareth and was brought up as a Jew. The Bible picks up the story when Jesus was in his early 30s. He was baptized in the river Jordan and spent

▲ JESUS
All that we know about Jesus's life comes from the accounts in the four gospels, the books of the Bible written specifically about Jesus.

▶ PARABLES
Jesus often told parables (stories about everyday life) to teach people about God in a way they could understand and remember. One of his most famous parables is the story of the good Samaritan. It tells the story of a man who was helped by the one person he thought was his enemy.

WEEKLY WORSHIP

Christians gather together to worship God on Sunday and at other important festivals. They usually meet in a church, but some groups meet in people's homes. The most important form of Christian worship is the service known as communion, mass, or the Eucharist. At holy communion, Christians share bread and wine, as Jesus did with his disciples at the Last Supper. Christian worship includes prayers, readings from the Bible, and singing religious songs called hymns.

◀ NOTRE-DAME CATHEDRAL
Huge cathedrals were built in Europe during the Middle Ages. One of the most beautiful is the Cathedral of Notre-Dame (Our Lady), in Paris, which was begun in 1163. It has many stained-glass windows.

▲ MODERN CATHEDRAL
Not all cathedrals are old. The Cathedral of Christ the King, in Liverpool, England, dates from 1967.

◀ A PARISH CHURCH
In Britain, most Christians worship at a small local church, with members of their parish (community).

40 days fasting in the desert in preparation for his work. Then he traveled around the country, teaching people about God, healing the sick, and performing miracles. He was accompanied by a group of twelve disciples (followers). Jesus told people that God's kingdom was coming and that they should ask God's forgiveness so they could be saved. Jesus became very popular, and vast crowds of people came to hear him preach. However, he faced opposition from the Jewish religious authorities, who saw him as a threat.

After three years, Jesus traveled to Jerusalem for the Jewish festival of Pesach (Passover). According to the Bible he rode a donkey into the city, cheered on by crowds who threw palm branches in his path. Later in the week, Jesus and his disciples ate *seder* (the Pesach meal) together. This is now known as the Last Supper. Jesus shared bread and wine with his disciples. Later that night, Jesus was arrested, tried, and found guilty by the religious authorities. The Roman governor of the province, Pontius Pilate, sentenced him to death. The following day, Jesus was forced to carry a wooden cross through the streets of Jerusalem to a place outside the city walls, where he was crucified. He died in the afternoon, and was buried by his friends and followers.

Three days later Jesus's followers discovered that his tomb was empty. An angel told them that Jesus was alive again. Jesus himself appeared to his astonished disciples on many occasions over the next few weeks. Forty days later, he was taken up into heaven. This marked the end of his life on Earth, but Christians believe that Jesus is still alive in heaven.

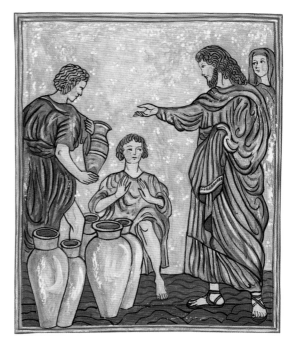

▲ THE WEDDING AT CANA
In the three years of his teaching, Jesus performed many miracles. His first was to turn jars of water into wine at a wedding. Jesus healed many people, and even brought a dead man, Lazarus, back to life. He also used miracles to demonstrate his power over nature—for example, by calming a storm.

▲ HOLY COMMUNION
The bread and wine that Christians receive at communion represent the body and blood of Jesus. At the Last Supper, Jesus told his disciples to think of bread and wine in this way.

▼ FORMS OF WORSHIP
There are many styles of Christian worship. The Baptist Church, founded around 1611, is known for its lively services. Baptists celebrate Jesus with joyful singing—some with dancing.

Key Dates

- c.6–7B.C. Jesus is born in Bethlehem. His family flees to Egypt to escape King Herod.

- c.4B.C. King Herod dies and Jesus's family returns to Nazareth.

- c.A.D.5–6 With his family, Jesus visits the temple at Jerusalem, where he is dedicated to God.

- c.A.D.28 Jesus is baptized in the river Jordan and starts his public teaching.

- c.A.D.30 Jesus is crucified in Jerusalem, but is resurrected after three days. About 40 days later he ascends into heaven.

The Christian Scriptures

▲ GUTENBERG BIBLE
In the Middle Ages, when all books had to be copied out by hand, Christian monks produced some beautiful Bibles. The first printed edition was the Gutenberg Bible of 1455.

THE CHRISTIAN HOLY BOOK is the Bible. Christians believe that although the Bible was written by people, it was inspired by God. It is a collection of books written by different authors. These books are divided into two sections, the Old and New Testaments. The Old Testament consists of the Jewish scriptures. The New Testament deals with the life and teachings of Jesus Christ and the story of the early Christian Church. All 27 books in the New Testament were written by early followers of Jesus, roughly between A.D.45 and A.D.97.

The first four books of the New Testament are the gospels of Matthew, Mark, Luke, and John. The word "gospel" means "good news" and refers to the good news that Jesus was the long-awaited Messiah. Together the gospels tell the story of Jesus's life. All four of the gospel writers were closely involved with Jesus or with his followers. Matthew and John were two of Jesus's disciples. Mark was probably a translator for Peter, another of the 12 disciples. Luke was a friend of Paul's. Paul was not a disciple. He was a Jew who had persecuted the Christians but converted to Christianity after seeing a vision on the road to Damascus. After this, Paul traveled widely spreading the Christian message.

Each of the gospels tells the life of Jesus from a different viewpoint. All four concentrate on Jesus's ministry, his time teaching in Galilee, and on the events of the last week of his life.

The fifth book of the New Testament, *The Acts of the*

◀ ST. ANDREW AND ST. JAMES
The first four disciples that Jesus recruited were Peter, Andrew, James, and John. After Jesus's death, they carried on preaching his message. Some died for their religion. King Herod Agrippa I of Judah had James beheaded around A.D.44, and Andrew was crucified (in modern-day Turkey) in the A.D.60s.

THE CHRISTIAN YEAR

Christians celebrate many festivals. Most commemorate events in Jesus's life. In some churches, saints are celebrated on the particular days dedicated to them. Festivals are marked with special church services and with other customs, such as giving Christmas presents or Easter eggs.

▲ EASTER EGGS
In some countries it is traditional to give and receive eggs at Easter, as a symbol of new life. Easter eggs may be real or made of wood or chocolate.

◀ THE NATIVITY
At Christmas, Christian homes and churches often display models of the nativity, Jesus's birth in the stable in Bethlehem.

▲ PALM SUNDAY
Shortly before his death, Jesus rode into Jerusalem on a donkey. He was greeted by crowds of people, who laid palm branches in his path. Christians remember this event on Palm Sunday. At some churches, small crosses made of palm leaves are handed out to worshipers.

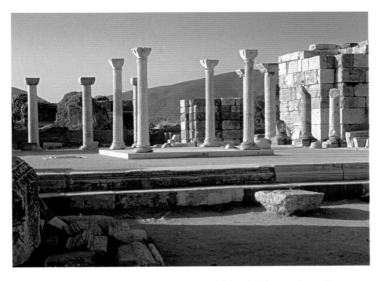

Apostles, was written by Luke, the author of the third gospel. It tells what happened in the 30 years after Jesus's ascension into heaven. *Acts* describes the missionary work of the apostles, Jesus's specially appointed helpers, the life of the early Christian Church, and Paul's travels.

The next 21 books are letters from the early Christian leaders to the newly founded churches, giving them advice and encouragement. Paul is believed to have written 13 of the letters. Other authors include the disciple Peter and Jesus's brother James.

The final book of the Bible is the *Book of Revelation*. The writer, John, who may be the same John who wrote the fourth gospel, describes what will happen at the end of the world.

▲ A FRANCISCAN FRIAR
Monks or friars try to spread the Christian message by setting a good example. Francis, who later became a saint, founded his order of monks in 1209. The Franciscans live in poverty and in harmony with nature.

▶ PENTECOST
A few days after Jesus had ascended into heaven, his disciples gathered together on the Jewish festival of Shavuot. The Bible says that they suddenly heard a sound like rushing wind. They saw tongues of flame which came to rest on each of them. They were all filled with the power of the Holy Spirit and began to speak in tongues (other languages). Christians celebrate this event at the festival of Pentecost, or Whitsunday.

Christian Festivals

- December 25—Christmas (celebrates Jesus's birth)

- March/April—Lent (a 40-day fast that ends on Easter Sunday)

- March/April—Maundy Thursday (held the Thursday before Easter to celebrate the Last Supper)

- March/April—Good Friday (marks the crucifixion of Jesus)

- March/April—Easter Sunday (celebrates Jesus's resurrection)

- May/June—Pentecost or Whitsunday (celebrates the event in which the disciples received the Holy Spirit)

Islam

ISLAM WAS FOUNDED by the prophet Muhammad. It began in the cities of al-Madinah (Medina) and Makkah (Mecca) in modern-day Saudi Arabia in about A.D.620. Muhammad received revelations from Allah (God) and began to preach his message.

Muhammad died in A.D.632, and within a few years the peoples of the Arabian peninsula had converted to Islam. The new religion soon had followers as far west as the Atlantic coast of Africa and as far east as India. Today, Islam is the world's second-largest religion, with more than a billion followers spread over almost every country.

The word "Islam" means "surrender to the peace of Allah." Muslims (followers of Islam) give themselves up to Allah's will. They believe that Allah is the one God, and that Muhammad was Allah's messenger.

Muslims believe that Allah sent many prophets (messengers) before sending Muhammad. These include holy men recognized by Jews and Christians, such as Adam, Ibrahim (Abraham), Musa (Moses), Dawud (David), and Isa (Jesus). Muhammad received revelations from Allah through the Angel Jibril (Gabriel) from the age of 40. He told his followers about these revelations. They were eventually written down in the Islamic holy book, the Qur'an.

Muslims believe that their faith is the final revelation of Allah. Every aspect of Muslim life is governed by the Five Pillars of Islam, duties that unite Muslims all over the world into a single community.

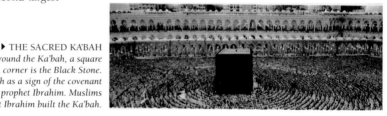

▶ THE SACRED KA'BAH
The Great Mosque at Makkah is set around the Ka'bah, a square building made of gray stone. In its eastern corner is the Black Stone. Muslims believe this fell to Earth as a sign of the covenant (agreement) between Allah and the prophet Ibrahim. Muslims believe that Ibrahim built the Ka'bah.

THE FIVE PILLARS OF ISLAM

Islam rests on five duties that all Muslims must obey and carry out. These are called the Five Pillars (supports) of Islam. They are based on the Qur'an and the actions of Muhammad. They give a sense of purpose to every Muslim's life.

◀ SHAHADAH
The first pillar is *shahadah*. This is the Muslim statement of faith—that Allah is the one true God and that Muhammad was his prophet. This belief is stated each day in the call to prayer.

◀ SALAH
The second pillar is *salah*, the prayers that Muslims say five times a day. Wherever they are in the world, Muslims face toward the sacred Ka'bah in Makkah when they pray.

▼ CHARITY SCHOOL, OMAN
Every Muslim must give one-fortieth of his or her annual income to charities such as this religious school. This is called *zakat*, and is the third pillar.

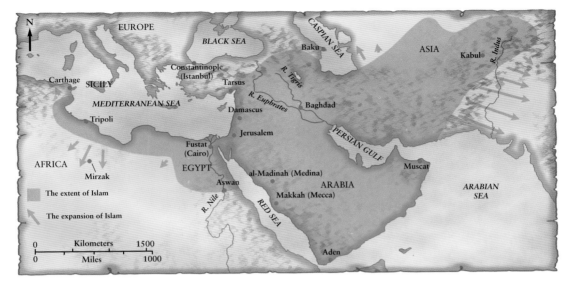

▶ HOLY SITE
*Al-Aqsa (the Dome of the Rock)
in Jerusalem is where Muhammad
ascended into heaven in A.D.619 to
meet Allah. It is sacred to Jews and
Christians, too, as the ancient site
of Solomon's temple. Other holy
Muslim sites are the Great Mosque
at Makkah and the tomb of
Muhammad at al-Madinah.*

▲ THE ISLAMIC WORLD
*Islam began in the cities of Makkah
and al-Madinah. It became the
chief religion of the Arabian
peninsula, spreading into Persia
(modern-day Iran), Mesopotamia
(modern-day Iraq), and North
Africa. During the 1100s and
1200s, Christian knights known
as Crusaders recaptured Jerusalem
from Muslim control, but they
failed to hold their gains for long.*

▼ ID-UL-FITR
The fourth pillar is *sawm* (fasting).
During the month of Ramadan, Muslims
do not eat or drink during daylight hours.
Muslims celebrate the end of Ramadan
with a feast. They call this festival
Id-ul-Fitr.

▶ PILGRIMS
During their lifetime all healthy Muslims
must make at least one *hajj* (pilgrimage)
to Makkah during the 12th month of the
Islamic year. The *hajj* is the fifth pillar.

Key Dates

- A.D.570–632 Life of Muhammad.

- A.D.622 Muhammad's hijrah (flight)
  from Makkah to al-Madinah.

- A.D.630 Muhammad conquers Makkah.

- A.D.634 Muhammad's successor,
  Abu Bakr, conquers Arabia.

- A.D.638 Arab armies capture Jerusalem.

- A.D.651 Arab armies overrun Persia.

- A.D.711 Arab armies reach India.

- A.D.732 Arab armies conquer Spain.

- 1453 Muslim Ottoman Turks
  capture Constantinople.

- 1492 Last Muslim armies retreat
  from Spain.

The Life of Muhammad

▲ MIHRAB TO MAKKAH
Makkah is sacred to Muslims because it was there, in A.D.610, that Muhammad had his first vision of the Angel Jibril. Mosques, such as this one at Aleppo, Syria, always feature a mihrab *(an alcove in the wall that shows the direction of Makkah).*

MUHAMMAD WAS BORN in the Arabian city of Makkah in A.D.570. He was orphaned as a child and brought up by his grandfather and then his uncle. He worked as a desert trader, and in A.D.595 married Khadijah, a wealthy widow. Muhammad became wealthy and well-respected in the city. However, he was increasingly concerned about the worship of pagan gods at the Ka'bah, the sacred house said to have been built by Ibrahim. Muhammad used to go and pray and meditate in the mountains at Hira, outside Makkah. In A.D.610 he was meditating when the

▶ HARUN AL-RASHID
In A.D.750 the Abbasid Dynasty took control of the Muslim world. They moved the capital from Damascus (in modern-day Syria) to Baghdad (in modern-day Iraq). Under Caliph (leader) Harun Al-Rashid (A.D.786–809), Baghdad became the center of Islamic arts and learning.

ISLAMIC WORSHIP

The center of the Islamic religion is the mosque. It is a space for prayer, worship, teaching, and study. It also acts as a community center for local Muslims. The main weekly service is usually held on Friday afternoon, but the mosque is open throughout the week for constant prayer and study.

◀ MOSQUE
Most mosques contain an outer courtyard with running water for *wudu* (washing before prayer). Inside is an area for prayer, with a pulpit and lectern.

▶ THE MINARET
Each mosque has a minaret (tower). A man called a *mu'adhin* or *muezzin* climbs it five times each day and calls Muslims to prayer.

▼ WOMEN AT WORSHIP
Muslim men and women pray separately. Most women worship at home, but some mosques have special areas reserved for women.

◀ PREACHING THE MESSAGE
This Turkish manuscript dates to the 1500s. It shows the Prophet Muhammad preaching to the people of Makkah after his first vision.

hijrah (emigration), marks the start of the Islamic Era. All Muslim calendars are dated A.D. (*Anno Hegirae* is Latin for "year of the *hijrah*"). The year A.D.2000 is 1421A.H. in the Muslim calendar.

By A.D.630 Muhammad had a strong enough following to return in triumph to Makkah. He forgave his former enemies,

Angel Jibril appeared to him and told him he would be Allah's messenger. Muhammad had other revelations for the rest his life. These include his famous night journey of A.D.619, when Jibril took him to Jersualem and then up to heaven to meet Allah. Muhammad tried to preach Allah's message to the people of Makkah, but they did not want to listen. In A.D.622 Muhammad fled the city and moved to al-Madinah. The people there did listen, and al-Madinah became the first Islamic city. For this reason, Muhammad's flight from Makkah, known as the

and many became Muslims. After Muhammad's death in A.D.632, Islam became the major religion of the Middle East and North Africa. However it soon split into two groups, Sunnis and Shi'ahs. The two groups have many beliefs in common, but the Sunnis believed that Muhammad's successors should be chosen by the Muslim community. The Shi'ahs believed that only the descendants of his cousin and son-in-law, Ali, could follow him. Most Muslims today are Sunnis. Ten percent are Shi'ahs, and they live mainly in Iran.

◀ IMAM
The main official at the mosque is called the *imam* (chief). He leads the prayers. Sermons are read by the *khatib* (preacher).

▶ SAJJADA
Muslims use a *sajjada* (prayer mat) to make sure that they pray on a clean space. Many mats have a picture of a mosque. Some feature an inbuilt compass, so that the user always knows the direction of Makkah and which way to face as he prays.

Key Dates

- A.D.595 Muhammad marries Khadijah, a wealthy widow.

- A.D.610 Muhammad's vision of Jibril in a cave on Mt. Hira.

- A.D.619 Muhammad's Night Journey with Jibril to Jerusalem.

- A.D.622 Muhammad's *hijrah*.

- A.D.630 Muhammad captures Makkah.

- A.D.632 Muhammad dies in Makkah and is buried in al-Madinah.

- A.D.632 Abu Bakr becomes the first caliph (Muslim ruler).

- A.D.680 Sunni-Shi'ah split.

The Qur'an

◄ CALLIGRAPHY
Muslims are forbidden to depict Allah or Muhammad in paintings. They decorate the Qur'an with geometric or floral designs and with intricate calligraphy (writing). This lettering is the Arabic script for "Allah."

MUHAMMAD TOLD his followers all the teachings that Allah had passed on to him through the Angel Jibril. They learned his revelations by heart and dictated them to scribes, who wrote them down in what became the Qur'an, which means "revelation." Muslims believe that earlier messages from Allah to his prophets had been corrupted or ignored. They believe that the Qur'an is the true word of Allah. Because it was spoken by Muhammad in Arabic, the Qur'an can be written and recited only in Arabic, regardless of the language of the believer. Muslims believe that the Qur'an is perfect, and therefore it cannot be translated into any other language, only interpreted.

Copies of the Qur'an are always beautifully illustrated. Muslims believe that making the word of Allah beautiful is in itself an act of worship.

The Qur'an is divided into 114 *surahs* (chapters). It starts by saying that Allah is the one true God. Then it discusses Allah's role in history and Muhammad's role as Allah's prophet. The Qur'an describes Allah's last judgment on his people and the need to help other people. It tells Muslims how to behave, as well as how to treat other people and animals. However, not everything is covered by the Qur'an, so Muslims also study the *Sunnah*, too. This book contains accounts of the words and deeds of Muhammad and his close followers. The *Sunnah* helps Muslims to gain a clear understanding of the Qur'an. Muslim laws are taken from both the Qur'an and the *Sunnah*. These laws, known as the *Shari'ah*,

◄ PATHWAY TO ALLAH
Islamic law is known as the Shari'ah. This is an Arabic word meaning a track that leads camels to a water hole. In the same way, Muslims who obey the Shari'ah will be led to Allah. The Shari'ah guides Muslims in their faith and behavior. It is taught in law schools, such as this one, throughout the Islamic world.

THE SUFIS

Sufis are Muslims, who can be either Sunnis or Shi'ahs. They place complete obedience and trust in Allah. They try to get closer to Allah through dance and music. Sufi beliefs are passed down through the generations by saints and teachers. Many Sufis are involved in education and community work.

► SOULFUL SINGER
Sufis believe that music is both a path to Allah and a means of spiritual healing. They sing *qawwalis*, trancelike hypnotic songs that build up to an ecstatic climax. *Qawwali* singers such as Nusrat Fateh Ali Khan have achieved international fame.

▲ DERVISHES
Some Sufis dance and spin to forget the things around them and get closer to Allah. They are known as Whirling Dervishes.

▲ A SUFI
No one really knows how Sufis got their name. The word might come from *suf*, a basic woolen garment that early Sufis wore. Sufis turn their back on the world. They do not own many possessions, and they often take vows of poverty.

provide detailed instructions to Muslims as to how to lead a good life. Sunni Muslims follow one of four different schools, or interpretations, of the *Shari'ah*. The Shi'ahs also follow the teachings of the first *imams*, the spiritual leaders descended from Ali, Muhammad's cousin. They follow the teachings of individual thinkers, too. The greatest thinkers are known as *ayatollahs* (signs of Allah).

◀ THE QUR'AN
The Qur'an was prepared in about A.D.650 by Uthman, the third successor to Muhammad. Muslims consider it to be the perfect word of Allah. Only Muslims who have been ceremonially washed can touch it.

▶ SHI'AH LEADER
Muslims interpret the Qur'an in different ways. Ayatollah Khomeini was leader of Iran between 1979 and 1989. He interpreted the Qur'an very strictly. During his decade of power, he applied its teachings to every aspect of political and social life in his country.

▼ QAWWALI SHRINE, DELHI
One of the main Sufi shrines, dedicated to the Sufi saint Nizamuddin Awliya, is in Delhi, India. Its community of *qawwali* singers trace their ancestors back to Amir Khusrau (1253–1325). He was the founder of *qawwali* music.

▲ THE SIMURG
Sufis use a mythical bird, the *simurg*, to symbolize their search for unity with Allah. Its name is Persian for "30 birds." The *simurg's* multicolored feathers represent every other bird that there is.

The Islamic Year

The Islamic calendar has 12 lunar months, each with 29 or 30 days.

- Muharram is the first month.

- Muslims celebrate the birthday of Muhammad on the 12th day of Rabi'I, the third month.

- Ramadan is the ninth month, when Muslims fast during daylight hours.

- Id-ul-Fitr (the breaking of the fast) is celebrated at the start of Shawal, the tenth month.

- Dhul-Hijjah, the 12th month, is when Muslims make their *hajj* (pilgrimage) to Makkah.

Modern Religions

▲ MARY BAKER EDDY
Christian Scientists believe that illness can be cured by prayer and so believers do not take medicines or even accept blood transfusions. The religion was founded by the American Mary Baker Eddy (1821-1910).

▶ MORMONS
The Church of Jesus Christ of Latter-Day Saints is better known as the Mormons. Their name comes from the Book of Mormon, which their founder, Joseph Smith (1805–44), claimed to have translated under God's guidance. Mormons believe the book is equal to the Old and New Testaments of the Bible. Here you can see the first Mormon church leaders.

THE MAJOR RELIGIONS of the world were all formed more than 1,350 years ago. New religions are still being founded today, as people seek fresh answers to the age-old questions about the meaning of life and our place in the world. Some new religions, such as the Baha'i faith, are born out of existing ones. Others, such as the Moonies, are created by a visionary leader, who starts a completely new faith. All new religions borrow elements from existing ones and add new ideas of their own.

Both Islam and Christianity have inspired new religions. The Baha'i faith began in Iran in 1844, when a Shi'ah Muslim, Siyyid Ali-Muhammad, announced he was a *Bab* (gate) through which Allah communicates with his people. He predicted that a new prophet would arrive to lead Allah's people. Baha'is believe that Baha'u'llah (1817–92) was that prophet. Baha'u'llah was persecuted throughout the Middle East. Eventually he was exiled to Acre, in what is now Israel. From there, the Baha'i faith has spread throughout the world.

Christianity produced the Mormons and the Jehovah's Witnesses. Both of these believe that the second coming of Jesus Christ is close, a belief shared

RASTAFARIANISM

Rastafarians believe that they are the descendants of the 12 tribes of Israel. They worship the Hebrew God, whom they call Jah. They believe that the white world is godless, and that black people will eventually return to Africa to achieve their freedom. Their messiah, after whom they take their name, is Haile Selassie, the only black leader in Africa to keep his country independent of white, European rule.

◀ THE ETHIOPIAN FLAG
The green, yellow, and red colors on the flag of Ethiopia have been adopted by Rastafarians as their own personal colors. They have also added black, which appears on the flag designed by Marcus Garvey.

◀ DREADLOCKS
Rastas wear their hair in dreadlocks. The style is inspired by the description in the Bible of the mane of the Lion of Judah. It is also an outward sign that Rastas refuse to conform to the expectations of white people.

▶ BLACK ACTIVIST
In 1914 Jamaican-born Marcus Garvey set up the Universal Negro Improvement Association. He urged black people to assert themselves and return to Africa. He said a Black Messiah would appear there to redeem (save) black people.

◀ THE MOONIES
The Unification Church was founded in Korea by Sun Myung Moon in 1954. The Moonies hold mass weddings, at which the couples are purified so that their children will be born without sin.

▲ THE RAELIANS
The UFO writer Claude Vorilhon formed the Raëlian cult in 1973. He also renamed himself Raël. Raëlians believe that one day extraterrestrials will land on Earth. According to Raël, these aliens are what we have mistaken for gods or God in all the world's religions. The Raëlian symbol represents star systems inside bigger star systems.

by the Seventh Day Adventists and other new Christian churches. Rastafarians believe in the Old Testament but worship a visionary leader, the Ethiopian emperor Haile Selassie.

Although all the new religions are very different, they often share two central beliefs. The first is the idea that a new messiah or prophet has arrived to lead the people. The second is that the end of the world is coming soon. New Christian religions also believe that Jesus Christ will return to lead the world for 1,000 years, a belief known as millennarianism. Members of cults such as Heaven's Gate try to speed up the process of the end of the world with mass suicides.

Whatever their beliefs and differences, the new religions show us that as long as there is suffering and cruelty in the world, people will continue to look for new ideas and beliefs that make sense of the world.

▼ THE BLACK MESSIAH
Haile Selassie (Might of the Trinity) was the emperor of Ethiopia from 1930 until 1974. He was also known as Prince Ras Tafari. Rastafarians believe that he was the Black Messiah prophesied in 1916 by the black Jamaican activist Marcus Garvey.

▲ BOB MARLEY
Reggae is a music style that grew up in Jamaica in the 1950s and 1960s. It gained worldwide fame through the singing of Bob Marley. Many reggae stars are rastas. They sing about their faith in their songs.

Key Dates

- 1830 Joseph Smith translates the *Book of Mormon*.

- 1863 Baha'u'llah declares that he is the new prophet.

- 1870s Charles Taze Russell forms the Jehovah's Witnesses.

- 1930–74 Haile Selassie (Ras Tafari) rules Ethiopia.

- 1954 L Ron Hubbard founds the Church of Scientology.

- 1954 Sun Myung Moon founds the Unification Church in Korea.

- 1977 Marshall Applewhite founds the Heaven's Gate cult.

EXPLORATION AND DISCOVERY

BY SIMON ADAMS

Questing has been part of human nature since earliest times, from the search for food to the thirst to conquer new lands. This section looks at the whole history of exploration, from its golden age to missions into space.

Journey without End

▲ SCIENCE
Explorers in the 18th century set out to record the world they found. Illustrators were taken on expeditions to catalog the wildlife of the islands that they discovered.

▼ KEY DATES
The panel charts voyages of discovery on Earth, from the first sea voyages in the Mediterranean 3,500 years ago to the conquest of the South Pole in 1911.

EVER SINCE THE FIRST PEOPLE walked on the Earth they have explored the world they lived in. In the beginning, hundreds of thousands of years ago, this was to hunt and gather food; later on it was to find new pastures for their animals. But food was the reason for exploring, and people rarely went far from the place they were born.

When the first civilizations began, in the Middle East, people began to live in towns and cities. Farmers grew crops, and traders bought and sold goods that were not available in their own area. It was these intrepid merchants, from ancient civilizations like Phoenicia and Egypt, who were the first explorers. The Phoenicians sailed out from the Mediterranean into the North Atlantic, while the Egyptians ventured south into the Indian Ocean, looking for opportunities to trade and to establish permanent trading posts or colonies.

Throughout history trade has remained the driving force of discovery. It was the search for a new trade route to China and India that sent Vasco da Gama around Africa into the Indian Ocean, and Columbus across the Atlantic. Explorers like Hudson and Bering braved the Arctic Ocean trying to find ways around the top of North America and Siberia. And it was trade that sent Magellan around the world and European sailors into

▼ CONVERSION
Many European explorers set out to convert the local people they encountered to Christianity.

EUROPE

Phoenician galley

c.1400B.C. Phoenician sailors explore Mediterranean.

c.330B.C. Pytheas sails from France to Thule.

A.D.300s First Barbarian invasions of Roman Empire.

1419 Henry "The Navigator" establishes school of navigation in Portugal. *Pilgrims*

ASIA

c.500B.C. Silk Road opened.

138B.C. Chang Ch'ien, from China, travels into Central Asia.

A.D.399 Fa Hsien travels from China to India and Ceylon.

1099 First Christian crusaders visit Palestine.

1271–95 Marco Polo visits China.

1325–54 Ibn Battuta, from Algeria, travels around Islamic world.

1405–33 Zheng He, from China, leads expeditions to Southeast Asia.

Caravanserai on the Silk Road

1498 Da Gama, from Lisbon, Portugal, sails to India.

1549 Xavier, a Spanish Jesuit, goes to Japan as a missionary.

1594–97 Barents, a Dutch mariner, explores Arctic Ocean.

1725–29 Bering, from Denmark, crosses Siberia.

1734–42 Teams of explorers map Siberian coast and rivers.

1878–79 Nordenskjöld, from Finland, discovers the Northeast Passage.

Inuit igloo

AFRICA

Timbuktu

c.1490B.C. Egyptians sail to Punt.

c.600B.C. Phoenician fleet sails around Africa.

c.500B.C. Hanno, from Carthage in modern Tunisia, explores coast.

A.D.1480s Portuguese cross the Equator and sail around Cape of Good Hope.

1768–73 Bruce, from Scotland, searches for source of the River Nile and discovers Lake Tana.

▼ NAVIGATION
The first explorers had little to help them navigate, apart from the positions of the Sun, Moon, and stars, and had to stay close to land. The development of instruments like the magnetic compass, astrolabe, and quadrant made navigation easier and more exact.

the Pacific Ocean to the rich spice islands of Southeast Asia.

Explorers also set out seeking fame and fortune and for political advantage—to conquer new lands for their king and country. Many European explorers traveled out of religious conviction, attempting to convert other races to Christianity. But by the 18th century, it was scientific curiosity that sent Cook into the Pacific Ocean and Bates into the Amazon rainforest.

Today there are few places left on Earth that have not been fully explored. There are unexplored mountains in Tibet, and the ocean floor remains largely undiscovered, but now our attention has turned to the skies and space. Unmanned space probes explore the planets of our solar system and the wider reaches of our galaxy of stars, looking for life on other planets. Exploration has come a long way since those early sailing ships left the shores of Phoenicia and Egypt more than 3,500 years ago.

▲ TRADE
The Dutch East India Company was a powerful trading organization. By 1700 it had control of the valuable cinnamon, clove, and nutmeg trade in the East. It established trading posts throughout Asia and ruled what is now called Indonesia.

1795–1806 Park, from Scotland, explores the River Niger.

1841–73 Livingstone, from Scotland, explores southern and central Africa.

1844–45 Barth, from Germany, explores the Sahara Desert region.

1858-63 Englishman John Speke discovers the source of the River Nile.

1874–77 Stanley, from Wales, sails down Congo River.

Stanley's hat

AMERICA and the ARCTIC

A.D.980s–90s Vikings settle in Greenland and explore parts of North America.

1492 Columbus, from Italy, finds the West Indies.

1497 Cabot finds Newfoundland.

1502 Amerigo Vespucci, from Italy, explores South America.

1513 Balboa sights Pacific Ocean.

1519–33 Spanish conquer Aztecs.

1535–6 Cartier, from France, journeys up St. Lawrence River.

1603–15 Champlain explores Canada and founds Quebec.

1610–11 Englishman Henry Hudson searches for Northwest Passage.

1680–82 La Salle, from France, sails down Mississippi River.

1800s Several scientific expeditions explore the Amazon.

1804–06 Americans Lewis and Clark explore Louisiana Purchase.

1903–06 Amundsen, from Norway, finds the Northwest Passage.

1908 Peary, from the United States, reaches North Pole.

Lewis and Clark

AUSTRALASIA and the ANTARCTIC

c.1000 B.C. Polynesians settle in Tonga and Samoa.

Boomerang

A.D.400 Polynesians reach Easter Island and Hawaii.

c.1000 Maoris settle in New Zealand.

1520–21 Magellan crosses Pacific on his round-the-world voyage.

1605 Jansz explores Queensland.

1642–43 Dutchman Tasman discovers New Zealand.

1770 Cook lands in Australia.

1828–62 Interior explored.

1911 Amundsen reaches South Pole.

Egyptians, Phoenicians, and Greeks

▲ BABOON
The Egyptians brought live baboons and cheetahs back from Punt, as well as leopard skins.

PEOPLE HAVE BEEN EXPLORING the world since ancient times. The earliest civilizations grew up in the Middle East thousands of years ago. Merchants began to trade with far-off cities so that they could get hold of goods that were not available in their own land. Gold, spices, and craftworks were bought and sold. The easiest way to make long journeys to other countries was by sea. The traders had no maps to guide them, so they had to discover the best routes for themselves. They soon learned about the winds and sea currents that would help their voyages and which seasons were best to travel in.

The ancient Egyptians lived along the banks of the River Nile. They had plenty of food

and other goods, so traders did not venture very far. But eventually the traders wanted to find new markets, and this tempted them to explore farther afield. They started to sail ships out into the Mediterranean and the Red Sea.

In 1490B.C., Queen Hatshepsut of Egypt ordered a fleet to sail down the Red Sea in search of new lands. The fleet reached a place called Punt (modern Somalia or somewhere farther down the coast of East Africa). The sailors returned with ivory, ebony, spices, and myrrh trees—a present from the people of Punt. Other expeditions explored the interior of North Africa.

Phoenician sailors began to explore the Mediterranean Sea in about 1400B.C. The Phoenicians lived in cities along the coast of what is now Lebanon, at the eastern end of the Mediterranean. They were skilled seafarers and soon started to establish prosperous trading colonies throughout the region. One Phoenician fleet even sailed around Africa on behalf of an Egyptian pharaoh. In 500B.C. a man named Hanno sailed from Carthage, a Phoenician colony in North Africa, as far as modern Senegal, a journey of

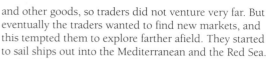

▸ A PHOENICIAN SHIP
Phoenician ships were short, broad, and strong. They were built from cedar, which grew on the mountain slopes of Phoenicia. A single sail and oars powered the ship along.

SAILING THE MEDITERRANEAN
Phoenicia had little arable land, and so in 1400B.C. its people turned to the sea for a living. They became excellent seafarers, sailing great distances in search of new markets. They established colonies as far away as North Africa and Spain. Egyptians and Greeks also began to explore by sea.

◂ PHOENICIAN TRADERS
The Phoenicians traded grain, olive oil, glassware, purple cloth, cedar wood, and other goods throughout the Mediterranean area. They were somewhat like traveling shopkeepers.

▾ MUREX SHELL
One of the most precious items traded by the Phoenicians was purple cloth. The dye for the cloth was made from murex shells. Up to 6,000 shells were crushed to make 16 ounces of dye.

▸ PHOENICIAN GLASS
The Phoenicians were good at making glass items, such as vases and jewelry. Sand and soda were mixed to make a paste, which was colored with pigment and fired at a high temperature.

Warehouse

Single sail

▼ **EGYPTIAN PORT**
In Egypt, shallow-bottomed boats made of reeds, with a single sail, carried goods and passengers along the River Nile. After about 2700 B.C. the Egyptians began to build wooden boats, which were stronger and could cross seas to foreign lands.

2,500 miles. Other Phoenician traders sailed to Britain, buying tin in Cornwall.

The Greeks also founded colonies throughout the Mediterranean. The Phoenicians were their great rivals, because they were so successful at trading by sea. Greek merchants wanted some of the business for themselves. In 330 B.C., an explorer named Pytheas sailed to Britain, possibly to try to get access to the profitable tin trade.

▶ **PYTHEAS**
One of the most amazing voyages of ancient times was made by a Greek astronomer named Pytheas. In 330 B.C. he set sail from Marseille in southern France, which was a Greek colony. He headed around Spain and then north to the British Isles, where he reported that the local people were friendly. Pytheas continued his voyage farther north to the land of Thule. Thule was probably Norway or Iceland. Pytheas noted that in Thule the sun never set. (In these countries it does not get dark in summer.)

Key Dates

- 1490 B.C. Egyptians sail to Punt.

- 1400 B.C. Phoenician traders explore the Mediterranean Sea and the eastern Atlantic Ocean.

- 1000 B.C. First Phoenician colony established on Cyprus.

- c.800 B.C. Greeks set up colonies in the eastern Mediterranean.

- 814 B.C. Phoenicians found Carthage in North Africa.

- c.600 B.C. Phoenician fleet sails around Africa.

- 500 B.C. Hanno explores the coast of West Africa.

- 330 B.C. Pytheas sails to Thule.

Europe and Asia

▲ SILKWORM
A silkworm feeds on a mulberry leaf. The Chinese began cultivating silkworms for silk over 4,500 years ago.

IN ANCIENT TIMES there was not much contact between Europe and Asia. In Europe the flourishing trading empires of the Phoenicians and Greeks were centered on the Mediterranean Sea. In eastern Asia the Chinese had their own trading centers. In between the two continents were the deserts, mountains, and arid plateaus of central Asia.

The Chinese were famous for making beautiful silk fabric. A few hardy traders made the long journey between Europe and China along a route known as the Silk Road. They bought bales of silk from Chinese merchants to take back with them. There are records of Chinese silk being sold in the Greek city of Athens as early as 550 B.C.

Two hundred years later, King Alexander of Macedon (later known as Alexander the Great) invaded the huge Persian Empire, which extended into central Asia. Many scholars and historians went with him. They began to explore the vast regions that Alexander had conquered, and learned a lot about them.

When Alexander died his empire broke up. But links between Europe and Asia became stronger over the next century. The empires of different rulers lay all along the Silk Road. The Romans controlled Europe, the Parthians ruled Persia, and the Kushans dominated central Asia. In China the country became united for the first time under the first Ch'in emperor in 221 B.C. These four empires spanned the length of the Silk Road, and for more than 400 years there was uninterrupted trade between East and West. Few Roman merchants visited China, but a wide variety of goods flowed along the Silk Road in both directions.

There was also a thriving sea trade across the Indian Ocean between Egypt and India, and from there on to China. This too helped to increase international trade and contacts.

▶ TRADERS
The Silk Road was a busy route. Merchants from Europe, the Middle East, central Asia, and China used it on trips to buy and sell goods. However, not many of them ever traveled along its entire length.

FROM WEST TO EAST

The major trade route between China and Europe was known as the Silk Road, because Chinese silk was brought along it by traders returning to Europe. In exchange, China received gold and silver, cotton, and a wide variety of fruits and other produce.

▼ ALEXANDER THE GREAT
Alexander was only 20 when he succeeded his father as king of Macedon in 336 B.C. By the time of his death, 13 years later, he had conquered an empire that stretched from the Adriatic Sea in southern Europe to the mouth of the River Indus in India.

◀ BEASTS OF BURDEN
Donkeys, horses, and two-humped Bactrian camels were all used on the Silk Road. They worked hard carrying the traders and their cargoes.

▲ JADE
Jade was the most precious substance known to the Chinese. They carved it into elaborate and intricate ornaments and utensils, such as this brush-washer.

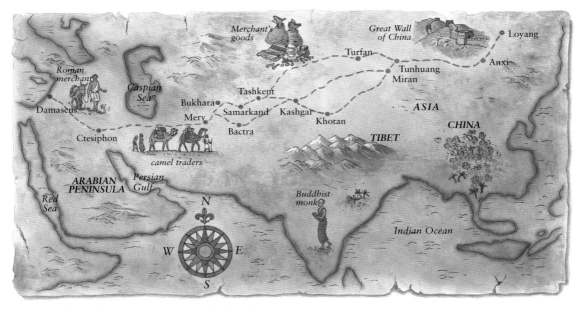

The Silk Road was also important in linking the different Asian empires together. Buddhist monks brought their religion from India into China in about A.D.100. Chinese explorers journeyed into neighboring countries, which helped to strengthen religious and trading ties between them. Chang Ch'ien, a court official, traveled into central Asia in 138B.C. A monk named Fa Hsien visited India and Sri Lanka in A.D.399. However, by A.D.400 these ties had weakened. Civil war

▲ THE SILK ROAD
The Silk Road started in the Chinese capital of Loyang and ran westward across northern China and central Asia to Ctesiphon on the River Tigris in southwest Asia. It later continued to the Mediterranean. It was not a single road, but a series of well-marked routes. Traders using them were fairly safe from attacks by robbers.

broke out in China, and barbarian invaders and nomads from central Asia overran the Silk Road. By A.D.450 the links between East and West were broken.

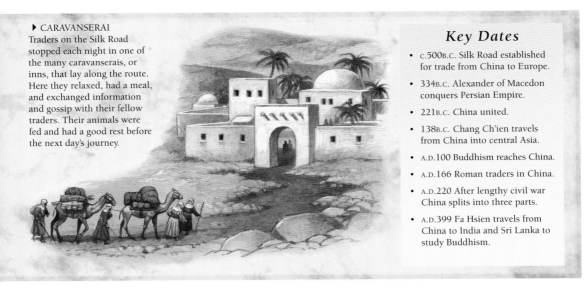

▶ CARAVANSERAI
Traders on the Silk Road stopped each night in one of the many caravanserais, or inns, that lay along the route. Here they relaxed, had a meal, and exchanged information and gossip with their fellow traders. Their animals were fed and had a good rest before the next day's journey.

Key Dates

- c.500B.C. Silk Road established for trade from China to Europe.

- 334B.C. Alexander of Macedon conquers Persian Empire.

- 221B.C. China united.

- 138B.C. Chang Ch'ien travels from China into central Asia.

- A.D.100 Buddhism reaches China.

- A.D.166 Roman traders in China.

- A.D.220 After lengthy civil war China splits into three parts.

- A.D.399 Fa Hsien travels from China to India and Sri Lanka to study Buddhism.

The Invasion of Europe

▲ GOTHIC ART
This illuminated manuscript from the 1100s is by the Goths. They were the first Germanic people to become Christians. Many years later an ornate style of art developed, based on original Gothic designs.

THE CITY OF ROME started off as a small cluster of villages in the hills around the River Tiber in central Italy. By 500 B.C. it had grown into the most powerful city in Italy. Rome declared war on its main rival, the Phoenician city of Carthage. Carthage was defeated, and the Romans built an empire that spanned the Mediterranean. By the reign of Emperor Trajan (A.D. 98–117), the Roman Empire stretched from Portugal to Mesopotamia, and from the Sahara Desert to the border between Scotland and England.

The long eastern frontier of the Romans' vast empire was easy to invade. In A.D. 300, the Huns, from the vast steppes of central Asia, began to head westward into southeast Europe, in search of new pastures. This pushed the Germanic tribes living there (including the Goths, Visigoths, Vandals, Alans, and Franks) across the Roman frontier.

At first the various tribes lived peacefully in the Roman Empire. But in A.D. 378 fighting broke out, and the Visigoths defeated the powerful Roman army in the Balkans. From there the Visigoths moved farther into the Roman Empire. They successfully attacked Rome in A.D. 410 and continued westward to settle in Spain. The Franks and

▼ ROME DESTROYED
In AD 410 the Visigoths captured and plundered Rome, killing many of its inhabitants. The Vandals did the same in AD 455. But Rome continued as a thriving city until AD 546, when the Ostrogoths captured it and expelled its entire population, leaving it in ruins.

THE DARK AGES

The period after the fall of the Roman Empire is often called the Dark Ages. This is because Europe became a poorer place. People managed to grow enough food, but trade and commerce declined rapidly. Europe seemed to be taking a step backward from the great culture and prosperity enjoyed by the Romans. However, learning and scholarship continued in monasteries everywhere. Christianity became the main religion of Europe, and the new rulers of Europe soon developed cultures of their own.

▶ LINDISFARNE
In monasteries such as Lindisfarne Priory, in northeast England, monks kept education alive during the times known as the Dark Ages.

▲ MAUSOLEUM
The barbarian invaders of Europe soon adopted Roman customs. This mausoleum was built in the Roman style in A.D. 526 in Ravenna, northern Italy, as the burial place of Theodoric, an Ostrogoth chief.

▲ ENAMELED BROOCH
Many of the barbarian invaders were skilled craftworkers, as can be seen from this brooch.

Vandals crossed the River Rhine and invaded Gaul (France). The Vandals kept going south until they reached North Africa. Finally the Huns, led by Attila, arrived in Europe. The Romans managed to defeat Attila in A.D.453 with the help of friendly Germanic tribes, but by then their empire was weak and exhausted.

In A.D.476 the last Roman emperor was removed from power. Rival invading tribes fought over the remains of the Roman Empire. The Romans called the invaders barbarians, but many were educated people looking for a safer land to live in.

The old Roman Empire was swept away, but the tribes of Europe remained disunited for several hundred years. Then in A.D.800 Charlemagne, a Frankish king from northern Europe, was crowned "Holy Roman Emperor" by the pope in Rome. By that time Christianity was the main religion across Europe. Between them, the pope and Charlemagne brought some unity to the peoples of western Europe.

▲ ROMAN RUINS
After the collapse of the Roman Empire many of its impressive buildings, such as this forum, fell into disuse. The stone was removed to construct new buildings, and the roofs were left to rot and fall in.

▲ CHARLEMAGNE
In A.D.768 the Frankish leader Charlemagne began to conquer a vast empire that included modern France, Germany, the Low Countries, and Italy. The new empire reunited western Europe for the first time since the fall of the Roman Empire.

Key Dates

- 264–146B.C. Rome overthrows Carthage after three wars.

- A.D.300s Germanic tribes begin to enter Roman Empire.

- A.D.378 Visigoths defeat Roman army in the Balkans.

- A.D.410 Visigoths ransack Rome.

- A.D.455 Vandals plunder Rome.

- A.D.476 Roman emperor deposed.

- A.D.546 Ostrogoths destroy Rome.

- A.D.768 Charlemagne, Frankish leader, begins to reunite Europe.

- A.D.800 Charlemagne is crowned emperor by the pope in Rome.

The Vikings

▲ BROOCH
Lavishly decorated clasps and brooches made of bronze, silver, and gold were used to hold clothes in place.

THE VIKINGS SEEMED to come from nowhere. Setting out from Norway and Denmark, they suddenly became a frightening force that dominated the northern seas, from the Atlantic Ocean to the Black Sea. They struck terror into all those they met on land. The records kept by Christian monks describe them as ruthless fighters who plundered towns and slaughtered all the inhabitants. Few towns managed to hold off these ferocious invaders.

The name "Viking" means "men of the creek," and they came from the fjords and lowlands of Scandinavia, in the north of Europe. Although the Vikings have a reputation for cruelty, they were a talented people. They were skilled shipbuilders and navigators and excellent engineers and craftworkers. They had a rich tradition of myths and legends and had worked out a fair system of rules for the way their people lived.

In about A.D.790, parties of Vikings began to leave their homeland, launching their boats into the open sea. No one is quite sure why they began to do this. Some

▼ VIKING SAILORS
Much of the Vikings' homeland was mountainous, with few roads. They used their boats to travel the fjords and the open seas.

historians believe that overcrowding in the country drove out the younger sons, who had nothing to inherit from their fathers. Or perhaps the climate was getting colder and harvests often failed, leading people to search for new sources of food.

Vikings from Norway and Denmark crossed the North Sea to raid Britain, Ireland, and northern France. They ventured across the North Atlantic to Iceland, Greenland, and the east coast of North America. Vikings from Sweden preferred trading with other

THE VIKING WAY OF LIFE

There were three classes of Vikings—slaves, who did most of the work, freemen, and nobles, who were the rulers. Nobles had to obey rules made by the Thing, a local assembly where freemen could discuss these rules. But by about 1050, powerful kings ruled most Viking lands. The Things were no longer so important, and their role gradually declined.

◄ CLOTHES
Clothes were made from wool or flax spun on a vertical loom. Women wore a long dress with a shorter tunic on top. Men typically wore trousers, a shirt, a tunic, and a cloak.

▶ LEIF ERIKSSON
Vikings living in the colony of Greenland heard stories of a flat land to their west covered with trees. In A.D.992 Leif Eriksson set out due west, and found what was probably Baffin Island. He then sailed south past Labrador and Newfoundland, in eastern Canada, to a place he named Vinland, the "land of wine," as he found so many shrubs and wild berries there.

◄ RUNES
The Vikings used an alphabet system based on runes, which were usually carved in wood or on pieces of stone. Calendars, bills, accounts, and even love messages were all written in runic script.

Single mast stepped, or mounted,
in the middle of the boat

▲ BOAT BUILDING
*Ships were built from local wood. Solid beams
of oak were used for the keel and cross beams,
lighter planks of ash and pine for the sides.*

countries to conquering them. They sailed east, across
the Baltic Sea and down the rivers of Russia to the
Black Sea and the Mediterranean. They even reached
the city of Baghdad on the river Tigris in modern Iraq.

At first the Vikings plundered the lands they visited,
taking their booty home. But gradually they started to
establish trading posts in places such as Dublin in
Ireland and Kiev in Ukraine. Soon they began to marry
the local people and settle down. Many converted to
Christianity. The Viking raids were over.

Key Dates

- A.D.793 Vikings attack
  Lindisfarne Priory in northeast
  England. It is their first major
  raid on England.

- A.D.815 Vikings from Norway
  settle in Iceland.

- A.D.841 Foundation of Dublin.

- A.D.855 Vikings sail up the river
  Seine in France and raid Paris.

- A.D.911 Vikings settle in
  Normandy, France.

- A.D.982 Eric the Red begins his
  epic voyage to Greenland.

- A.D.992 Leif Eriksson leaves
  Greenland and sails to Vinland.

▲ VIKING EXPEDITIONS
Viking traders from Sweden sailed down the rivers of Russia. Others sailed around the
Atlantic coast into the Mediterranean. Eric the Red was expelled from the Viking
colony on Iceland and sailed to Greenland, and Leif Eriksson voyaged to Vinland.

The Polynesians

THE ISLANDS OF THE South Pacific were uninhabited until about 3,000 years ago. Then the first Polynesians arrived to live there. We do not know much about these people. Historians think that they originally came from Asia or America.

Over the next 2,000 years the Polynesians slowly spread out across the vast South Pacific Ocean. They sailed north to Hawaii, east to Easter Island, and, finally, south to New Zealand. They were probably the greatest explorers and navigators in history. When Europeans first visited the region in the 1500s, they got a surprise. They could not believe that the

▶ GIANT STATUES
Easter Islanders erected 600 giant carved statues across their small island between A.D. 1000 and 1600. No one knows what these statues were for or how the islanders managed to move and erect the huge stones.

Polynesians, who they thought were a very primitive people, could have developed such advanced skills.

The immense Pacific Ocean is scattered with islands, but these make up only a minute part of its total area and lie hundreds of miles apart from each other. The rest is open sea, and it is easy to sail for days without sighting any land. The Polynesians did not have any maps or modern navigation equipment, but they successfully explored the entire ocean in their sturdy canoes. They settled on almost every island, finding them by following migrating birds and by watching changes in wind direction and wave pattern.

The Polynesians gradually built up a detailed knowledge of where each island was and how they could find it again in the future, using the Sun, Moon, and stars as navigation aids. They gave each island its own "on top" star. Sailors knew that when this was directly over their boat, they were on the same latitude as the island. Using the position of the Sun, they sailed due east or west until they reached land. Sirius, for example, was the "on top" star for Tahiti.

All this information was passed down

ASIAN OR AMERICAN?
Some historians think that the Polynesians originally came from Southeast Asia, but there are many similarities between the cultures of Polynesia and Peru. One modern explorer from Norway named Thor Heyerdahl set out to prove that Polynesians could have come from South America. He built a raft like those used by early settlers and sailed from Peru to the South Pacific.

◀ KON-TIKI
Thor Heyerdahl's raft was called *Kon-Tiki* after the Peruvian sun god. The god was believed to have migrated to the Pacific islands. The raft measured 45 feet long and 18 feet wide and was made of balsa wood and bamboo.

▼ THOR HEYERDAHL
Thor Heyerdahl was born in 1914 and studied zoology and geography at college. He became fascinated by Polynesia and lived for two years in Tahiti.

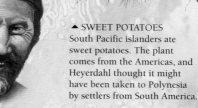

▲ SWEET POTATOES
South Pacific islanders ate sweet potatoes. The plant comes from the Americas, and Heyerdahl thought it might have been taken to Polynesia by settlers from South America.

▼ POLYNESIAN BOAT
Polynesian canoes were up to 100 feet long. They were built with two hulls or a single hull and an outrigger. The sails were made from coconut-palm leaf matting sewn together.

▲ PACIFIC ISLANDS
There are about 20,000 islands in the Pacific Ocean. Most are either high volcanic peaks or low coral reefs. Apart from New Zealand, the vast majority are small, some only a few miles across.

Canoe steered
by single oar

Outrigger

Main hull

through the generations and recorded on a chart made of palm sticks tied together with coconut fiber. The framework of sticks represented distance, and shells threaded on the sticks showed where the islands were.

The Polynesians used these simple but effective charts to make accurate voyages across vast expanses of ocean. They took colonists and supplies to newly discovered islands and brought back fish and other goods.

◄···· Route of the *Kon-Tiki* 1947

N

Hawaiian
Islands

Pacific Ocean

New
Guinea

Solomon
Islands

Phoenix
Islands

Marquesas
Islands

SOUTH
AMERICA

Western
Samoa

Society
Islands

Tuamotus

Callao

Vanuatu

Fiji

Samoa

Cook
Islands

AUSTRALIA

New
Caledonia

Tonga

Easter
Island

New
Zealand

Polynesian Triangle

| 0 | Kilometers | 3200 |
| 0 | Miles | 2000 |

▲ THOR HEYERDAHL'S VOYAGE
In 1947 *Kon-Tiki* set sail from Peru. It steered westward, making use of the winds and sea currents. After a voyage of 4,290 miles, lasting 101 days, Thor Heyerdahl reached the Tuamotu archipelago in the South Pacific.

Key Dates

- 1000 B.C. Polynesians begin to settle in Tonga and Samoa.

- 150 B.C. Settlers leave Samoa for Marquesas Islands.

- A.D. 400 Polynesians reach Easter Island in the east and the Hawaiian Islands in the north.

- 1000 Polynesian Maoris settle in New Zealand.

- 1000–1600 Statues built on Easter Island.

- 1947 Thor Heyerdahl's *Kon-Tiki* expedition from Peru to the South Pacific.

Crossing the Deserts

▲ THE DESERT
The deserts of North Africa and Arabia are a mixture of rocky plains, sand dunes, and high mountains.

IN A.D.622 ARABIA GAVE birth to a new religion called Islam, which soon became the main religion there. Islam was founded by the Prophet Muhammad, who died in A.D.632. Within a few years an Islamic Empire stretched from the Atlantic Ocean across North Africa and the Middle East to the borders of India. Much of the Islamic world was desert, including the Sahara Desert in North Africa, which is the biggest in the world.

The Arabs dominated the Islamic Empire, conquering other lands. Soldiers and missionaries spread Islam to all the people they conquered. The Arabs were great travelers. Merchants and traders followed the soldiers into the new lands in search of markets to exploit and goods to trade. Scholars and scientists traveled to increase their knowledge of the world. Every Muslim (a believer in Islam) also made a once-in-a-lifetime pilgrimage to the holy city of Mecca in Arabia. As a result, towns and cities were bustling with travelers stopping to rest for the night after a long day's journey. Markets and public places were full of people telling stories about faraway cities and strange lands they had visited.

▲ MUSLIM TRAVEL
Muslim travelers felt at home wherever they went in the Islamic world, since everyone spoke the common language of Arabic and all were followers of Islam. Travelers got a warm welcome at every town.

MUSLIM TRAVELERS

There are many reasons why the Muslims were great travelers. One was because of Islam. It was the duty of all Muslims to make a pilgrimage to the holy city of Mecca. People also traveled on business or because they were curious about other places.

▲ MUSLIM PRAYER CASE
Muslims carried verses from their holy book, the Koran, in prayer cases. These were often carved and decorated.

◀ SALT
Salt occurs naturally throughout the Sahara Desert, and was much prized as a food preservative. Camel trains were used to bring the mineral to the Mediterranean for shipment to Europe.

▼ IBN BATTUTA
Ibn Battuta was born into a wealthy, educated family in Tangier, North Africa, in 1304. After a pilgrimage to Mecca in 1325, he was inspired to devote his life to travel. After his final journey in 1352–53, he recorded his adventures in a book called the *Rihlah*, which means "Travels." He died in 1368.

◀ ARAB DHOW
The main type of ship used by the Arabs for their travels was the dhow. It had one or two masts and a triangular sail bent on to a spar. This was called a lateen sail.

▲ SHIP OF THE DESERT
Camels can travel for many days without food or water. Fat stored in their humps gives them energy when food is scarce.

Many Muslims left records of their travels. One of them, Ibn Battuta, was the greatest traveler of his age. The geographer Al Idrisi (1100–65) used his explorations to produce a book on geography and two large-scale maps of the world. Al Idrisi even sent out scientific expeditions to explore northern Europe and other areas unfamiliar to the Arabs.

At first Arabs avoided the Indian Ocean, calling it the "Sea of Darkness." But then they developed the dhow, a versatile ship that could carry large cargoes, but which needed only a small crew. Astrolabes, quadrants, and other devices were used to navigate. At that time, most European people thought that the world was flat and that it was unsafe to venture far beyond land. The Arabs were sailing across the Indian Ocean to purchase silks and spices from India, Indonesia, and China, and traveling vast distances as traders, pilgrims, or adventurers.

▼ THE TRAVELS OF IBN BATTUTA
Ibn Battuta spent a total of 28 years traveling to find out more about the world. He explored the entire Islamic Empire, as well as much of Europe, Southeast Asia, and China. He covered a total distance of 74,970 miles.

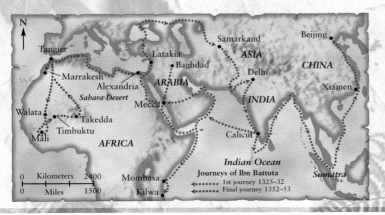

Key Dates

- A.D.622 Muhammad and his followers flee persecution in Mecca and go to Medina, starting the Islamic religion.

- A.D.632 Death of Muhammad.

- A.D.634–50 Muslims conquer Middle East.

- A.D.650 The Koran (the sacred book of Islam) is written.

- A.D.712 Islamic Empire extends east to Spain and west to India.

- 1200s The dhow sailing boat is developed.

- 1325–53 Ibn Battuta travels around the Islamic world.

The Chinese Empire

▲ PORCELAIN
The Chinese invented a new type of pottery called porcelain. It is very fine and hard, and light can shine through it.

DURING THE 1200s, a new threat emerged from the empty, hostile grasslands or steppes of central Asia. It was the Mongols, a nomadic people who were skilled horsemen and warriors. They conquered most of Asia and eastern Europe in a series of brilliant military campaigns led by their ruler, Genghis Khan, and his successors. Their empire stretched from the eastern frontier of Germany to Korea, and from the Arctic Circle to the Persian Gulf. It was the biggest empire the world had ever seen. Although the Mongols had a reputation for extreme violence, they kept strict law and order throughout their empire and encouraged trade. The main trade link between Europe and Asia—the Silk Road—had fallen into disuse after the collapse of the Roman Empire and the Han dynasty in China. The Silk Road was now in the Mongol Empire. The Mongols made sure that the road was safe to use.

Two Venetian merchants, Niccolò and Maffeo Polo, were among the first traders to travel its entire length. The Mongol ruler of China, Kublai Khan, welcomed them to his court, as he was fascinated by the foreigners and the mysterious lands they came from. When the Polos returned home, they promised him that they would serve as his envoys to the pope in Rome and would arrange for 100 theologians to go to China to discuss Christianity with Mongol philosophers. Kublai Khan gave them a golden tablet inscribed with the imperial seal to guarantee them good treatment and hospitality while in Mongol territory.

When the Polo brothers returned to China, they took Niccolò's son Marco with them. He served Kublai

▲ VENICE
The port of Venice in Italy was the richest city in Europe in the 1200s. It controlled much of the trade in the Mediterranean. It was from here that the Polo brothers set out on their travels.

CHINESE VOYAGES

In 1368, nearly a century after Marco Polo's amazing reports of the court of Kublai Khan, the Mongols were thrown out of China. To try to restore China's prestige in Asia, the new Ming dynasty sent Admiral Zheng He (1371–1433) on a series of seven diplomatic journeys through the whole region.

◀ GIRAFFES
The cities of East Africa did a lot of trade with China. Their ambassadors visited China in 1414 and presented the emperor with gifts, including a giraffe.

▲ CHINESE JUNKS
Zheng He commanded a fleet of ocean-going junks. These were two-masted ships that could carry large cargoes. Some junks were five times larger than European ships of the time.

◀ MARCO POLO
The explorer Marco Polo (1254–1324) was born in Venice and traveled to China in 1271. He stayed there for 20 years. On his return he was imprisoned in Genoa, which was at war with Venice. He dictated an account of his travels to a fellow prisoner. Il milione (The Travels) was read throughout Europe.

Khan for the next 20 years and traveled throughout eastern Asia. When Marco Polo returned to Europe, he wrote a book about his epic journeys. He described the fabulous court of Kublai Khan, and he praised the artistic and technological achievements of Mongol China. However, some modern scholars believe that Marco Polo did not go to China but wrote his book after reading other people's reports.

▲ KUBLAI KHAN
The Mongol ruler of China, Kublai Khan, was a highly intelligent and civilized man. His summer palace at Shangdu, where he welcomed the Polos to China, and his court in Cambaluc (Beijing) were both magnificent buildings.

▼ MARCO POLO'S ROUTE
In 1271 the Polo family set out from Europe along the Silk Road, taking over three years to reach China. There they stayed for 20 years, while Marco traveled around the vast Mongol Empire. They returned to Europe across the Indian Ocean in 1295.

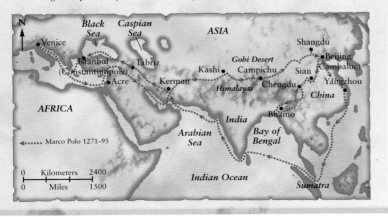

Key Dates

- 1211 Genghis Khan begins invasion of China.

- 1234 Mongols overrun northern China.

- 1260–94 Mongol leader Kublai Khan rules China.

- 1261–69 Polo brothers travel to China.

- 1271–95 Marco Polo travels throughout the Mongol Empire.

- 1368 Mongols thrown out of China by the Ming dynasty.

- 1405–33 Zheng He leads seven expeditions to Southeast Asia and Indian Ocean.

Travelers in Europe

▲ CITY OF DANZIG
The ship on Danzig's official seal shows membership of the Hanseatic League, a network of trading cities in northern Europe.

TODAY WE KNOW OF Europe as a busy place with a huge population. However, a thousand years ago Europe was a very different place indeed.

In the year 1000 the total population of western Europe was fewer than 30 million, which is about half that of modern France. Only a handful of cities, including Paris, Milan, and Florence, had more than 40,000 people. Most had fewer than 10,000 inhabitants. Roads were rough and uneven, and much of the countryside was covered in thick forests. Bandits lay in wait to rob travelers. Yet despite these problems, a surprising number of people ran the risk of getting lost or being robbed and took to the roads.

Pilgrims journeyed in great numbers to holy sites, such as the shrine of St. James in Santiago de Compostela, northern Spain. Some went even farther afield, to Jerusalem in the Middle East. Armies of Crusaders assembled to reconquer the Holy Land from its Muslim occupiers. National armies marched off to fight wars on behalf of their kings. Merchants and traders traveled from town to town, buying and selling goods at the increasing number of trade fairs held in northern France, Germany, and Flanders (Belgium). Government and church administrators moved from town to town on official business. Scholars often passed

▼ PILGRIMAGES
Pilgrims traveled to the great religious shrines in large groups, telling each other stories and singing songs to pass the time.

THE CRUSADES
Between 1095 and 1444, armies of Christian knights went to Palestine in the Muslim Empire. They intended to secure the Christian holy places against Muslim control. The First Crusade successfully captured Jerusalem. In 1291, the last Crusader stronghold was lost. Later Crusades all ended in failure.

◀ THE CRUSADERS
Crusading knights and soldiers were inspired by religious devotion. They also followed a code of conduct called chivalry, which meant that they pledged to be brave and loyal to their lord and to protect women.

▲ RICHARD I
Many kings and princes joined the Crusades. Richard I of England (ruled 1189–99) took part in the Third Crusade.

▼ HEIDELBERG
Heidelberg and other fortified towns throughout Germany were good centers for recruiting men for the Crusades. All types of people went, commoners and knights, to spread Christianity through the Holy Land.

from one university to another for their studies. Craftworkers and builders made their way to the cities where new cathedrals were being built.

Most people traveled on foot or, if they were rich, on horseback, but progress was slow, and it could take up to a week to travel 100 miles. Every night they stopped at village inns. Yet travelers were a small minority of the population. The vast majority of people never left the place where they were born. For them, the next town was like a foreign land.

▲ HERRING
The coastal cities of northern Europe, especially Amsterdam and Lübeck, grew rich from fishing. Salted herring and other fish were sent to markets in England and Flanders in exchange for wool, cloth, pewter, and other goods.

◀ MARKETS
Every town had a regular market, where local agricultural produce was bought and sold. Some of these markets developed into large commercial trade fairs. Merchants from all over Europe would come to trade in goods from Europe, the Arab world, and Asia.

▼ KRAK DES CHEVALIERS
The Crusaders built castles throughout Palestine to secure their conquests against Muslim invaders. The most impressive was Krak des Chevaliers, which is in present-day Syria. It eventually surrendered to Muslim armies in 1271.

Key Dates

- 1095 Pope Urban II calls for a Crusade to defend the Church.

- 1099 Crusaders capture Jerusalem and set up Crusader kingdoms throughout Palestine.

- 1187 Muslim leader Saladin retakes Jerusalem and overruns most of the Crusader kingdoms.

- 1189–92 Third Crusade recaptures Acre from Saladin.

- 1241 Hamburg and Lübeck set up the Hanseatic League.

- 1291 Acre, the last Crusader stronghold in Palestine, is lost.

- 1444 Final Crusade.

The Portuguese

▲ DA GAMA
In May 1498 the Portuguese navigator Vasco da Gama (1460–1524) became the first European to reach India by sea.

PORTUGAL IS ON THE EXTREME west of Europe, facing the Atlantic Ocean. The Portuguese relied on the sea to give them a living. Traditionally, they had fished and traded northward along the Atlantic coast with France and Britain. But during the 1400s they turned their attention south and started looking at Africa.

The Portuguese wanted to explore Africa for two main reasons. They aimed to convert the Moors (the Muslim people of North Africa) to Christianity. They were also going to search for gold and other riches. To do this they needed better ships than the inshore, open boats they usually sailed. They developed the caravel, which was able to withstand the storms and strong currents out at sea.

Caravels allowed the Portuguese to venture farther and farther from their own shores. Expeditions boldly set off down the African coast, erecting *padrãoes*, or stone pillars with a Christian cross on the top, to mark their progress. By 1441 they had reached Cape Blanc in what is now Mauritania. By 1475 they had sailed

▲ CARAVEL
The development of the small but sturdy caravel enabled the Portuguese to leave coastal waters and venture out into the open seas. A caravel was about 65 feet long and held a crew of 25.

around West Africa and along the coast to the Gold Coast (Ghana) and Cameroon.

By now the Portuguese had an extra reason to voyage south. In 1453 the Ottoman Turks had captured the Christian city of Constantinople, which was the gateway to Asia, and closed the Silk Road to China. Europeans needed to find a new way to get to the wealth of the East. In 1482 Diego Cão was the first

NAVIGATION

The first sailors navigated by sailing along the coast from one landmark to the next. Once out of sight of land, they could not do this! Portuguese sailors learned how to use the positions of the Sun and stars to calculate where they were. With the aid of compasses, astrolabes, quadrants, sand glasses, and nocturnals, they were able to navigate over long distances with increasing accuracy.

◄ PRINCE HENRY "THE NAVIGATOR"
Prince Henry (1394–1460) was the son of King John I of Portugal. He was keenly interested in the sea and supported many voyages of exploration. He set up a school of navigation, astronomy, and cartography (mapmaking) to educate captains and pilots. These skills enabled Portuguese sailors to explore the coast of Africa.

▶ SAND GLASS

Sailors told the time with a sand glass. The sand took 30 minutes to run to the bottom and it was then turned over. To calculate the ship's speed, they floated a knotted rope beside the ship, and worked out how long it took to pass each knot.

▲ NOCTURNAL
The old way of telling the time, by the position of the Sun, did not work at night. The development of the nocturnal during the 1550s solved this problem. By lining it up with the Pole Star and two stars close to it, sailors could tell the time to within ten minutes.

European to cross the Equator. On his second voyage in 1485–86 he sailed as far south as the Namib Desert. He thought that the African coast was endless and that there was no way round it toward Asia. But in 1487–88 Bartolomeu Dias proved him wrong when he sailed around the stormy Cape of Good Hope into the Indian Ocean. He was the first Portuguese explorer to enter these waters. Although Dias wanted to go on, his exhausted crew made him turn back. Ten years later Vasco da Gama achieved the Portuguese dream. He rounded the tip of Africa with a fleet of four ships. After sailing up the east coast, he headed across the Indian Ocean. In May 1498 he arrived in the busy trading port of Calicut in the south of India. He had discovered a new route to Asia.

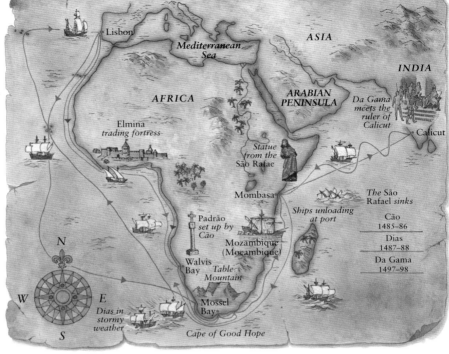

Lisbon

Mediterranean Sea

ASIA

INDIA

AFRICA

ARABIAN PENINSULA

Da Gama meets the ruler of Calicut

Calicut

Elmina *trading fortress*

Statue from the São Rafae

Mombasa

Ships unloading at port

The São Rafael sinks

N

W   E

S

Padrão set up by Cão

Mozambique (Moçambique)

Walvis Bay   Table Mountain

Mossel Bay

Dias in stormy weather

Cape of Good Hope

Cão 1485–86

Dias 1487–88

Da Gama 1497–98

▲ THE ROUTE TO INDIA
By slowly mapping the coast of Africa, the Portuguese discovered a route that took them around the Cape of Good Hope to East Africa and then, using the westerly winds, across the ocean to India. Once the coast was mapped, later voyages could take a more direct route.

▶ USING A COMPASS
The magnetic compass was developed by both the Chinese and the Arabs. It was first used in Europe during the 1200s. By lining up the compass with the magnetic North Pole, sailors could tell which direction they were sailing in. However, early compasses were often unreliable and were easily affected by other iron objects on board ship. As a result, many ships headed off in the wrong direction. By the time of Henry the Navigator in the 1400s, compasses were much improved.

Key Dates

- 1419 Prince Henry establishes a school of navigation.

- 1420s First voyages south to southern Morocco.

- 1475 Portuguese sailors map the African coast from Morocco to Cameroon.

- 1482 Diego Cão crosses over the Equator.

- 1485–86 Diego Cão sails south to Namibia.

- 1487–88 Bartolomeu Dias sails around Cape of Good Hope.

- 1497–98 Vasco da Gama sails around Africa to India.

Christopher Columbus

▲ COLUMBUS
Christopher Columbus (1451–1506) was born in the Italian port of Genoa. He was named after St. Christopher, the patron saint of travelers. His discoveries included Cuba and the Bahamas.

FOR CENTURIES EUROPEANS believed that the world consisted of just three continents—Europe, Africa, and Asia. They thought that the whole of the rest of the world was covered by sea.

The traditional route to Asia had always been overland along the Silk Road. During the 1400s, the Portuguese discovered a way of getting there by sea, sailing south and east around the coast of Africa. Then an Italian named Christopher Columbus worked out that it should be possible to get to Asia by sailing west, across the great Atlantic Ocean.

Columbus devoted his life to finding this sea route to the riches of Asia. At first, people thought that it was a stupid idea, and Columbus could not get any support. But in 1492 Queen Isabella of Spain agreed to give him money to make the voyage on behalf of Spain. He set out with three ships in August 1492, and after 36 days landed in what we now call the Bahamas. Sailing southeast, he passed Cuba and Hispaniola (present-day Haiti) before returning home in triumph in March 1493.

▼ LANDING IN AMERICA
When Columbus and his crew landed on Watling Island in the Bahamas, he claimed the island for Spain and renamed it San Salvador "in honor of God who guided us and saved us from many perils."

Columbus was convinced that he had found a new route to Asia. Although he was disappointed that the new lands were not full of gold, he set off again later in the year to confirm the discoveries of his first voyage.

Columbus made four voyages west across the Atlantic, establishing Spanish colonies on the islands he passed and claiming the region for Spain. Right up to

THE NEW WORLD?

The lands visited by Columbus disappointed him, for he did not find the walled cities and fabulous wealth of China and Japan that he expected. Yet he remained convinced that he had sailed to Asia and never realized that what he had discovered was a continent previously unknown to Europeans.

◄ NATIVE AMERICANS
The Arawak peoples of the West Indies lived off the abundant fruits and berries of the islands. They lived in shelters that they built out of palm leaves and branches. Most people did not wear anything, although some wore clothes for ceremonies.

◄ FERDINAND AND ISABELLA
When Ferdinand of Aragon married Isabella of Castile in 1469, Spain became a united country for the first time since the Roman Empire. Isabella sponsored Columbus's first voyage.

▼ TOBACCO
While in Cuba, Columbus saw the Arawak people roll the dried leaves of the tobacco plant into a tube, set light to it, and smoke it. Smoking soon became a popular pastime throughout Europe. Below you can see tobacco leaves being dried in a shed.

▲ COCONUT PALMS
During his travels, Columbus saw many crops unknown to Europeans, including coconuts, pineapples, potatoes, and corn.

▼ THE *SANTA MARIA*
Columbus's flagship was the Santa Maria, a three-masted, square-rigged cargo ship capable of holding up to 40 crew. The other two ships, the Niña and Pinta, were much smaller.

his death in 1506, he remained convinced that he had sailed to Asia, although he failed to find proof. Because he had sailed west, the new islands he had come across became known as the West Indies.

Few people accepted his claims. In 1502 Amerigo Vespucci (1451–1512) returned to Europe from an expedition down the east coast of South America. He was certain that the lands were not part of Asia but part of a continent unknown to Europeans. He called it *Mundus Novus*—the New World. In 1507 a German geographer, Martin Waldseemüller, renamed it America in honor of Amerigo Vespucci. What Columbus had actually discovered was of far greater importance than a lengthy sea route to Asia. By sailing west, he had stumbled upon the American continent. As a result, within a few years the history of both America and Europe was completely transformed.

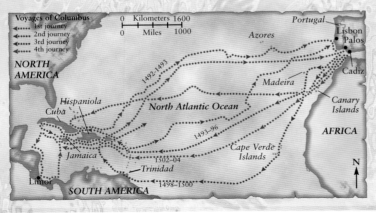

▼ THE VOYAGES OF COLUMBUS
Over the course of four voyages, Columbus sailed around most of the Caribbean islands and explored the coasts of South and Central America, believing that he had discovered a new route to Asia.

Voyages of Columbus
◄····· 1st journey
◄····· 2nd journey
◄····· 3rd journey
◄····· 4th journey

NORTH AMERICA

Hispaniola
Cuba
Jamaica
Limor
SOUTH AMERICA
Trinidad

North Atlantic Ocean

Portugal
Lisbon
Palos
Azores
Cadiz
Madeira
Canary Islands
Cape Verde Islands
AFRICA

1492–1493
1493–96
1502–04
1498–1500

0 Kilometers 1600
0 Miles 1000

N

Key Dates

- 1492–93 Columbus makes his first voyage to the West Indies, finding the Bahamas, Cuba, and Hispaniola.

- 1493–96 His second voyage takes him throughout the West Indies. He builds settlements on Hispaniola and explores Jamaica.

- 1498–1500 On the third voyage he sails between Trinidad and South America and is the first European to land in South America.

- 1502–04 Fourth voyage, along the coast of Central America.

Conquering the New World

IN THE YEARS AFTER THE HISTORIC voyages of Columbus a wave of Spanish explorers descended on Central and South America. They were searching for treasure.

Vasco de Balboa (1475–1519) was one of these adventurers. He was a colonist living in Hispaniola (Haiti), who fled to Central America to escape his debts. In September 1513 he set off into the interior of the country in search of gold. Twenty-seven days later he gazed westward across a vast sea, becoming the first European to look at the eastern shore of the Pacific Ocean.

◂ KNIFE
The Aztecs were skilled craftworkers. They used wood inlaid with gems and pieces of shell and turquoise to make the handle of this sacrificial knife. This knife was given as a gift to Hernán Cortés.

In November 1518 a second expedition left the Spanish colony of Santiago in Cuba, bound for Mexico. Previous expeditions had reported that there were vast temples and huge amounts of gold there. The 11 ships and 780 men were commanded by Hernán Cortés, a Spanish lawyer who had gone to the West Indies to seek his fortune. Cortés sailed along the coast for some months, raiding local towns and gaining valuable intelligence, then set off inland to the Aztec capital of Tenochtitlán.

Although the Aztecs were immensely skilled people, they were no match for the Spanish. The Aztecs had no gunpowder, and horses were unknown in the Americas. Cortés enlisted the help of the Aztecs' many enemies, then entered the city and captured its ruler, Montezuma. Cortés finally secured Tenochtitlán in August 1521, with only 400 men. The mighty Aztec Empire now became the province of New Spain.

Soon, rumors began to circulate about another rich empire, this time in South America. In 1530 Francisco Pizarro set out to conquer it with only 168 soldiers. The Inca Empire he found was weakened by civil war and an epidemic (probably smallpox). Once again, the Spanish soldiers overwhelmed the enemy. By 1532 the vast Inca Empire was defeated and its huge reserves of gold and silver were now under Spanish control.

◂ MONTEZUMA'S HEADDRESS
The Aztecs and Incas hunted tropical birds for their feathers. The quetzal's bright green feathers were highly prized and used in the headdress of Montezuma, the last Aztec ruler.

THE INCAS

The Incas were a hill tribe from Peru. Over the course of 300 years, they came to dominate the whole of the Andes mountains. By 1500 their empire stretched nearly 2,500 miles. Although they had no wheeled transportation, they built a huge network of roads and large cities of stone. They seem to have had no alphabet, so could not read or write. Despite this, their civilization was as advanced as any in Europe. The Incas were overthrown by Pizarro's small army.

▴ PIZARRO
The Spaniard Francisco Pizarro (1475–1541) went to the Americas to seek his fortune. He was spectacularly successful, crushing the powerful Inca Empire.

▸ QUIPU
Special officials kept records of taxation, population figures, and other statistics on quipus. A quipu is a series of vertical knotted strings, of varying length and color, that hang from a horizontal cord. The length and color of each string, its position, and the type of knot record the information.

◂ GOLD LLAMA
Llamas were valued by the Incas for their meat and wool and as beasts of burden. Gold figurines were made to show their importance.

◀ TENOCHTITLAN
The Aztecs' capital city had a population of 200,000, more than in any Spanish city, yet Cortés and his 400 men managed to capture it using trickery and deceit.

Cortés, Pizarro, and the other adventurers were *conquistadores,* which means conquerors in Spanish. The conquistadores were brutal and often dishonest. They went in search of wealth and to convert everyone they met to Christianity. Their conquests stretched the length of the Americas, from Mexico to Chile. Within 50 years of the expedition by Columbus, the Americas were under European control.

▶ MACHU PICCHU
The Incas established the city of Machu Picchu in a strategic position, protected by the steep slopes of the Andes Mountains. It was built of stone blocks fitted together without mortar. Temples, ceremonial places, and houses made up the 143 buildings. The city was so remote that the Spanish failed to discover it, and it was forgotten until an American explorer found it in 1911. It is located in south Peru.

Key Dates

- 1100s Incas start to dominate central Peru.

- 1325 Aztecs found the city of Tenochtitlán.

- 1430 Incas begin to expand north along the Andes.

- 1450s Incas build Machu Picchu.

- 1500 Aztec and Inca empires at their greatest extent and power.

- 1513 Vasco de Balboa first sees Pacific Ocean.

- 1521 Spanish capture Tenochtitlán and take over the Aztec Empire.

- 1532 Inca Empire conquered and under Spanish control.

Around the World

▲ FERDINAND MAGELLAN
Magellan (1480–1521) was a Portuguese sailor who quarreled with the Portuguese king and left the country in 1514 to work for the King of Spain. His round-the-world fleet sailed under the Spanish flag.

EUROPEAN NATIONS WERE entranced by stories about the vast wealth of Asia. Travelers and merchants told of treasures in India, China, Japan, and the spice-rich islands off their coasts. Throughout the 1500s sailors made epic voyages to seek out new routes to this wealth.

After the voyages of the Portuguese to the Indian Ocean and Columbus to America, Spain and Portugal made the Treaty of Tordesillas in 1494. The two countries divided the undiscovered world between them. They drew a line on a map and agreed that everything to the west of it was the property of Spain and everything to the east belonged to Portugal. South America was cut in half by the line.

Spanish explorers still wanted to find a new route to Asia by going west, as Columbus had tried to do. Columbus had discovered America when he went west, although he thought it was Asia. His successors had to find a way around America in order to get to Asia. In 1519 Ferdinand Magellan left Spain with five ships and 260 men to find a route to the rich Spice Islands (the

Moluccas, now part of Indonesia). In 1520 he sailed through the straits at the tip of South America and into the Pacific Ocean. He sailed northwest and in 1521 reached the Philippine Islands.

Magellan never reached the Spice Islands, because he was killed in a skirmish in April 1521. But one of his ships managed to get there. The *Victoria* was captained

PRIVATEERS AND PIRATES

Treasure ships heading for Spain laden with riches were soon noticed by Spain's main enemies, France and England. In wartime, both nations allowed privately owned ships (known as privateers) to attack Spanish ships and keep the booty. However, privateers often attacked in peacetime. Illegal pirate ships also joined in. Spain considered everyone who attacked one of its ships to be a pirate.

▲ JOLLY ROGER
During the 1600s, pirate ships began to fly the Jolly Roger—a black flag with a skull and crossbones on it—to show other ships their hostile intent. Each pirate ship had its own flag, but the most feared was the plain red flag, which meant death to every sailor who resisted a pirate takeover.

▼ DOUBLOONS
The Spanish mined precious gold and silver in the Americas. Some was made into coins to take to Spain. Gold was minted into doubloons, silver into pieces of eight.

▶ PIRATES
Pirates faced death if they were captured. Escaped slaves and convicts often became pirates. When they were attacked by a pirate ship, sailors often joined the pirates, hoping to get rich.

◄ AROUND THE WORLD
Both Magellan and Drake sailed in a westerly direction. From Europe their voyages took them to the south Atlantic Ocean, around Cape Horn, across the Pacific and Indian oceans, then back via the Cape of Good Hope and Atlantic.

▲ THE *GOLDEN HIND*
Francis Drake's flagship, the Golden Hind, *was originally called the* Pelican. *It had three masts and was the largest of the five ships in the fleet.*

by Juan de Elcano (1476–1526). When the crew reached the Spice Islands they loaded the ship with spices and headed home across the Indian Ocean.

In trying to find a westerly route to the Spice Islands, Magellan and his sailors had inadvertently become the first people to circumnavigate the Earth. Others followed Magellan. Francis Drake (1543–96) was an English seafarer and pirate with a successful record of raiding Spanish ships. In 1577 he set off to explore the Pacific Ocean, attacking Spanish treasure ships and collecting their gold as he went. In the Spice Islands he bought about 6 tons of valuable cloves. When he returned to England, this treasure was worth about $16 million in today's money.

▶ SPICES
Spices were highly valued in Europe for flavoring meat after it had been salted to preserve it, as well as for adding flavor to other foods and drinks. Cloves, nutmeg, cinnamon, pepper, and other spices all grew wild in the Far East. They had also been cultivated for centuries and were sold in markets as they are today.

cloves

cinnamon

Key Dates

- 1519–21 Magellan sails from Spain to the Philippines across the Pacific Ocean.

- 1521–22 Juan de Elcano completes the first circumnavigation of the world.

- 1520s First treasure ships bring Aztec gold back to Spain.

- 1545 Silver discovered in vast Potosí mine in Bolivia. It was the world's biggest single source of silver for the next 100 years.

- 1545 Major silver mine opened in Zacatecas, Mexico.

- 1577–80 Drake is the second person to sail around the world.

Into Canada

▲ JOHN CABOT
The adventurer John Cabot (1450–99) was probably born in Genoa in Italy. He traded in spices with the Arabs before moving to England.

IN ABOUT 1494 AN ITALIAN merchant named John Cabot arrived in England. Like Columbus, he planned to sail west across the Atlantic in search of the Spice Islands of eastern Asia. However, he proposed to make the voyage at a more northerly latitude, making the journey shorter. Cabot needed to find someone to finance his trip. After rejection by the kings of both Spain and Portugal, Cabot took his idea to King Henry VII of England. Henry had previously refused to sponsor Columbus. This time he was aware of the riches of the New World and was eager to support Cabot so that he could profit from any discoveries.

In May 1497 Cabot set sail from Bristol on board the *Matthew*. A month later he landed in Newfoundland, off the east coast of Canada, which he claimed for England. He had not found Asia, nor had he found wealth, but he had discovered rich fishing grounds and lands not yet claimed by Spain.

The French set out to explore these new lands. In 1534 Jacques Cartier (1491–1557) sailed from St. Malo. Like Cabot, he too was searching for a new, northerly route to Asia. He sailed around the mouth of the great St. Lawrence River, and the following year he returned to sail up it to present-day Montreal. He struck up good relations with the Huron Indians who lived there, who told him about the riches of the kingdom of Saguenay, farther west up the St. Lawrence. In 1541 Cartier decided to return to find Saguenay. But not surprisingly he failed to do so, because Saguenay was an imaginary place. The Hurons had made up the story about this marvelous

◄ MONTREAL
When Cartier sailed up the St. Lawrence River in 1535, he got as far as the wooden-walled Huron village of Hochelaga. Cartier climbed the hill behind it, naming it Mont Réal (Mount Royal), the present-day Montreal.

NATIVE AMERICANS
Numerous tribes of Native Americans lived in the woods and plains of the St. Lawrence valley. Five of the main tribes—the Mohawk, Onondaga, Seneca, Oneida, and Cayuga—joined together to form the Iroquois League in the early 1600s to protect themselves from other powerful tribes in the area.

◄ A HURON BRAVE
The Hurons welcomed the French to North America, trading furs and other goods with them and acting as guides and advisers. They also enlisted the French to help fight their wars with the Iroquois, who were their deadly enemies.

▼ FUR TRADE
The rivers and woods of Canada teemed with wildlife, providing furs for clothing and meat for food. Animal pelts, particularly from the seal, otter, and beaver, were prized by the Europeans. They traded guns and other goods to obtain the skins from the Native Americans.

▲ A SCALP
Fierce warfare between the different tribes was common. The most important trophy a brave could win in battle was the scalp of his opponent. Skin and hair were removed in one piece and then displayed on a wooden frame.

▶ QUEBEC

When Champlain visited Canada in 1608, he built a wooden fort on a hill overlooking the St. Lawrence River at a point where it narrowed considerably. The Native Americans called the place Kebec, and today it is known as Quebec.

Fort built of wood

Balcony for strategic lookout

Cannon positioned for quick firing

Bridge for crossing the St. Lawrence

kingdom, full of treasures, to please their French visitors!

Fur traders and fishermen followed Cartier's route up the St. Lawrence. But it was not until the next century that the French abandoned their search for a new route to Asia and began to settle in Canada. Samuel de Champlain (1567–1635) explored the east coast of North America and went inland as far as the Great Lakes. In 1608 he founded the city of Quebec, the first permanent French settlement in North America. The continent was now open for European colonization.

▼ EXPLORING CANADA

After John Cabot's exploratory voyage in 1497, the Frenchmen Jacques Cartier and Samuel de Champlain explored the valley of the St. Lawrence River and claimed the region for France. Champlain founded the city of Quebec.

NORTH AMERICA

Labrador

Gulf of St. Lawrence

North Atlantic Ocean

British Isles

Lake Huron

Quebec

Montreal

Newfoundland

Bristol

France

Lake Erie

Lake Champlain

Nova Scotia

EUROPE

| 0 | Kilometers | 1600 |
| 0 | Miles | 1000 |

◄···· Cabot 1497
◄···· Cartier 1535–36
◄···· Champlain 1608–16

Key Dates

- 1497 John Cabot claims Newfoundland for England.

- 1534 Jacques Cartier explores St. Lawrence estuary in Canada.

- 1535–36 Cartier sails up St. Lawrence as far as Montreal.

- 1603 Champlain sails up the St. Lawrence to Montreal.

- 1604 Champlain explores from Nova Scotia to Cape Cod.

- 1608–09 Champlain founds settlement of Quebec.

- 1615 Champlain explores Lakes Huron and Ontario.

The Northwest Passage

▲ POLAR BEARS
Polar bears were a constant threat to Arctic explorers, although their meat was a useful supplement to rations.

WHEN SPAIN AND Portugal divided up the undiscovered world between them in 1494, other European nations were prevented from sailing to Asia around the south of Africa or America. The Pope had split the world between Spain and Portugal, whose ships stopped British and Dutch traders from sailing south across the Atlantic. The only way left for the British and Dutch was to sail around the top of the world. For more than 300 years, explorers had tried to find a route through the Arctic Ocean, either around Canada, or around Siberia. Their efforts, however, proved fruitless.

In 1576 Queen Elizabeth I of England sent Martin Frobisher off to find a northwest passage to China. He reached Baffin Island, then returned home with rocks of gold. These turned out to be iron pyrites, or "fool's gold," and had no value.

The Englishman Henry Hudson was an experienced navigator who discovered a big river on the east coast of America in 1609. It was named the Hudson River after him. But he could not find a northwest passage either.

In 1610 he sailed his ship *Discovery* around northern Canada before heading south toward what he hoped would be the Pacific Ocean. In fact it turned out to be the vast but landlocked bay now called Hudson Bay. His crew refused to continue and mutinied, setting Hudson and the loyal members of his crew adrift in an open boat.

Over the next two centuries, a number of expeditions mapped the north coast of Canada but failed to make much headway through the maze of Arctic islands. Interest in the project faded. Then in 1817 the British government offered a prize of £20,000 to whoever could find a northwest passage. Many explorers set out but failed to find it. In 1844 the British Royal Navy organized a big expedition led by

▲ THE ARCTIC
The seas to the north of Canada are filled with islands. Between them are narrow channels which freeze solid every winter and are full of floating pack ice and icebergs during the short summer.

THE INUIT
The Inuit peoples of northern Canada and Greenland encountered by the polar explorers were well adapted to the cold conditions they lived in. During the summer months, they moved near the coast, building up food reserves for the long winter ahead. They hunted fish, caribou, seals, polar bears, and whales. Every part of the animal was used for food, clothing, fuel, shelter, and weapons.

▲ INUIT CARVINGS
Inuits carved real and mythical animals out of walrus ivory, caribou antlers, and bone from seal or whales.

◄ IGLOOS
Inuits made their igloos or snow houses out of blocks of packed snow built into a low dome. The warmth inside the igloo melted the edges of the blocks, which then froze together in the cold air outside.

▼ HUNTING SEALS
The Inuits caught seals by waiting patiently by a hole in the ice. Eventually a seal would come up for air. They then harpooned it, dragged it out of the freezing water, and loaded it onto a sledge.

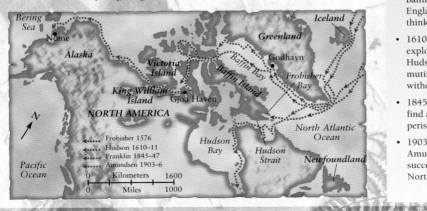

◀ MUTINY
In June 1611 the crew of Hudson's ship Discovery *mutinied in Hudson Bay. They put Hudson, his son and his loyal crew in an open boat with no oars. They were left to die.*

John Franklin. But he fell victim to the extreme cold and died in 1847, along with all his men.

Over the next decade, more than 40 expeditions went to look for Franklin. In 1859 the last message he left was found on King William Island. Some of those ships found the Northwest Passage, although none sailed through it. It was not until 1906 that the Norwegian polar explorer Roald Amundsen sailed from east to west along the north coast of Canada to the Pacific Ocean. By then, Spain and Portugal no longer controlled the southern seas, and the Panama and Suez canals were open for international shipping. The Northwest Passage was now just a long stretch of icy, treacherous water and of no commercial or political interest whatsoever.

▼ THE NORTHWEST PASSAGE
It took more than 300 years for explorers to navigate the Northwest Passage, and many died in the attempt. Finally, Roald Amundsen succeeded in 1906. By that time, there were easier ways of getting to Asia.

Map labels:
Bering Sea
Nome
Alaska
Victoria Island
King William Island
Gjoa Haven
NORTH AMERICA
N
Pacific Ocean
Iceland
Greenland
Godhavn
Baffin Bay
Baffin Island
Frobisher Bay
North Atlantic Ocean
Hudson Bay
Hudson Strait
Newfoundland

Frobisher 1576
Hudson 1610–11
Franklin 1845–47
Amundsen 1903–6

0   Kilometers   1600
0   Miles   1000

Key Dates

- 1576 Martin Frobisher lands on Baffin Island and returns to England with rocks that he thinks are gold.

- 1610–11 Henry Hudson explores the vast, inland Hudson Bay, but his crew mutiny and return home without him.

- 1845–47 John Franklin tries to find a northwest passage but perishes in the attempt.

- 1903–06 Norwegian Roald Amundsen makes the first successful voyage along the Northwest Passage.

The Northeast Passage

▲ SEALS
Siberian peoples and explorers seeking the Northeast Passage, hunted seals for food. Their skins also had many uses.

WHILE ENGLISH SAILORS concentrated on finding a northwest passage around the north of Canada, the Dutch were seeking a northeast passage to the north of Russia and Siberia. The Dutch were good sailors, and their fishing and whaling fleets regularly sailed in the Arctic Ocean, but even so they were unsure whether a northeast passage really did exist.

The Dutch followed in the wake of the Englishman Hugh Willoughby (1510–54), who had succeeded in sailing as far as the large island of Novaya Zemlya. But on his return journey, he perished in the pack ice off Murmansk on the Kola Peninsula.

In 1594 the Dutch mariner Willem Barents (1550–97) set sail on the first of his expeditions to find the Northeast Passage. He too was unsuccessful, although on his third voyage in 1596 he discovered Bear Island, which got its name after his crew had a fight with a polar bear. He also found the rich fishing grounds of the Spitsbergen archipelago, which was to become hugely profitable for Dutch hunters of whales, seals, and walruses. Then Barents's ship became trapped and damaged by the winter pack ice. He set off to row

▲ SIBERIA
The northern coast of Siberia lies inside the Arctic Circle. Here the temperature barely reaches above freezing point in summer and drops far below it in winter. Little grows in such an inhospitable landscape, although animals such as reindeer live there.

and sail the 1,590 miles to Kola, but died of starvation at sea. His crew survived and managed to return home once the ship was free.

After the failure of Barents's trip, there were no more expeditions until the Russian explorer Semyon Dezhnev (1605–72) sailed around the eastern tip of Siberia into the Pacific Ocean, proving that Asia and America were not joined. This knowledge did not reach Europe for

THE ARCTIC OCEAN

Although the waters north of Siberia do not freeze over as much as those north of Canada, the Arctic Ocean is still a harsh place. The ice-free summer months are short, and ships risk being caught and trapped in pack ice during the winter, which can last for up to nine months.

◄ THE *VEGA*
The 300-ton *Vega* was built in Germany as a whaling ship. It was constructed of oak with an outer skin of tougher wood to protect it against the ice. The ship had sails and a powerful steam engine. Nils Nordenskjöld made the first successful transit of the Northeast Passage in it during 1878–79.

◄ ICEBREAKER
Today the Northeast Passage is kept reasonably free of ice by a fleet of ice-breakers. These specially strengthened ships clear a passage to allow shipping through the pack ice.

▶ WHALES
The first people to explore the Arctic Ocean were whalers (whale hunters) from ports in northern Europe. They sailed the ocean in reinforced ships. Whales were caught for their meat, blubber, and bone.

◀ AN ARCTIC SHELTER
In the winter of 1596 the ship of Barents and his crew of 20 men was trapped by ice in the Arctic. The men survived by building a hut out of driftwood. It measured 33 feet x 20 feet and contained a fireplace, with a chimney to escape through if the hut was buried by snow. It even had a primitive Turkish bath made out of a barrel.

Icicles hanging on the bunk beds

Chimney to escape through if snow blocked the door

Turkish bath made of a barrel

great rivers and forests of Siberia might be a rich hunting ground. In 1878 the Finnish polar explorer Nils Nordenskjöld (1832–1901) set out from southern Sweden on board his ship, the *Vega*. Keeping close to the Siberian coast, he voyaged east until ice near the Bering Strait blocked his way. The following July he sailed into the Pacific Ocean. The quest was over and the Northeast Passage was now open for commerce.

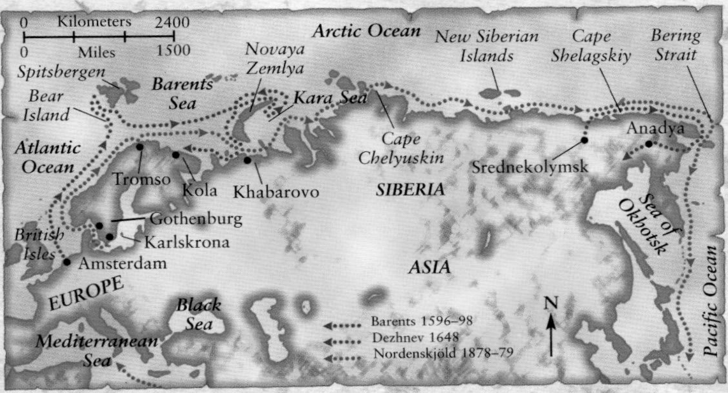

many years, and the Arctic Ocean was mainly left to the Siberians to fish. It was not until the late 1800s that there was interest in the Northeast Passage again, when Russia and other European countries realized that the

▲ THE NORTHEAST PASSAGE
For more than 300 years, explorers sailed northeast from Europe in the hope of finding a way along the top of Siberia and around into the Pacific Ocean. They were looking for an easy way to the riches of Asia.

Key Dates

- 1554 Hugh Willoughby reaches Novaya Zemlya.

- 1594 Barents sails into Kara Sea east of Novaya Zemlya.

- 1595 Barents's second voyage ends in failure in the Kara Sea.

- 1596 Barents discovers Bear Island and the rich fishing grounds of Spitsbergen.

- 1597 Barents dies on the sea that now bears his name.

- 1648 Semyon Dezhnev sails around eastern tip of Siberia.

- 1878–79 Nils Nordenskjöld navigates the Northeast Passage.

Exploring Asia

A T THE START of the 1700s Russia had a dynamic ruler, Czar Peter I. He built up a big navy and army, reorganized the government, and constructed the country's new capital of St. Petersburg. In previous years Russia had extended its territory right across Siberia to the shores of the Pacific Ocean. However, few Russians had any idea what their new land contained, or whether it was joined to America, so Peter the Great decided to find out.

Vitus Bering (1681–1741) was born in Denmark. He was a superb administrator, and Peter invited him to help modernize the Russian navy. In 1724 Peter appointed him to lead a large expedition across Siberia. The expedition left St. Petersburg in 1725 and reached the Pacific Ocean two years later. There Bering and his men built a ship, the *St. Gabriel*, and sailed up the coast and into the Arctic Ocean. From what he saw, Bering was satisfied that Siberia and America were not linked. He returned to St. Petersburg in 1730. In 1732 Bering was put in charge of a huge new undertaking. The Great

Northern Expedition consisted of more than 3,000 men, including 30 scientists and 5 surveyors, with 13 ships and 9 wagonloads of scientific instruments. Its task was to explore the entire northern coast of Siberia as well as the seas to its east.

Over the next ten years five teams mapped the northern coast and the great rivers that flowed north through the country toward it. Bering concentrated on the seas beyond Siberia. This time he sailed across the Pacific to Alaska, returning to the Kamchatka Peninsula along the string of islands called the Aleutian Islands.

▲ CROSSING SIBERIA
Travelers in Siberia used teams of trained reindeer or huskies to pull sledges bearing food and other provisions. People sometimes wore wide snowshoes to stop themselves from sinking into the snow.

EASTERN ASIA
During the 1500s, Europeans began to travel to China and Japan. Most were Jesuit missionaries, who were trying to convert people to Christianity. However, eastern Asia was still mainly closed to foreigners, and little was discovered about these strange and distant lands.

◀ JESUIT PRIEST
The Jesuits are a Roman Catholic religious order formed in 1534 by Ignatius Loyola. Their first main aim was to convert Muslims to Christianity, but they soon expanded their work, opening missions in India and China.

▲ FRANCIS XAVIER
Francis Xavier (1506–52) was a Spanish Jesuit who traveled around India before visiting Japan in 1549. He admired Japanese people for their sense of honor, and he made many converts.

▶ PRAYER WHEEL
Siddhartha Gautama was an Indian prince who became known as the Buddha. The religion of Buddhism is based on his teachings. From about 400 B.C. it began to spread throughout eastern Asia. Many Tibetan Buddhists use a prayer wheel for saying their prayers.

▲ HUNTERS' PREY
The Siberian tiger lives in southeast Siberia,
near the border with China. Its pelt (skin) was
much prized by fur trappers.

▶ DEATH OF BERING
In 1741 Bering started the voyage back from
the Aleutian Islands off Alaska. He reached an
island near the Kamchatka Peninsula,
where he died of scurvy and exposure.
The island is now named after him.

Bering died in 1741, before the expedition was finished, but he achieved a great deal. His team had mapped Siberia and opened up both Siberia and Alaska to Russian fur traders. By 1800 Alaska was part of the Russian Empire. Although Semyon Dezhnev had discovered a century earlier that Siberia and America were separated by sea, he left no records, and few people were aware of his work. Bering confirmed these findings, so in his honor, the strait between the two continents is named the Bering Strait.

▶ LHASA
In Tibet, the isolated city of Lhasa was the center of Tibetan Buddhism. In 1658 the German Jesuit John Grueber (1623–80) and the Belgian Albert d'Orville (1621–62) set out from China to find an overland route to India so as to avoid hostile Dutch ships on the sea route. In 1661 they entered Lhasa— the first Europeans to set eyes on the mystical city with its palaces and great temple complexes.

Key Dates

- 1549 Francis Xavier in Japan.

- 1661 Grueber and d'Orville visit Lhasa in Tibet.

- 1725–29 Bering crosses Siberia and explores the sea between Siberia and Alaska.

- 1732 Bering organizes Great Northern Expedition.

- 1734–41 Bering crosses Siberia and explores coast of Alaska.

- 1734–42 Five teams of explorers map the northern Siberian coast and the Ob, Yenisei, and Lena rivers.

Advancing into America

▲ JEFFERSON
In 1803 President Thomas Jefferson bought the Louisiana territory from France, more than doubling the size of the U.S.

Two hundred years after Columbus landed in the West Indies, Europeans still knew surprisingly little about the enormous American continent to the north. The Spanish explored Florida and the Gulf of Mexico, the English established colonies on the east coast, and the French sailed up the St. Lawrence River and settled in Canada. But the vast lands that lay in between remained a mystery.

In 1541 the Spaniard Hernando de Soto set out to explore Florida and became the first European to set eyes on the wide southern reaches of the Mississippi River. Unfortunately he died soon afterward and the Spanish failed to explore further. More than a century later, hundreds of miles to the north, Louis Jolliet (1645–1700) and the French Jesuit missionary Father Jacques Marquette (1637–75) discovered a route to the Mississippi River from the Great Lakes. They explored the river as far south as Arkansas. However, it was another Frenchman, Robert de la Salle (1643–87), who became the first European to sail down the river to its mouth on the Gulf of Mexico. He claimed the land in

▶ SACAJAWEA
In 1804 Lewis and Clark were joined by Sacajawea, a member of the Shoshone tribe. She spoke many native languages and acted as the interpreter on the expedition.

this area for his country, naming it Louisiana after the French king, Louis XIV.

Over the next century, European influence in North America changed considerably. The Spanish still controlled Mexico and Florida, but in 1760 the English had thrown the French out of Canada. Most importantly, the English colonists rebelled against their own country and set up an independent United States which stretched from the Atlantic coast to the east side of the Mississippi River. West of the Mississippi lay the huge Louisiana territory, which in 1803 the United States purchased from France.

U.S. President Thomas Jefferson wanted to find out more about this vast new Louisiana Purchase, as it was known. In 1804 he sent two men to explore it. They were his personal secretary, Meriwether Lewis (1774–1809), and William Clark (1770–1838), a former

THE NEW CONTINENT
The Spanish were the first Europeans to explore North America, moving northward from their empire in Mexico. Pánfilo de Narváez (1470–1528) explored the Gulf of Mexico, while Hernando de Soto (1500–42) became the first European to see the Mississippi River in 1541. These were the first of many people to push across this huge new continent.

▲ CABEZA DE VACA
Alvar Nuñez Cabeza de Vaca (1490–1556) sailed with De Narváez around the Gulf of Mexico. The fleet was wrecked off Texas in November 1528, but Cabeza de Vaca was saved by Yaqui tribesmen. He stayed with them for five years, then set out on foot through Texas and across the Rio Grande into Mexico, reaching the safety of Mexico City in 1536.

▶ THE MISSISSIPPI RIVER
The mighty Mississippi River flows south through the United States to the Gulf of Mexico. The discovery of its northern reaches by Jolliet and Marquette opened up America to European explorers and settlers.

◀ BISON
For 350 years European settlers hunted the bison herds of the plains almost to extinction, wiping out the Native Americans' main source of food and clothing.

army officer. Over the course of two years, they traveled from St. Louis up the Missouri River, over the Rockies, and down the Columbia River to the Pacific coast, before returning to St. Louis.

The success of the expedition convinced the U.S. government that Louisiana was suitable for people to live in. Within a generation, settlers were pouring across the Mississippi to start a new life on the Great Plains and the Pacific coast. The expansion of the United States across the continent was gaining momentum.

▲ SHOOTING RAPIDS
Lewis and Clark used canoes to navigate the dangerous Missouri, Columbia, and Yellowstone rivers.

▶ GRIZZLY BEARS
Bears were a menace to the expedition. One chased six men from Lewis and Clark's party into the Missouri River.

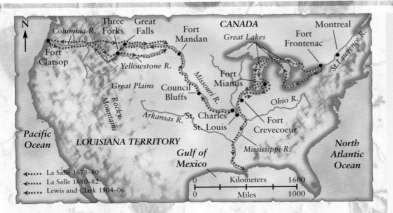

▲ SPREADING OUT ACROSS AMERICA
Robert de la Salle's two voyages around the Great Lakes and down the Mississippi River and the expedition of Lewis and Clark up the Missouri River did much to open up North America to traders and eventually to settlers.

Key Dates

- 1527–28 De Narváez explores the Gulf of Mexico.

- 1528–36 De Vaca explores Texas.

- 1541 De Soto is first European to see the Mississippi.

- 1672 Marquette and Jolliet explore the upper Mississippi.

- 1678–80 La Salle explores the Great Lakes.

- 1680–82 La Salle sails down Mississippi to Gulf of Mexico and claims the region for France.

- 1804–6 Lewis and Clark explore the Missouri River and routes to the Pacific.

Across the Pacific

▲ ABEL TASMAN
The two voyages of Abel Tasman did much to map the uncharted lands of the southern oceans.

EVER SINCE THE time of the ancient Greeks, people in Europe had imagined that there was a great continent lying on the other side of the world. They reasoned that since there was a Eurasian continent in the northern hemisphere, there must be a similarly large continent in the southern hemisphere, in order to balance the world! The only problem was that no one had ever managed to discover where this southern continent actually was.

Several sailors employed by a trading organization, the Dutch East India Company, stumbled across unknown land during their voyages. In 1605 Willem Jansz (1570–1629) sailed south from New Guinea and found the northern tip of Australia. In 1615 Dirk Hartog (1580–1630), traveling to Indonesia, sailed too far east and landed in Western Australia. Both sailors reported that this new land was too poor to bother with. So the Dutch East India Company took no further action, as it was interested in trade, not exploration.

In 1642 the company changed its mind and began to search for Terra Australis Incognita, or "unknown southern land." In 1642–43 Abel Tasman (1603–59)

▲ TASMANIA
When Tasman landed on a new island in November 1642, he named it Van Diemen's Land, after the governor-general of Batavia in the East Indies. It was later renamed Tasmania, after Tasman.

sailed around the Indian and Pacific oceans in a huge circle without discovering a southern continent, although he did find the island later named after him—Tasmania—and New Zealand. In 1643–44 he explored the Australian coastline that Jansz and Hartog had found. Tasman thought that the land to the south of

THE SOUTH PACIFIC

Although both Magellan and Drake crossed the Pacific, their routes took them north of the many island groups. During the following centuries these islands were gradually reached by Europeans: Alvaro de Mendaña (1541–95) reached Tuvalu and the Solomon Islands; Pedro Quirós (1565–1614) got to Vanuatu; and Tasman saw Fiji and Tonga. Louis Bougainville (1729–1811) mapped the region but did not reach eastern Australia because the Great Barrier Reef was in the way.

◀ THE GREAT BARRIER REEF
This 1,200 mile-long coral reef runs along the coast of northeast Australia. It is made up of the skeletons of millions of tiny sea creatures and is home to lots of marine life. It prevented Bougainville and other explorers from landing in Australia.

◀ THE SOLOMON ISLANDS
The first South Pacific islands to be explored by Europeans were the Solomon Islands, off the coast of New Guinea, which were found by De Mendaña in 1568. Over the next 200 years the rest of the islands in the region were slowly explored and mapped by visiting Europeans.

▶ BOUGAINVILLEA
On his round-the-world voyage Louis Bougainville took a botanist with him. One of the plants they brought back to Europe was a flowering climber now named bougainvillea in his honor.

▶ DUTCH EAST INDIA COMPANY
In 1602 the Dutch set up a company to coordinate their trading activities in the East Indies. They established trading posts, like the one pictured here, in India, China, and Japan, soon controlling the local spice trade.

New Guinea was not part of a southern continent, but he did not find out whether it was connected to New Guinea or whether it was an island.

Strangely enough, Luis Torres (c.1570–1613) had already proved that New Guinea was an island. In 1607 he sailed right around New Guinea through the strait that now bears his name, showing that it was an island. Therefore the land to its south, Australia, could not be attached to it. However, Tasman did not realize the significance of this discovery, so the mystery concerning the great southern continent, and the unnamed land that lay above it, remained unsolved.

▼ TASMAN AND BOUGAINVILLE
Neither Abel Tasman nor Louis Bougainville actually landed in Australia, although both did much to increase knowledge of the continent. Bougainville's voyage around the world established a French presence in the South Pacific.

Key Dates

- 1567–69 De Mendaña discovers the Solomon Islands.

- 1602 Dutch East India Company is established.

- 1605 Willem Jansz explores Queensland.

- 1615 Dirk Hartog discovers Western Australia.

- 1642–43 Tasman discovers Tasmania and sees New Zealand and the Fiji Islands.

- 1643–44 Tasman maps north coast of Australia.

- 1766–69 Louis Bougainville circumnavigates the world.

Captain Cook

▲ CAPTAIN COOK
James Cook (1728–79) sailed in the merchant navy for ten years and became an experienced navigator and seaman before he joined the British Royal Navy in 1755.

B Y THE 18TH CENTURY Europeans were still not sure of the shape and size of the strange land—*Terra Australis Incognita*—in the southern hemisphere. They did not even know for sure whether this mysterious new continent actually existed. By now, the British had overtaken the Dutch as the major trading nation in the world, and their Royal Navy ruled the waves. In 1768 the British Navy sent an expedition to the South Seas to search for the southern continent. James Cook was the ideal choice to lead it—he was an expert in navigation and an experienced seaman, having spent more than ten years on merchant ships.

Cook set sail from Plymouth, England, in August 1768. In April 1769 he reached Tahiti, where he and his crew were impressed by the warm climate and the beautiful plants and wildlife. Then he sailed southwest to New Zealand, the west coast of which had been discovered by Tasman. By steering a course in the shape of a figure eight, he found that New Zealand was two islands, not one. Cook continued west, landing at a place that is now called Botany Bay, in Australia, which he claimed for Britain. He then sailed up the coast until he got to the Great Barrier Reef, where his ship, the *Endeavour,* ran aground and had to be repaired. He then went through the Torres Strait and home to England across the Indian and Atlantic oceans. Cook made two more voyages to the South Seas. His second trip, in 1772–75, took him toward the South Pole, which was where Cook thought the southern continent lay.

▼ BAY OF ISLANDS, NEW ZEALAND
Cook visited many fine harbors on his voyages to New Zealand. The Bay of Islands, shown below, is on New Zealand's North Island.

THE SOUTH SEAS
Everywhere Cook went he was greeted with strange and wonderful sights. He found many animals and plants previously unknown to Europeans and met many different people. Although the Polynesians were mainly friendly, the Maoris of New Zealand were somewhat more suspicious.

▼ MAORI CANOES
The Maoris were skilled seamen. They greeted Cook on his arrival in New Zealand with a fleet of intricately decorated and carved canoes that were able to carry up to 100 warriors.

▶ LIME
During long voyages, most sailors developed scurvy, a disease caused by a lack of vitamin C in their diet. Cook solved this problem by feeding the crew with vitamin C-rich pickled cabbage, vegetables, and limes.

▲ KANGAROOS
Cook's crew were the first Europeans to see a kangaroo, but they could not decide what type of animal it was. In the end they decided that it was "some kind of stag."

◀ HONEYSUCKLE
Sydney Parkinson was an illustrator who went on the voyage. He drew many of the exotic plants that he saw on the journey. One was a type of honeysuckle.

His final voyage, in 1776–79, took him north in a search for an inlet into the Arctic Ocean.

Cook met a tragic end when he was killed in Hawaii after a scuffle broke out on the beach. But in his three voyages, Cook finally proved that Australia and New Zealand were separate islands and not part of a larger southern continent. When a landmass was later discovered around the South Pole, Antarctica was identified as the true Terra Australis Incognita. The vast amount of scientific, botanical, and navigational information Cook brought back from the South Seas was equally important. As a result of his work, exploration turned from adventure into scientific discovery.

Artist records plant information

Sorting animal skins and specimens

▶ THE *ENDEAVOUR*
When he was in the merchant navy, Cook sailed colliers, or coal ships, out of his home port of Whitby, Yorkshire. He therefore chose a converted collier, the Endeavour, *to sail around the world in. The ship was slow but tough and spacious, with enough room for the 94 crew and their supplies.*

▼ COOK'S VOYAGES
Over the course of three voyages, between 1768 and 1779, Cook explored much of the Pacific Ocean, including eastern Australia, which he named New South Wales. He also discovered many islands, including Hawaii, where he was eventually murdered.

Voyages of James Cook
••••◄ 1st journey 1768–71
••••◄ 2nd journey 1772–75
••••◄ 3rd journey 1776–79

0 Kilometers 3200
0 Miles 2000

N

EUROPE
ASIA
AFRICA
EAST INDIES
Torres Strait
Fiji
Pacific Ocean
Tahiti
Indian Ocean
Hawaiian Islands
NORTH AMERICA
Atlantic Ocean
SOUTH AMERICA
Tierra Del Fuego
Cape Horn
Kerguelen Islands
AUSTRALIA
New Zealand
Cape of Good Hope
ANTARCTICA

Key Dates

- 1755 Cook joins the Royal Navy and rises in rank to captain.

- 1768–71 On his first voyage, Cook sails round New Zealand and explores the east coast of Australia, claiming it for Britain.

- 1769 Cook discovers the island of Tahiti

- 1772–75 Cook's second voyage takes him south toward Antarctica.

- 1776–79 His third voyage heads north into the Arctic Ocean, and he discovers Hawaii on the way.

- 1779 Cook is killed in a violent skirmish on a beach in Hawaii

Trekking across Australia

ABORIGINAL ART
Aborigines believe that their Ancestral Beings shaped the land and created life in a period known as Dreamtime. These Beings live on in spirit form and are represented through paintings at sacred sites, such as caves and rocks.

AFTER COOK LANDED in Botany Bay, Europeans began to settle in Australia. But ninety years later they still knew little about their new country. The first settlers were convicts sent out from Britain to serve their prison sentences in Fort Jackson, now the city of Sydney. They were soon joined by farmers looking for a new start in a foreign land. There was plenty of land for everyone, so few ventured far inland from the coast.

Some intrepid explorers did investigate further, following the coastline or river valleys. In 1828 Charles Sturt (1795–1869) discovered the Darling River and then followed the Murray River to the sea. In 1844 he headed up the Murray inland. In 1840–41 Edward Eyre (1815–1901) walked along the southern coast from the town of Adelaide to find a route to the Western Australian settlement of Albany. Even by the late 1850s,

▶ CAMELS
Camels were imported from India for Burke and Wills's expedition. They proved unsuitable and most eventually ended up as food for the explorers. Descendants of those that survived still live in the outback.

the settlers still did not know what lay in the interior of their enormous country. Some thought there was a huge inland sea, while others feared it was nothing but desert. In 1859 the South Australian government offered a prize to the first person who crossed the continent from south to north.

Two expeditions set out to claim the prize. The first was led by Robert O'Hara Burke (1820–61), who was more of an adventurer than an explorer, and his young companion William Wills (1834–61). This was the biggest and most expensive expedition

EARLY AUSTRALIA
The Aborigines, or Native Australians, arrived on the continent more than 40,000 years ago. They lived in isolation from the rest of the world, existing by hunting and gathering their food, catching kangaroos and other animals and harvesting wild plants, nuts, and berries to eat. They were pushed off their native lands when the Europeans started colonizing Australia.

▼ ULURU
The name Uluru means "great pebble." It is a vast sandstone rock in central Australia which is more than 1.5 miles long and is sacred to the local Aranda Aborigines. It is also known as Ayers Rock.

▲ BOOMERANG
Aborigines hunted wild animals by throwing a boomerang at them. It returned to the thrower if it did not hit the target. Boomerangs were often patterned like this one.

◀ MODERN ABORIGINES
After the arrival of Europeans in 1788, Aborigines were reduced to second-class citizens in their own country. About 250,000 Aborigines live in Australia today.

▶ **INTO AUSTRALIA**
Despite their extensive knowledge of the coastline of Australia, few of the early settlers knew what lay inland. Over the course of 30 years a number of expeditions set out to explore and map the interior. By 1862 the continent had been successfully crossed from south to north by Burke and Wills, although they died on the way back.

Map labels:

Stuart 1828–30
1844-45
Eyre
1840–41
Stuart
1862
Burke and Wills
1860–61

Darwin

Aborigines set fire to the bush to stop Stuart's advance into their land

Daly Waters

N

W   E

S

Flinders

Stuart reaches the center of Australia

Tennant Creek

Cooper's Creek

Ashburton

Alice Springs

Burke and Wills find a note from the support party

Murchiso

Kangaroo

AUSTRALIA

Oodnadatta

Eyre digs to find water

Darling

Ceduna

Menindee

Burke and Wills set out

Perth

Adelaide

Sydney

Albany

Melbourne

ever organized in Australia. It consisted of 15 men, accompanied by camels and horses. It went north from Melbourne to the Gulf of Carpentaria. But the expedition was badly organized and both Burke and Wills died on the long journey back south.

John Stuart (1815–66) was more successful. He was an experienced explorer who knew how to survive in the outback. He set out from Adelaide to try to cross the continent but was turned back by Aborigines. He set

out again but was blocked by long stretches of thorny bushes. Finally, in July 1862, he succeeded in reaching Darwin. Stuart proved that the interior of Australia was indeed desert, but his journey opened up the interior for settlement and farming.

▲ **PROSPECTING**
The discovery of gold in Australia in 1851 brought a rush of prospectors from Europe and America, but few people struck it rich.

▼ **NED KELLY**
Many bushrangers, or outlaws, lived in the Australian outback. The most famous of these was Ned Kelly (1855–80), whose gang of robbers killed three policemen and robbed several banks before Kelly was finally caught and hanged in Melbourne. Kelly, who wore a tin hat to protect himself, soon became a national hero for many people.

Key Dates

- 1770 Cook lands in Botany Bay.

- 1788 First convicts to Australia.

- 1828–30 Charles Sturt crosses the Blue Mountains and reaches the Darling River.

- 1840–41 Edward Eyre walks along the south Australian coast from Adelaide to Albany in Western Australia.

- 1844–45 Sturt travels into central Australia.

- 1860–61 Burke and Wills cross Australia from south to north.

- 1862 On his third attempt, John Stuart crosses Australia from Adelaide to Darwin.

The Amazon

▲ JAGUAR
Alfred Wallace met a jaguar, a tree-climbing big cat, when he was exploring the River Orinoco.

DURING THE 1700S A NEW TYPE of explorer emerged. While most explorers set out to make their fortune, either by finding gold or by opening up new and profitable trade routes, this new breed of explorer wanted to expand the scope of scientific knowledge.

This was a period of great scientific and intellectual debate across Europe. Scientists such as Galileo and Newton had already worked out the laws of the natural world—the movement of the planets and how motion and gravity worked. Now philosophers began to challenge existing religious beliefs with the power of human reason, or rationality. In France a

▶ UNKNOWN TRIBES
Explorers of the Amazon jungle discovered many tribes of people unknown to Europeans. But the arrival of settlers, and exposure to their diseases, soon killed off many of these native South American tribes.

group of intellectuals compiled a 35-volume *Encyclopédie* of all knowledge. This new thinking was called "The Enlightenment." It influenced explorers, who now searched for knowledge, not for gold or glory.

South America had barely been explored since the Spanish and Portuguese conquered it in the 1500s. Two hundred years later scientists started to examine this rich and varied continent. In 1735 the French mathematician Charles-Marie de la Condamine (1701–74) went to Ecuador to record the shape and size of the Earth—the science of geodesy—by calculating its width at the equator. He was so enthralled by the wildlife there that he stayed for another ten years.

At the end of the century, the German naturalist Alexander von Humboldt (1769–1859) and the French naturalist Aimé Bonpland (1773–1858) trekked up the River Orinoco and along the Andes mountains to study plant life. Over the course of five years they recorded more than 3,000 previously unknown plant species and gathered many samples. Fifty years later two pioneering English naturalists, Henry Bates (1825–92) and Alfred Wallace (1823–1913), ventured into the

THE AMAZON RAINFOREST

Even now, scientists have no idea how many different plants and animals live in the Amazon rainforest, as new species are constantly being discovered. Two hundred years ago the first European travelers were amazed at the sheer variety of wildlife they found and fascinated by the tribes of people they met living deep in the jungle.

▲ ALEXANDER VON HUMBOLDT
German naturalist Alexander von Humboldt traveled extensively throughout South America, examining plants and wildlife as well as the landscape and climate. The cold sea current that flows up the west coast of South America is named in his honor.

▲ RECORDING NATURE
In the days before photography, explorers recorded what they saw by drawing it. In his sketchbooks, Henry Bates drew hundreds of the butterflies and other insects he saw on his travels.

◀ CINCHONA
Among the many new plants discovered by Aimé Bonpland was the cinchona tree. Its bark was used to make quinine, a natural cure for malaria, one of the most deadly tropical diseases.

Amazon rainforest. When Bates returned to England in 1859, he took with him more than 14,000 insects and other specimens. Another scientist, Richard Spruce (1817–93), went back to England in 1864 with more than 30,000 plant specimens.

As a result of this scientific activity people became far more aware of the variety of life on Earth. New animals and plants were discovered, and medicines developed from some of the plants. The age of the scientific explorer was now well under way.

▶ TOUCAN ATTACK
Although toucans are normally shy and nervous, they can be aggressive. When naturalist Henry Bates attempted to capture one, he was attacked by a flock of its fellow birds.

▲ RIVER AMAZON
The Amazon in South America is the second-longest river in the world and runs east from the Andes Mountains, through Brazil to the Atlantic Ocean. It flows through the world's largest rainforest, which is home to many exotic animals and plants.

◀ COLLECTING RUBBER
Rubber is made from latex, a sticky white liquid drained from the trunk of the rubber tree and collected in pots. Columbus saw locals playing with a rubber ball, but la Condamine was the first European to take rubber back home, in 1744.

▲ TREE FROG
Tree frogs were among the many new and exciting species that European naturalists encountered for the first time in the rainforest.

Key Dates

- 1735–44 La Condamine studies the shape of the Earth at the Equator. He stays there to watch the wildlife.

- 1799–1804 Alexander von Humboldt and Aimé Bonpland study botany along the River Orinoco and in the Andes.

- 1848–59 Amazon explored by Alfred Wallace and Henry Bates.

- 1849–64 Richard Spruce travels up the Amazon, collecting 30,000 plant specimens.

- 1852 Wallace returns to England, but all his specimens are lost in a fire on board ship.

Deep inside Africa

▲ RICHARD BURTON
Richard Burton was a fearless explorer. In 1853 he dressed up as an Arab and visited the holy city of Mecca, in Saudi Arabia, which was closed to non-Muslims.

THE ONLY PART OF AFRICA known to Europeans was its coastline, which for most of its length was an inhospitable place. There were few natural harbors, and much of the coast was either dry desert or wet jungle. Many of the rivers flowed out into the sea through swampy deltas. As a result, the interior of Africa was too difficult for European travelers to get into.

During the late 1700s Europeans began to venture inland, exploring both the major rivers and the vast Sahara Desert. In 1770 James Bruce (1730–94) discovered Lake Tana in the east, in what is now Ethiopia. He realized that it was the source of the Blue Nile, one of the main tributaries of the great River Nile. In the west, Mungo Park (1771–1806) set out in 1795 to explore the mysterious, little-known River Niger, which flowed

inland and never seemed to reach the sea. He discovered that the river actually flowed east, not west as had always been thought, and that it turned south near Timbuktu. However, he was not clear what happened to it after that. He drowned when his canoe was ambushed by tribesmen.

Over the next fifty years attention turned to the Sahara Desert. In 1828 a French explorer named René Caillié (1799–1838) became the first European to survive a secret visit to the legendary and forbidden city of Timbuktu,

◀ TIMBUKTU
During the 1300s the city of Timbuktu became a prosperous center for trade across the Sahara Desert. Over the centuries, the city became famous for its wealth and learning, although no European had ever visited it.

THE SLAVE TRADE
The first black slaves were shipped out of Africa by the Arabs more than 1,000 years ago. Local rulers grew rich by selling captured enemies into slavery. In 1482 the Portuguese opened a trading post for exporting slaves to the New World. Other European nations joined in. From 1701 to 1810 more than seven million Africans were sent to the Americas. In the early 1800s slavery was abolished in Europe, but the Arabs continued the trade until 1873, when the main slave market in Zanzibar was closed.

▼ LIFE OF A SLAVE
Slaves worked very long hours, six days a week on the plantations of the New World. If a slave tried to escape, they were made to wear a heavy iron collar with long spikes, which made it difficult for them, if they tried again, to escape to freedom through the undergrowth.

▼ SLAVE SHIPS
Slaves were packed into the holds of ships for transportation across the Atlantic. Conditions were bad and more than one million people died on the way.

▲ CATCHING SLAVES
In West Africa armed slave traders captured young African men and took them to the slave ports ready for export.

▶ INTO AFRICA

From the 1760s onward, Europeans made determined attempts to explore the interior of Africa. The major rivers of the Niger and Nile were mapped and the great Sahara Desert was thoroughly explored. The south of the continent, however, remained largely unknown.

which as a Muslim city was closed to Christians. He was very disappointed to find that it was full of mud huts, not rich buildings, and few people believed him when he returned to France. His story was confirmed, however, by the German explorer Heinrich Barth (1821–65), who explored the entire region thoroughly for the British government during the 1850s.

In 1857 two hardy British explorers, Richard Burton (1821–90) and his friend John Speke (1827–64), set out to solve one of the great African mysteries—the source of the river Nile. They explored the great lakes in East Africa, but Burton fell ill and Speke continued alone. After two attempts, he discovered that the Nile flowed out of the northern end of Lake Victoria (which Speke named after the reigning British queen) and over the mighty Ripon Falls. The interior of Africa was slowly giving up its secrets.

Tangier
Rabat
Fez
Tripoli
Alexandria
Cairo

Barth crosses the Sahara

AFRICA
Timbuktu
Segu
Agadez
Kano

Jedda
Khartoum
Massawa

Burton and Speke search for the source of the Nile

Park arrives at Segu but turns back

Gondokoro
Lake Victoria

Congo

Bruce
1768–73

Park
1795–1806

Caillié
1827–28

Barth
1844–55

Burton and Speke
1857-63

Lake Tanganyika
Tabora

Victoria Falls

N
W
E
S

Zulu warrior

Cape Town

▲ TRANSPORTATION
The slave traders rarely traveled into the interior of Africa. Slaves would be brought to the coast for sale by tribal leaders who had enslaved their enemies. The slaves would either have been forced to walk to the coast or taken in canoes such as this one.

▼ SAHARA DESERT
Even the vast Sahara Desert was not a barrier to slave traders who would take caravans of slaves across the desert, empty but for occasional rock formations like this one.

Key Dates

- 1768–73 James Bruce searches for the source of the Nile.

- 1795–1806 Mungo Park explores the River Niger.

- 1827–28 René Caillié becomes the first European to visit the city of Timbuktu.

- 1844–55 Heinrich Barth travels across the Sahara Desert.

- 1857–58 Richard Burton and John Speke explore the great lakes of East Africa.

- 1858–63 John Speke investigates the Nile and eventually discovers its source.

Livingstone and Stanley

▲ LION ATTACK
In 1844 Livingstone was attacked by a lion, which mauled his left shoulder. Although he eventually got better, he never regained the full use of his left arm.

ONE MAN MORE THAN any other transformed European knowledge about Africa—David Livingstone (1813–73). He started out as a missionary and doctor, and went to Africa to convert the local people to Christianity and to improve their lives through medicine and education. Once in Africa, however, Livingstone became curious about everything he saw and began to travel extensively. He recorded it all in three large books, totaling more than 750,000 words, which made him and his journeys world-famous. But today some people think that his travels were not such a good thing, because he paved the way for the European colonization and exploitation of Africa.

Livingstone was born in Scotland and arrived in Cape Town on the Cape of Good Hope in 1841. From there he traveled to the mission station of Kuruman, on the edge of the Kalahari Desert. Here he met his future wife, Mary, and had a family. Together they established more missions, but Livingstone soon got restless and sent his wife and children back to England so that he could continue to explore by himself.

In 1851 he discovered the river Zambezi, which was previously unknown to people in Europe. Between 1852 and 1856 he became the first European to cross the continent from east to west, exploring the length of the Zambezi as he went. He then investigated the eastern coast and in 1865 set out to find the source of the river Nile. For a while, nothing was heard of him. An American newspaper, *The New York Herald*, sent a reporter, Welsh-born Henry Stanley (1841–1904), to find Livingstone.

◀ RIVER SCARES
Livingstone made many of his journeys by boat, braving rapids, waterfalls, and even hippopotamuses. On one occasion, his boat crashed into a hippo and overturned it, causing him to lose much of his equipment.

THE INTERIOR OF AFRICA

John Speke, who discovered the source of the river Nile, described Africa as an upside-down soup plate—a rim of flat land around the edge with a sharp rise up to a central plateau. Rivers flowing from the interior often crashed over rapids or waterfalls, and explorers had to carry their boats around them. Wild animals and hostile locals added to the problems.

◀ VICTORIA FALLS
On November 17, 1855, Livingstone came up against a huge waterfall on the river Zambezi. Clouds of water vapor gave it its local name of Mosi-oa-tunya, or "the smoke that roars." Livingstone named the falls after Queen Victoria of Britain, the only English name he gave to any discovery.

▲ STANLEY'S HAT
Stanley wore a hat like this one, and Livingstone a flat cap, at their famous meeting at Ujiji.

▲ ZULU WOMEN
The Zulus of southern Africa were a warlike people. Under their leader, Shaka, they built a powerful nation in the region in the early 1800s. Today there are more than seven million Zulu people living in South Africa.

◀ "DR. LIVINGSTONE, I PRESUME?"
*In March 1871 Henry Stanley set out from
Zanzibar to find Dr. Livingstone. Stanley
was an adventurer, who was probably
motivated by fame and fortune. Eight
months later he heard from
local people that Livingstone had recently
returned to Ujiji, on the shores of
Lake Tanganyika. Stanley rushed
to meet the ailing Livingstone,
greeting him on November 10
with the now famous words
"Dr. Livingstone, I
presume?" "Yes," replied
the explorer.*

He managed to track him down eight months later. Stanley returned twice to Africa, once to explore the Great Lakes region and sail down the last great unknown river in Africa, the river Congo (now Zaïre). Then, after working for the Belgian king in the Congo, he went to rescue Emin Pasha, the British governor of Equatoria (north of the Great Lakes), who was besieged by enemy tribespeople. Stanley's expeditions helped both Britain and Belgium establish colonies in central Africa, and by the time he died in 1904, almost all of Africa was under European control.

▶ DR. LIVINGSTONE AND MR. STANLEY
Between them Livingstone and Stanley explored much of central and southern Africa. They also navigated the two great and previously unknown African rivers—the Zambezi and Congo (now Zaïre)—although neither proved very easy to navigate. They also explored the Great Lakes region, confirming the source of the river Nile and settling disputes about how the different lakes drained into each other.

AFRICA

Kilometers 0 — 1200
Miles 0 — 750

White Nile
N

Livingstone Falls
L. Victoria
Stanley Falls
Cabinda
Nyangwe
Ujiji
Indian Ocean
Boma
L. Tanganyika
Zanzibar
Comoro Islands
Luanda
Victoria Falls
L. Nyasa
Sesheke
R. Zambezi
Quelimane
Kalahari Desert
Atlantic Ocean
Kuruman
Port Elizabeth
Cape Town

David Livingstone
1st expedition 1841–52 •••••
2nd expedition 1852–56 •••••
3rd expedition 1858–64 •••••
4th expedition 1865–73 •••••

Henry Morton Stanley
1st expedition 1871–72 ◀•••
2nd expedition 1874–77 ◀•••
3rd expedition 1887–89 ◀•••

Key Dates

- 1841–52 Livingstone explores southern Africa.

- 1852–56 Livingstone goes down the river Zambezi. Discovers Victoria Falls.

- 1858–64 Livingstone explores Lake Nyasa and eastern coast.

- 1865–73 Livingstone goes to the Great Lakes and disappears.

- 1871–72 Stanley looks for Livingstone. Finds him in Ujiji.

- 1874–77 Stanley goes down the river Congo to Cabinda in west.

- 1887–89 Stanley rescues besieged Emin Pasha.

The North Pole

IN 1881 A SHIP, the *Jeannette*, sank off the coast of Siberia. Three years later the wreckage turned up 3,000 miles away on the coast of Greenland, right on the other side of the Arctic Ocean. This extraordinary event caused great confusion, because everybody knew that the Arctic Ocean consisted of a thick layer of pack ice. How had the wreckage managed to travel such a great distance? And how had it moved through the ice?

The Norwegian explorer Fridtjof Nansen (1861–1930) decided to find out. He calculated that the wreckage could have been moved only by a powerful ocean current which had pushed it along in the ice. Nansen designed a boat, the *Fram*, which he intended to steer into the ice and allow the currents to move, just as they had the *Jeannette*. He worked out that the currents would carry

him close to the North Pole, in the middle of the Arctic Ocean. For three years, the *Fram* drifted in the ice from Siberia to the Spitsbergen islands to the east of Greenland. Although he failed to reach the North Pole, Nansen did prove that there was no land under the North Pole—it was just ice.

Nansen was not the first explorer to try to reach the North Pole. Between 1861 and 1871 an American, Charles Hall (1821–71), made three attempts on foot, dying after his last journey. But it was Nansen's voyage that raised huge international interest in the North Pole and a race to get there first began.

In 1897 the Swedish engineer Salomon Andrée tried to fly to the North Pole in a balloon, but he perished soon after taking off from Spitsbergen. Robert Peary (1856–1920) was more successful. He was an American explorer who made his first visit to the Arctic in 1886. For the next 22 years he devoted

◀ HUSKIES
Husky dogs have a thick, double coat of fur which helps to keep them warm in the extreme cold and snowy conditions of the Arctic. They can be trained to pull sledges of equipment over the ice.

WHAT'S IT LIKE AT THE NORTH POLE?

The North Pole is located in the middle of the Arctic Ocean, which is covered with pack ice all year round. Because the ice floats on top of the ocean currents, it is broken up and jagged, often rising to ridges 33 feet or more high.

▼ PEMMICAN
An ideal food for a long Arctic expedition is pemmican. It is made from dried, shredded meat mixed with melted fat. It is full of calories and lasts for years.

▲ SEALSKIN
The first European travelers in the Arctic wore layers of woolen clothes, which failed to protect them from the cold. Later, they learned to wear Inuit-style animal-skin clothes, such as this sealskin hood.

▲ REFUELING AT THE NORTH POLE
Airplanes play a vital role in bringing in supplies to the North Pole. American explorers Richard Byrd and Floyd Bennett reached the North Pole by airplane in 1926.

◀ THE *FRAM*
Nansen needed a very strong ship for his plan. The Fram was specially designed to be frozen into the Arctic ice so that it could then float with the currents across the Arctic Ocean without being damaged. Nansen hoped that the ice-bound ship would drift toward the North Pole. The ship went right across the Ocean, but it didn't get as near to the Pole as Nansen had hoped.

Icebergs and frozen pack ice pile up on either side of the Fram

Hull built to withstand the huge pressure of the ice

himself to polar exploration, returning year after year, each time getting closer to his goal of reaching the North Pole. In 1908 he set off up the west coast of Greenland and established a base camp at Cape Columbia on Ellesmere Island. His six-strong team set off from there, making a mad dash and reaching the

North Pole on April 6, 1909. They then hurried back to base camp. The top of the world had been conquered.

Some people doubted that Peary had reached the North Pole, since he made the return journey in record time, covering 70 miles in one day. Nowadays most people think that Peary did indeed reach the Pole.

▼ USS *NAUTILUS*
In 1958 a U.S. nuclear-powered submarine, the U.S.S. *Nautilus*, sailed under the polar ice cap. It left Point Barrow in Alaska and sailed the 1,820 miles to Spitsbergen in the North Atlantic Ocean in four days. The submarine, which was 300 feet long and had a crew of 116, passed directly under the North Pole.

Key Dates

- 1871 Charles Hall sails up the west coast of Greenland and gets nearer to the North Pole than anyone before him.

- 1893–96 Fridtjof Nansen sails the *Fram* into the polar ice and drifts toward the North Pole, but fails to reach it.

- 1897 Salomon Andrée attempts to reach the Pole by balloon, but dies in the attempt.

- 1908–09 Robert Peary reaches the North Pole.

- 1958 U.S.S. *Nautilus* sails under the polar ice cap.

Race to the South Pole

AFTER ROBERT PEARY MADE his successful attempt on the North Pole in 1909, all eyes turned toward the South Pole. Because it was the last unconquered place on Earth, the South Pole held a huge attraction for explorers, but it was a daunting place to visit.

Unlike the North Pole, the South Pole is covered by land. The vast, frozen continent of Antarctica is the coldest place on Earth, with ridges of mountains and large glaciers, making traveling extremely difficult. In addition, the land is surrounded by pack ice and icebergs that stretch far into the Southern Ocean. Two people prepared themselves to conquer this icy wilderness. The first was Robert Scott, a British explorer who had visited the region in 1901–4 and came to think of the continent as his to conquer. As his intention to

▶ ROALD AMUNDSEN
Norwegian polar adventurer Roald Amundsen (1872–1928) was a skilled explorer and had three impressive records to his name. He was the first person to sail through the Northwest Passage, in 1903–6, the first person to reach the South Pole, in 1911, and the first person to fly an airship across the North Pole, in 1926.

lead an expedition to the South Pole became known, a second explorer, the Norwegian Roald Amundsen, joined the race. He kept his plans secret to prevent Scott from speeding up his preparations. Amundsen, too, was an experienced polar explorer, and far better equipped and prepared than Scott.

Both expeditions arrived in Antarctica in January 1911 and spent the winter on either side of the Ross Ice Shelf. Amundsen, however, had left two weeks before Scott and was 68 miles closer to the Pole. He was also better prepared, having already made several journeys to leave food stores at stages along the route. His five-strong party made fast progress, climbing the steep Axel Heiberg glacier onto the plateau surrounding the

◀ PENGUINS
The Antarctic is home to several different species of penguin. Penguins cannot fly, but use their wings as flippers to swim.

SCOTT'S JOURNEY
In 1910 Robert Scott set out for Antarctica on board the ship *Terra Nova*. After spending the winter at Cape Evans, he set out for the South Pole in November 1911. Unlike his rival Amundsen, Scott used ponies as well as dogs to haul the sledges, but the ponies died in the cold. As a result, the party of five made slow progress and were devastated to discover, when they reached the South Pole on January 17, 1912, that Amundsen had beaten them to it. All five died on the return journey.

▲ ROBERT SCOTT
The naval officer Robert Scott (1869–1912) led a scientific expedition to Antarctica in 1901. His ill-fated expedition to the Pole in 1910–12 captured the imagination of the world.

◀ CHEMISTRY SET
Scott's expeditions were scientific as well as exploratory. His team carried this chemistry set with them when they set off in 1910.

▶ SCOTT'S BASE CAMP
Scott established his base camp at Cape Evans, on the east side of the Ross Ice Shelf. Here he and his team spent the winter of 1911, planning their route to the Pole, studying maps, and also writing letters and reports.

▶ BATTLING ACROSS A FROZEN LAND
Amundsen and his party were well equipped to endure the cold conditions and were all expert skiers. They used husky dogs to pull their sledges. As food and other provisions were used up and the sledges got lighter, unwanted dogs were shot and eaten, reducing the amount of food required for the expedition. As a result, Amundsen and his team traveled far faster than Scott's team.

South Pole. They arrived at the Pole on December 14, 1911. Scott set out on November 1, 1911, but encountered far worse weather and made slow progress, finally getting to the Pole a month after Amundsen, on January 17, 1912.

Amundsen's expedition skills and equipment ensured that all his party returned home safely. Sadly, Scott and his team all perished, three of them within 11 miles of a supply depot equipped with food and other life-saving provisions. The race to the South Pole was over, but although Amundsen claimed the prize, Scott has continued to hold a special fascination for people, because of the tragic ending to his expedition.

▼ RESEARCH STATION, ANTARCTICA
In 1959 an agreement was made to reserve Antarctica for scientific research. Today, 18 nations have scientific bases there to conduct research into the environment, wildlife, and weather. In 1987 scientists found a hole in the ozone layer above Antarctica. The ozone layer protects the earth from the harmful rays of the sun.

Key Dates

- 1840 Antarctic coastline visited by James Wilkes and Jules Dumont d'Urville.

- 1841 James Ross from Britain explores the Ross Sea and its vast ice shelf.

- 1901–04 Scott explores the Antarctic coast and Ross Sea.

- 1908 Ernest Shackleton gets within 112 miles of the Pole.

- 1911 Roald Amundsen reaches the South Pole.

- 1912 Scott gets to the Pole but the team dies on return journey.

Seas, Summits, and Skies

▲ CHARLES LINDBERGH
The first solo flight across the Atlantic was made by 25-year-old Charles Lindbergh in 1927, when he flew the Spirit of St. Louis *from New York to Paris in 33 hours.*

WITH THE CONQUEST of the South Pole in 1911, an age of exploration came to an end. All the major undiscovered parts of the world had now been explored. But eight years earlier, in 1903, a new method of transportation had made its début. Orville and Wilbur Wright took to the skies over North Carolina in the airplane they had built, called the *Flyer.* Powered aircraft created new opportunities for exploration and discovery, and in the first 30 years of the 20th century a series of epic flights took place.

Louis Blériot made the first crossing of the English Channel in 1909. The first non-stop journey across the North Atlantic, from Newfoundland to Ireland, followed a decade later. It was made by John Alcock and Arthur Brown. Charles Lindbergh flew solo over the Atlantic in 1927, and Amy Johnson made the first solo flight by a woman, from Britain to Australia in 1930. These and other historic flights opened up the skies to commercial travel, and airlines began regular

▲ BALLOONING AROUND THE WORLD
In 1999 Brian James and Bertrand Piccard became the first people to circumnavigate the world non-stop in their balloon, the Breitling Orbiter 3. *The pair set off from Switzerland and used the jet streams in the upper atmosphere to glide eastward around the world.*

flights between the major cities of the world. People were now able to travel to faraway places without spending months at sea in order to get there.

As a result, more and more people decided to travel to other countries and explore the world for themselves. The growth in foreign travel led to a change in the nature of exploration. Now explorers took to the

HIGHS AND LOWS
Although nearly three-quarters of the world's surface is covered by sea, we still know very little about what lies beneath the ocean's surface. The development of underwater craft enabled explorers to study the seas in greater detail. At the other extreme, the highest places on the earth's surface have similarly fascinated explorers.

▲ THE *TRIESTE*
The *Trieste* bathyscaphe was designed to withstand the great pressure under the sea. In 1960 Jacques Piccard descended nearly 7 miles into the Marianas Trench in the western Pacific Ocean, setting a world record that survives today.

▶ JACQUES COUSTEAU
One of the world's most famous ocean explorers, Jacques Cousteau (1910–97) invented the aqualung in 1943 to help divers breathe underwater. It was an air tank connected to a face mask.

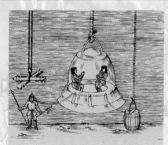

▲ DIVING BELL
Edmund Halley invented the diving bell in 1690. It consisted of a watertight barrel anchored to the sea floor by heavy weights. Barrels of air were lowered and connected to the bell to supply the divers with fresh air.

▼ AMY JOHNSON
In 1930 the English pilot Amy Johnson (1903–41) flew single-handed from Britain to Australia in just 17 days. She had learned to fly only two years earlier. Amy went on to become the first woman to fly solo across the Atlantic and also made solo trips to India and Japan.

air, surveying lands by airplane and producing detailed maps by aerial reconnaissance. For those expeditions still on foot, supplies and reinforcements could now be airlifted in, and any casualties flown out for medical treatment. As a result, explorers face less physical danger than they used to, and their emphasis has shifted away from exploration from its own sake toward exploration for scientific reasons. Today, teams of scientists investigate the impact of global warming in Antarctica, for example, or the effects of the climate change in the Pacific Ocean. They use highly complex scientific instruments and techniques, and have a support team ready to fly them out of danger at a moment's notice.

▶ MOUNT EVEREST
Climbing to the summit of the highest peak on Earth has always fascinated mountaineers. Mount Everest (29,000 feet) lies between Nepal and Tibet, and mountaineers found it a very difficult challenge. Thirteen expeditions tried to reach the summit before the New Zealander Sir Edmund Hillary (born 1919) and the Nepalese Tenzing Norgay (1914–86) succeeded on May 29, 1953. Within a year, most of the other major Himalayan peaks were also conquered by European mountaineers.

Key Dates

- 1903 Wright brothers' flight.
- 1909 Louis Blériot flies nonstop across the English Channel.
- 1919 Alcock and Brown cross the Atlantic.
- 1927 Charles Lindbergh crosses the Atlantic.
- 1930 Amy Johnson flies single-handed from Britain to Australia.
- 1953 Everest conquered.
- 1954 Italians climb K2—world's second-highest mountain.
- 1960 Jacques Piccard descends to record depths below the sea.

Blasting into Space

ON OCTOBER 4, 1957 an aluminum sphere no bigger than a large beachball was launched into space by the USSR. It measured 23 inches across and had four antennae trailing behind it. It orbited the Earth once every 96 minutes. This was *Sputnik I*, the world's first artificial satellite, and it began a period of intense space exploration and discovery that continues to this day.

Modern rocket technology had made it possible to travel out of the Earth's atmosphere and into space. It then became easier to fly to the Moon and to examine our closest planet neighbors in the solar system. Scientists wanted to find out the answer to some of the oldest questions on Earth—is there life elsewhere in the universe?

▲ FLOATING IN SPACE
Astronauts are able to venture outside their spacecraft to do repairs or to help it dock with another craft. They must be tethered to their own craft to stop them from drifting off into space.

▲ LAUNCH SITE
A rocket needs huge power to lift it and its load off the launch pad. Once in space, the rocket is no longer needed and falls away, leaving the spacecraft or satellite to continue on its own.

▶ MOON LIVING
Astronauts lived in this lunar module when they landed on the Moon. When they were ready to leave, the module blasted off to rejoin the orbiting main spacecraft.

THE SPACE RACE

The former USSR launched the world's first satellite in 1957, beginning a space race with the U.S. that lasted until 1969. The Americans feared that the USSR would use space for military purposes, and wanted to prove that the U.S. was the world's leading superpower. The race ended when the U.S. landed a man on the Moon. Today the two countries cooperate on missions.

▶ SPACE FOOD
Prepackaged, specially prepared food is taken on space missions. It requires heat or water to make it edible. Fresh foods are rarely taken because they do not keep well.

◀ YURI GAGARIN
The first human to go into space was the Russian cosmonaut Yuri Gagarin (1934–68). On April 12, 1961 he orbited the Earth once while on board *Vostok I*, returning to Earth after 108 minutes in space. Gagarin became a hero throughout the USSR and was given many national honors.

▲ DOG IN SPACE
The first living creature in space—a Russian dog named Laika—was launched into space on board *Sputnik 2* in November 1957 and remained in orbit for two days. Many other creatures, such as monkeys and jellyfish, have made the trip.

◄ MOON WALK
Neil Armstrong became the first person to walk on the Moon on July 24, 1969 . He said, "That's one small step for man, one giant leap for mankind." Today, only 12 astronauts, including Buzz Aldrin, pictured, have been there.

▼ WORKING IN SPACE
The space shuttle is launched like a rocket, but returns to Earth like a plane. It can then be used again. In space the shuttle is used for launching, repairing, and recovering satellites and for further scientific research.

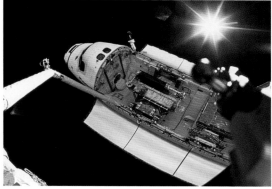

How and when were the Earth, and the universe itself, formed? They also wanted to explore the nearest planets and find out more about them.

This combination of technology and curiosity has sent men to the Moon and unmanned spacecraft to examine every planet in the solar system. Weather, communication and spy satellites now orbit the Earth

in huge numbers. At least two new satellites are launched each week. Orbiting telescopes send back detailed information about distant stars, and permanent space stations enable astronauts to spend many months in space. Gradually a more complete picture is being built up about our solar system and its place in the universe, and new discoveries are made every year.

▼ THE HUBBLE TELESCOPE
In 1990 the *Hubble* space telescope was launched into orbit high above the Earth. It sends back X-ray and other photographs free from interference or distortion by the Earth's atmosphere.

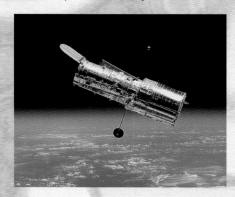

▲ THE GALAXY
The exploration of space has told scientists more about our own galaxy (the Milky Way) and the millions of stars it contains. By observing how these stars are born and die, scientists have begun to understand how the universe itself was formed.

Key Dates

- 1957 Russians launch *Sputnik I*, the first satellite, into space.

- 1960 First weather, navigation, communication satellites (U.S.).

- 1961 Soviet cosmonaut Yuri Gagarin is first person in space.

- 1966 *Luna IX* lands on Moon.

- 1969 Neil Armstrong is first person to walk on the Moon.

- 1970 USSR launches *Salyut I*, the world's first space station.

- 1981 *Columbia* space shuttle.

- 1983 *Pioneer 10* is first space probe to leave solar system.

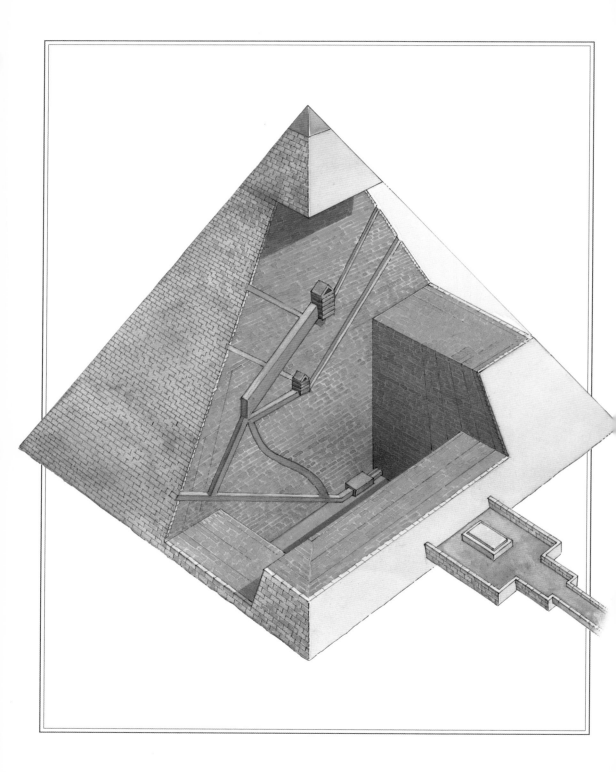

SCIENCE AND TECHNOLOGY

BY JOHN FARNDON

*Scientists have changed the face of the planet,
from the astronomers of ancient Greece to
today's genetic engineers. This section explores
how human beings have sought to master their
world through new technologies.*

The Quest for Knowledge

▲ PYTHAGORAS
Great thinkers such as Pythagoras of Samos (560–480B.C.) are essential to scientific progress. Without the input of people like Pythagoras, Albert Einstein and Louis Pasteur there would be no scientific advances at all.

▼ KEY DATES
This panel charts the progress of science through the ages, from the invention of the wheel to the creation of the World Wide Web.

SCIENCE AND TECHNOLOGY SEEM VERY modern ideas, but humans have been striving to understand the world and inventing machines to help them ever since they first walked on the Earth 30,000 years ago.

The earliest people lived simply by hunting animals and gathering fruit, and there was no need for science to be anything but basic. But as people settled down to farm, around 10,000 years ago, the first towns and cities were built in the Middle East, and life became much more complicated. At once science and technology began to develop apace to meet their varied needs. The Babylonians, for instance, created numbers and mathematics to keep track of goods and taxes. The Egyptians studied astronomy to help them make a calendar. And the astonishing achievements of Greek thinkers like Archimedes and the engineers of the Roman Empire laid the foundations of modern science and technology.

Their achievements were almost lost with the collapse of the Roman Empire, which plunged Europe

▼ OVERCOMING PROBLEMS
Most of the great explorers had used square-sailed ships, which were limited in their manoeuvrability. The development of new technology, such as this caravel with its triangular sails which could sail almost directly into the wind, opened up new possibilities.

EUROPE

c.3200B.C. The wheel is invented in Sumeria.

c.2500B.C. The ancient Egyptians devise a 365-day calendar.

c.1500B.C. The Babylonians develop numbers.

c.300B.C. Euclid writes *Elements of Geometry*.

c.250B.C. Archimedes establishes the mathematical rules for levers.

221–206B.C. The Great Wall of China is built.

A.D.130 Galen writes his medical books.

140 Ptolemy writes *Almagest*.

c.850 Al-Kharwarizmi introduces algebra.

1492 Christopher Columbus sails across the Atlantic.

1543 Copernicus shows that the Earth circles the Sun.

1610 Galileo spies Jupiter's moons through a telescope

1628 Harvey shows how the heart circulates blood.

1661 Boyle introduces the idea of chemical elements and compounds.

1686 Newton establishes his three laws of motion and his theory of gravity.

1698 Savery invents the first practical steam engine.

1735 Linnaeus groups plants into species and genera.

1752 Franklin shows that lightning is electricity.

1783 The Montgolfier brothers' balloon carries two men aloft.

1789 Lavoisier writes the first list of elements.

1804 Trevithick builds the first steam locomotive.

1808 Dalton proposes his atomic theory of chemical elements.

1830 Faraday and Henry find that electricity can be generated by magnetism.

1825 The first passenger railroad, from Stockton to Darlington, in England.

◄ FIRST CARS
The invention of the automobile has had a huge impact on transport throughout the world. The slow and noisy early cars have been replaced by quieter, safer and more economical models. Prices have come down, and the range of makes is now greater than ever. The car has, in fact, been so successful that many countries are now trying to limit car ownership because of the impact on the environment.

into the Dark Ages. But scientific thought continued to flourish in the Islamic east and farther east in China. And as eastern ideas gradually filtered into Europe in the 15th century, European scholars began to rediscover Greek and Roman science and make new discoveries of their own.

The next 100 years brought great shocks to established ideas. First, in 1492, Columbus sailed across the Atlantic to discover a whole new, undreamed-of land. Then, in 1543, Copernicus showed that the Earth, far from being the center of the Universe, was just one of the planets circling around the Sun.

Deep thinkers realized that ancient ideas could not necessarily be trusted: the only way to learn the truth was to look and learn for themselves. Observation and experiment became the basis of a new approach to science which has led to a huge range of discoveries such as Newton's laws of motion, Dalton's atoms, Darwin's theory of the evolution of life, and many more—right up to recent breakthroughs in the science of genetics. Trade and industry, meanwhile, have fueled a revolution in technology, which began with the steam-powered factory machines of the late 18th century and continues to gather pace with the latest computer technology of today.

▼ MIR
Despite a number of mishaps, the Soviet Mir spacecraft stayed up in space for over 13 years, between 1986 and 1999, and made more than 76,000 orbits of the Earth. It was a temporary home to many astronauts—and Russian Valery Polyakov spent a record 437 continuous days aboard.

1856 Mendel discovers the basic laws of heredity.

1858 Darwin and Wallace suggest the theory of evolution by natural selection.

1861 Pasteur shows that many diseases are caused by germs.

1862 Lenoir builds the first internal combustion engine car.

1862 Maxwell proposes that light is electromagnetic radiation.

1876 Alexander Graham Bell sends the first telephone message.

1888 Hertz discovers radio waves.

1895 Röntgen discovers X-rays.

1897 Thomson discovers electrons, and Becquerel discovers radioactivity.

1898 Marie and Pierre Curie discover the radioactive elements radium and polonium.

1900 Planck suggests quantum theory.

1903 Orville and Wilbur Wright make the first controlled, powered flight.

1905 & 1915 Einstein's special and general theories of relativity.

1908 Ford's Model T, the first mass-produced car.

1911 Rutherford shows that atom has a nucleus circled by electrons.

1923 Wegener suggests continental drift.

1927-9 Hubble realizes that there are other galaxies and that the universe is expanding.

1928 Fleming discovers penicillin.

1935 Carothers develops nylon.

1939 Hahn and Strassman split a uranium atom.

1945 The USAF drops atomic bombs on Nagasaki and Hiroshima.

1948 Shockley, Bardeen, and Brattain invent the transistor.

1953 Crick and Watson show that DNA, the gene molecule in living cells, has a double-spiral shape.

1957 Sputnik is the first spacecraft to orbit the Earth.

1969 Armstrong and Aldrin are the first men on the Moon.

1989 Berners-Lee creates the World Wide Web.

Inventing Mathematics

▲ CUNEIFORM
The first writing came hand in hand with the development of numbers. This is Sumerian cuneiform (wedge-form) writing.

PEOPLE PROBABLY LEARNED TO count using numbers many, many thousands of years ago. In fact, even small animals have a basic number sense. Birds usually know how many babies they have, for example. However, it was only when primitive hunters began to settle down and farm, around 10,000 years ago, that people started to think in terms of larger numbers. Then, for the first time, people needed to count things properly. They needed to count how many sheep they were selling at the market, how many bags of wheat they were buying, and so on. So the first farms and the first towns appeared in the Middle East, together with the first numbers, in the ancient civilizations of people such as the Sumerians.

People probably started by counting on fingers. This idea worked well, as it still does today, but fingers do not help you to remember how many. So people began to make the first number records by dropping stones, shells, or clay disks one by one into a bag. In Sumeria, about 6,000 years ago, someone had the bright idea of making scratch marks on a clay tablet—one mark for each thing they were counting. Soon the Babylonians learned to use different-shaped marks for larger numbers. This system is still the basis of our modern number system—except that instead of using different marks for larger numbers, we simply use a different symbol for each number up to nine, and then put the symbols in different positions for the larger numbers.

The early civilizations also developed mathematical skills. First, there was arithmetic. This is the art of working things out by numbers —by addition, subtraction, multiplication, and division. Arithmetic is the oldest of all the mathematical skills. We know that the Babylonians and Sumerians were skilled in arithmetic at

◀ SUMERIAN ACCOUNTANTS
The accountants of the ancient civilization of Sumeria may have written down the first numbers over 6,000 years ago. To keep track of tax accounts and payments, they scratched marks on soft clay tablets. The tablets hardened to make a permanent record.

THE GREAT GEOMETERS
The first great masters of geometry were the ancient Greeks, such as Pythagoras, Eudoxus, and, in particular, Euclid, who lived between about 330 and 275B.C. Geometry is actually a Greek word meaning "earth measurement." Euclid's book *Elements* was such a brilliantly thorough study of geometry that it became the framework for geometry for thousands of years. Even today, mathematicians still refer to all the geometry of flat surfaces—lines, points, shapes, and solids—as Euclidean geometry.

▶ EARLY GEOMETRY
Most basic geometry is about lines and the angles between them—and how they make up two kinds of shape, or figure: circles and polygons. The Greek geometers used to analyze these shapes in particular ways. They might try to calculate the area of a triangle, for instance, or work out the relationship between particular angles.

Right-angled triangle

A B C

◀ PYTHAGORAS
Pythagoras of Samos (560–480B.C.) was one of the first great mathematicians. He is a rather mysterious figure, who believed that numbers were the perfect basis of life. He is most famous for his theory about right-angled triangles. His theory showed that if you square the two sides next to the right angle, the two add up to the third side squared. (Squaring simply means multiplying a number by itself.) This was expressed by Pythagoras in the following, famous, formula;

$$A{\times}A + B{\times}B = C{\times}C$$
or
$$A^2 + B^2 = C^2$$

least 5,000 years ago. Babylonian schoolchildren learned how to multiply and divide, and they used arithmetical tables to help with complex sums.

Arithmetic was developed to keep the accounts that were the key to power in the ancient civilizations. Accounts and arithmetic were vital. For example, they helped to work out how much tax people owed. Many of those skilled in arithmetic were highly honored. In fact, they were often feared, for when mathematicians first learned to make quick mathematic calculations it seemed like magic. The arithmetic processes developed in ancient China seemed so tricky and clever that they were still being used by Chinese "mind-readers" in the variety shows of Europe in the early 20th century.

Another skill was geometry, which is the mathematics of shapes. It was probably first invented to help people work out the area of their land. Geometry was developed by the ancient Egyptians over 4,000 years ago to help them build perfect pyramids.

▼ THE PERFECT PYRAMID

The Great Pyramids of ancient Egypt still astonish us with their geometric precision, and an amazing discovery showed us just how the Egyptians did it. In 1858, while vacationing in Egypt, the Scottish historian Alexander Rhind bought an ancient papyrus written by an Egyptian scribe named Ahmes around 1650B.C.. The Rhind Papyrus showed that the ancient Egyptians knew a great deal about the geometry of triangles, which is vital in building the pyramids. For example, they knew how to work out the height of a pyramid from the length of its shadow on the ground.

◀ TRIANGULAR FRIEZE

The ancient Greeks were fascinated by perfect geometric shapes, which is reflected in their elegant temples. These graceful buildings were among the first to be built using geometric rules, with beautifully proportioned rectangles crowned by triangular friezes. At this time, geometry not only was used in the building of temples, it was the basis for practical engineering too. In fact, much of our knowledge of geometry is based on the theories of ancient Greeks.

Key Dates

- 1500B.C. Babylonians develop a number system.

- 530B.C. Pythagoras devises his theory about right-angled triangles.

- 300B.C. Euclid writes his *Elements of Geometry*, the most influential mathematics book ever written.

- 300B.C. The Hindus develop their own number system.

- 220B.C. Archimedes finds a way of measuring the volume of spheres.

- 200B.C. Appolonius analyzes slices across cones—parabolas and ellipses.

- A.D.662 Hindu number system develops into decimal system we now use.

Star Gazing

A STRONOMY DATES BACK TO the earliest days of humankind, when prehistoric hunters gazed up at the sky to work out which night might give them a full moon for hunting. When people began to settle down to farm, 10,000 years ago, astronomy helped farmers to know when seasons would come and go. Indeed, astronomy played such a vital role in early civilizations that astronomers were often high priests. Many ancient monuments have strong links with astronomy. The standing stones in Stonehenge in England, for instance, are aligned with the rising sun on the solstices, the longest and shortest days of the year. Shafts in Egypt's Great Pyramids point at the star group called Orion.

▲ PTOLEMY
Ptolemy was the great Alexandrian astronomer whose books were the definitive guide to astronomy for 1,500 years.

By the time the ancient Greek astronomer Hipparchus of Rhodes (170–127B.C.) began to study the sky, astronomy was already an ancient art. Hipparchus was a skilled observer, but much of his work was based on old Babylonian records rescued from the ruins of the Persian Empire by Alexander the Great. Even so, his achievement was stupendous. He was the first great astronomer, and he laid the foundations for astronomy for almost 2,000 years.

Excited by spotting a new star in 134B.C., Hipparchus began to make a catalog of the 850 stars whose positions were then known. This catalog, adapted by Ptolemy, was still being used in the 16th century. Hipparchus also compared stars by giving each one a "Magnitude" from one to six, depending on how bright it looked. The

▲ PTOLEMY'S MAP
Early European maps were based on a work called Geography, *by the astronomer Ptolemy. It was because Ptolemy underestimated the size of the world that Columbus set out for Asia, sailing west across the Atlantic. This, then, inspired his discovery of the Americas.*

THE CONSTELLATIONS

To help find their way around the night sky, astronomers in ancient Babylon and Egypt looked for patterns of stars, or constellations. They named each star pattern after a mythical figure. On star maps, you often see these figures drawn over the stars, as if the stars were a giant "painting by numbers" book.

There is no real link between the stars in a constellation; they simply look close together. But the system is so effective that astronomers still use it, though they have added a few extra constellations. Each ancient civilization had its own names for constellations, and the names we use today come from Greek myths. The names are written, not in Greek, but in their Roman (Latin) equivalent, such as Cygnus (the Swan) and Ursa Major (the Great Bear).

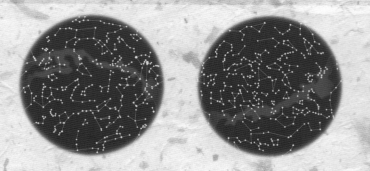

▲ NORTHERN HEMISPHERE
These are some of the 88 constellations, or star groups, that are recognized by astronomers today. There are many other stars in the sky; the constellations simply make groups of the brightest stars.

▲ SOUTHERN HEMISPHERE
A different set of constellations is visible from the Southern Hemisphere (half of the world). Indeed, many, such as Crux (the Southern Cross), would have been completely unknown to ancient Greeks.

▼ CLAY TABLETS
Many of the earliest astronomical records were kept by the Babylonians, who kept records on clay tablets like this one.

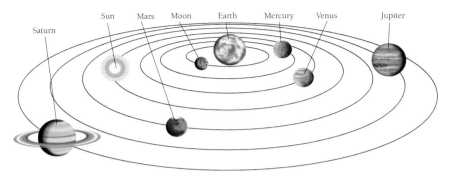

brightest star is Sirius (the Dog Star), which he called a First-Magnitude star; the faintest star was called a Sixth-Magnitude star. The idea of star magnitude is very important to astronomers even today, although the scale has been refined.

Hipparchus measured things in the sky very exactly, considering that he had only his own eyes to guide him. He made some amazingly precise measurements of the movements of the heavens. He calculated the length of a year, for instance, to within less than seven minutes. He also discovered that the relative positions of the stars on the equinoxes (March 21 and September 23) slowly shift around, and worked out that they take 26,000 years to return to the same place.

Sadly, hardly any of Hipparchus' work survives as he

▲ THE WANDERERS
Early astronomers such as Ptolemy knew that the world was round, but they believed that the Earth was the center of the Universe and everything revolved around it. They knew of only five planets—Mercury, Venus, Mars, Jupiter, and Saturn.

The early astronomers had no telescopes, so the planets looked just like stars, only they were brighter. What makes planets different is that the position of the stars in the night sky is fixed and they move only as the Earth turns. The planets, however, wander through the sky like the Sun and the Moon. This is why they are called planets, which is the Greek word for "wanderers."

wrote it. We know of it because it was developed by the astronomer Ptolemy (A.D.90–170), who wrote four books summarizing Greek astronomical ideas in the 2nd century A.D., including *Almagest* (Arabic for "The Greatest"). These books became the cornerstone of Western and Arab astronomy until the 16th century.

◀ EGYPTIAN ASTRONOMY
Here you can see an Egyptian drawing of the goddess Nut holding up the sky. The ancient Egyptians relied on astronomy to give them times and dates. They performed some religious ceremonies, for instance, at certain times during the night when the constellations reached a particular place in the sky.

The most important date was the time when Sirius, the brightest star in the sky, appeared after being hidden behind the Sun for many months. This date was important as it coincided with the annual floods of the river Nile, which made the Egyptian soils fertile.

Key Dates

- 2800B.C. The ancient Egyptian astronomer Imhotep aligns the first great pyramid perfectly with the Sun.

- 2500B.C. The ancient Egyptians devise a 365-day calendar.

- 550B.C. Greek astronomer Anaximander suggests that the Earth is a globe hanging in space.

- c.200B.C. Eratosthenes calculates the size of the Earth.

- 134B.C. Hipparchus catalogs 850 stars and devises a magnitude scale for stars.

- A.D.140 In *Almagest* Ptolemy describes the motions of the planets and catalogs stars and planets.

The First Scientist

▲ ARCHIMEDES
The great scientist Archimedes was killed when the Romans invaded Syracuse. Some say he was then working on a theory.

ARCHIMEDES WAS THE WORLD'S first great scientist. Of course, others had studied scientific subjects before, but Archimedes was the first to think about problems in the scientific way that we now take for granted. He came up with abstract theories that could be proved or disproved by practical experiments and by mathematical calculations.

Archimedes lived in Syracuse in Sicily, which was a Greek colony at the time. He was born there around 285B.C., and spent most of his life in the city studying geometry and inventing all kinds of fantastic machines. These included the famous Archimedes' screw (a device for pumping water) and many war machines which he built for the defense of Syracuse. Archimedes was regarded with awe in his lifetime, and there are many stories about him.

The most famous is about a task that the king of Syracuse once set him. The king wanted to know if his crown was pure gold—or if the crafty goldsmith had mixed in some cheaper metal, as he suspected. Archimedes was thinking about

this tricky problem in his bath one day when suddenly he noticed how the water level rose the deeper he sank into the bath. The story goes that he leaped out of his bath and ran naked through the streets to the king, shouting at the top of his voice "Eureka! Eureka!," which means "I've got it! I've got it!" Later, he showed the king his idea. First, he immersed in water a piece of gold that weighed the same as the crown. Then he immersed the crown itself and discovered that the water level was different. Archimedes then concluded that the

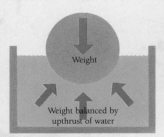

◄ ARCHIMEDES' SCREW
Archimedes' screw is a very simple but effective pump. Inside a tube is a spiral, which scoops up the water as someone turns the handle at the top. Such pumps are still in use 2,000 years later in some places in the Middle East. They lift water from irrigation canals and rivers onto dry fields.

FLOATING AND SINKING
One of Archimedes' great breakthroughs was the discovery that an object weighs less in water than in air—which is why you can lift a quite heavy person when in a swimming pool. The reason for this "buoyancy" is the natural upward push, or upthrust, of the water.

When an object is immersed in water, its weight pushes down. But the water, as Archimedes realized, pushes back up with a force equal to the weight of water the object pushes out of the way. So the object sinks until its weight is exactly equal to the upthrust of the water, at which point it floats. So objects that weigh less than the water displaced will float, and those that weigh more will sink.

Weight

Weight balanced by
upthrust of water

▲ BUOYANCY
If you drop a barrel weighing 100g into water, it will sink until it displaces (pushes out of the way) a volume of water weighing 100g. It floats at this point because the upthrust created by pushing 100g of water out of the way exactly balances with the weight of the barrel.

▲ WHY SHIPS FLOAT
When the first iron ships were made in the 19th century, many people were convinced they would sink, because iron is too heavy to float. They were right; iron is too heavy to float. But iron and steel ships float because their hulls are full of air, and so they can safely sink until enough water is displaced to match the weight of the iron in the hull.

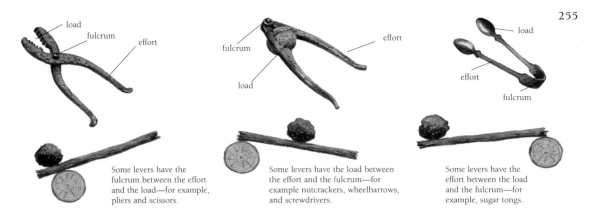

Some levers have the fulcrum between the effort and the load—for example, pliers and scissors.

Some levers have the load between the effort and the fulcrum—for example nutcrackers, wheelbarrows, and screwdrivers.

Some levers have the effort between the load and the fulcrum—for example, sugar tongs.

crown was not pure gold, because the difference in water levels showed that the crown had a different volume from the gold, although they were the same weight. This proved that it must have included a different metal. The goldsmith was executed.

Whether this story is true or not, it is typical of Archimedes' amazingly neat and elegant scientific solutions to awkward questions. He also tried to approach problems mathematically. He was probably not the first to realize that if you put a weight on each end of a seesaw, the lighter weight must be farther away if the two weights are to balance. Archimedes, though, showed that the ratio of the weights goes down in exact mathematical proportion to the distance they must be from the pivot of the seesaw—and he proved this also mathematically. In the same way, he had the brilliant insight that every object has a center of gravity—a

▲ LEVERS AND FORCES
Archimedes' brilliant insight was to analyze mathematically an everyday tool such as a lever. If a lever, such as a plank of wood, pivots around one point, called the fulcrum, the effort you apply on one side of the fulcrum can move a load on the other side. What Archimedes found was that the load you could move with a certain amount of effort depended exactly on the relative distance of the effort and load from the fulcrum. Working out load, force, distance and so on mathematically is now one of the cornerstones of science.

single point from which all its weight seems to hang— and he proved it mathematically.

Sadly, much of Archimedes' work has been lost. Yet his approach to science—using mathematics to understand the physical world—is the basis of the most advanced science today. Almost 1,900 years after Archimedes' death, the great Italian scientist Galileo said, "Without Archimedes I could have achieved nothing."

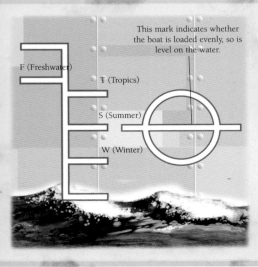

This mark indicates whether the boat is loaded evenly, so is level on the water.

F (Freshwater)

T (Tropics)

S (Summer)

W (Winter)

◀ PLIMSOLL MARK
The density of water (how tightly together its particles are packed) changes depending on its temperature and on whether it is fresh (non-salty) or sea water. Ships float higher in cold or salty water because it is more dense and creates more upthrust.

Some ships are marked with a set of lines, called a Plimsoll mark, to show the safe levels to which cargo can be loaded on board —in the tropics, in freshwater, in summer, and in winter.

Key Dates

- c.450 B.C. Empedocles suggests that all substances are made from four elements: earth, air, fire, and water.

- c.335 B.C. Theophrastus writes the first scientific book on plants.

- c.350 B.C. Aristotle lays down rules for science.

- 250 B.C. Archimedes discovers principles of buoyancy and forms mathematical rules for levers.

- c.A.D.70 Hero of Alexander invents a pump, a fountain, and a steam turbine.

- c.A.D.100 Chinese thinker Zhang Heng makes a seismoscope to record earthquakes.

Roman Engineers

▲ ROMAN BUILDINGS
This temple is an excellent example of Roman architecture. To create buildings such as this, the Roman's would use bricks to form a strong and long-lasting structure.

ANCIENT ROME HAD few of the great thinkers that made ancient Greece so remarkable. However, it had many clever, practical men, and the Romans were the greatest engineers and builders of the ancient world. Their bridges, roads, and aqueducts are marvels of ingenious, efficient large-scale construction, and many of them are still standing today, over 2,000 years later. Some, such as the eight aqueducts that supply Rome with water, are still in use, working as well as they ever did. It is hard to imagine many modern structures lasting so long.

Much of the Romans' engineering was connected with their military conquests, and engineers traveled with the armies to build roads and bridges. A sound knowledge of engineering was an essential skill for an officer, and soldiers provided much of the labor for the major construction works. Whenever the Romans conquered a new territory, one of the army's first tasks was to lay out cities to a standard plan, build roads to supply the army, and lay on a clean water supply.

The Romans inherited some of their construction techniques from the Greeks and the Etruscans. They added to the Greek knowledge and pushed Greek techniques to new levels, adding a number of features of their own. One of the keys to Roman engineering was the arch. The arch is a simple but clever way of making strong bridges. A flat piece of stone across two posts can take only so much weight before snapping. But in an arch the stones are pushed harder together when weight is placed on them, so the arch actually becomes stronger.

Hot air circulates under the floor and around the walls.

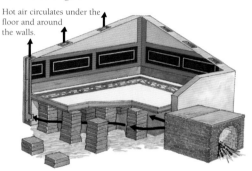

▲ UNDERFLOOR HEATING
We tend to think of central heating as a modern invention, but many Roman villas (houses) had a space under the floor called a hypocaust. Warm air from the hot bricks of a furnace circulated through this space, keeping the floor warm and the house very cozy.

ROMAN ROADS

None of the Romans' engineering achievements has had more impact than their road system. The Romans began building roads in 334B.C., and by the time their empire was at its peak they had laid down more than 53,000 miles of roads, including the famous Appian Way running 410 miles through Italy.

During this time most roads were simple, rough dirt tracks, which were impassable with mud in winter. By contrast, the Romans laid smooth, hard-surfaced roads which cut as straight as an arrow across marshes, lakes, gorges, and hills. Using these roads, their soldiers could move around the empire with astonishing speed.

▲ ROMAN ROUTES
Even today, roads in many parts of the world quickly become impassable in bad weather. The Romans, however, built their roads to be used in all seasons. They built strong stone bridges high above rivers, and raised roads, on embankments called aggers, above ground that was liable to flooding. They even made grooves in the road to guide trucks.

Another feature of Roman engineering was cement. The Romans made bricks on an unprecedented scale, and Roman bridges and buildings are the first great brick structures. At first, the structures were mortared together with a mixture of sand, lime, and water. In the 2nd century B.C. a new ingredient was added: volcanic sand found near the modern town of Pozzuoli in Italy. This ingredient, now called pozzolana, turned mortar into an incredibly tough cement which hardens even underwater. Pozzolanic mortars were so strong and cheap that the Romans began to build with cement only and dispense with the bricks. Eventually, they added stones to make concrete.

With the arch and pozzolanic cement, the Romans could build bridges and aqueducts on a massive scale, such as the famous Pont du Gard, near Nîmes in France, and the 2,560-foot-long Segovia aqueduct in Spain. The fact that these bridges have survived almost 2,000 years testifies to both their strength and their durability.

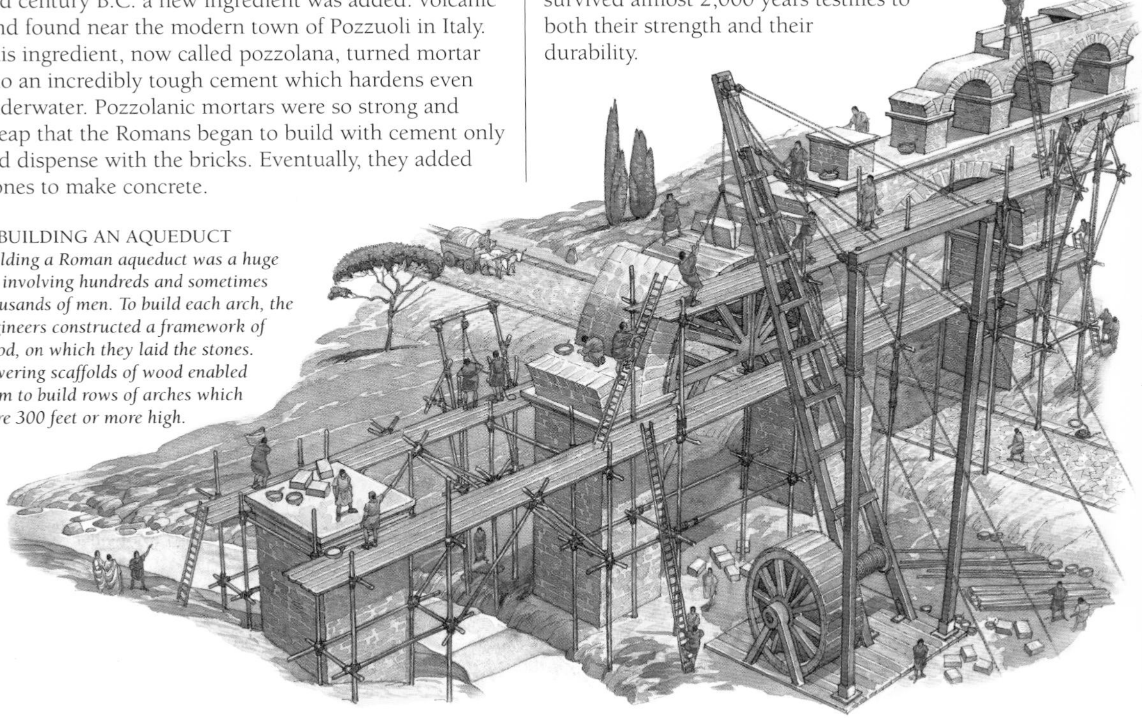

▶ BUILDING AN AQUEDUCT
Building a Roman aqueduct was a huge job involving hundreds and sometimes thousands of men. To build each arch, the engineers constructed a framework of wood, on which they laid the stones. Towering scaffolds of wood enabled them to build rows of arches which were 300 feet or more high.

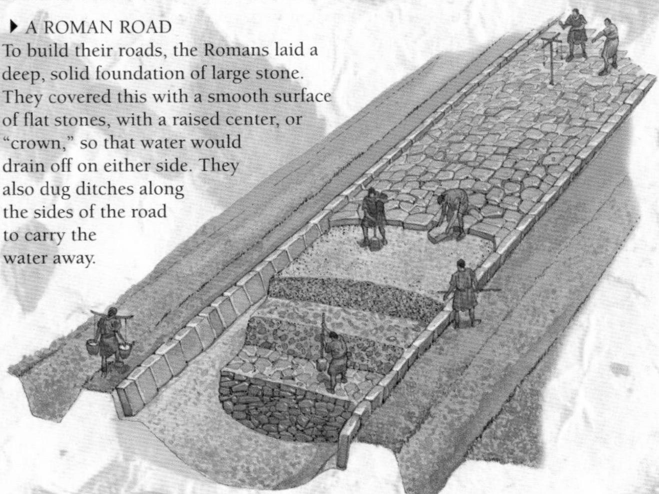

▶ A ROMAN ROAD
To build their roads, the Romans laid a deep, solid foundation of large stone. They covered this with a smooth surface of flat stones, with a raised center, or "crown," so that water would drain off on either side. They also dug ditches along the sides of the road to carry the water away.

Key Dates

- c.3200B.C. The wheel is invented in Sumeria.

- 2800B.C. The ancient Egyptians build the first pyramid.

- 1470B.C. Pharaoh Sesostris builds first Suez Canal, linking the Nile River to the Red Sea.

- 480B.C. Xerxes of Persia builds a bridge of boats across the Hellespont.

- 312B.C. The Appian Way, the first great Roman road, is built.

- 221–206B.C. The Great Wall of China is built.

- c.A.D.200 By this time the Romans have built over 53,000 miles of roads.

Where and When

▲ SHIP'S COMPASS
The compasses that ships use utilize a suspended, magnetized needle that aligns itself in a north-south direction with the Earth's magnetic field.

I N THE MIDDLE AGES THE Europeans knew little of the world. Maps were inaccurate and showed Asia, to the east, only vaguely. To the south, Africa faded off into a mystery land filled with monsters and dangerous peoples. To the west there was nothing at all. It was still not absolutely certain that the world was round. Perhaps the world ended in empty space? Even charts of Europe itself were so inaccurate and navigation methods so unreliable that ships stayed in sight of land to be sure of finding their way.

Then, in the 14th century, the great Mongol Empire in Asia collapsed. The roads to China and the East, along which silks and spices were brought, were cut off. So bold European mariners set out westward to find their way to the East by sea. From 1400, ship after ship sailed from Europe. At first they ventured south around the unknown west of Africa in small ships called caravels. Many of these mariners were Portuguese, sent out by Prince Henry "the Navigator" (1394–1460) from his base at Sagres. They pushed on, cape by cape, until Bartolomeu Dias rounded Africa's southern tip in 1488. Nine years later, Vasco da Gama sailed right around to India. In the

▼ THE CARAVEL
Up until the 15th century, most European ships were square-rigged, which meant that they could sail only in much the same direction as the wind. Most of the great explorers, including Columbus, used a small revolutionary ship called a caravel, which had triangular "lateen" sails adopted from Arab dhows. With these sails, a caravel could sail almost directly into the wind.

THE SEARCH FOR LONGITUDE

Finding longitude was a problem in navigation for a long time. In theory you can work it out from the Sun's position in the sky, comparing this to its position at the same time at a longitude you know. However, you must know the exact time. Huygens had made an accurate pendulum clock in the 1670s, but it was too sensitive to keep good time aboard a tossing ship. The solution was the chronometer, a very accurate, stormproof clock made in the 1720s by John Harrison (1693–1776). It used balance springs, rather than a pendulum, to keep time.

◀ HUYGENS'S CLOCK
The pendulum clock, invented by Christiaan Huygens in the 1670s, was the world's first accurate timepiece.

◀ HARRISON'S CHRONOMETER
It took John Harrison decades to persuade the authorities that his chronometer was indeed the solution to the longitude problem. This is his second version.

▲ LATITUDE
Latitude says how far north or south you are in degrees. Lines of latitude are called parallels because they form rings around the Earth parallel to the Equator. You can work out latitude from the Sun's height in the sky at noon. The higher it is, the nearer the Equator you are.

▲ LONGITUDE
Longitude says how far east or west you are in degrees. Lines of longitude, or meridians, run from pole to pole, dividing the world like orange segments. You can work out your longitude from the time it is when the Sun is at its highest.

meantime, in 1492, Christopher Columbus took a great gamble and set out west across the open Atlantic, hoping to reach China. Instead, he found the New World of the Americas waiting to be explored. Finally, in 1522, fewer than 90 years after the voyages of discovery had begun, Ferdinand Magellan's ship *Victoria* sailed all the way around the world. Now there could be no doubt: the world is round.

Maps improved vastly as each voyage brought new knowledge, and map "projections" were devised to show the round world on flat paper and parchment. Yet these early projections helped sailors little, since a straight course at sea was an elaborate line on the map. In 1552 the Dutch mapmaker Gerhardus Mercator invented a new projection. It treated the map of the world as if it were projected onto a cylinder, which could then be rolled out and laid flat. Although Mercator's projection made countries near the poles look far too big, it enabled sailors to plot a straight course by compass simply by drawing a straight line on the map.

At the same time, navigation at sea made startling progress. Early sailors had steered entirely by the stars—they had only a vague idea where they were during the day, and no idea at all if the sky clouded over. From the 12th century on, European sailors used a magnetic needle to find north at all times. This however, gave them only a direction to steer; it did not tell them where they were. From the 14th century, sailors used an astrolabe to get an idea of their latitude—how far north or south of the Equator—by measuring the height of a star or the Sun at noon. The great breakthrough came with the invention of the cross-staff in the 16th century. Sailors used it to measure the angle between the horizon and the Pole Star and so work out their latitude precisely. Now the problem was longitude—how far east or west they were. For centuries, the only way to work out a ship's longitude was to guess how far it had come by "dead reckoning." This involved trailing a knotted rope in the water to keep a constant track of the ship's speed. However, this was not very accurate, so the problem of longitude was to tax some of the greatest minds over the next few centuries.

▶ GREENWICH
The great observatory at Greenwich, London, was set up in 1675. Its brief from King Charles II was to map the movements of the heavens so accurately that the longitude problem could be solved. The problem was not solved here, but the observatory sits on the Prime Meridian, the first line of longitude.

▲ HOW FAR NORTH?
The mirror sextant was developed in the mid-1700s from the cross-staff to measure latitude accurately. It became the main navigation aid for sailors until the days of electronic technology after World War II. It has one mirror which you point at the horizon and another mirror which you adjust until the Sun (or a star) is reflected in it at exactly the same height as the horizon. The degree of adjustment you need to make to the second mirror gives the latitude. The sextant gets its name from its shape, which is one-sixth of a circle.

Key Dates

- 1488 Bartolomeu Dias sails around the southern tip of Africa.

- 1492 Christopher Columbus sails across the Atlantic.

- 1497 Vasco da Gama sails around Africa to India.

- 1497 John Cabot discovers Canada while trying to find a way to Asia.

- 1501 Amerigo Vespucci realizes that South America is a whole new continent.

- 1513 Vasco de Balboa of Spain sails on the Pacific Ocean.

- 1519 Ferdinand Magellan leads the first voyage around the world.

The Great Anatomists

Nothing is closer to us than the human body, yet it has taken as long to explore it as it has to explore the Earth. For thousands of years medicine was based as much on superstition as on research. The first

doctor that we know about was Imhotep, who lived in ancient Egypt 4,600 years ago. People traveled from far and wide to be treated by him, and after his death he was declared to be a god. The greatest physician of the ancient world was the Roman Galen, born around

▲ LEONARDO DA VINCI
Da Vinci (1452–1519) is best known for his few master paintings, such as the Mona Lisa *and the* Last Supper. *His curiosity led him to study everything from human anatomy to astronomy with the same remarkable insight.*

▼ DA VINCI'S ANATOMICAL DRAWINGS
To draw human figures exactly, many artists in the Renaissance began to study human anatomy for themselves. Some, such as Da Vinci, made their own dissections, and their knowledge of the human body often outstripped that of physicians.

THE POWER OF THE MICROSCOPE

Until the microscope was invented, in around 1590, people never suspected that many things were far too small for the eye to see. Soon, using a simple microscope made with a drop of water, the Dutch scientist Anton van Leeuwenhoek found that the world is full of tiny microorganisms such as bacteria.

In the 1660s the Italian physician Marcello Malpighi (1628–1694) began to use a microscope to study the human body. He made many discoveries of tiny structures such as the tastebuds on the tongue. He did not, however, restrict himself to the study of humans, but he studied plants and animals in great detail as well.

▼ MICROSCOPES
Early microscopes magnified things many times by combining two lenses. One lens, called the objective lens, bends light rays apart to create an enlarged image; but this image is still very small. A second lens, called the eyepiece lens, acts like a magnifying glass to make this tiny image visible.

A.D.130. Like his contemporaries, Galen learned about the body by studying ancient manuscripts, but he also took a scientific approach and cut up animals to see how their bodies worked. He recorded his findings in many books describing the skeleton, the muscles, and the nerves. Respect for Galen was so great that for more than 1,000 years, doctors would consult Galen's books rather than look at a body.

During the Renaissance in Italy in the 15th and 16th centuries, physicians began to consider that it might be better to look at real bodies, rather than at Galen's texts. They retrieved dead bodies from graveyards and cut them up to see exactly how they were put together. This is called dissection. The focus of this revolution was the University of Padua, where a brilliant German, Andreas Vesalius (1514–1564), was professor of surgery and anatomy. (Anatomy is the study of the way the human body is put together.) When dissection had been done in the past, it was usually done for the physicians by a butcher. Vesalius, though, began dissecting corpses himself, and he asked the Flemish artist Jan van Calcar to draw very accurately what he found. In 1543, Vesalius published his findings in a textbook of anatomy called *De Humani Corporis Fabrica* ("On the Structure of the Human Body"), which became the most influential medical book ever written.

Inspired by Vesalius's work, other physicians began to make their own dissections. Piece by piece, a very detailed picture of human anatomy began to build up. In the 1550s, for instance, Vesalius's colleague Gabriel Fallopio (1523–1562) discovered the tubes that link a

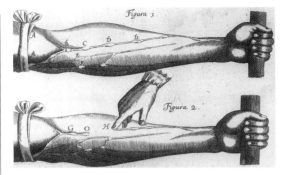

▲ BLOOD CIRCULATION
The English physician William Harvey (1578–1657) was one of the many great scientists who studied at the University of Padua in the 1500s and 1600s. Harvey's great insight was to realize that blood flows out from the heart through arteries and back through veins, making a complete circulation of the blood.

female's ovaries to the uterus. These are now known as the Fallopian tubes. He also identified various other parts of the female reproductive system. Another colleague, Matteo Corti, discovered minute structures in the inner ear.

Gradually, physicians began also to learn about physiology (the science of the workings of the body). In 1590, for example, Santorio Sanctorius showed how to measure pulse and body temperature. In 1628 William Harvey showed that the heart is a pump and that blood circulates round and round the body. In this way the foundations for our current knowledge of the human body were built bit by bit.

▶ MALPHIGI
Marcello Malpighi was the first person to apply the power of the newly invented microscope to the human body. He made the first microscopic studies of human tissues, discovering the tiny structures present in the body. In 1661 Malpighi discovered capillaries, the minute blood vessels that were the missing link in Harvey's blood circulation.

Key Dates

- c.480B.C. Hippocrates, one of the first great doctors, practices in Greece.

- c.A.D.130 Galen writes his medical treatises.

- 1543 Vesalius publishes his book *De Humani Corporis Fabrica*.

- 1550 Gabriel Fallopius studies the human body in minute detail.

- 1590 Santorio Sanctorius creates science of physiology and shows how to measure pulse and temperature.

- 1628 William Harvey shows how the heart circulates blood.

- 1661 Marcello Malpighi sees tiny blood vessels called capillaries under a microscope.

Sun and Earth

▲ COPERNICUS
The astronomer Copernicus spent most of his life studying old astronomical texts at Frauenberg Cathedral in Germany. His radical theories shook the world.

UNTIL THE 16TH century, nearly everyone was certain that the Earth was at the center of the Universe and that the Moon, the Sun, the planets, and the stars revolved around it. Then a Polish astronomer, Nicolaus Copernicus, began to think there was something strange about the path of the planets through the sky.

Most of the time, the planets follow a smooth, curved path, but every now and then some of them perform a small backward loop through the sky. Ancient astronomers, including the brilliant Ptolemy, had explained this by suggesting that everything in the Universe worked by an ingenious system of epicycles, or wheels within wheels. This elaborate system did not quite ring true with Copernicus. He noted, for example, that the stars seem sometimes nearer and sometimes farther away. "Why should this be?" he asked.

Then Copernicus had a simple but brilliant idea. What if the Earth was not the fixed center of the Universe but was one of the planets revolving around

▲ ORRERY
Once people accepted the idea that the Earth was just one of the planets circling the Sun, they became fascinated by how this system worked. In 1710 a Scottish clockmaker named George Graham built a clockwork model to show how the planets moved. He built the model for his patron, the 4th Earl of Orrery. Orreries, as they came to be known, were soon very popular.

the Sun? Then the strange movement of the planets and the varying distance of the stars would be explained very simply. He wrote his ideas in a book called *De Revolutionibus Orbium Coelestium* ("On the Revolutions of the Heavenly Spheres"), which was published just after he died in 1543.

GALILEO'S TELESCOPE

Galileo did not invent the telescope, but he was the first person to make one for looking at the night sky. He encountered an extraordinary amount of prejudice and skepticism. One professor said that he refused to waste his time looking through this silly device "to see what no one but Galileo has seen. Besides, it gives me a headache." "It's all a trick!" said others.

When an excited Galileo tried to show the professors at Bologna the four moons of Jupiter which he had seen through his telescope, all the "most excellent men and noble doctors" insisted that "the instrument lies!" Father Clavius, the professor of mathematics, laughed and said he would show them the moons of Jupiter, too, if he had time to paint them onto the lens.

▲ GALILEO
Galileo Galilei (1564–1642) was one of the greatest scientists of all time. He made many important scientific discoveries, but none that caused as much controversy as his support for Copernicus's ideas.

▶ POWERFUL TELESCOPES
In 1609 Galileo heard of the invention of the telescope in the Netherlands. He quickly learned how to make his own telescope. His telescopes were increasingly powerful, magnifying up to 20 times.

No single idea in history has changed our view of the Universe, and our place in it, quite so much. At first, only a few astronomers paid much attention to Copernicus's new theory. After all, people had been publishing crazy ideas for centuries. Then early in the 17th century, the famous Italian scientist Galileo began to look at the night sky with a new device called a telescope. What Galileo saw through his telescope proved that Copernicus's ideas were not just an interesting theory—they were really true.

Galileo saw two things that confirmed this view for him. The first was the fact that he could see four moons circling Jupiter—the first proof that the Earth is not at the center of things. The second was the fact that he could see that Venus has phases like our Moon. (Phases are the way the Moon seems to change shape as we see its bright sunlit side from a different angle.) The nature of Venus's phases showed that it must be moving around the Sun, not the Earth.

Catholic teaching at that time was based on the idea that the Earth was the fixed center of the Universe. When Galileo published his findings in a book called *The Starry Messenger* in 1513, he was declared a heretic by the cardinals in Rome. When threatened with torture, Galileo was forced to deny that the Earth moves. Legend says that he muttered *"Eppur si muove"* ("Yet it does move") later. The Catholic Church did not retract its sentence on Galileo until October 13, 1992.

▼ COPERNICUS'S MAP OF THE HEAVENS
Copernicus's map showed that the Earth was not at the center of the Universe and gave us the "heliocentric," or Sun-centered, Universe. Now we know, of course, that not even the Sun is the center of the Universe. It is just one of many billions of stars.

◄ JUPITER'S MOONS
In January 1610, Galileo was looking at the planet Jupiter through his telescope when he saw what could only be four tiny moons circling it. Up until then, most people thought everything in the Universe circled the Earth. Yet here were four moons circling just one of the planets in the solar system. Jupiter is now known to have 16 moons. The four that Galileo saw are called Galilean moons.

Key Dates

- 300B.C. Greek astronomer Aristarchus suggests that the Earth revolves around the Sun.

- 1543 Copernicus suggests that the Earth circles the Sun.

- 1550 Johann Kepler recognizes that the planets follow elliptical, not circular, paths.

- 1610 With his telescope Galileo sees mountains on the Moon and four moons orbiting the planet Jupiter.

- 1665 Isaac Newton uses the theory of gravity to explain how the planets move.

- 1781 William Herschel discovers the planet Uranus.

Force and Motion

▲ ISAAC NEWTON
Isaac Newton (1642–1727) showed the link between force and motion in his three laws of motion. He realized that a force he called gravity makes things fall and keeps the planets orbiting the Sun.

THE 17TH CENTURY WAS THE first real age of science, when brilliant men such as Galileo, Huygens, Boyle, Newton, Liebnitz, and Leeuwenhoek made many important discoveries. Of all their achievements, however, perhaps none was as important as the understanding of forces and motion.

The philosophers of ancient Greece had known a great deal about "statics"—things that are not moving. When it came to movement, or "dynamics," however, they were often baffled. They could see, for instance, that a plow moves because the ox pulls it and that an arrow flies because of the force of the bow. But how, they wondered, did an arrow keep on flying through the air after it left the bow—if there was nothing to pull it along? The Greek philosopher Aristotle made his commonsense assertion that you must have a force to keep something moving—just as your bike will slow to a halt if you stop pedaling.

Yet common sense can be wrong, and it took the genius of Galileo and Newton to realize it. After a series

▼ THE TOWER OF PISA
Galileo was the first to appreciate that gravity accelerates any falling object downward by exactly the same amount. In other words, things will fall at the same speed no matter how heavy they are. Legend has it that he demonstrated this by dropping two objects of different weights from the Leaning Tower of Pisa in Italy. The two objects would have hit the ground at the same time.

NEWTON AND GRAVITY
No one knew why planets circle around the Sun or why things fall to the ground until one day around 1665, when Newton was thinking in an orchard. As an apple fell to the ground, Newton wondered if the apple were not just falling but actually being pulled to the Earth by an invisible force. From this simple but brilliant idea, Newton developed his theory of gravity, a universal force that tries to pull all matter to together. Without gravity, the whole Universe would disintegrate.

Newton showed that the force of gravity is the same everywhere, and that the pull between two things depends on their mass (the amount of matter in them) and the square of the distance between them.

PHILOSOPHIÆ
NATURALIS
PRINCIPIA
MATHEMATICA

Autore J.S. NEWTON, Trin. Coll. Cantab. Soc. Mathese Professore Lucasiano, & Societatis Regalis Sodali.

IMPRIMATUR
S. PEPYS, Reg. Soc. PRÆSES.
Jul. 5. 1686.

LONDINI
Jussu Societatis Regiæ ac Typis Josephi Streater. Prostat apud plures Bibliopolas. Anno MDCLXXXVII.

▲ NEWTON'S PRINCIPIA
Newton's *Philosophiae naturalis principia mathematica* (The Mathematical Principles of Natural Philosophy), in which he set out the laws of motion, is the most influential science book ever written.

▶ BAROMETER
By the mid-1600s scientists knew about force and motion and about gravity. The picture of what made things move was completed when they learned about pressure. In 1644 one of Galileo's students, Evangelista Torricelli, showed that air is not empty space but a substance.

In a famous experiment, Torricelli showed that air has so much substance it can press hard enough to hold up a column of liquid mercury in a tube. In this experiment, Torricelli made the first barometer, the first device for measuring air pressure. Before long, he realized the value of the barometer for forecasting weather.

of experiments—notably rolling balls down slopes—Galileo realized that you do not need force to keep something moving. Exactly the opposite is true. Something will keep moving at the same speed unless a force slows it down. This is why an arrow flies on through the air. It falls to the ground only because the resistance of the air (a force) slows it down enough for gravity (another force) to pull it down. This is the idea of inertia. Galileo realized that there is no real difference between something that is moving at a steady speed and something that is not moving at all—both are unaffected by forces. But to make the object go faster or slower, or begin to move, a force is needed.

Further experiments, this time with swinging weights, led Galileo to a second crucial insight. If something moves faster, then the rate it accelerates depends on the strength of the force moving it faster

and how heavy the object is. A large force accelerates a light object rapidly, while a small force accelerates a heavy object slowly.

Galileo's ideas made huge leaps in the understanding of force and motion. In 1642, the year he died, another scientific genius, Isaac Newton, was born. It was Newton who drew these ideas together and laid the basis of the science of dynamics. In his remarkable book *Philosophiae naturalis principia mathematica* ("The Mathematical Principles of Natural Philosophy"), published in 1684, Newton established three fundamental laws, which together account for all types of motion.

The first two laws were Galileo's two insights about inertia and acceleration. Newton's third law showed that whenever a force pushes or pulls on one thing, it must push or pull on another thing equally in the opposite direction (see below). Newton's three laws gave scientists a clear understanding of how force and motion are related and a way of analyzing them mathematically. Morever, together with Newton's insight into the force of gravity (the pull between two things), these laws seemed to account for every single movement in the Universe, large or small—from the jumping of a flea to the movements of the planets.

◄ WEIGHTLESSNESS
In a spaceship orbiting the Earth, the crew floats weightless. You might think that gravity is not working, just as Newton had predicted. The reality is that gravity is in fact still acting as a force, but the spaceship is hurtling around the Earth so fast that its effects are cancelled out.

▼ THE THREE LAWS
Newton's laws of motion are involved in every single movement in the Universe. They can be seen in action in a frog jumping from a lily pad.

Newton's first law says that an object accelerates (or decelerates) only when a force is applied. In other words, you need force to make a still object move (inertia) or to make a moving object slow down or speed up (momentum). To jump from the lily pad, the frog needs to use the force of its leg muscles.

The second law says that the acceleration depends on the size of the force and the object's mass. So the frog will take off faster if it gives a stronger kick (or is less heavy).

The third law says that when a force pushes or acts one way, an equal force pushes in the opposite direction. So as the frog takes off, its kick pushes the lily pad back.

Key Dates

- 1638 Galileo publishes his theories on speed and forces.

- 1644 Evangelista Torricelli demonstrates the reality of air pressure and invents the barometer.

- 1646 Blaise Pascal shows how air pressure drops the higher you go.

- 1650 Otto von Guericke invents the air pump.

- 1660 Robert Boyle shows how the volume and pressure of a gas vary.

- 1686 Newton publishes his work *The Mathematical Principles of Natural Philosophy*. It contains his theory of gravity and three laws of motion.

Atoms and Matter

▲ JOSEPH PRIESTLEY
Joseph Priestley (1733–1804) is the English scientist who discovered the gas in air that Lavoisier later called oxygen. This is the gas we need to breathe and fire needs to burn.

THANKS TO NEWTON AND Galileo, scientists in the 17th century knew a lot about how and why things moved; but they knew little about what things are made of. In ancient Greece 2,000 years earlier, philosophers thought all substances were made of just four basic things, or elements—earth, water, air, and fire. In the Middle Ages men called alchemists had tried heating and mixing substances to see how to change one into another. They discovered new substances such as nitric acid and sulfuric acid, but they still agreed with the idea of four elements.

The first chemist to really doubt this idea was the Irishman Robert Boyle (1627–1691), who carried out experiments with all kinds of substances. In his book *The Sceptical Chemist*, Boyle suggested that everything is made from a handful of basic substances, or "elements," each made up from a tiny lump called an "elementary corpuscle." Boyle believed that all the substances in the world are compounds made from these corpuscles joined together in different ways.

▼ LAVOISIER IN HIS LABORATORY
Lavoisier's carefully weighed experiments showed that air, one of the four basic elements of the ancient Greeks, is actually a mixture of different gases, mainly oxygen and nitrogen. He also showed that another of the basic elements, water, is a compound of hydrogen and oxygen.

DALTON AND ATOMIC THEORY

The idea that all matter is really made of tiny particles called atoms was first suggested by the Greek philosopher Democritus in the 5th century B.C. Later, in the 17th century, it was championed by Boyle, with his elementary corpuscles.

The English chemist John Dalton (1766–1844) put forward the first real atomic theory and gave the first proof of it. By comparing the relative weights of the elements in different samples of different compounds (chemical combinations of elements), Dalton was able to deduce how much an atom of each element actually weighs.

DALTON'S MODEL OF WATER MOLECULES

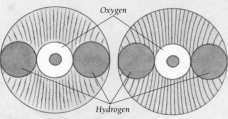

Oxygen

Hydrogen

▲ DALTON'S ATOMIC MODEL
Dalton's theory showed that compounds are formed when the atoms of one element join with the atoms of another. Dalton believed that water was made when a hydrogen atom links with an oxygen atom. Italian physicist Amedeo Avogadro later showed that each atom of oxygen joined with two hydrogen atoms, not one, to make water.

▼ DALTON'S ELEMENTS.
In 1808 Dalton published the first list of chemicals, complete with his estimated weights for individual atoms, or "atomic weights."

▶ MINER'S FRIEND
With the idea of chemical elements established, chemists raced to discover new ones. Dalton's 1803 notebooks show just 20 elements. By 1830 chemists knew of 55. Flamboyant English scientist Humphry Davy (1778–1829) discovered sodium and potassium and showed that chlorine and aluminum were elements. Davy is best remembered for inventing the miner's safety lamp, which greatly reduced the risk of explosions underground.

The alchemists believed that one substance could be changed into another—that was why they had searched for the "philosopher's stone," a substance that would transform ordinary "base" metal into gold. If Boyle's theory of elements were true, the alchemists were wrong; substances could only be mixed together differently but not actually changed. The scene was set for a controversy that raged throughout the 18th century.

The debate focused on burning. If you look at wood turning to ash as it burns, or at metal turning rusty, the alchemists argued, it seems quite clear that substances can change. An alchemist named Georg Stahl suggested in the early 18th century that anything burnable contains a special "active" substance called phlogiston, which dissolves into the air when it burns. If this is so, anything that burns must surely become lighter as it loses phlogiston. Does this happen?

A French chemist, Antoine Lavoisier (1743–1794), realized that the way to settle the argument was to weigh substances carefully before and after burning. In a brilliant experiment, Lavoisier burned a piece of tin inside a sealed container. The tin was actually heavier after burning—contrary to the phlogiston theory—but the air became lighter. So there was really no change in weight at all—substances were simply changing places! It was also clear that instead of losing something (phlogiston) to the air, the tin was taking something from it. Lavoisier later realized this was the gas oxygen, which had recently been discovered in England by scientist Joseph Priestley.

Lavoisier's experiment was a turning point in our understanding of matter, for three reasons. First, it put accurate scientific measurement firmly at the heart of chemistry. Second, it demolished the phlogiston theory and showed that burning is a process involving oxygen. Third, it showed that substances do not change even in a process as dramatic as burning; they simply change places. So Lavoisier put Boyle's idea of elements firmly on the map. Indeed, he made the first real list of chemical elements. Quite rightly, he has been called the father of modern chemistry.

◀ MENDELEYEV
Dmitri Mendeleyev was a Russian chemist who lived from 1834 to 1907. In the 1860s he realized that if the 60 elements known then were arranged in order of increasing atomic weight, then elements with similar chemical characteristics could be arranged in eight neat vertical groups. This arrangement, later known as the periodic table, has become central to our understanding of the elements. Scientists today continue to use Mendeleyev's table to assist them in their work and experiments.

Key Dates

- 1661 Robert Boyle introduces the idea of elements and compounds.

- 1756 Joseph Black deduces the presence of carbon dioxide in the air.

- 1774 Joseph Priestley discovers many new gases, including ammonia.

- 1784 Henry Cavendish shows that water is a compound of hydrogen and oxygen.

- 1789 Lavoisier writes the first list of elements and disproves the phlogiston theory.

- 1808 John Dalton proposes his atomic theory of chemical elements.

- 1818 Jöns Bezelius publishes the first table of atomic weights for the elements.

Factory and Furnace

▲ IRON BRIDGE
Iron was the new material of the Industrial Age. In 1779 the first all-iron bridge was built in Coalbrookdale in England.

UNTIL 1750, MOST people lived in country villages, raising animals and growing crops. Then two great revolutions started in Britain and changed things forever. A revolution in farming drove poor laborers off the land. A revolution in industry saw cottage crafts give way to great factories. People who were driven off the land came to work in the factories, and the first great industrial cities grew up.

These revolutions were fueled by the growth of European colonies and trade around the world. Colonies were vast new markets for goods such as clothes and eating utensils. In the past, people had made things slowly by hand. Now enterprising men realized they could make a fortune by producing huge quantities of goods quickly and cheaply for the new markets. They began to invent machines to speed things up, increase production, and reduce the number of people to be paid.

At first, the clothing industry was the main focus. Traditionally, yarn had been made by spinning together fibers, such as cotton, with a foot-driven spinning wheel. Cloth was woven from yarn on a loom, by hand. Then in

THE COMING OF WATERWAYS
The traditional horse and cart could not transport all the goods produced by the new factories, and within a few decades thousands of miles of canals were built across Europe. Using thousands of construction workers, these canals were then the biggest, most complex things ever built by humans.

▶ NEWCOMEN'S ENGINE
Newcomen's 1712 beam engine was the first practical steam engine. Steam drove a piston up and down to rock the beam which pumped water from the mines. It used a lot of coal but worked.

◀ SEVERN CANAL
The great canal-building era began in 1761 with James Brindley's Bridgewater Canal from Manchester, England. Soon the Grand Trunk Canal linked the rivers Mersey and Trent, and the Severn Canal linked the Thames and Bristol Channel. The area around Birmingham became the hub of a national canal network.

1733, John Kay built a machine called a flying shuttle. Kay's shuttle wove cloth so fast that the spinners could not make enough yarn. In 1764 Lancashire weaver James Hargreaves created the spinning jenny to spin yarn on eight spindles at once. This was a machine for home use, but a bigger breakthrough was Richard Arkwright's water frame of 1766. The water frame was a spinning machine driven by a water wheel. In 1771 Arkwright installed a series of water frames in a mill in Cromford in Derbyshire, England, to create the world's first large factory.

The early factories were water powered, but could they be powered by steam? Steam would be more powerful and there would be no need to locate factories by rivers. Thomas Savery had created a steam engine for pumping water out of mines in 1698, and a version developed by Newcomen in the 1720s was installed in many mines. Newcomen's engine was expensive to run, but in the 1780s James Watt created a cheaper engine. It gave power anywhere, and steam engines soon took over in factories.

The success of steam power depended on machine tools to shape metal, such as John Wilkinson's 1775 metal borer, and on iron and coal. Coal produced heat to make, or "smelt," iron. In the past iron had been smelted with charcoal. Then, in 1713, Abraham Darby found out how to smelt with coke, a kind of processed coal. Soon huge amounts of iron were churned out by coke-smelters. The combination of big steam-powered machines, cheap iron and coal proved unstoppable, and the quiet rural ways gave way to the big cities and noisy factories.

▼ THE INDUSTRIAL TOWN
The vast new towns of the Industrial Revolution, such as Birmingham and Leeds, were different from any town before. Noisy, smoky factories loomed over neatly packed rows of tiny brick houses—home to tens of thousands of factory workers. The coming of the railroads in the 1840s completed the picture.

▶ ARKWRIGHT'S WATER FRAME
The Industrial Revolution got under way with the invention of numerous ingenious machines for making cloth. The crucial breakthrough was the move from machines powered by humans or horses alone, to machines powered first by massive waterwheels and later by steam. The invention of a cotton-spinning machine called a frame, by Sir Richard Arkwright (1732–1792) in 1766, was a turning point. Arkwright had originally designed the spinners to be turned by horsepower. Then in 1771 he adapted the machine to run on water power, which is why it came to be called the water frame.

Key Dates

- 1698 Thomas Savery invents the first practical steam engine.
- 1722 Thomas Newcomen improves the steam engine.
- 1733 John Kay invents the flying shuttle weaving machine.
- 1764 James Hargreaves invents the spinning jenny to spin yarn.
- 1766 Richard Arkwright invents the water frame for spinning by water power.
- 1782 James Watt creates a cheap-to-run steam engine for powering machines.
- 1794 Eli Whitney patents his cotton gin, for removing seeds from cotton.

The Charged World

▲ MICHAEL FARADAY
(1791–1867)
The son of a blacksmith, Michael Faraday grew up to become one of the greatest experimental scientists of all time. He laid the foundation of our knowledge of electricity and magnetism.

IT WOULD BE HARD TO IMAGINE a world without electricity. Not only is it the energy that powers everything from toasters to televisions, but it is one of the fundamental forces in the Universe, holding all matter together. Yet until the late 18th century, scientists knew almost nothing about electricity. The ancient Greeks knew that when you rubbed a kind of resin called amber with cloth it attracts fluff. The word "electricity" comes from *elektron*, the Greek word for amber. For thousands of years amber attraction was considered a minor curiosity.

In the 18th century scientists such as the French chemist Charles Dufay (1698–1739) and the English physicist Stephen Gray (1666–1736) began to investigate electricity. They soon discovered not only that various substances could conduct (transmit) the same attraction to fluff as amber, but also that rubbing two similar substances together made them repel, not attract, each other. This attraction and repulsion came to be called positive and negative electrical "charge."

▶ THE DYNAMO
The discovery of the link between electricity and magnetism led to the development of the dynamo. It could generate electricity by turning magnets between electrical coils. In 1873 the Belgian Zénobe Gramme built the first practical generator. By 1882 power stations were supplying electric power to both New York and London.

By the mid-1700s some machines could generate quite large charges when a handle was turned to rub glass on sulfur. The charge could even be stored in a special glass jar called a Leyden jar—then suddenly let out via a metal chain to create a spark. Seeing these sparks, the American statesman and inventor Benjamin Franklin (1706–1790) wondered if they were the same as lightning. He attached a metal chain like that of a Leyden jar to a kite sent up in a thunderstorm. The lightning sent a spark from the chain—only much bigger than expected; and Franklin was lucky to survive.

ELECTRICAL PROGRESS

Faraday's and Henry's discovery of a way to generate electricity may have transformed our lives more than any other single scientific discovery. For thousands of years, people had seen at night by candlelight, kept in touch with messages carried on foot or horseback, and heard music only when someone played an instrument near them. The discovery of electricity changed all this.

◀ VOLTAIC PILE
Volta's pile, or battery, was invented in 1800. It was the first source of plentiful electricity.

▲ EDISON'S PHONOGRAPH
The first record player, Edison's phonograph of 1877, was mechanical. The arrival of electrical sound recording in the 1920s, including sound on TV and film, made sound and music more accessible.

▲ EDISON'S ELECTRIC LIGHTBULB
The electric lightbulb was invented independently by Sir Joseph Swan, in Britain, in 1878 and by Thomas Edison in the United States, in 1879.

▶ FARADAY AT WORK
Michael Faraday spent his life working at the Royal Institution in London, where his exciting and brilliantly clear public demonstrations of the latest electrical discoveries were famous. For one show he built a big metal cage. He stepped inside it with his instruments, while his assistant charged up the cage to 100,000 volts —a terrifying crackle of sparks ran around it. Faraday knew that he would be safe inside the cage because the charge courses around the outside. Such electrically safe cocoons are now called Faraday cages.

People were so excited by Franklin's discovery that demonstrations of electrical effects became very fashionable. When Italian anatomist Luigi Galvani (1737–1798) found that a dead frog's legs hung on a railing twitched in a thunderstorm, people wondered if they had found the very force of life itself—animal electricity. Alessandro Volta (1745–1827) realized that it was not a "life force" that made the electricity that twitched the frog's legs, but simply a chemical in the metal railing. Soon scientists realized that an electrical charge could be made to flow in a circular path from one side, or "terminal," of a battery to the other.

The real breakthrough, however, was the discovery of the link between electricity and magnetism. In 1819, Danish physicist Hans Øersted suggested that an electrical current has a magnetic effect, turning the needle of a compass. Little more than a decade later Joseph Henry (1797–1878) in the United States and Michael Faraday (1791–1867) in Britain proved that the opposite is, in fact, true—that it is actually a magnet that has an electrical effect. When a magnet is moved near an electric circuit, it generates a surge of electricity in the circuit. Using this principle—called electromagnetic induction—huge machines could be built to generate large quantities of electricity. The way was now open for the development of every modern appliance from electric lighting to the Internet.

▲ ALEXANDER GRAHAM BELL
Bell (1847–1922) was the Scottish-born American inventor of the telephone and a pioneer of sound recording.

▼ THE FIRST TELEPHONE
When Alexander Bell invented the telephone in 1876, electric telegraphs were already widely used to send messages along an electric cable, simply by switching the current on and off. Bell found a way of carrying the vibrations of the voice in a similar electric signal.

Key Dates

- 250 B.C. Parthians invent the battery.
- 1710s Stephen Gray transmits electricity 328 feet along a silk thread.
- 1752 Benjamin Franklin shows that lightning is electricity.
- 1800 Alessandro Volta makes the first modern battery.
- 1819 Hans Øersted discovers that an electric current creates a magnetic field.
- 1820 Georg Ohm shows that the flow of an electric current depends on the resistance of a wire.
- 1830 Joseph Henry and Michael Faraday discover how an electrical current can be generated by magnetism.

Steam Power

▲ TREVITHICK'S STEAM
LOCOMOTIVE
*The age of modern powered land
transportation began in 1804 with
Trevithick's locomotive, the world's
first steam railroad locomotive. It
ran on a mine track in Wales.*

FOR TENS OF thousands of years, human beings had managed with the power provided by wind, water, or sheer muscle. Then with the Industrial Revolution of the 18th century came the first steam engines, bringing huge amounts of controllable, and reliable, power.

The idea of using steam for power dates back to the 1st century A.D., to an ancient Greek mathematician named Hero, from Alexandria in Egypt. He came up with the idea of using jets of steam to rotate a kettle-like vessel. However, it was not until the 18th century that steam engines became a practical reality.

Most of the early steam engines, including those built by James Watt, were fixed engines, which provided power for working machines and pumps in factories and mines. Then in 1769 a French army engineer named Nicolas-Joseph Cugnot (1725–1804) built a massive three-wheeled cart that was driven along by a steam engine at walking pace.

The problem with using steam to drive vehicles such as this was that steam engines were incredibly heavy. Weight, though, would not be a problem in boats. In 1783 the Marquis Claude de Jouffroy d'Abbans, a French nobleman, built a steamboat which churned up the Saone River near Lyons, in France, for 15 minutes before the pounding of the engines shook it to bits. The boat sailed only once, but in 1787 John Fitch, an American inventor, made the first successful steamboat with an engine driving a

THE FIRST PASSENGER RAILROADS
The first steam locomotives were built to haul coal trucks around mines. On September 27, 1825, a father and son, George and Robert Stephenson, ran the first passenger train from Darlington to Stockton in the north of England. More than 450 people rode in the train's open wagons that day, pulled by the Stephensons' locomotive *Active* (later renamed *Locomotion*), and the 8-mile journey was completed in just 30 minutes. The railroad age had begun.

▲ THE ROCKET
In Stephenson's famous *Rocket*, the cylinder that drove the wheels was almost horizontal. This made it so powerful that it easily won the first locomotive speed trials in 1829.

▲ THE LIVERPOOL AND MANCHESTER
The 40-mile-long Liverpool and Manchester railway, which opened on September 15, 1830, was the first real passenger railroad. On the opening day, it also claimed the first railroad casualty: Home Secretary William Huskisson was killed under the wheels of a locomotive.

series of paddles on each side of the boat. In 1790 Fitch started the world's first steam service on the Delaware River. In 1802, in Scotland, another steam pioneer, William Symington (1763–1831), built a steam tug, the *Charlotte Dundas*. It was so powerful that it could pull two 70-ton barges.

The steamboat really arrived when American engineer Robert Fulton (1765–1815) made the first successful passenger steamboats in 1807. They carried people 150 miles up the Hudson River between New York City and Albany. This journey, which took four days by sailing ship, took Fulton's steamboats less than a day.

Three years earlier, British engineer Richard Trevithick had shown that heavy steam vehicles—or "locomotives" —could move more easily on rails. In 1804 he fired up the world's first steam railroad locomotive, in Wales.

Even rails did not solve the problem at once, because Trevithick's locomotive cracked the cast-iron tracks. But cast-iron rails were soon replaced with wrought-iron and, later, steel rails, which could take more weight. Within 15 years steam locomotives were running on short railroads all over Britain. In 1831 the first regular steam railroad service in the U.S. began, in South Carolina. The age of steam travel had begun.

▲ H.M.S. *THESEUS*
Steamships gained in power and reliability, and in the 1880s many navies began to build steam-power warships like H.M.S. Theseus.

◀ *THE GREAT EASTERN*
In 1819 the New York-built Savannah, *a sailing ship equipped with a steam engine, made the first Atlantic crossing using steam power. The age of regular transatlantic steam passenger services began in 1837 with the launch of the* Great Western, *one of three giant steamships designed by British engineer Isambard Kingdom Brunel. Brunel's* Great Eastern, *launched in 1858, was the biggest ship launched in the 1800s—692 feet long and weighing almost 19,000 tons.*

▶ STEAM SPEED
Steam locomotives were the cutting edge of technology in Victorian Britain. Brilliant men such as James Nasmyth (1808–1890) went into locomotive design in the same way that talented designers are now drawn into electronic and space technology. As a result, steam locomotives rapidly became more and more efficient.

In the U.S., railroads helped to open up the West, cutting journeys of weeks down to a few days. Safety features, such as George Westinghouse's air brake (1872), brought greater speeds —by the 1880s, up to 60mph.

Key Dates

- 1783 Claude d'Abbans sails the first steamboat on the Saone near Lyons, in France.

- 1804 Richard Trevithick builds first steam-powered railroad locomotive.

- 1807 Robert Fulton opens the first passenger steamboat service.

- 1819 The *Savannah* makes the first steam-powered crossing of the Atlantic.

- 1823 George and Robert Stephenson begin to build railroad locomotives.

- 1825 Stockton and Darlington railroad opens in England.

- 1869 The first transcontinental railroad in the United States is completed.

The Story of Life

▲ CHARLES DARWIN
Charles Darwin (1809–1882) was one of the most influential scientists of his day. His theory of evolution is one of the most important ever scientific breakthroughs.

IN THE 18TH CENTURY travelers returning to Europe brought news of thousands of previously unknown plants and animals which they had found on their travels around the world. To try to make sense of these finds, the great Swedish botanist Carl Linnaeus (1707–1778) devised a system of classifying plants and animals into the many species and genera (groups of species) that we still use today.

People began to wonder how all this variety of life had come to be. Perhaps the variety had developed, little by little, over time; but how did this gradual development, or evolution, work? How did new species appear? In 1808 a French naturalist named Jean Lamarck suggested that it happened because animals can change during their lives. For example, organs and

muscles that are used a lot become stronger. In this way useful developments are then passed on to an animal's offspring. This was the first proper theory of evolution, but few people were convinced, for they could see that strong parents could produce weak offspring.

▼ DINOSAUR SKELETON
Darwin's theory of evolution arose partly from the first discovery in the 1820s and 1830s of the fossilized bones of huge extinct reptiles which came to be called dinosaurs. In 1824, William Buckland found the jaw of Megalosaurus. The following year, Gideon Mantell found a giant tooth of a creature he called Iguanodon. Soon many more dinosaur fossils were found.

DARWIN'S THEORY
Darwin's theory depends on the fact that no two living things are alike. Some may start life with features that make them better able to survive. For example, an animal might have long legs to help it escape predators. Individuals with such valuable features have a better chance of surviving and having offspring that inherit these features. Slowly, over many generations, better-adapted animals and plants survive and flourish, while others die out or find a new home. In this way, all the millions of species that we know about today gradually evolved.

▼ THE EVOLUTION OF THE HORSE
Species may die out, but they leave behind similar but better-adapted offspring species. The earliest horse, called Eohippus or "dawn horse," was tiny—only 10–20 inches high at the shoulder—and had four toes on each of its front feet. Fossils have shown that a chain of about 30 species, spread over 60 million years, led step by step from Eohippus to the modern horse. Each species is slightly bigger and has fewer toes than its ancestors.

Hyracotherium   *Mesohippus*   *Merychippus*   *Equus*

In the 1820s and 1830s geologists and naturalists made a series of discoveries that were to pave the way for a new theory of evolution, proposed by Charles Darwin. Geologists discovered that the Earth was much older than had previously been thought, and that the landscape of today has evolved over millions of years. At the same time, naturalists discovered more fossils of long-dead creatures, including dinosaurs, showing that many more species had once lived on Earth than are alive today.

Charles Darwin made a long trip around the world on a ship called the *Beagle*, on which he was employed as a botanist. He began to develop a theory of evolution that depended on species' developing as gradually as the landscape. He found an explanation for how this happened in the ideas of the economist Thomas Malthus, who suggested that when populations grow too big for the available resources the weak slowly die out. In the same way, Darwin suggested, species slowly

▲ THE VOYAGE OF THE *BEAGLE*
Between 1831 and 1836, Darwin traveled aboard H.M.S. Beagle as it voyaged around the world on a scientific expedition. He studied plants and animals everywhere the ship landed, including on the Galapagos Islands in the Pacific. While Darwin was sorting through the material that he brought back, he developed the idea of evolution.

◀ UNIQUE WILDLIFE
This is a giant tortoise that lives on the Galapagos Islands ("Galapagos" means "giant tortoise"). Here Darwin found wildlife unique to the islands.

evolve by natural selection as they compete for limited resources—with only the fittest surviving.

The English naturalist Alfred Wallace (1823–1913) independently proposed a theory of evolution similar to Darwin's, and they published their ideas jointly in 1858. It was Darwin's research that gave the theory substance, which is why it is called Darwin's theory. Many people were shocked by Darwin's ideas, but his evidence was hard to ignore, and his theory gradually gained acceptance. Most scientists today see it as one of the greatest-ever scientific breakthroughs.

These finches have longer, thinner beaks for catching insects.

These finches have short, stout beaks for cracking seeds. The bird on the right, has evolved a slightly longer beak as it eats both insects and seeds.

▲ THE GALAPAGOS FINCHES
When Darwin landed in the Galapagos Islands in the Pacific he found slightly different species of finch on each island. These small but significant variations made it clear to Darwin that species must gradually change through time. He thought that species changed in different ways in different places, even if they start the same.

Key Dates

- 1735 Carl Linnaeus groups plants into different species, and subgroups.

- 1788 James Hutton realizes that the Earth is many millions of years old.

- 1801 Jean Lamarck proposes that animal species evolve in response to their habitat.

- 1820s William Buckland and Gideon Mantell discover the first fossils of dinosaurs.

- 1830 Charles Lyell's *Principles of Natural Geology* shows that landscapes evolved gradually.

- 1858 Charles Darwin and Alfred Wallace suggest the theory of evolution by natural selection.

On the Road

▲ THE MODEL T
Cars were toys for the rich in the early days. Then the age of mass motoring dawned in 1908, when Henry Ford launched the Model T Ford, the world's first mass-produced car. By assembling the car from standardized parts on a moving production line, Ford workers could make a Model T so cheaply that people barely able to afford a horse and buggy could easily buy a car. Within five years, 250,000 Americans owned a Model T.

THE STORY OF THE automobile really began in the summer of 1862, when Frenchman Étienne Lenoir drove his small self-propelled cart out through the forests of Vincennes, near Paris, with its small engine slowly thumping. Lenoir's was not the first powered car, however. At the Chinese court a Jesuit priest, Padre Verbiest, had built one as long ago as 1672. Nicolas Cugnot built one in 1769, and over the next 100 years there were many others, including Goldsworthy Gurney's steam carriages (1829), which ran between London and Bath. The problem was that all of these vehicles were powered by steam engines, which tended to be either cumbersome or very expensive to make.

Lenoir's breakthrough was to make a neat little engine that worked by internal combustion—that is, by

▲ FIRST CARS
The idea of steam cars seems quaint nowadays, but many of the first successful automobiles were driven by steam. The steam engine was, after all, a tried and tested form of engine.

burning gas inside a cylinder. Lenoir's gas internal combustion engine was much lighter because it needed neither a tank of water nor a bunker of coal. He set up his engine on an old horse cart so that it drove the

HISTORY OF CARS

Cars have come a long way Since the Benz Motorwagen rolled out of the works in 1888. The earliest cars were built one by one for the rich, but the Ford Model T showed that mass production was the way forward. By the 1930s, mass production enabled many ordinary people to afford cars, but the rich still had individually-built beauties. Cars then were designed mostly by experience and trial-and-error. Car design today relies more on the computer.

▲ 1886 DAIMLER
Gottlieb Daimler was one of the pioneers of motoring. Unlike Benz, who set out to build a motor vehicle from scratch, Daimler fitted an engine to a horse carriage. Like many of the first cars, this had wooden-spoked wheels like a horse cart.

▼ 1901 OLDSMOBILE
This was one of the most popular cars of its time. The Oldsmobile was made by the American Ransom Eli Olds (1864–1950). His 1901 Oldsmobile was steered with a tiller like a boat, rather than with a steering wheel. Many early cars used this means of steering.

▲ MORRIS OXFORD
Millions of Americans had their own cars by the 1920s, thanks to Ford. In the rest of the world cars were still costly. Prices did come down, and soon middle-class families were buying modest sedans such as the Austin Ten, the Opel Kadett, and the Morris.

◀ MAN WITH FLAG
After a few early accidents, cars were seen as highly dangerous machines. For 30 years from 1865, the British "Red Flag" Act required motor vehicles to be preceded by a man on foot waving a red flag. It was not until 1896 that this restriction was lifted and the speed limit raised to 12mph. New York had a Red Flag Act until 1901.

wheels via a chain around the axles. Another Frenchman, Alphonse Beau de Rochas, soon improved the efficiency of Lenoir's engine by using an extra movement, or "stroke," of the piston to squeeze the gas before burning it, making a four-stroke engine. Four-stroke engines are the engines still used in most cars today.

A few years later an Austrian named Siegfried Marcus managed to make an internal combustion engine that ran on gasoline instead of gas. His secret was to create a simple but ingenious device called a carburetor, which turned the gasoline into vapor. In 1873, Marcus built what is now thought to be the world's oldest gasoline-engine car.

It had wheels like a cart but a small steering wheel. It looked more like a car than a horse cart with an engine.

Despite these successes, gasoline-engine cars were still at the experimental stage. Many people believed that the future of the car lay with tried and tested steam engines. Indeed, the land speed record was broken in 1906 not by a gasoline-engine car but by a steam car, the Stanley Steamer, traveling at an astonishing 128mph! The breakthrough for the gasoline engine came with the three-wheel car developed by German engineer Karl Benz and his wife Berta in the 1880s. In 1888, the Benz Patent-Motorwagen became the first automobile ever made for sale to the public. It was such a success that within a decade the Benz factory in Mannheim was turning out 600 cars a year. The automobile age had begun.

▲ FUTURISTIC CAR
Automobile manufacturers are always trying to improve their cars. Top speed, fuel economy, safety, and good looks are all important factors to consider. Manufacturers need to make a car that balances these elements.

▲ VOLKSWAGEN BEETLE
The biggest-selling car ever, the Volkswagen "Beetle," was developed in Germany in the 1940s as a compact and affordable "people's car."

▲ MORRIS MINI
The 1959 Mini was the first tiny family car. To save space, its designer Alex Issigonis placed the engine across the car, to drive the front wheels.

▶ MCLAREN F1
Plans for Gordon Murray's McLaren F1—designed to be the ultimate road-going car— were released to the public in March 1989. It has a top speed of 231mph.

Key Dates

- 1672 Padre Verbiest builds the world's first steam carriage in China.

- 1769 Nicolas Cugnot builds a three-wheeled steam carriage.

- 1862 Étienne Lenoir builds the first vehicle powered by an internal combustion engine.

- 1865 Alphonse Beau de Rochas builds first four-stroke internal combustion engine.

- 1873 Siegfried Marcus builds the first gasoline-powered car.

- 1888 Karl Benz builds the world's first gasoline-engine car for sale.

- 1908 Henry Ford launches the first mass-produced car, the Ford Model T.

Off the Ground

▲ ORVILLE WRIGHT
Orville Wright was at the controls of his plane, the Flyer, for the world's first controlled flight. The younger of the two Wright brothers, he was born in 1871, in Dayton, Ohio, and died in 1948.

THERE WAS PROBABLY NEVER a time when people did not look up and long to fly like the birds. In ancient Greece there was a myth about an inventor named Daedalus, who made himself wings of feathers and flew high in the sky. Long after, there were those who believed they could mimic the birds and their flapping wings. In the Middle Ages, many reckless pioneers strapped on wings and launched themselves over cliffs and from high towers—only to plummet to the ground.

In the 15th century the brilliant Italian artist and thinker Leonardo da Vinci designed a flying machine with pedal-power wings, which he called an "ornithopter." It was never built and would never have flown, because it was far too heavy. Men did get off the ground every now and then. In ancient China, over 3,000 years ago, the military lifted lookouts aloft on giant kites.

In 1783 two men were carried high in the air over Paris in a giant paper balloon made by the Montgolfier brothers. It was filled with hot air, which rises because it is less dense than cold air. Both kites and balloons were at the mercy of the wind, however, and many inventors believed the future of flight lay with wings.

The great pioneer of winged flight was the British engineer George Cayley (1773–1857). After a series of experiments with kites, Cayley worked out that a wing lifts because its curved upper side boosts air pressure underneath and reduces it above. All modern airplanes are based on the kite-like model glider Cayley built in 1804, with its up-angled front wing and stabilizing tail. In 1853, at the age of 80, he built a full-size glider which is said to have carried his terrified coachman through the air for several hundred yards.

After Cayley, various experimenters tried their luck with gliders. No one

▶ THE WRIGHT BROTHERS' FIRST FLIGHT
One of the secrets of the Wright brothers' success at Kitty Hawk was their development of a way to stop the plane from rolling from side to side—something that had proved the downfall of many earlier planes. Their Flyer had wires to "warp," or twist, the wings to lift one side or the other. This meant that it could not only fly level but also make balanced, banked turns.

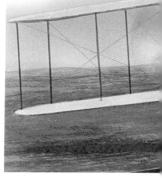

FLYING AHEAD

When Wilbur Wright took their plane, the *Flyer,* to France in 1908, it was clear that the Wrights were far head of pioneers in Europe, such as Louis Blériot. Before long, airplanes were making rapid progress everywhere. On July 25, 1909, Blériot flew across the English Channel. The military demands of World War 1, which began in 1914, gave a tremendous boost to aircraft development. By the time the war was over in 1918, airplanes were reliable enough for the first regular passenger flights to begin.

▶ FIRST HANG-GLIDER
The Wright brothers' ideas on control in flight were preceded in the 1890s by Otto Lilienthal's pioneering flights with craft such as hang gliders. Sadly, Lilienthal was killed flying in 1896.

▲ 1917 BIPLANE
The fighter aircraft of World War I were incredibly flimsy machines, made of fabric stretched over a wooden frame. Most were biplanes—they had two sets of wings—because single wings were far too fragile.

▲ JUMBO JET
The age of mass air travel began with the first jet airliner, the Comet 4, in 1952. Now millions of people fly each year in giant jets such as the Boeing 747 jumbo jet. These planes fly high above the clouds and winds so that the journey is smooth and comfortable.

had any idea how to control their craft in the air until, in the 1890s, a brave young German named Otto Lilienthal built a series of fragile gliders somewhat like modern hang gliders. He succeeded in making the world's first controlled flights in them.

With a glider, a person could fly on wings at last, but not for long. What was needed for sustained flight was an engine. As long ago as 1845 two Englishmen, William Henson and John Stringfellow, built a working model of a plane powered by a lightweight steam engine, which may well have made a successful trial

flight. Steam engines were too weak or too heavy, however, and it was the development of the gasoline engine that proved to be the breakthrough. Even with a gasoline engine, a single wing did not provide enough lift, so experimenters tried adding more and more wings.

Then, one cold Thursday in December 1903 at Kitty Hawk, North Carolina, a gasoline-engine, biplane (double-winged) flying machine built by the brothers Orville and Wilbur Wright rose shakily into the air. It flew 131 feet and then landed safely. It was the world's first controlled, powered, sustained flight.

▼ CONCORDE
By the time the Anglo-French Concorde was built in the 1960s, millions of people were being zoomed around the world each year in high-speed jet airliners. For four decades, Concorde carried passengers at supersonic speeds—that is, well above the speed of sound.

▶ STEALTH BOMBER
In 1988, after years of secret development, the U.S. Air Force unveiled its B-2 "stealth" bomber—the most advanced military plane in the world at the time. This sinister-looking aircraft is designed to fly at incredibly high speeds at low altitudes—and be almost invisible to enemy radar. A few years later, it was joined by the F-117 "stealth" fighter. Stealth bombers were used heavily in 1999 in the U.S. bombing raids on Serbia and Kosovo.

Key Dates

- 1783 Two men fly in the Montgolfier brothers' hot-air balloon.

- 1804 George Cayley builds a model kite with wings and a tail.

- 1853 Cayley builds a full-size glider.

- 1890 Clement Ader makes the first powered flight in a steam-powered plane, the *Eole*.

- 1896 Samuel Langley flies about half a mile in his steam-powered *Aerodrome*.

- 1903 Orville and Wilbur Wright make the first controlled, powered flight in the *Flyer*.

- 1909 Louis Blériot flies across the English Channel.

Rays and Radiation

▲ SEE-THROUGH HAND
X-rays can reveal the bones inside a living hand because the rays shine through skin and muscle and are blocked only by bone.

I N 1864 THE SCOTTISH scientist James Clark Maxwell made the brilliant deduction that light is a kind of wave created by the combined effects of electricity and magnetism. He also predicted that light might be just one of many kinds of "electromagnetic" radiation. Scientists were keen to find out, and in 1888 German physicist Heinrich Hertz built a circuit to send big sparks across a gap between two metal balls. If Maxwell was right, the sparks would send out waves of electromagnetic radiation. But they might not be visible like light. So Hertz set up another electric circuit to detect them. The waves created pulses of current in this circuit, which Hertz saw as tiny sparks across another gap. By moving the receiving circuit, he worked out just how long the waves were. They proved to be much longer than light waves; they are now known as radio waves.

About the same time, others were experimenting with discharge tubes. Scientists had known for 100 years or more that a bottle from which air is sucked glows eerily if you put electrodes (electric terminals) into it and fire a spark between them. Discharge tubes gave a near-perfect vacuum (space without air), and the spark between the electrodes made the tube glow brightly. Sometimes even the

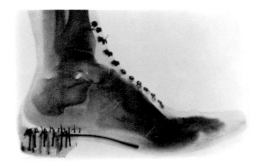

▲ FIRST X-RAY
In 1895, Röntgen shone X-rays through his wife's shoe to make a photo of the bones of her foot inside the shoe.

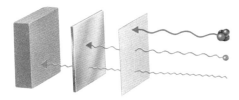

▲ RADIOACTIVITY
We now know that radioactivity is three kinds of particle shot out by atoms as they disintegrate naturally: alpha, beta, and gamma particles. Each kind of particle has the power to penetrate different materials.

THE TV TUBE
The cathode-ray tube did not lead only to the discovery of electrons and radioactivity. Most TV and computer screens are also cathode-ray tubes. The stream of electrons discovered by Thomson is what makes your TV or computer screen glow.

▼ PRISM AND SPECTRUM
In the 1600s Newton showed that light is made of a spectrum, or range, of different colors. We now know that light itself is part of a much wider spectrum of electromagnetic radiation. The radio waves that beam out TV signals are just part of this spectrum.

▲ BAIRD'S TELEVISION ATTEMPTS
John Logie Baird (1888–1946) was the Scottish inventor who made television a reality. It had no single inventor, but it was Baird who made the the first true TV pictures in 1926. Baird transmitted TV pictures by telephone line from London to Glasgow in 1928.

▶ THE CURIES IN THEIR LABORATORY
The Curies were among the greatest of all scientific experimenters. Their combination of brilliant insight and exact, patient work led them not only to discover the true nature of radioactivity— radiation from atoms—but to prove it, too.

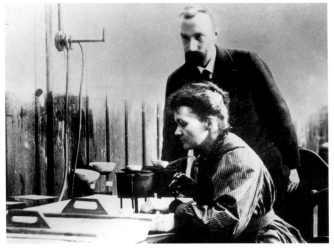

glass glowed. The glowing was named "cathode rays" because it seems to come from the negative terminal, or cathode. If the tube was empty, how was the spark crossing from one electrode to another? In 1897, J. J. Thomson guessed that the spark was a stream of tiny bits of atoms, which he called electrons. For the first time, scientists saw that the atom is not just a solid ball, but contains smaller, subatomic particles.

Meanwhile, in 1895 the discharge tube helped Wilhelm Röntgen to discover another kind of radiation. Röntgen found that, even when passed through thick cardboard, some rays from the tube made a sheet of fluorescent material glow. Although cardboard could block out light it could not stop these new mystery rays, which he called X-rays. He went on to take a picture of the bones in his wife's foot by shining X-rays through it and onto a photographic plate.

In the same year French scientist Henri Poincaré was wondering why the glass in discharge tubes often glowed, as well as the sparks. Perhaps radiation might be emitted not only by electricity but by certain substances, too. Soon, Antoine Becquerel discovered this when he left uranium salts in a dark drawer on photographic paper. A few weeks later there was a perfect image of a copper cross that had been lying on the paper. There was no light or electricity to form the image, so where was the radiation coming from?

Marie and Pierre Curie soon found that the intensity of radiation was in exact proportion to the amount of uranium. They realized that it must be coming from the uranium atoms themselves, and called this atomic radiation "radioactivity." In fact, not only uranium but also many other elements are radioactive, including two new elements discovered by the Curies—radium and polonium. Since this crucial discovery, many uses for radioactivity have been found, but so too have its dangers. Marie Curie herself died of cancer brought on by overexposure to radioactivity.

▲ BAIRD'S SPINNING DISK
Modern TVs work by scanning streams of electrons back and forth inside a cathode-ray tube. Baird's system was entirely mechanical, using a rapidly spinning disk drilled with holes. The holes let different parts of the picture shine through onto different light-sensitive electric cells.

Key Dates

- 1864 James Clerk Maxwell says that light is electromagnetic radiation.

- 1888 Heinrich Hertz discovers radio waves.

- 1895 Wilhelm Röntgen discovers X-rays.

- 1897 J. J. Thomson discovers electrons.

- 1897 Antoine Becquerel discovers radioactivity.

- 1898 Marie and Pierre Curie discover the radioactive elements radium and polonium.

- 1898–1900 Ernest Rutherford finds that radioactivity is emissions of alpha, beta, and gamma particles.

Space and Time

▲ MICHELSON
Albert Michelson (1852-1931) became the first American scientist to win the Nobel Prize in 1907.

I N 1905, A TALENTED YOUNG scientist named Albert Einstein came up with his special theory of relativity. The theory is not easy to understand, but it has revolutionized the way in which scientists think about space and time. Its origins date back to 1610, when Galileo was thinking about how things moved and described a ship at sea. Shut yourself in a cabin with a tank containing fish, suggested Galileo, and you will see that the fish swim in all directions just as easily when the ship is moving as when it is at anchor. For the fish, the ship's motion is irrelevant. In the same way, when you walk around, you are never aware that the ground beneath your feet is a planet whizzing through space at 62,000mph. So we can detect movement through space only in relation to something else.

Half a century later, a Dutch astronomer named Owe Roemer added another dimension to the picture—time. Roemer realized that because the light from Jupiter took ten minutes to travel across space to the Earth, he was seeing the eclipse of Jupiter's moons, in 1676, ten minutes

▲ EINSTEIN AND E=MC²
Einstein's theory of relativity is not just about space and time; it involves energy too. Energy is how vigorously something can move. Something moving fast clearly has a lot of energy, called kinetic energy. The energy of a heavy ball perched on a hilltop is called potential energy. Scientists knew that kinetic and potential energy are interchangeable—the ball might roll downhill, for example.

Einstein went further and showed that mass, energy, and movement are interchangeable. They are swapping over all the time—energy into mass, mass into movement, and so on. Since light is the fastest moving thing, it clearly plays an important role in the relationship between energy, mass, and movement. Einstein linked them in a famous equation: energy equals mass times the speed of light squared, or E=mc². This equation shows how a very little mass can give an enormous amount of energy.

TIME MACHINES
Ever since people realized, earlier this century, that time is just a dimension, many have fantasized about the possibility of traveling backward or forward in time. Stories such as H. G. Wells's *The Time Machine* and films such as the *Back to the Future* series center on amazing time machines that can whisk you millions of years into the past or the future, or in some cases just a few minutes or days. Scientists are now beginning to think these may not be just pure fantasies. If time is just another dimension, like length and breadth, what is to stop us from traveling in time to visit the past or the future, just as we travel through space? Einstein himself said it was impossible, and though some scientists think we could do it by bending space–time in some way, no one has yet come up with any convincing ideas of just how it might be possible.

◀ DOCTOR WHO'S TARDIS
The popular British television series Doctor Who had the time-traveling Doctor moving around time and space in his TARDIS, which was disguised as a police phone booth. TARDIS stands for "Time And Relative Dimensions In Space." The TARDIS is remarkable because it warps space and time and because it is many times larger inside than it appears to be on the outside.

▶ THE FOURTH DIMENSION

Einstein's proof that everything is relative upsets our commonsense idea of time. We see time passing as one thing happening after another—as the hands tick around on a clock. It seems that time can move in only one direction, from past to future. But many laws in science, such as Newton's laws of motion, work just as well whether time goes backward or forward. In theory, time could run backward just like a video replay. Einstein's theory showed that this is not just theory, but reality. Many scientists now prefer to think of time, not as a one-way train, but as a dimension, like length, depth, and breadth. The three space dimensions—length, breadth, and depth—combine with the time dimension to make the fourth dimension of space–time.

after it actually occurred. In the same way, when we see a star four million light-years away, we see it as it was four million years ago. Someone elsewhere in the Universe would see the eclipse at a different time. So the timing of events depends on where you are. If this is true, how do you know which is the right time? Is it the time you set on your watch, or the time your friend on a distant planet sets? The fact is, you do not know. You can tell the time only in relation to something else, such as the position of the Sun in the sky or the position of a distant star.

Despite this, 120 years ago most people were sure that behind all this relative time and space there was real, or "absolute," time and real movement. In 1887, two American scientists, A. A. Michelson and E. W. Morley, set out to prove it with an ingenious experiment. They reasoned that a beam of light moving the same way as the Earth should whizz along slightly slower than one shooting past the opposite way—just as an overtaking bike passes you more slowly than one coming toward you at the same speed. So, they tried to measure the speed of light in different directions. Any difference would show that the Earth was moving absolutely. Yet they detected no difference in the speed of light, in whichever direction they measured it.

Einstein then came to a startling conclusion, which he published as his theory of special relativity. It demolished the idea of absolute time and space forever. Einstein showed not only that light is the fastest thing in the Universe—but that it always passes you at the same speed, no matter where you are or how fast you are going. You can never catch up with a beam of light. Einstein realized that every measurement must be relative, because not even light can help to give an absolute measurement.

◀ KILLING YOUR GRANDPARENTS

A famous argument against the possibility of time travel is about killing your grandparents. The argument asks, what if you traveled back in time to before your parents were born and killed your grandparents? Then neither your parents nor you could have been born. But if you were never born, who killed your grandparents? This kind of problem is called a paradox. Some scientists get around it with the idea of parallel universes, different versions of history that all exist at the same time, running in parallel.

Key Dates

- 1610 Galileo suggests the idea of relative motion.

- 1676 Owe Roemer realizes that light takes time to reach us across space.

- 1887 Michelson and Morley show that the speed of light is the same in all directions.

- 1900 Max Planck invents quantum theory to explain why radiation varies in steps rather than continuously.

- 1905 Albert Einstein publishes his special theory of relativity.

- 1915 Einstein publishes his general theory of relativity.

The Big Universe

▲ EDWIN HUBBLE
Hubble (1889–1953) was an exceptional man. He had trained at Chicago and Oxford in law, and then taken up professional boxing, before turning to astronomy.

UP UNTIL THE 20TH century, astronomers thought the Universe was little bigger than our own Milky Way Galaxy, with the Sun at its center. All the Universe consisted of, they thought, were the few hundred thousand stars they could see with the most powerful telescopes of the day. The largest estimates put the Universe at no more than a few thousand light-years across (one light-year is 5,876 billion miles, the distance light travels in a year). There were fuzzy spiral patches of light they could see through telescopes, but these were thought to be clouds of some kind. They were called spiral nebulae, from the Greek word for "cloud."

In 1918 an American astronomer named Harlow Shapley made an astonishing discovery. Shapley was working at the Mount Wilson Observatory near Los Angeles. He was studying ball-shaped clusters of stars called globular clusters through the observatory's powerful telescope. He wondered why they seemed to be concentrated in one half of the sky and guessed that this is because the Earth is not at the center of the

Galaxy, as had been thought—but right out at the edge, looking inward. He also realized that if this is so, then the Galaxy must be much, much bigger than anyone thought—perhaps as big as 100,000 light-years across.

The discoveries that we are not at the center of the Galaxy but at the edge and that the Galaxy is gigantic were in some ways as dramatic as Copernicus's discovery that the Earth is not at the center of the Solar System. Even as Shapley was publishing his ideas, a new and even more powerful telescope was being installed at Mount Wilson. It enabled a young

▲ THE ANDROMEDA GALAXY
The Andromeda Galaxy is the nearest galaxy beyond our own, and the only one visible with the naked eye. But as Hubble's study of Cepheid variable stars within it showed, even this nearby galaxy is over two million light-years away. Thousands of other galaxies, which are visible only through powerful telescopes, are many billions of light-years away.

BIG BANG

Hubble's discovery that the Universe is getting bigger led to an amazing theory about the history of the Universe. If the Universe is expanding as Hubble showed, it must have been smaller at one time. Indeed, all the signs are that it was once very, very small indeed—perhaps smaller than an atom. The Universe began with an unimaginably gigantic explosion called the Big Bang. It was so big that the galaxies are still being flung out from it today.

◀ THE AFTERGLOW OF THE BIG BANG
The Big Bang theory seemed a very good explanation of the way the Universe is expanding. But there was little real proof until 1992, when the Cosmic Background Explorer (COBE) took a picture of the whole sky showing the microwave radiation coming toward us from all over space. This radiation is the afterglow of the Big Bang, and the slightly uneven pattern shown by the COBE picture confirmed astronomers' theories. Without this unevenness the galaxies could never have formed, so the Big Bang theory would not be correct.

▶ THE STORY OF THE UNIVERSE

By calculating back from the speed of the galaxies, we can estimate that the universe began about 14 billion years ago. Gradually, astronomers have been piecing together the history of the Universe, from the time the first stars and galaxies formed, perhaps 13 billion years ago, through the beginnings of the Earth 4,567,000,000 years ago, the beginning of life some 3,500,000,000 years ago, and the age of the dinosaurs 210–65,000,000 years ago, down to the modern age.

astronomer named Edwin Hubble to make even more astonishing discoveries.

Using the new telescope, Hubble began to look at the spiral nebulae—in particular the nebulae we now know as the Andromeda Galaxy. He could see that it was much more than a fuzzy patch of light and actually contained stars. Among these stars he could see special stars called Cepheid variables, which are so predictable in their brightness that we can use them as distance markers in the sky. The Cepheid variables showed Hubble that Andromeda is several hundred thousand light-years away—far beyond the edge of the Galaxy.

Soon it became clear that many of the fuzzy patches of light in the night sky were other galaxies of stars, even farther away. Suddenly the Universe seemed much, much bigger than anyone had dreamed of. In 1927 Hubble made an even more amazing discovery. While studying the light from 18 galaxies,

he noticed that the light from each one had a slightly different red tinge. He realized that this was because the galaxies are zooming away from us so fast that light waves are actually stretched out and become redder. Remarkably, the farther away the galaxies are, the faster they seem to be moving away from us. Hubble realized that this is because the Universe is expanding.

So within ten years the Universe, which was thought to be just a few thousand light-years across, was found to be many millions, and it was known to be growing bigger at an absolutely astonishing rate. Astronomers can now see galaxies 13 billion light-years away— zooming away from us at nearly the speed of sound.

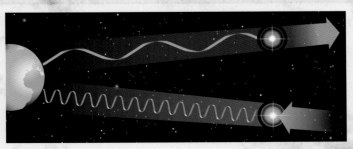

▲ RED SHIFT

We know galaxies are speeding away from us because their light is "red-shifted." If a light source is rushing away, each light wave is sent from a little farther on—and so gets stretched out. As the light waves are stretched out, the light appears redder. The most distant galaxies have such huge red shifts that they must be moving very, very fast. Red shift is based on the observation by Austrian physicist Christian Doppler (1803–1853) that sound waves moving away are stretched out in the same way. The roar of a train coming toward you is high-pitched. As it zooms on past and away, the pitch drops as the sound waves become longer.

Key Dates

- 1918 Harlow Shapley shows that Earth is on the edge of the Galaxy.

- 1929 Hubble shows that Andromeda is a galaxy beyond our own.

- 1927 Hubble realizes that other galaxies are flying away from us— and the Universe is expanding.

- 1927 Abbé George Lemaitre proposes that the Universe began in a Big Bang.

- 1948 Alpher and Herman suggest that the Big Bang left behind weak radiation.

- 1964 Penzias and Wilson detect weak cosmic background radiation, providing evidence for the Big Bang.

Miracle Cures

▲ ALEXANDER
FLEMING
*The discovery of penicillin,
the first antibiotic, by
Scottish bacteriologist
Alexander Fleming (1881–
1955) was one of the great
medical breakthroughs of
the 20th century. For the
first time doctors had a
powerful weapon against a
wide range of diseases.*

IN 1900 DISEASE WAS A frighteningly normal part of life—and death. Few large families of children ever grew up without at least one of them dying. The introduction of vaccination began to save many people from catching diseases such as smallpox. Doctors could do very little once anyone actually became ill, except tend them and pray. To catch a disease such as tuberculosis or syphilis was very likely to be a death sentence.

The main reason for doctors' helplessness in the face of infectious (catching) diseases was the fact that they had no idea what caused them. Then, in the late 19th century, thanks to the work of scientists such as Louis Pasteur, it finally became clear that it was tiny, microscopically small germs such as bacteria and viruses that were to blame.

Gradually medical scientists, especially those in Germany, began to realize that it might be possible to fight infectious disease with chemicals that targeted the germs but left the body unharmed. A very dedicated scientist named Paul Ehrlich believed that the key was to find chemical "magic bullets" that could be aimed at

▲ ERNST CHAIN
*Along with Howard Florey, Chain continued the research
into penicillin that had been started by Alexander Fleming.
The value of the three men's work was recognized in 1945
when they were awarded the Nobel Prize for Medicine.*

ANTIBIOTICS

Antibiotics work by attacking germ cells, but not body cells, and they have proved remarkably effective at treating a variety of bacterial diseases, including pneumonia, meningitis, scarlet fever, syphilis, tuberculosis, and other infections. There are at least 70 useful antibiotics. Most are used against bacterial infections, but some attack fungal diseases and a few are designed to work against cancer. Diseases caused by viruses, however, cannot be treated by antibiotics in any way.

▼ HOW ANTIBIOTICS WORK
Antibiotics fight germs in a number of ways. Some antibiotics make the germ cell's skin leak vital nutrients or let in poisonous substances, but they have no affect on human cell skins. Others, such as penicillin, work by stopping the germ cell's tough skin from forming. Human cells do not have the same tough skins, so they are left unharmed. A third kind of antibiotic, including streptomycin and rifampicin, interferes with chemical processes inside the germ cell.

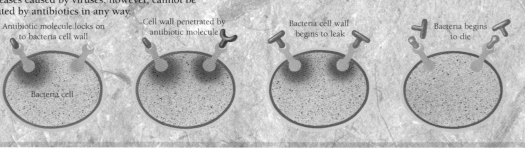

Antibiotic molecule locks on
to bacteria cell wall

Cell wall penetrated by
antibiotic molecule

Bacteria cell wall
begins to leak

Bacteria begins
to die

Bacteria cell

germs. With his colleague Sahachiro Hata, Ehrlich worked to find such a cure for syphilis—a terrible disease that had killed millions of people over the centuries. In 1910 he discovered the chemical arsphenamine, which was later sold under the name Salvarsan. It wiped out the germ that causes syphilis while leaving body cells virtually unharmed.

For the first time, doctors had a powerful weapon against a disease, and the search was now on for similar chemical treatments for other diseases. The early hopes were dashed, and it was not until the 1930s that scientists discovered a group of chemicals named sulfonamides that were deadly to a wide range of bacteria. In the meantime, a British scientist called Alexander Fleming had made a remarkable discovery.

In 1928 Fleming was working in his laboratory in St. Mary's Hospital, London, when he noticed a strange thing. He had been culturing (growing) the staphylococcus bacteria in a dish, and it had grown moldy. What was remarkable was that the bacteria seemed to have died wherever the mold was. Fleming had a hunch that this mold, called *Penicillium notatum*, could be useful against disease.

Fleming himself was unable to find out if his hunch was true, but ten years later Howard Florey, Ernst Chain, and others took up the idea and developed the first antibiotic drug, penicillin. "Antibiotic" means germ-attacking. Penicillin, one of the miracle drugs of the 20th century, has saved many, many millions of people from dying from a wide range of infectious diseases, including tuberculosis. Since then, thousands

▲ CLEAN BILL OF HEALTH
In the 1850s Austrian Ignaz Semmelweiss found that he could save women from dying in childbirth in hospital by getting his medical students to wash their hands to stop the spread of infection. Later, Joseph Lister introduced phenol to kill germs in surgery. These antiseptic (germ-killing) techniques were not miracle cures, but they made hospitals, such as this smallpox hospital, much, much safer.

of other antibiotic drugs have been discovered. In the early 1940s, for instance, the American scientist Selman Waksman found the antibiotic streptomycin in soil fungi. Some antibiotics come from nature, mainly molds and fungi, and some have been made artificially from chemicals. None has proved as effective and safe against such a broad range of diseases as penicillin.

◀ NEW DRUGS
In the past, drugs either occurred naturally or were created in the laboratory. In future, some may be created in cyberspace, as chemists put computer models of molecules together with models of body cells to see how they react, which is what this chemist is doing. Computers may be able to trawl through millions of different ways of putting atoms together very quickly to find the perfect "magic bullet" that targets the disease precisely.

Key Dates

- 1867 Joseph Lister shows the value of antiseptic surgery.

- 1860s Louis Pasteur insists that many diseases are caused by germs.

- 1876 Robert Koch proves that germs can cause disease.

- 1910 Ehrlich and Hata find that Salvarsan is a cure for syphilis.

- 1928 Florey, Chain, and others turn penicillin into the first antibiotic.

- 1942 Waksman discovers streptomycin.

- 1951 Frank Burnet discovers how the immune system attacks germs but not body cells.

Nuclear Power

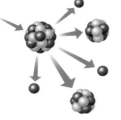

▲ NUCLEAR FISSION
In nuclear fission, an atom is split by the impact of a tiny neutron. As it splits into two smaller atoms, it releases a lot of energy and two more neutrons, which may split more atoms.

NO SCIENTIFIC DISCOVERY has been so awesome as that of nuclear energy, the energy in the nucleus of every atom in the Universe. Nuclear energy is not only the energy that makes nuclear weapons, it is the energy that keeps every star in the Universe burning. Until the 20th century, this vast power was undreamed of. Scientists knew that matter was made of atoms, but they thought atoms were no more lively than billiard balls. No one knew what energy really was.

Albert Einstein had a brilliant insight in his theory of special relativity of 1905. He showed that energy and matter are flip sides of the same basic thing, swapping back and forth all the time. His famous equation $E=mc^2$ gave this swap a real quantity. E is energy, and m the mass, or quantity, of matter; c is the speed of light, which is huge. If the mass of a tiny atom could be changed to energy, some scientists believed it would yield a huge amount of power.

At the same time, scientists such as Neils Bohr were probing the atom and finding that it is not just a ball. First, they found that it holds tiny electrons whizzing around a nucleus, or core, of larger

▼ NUCLEAR MUSHROOM
When a nuclear bomb explodes on the ground, a huge fireball vaporizes everything on the ground and turns it into a blast of hot gases and dust that shoots far up into the sky. When this blast reaches the stratosphere, one of the layers of the atmosphere that finishes 31 miles from the earth's surface, it begins to cool, and some of the gases condense into dust. As the dust begins to fall it billows out in a distinctive mushroom-shaped cloud. Often radioactive particles drop back to the ground.

THE MANHATTAN PROJECT
The bombs dropped on Hiroshima and Nagasaki were developed in a secret program, called the Manhattan Project, by a team at Los Alamos, New Mexico. On July 16, 1945, the Los Alamos team exploded the first atomic bomb in the desert, to the amazement of spectators in bunkers 5 ¹/₂ miles away.

The team achieved the critical mass of fission material (plutonium-239 and uranium-235) in two ways. One was to smash two lumps together from opposite ends of a tube, a system called "Thin Man." The other was to wrap explosive around a ball of fission material and smash it together ("Fat Man"). The Hiroshima bomb was a uranium-235 "Thin Man." The Nagasaki bomb was a plutonium -239 "Fat Man."

▲ J. ROBERT OPPENHEIMER
Oppenheimer (1904–1967) led the Los Alamos team, but he later opposed hydrogen bombs. These are powerful nuclear bombs based not on the fission (splitting) of atoms but on the fusion (joining together) of tiny hydrogen atoms.

▼ NAGASAKI
The effect of the nuclear bombs on Hiroshima and Nagasaki was so terrible that no one has used them in warfare again. The bombs obliterated huge areas of both cities and killed over 100,000 people instantly. Many of those who survived the initial blast died slow and painful deaths from the aftereffects of radiation.

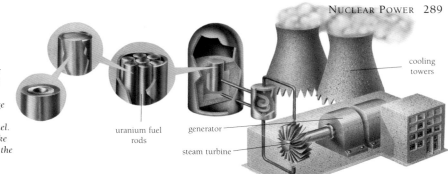

▶ NUCLEAR POWER
*A nuclear bomb is an
uncontrolled nuclear chain
reaction. In a nuclear power
plant, the reaction is slowed
down and sustained almost
indefinitely to provide a huge
amount of heat from just a
small amount of uranium fuel.
This heat boils water to make
steam, which drives around the
turbines (fan blades) that
generate the electricity.*

cooling
towers

uranium fuel
rods

generator

steam turbine

protons. Then, in 1932, James Chadwick discovered a
second kind of particle in the nucleus—the neutron.

At once, Italian atomic scientist Enrico Fermi tried firing
neutrons at the nuclei of uranium atoms. He found different
atoms forming and guessed that the neutrons had joined the
uranium atoms to make bigger atoms of an unknown
element, which he called element 93. But Fermi was wrong.
In 1939, German scientists Otto Hahn and Fritz Strassman
repeated Fermi's experiment. What they found was not a
new element but something even more astonishing—so
astonishing that Hahn hardly dared believe it. It was a
woman physicist, Lise Meitner who explained to the world
what Fermi, Hahn, and Strassman had done. They had split
the uranium atom in two, making smaller atoms including
barium. This splitting of the atom is called fission.

When the uranium atom split, it not only released a lot
of energy, but also split off two neutrons. What if these two
neutrons zoomed off to split two new atoms? These atoms
would then, in turn, release two more neutrons, which

would split more atoms, and so on. Scientists soon realized
that this could become a rapidly escalating chain reaction of
atom splitting. A chain reaction such as this would unleash a
huge amount of energy as more and more atoms split.

Normally, chain reactions will not start in uranium
because only a few uranium atoms are of the kind that splits
easily, namely uranium-235. Most are tougher uranium-238
atoms. To make a bomb or a nuclear power plant, you need
to pack enough uranium-235 into a small space to sustain a
chain reaction. This is known as the critical mass.

During World War II, scientists in Germany and the
United States worked furiously to achieve the critical mass;
neither wanted to be last to make the atomic bomb. The
Americans realized that another atom—plutonium-239—
might be used instead of uranium-235. At 3:45 p.m. on
December 2, 1942, a team in Chicago led by Fermi used
plutonium-239 to achieve a fission chain reaction for the
first time. In August 1945, American fission bombs
devastated the Japanese cities of Hiroshima and Nagasaki.

▲ NUCLEAR POWER PLANT
Nuclear reactions release huge amounts of energy, but they create dangerous radioactivity
too. Radioactivity can make people very ill or even kill them. Many people suffered
radiation sickness after the Hiroshima and Nagasaki bombs. Even nuclear power plants
can have dangerous leaks. A serious nuclear accident occurred when the Chernobyl
reactor, in the Ukraine, went wrong in April 1986, spreading radioactive material over a
vast area. The radioactive material produced by nuclear power plants must be stored
safely for hundreds of years until it loses its radioactivity.

Key Dates

• 1905 Einstein reveals the theoretical
  power of the atom in special relativity.

• 1911 Rutherford proposes that atoms
  have a nucleus, circled by electrons.

• 1919 Rutherford discovers the proton.

• 1932 Chadwick discovers the neutron.

• 1939 Hahn and Strassman split a
  uranium atom.

• 1942 Fermi's team achieves the first
  fission chain reaction.

• 1945 July 16: Oppenheimer's team
  explodes the first atomic bomb.

• 1945 August: U.S. Air Force drops
  atomic bombs on Nagasaki and
  Hiroshima.

Lifeplan

E VERY LIVING THING—EVERY human, animal, and plant—is made up from millions of tiny packages called cells. Inside each cell is a remarkable chemical molecule called DNA. It is the basis of all life. The DNA in human body cells not only tells each cell how to play its part in keeping the body alive but also carries all the instructions for making a new human being. The discovery of DNA's shape by James Watson and Francis Crick in 1953 was one of the major scientific breakthroughs of the 20th century, and the impact of their discovery on our lives has already been huge.

DNA (deoxyribonucleic acid) was discovered in 1869 by a Swiss student named Friedrich Miescher. Miescher was looking at pus on old bandages under a microscope when he saw tiny knots in the nucleus, or core, of

▲ DNA

DNA is one of the largest molecules known, weighing 500 million times more than a molecule of sugar. It is very thin, but very long— if stretched out it would be about 16 inches long. The molecule is usually coiled up, but it is made from two thin strands wrapped around each other in a twin spiral, or "double helix." It is somewhat like a long twisted rope ladder, with rungs made of chemicals called bases.

▲ FAMILY

Everyone has their own unique DNA, and it is so distinctive that it can be used to prove who you are, like a fingerprint. You get half your DNA from your mother and half from your father. There are sequences of bases in your DNA that are so similar to both your mother's and your father's that an analysis of your DNA proves who your parents are. DNA is also the reason why we all bear some resemblance to our parents.

the pus cells. His tutor, Ernst Hoppe-Sayler, analyzed these nuclear knots chemically and found that they were acidic, so they called the substance nucleic acid. No one at the time had much inkling of its real significance.

Seventy-six years later, in 1945, American bacteriologist Oswald Avery was studying influenza bacteria when he noticed that DNA could turn a harmless bacteria into a dangerous one—as if it were giving instructions. In 1952 Alfred Hershey and Martha Chase

THE CHEMICALS OF LIFE

The study of the chemicals of life, such as DNA, is called organic chemistry, or biochemistry. It can also be called carbon chemistry because, remarkably, all life depends on chemicals that include atoms of carbon. There are literally millions of these carbon compounds, because carbon atoms are uniquely able to form links with other atoms. Some, such as proteins and amino acids, are more important than others.

▶ NICOTINE MOLECULE

Many organic compounds are based on a ring, or hexagon, of six carbon atoms. This is a model of the compound nicotine, found in the dried leaves of the tobacco plant. It is a poison used as an insecticide. It is also the chemical in cigarettes that makes people addicted to smoking.

▼ PROTEINS

Proteins are the basic material of all living cells. They are built up from different combinations of chemicals called amino acids. All these amino acids are present in each cell, like these cells from around human teeth. To make a protein, DNA must instruct the cell to make the right combination of amino acids.

showed that this is just what DNA does. Once DNA's importance became clear, the race was on to find out how it worked. It was crucial to discover the shape of this long and complex molecule. In 1952 Rosalind Franklin, a young woman working at Imperial College in London, photographed DNA using X-rays, but she could not figure out its structure. The young American Watson and Englishman Crick were then working on DNA at the Cavendish Laboratory in Cambridge, England. When they saw Rosalind Franklin's photographs, they suddenly realized that the DNA molecule is shaped like a double helix—that is, like a rope ladder twisted in a spiral.

After this great discovery, biochemists began to take DNA apart piece by piece under microscopes, then put it together again to find out how it gave instructions. The search focused on the four different chemicals making up the "rungs" of the ladder: guanine, cytosine, adenine, and thymine. Erwin Chagraff found that these four "bases" pair up only in certain ways—guanine links only with cytosine; adenine only with thymine.

It soon became clear that the key to DNA lies in the order, or sequence, of the bases along each of the molecule's two long strands. Like the bits of a computer, the sequence of bases works as a code. The bases are like letters of the alphabet, and the sequence is broken up into "sentences" called genes. The code in each gene is the cell's instructions to make a particular protein, one of the basic materials of life. The complete gene code, or genetic code, was finally worked out in 1967 by American biochemists Marshall Nirenberg and Indian-American Har Khorana— work that earned them the Nobel Prize.

▲ STAYING ALIVE
Not only humans, but every living thing in the world has a DNA molecule in each of its body cells. This remarkable molecule tells the cell exactly what to do in keeping the living thing's body together, whether it is a bear or a salmon. It is also a complete copy of instructions for making an entirely new bear or salmon.

▲ THE GENETIC CODE
The key to the DNA code lies in the sequence of chemical bases along each strand, shown here in the form of a DNA fingerprint. These bases are a bit like letters of the alphabet, and the sequence is broken up into "sentences" called genes. Each gene provides the instructions to make a particular set of proteins.

Key Dates

- 1869 Miescher discovers DNA.

- 1945 Avery discovers that DNA issues life instructions to living things.

- 1952 Hershey and Chase show that DNA carries genetic instructions.

- 1953 Watson and Crick show that DNA has a double-helix (spiral) structure.

- 1954 Chagraff shows that DNA's four "bases" join together only in certain ways.

- 1961 Brenner and Crick show how so-called "letters" in the DNA code are formed by triplets of bases.

- 1967 Nirenberg and Har Khorana show how the genetic code works.

The Power of the Processor

▲ MICROCHIP
Microprocessors are made from thousands of tiny transistors joined in circuits and printed onto a tiny slice of silicon, or silicon chip. The biggest parts of a chip are not its circuits and switches—the tiny patch in the center—but the connecting teeth along its sides.

THE COMPUTER'S ORIGINS date back 5,000 years when people in Asia used abacuses to do sums. An abacus is a simple frame with rows of sliding beads, but a skilled user can do complex computations very quickly. In the 1600s, men such as French mathematician Blaise Pascal, built adding machines with gears and dials.

The first real computer was an "analytic engine" designed in the 1830s by Englishman Charles Babbage along with the poet Byron's daughter Ada Lovelace. This machine would have used cards punched with holes to control the movement of rods and gears, and so make complex calculations. Crude mechanical systems though, were not up to the task, and Babbage never built it.

During the next 100 years, people built increasingly clever calculators using punch cards to control rods and dials. These were just adding machines and could not do the complex sums we expect of a computer. Mechanical devices were too big and noisy. In 1944, Howard Aiken and IBM did build a basic computer using punch cards, but it was over 49 feet long and had less computing power than a modern pocket calculator!

The way forward for computers was to replace mechanics with electronics. Electronics are at the heart of most modern technologies, from CD players to rocket-control systems. They work by using electricity to send signals. Inside every electronic device there are lots of small electric circuits, which continually switch on and off telling the device what to do. Unlike electric light switches on the wall, electronic switches work automatically.

The first electronic device, called a valve, was invented in 1904. It looked like an electric lightbulb and was used in radios and TVs. In 1939 American physicist John Atasanoff built a valve computer at Iowa University. A few years later, during World War II, an English mathematician named Alan Turing developed a giant valve

◀ VIRTUAL REALITY
Virtual reality (VR) systems build a picture electronically to create the impression of a real 3D space. They were developed in the 1960s in simulators that taught jet pilots how to fly. With VR, people can operate a computer-guided device in dangerous or difficult places, for example in an underwater wreck or inside the body.

THE TRANSISTOR

In the 1940s, TVs and other electronic devices relied on huge, hot-running glass tubes (somewhat like lightbulbs) for fine control over electric currents. Then John Bardeen and his colleagues showed that the same control could be achieved with tiny, solid lumps of semiconductor materials—special materials such as germanium and silicon that conduct electricity only when warmed up by another electric current. The development of integrated circuits and microchips, on which all modern electronic technology relies, stems from this discovery.

◀ BARDEEN AND COLLEAGUES
The transistor was created by three scientists working together at the Bell Laboratories in 1948 —John Bardeen, William Shockley, and Walter Brattain.

Random Access Memory (RAM)

screen

keyboard

Read Only Memory (ROM)

computer called Colossus to break the secret German "Enigma" codes. Turing also created many of the basic rules of computing. Valves were used in the first electronic computers built for sale in the early 1950s, called first-generation computers. However, the valves were big, got very, very hot, and kept failing.

The big breakthrough came when valves were replaced with transistors. Transistors are switches, like valves, but they are made from special "semiconductor" materials, such as silicon and germanium, which can change their ability to conduct electricity. Transistors are lumps of these material inserted with electrodes (conductors). These can be very small and robust.

With transistors, computers moved on to the second and third generations in the 1950s and 1960s, but they were still small and expensive. Then, in 1958, American Jack Kilby put the connections for two transistors inside one 3/8-inch-long crystal of silicon—he had made the world's first integrated circuit, or microchip.

Soon microchips were getting smaller and smaller, and electronic circuits became increasingly complicated as scientists discovered new ways of squeezing more and more components into a single chip. Nowadays, microchips, or silicon chips, range from simple circuits for electric teakettles to complex

high-speed microprocessors with millions of transistors capable of running computer programs at very high speeds.

With integrated circuits, computers could start to be miniaturized. Heat ceased to be a real problem, and a great deal of computing power could be packed into a tiny space. The first computer based on a microprocessor was the Intel (1974), which moved computers into the fourth and fifth generations. Since then, they have progressed in leaps and bounds in terms of reliability, speed, and power. Today's computers are packed into such compact and inexpensive packages that the average household in most developed countries can now have its own high-powered computer.

◀ COMPUTER GRAPHICS
The sophisticated graphics (pictures) now seen on ordinary home computers require levels of computing power that would have been envied by the scientists guiding spacecraft through the Solar System just 15 years ago. Every computer we use is still built around the microprocessor.

◀ SCREEN AND KEYBOARD
The keyboard and TV-like screen of the computer are so familiar that we take them for granted. Flat screens which are thin enough to hang on the wall have already been developed. So, too, have voice-operating systems that may make the keyboard redundant.

◀ ELEMENTS OF A COMPUTER
Inside a computer are a number of microchips. Some of a computer's memory, called the ROM (read-only memory), is built into these microchips. A computer also has chips for RAM (random-access memory), which takes new data and instructions whenever needed. Data can also be stored on magnetic patterns on removable disks, or on the laser-guided bumps on a CD.

At the heart of every computer is a powerful microchip called the central processing unit (CPU). The CPU is the part that works things out, within guidelines set by the ROM, and processes and controls all the programs by sending data to the right place in the RAM.

▲ TRANSISTOR
The modern computer was born when the transistor was invented in 1948. Modern microprocessors contain millions of transistors packed onto tiny silicon chips, but they still work in the same way as this single transistor.

Key Dates

- 1642 Pascal invents an adding machine.
- 1835 Babbage begins to build his programmable analytic engine.
- 1847 George Boole devises the basis of computer logic.
- 1930 Vannevar Bush builds a mechanical computer.
- 1937 Atsanoff builds a digital electronic computer.
- 1939 Aiken builds a valve computer.
- 1948 Shockley, Bardeen, and Brattain invent the transistor.
- 1958 Jack Kilby invents silicon chip.

Space Age

▲ THE EARTH
FROM SPACE
*Viewing the Earth from
space has been one of the
most extraordinarily
powerful experiences of
the space age. It makes
clear what we had never
been able to see before—
that the Earth is an
almost perfect sphere. It
has also made us much
more aware of the frailty
of our planet.*

THE CONQUERING OF SPACE has been one of the great human achievements of the 20th century. What was barely a fantasy 100 years ago is now an everyday reality. Over 100 artificial satellites are launched into space every year, manned space flights are commonplace, and space probes have visited all but one of the planets in the Solar System. The *Mir* space station was recently abandoned after 13 years as an orbiting laboratory in space.

The space age began on October 4, 1957 when the Soviet Union launched *Sputnik* (later called *Sputnik 1*). It was blasted straight up by powerful rockets, and as the rockets fell away *Sputnik* soared on upward, leveled out, and hurtled into the first-ever orbit of the Earth. A month later, the first living creature went into space in *Sputnik 2*—a dog called Laika. Sadly, Laika never came back.

On April 12, 1961, brave Russian

cosmonaut Yuri Gagarin went up in *Vostok 1* to become the first man in space. *Vostok 1* took Gagarin once around the Earth before re-entering the atmosphere and parachuting into the ocean. A few months later U.S. astronaut Alan Shepard went up, and in June 1963 Valentina Tereshkova became the first woman in space in *Vostok 6*. In 1965, Russian Alexei Leonov stepped outside a spacecraft in space, floating on the end of a cable.

During the early years of the space age, the United States and Soviet Union were engaged in a bitter rivalry called the Cold War. Each was determined to beat the other in the "space race." Throughout the 1960s and 1970s, each nation was spurred on to ever more spectacular and showy

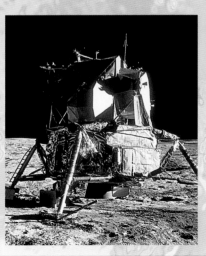

◄ GAGARIN
*Born of a poor Russian
farming family, Yuri Gagarin
became the most famous
person in the world in 1961
when Vostok 1 made him
the first man in space. His
flight around the Earth
lasted just 1 hour 48
minutes, but it was a
spectacular moment in
human history. Sadly,
Gagarin died only seven
years later at the age of 34
while testing a new plane.*

EXPLORING SPACE

On July 17, 1969, the giant *Saturn V* rocket launched three astronauts toward the Moon on the *Apollo 11* mission. Three days later, the Apollo command module was circling the Moon. While Michael Collins stayed in the command module, Neil Armstrong and Buzz Aldrin went down to the Moon's surface in the lunar module. On July 20, Neil Armstrong opened the hatch and climbed out onto the Moon.

▶ THE LUNAR MODULE
Armstrong and Aldrin went down to the Moon's surface in the tiny lunar module, which was little bigger than a trailer. When it landed, four legs supported it on big pads on the soft, dusty surface.

▲ FIRST STEPS
Neil Armstrong was the first man on the Moon. As he climbed down the ladder of the lunar module and stepped onto the Moon's surface, he said these now-famous words: "That's one small step for a man, one giant leap for mankind."

▶ MIR
Despite a number of mishaps, the Soviet Mir spacecraft stayed up in space for over 13 years, between 1986 and 1999, and made more than 76,000 orbits of the Earth. It was a temporary home to many astronauts—and Russian Valery Polyakov spent a record 437 continuous days aboard.

achievements. Both the United States and the USSR sent probes to the same planets, including Venus (the American *Mariners* and the Soviet *Veneras*) and Mars. Both sent probes to the Moon. Then, in July 1969, the Americans went ahead by putting men on the Moon. The Soviets could go no better, but within two years they launched *Salyut 1*, the first space station.

Although these achievements were spectacular, the space race cost the two superpowers a fortune, and by the end of the 1970s it began to slow down. Today the Cold War is over, cooperation in space is the spirit of the day, and the Americans and Russians are working with Canada, Europe, and Japan to build a huge international space station (ISO), which is being assembled in space piece by piece.

One cause of controversy among those involved in space exploration has been whether to focus on manned or unmanned exploration. Unmanned probes are cheaper, safer, and faster than manned vehicles and can make trips far too risky for human beings to attempt. No manned probe is ever likely to descend into Saturn's atmosphere or venture out beyond the edge of the Solar System—partly because manned spacecraft must return.

Unmanned probes have already visited most of the Solar System's planets. They have landed on Mars and Venus and they have told us a huge amount about all the planets. Unmanned probes can never give as full a picture as human observers, and cannot react so well to unexpected events. Manned spacecraft have been sent to the Moon, but sending people to the planet Mars is far trickier. Even the journey itself would take many months and would be a tremendous ordeal for astronauts. Most experts think astronauts may land on Mars by 2020.

▼ THE SPACE SHUTTLE
Early spacecraft were usable only for one flight, but the U.S. space shuttle of 1981 was the first reusable craft, landing again with the aid of plane-like wings. It made short flights in space much easier.

▲ MARS LANDING
No manned spacecraft has landed on another planet, but many unmanned probes have landed on Mars. In July 1997, the U.S. *Mars Pathfinder* touched down on Mars and beamed back "live" TV pictures from the planet. Two days later, it sent out a wheeled robot vehicle called *Sojourner* to survey the surrounding area.

Key Dates

- 1957 *Sputnik* is the first spacecraft to orbit the Earth.
- 1957 Laika the dog is the first living creature in space.
- 1961 Yuri Gagarin is the first man in space.
- 1961 Alan Shepard is the first American in space.
- 1963 Valentina Tereshkova is the first womna in space.
- 1965 Alexei Leonov does the first space walk.
- 1969 Neil Armstrong and Buzz Aldrin are the first men to land on the Moon.

Instant Contact

▲ TELEPHONES
Since its invention by Alexander Graham Bell in 1876, the telephone has become a vital part of our lives, giving us the instant contact we now take for granted.

THE AGE OF INSTANT communication began when American painter and inventor Samuel Morse invented the electric telegraph in the 1830s. The telegraph linked two places by electric wire. By simply switching the current rapidly on and off, one could send a message in a code of pulses, called Morse code. For the first time, people could send messages almost instantly over long distances. On May 24, 1844, Morse sent this message from Washington, D.C., to Baltimore over the world's first commercial telegraph line: "What hath God wrought?"

Newspapers quickly began to use the Morse telegraph to send news stories, and by the 1860s the telegraph was the main means of long-distance communication in the United States, linking all major cities. Thanks to the backing of American banker Cyrus W. Field and British physicist Lord Kelvin, a telegraph cable was laid all the way under the Atlantic

in 1866. The benefit was instant. Once, even urgent messages between London and New York had taken weeks to get through. Suddenly, via the transatlantic cable, contact was almost instant.

However, messages still had to be transmitted in an elaborate code. A few years later, in Boston, the Scotsman Alexander Graham Bell found a way to transmit not just single pulses, but multiple pulses down the telegraph wire. In 1875 he found a way to transmit all the vibrations made by sounds as multiple pulses. On March 10, 1876, he transmitted human

▼ THE INVENTION OF RADIO
The telegraph and the telephone rely on a physical connection by wire. In 1895 Guglielmo Marconi transmitted a Morse message across empty space using pulses of radio waves.

INTERNET
The Internet is a vast network linking millions of computers around the world. It transmits huge amounts of information, including words, images, and sounds. It began in the 1960s when the U.S. army developed a network called ARPAnet to link military and government computers in case of nuclear war. Soon places such as universities developed their own networks.

In 1983, the university networks merged with ARPAnet to form the Internet. Now anyone with a computer, a modem, and a phone line can join. Originally the Internet was used just for electronic mail (e-mail) and transferring files. But there was a huge explosion of interest in the Internet after Tim Berners-Lee of the CERN laboratories in Switzerland developed the World Wide Web in 1989 for finding your way around Internet sites.

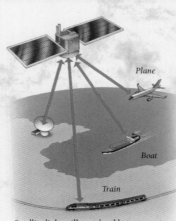

Plane

Boat

Train

Satellite links will soon be able to connect you to the Internet wherever you are.

◀ THE NET
Just as you can talk on the phone, so computers can talk to each other on the Internet. Every computer has its own "address" where it can receive messages, like a telephone number. Computers that have a "site"—a window of information open to all—have a website address, too.

When you access the Net, your computer connects via a local phone line to a big computer called a net provider. This, in turn, is linked to a bigger computer called a main hub. Each main hub is connected to about 100 other main hubs around the world. Some messages travel between main hubs by phone lines and others are linked by satellite. Either way, they are incredibly fast and are called "fast-truck connections."

speech for the first time, saying to his colleague in another room: "Watson, come here. I want you!" By the end of the 19th century every major city in the world was linked by telephone.

Over the next 90 years, nearly every household in North America and Europe acquired a phone. People took it for granted that they could pick up the phone and chat to friends at opposite ends of the country. When it came to international calls, there were often long delays—either because the line was crowded or because the signal took time to get through. Also, some countries did not have a cable link.

When the space age dawned in the 1960s, communications companies were quick to take advantage of the satellites being fired up into space. Telephone signals were translated into microwaves (like the rays in a microwave oven) and bounced around the world off satellites. Suddenly even the most out-of-the-way places could join the telephone network cheaply, and people could speak almost instantly to people across the far side of the world. Communications satellites not only transmit telephone messages instantly; they also handle TV and radio signals.

The telephone network was speeded up even further when fiber-optic cables began to be used in the 1970s. A laser or a light-emitting diode (LED) translates the electric signals of a telephone call into light impulses.

These are shone along a thin, transparent glass or plastic strand called an optical fiber. The light impulses are reflected off the internal surfaces of the fiber, and so they travel much faster and more cleanly than a conventional electric signal.

In the early 1980s several companies had begun to market cellular telephones, which used no wires at all. They sent and received messages via microwaves sent to special receiving stations. By the mid-1990s, a huge number of people used the compact mobile phones developed from these first bulky cell phones. The great revolution of the 1990s has been the Internet, which links computers all around the world using the telephone network.

▲ COMMUNICATIONS SATELLITE
Since the first communications satellite, called Telstar, was launched in 1962, satellites have dramatically accelerated the speed and ease with which all kinds of messages—from telephone conversations to TV broadcasts —can be beamed around the world.

▶ THE WORLD WIDE WEB
The World Wide Web is an amazingly clever way of finding your way around information on all the computers in the Internet. The information you can reach is set up as "sites" on all the millions of individual computers in the Net. The Web makes "hyperlinks" (fast links) to all the sites that contain the word you select. To find the right sites, you need a browser, which is a computer program that searches the entire Net.

Key Dates

- 1844 Morse sends the first telegraph message.
- 1866 The first telegram is sent through the transatlantic cable.
- 1876 Bell sends the first telephone message.
- 1963 The first communications satellite is launched.
- 1960s The U.S. military develops ARPAnet to link computers.
- 1983 ARPAnet merges with university links to form the Internet.
- 1989 Tim Berners-Lee develops the World Wide Web.

The Moving Earth

▲ LYSTROSAURUS
Finding fossils of Lystrosaurus in Antarctica was crucial evidence for the theory that the continents were once joined. Lystrosaurus is a reptile known to have lived in China, Africa, and India 200 million years ago—and the best explanation for finding fossils in all four places is that all four places were once joined together.

IN RECENT YEARS geologists have made the startling discovery that the Earth's surface is broken into 20 or so giant slabs called "tectonic plates." Even more startling is the fact that these plates are moving slowly around the Earth. As they move, the plates carry the oceans and the continents with them, so that they drift around the world. This discovery revolutionized our understanding of the Earth's surface, showing us why and where earthquakes and volcanoes occur and a great deal more.

The idea that the continents have moved is so astonishing that when a young German meteorologist named Alfred Wegener (1880–1930) first suggested it in 1923, he was ridiculed. "Utter damn rot!" sneered the President of the American Philosophical Society.

Yet it was not an altogether new idea. In the 17th century the English thinker Francis Bacon had noticed how strangely alike the coasts of South America and

◄ KOBE QUAKE
The idea that tectonic plates move has transformed scientists' understanding of how earthquakes happen. One day they may be able to predict earthquakes such as the one that hit Kobe, in Japan, in 1996.

Africa are, and in the early 19th century a German explorer had noticed remarkable similarities between the rocks of Brazil and those of the African Congo. No one thought much of this until naturalists found not only identical turtles, snakes, and lizards in both South America and Africa, but fossils of the ancient reptile Mesosaurus in both Brazil and South Africa.

The accepted explanation was that the continents had once been joined by necks of land that had since vanished. The evidence was weak, but by the time Wegener came up with his theory, the idea of land bridges was firmly entrenched. Wegener's theory was that all the continents had once been joined in a single huge landmass which he called Pangaea, which had split up hundreds of millions of years ago.

Only in the 1950s, when geologists began to explore the ocean floor, did evidence in favor of Wegener start to emerge. First, oceanographers found a great ridge

EARTHQUAKE AND VOLCANO ZONES

Soon after the idea of tectonic plates was developed, geologists realized that the world's major earthquake and volcano zones coincide with the boundaries between the plates. It has now become clear that most major earthquakes are triggered by the immense forces generated as plates grind together. When one plate drags past another, the rock on each side of the boundary bends and stretches a little way, then may snap suddenly. This sudden rupture sends shock waves, called seismic waves, shuddering through the ground, causing earthquakes.

▶ MONITORING VOLCANOES
Most of the world's most explosive volcanoes occur in an arc along the edge of what are called "convergent" plate margins (places where two tectonic plates are coming together). Volcanologists learn about volcanoes from studying less-violent volcanoes away from plate margins and above hot spots in the Earth's interior, such as this one.

◀ ERUPTING VOLCANO
Here you can actually see the molten lava exploding from the Earth's crust, where the pressure has become too great.

switches in the Earth's magnetic field, and so the stripes recorded the spreading of the ocean floor like the growth rings in a tree. A few years later, scientists on the research ship *Glomar Challenger* found that rocks got older the farther away from the ridge they were.

If Hess's theory that the ocean floor is spreading was right, then it seemed likely that Wegener's theory of continental drift was right too. In the 1980s geologists began to measure the distance between continents with astonishing accuracy, using laser beams bounced off satellites. They found that the continents really are moving, but the speed of this movement varies from place to place. North America and Europe are moving over 3/4 inch farther apart every year, which is faster than the rate at which a fingernail grows.

winding along the middle of the ocean floor through all the world's oceans, like a seam on a baseball. At the crest of this ridge was a deep central rift, or canyon.

In 1960 an American geologist, Harry Hess, stunned geologists by suggesting that the ocean floors might not be fixed, but were spreading rapidly from the mid-ocean ridge. As hot material wells up from the Earth's interior through the ridge's central rift, Hess suggested, it pushes the two halves of the ocean apart. Geologists were skeptical until, in the late 1960s, Frederick Vine and Drummond Matthews found stripes of strong and weak magnetism in the rocks on either side of the ridge. These stripes, they realized, must indicate ancient

▼ KINDS OF VOLCANO
The movement of the plates creates different kinds of volcano. Where the plates are pulling apart—long the mid-ocean ridge, for instance—volcanoes ooze lava gently all the time, often bubbling up through the gap. The lava often flows out to form shallow shield volcanoes. Where the plates are pushing together, volcanoes are much more unpredictable and explosive— thick magma piles up steep, cone-shaped volcanoes.

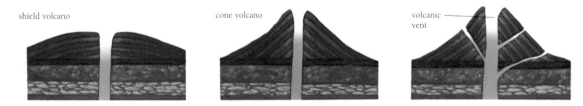

shield volcano   cone volcano   volcanic vent

▶ QUAKE WATCH
All around the world seismographic stations, such as the one shown here, are continually monitoring the earthquake vibrations generated as the Earth's tectonic plates grind together. The most violent earthquakes tend to occur in places where plates are sliding past each other—for example, along the San Andreas fault in California—or where one plate slides under another.

Key Dates

- 1923 Alfred Wegener suggests the idea of continental drift.

- 1956 Maurice Ewing, Bruce Heezen, and Marie Tharp discover the mid-ocean ridge.

- 1960 Harry Hess suggests that the ocean floors are spreading away from the mid-ocean ridge.

- 1963 Frederick Vine and Drummond Matthews find proof of ocean floor spreading in magnetic reversals in sea-bed rocks.

- 1967 Discovery of Lystrosaurus fossils in Antarctica.

- 1983 Satellites measure how fast tectonic plates are moving.

Artificial Materials

▲ ETHYLENE MOLECULE
Ethylene is a gas extracted from oil and natural gas. Ethylene molecules are made from four hydrogen atoms and two carbon atoms. Long chains of these molecules are put together to make polyethylene.

IN THE PAST, PEOPLE MADE things largely with natural materials such as wood and wool. During the 20th century, scientists developed an increasing range of synthetic, or manufactured, materials with properties that natural materials could not possibly match.

One of the biggest groups of synthetic materials is plastics, which are used in everything from spacecraft and car parts to bottles and artificial body parts. Plastics are incredibly light and can be molded into any shape. What gives plastic its special quality is the shape of its molecules (the smallest particles). With only a few exceptions, plastics are made from long organic (natural) molecules called polymers, which are made from lots of smaller molecules called monomers. Polyethylene, for instance, is a chain of 50,000 tiny molecules of an oil-extract called ethylene.

A few polymers, such as the tough fiber in plants known as cellulose, occur naturally. In the mid-1800s, scientists already knew that cellulose could be made into a brittle substance called cellulose nitrate. Then, in 1862, British chemist Alexander Parkes discovered that by adding camphor he could make cellulose nitrate tough but bendy and easy to mold. The new material "Parkesine" never took off, but in 1869 American John Hyatt created a similar substance called celluloid. At first it was used simply to make billiard balls, but when Kodak started to make photographic film with it in 1889, its success was assured.

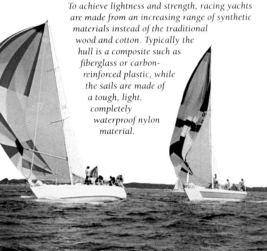

▼ RACING YACHT
To achieve lightness and strength, racing yachts are made from an increasing range of synthetic materials instead of the traditional wood and cotton. Typically the hull is a composite such as fiberglass or carbon-reinforced plastic, while the sails are made of a tough, light, completely waterproof nylon material.

POLYMER QUALITIES

Some polymers, such as the cellulose in wood and cotton, occur naturally, but most are now manufactured. They are all long chains of smaller molecules, altered slightly and repeated many times. In many polymers, the long molecules get tangled up like spaghetti, and it is the way they are tangled that gives a polymer its strength. If the strands are held tightly together, the result is a stiff plastic such as Lucite. If the strands slip over one another easily, it makes a bendy plastic such as polyethylene. Forcing the molecules through tiny holes lines them up to form a fiber such as nylon.

▶ LAVA LAMP
Plastics are easy to mold into almost any shape while warm, and once set, they hold their shape well. The clear cover for this lamp is molded plastic—typical of the fashion for molded plastic in the 1960s and 1970s.

◀ PVC
Polyvinyl chloride (PVC) is a synthetic polymer introduced in the 1920s. It can be either rigid or flexible. Rigid PVC is used for making objects such as bottles. Flexible PVC is used for making raincoats, garden hoses, and electrical insulation.

Since then, hundreds of plastics and other synthetic polymers have been developed, including Plexiglas, polyethylene, vinyl, cellophane, and a huge range of artificial fibers. The first of the synthetic fibers was nylon, which was created in the 1930s by Wallace Carothers, a chemist with the Du Pont company. In the 1920s, Carothers had found a way of making fibers out of very long polymer molecules stretched out in a machine called a molecular still. The stretching made the fibers strong and elastic, but they melted at very low temperatures. In 1935 he tried using a combination of chemicals called polyhexamethylene adipamide, which came to be called nylon.

Within a few years, Du Pont researchers had found a way of making the basic ingredients from petroleum, natural gas, and agricultural byproducts, and the first nylon products went on sale in 1939. People were so excited by this amazing new material that nylon mania swept the United States, and by the end of World War II everyone was wearing nylon-based clothes, and nylon stockings were a must for every woman. Nylon's

◀ RACING CYCLIST
Lightness really counts for a racing cyclist. This world-beating bike, instead of being made of metal like most bikes, is molded from carbon-reinforced plastic, which is far lighter than metal. Even the weight of the cyclist's clothes, shoes, and helmet is important. The synthetic fiber Lycra meets these requirements perfectly, in a way that no natural material can match.

toughness, elasticity, and moldability soon made it valued for furnishings, cars, and machinery as well as for clothes.

Since the introduction of nylon a whole new range of artificial fibers has been developed, including polyesters and Lycra, with a huge variety of uses. The big new area of polymer-based synthetic materials is "composites," which are made by combining two substances to obtain a material that has the qualities of both. Typically, one of the materials is a polymer. In carbon-reinforced plastic, tough carbon fibers are set within a polymer to make an amazingly strong but light material which is used to make anything from tennis rackets to racing car bodies. Kevlar, developed by Du Pont in 1971, is a composite based on nylon fibers set inside another polymer.

▶ PLASTIC DUCK
Plastics are so easily molded and so easy to make in bright colors that they have become very popular materials for making toys.

▲ BAKELITE
Bakelite was the first entirely synthetic plastic, invented by Leo Baekeland in 1909. It was made by treating phenol resin made from coal tar with formaldehyde. Like earlier plastics, it could be molded, but once molded, it set hard and was heatproof. Bakelite was also a good electrical insulator, so it was used for switches and plugs. It was also used to make radios, telephones, kitchenware, cameras, and much more.

Key Dates

- 1862 Alexander Parkes invents Parkesine, the first artificial polymer.
- 1869 John Hyatt invents celluloid.
- 1889 Kodak uses celluloid to make photographic film.
- 1909 Leo Baekeland invents Bakelite, the first entirely synthetic plastic.
- 1920 PVC is developed.
- 1935 Carothers develops nylon.
- 1939 Du Pont launches nylon.
- 1950s Carbon-fiber materials introduced.
- 1971 Kevlar created by Du Pont.

Life Changing

▲ G.M. TOMATOES
Many foods in our shops are already made with crops that have been genetically modified in some way. The genetically modified (G.M.) foods look no different from other foods.

During the 1950s, scientists discovered that all the instructions for life were carried in genetic code on the remarkable DNA molecule coiled inside every living cell. It took a while to crack the genetic code, but as they finally did, scientists began to realize that they might be able to manipulate it as a means of changing life's instructions.

In 1971, American microbiologists Daniel Nathans and Hamilton Smith discovered some chemicals called restriction enzymes. Restriction enzymes are like biological scissors, and they can be used to snip DNA in particular places. Other scientists soon found a biological glue— another enzyme, called DNA ligase, which can stick DNA back together. A few years later, American biochemist Paul Berg realized that by using restriction enzymes to cut DNA, and DNA ligase to glue it back together again, it would be possible to create entirely new and different DNA molecules. He called these new molecules "recombinant DNA." The remarkable thing about recombinant DNA was that it could be made to order, which made it completely different from anything that had ever existed before. This discovery was the beginning of what is now called genetic engineering. Scientists soon found, for example, that they could turn bacteria into protein factories by altering their genes. They simply extracted the DNA from the bacteria,

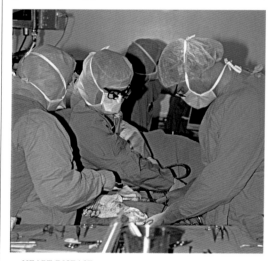

▲ HEART DISEASE
Many illnesses are inherited in the genes from parents; for example, a predisposition to heart disease can be inherited. One key area of genetic research focuses on ways of manipulating genes to cure genetic disorders such as these.

PERFECT REPLICAS
Usually each plant and animal has its own unique genes, which are different from those of every other plant and animal. You have a mix of genes from your mother, father, and grandparents, plus some that are your own and no one else's. "Cloning" means creating an organism (living thing) with exactly the same genes as another. The first clone was made when John Gurdon put the nucleus from a tadpole's gut cell, complete with DNA, into a frog's egg. The egg grew into a new tadpole, identical to the first.

Normally, new organisms grow from sex cells (from both parents) in which genes are mixed up. The DNA in each cell is a complete set of genes. Cloning uses the DNA from any body cell to grow a new creature. Since the new creature has the same genes, it is a perfect replica.

◄ DOLLY THE SHEEP
In 1997 Ian Wilmut and colleagues at Edinburgh's Roslin Institute made the first clone of an adult mammal. The clone was a sheep called Dolly. Scientists had thought adult mammals could not be cloned, but Dolly proved otherwise. Dolly grew from the nucleus of a cell taken from the teats of a Finn Dorset ewe and inserted in an egg in the womb of a Scottish Blackface ewe. The egg grew there to be born as a lamb with identical genes to the Finn Dorset ewe.

cut the right gene out of their DNA, inserted the one for the protein, and put it back in the bacteria. As the bacteria multiplied they would become a growing factory for the protein.

One valuable protein soon made like this was interferon. Interferons are proteins made by the human body which protect us against some viruses. However, the body makes only a tiny amount. By inserting doctored DNA into bacteria, it is possible to make lots of interferon reasonably cheaply. In the 1980s, scientists found how to use bacteria to make enzymes for detergents and melanin for suntan lotion, and also how to heighten the resistance of crops to pests and disease. Later, they discovered how to use sheep to produce insulin in their milk for diabetics. Scientists began to realize that there is no reason why, in future, we should not be able to transfer any gene from one living thing to another by using recombinant gene techniques. Soon they were investigating how to get bacteria and other living things to make certain substances, and many other things. Some scientists, for instance, began to work on how genetic disorders—illnesses inherited from your parents via your genes—might be cured. Others looked at how the genes of crops and farm animals might be modified to give them particular qualities. By adding to crops the genes from plants known to be distasteful or poisonous to crop pests, it might be possible to make crops pest resistant. The antifreeze genes from Antarctic fish, could be used to make other crops frost-resistant. However, as such experiments in the genetic modification of crops continued, they began to cause some public concern.

▶ G.M. CROPS
The idea of genetic modification of crops has become a topic of heated debate. Many scientists believe that genetic modification could dramatically boost crop production and reduce the need for pesticides. Others believe that the introduction of unnatural genes might have a devastating effect on natural ecosystems.

▼ IDENTICAL TWINS
Identical twins are the nearest nature provides to human clones. In theory, they both have identical genes because they grow from the same egg, which splits in two. In practice, however, many small differences appear as the twins develop inside their mother's womb.

Key Dates

- 1967 Gurdon creates the first clone, from a tadpole.

- 1970 Khorana creates the first truly artificial gene.

- 1971 Nathans and Smith discover restriction enzymes to snip DNA.

- 1973 Paul Berg discovers recombinant DNA techniques.

- 1973 Boyer uses recombinant DNA to create a chimera (combination of two species).

- 1975 Milstein produces the first monoclonal (single-cell clone) antibodies.

- 1997 Wilmut and colleagues clone Dolly the sheep, the first adult mammal clone.

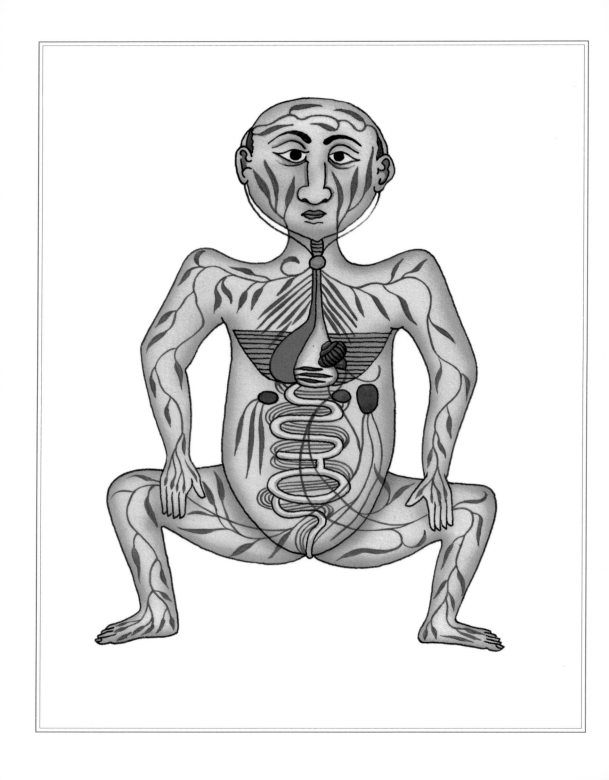

THE STORY
OF MEDICINE

BY BRIAN WARD

From prehistoric skull-drilling to laboratory-grown body parts, humans have made great advances in medicine. This section shows how, over the ages, mastery of medicine has enabled humans to live longer, more comfortable lives.

A Healthy Mind and Body

W hat is medicine? And what is health? In different cultures and at different times you would have received widely varying answers to these questions. In the modern Western medical tradition, the main objective is first to get rid of disease, and then to keep people healthy. In earlier times, Western medicine depended on a muddled mixture of prayer, folk remedies, and theories going back to the Arab civilizations and beyond that to the ancient Greeks. True advances in medical care did not take place until the 1800s, and it was not until the 1900s that medicine was able to reduce the high death rates caused by infections. Eastern medicine took a different line, which was that the whole body had to be treated in order to keep it healthy and to prevent disease from appearing. Now, in the 2000s, Western medicine has begun to accept the idea of keeping the whole body healthy.

Disease is a state in which the body does not function properly, but it is harder to define health. A person aged 70 or more may feel that they are in perfect health, but a younger person would not be happy to experience the aches, pains, and breathlessness that often accompany aging. So health needs to be considered in terms of our expectations

▲ TRADITIONAL MEDICINES
Chinese medicine developed from a totally different background from science-based Western medicine. It treats the whole body by restoring the balance of forces flowing within it. There is growing interest in this and other forms of traditional medicine.

▼ KEY DATES
The panel charts the history of medicine, from the earliest uses of herbs and magic as cures, to the invention of state-of-the-art technologies.

▼ CAUTERIZING IRON
Medical techniques become outdated as better knowledge and technology lead to an improved way of doing things. For centuries, a red-hot iron was used to seal or cauterize the blood vessels and prevent bleeding after surgery. This agonizing process usually led to infection. Today, high-tech laser beams seal a wound safely and painlessly.

ANCIENT TIMES

15,000B.C. Cave paintings in France show shamanic rituals.

2700B.C. Legendary Shen Nong discovers herbalism.

2600B.C. Imhotep describes ancient Egyptian medicine.

c.2000B.C. Legendary date for the writing of the *Nei Ching*.

c.1700B.C. Code of Hammurabi lays down laws for doctors.

Hammurabi, king of Babylon

1550B.C. Ebers papyrus records Egyptian medical practices.

1200B.C. Asclepius sets up healing centers in ancient Greece.

460B.C. Birth of Hippocrates, who founds Greek medicine.

Hippocrates

c.300B.C. The medical school and library at Alexandria are founded.

A.D.40–c.90 Dioscorides writes manual of herbal medicine.

A.D.129-216 Galen enlarges on earlier Greek writings and begins experimental medical studies.

THE MIDDLE AGES

A.D.832 Non-Islamic medical texts are translated in Baghdad.

c.A.D.800 Rhazes prepares his medical compendium.

c.A.D.1000 Avicenna produces the *Canon of Medicine*.

1100–1300 Medical schools are founded throughout Europe.

1215 The Pope decrees that all doctors need Church approval.

c.1200–1300 Professional medical organizations are set up.

1258 Medical texts preserved by the Arabs flow back to the West.

Paracelsus

THE RENAISSANCE

1527 Paracelsus lays the ground for studies into chemical treatment of diseases.

1543 Vesalius publishes accurate illustrations of human anatomy.

1628 William Harvey publishes his theory of blood circulation.

1665 King Charles II and the royal court flee London during the Great Plague.

for normal life. Even aging itself is thought of almost as a disease in some Western cultures, where people are living longer. Thanks to modern medicine, today people can live an active life into extreme old age, while in earlier times they might have been crippled by heart disease or arthritis. However, in some developing countries where malnutrition and infection are common, 40 years is still considered to be a good life expectancy.

Killer diseases, which used to wipe out as many as half of the children in a family, have been brought under control by drugs and vaccination in Western countries. However, nature still has a few surprises for modern medicine. New diseases such as AIDS have appeared, and these are not yet under control. Some of the old, familiar microbes have found ways to beat modern antibiotics and are threatening health once more. The only real conquest of a disease has been the eradication of smallpox. There are a few more diseases, such as polio, measles, and leprosy, that may be conquered soon.

Medicine has made other huge advances. Doctors have the technology with which to examine almost every part of the body. Scientists are beginning to understand the complex chemical reactions that power the body. Surgery, which has been performed for thousands of years, has made great leaps with the techniques for transplantation of body organs and artificial organs. One thing is certain—no one can be sure what advances medicine will make in the future.

▲ HIV VIRUS
Recent understanding of the structure of viruses, such as HIV, has revealed how they overcome the body's natural immune defenses. Research into viruses can reveal their weak points, so that effective drugs can be designed to attack them.

MODERN TIMES

1673 Van Leeuwenhoek makes the first microscope and discovers microbes.

1714 Gabriel Fahrenheit invents the mercury thermometer.

1796 Edward Jenner vaccinates against smallpox using cowpox.

1819 René Laënnec introduces the first stethoscope.

Laënnec's stethoscope

1847 Ignaz Semmelweiss demonstrates that infection is spread by unwashed hands.

1853 Queen Victoria uses chloroform as an anesthetic during childbirth.

chloroform mask

1854 John Snow demonstrates that cholera is spread through contaminated drinking water.

1865 Joseph Lister carries out the first operation using carbolic acid as an antiseptic.

1878 Louis Pasteur presents his case for the germ theory of infection.

1882 Robert Koch discovers the tubercle bacillus that causes TB.

1885 Louis Pasteur successfully tests his rabies vaccine.

1895 X-rays are discovered by Wilhelm Röntgen.

1898 Marie Curie discovers the radioactive element radium.

1901–2 Blood groups are described by Karl Landsteiner, making transfusion practical.

1902 Frederick Treves makes removal of the appendix a popular treatment for appendicitis.

Marie Curie

1928 Alexander Fleming discovers penicillin.

1953 James Watson and Francis Crick discover the structure of DNA.

DNA

1954 The first successful kidney transplant is performed.

1955 Jonas Salk introduces the first polio vaccine.

1961 Thalidomide (a sedative) is withdrawn after causing birth defects.

1964 Christiaan Barnard carries out the first heart transplant.

1974 The last natural case of smallpox occurs.

1983 HIV is identified in France and the United States.

Earliest Medicine

ARLY PEOPLE'S REMAINS contain evidence of attempts at medical care. The most striking of these are skulls with neatly drilled or cut holes. The process of making these holes is called trepanning. The holes may have been made to allow a disease to escape from the body. Trepanned skulls have been found in Europe and in South America. Remarkably, some of them show signs that the cut edges of bone had healed, so the patient had survived for some time after the operation. Some even show evidence of being trepanned on several different occasions.

Herbal medicine was probably also practiced from the earliest times. It can still be seen in the great apes, such as chimpanzees. Chimps sometimes chew herbs that are not part of their normal diet, probably for their medicinal effects. The remains of herbs are not uncommon in ancient burials, and have also been found in association with the burials of Neanderthals,

▲ TREPANNING TOOLS
Stone Age people used a drill to cut a hole in the skull. This was a wooden stick with a sharpened piece of flint at the tip. Flints were later used with a bow drill. Sometimes the drill was tipped with volcanic glass or even a shark's tooth.

who were ancient relatives of modern people.

Although prehistoric people must have suffered from many diseases, they probably did not experience the rapidly spreading infections that later caused epidemics. They lived in small groups, so there were not enough people for diseases to spread quickly.

By 3000B.C. people were beginning to live in huge cities, such as Babylon. Epidemic diseases appeared, many of which are recorded in ancient documents. By about 1700B.C. Babylonian doctors had to follow a number of laws. These were written down in the Code of Hammurabi. One practice was to sacrifice animals and look at their organs to foretell if the patient would die.

The ancient Egyptians left careful records that describe a whole range of medical

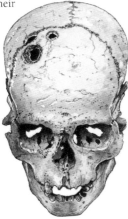

▶ HOLES IN THE HEAD
This skull was found in Jericho and dates to 2000B.C. It has three carefully cut trepanning holes, together with a healed hole. The holes are round, which tells us that they must have been drilled into the skull. In other skull finds, there are square holes, which were cut out with a knife.

MESOPOTAMIA AND EGYPT

The oldest surviving medical text is the Ebers papyrus from Egypt. It dates back to about 1550B.C. This papyrus scroll is more than 66 feet long and describes many diseases and remedies. It includes over 700 drugs and 800 medicine recipes. There is even a cure for crocodile bites. The Ebers papyrus has instructions for mixing up these medicines into ointments, poultices (compresses), pills, and inhalations. There are also descriptions of protective amulets (charms) and spells. Many of the medicines would have had little effect, but some were drugs still familiar today, including opium and cannabis.

▼ THE FIRST DOCTOR
Imhotep was an ancient Egyptian scribe and priest who lived 4,500 years ago. He left many detailed descriptions of diseases and treatments. After his death, he was made into a god.

◀ SURGICAL TOOLS
These bronze and copper knives are from ancient Mesopotamia. They may have been used to remove organs from dead bodies.

▶ CODE OF CONDUCT
Hammurabi, king of Babylon, laid down 17 rules for doctors in the Code of Hammurabi, his collection of all Babylonian laws. The rules included guidelines on punishments for doctors if their treatment did not work.

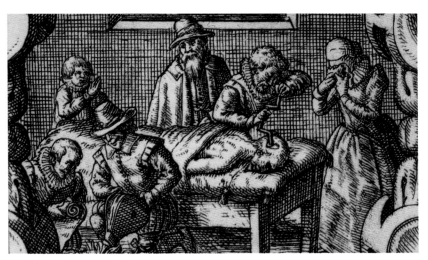

◀ TREPANNING IN PROGRESS
This picture from the 1500s shows a doctor trepanning his patient. In the ancient world, trepanning was often carried out to release spirits from the brain. Trepanning is extremely dangerous because it allows bacteria to come into contact with the brain surface. Many patients must have died.

▼ MEDICINE IN THE WILD
Animals such as this baby gorilla search out medicinal herbs in order to treat their ailments. Even carnivores, such as cats, sometimes chew leaves and stems. This may be a way to obtain extra nutrients.

procedures and drugs. Egyptian doctors began to specialize in treating particular organs or diseases. The most famous was Imhotep, who was also a high priest, an architect, and an astrologer. The Egyptians believed that spirits crept into the body and caused disease. They used surgery to set broken bones and sew up wounds. However, they took little interest in internal anatomy (the inside workings of the human body). This is surprising, as they must have learned about it through their interest in mummifying (preserving) the bodies of the dead. Most Egyptian medicine consisted of herbal treatments.

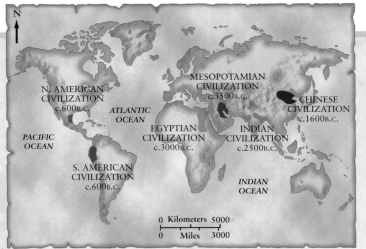

Key Dates

- 10,000–2000B.C. Evidence of ancient Egyptian medical practice.

- 5000B.C. Trepanned skull at Ensisheim, France, is the oldest evidence we have of trepanning.

- c.2686–2613B.C. Life of the Egyptian doctor, Imhotep.

- 1792–1750B.C. Hammurabi rules in Babylon.

- 1550B.C. The Ebers papyrus is written in Egypt.

- 650B.C. Mesopotamian clay tablets describe herbal cures and accurately describe a *migtu* (epileptic seizure).

▲ EARLIEST MEDICINE
Finds and written records provide evidence of medicine practiced by the civilizations shown here, but it is almost certain that medicine was known in all ancient cultures.

Shamans and the Supernatural

As isolated communities developed, so did the idea of an individual who could combine the function of healer with the ability to speak to the gods and spirits. In some early French cave paintings, made about 17,000 years ago, there are pictures of men in animal masks performing ritual dances. These are what we call shamans, and they still exist in many cultures around the world. Shamans are found in Arctic regions and especially in Siberia, among some Native North Americans and South Americans, in Southeast Asia, and in the Pacific Islands. In West Africa, shamans are often known as medicine men or witch doctors. Their activities include medical treatment with drugs and prayer, and sometimes the laying of curses on an enemy. People believe that shamans also have the power to cause illness, to ensure fertility or the birth of male children, and to prevent disease by the use of ointments, talismans (charms), and fetishes (magical objects). Shamans are thought to talk with gods, spirits,

▲ ASHANTI DOLL
Shamans heal by magic. They often use dolls to represent their patients or to represent the spirits that will aid in the healing ceremony.

▸ SHAMAN HEALING CEREMONY
During the healing ritual, such as this ceremony in Cameroon, West Africa, the shaman dances around the patient and chants prayers to the spirits.

NATIVE AMERICAN MEDICINE

All the Native American tribes had shamans. Those of the Ojibwa tribe formed secret societies and even specialized in particular types of medicine, such as herbalism. Disease was often seen as punishment for bad behavior or for not worshiping the spirits properly. The Navajo cure was to appeal to the spirits by means of songs, dance, prayer, sweat baths, massage, and making sand paintings. Noisemakers were flat pieces of wood, tied to cord that made a roaring sound when whirled around at high speed. They were used to invoke (call up) wind or rain and drive out evil spirits.

▸ MEDICINE MAN
There were over 300 different tribes of Native Americans, and they all had different traditions. This medicine man is from the Blackfoot tribe, who lived on the northwestern part of the Great Plains, in what is now the state of Montana.

◂ MAGIC NECKLACE
This magical amulet was worn by an Apache medicine man. It is made from glass beads and human teeth, some of which are still embedded in part of the jawbone.

and the dead. They often ask the spirits for special favors, such as a good harvest or victory in battle over other villages or tribes.

The shaman usually acts as a local religious leader. Shamanism is not organized like the major world religions. It is a collection of a whole range of folk beliefs and myths. The shaman is able to leave his body and enter a trance, in which he does not appear to be aware of what is going on around him. He does this through the use of drugs, dancing, music, or, sometimes, an epileptic fit.

In most cultures where shamans exist, illness is blamed on the soul's leaving the body. In a trance, the shaman finds the soul, which may have been stolen by witchcraft or magic, and persuades it to return to the body. This is a long process, often made dangerous by the use of drugs. If the patient dies, the shaman has to make a treacherous voyage to take the soul of the dead person safely to its new home.

Sometimes an illness is blamed on an object that has been put inside the sick person by magic. In these cases the shaman sucks hard at the affected area, then spits out pieces of wood or stone. These are said to be the cause of the problem. Shamans use various types of instruments and charms for their cures, such as hollow bones to suck out poison, sharp flints for cutting the skin and causing bleeding, and, often, masks and other ritual clothing.

◀ BAHUNGANA FETISH
A fetish is an object believed to possess magical powers. This one has a medicine bag like a shaman uses. It is covered with figures which help to give it its power.

▶ YOMBE FETISH
This fetish comes from the Yombe tribe of the Republic of Congo. It can be used to cure or curse, by driving nails into the image during a magical ritual. The nails are pushed into the part of the body that needs to be made better or harmed.

▼ SQUAWROOT
North American medicine men used the roots of the black cohosh, or squawroot, as a painkiller. It has now been adopted by Western herbalists.

▶ SAND PAINTING
Navajo Native Americans used grains of colored sand to create magical pictures called sand paintings. Some were big enough for the sick person to sit in the middle of them during the healing ceremony.

Key Dates

- 15,000B.C. French cave paintings show evidence of ritual dances.

- c.3000B.C. An amber horse from this date shows the use of amulets to ward off evil spirits and sickness.

- A.D.1492 Christopher Columbus "discovers" the Americas.

- 1520s Cabeza de Vaca witnesses medicine men curing the sick by blowing on the patient.

- 1800s Tradition of medicine men disappears as European settlers destroy and fragment Native American tribes.

Ayurvedic Medicine

THE *VEDAS* are a series of Hindu texts written in India between 1200B.C. and 900B.C., though they are probably based on much older stories. In among the religious parts of the *Vedas* are explanations of the workings of the body and detailed descriptions of diseases, including dropsy and tumors. Treatments recommended in the *Vedas* included herbal remedies and also prayers and magic rituals to expel demons. Vedic medicine was practiced up to around 1000BC.

After 1000B.C. a new school of medicine emerged in India, still based on the *Vedas* but drawing in beliefs from other systems, such as Buddhism. This is known as Ayurvedic (knowledge of life) medicine. Its principles were written down in two influential books. These were the *Caraka-samhita* and the *Sushruta-samhita*, written by two doctors named Caraka and Sushruta. Both believed that desires upset the body's balance, so they have to be satisfied in moderation. The Hindus believed that the body was built from three essences, or elements. These were air or breath, phlegm, and bile. They had to be in balance, for a person to enjoy good health. The essences interacted to produce the body's flesh, fat, marrow, blood, bone, chyle (fatty fluid), and semen. Ayurvedic treatment involved restoring the balance of the essences, with a combination of prayer, herbal medicine, diet, and, sometimes, surgery.

Indian doctors were very skilled in making a diagnosis (identifying a disease). As apprentices, they had to memorize passages from the *Vedas*. During the examination of the patient, appropriate verses would come to mind. The verses helped the doctor to

▲ FIRE AND FEVER
Agni was the Hindu god of fire. People prayed to him in cases of fever.

▶ LOTUS POSITION
Meditation (deep thought) and exercise are important parts of Indian medicine. The lotus position is one of the poses used in yoga during meditation. Practicing yoga helps the body to reach a state of spiritual enlightenment and keeps the three essences in balance.

INDIAN SURGERY

Hindu surgeons developed the first forms of plastic surgery. They were able to completely reconstruct a nose, which was often amputated (cut off) as a form of punishment. They performed skin grafts by taking pieces of skin tissue from other parts of the body and fixing them onto the damaged area. Quills were placed inside the nostrils so that the patient could breathe while the wounds healed. Western surgeons were astonished at their skill. After an account of this technique was published in 1794, it was introduced to Europe, and called the "Hindu method."

gripping tool

fine scissors

heavy scissors

gripping tools

◀ SURGICAL TOOLS
Ayurvedic doctors developed some sophisticated surgical techniques. They used steel instruments, such as these, dating from about A.D.1100, to carry out their operations. Steel does not rust, which makes these instruments far more hygienic.

make a proper diagnosis and suggest the right treatment. There was a large range of herbal medicines to choose from, as well as drugs prepared from animal parts or minerals. Drugs used included the dung or urine of elephants and the eggs of peacocks and crocodiles.

Partly for religious reasons, hygiene was very important to Ayurvedic surgeons. Doctors stressed the importance of washing the body and cleaning the teeth regularly.

Hindu surgeons were highly skilled. Operations included removing tumors and cataracts, repairing broken bones, stitching wounds, and performing caesarean births and amputations. They were even able to remove bladder stones. Thanks to their good hygiene, surgeons in India in 800B.C. had a higher survival rate among their patients than those in Europe up until the 1800s.

▲ MODELING THE BODY
Ayurvedic practitioners developed a plan of the inside workings of the body. It mapped a whole system of furnaces, tubes, and valves. These had no basis in reality, because Hindus were forbidden by their religion to cut open a dead body.

▲ LORD BRAHMA HOLDS COURT
Ayurvedic medicine was said to have been developed by Brahma, one of the Hindu trinity of ruling gods. The Vedas are a whole body of knowledge containing religious and philosophical teaching, as well as information on medicine.

▼ DR. ANT
Wounds were "stitched" by the use of fierce biting ants. The ants gripped the edges of the wound and held them tightly together.

▶ NOSE REBUILDING
Ayurvedic surgeons developed the techniques of plastic surgery. They knew that it was essential to keep a bridge of living tissue in the skin flap which they used to reconstruct a nose. This maintained the blood supply and prevented the grafted tissue from dying.

skin flap

skin flap

quills

Key Dates

- 1200–900B.C. The *Vedas* written.

- 200B.C. First descriptions of yoga techniques are written down in the *Yoga-sutras*.

- A.D.100 Final version of the *Caraka-samhita* is written.

- A.D.600s Final version of the *Sushruta-samhita* is written.

- A.D.1000s Islamic invaders bring new medical practices to India.

- 1500s European settlers bring Western medical ideas to India.

- 1793 British doctors first observe Hindus performing reconstructive surgery.

Chinese Medicine

CHINESE MEDICINE developed over thousands of years, almost without any outside influences from other medical systems. The *Nei Ching* (Book of Medicine) is an ancient medical work. According to legend, it was written over 4,000 years ago by the Yellow Emperor, Huang Ti. The book was more likely to have been written some time about 200B.C., but it has formed the basis for most Chinese medical literature since.

Chinese medicine is based largely on the concept of *yin* and *yang*, which stand for opposing states and conditions. *Yin* represents states such as feminine, dark, and wet. *Yang* represents the opposing states of masculine, light, and dry. In the *Nei Ching*, *yin* and *yang* are said to control the body, which is thought of as a tiny country with rulers and administrators. The "country" also has a communication system of 12 rivers, based on the great rivers of China. These rivers divide into much smaller channels which carry blood and *ch'i* (vital energy).

These channels connect organs to one another. For example, the kidney connects to the ear, the lungs to the nose, and the heart to the tongue. When these channels are in good working order, the body is healthy. Points along the channels can be used to influence the flow of *ch'i*.

As with Hinduism, Chinese religions discouraged dissection. For this reason, medicine was based largely

▲ YIN AND YANG
The symbol for yin and yang represents the rule of opposites which is so important in Chinese medicine. Yin is the force that represents qualities such as darkness. Its opposite, yang, stands for qualities such as light. Chinese medicine attempts to restore the balance between these opposites.

▶ HUANG TI
The Empero, Huang Ti, lived from 2698B.C. to 2598B.C. He was said to be the author of the great Chinese medical work called the Nei Ching. This forms the basis of all Chinese medicine.

RESTORING THE BALANCE

The Chinese doctor was paid only as long as his patient remained healthy. So if a patient became ill, it was very important to restore the balance of *ch'i* and other elements within the body. This was done with a mixture of exercise, contemplation (thought or meditation), diet, and other means. Many Chinese drugs were made from ingredients that were believed to have special effects. For example, organs from a tiger were thought to pass on some of that animal's power.

▶ DOCTOR AND PATIENT
Traditional Chinese medicine involves long discussion between the doctor and patient. The doctor treats the whole body, not just a small diseased part.

◀ MAMMOTH TEETH
So-called dragon teeth are still ground up and widely used in Chinese medicine. Of course, there are no such creatures as dragons. Huge teeth taken from the dug-up remains of ancient mammoths are often used by pharmacists, but so are the teeth of many other extinct animals, including those of the huge ape *Gigantopithecus*.

▼ GINSENG
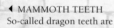
This root contains many substances that have powerful effects on the body. Extracts are widely used as a stimulant or tonic. The ginseng root may have appealed to early Chinese pharmacists because it looked a bit like a human body.

◀ PAGE FROM THE NEI CHING
The Nei Ching *explains how the forces* yin *and* yang *interact and affect the flow of* ch'i. *According to the* Nei Ching, *the human body, like all other matter, is made of five basic elements—fire, earth, water, metal, and wood.*

▶ SHEN NONG
This legendary emperor lived in about 2700 B.C. and is said to have discovered Chinese herbal medicine. He described 365 different medical plants. His teachings were written down about 2,000 years ago in a book called the Bencao Jing.

on these channels and their influences on the body. Treatments often involved the use of acupuncture, in which needles were inserted into one of the hundreds of points where *ch'i* channels were thought to run. This stimulated (perked up) the flow of *ch'i* and restored good health. Sometimes cones of dried herbs were burned on the skin at these points, for the same purpose. Acupuncture has been practiced for more than 4,500 years. It remains central to Chinese medicine and is also used in the West, especially as a treatment for pain and a cure for addiction (dependency on a drug).

Chinese medicine depends mostly on herbal remedies. Many of these herbs have been incorporated into Western medicine—among them castor oil, camphor, chaulmoogra oil to treat leprosy, and iron to

treat anemia. Ginseng is a widely known Chinese stimulant, used to keep a person alert.

The ancient Chinese invented vaccination as a way to treat smallpox. They injected a small amount of pus from a smallpox sore into healthy people. This gave them a mild form of the disease and made them immune (resistant) to full-blown infection. Europeans did not discover vaccination until the A.D. 1700s.

▲ CHANNELS OF CH'I
Acupuncture needles are inserted through the skin at points along lines called meridians (channels). The point where the acupuncturist inserts the needle may be a long way from the part of the body that needs treatment.

◀ ACUPUNCTURE NEEDLES
Acupuncturists (people who practise acupuncture) use very long needles. They may be inserted as deeply as 10 in. into the body. Then the needles are wiggled or twirled to restore the flow of *ch'i*. Modern acupuncturists often pass a small electrical current through the needle.

Key Dates

- 2700 B.C. Life of legendary emperor Shen Nong, who discovered herbal medicine.

- 2698–2598 B.C. The reign of Huang Ti, legendary founder of Chinese medicine.

- 200 B.C. The *Nei Ching* is written.

- A.D. 280 Wang Shu-ho writes his 12-volume *Mei Ching* (Book of the Pulse).

- 1601 Yang Chi-chou writes his ten-volume *Ch'en-Chiu Ta-Ch'eng*, describing acupuncture.

- 1600s The first descriptions of Chinese medical practice reach the West.

Hippocrates and the Greeks

▲ SERPENT AND STAFF
A snake coiled around a wooden staff was the symbol of the Greek physician Asclepius, who lived around 1200B.C. Even today, it is still used as a sign for the medical profession in many countries around the world.

THE ANCIENT GREEK DOCTOR Asclepius lived in about 1200B.C. According to legend, he was so successful in curing disease that he became a god. The sick went and slept in his temples, known as *asklepia*. They believed that Asclepius would cure them in the night. Diet and mineral baths were part of the cure, but treatment of disease was almost entirely a matter for prayer and magical rituals. However, from about 400B.C. Greek philosophers began to look for a more practical approach to disease.

The ancient Greeks had a great deal of contact with the Middle East and Asia, due partly to the conquests of Alexander the Great. In India they may have come across Vedic beliefs. This could explain how Greek philosophers came to believe that the universe was made up of four elements—air, earth, fire, and water. This led to the idea

▲ THE FOUR HUMORS
This medieval illustration shows the four humors. Greek philosophers held that the body was made up of these four elements—blood, phlegm, yellow bile or choler, and black bile or melancholy. These had to be kept in balance.

TREATING DISEASE

Hippocrates and his fellow doctors believed their job was to help the body to heal itself. Drugs were seldom used, although opium was used to relieve pain. Surgery was understood but was not very common. The Greeks have left behind detailed descriptions of trepanning, even advising surgeons to dip the knife or drill into cold water every now and then so it did not become too hot from rubbing against the bone. The writings of Hippocrates include a method for treating a dislocated (out of joint) shoulder which is still in use today. It is called the Hippocratic method.

▶ MANDRAKE
The root of the mandrake plant was believed to be a powerful magical charm because it looked rather like a human body. Mandrake is actually very poisonous.

▼ DOCTOR
Greek doctors traveled around to meet their patients, on trips called *epidemics*. They were skilled in examining patients and accurate in diagnosing diseases, but they had only limited treatments available.

▲ BLOODLETTING
A Greek vase, made in about 470B.C., shows a doctor preparing to bleed a patient by opening a vein. The blood would have been collected in the jar hanging on the wall behind them.

◀ FATHER OF MEDICINE
*Hippocrates was the greatest of the ancient
Greek doctors, and his influence persists to
this day. He is said to have written more
than 70 books on medicine and surgery.
The Hippocratic Oath (promise) outlined
the responsibilites that Hippocrates believed
doctors had to their patients and to society.
Doctors still try to live up to these today.*

▶ VOTIVE TABLET
*It was common to dedicate a tablet to the
gods in thanks for a cure. This votive tablet
is dedicated to Asclepius, probably in thanks
for treatment of varicose veins, which can be
seen on the leg that Asclepius is holding.*

that the body was made up of four humors (elements), too.

This belief was held by Hippocrates, the father of Western
medicine. He was born in Kos around 460 B.C. Little is known about
him. Even his surviving medical works were actually written by other
people. Hippocrates said that diseases had natural causes. He stressed
the importance of diagnosis and encouraged doctors to write down
all they could about how a disease developed. He thought the body
would heal itself and that this process could be sped up through
diet, exercise, and rest. These helped to restore the balance of the
humors. If the disease did not respond, humors were removed by
bloodletting (removing blood) or by making the patient sweat. These
treatments often worked, even though the reasoning behind them
was wrong. This is probably why the theory of humors survived into
the 1800s in Western medicine, and so did Hippocratic treatments.

▶ SPREAD OF
GREEK MEDICINE
Ancient Greek ideas
spread around the
Mediterranean, and
through the Middle
East and Egypt. In
turn, herbal remedies
and treatments from
these areas were
incorporated into
Greek medicine. Later,
after some initial
resistance, the
Romans also adopted
Greek methods of
medicine and surgery.

Map labels: ADRIATIC SEA, Rome, MACEDONIA, THRACIA, BLACK SEA, N, Mt. Olympus, Troy, Croton, GREECE, Pergamon, Epidauros, Athens, Ephesus, Sparta, Miletus, Acragas, Syracuse, MEDITERRANEAN SEA, CRETE, KOS, Salamis, CYPRUS, Cyrene, LIBYA, Alexandria, Memphis, EGYPT, R. Nile

0 Kilometers 500
0 Miles 300

Key Dates

- 1200 B.C. Asclepius sets up
  healing centers. He is later
  worshiped as a god.

- 490–430 B.C. Life of Empedocles,
  who described the four humors.

- 460–377 B.C. Life of Hippocrates.

- 429 B.C. An important medical
  school is founded at Cyrene.

- 356–323 B.C. Life of Alexander
  the Great, whose empire
  stretched as far as India.

- c.300 B.C. The famous medical
  school is founded at Alexandria.

- c.100 B.C. Greek doctors take
  their knowledge to Rome.

Roman Medicine

CELSUS
In around 25B.C., the Roman nobleman Celsus wrote his huge encyclopedia. One of its volumes, De medicina, *recorded all that was known about Greek and Roman medicine.*

THE FAMOUS GREEK school at Alexandria remained the center for medical teaching, even after the Romans conquered the Greeks. Asclepiades of Bithynia (in modern-day Turkey) lived from 124B.C. until 40B.C. He took Greek ideas about medicine to Rome. He did not believe in the healing power of nature, nor that humors caused disease. He recommended treatments such as poultices, massage, good diet, and plenty of fresh air. Asclepiades was also the first to study mental illness. He prescribed music, occupational therapy (work), and exercise, together with plenty of wine to sedate people (make them calm or sleepy).

The Romans employed mainly Greek doctors. Even then, many people preferred to treat ailments themselves with herbs and charms. Cornelius Celsus, a Roman nobleman, wrote a detailed history of medicine in about 25B.C. Doctors used this work up until the 1400s. It described diseases of the eyes, nose, and ears, hernias, bladder stones, and other common conditions.

CUPPING
The Romans and Greeks drew foul humors out of the body in a process called cupping. A piece of lint was set alight and placed inside a cup, which was pressed against the skin, an open wound, or a surgical cut. As the oxygen was used up the cup became a vacuum (airless space). This created suction (as in a vacuum cleaner) that sucked out the "vicious humors."

LEARNING FROM COMBAT

According to Galen, much disease resulted from an excess of blood, one of the four humors. This surplus blood might putrefy (rot) in some part of the body, and should be removed by bloodletting. Sometimes patients were even bled until they became unconscious. Like Galen's other teachings, bloodletting persisted until the 1800s, resulting in many unnecessary deaths.

ROMAN GLADIATOR
Before moving to Rome, Galen was physician to the gladiators in Alexandria. He must have gained useful experience of anatomy and surgery by treating these professional fighters.

BATTLEFIELD MEDICINE
The Roman army was the first to use doctors on the battlefield. They set up field hospitals to provide instant medical care.

SURGICAL HOOK
Roman surgeons used a bronze hook to tease apart the tissue during an operation. This kept the blood vessels and muscles out of the way and gave the doctor a clear view.

◄ PUBLIC BATHS
The Romans took great care of their bodies. They spent many hours in the public baths, soaking in hot water or enjoying a massage. This helped them to avoid infections caused by poor hygiene.

▼ ROMAN AQUEDUCT
Clean water supplies were an important public health measure introduced by the Romans. Aqueducts were bridges that carried supplies of fresh water from sources many miles away.

During the 1st and 2nd centuries A.D., many Greek doctors traveled to Rome. Claudius Galen moved to Rome in A.D.162 and went on to become the physician to five different Roman emperors. He was so influential that his writings were accepted for the next 1,500 years. Galen developed Hippocrates' theories about humors, but, unlike the Greeks, he believed in experimenting.

Human dissection was not permitted, so Galen learned about anatomy by dissecting monkeys and other animals. As a result, many of his assumptions were later proved wrong. Galen showed that blood ebbs and flows as the heart beats, but he never realized that it flows around the body. He wrote at least 350 books about medicine, some describing very complex operations. Galen's works were so respected that they went unchallenged for centuries. Even his mistakes were widely accepted up until the 1500s, when doctors

began to experiment once more.

While Greek influence accounted for most medical advances in Rome, the Romans made important advances in maintaining public health, which reduced infectious disease. Fresh water was piped into the cities, and public baths were built. There was proper sanitation and rubbish clearance. Clinics and hospitals were built, and there were also army doctors, who treated soldiers' battle wounds.

▲ FOLDING SCALPEL
The Romans used scalpels like this to cut open a body for surgery. It folded when not in use to prevent any accidental cuts.

▼ ARMY HOSPITAL
This model shows an army hospital, or *valetudinarium*. The Romans developed a sophisticated system of care for their soldiers. Hospitals on this scale did not appear again for nearly a thousand years.

Key Dates

- c.100–44B.C. Life of Julius Caesar, who employs doctors in the army.

- 53.BC.–A.D.7 Life of Cornelius Celsus, author of *De medicina*.

- A.D.40–c.90 Life of Nero's army surgeon, Dioscorides, who describes around 600 plants and over 1,000 drugs in his book *De materia medica*.

- A.D.77 Pliny the Elder's *Historia Naturalis* describes surgery and herbal remedies.

- c.A.D.100 Soranus writes about birth control and pregnancy.

- A.D.129–216 Life of Galen, who expands on Greek writings.

The Arab World

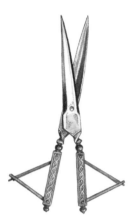

URING THE PERIOD of the Byzantine Empire (A.D.300–1453), the works of Greek and Roman doctors were collected together. Some appeared in the languages used at the fringes of the empire, such as Persian and Syrian.

▲ SURGICAL SCISSORS
Scissors were developed as a more precise way than knives or scalpels to cut through tissue.

▶ AVICENNA
Avicenna was a Persian doctor working within the Arab Empire. His book, the Canon of Medicine, *was used across the Middle East and Europe for centuries.*

Meanwhile the Arab Empire was growing in power and influence. It conquered Persia and Syria. At first, the Arabs favored their own traditional remedies, but as the power of the Islamic religion increased in the Arab Empire, many traditional treatments were lost. Doctors began to turn to ancient Greek ideas and translated Greek texts into Arabic. This enabled ancient Greek learning to spread throughout the Arab Empire, into Europe and around the Mediterranean.

Important centers of learning sprang up in Baghdad, Cairo, and Damascus in the Middle East, and in Toledo, Córdoba, and Seville in what is now Spain. Arab scientists and doctors published copies of the early medical works. Some of these were later translated into Latin and used in European medical schools from the 1200s.

Arab medicine did not contribute much new knowledge, but Arab writers made detailed descriptions of diseases and their diagnoses. Surgery suffered in early years, because dissection was banned, so little was known about anatomy. However, an Arab surgeon in Córdoba wrote a text on surgical techniques, and others developed techniques for surgery on the eye and the internal organs. The Arabs were interested in alchemy (trying to transform cheap metals into gold and searching for a source of eternal life). Their alchemical experiments led them to find many

MEDICAL PIONEERS

Not all of the medical scholars were Arabs. Many were Persians, Jews, or Christians living within the Arab Empire. Rhazes was a Persian who put together a huge medical compendium. Maimonides was a Jewish doctor born in the 1100s. He became physician to the Saracen ruler Saladin. His extensive writings on medicine were based on Greek ideas.

◀ RHAZES
The Persian physician Rhazes was born about A.D.865. He wrote more than 200 books on a huge range of subjects. He was admired for his medical care of the poor.

▲ EYE SURGERY
Cataracts is an eye condition that clouds the lens of the eye and eventually leads to blindness. Arab physicians developed a technique for dislodging the clouded lens and pushing it clear of the field of vision. This allowed some degree of sight to be restored.

drugs by accident. Alchemists also developed techniques for purifying chemicals that are still used today. Arab pharmacists compiled long lists of herbal remedies, gathered from the places they conquered. Some describe more than 3,000 different drugs, some of which were very unusual. The real value of Arab writings, however, was how carefully they recorded information. These great works were painstakingly copied and circulated throughout the Arab Empire.

◄ MIXING MEDICINES
Persian and Arab apothecaries (chemists) developed many methods for preparing medicines. These Persians are boiling the ingredients of a medicine over a brazier (a container of burning coals).

▼ PESTLE AND MORTAR
The simplest way to make up an herbal medicine was to grind its ingredients together using a pestle and mortar. This made a powder which could be mixed with water and drunk or made into a paste or ointment. The pestle and mortar are still in use today.

▼ MEDICINE IN THE ARAB EMPIRE
The Arab Empire spread widely around the Mediterranean and the Middle East and adopted the traditional remedies of the regions it conquered. Arab scholars preserved ancient Greek and Roman traditions and wrote down the newest medical discoveries.

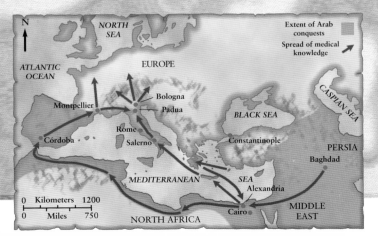

Key Dates

- A.D.620s Muhammad founds Islam.

- A.D.832 Baghdad is established as a center of learning.

- A.D.850 Muslim scholar at-Tabari compiles medical writings of Greece, Rome, Persia, and India.

- c.A.D.865–928 Life of Rhazes.

- A.D.980–1037 Life of Avicenna.

- 1174 Maimonides is appointed as court physician to Saladin.

- 1258 Mongol warriors sack Baghdad. Medical information preserved by the Arabs begins to flow back to the West.

Galen's Legacy

▲ URINE GAZING
During the 1200s and 1300s, there were few ways to diagnose a disease. One method was to examine the patient's urine. Its color, cloudiness, and even taste were carefully noted.

▶ MEDICAL GIANTS
In this edition of Galen's works published in 1528, Galen is shown with two other medical geniuses. Hippocrates is on the left and Avicenna on the right.

A FTER THE EMPEROR Constantine made Christianity the official religion of the Roman Empire, the power of Greek medicine and Galenic teaching began to fade. Once more, religion became more influential than practical medicine. Sickness was often seen as punishment from God for past sins. Prayer and pilgrimages to holy relics were the recommended cures for most diseases, and cults of healing saints sprang up.

The Church's opinion of medicine was summed up by St. Bernard, who lived from A.D.1090 until 1153. He said that going to the doctor was not proper behavior. Trying to cure a disease was seen as interfering with God's punishment. A dying person was more likely to call a priest than a doctor.

Christian saints became associated with different diseases. St. Christopher dealt with epilepsy, St. Roch was the patron saint of plague victims, St. Apollonia looked after those with toothache, and St. Margaret kept women safe during childbirth.

However, the sick did receive some practical care. Many monasteries offered care of the sick. Hospitals were built across Europe, often alongside healing shrines (holy places). Special hospitals were built for lepers, who were regarded with especial horror and considered "unclean."

Medical knowledge began to improve in the A.D.1000s, when

Tertius operum Galeni Tomus.

Hyppocr.   Galenus   Auicen.

Librorum principis medicorum Galeni, quos nuper insignes viri feliciffimis tralationibus illuftrarunt Tomus, exquiſitiſſima cura recognitus:Una cum indice re-cognitus:Una cum indice re-

FALSE BELIEFS
Throughout the Middle Ages, superstition formed part of medical practice. Herbals were books that listed the medicinal properties of plants. A few of these did have the promised effect, but most were useless. Bleeding, the use of leeches, enemas, and deliberate vomiting were all recommended. Following the ideas of Hippocrates, these methods were thought to restore the balance of the humors.

◀ LUNGWORT
Many plants were used in medicine on the basis of their appearance. This practice was known as the doctrine of signatures. The leaves of lungwort were thought to look like the lung, so this plant was used to treat lung disease.

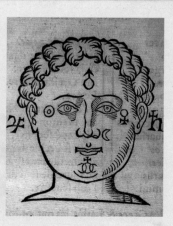

◀ ASTROLOGY
Astrology was thought to show a link between diseased body parts, different planets and star signs, and parts of the body. This is a chart showing planets' influences on the head.

▶ PURGING
Powerful drugs were given to cause vomiting. Throwing up was believed to rid the body of poisons.

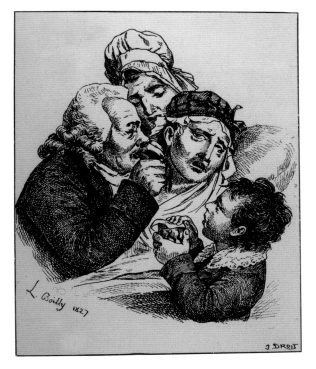

a small group of doctors began work at Salerno, in Italy. They formed an influential medical school and revived ancient ideas, especially those of Galen. People assumed Galen's teachings were accurate, even though some were changed or missed in translation and others had been wrong in the first place. Doctors treated their patients with diets and drugs, many of which were imported from the East.

Surgery became a separate branch of medicine and was carried out by barber-surgeons. Barber-surgeons provided a range of services. They cut hair, pulled out teeth, gave enemas (injected fluids into the rectum), and let blood.

At least one Greek technique was challenged. Hippocrates had recommended leaving open wounds to become septic. Henri de Mondeville, a French surgeon who lived from 1260 until 1320, had different ideas. He advised closing the wound as soon as possible and keeping it dry and covered to prevent infection. Thanks to de Mondeville, many limbs and lives were saved.

▼ CAUTERIZING IRON
To stop bleeding, medieval doctors used to apply a red-hot iron to coagulate (thicken) the blood. This caused agonizing pain. Cauterization was not very hygienic, and many wounds became infected.

▲ LEECHES
Bloodletting was a treatment for most illnesses. People often used freshwater leeches to suck out the blood. Recently, the use of leeches has been reintroduced as a way to reduce serious bruising.

▼ POMANDER
In medieval times, people thought that foul smells spread disease. Many carried scented pomanders about with them to drive these smells away. The simplest pomanders were oranges stuck with cloves.

▲ HOLY EYES
St. Lucy of Syracuse became the patron saint of eye disease. According to legend, she plucked out her own eyes but they grew back. Many sick people still pray to saints.

Key Dates

- 1100–1300 Medical schools and hospitals are founded throughout Europe.

- 1100s Trotula joins the Salerno medical school. She writes the first complete work on women's health and another on skin disease.

- 1200s–1300s Physicians and surgeons begin to form into professional organizations.

- 1215 Pope Innocent III decrees that all doctors must be approved by the Church and bans lepers from Churches.

- 1260–1320 Henri de Mondeville recommends closing wounds.

Renaissance Discoveries

THE RENAISSANCE was the period in European history that lasted from the 1400s until the 1600s. Before then, European medicine was based on theory rather than practice. Then Renaissance scientists and physicians began to question the old Greek writings on medicine. Some brave individuals even challenged the Church's teachings on the effect of the soul on the body. This change of approach was not the result of renewed interest in Greek and Roman medicine. It was led by people who rejected tradition and wished to discover and investigate. Scientists began to dissect human

▲ THERMOMETER
Unlike a modern one, this mercury thermometer from the 1400s had to be kept in the patient's mouth for up to 25 minutes.

▶ VESALIUS
This picture by Edouard Hamman was made during the 1800s. It shows how Vesalius dissected human bodies so that he could make extremely detailed anatomical drawings.

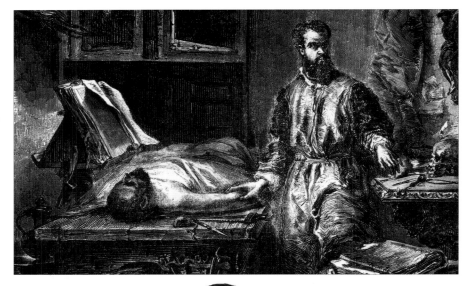

MEDICAL REVOLUTIONARIES
The ideas of Hippocrates and Galen had been followed for so long without question that it was difficult to abandon them. New ideas did not always offer a comforting solution to medical problems, and many traditional doctors did not welcome them. Despite opposition, revolutionary scientists and doctors persevered and made some ground-breaking discoveries.

▶ PARACELSUS
Paracelsus was a Swiss doctor. His belief in alchemy, which was unfashionable at the time, nevertheless led him to discover important new drugs. In this way, Paracelsus pioneered chemical treatment of disease.

▼ MARCELLO MALPIGHI
The Italian biologist and doctor Malpighi was able to complete part of the story of blood circulation. He discovered the capillary vessels that link arteries and veins, which Harvey had been unable to see.

▲ WILLIAM HARVEY
Harvey was the first person to prove that the heart pumped blood through the body, which he did by identifying the direction of blood flow. He even demonstrated his discovery to King Charles I of England.

bodies. The first anatomists were puzzled to see that their findings did not match Galen's descriptions. Their new knowledge led to great advances in surgery.

The greatest revolution in the understanding of anatomy and physiology came from the work of the Flemish physician Andreas Vesalius. In 1543 he published his detailed drawings of dissections of the human body. Vesalius was Professor of Anatomy at the University of Padua, Italy. One of his successors, Hieronymus Fabricius, studied the function of the valves in the veins and established that they made the blood flow in one direction. He tried to blend his findings with those of Galen, so he did not realize that the blood circulated through the body. One of his students, an Englishman named William Harvey, was able to contribute to the story by demonstrating the circulation of the blood. However, even Harvey missed the final link because he did not realize how blood passes from the arteries to the veins.

As people realized that many ancient manuscripts and descriptions were inaccurate, they collected new descriptions of medicinal plants in books called herbals. This led to the discovery of many plants and drugs previously unknown in Western Europe. These included the rhubarb root (first described in a Chinese herbal over 4,000 years earlier), which was used to cleanse the bowels. Explorers of the New World, especially the Spanish and Portuguese, brought back amazing new plants, while travelers to the Far East brought back new drugs and remedies too.

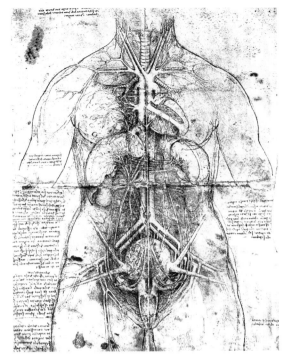

▲ THE MAJOR ORGANS OF THE BODY
Leonardo da Vinci's anatomical drawings were undoubted works of art. Often, however, they were highly inaccurate. Da Vinci made guesses rather than performing detailed dissections himself.

▲ AMBROISE PARÉ
Paré was a French army surgeon who came to realize that cauterizing wounds often resulted in the patient's dying. He developed a gentler form of dressing and tying off severed blood vessels, making a huge advance in surgical care.

▼ GIROLAMO FRACASTORO
This Italian formulated the idea that infection could spread from one person to another by physical contact, or through the air. He guessed that this might be caused by tiny living organisms, which he called "seeds." However, he could not prove his theory, so it was largely dismissed.

Key Dates

- 1482 Pope Sixtus IV allows the dissection of executed criminals.

- 1527 Paracelsus burns the books of Avicenna and Galen.

- 1537 Ambroise Paré develops his concept of wound care.

- 1540 Barber-Surgeons' Company is founded in England.

- 1546 Fracastoro publishes his theories on germs and disease.

- 1628 William Harvey publishes his theory of blood circulation.

- 1661 Marcello Malpighi publishes his theory on the circulation of the blood through the lungs.

Plague and Pestilence

▲ FLEA
Bubonic plague is spread by the bite of a flea that has fed on the blood of an infected rat. European towns and cities were infested with rats during the 1300s and 1400s.

IN A.D.540 A TERRIBLE DISEASE broke out in Europe. This epidemic is known as Justinian's Plague, after the Byzantine emperor at the time. So many people died that his empire was almost destroyed. During the 1300s, the plague reappeared in Europe. This outbreak is known as the Black Death, or bubonic plague. Between 1348 and 1351 it killed around 20 million people.

The plague had reached Constantinople in 1347, carried by traders fleeing from the advance of Mongol warriors from Asia. They brought the disease with them from the steppes (grasslands) where they originally lived. Although humans can catch it, plague is a disease of rodents, and especially of the black rat. Infected rats were bitten by fleas which fed on their blood. When the host rat died, the fleas looked for a new source of food. They bit people, who then became infected with the plague.

Infected people developed swellings around the neck, armpits, and groin, and bled beneath the skin, producing sores called buboes. They died at such a rate that bodies were just dumped in huge pits. Doctors were helpless to treat the plague. Isolating infected people did not help, because rats were everywhere. Once most of the rats died, the plague slowly vanished. However, it came back again at intervals. There was another serious outbreak during the 1800s. The plague is still around today—for example, in the United States.

Bubonic plague was not the only disease to strike Europe in the Middle Ages. Leprosy was common.

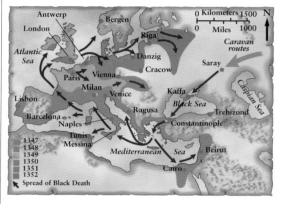

▲ SPREAD OF THE PLAGUE
In 1347 the bubonic plague arrived at the trading post of Kaffa (modern-day Feodosiya, in Ukraine). Merchants unwittingly carried the disease to Constantinople. From there, it soon spread rapidly throughout Europe.

THE BLACK DEATH
The mortality (death rate) from the Black Death was so huge that it changed the whole structure of European society. The ancient feudal system of serfs who worked their masters' land broke down. There were not enough people to work the land. Often, whole villages were abandoned. Wealthy people fled the cities as outbreaks of plague approached, but the rats traveled with them, so the disease continued unchecked.

▶ THE TOWN CRIER
"Bring out your dead" was the message called out at the height of the plague by the town criers. This was the only way of spreading news quickly, as most people could not read. Strangers were often barred from entering plague-free areas.

▲ FAST FUNERALS
People died from the plague in huge numbers. Only the rich were buried in individual graves like this one. Most bodies were dumped into huge communal graves, known as plague pits.

▶ THE TRIUMPH
OF DEATH
Pieter Bruegel painted his
Triumph of Death *in*
about 1562. It features
nightmarish skeletons
and gives some idea of the
hysterical fear caused by
the plague. The title of
the painting refers to the
commonly held belief that
the Black Death was a
victory for the forces of evil.

▼ PLAGUE VICTIM
This illustration appeared in
the Toggenberg Bible in the
1400s. It clearly shows the
huge buboes, or swellings,
that covered a plague
victim's body.

Although the disease is not very infectious, lepers were feared and treated as social outcasts. There were also epidemics of cholera and typhoid. Cholera was especially feared because it killed most people who caught it, and no one understood what caused it. It was caused by sewage and rubbish in rivers. People picked up the bacteria causing these diseases from contaminated drinking water and food.

Medicine was powerless against these epidemics, so prayer was the only option for the terrified people when disease broke out.

▶ PLAGUE HOUSE
The doors of houses where plague victims lived were marked with a red cross. Some houses were sealed up, even if there were healthy people still living inside.

◀ DR. DEATH
Plague doctors offered to cure or prevent the disease. To keep themselves clear of infection they wore strange costumes. They stuffed their headdresses with sweet-smelling herbs and carried amulets and pomanders.

Key Dates

- A.D. 540 Justinian's Plague attacks Constantinople.

- 1347 Plague reaches the Black Sea coast. It spreads all over Europe from Constantinople within two years.

- 1349 Jews are blamed for the plague and massacred in Strasbourg, Mainz, and Frankfurt.

- 1377 The port of Dubrovnik quarantines itself, followed by the Italian ports of Venice and Pisa, and by Marseilles, in France.

- 1665 The Great Plague attacks London. King Charles II and his court flee to the countryside.

Making a Diagnosis

Diagnosis is the skill of identifying a disease. It is carried out by observing signs and symptoms of the illness. Until recently there were few medical tests to help a doctor identify a disease. Instead, doctors talked to their patients, examined them, and looked at their behavior.

In Greece, at the time of Hippocrates, doctors tried to identify their patient's disease so they could reach their prognosis (say how the disease would develop). A doctor's reputation rested on how accurately he predicted whether the patient would recover or die. Hippocrates taught that every single observation could be significant. Greek doctors used all of their senses in making their diagnosis. Touch, taste, sight, hearing, and smell could all provide valuable clues. These principles still apply for modern doctors.

By Galen's time, taking the pulse had become a part of diagnosis. Galen gave instructions on how to take the

◀ CLINICAL THERMOMETER
The modern digital thermometer is quick and easy to use and is also extremely accurate. It does not contain the poisonous mercury used in traditional thermometers, which were fragile and easily broken.

▶ USING THE STETHOSCOPE
The stethoscope introduced by Laënnec in 1819 was awkward to use, because it was rigid. Unlike the modern stethoscope, which has a flexible rubber tube, it was not easy to move around in order to detect sounds in different areas.

TOOLS OF THE TRADE
Diagnosis improved with the invention of instruments that allowed the doctor to find out what was going on inside the body. A whole range of new observations could be made, and these were added to the findings from old methods, such as interviewing the patient. Better measurements of pulse rate, blood pressure, and temperature all helped toward accurate diagnosis.

◀ LAENNEC'S STETHOSCOPE
In 1819 the French physician René Laënnec introduced the first stethoscope. It was a wooden device, almost 9 in long, which amplified the sounds of the chest.

▼ THE STETHOSCOPE TODAY
The modern stethoscope is a simple, lightweight device. It allows doctors and nursing staff to listen to the sounds of the lungs and the heart. It often gives an early warning of illness.

early ophthalmoscope   *modern ophthalmoscope*

▲ EYE SPY
Doctors use instruments called ophthalmoscopes to examine a patient's eye. The earliest were little more than powerful magnifying glasses. The modern instrument has powerful lenses and lights that allow the doctor to see right to the back of the eyeball.

pulse. The findings could be described as "fast" or "normal."

In the Arab world, diagnosis involved careful examination of the affected parts, checking the pulse and examining the urine. Arab doctors did not disclose their findings to anyone else, in case they frightened the patient.

In most of Europe, diagnosis was rather haphazard, because disease was seen as a punishment from God. This meant its cause could not be questioned and the disease could not be treated, except with prayer. Sometimes the diagnosis was obvious to all, such as in cases of leprosy or plague, but even then the doctor was not able to cure the patient.

It was not until the 1700s that real advances were made in the art of diagnosis. In 1761, a Viennese doctor named Leopold Auenbrugger discovered that thumping on a patient's chest produced sounds that could indicate lung disease. The technique was reluctantly accepted

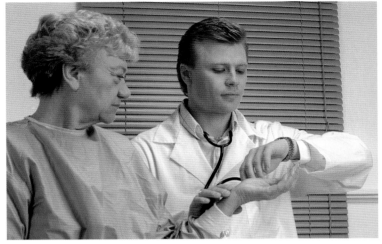

and is still in use today. However, most doctors did not perform physical examinations and still formed their diagnosis by interviewing the patient. Auscultation (sounding the chest) improved with the invention of the stethoscope in 1816. This also allowed doctors to hear the heart properly, and diagnose different heart diseases.

Examination of the urine was a popular method of diagnosis for all sorts of disease. Its color, odor, and even its taste were thought to reveal the state of the patient's health. Urine tests are still used in some forms of diagnosis today—for example to identify diabetes or pregnancy.

▲ COUNTING THE BEATS
Taking a person's pulse tells the doctor how fast the heart is beating. With each heartbeat, the arteries bulge slightly. The arteries at the wrist are very close to the skin surface, so the doctor can feel them bulge with his or her fingertip.

▲ UNDER PRESSURE
The sphygmomanometer is used to measure blood pressure. First the doctor puts an inflatable sleeve on the patient's arm. This is pumped up to close off the blood flow through the arteries. As the sleeve is slowly deflated, the device measures the blood pressure.

▼ BLOOD CHEMISTRY
Blood tests are used to measure changes in the chemical make up of the blood. These changes can indicate that a person is suffering from an infection, diabetes, or some other hormonal disorder, or that a woman is pregnant.

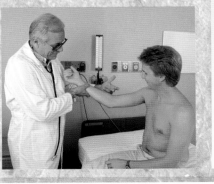

Key Dates

- 1714 Gabriel Fahrenheit invents the mercury thermometer.

- 1761 Leopold Auenbrugger publishes his findings on sounding the chest.

- 1819 René Laënnec introduces the first stethoscope.

- 1851 Hermann von Helmholtz invents the ophthalmoscope.

- 1868 Carl Wunderlich promotes widespread use of the thermometer.

- 1895 Wilhelm Röntgen discovers x-rays.

- 1896 Scipione Riva-Rocci invents the sphygmomanometer.

The Rise of Surgery

▲ JOHN HUNTER
Born in Scotland in 1728, John Hunter was very important to modern surgery. He changed people's views so that they saw it as a proper medical discipline. He put together a huge collection of medical specimens, which today is in the Hunterian Museum, in Glasgow.

SURGERY IS PROBABLY the oldest medical skill. Even pressing a hand over a cut to stop it from bleeding is a form of surgery. Prehistoric skeletons show signs of bone-setting to repair broken limbs, and holes drilled into skulls in the process of trepanning. Some ancient civilizations practiced very sophisticated surgery, with operations on the intestines, and even on eyes However, during the Middle Ages, the skill was almost lost. Surgery was not taught in most European medical schools. It was left to barbers and other unskilled people to carry out surgery, usually as a last resort. During the Renaissance, there were attempts to improve matters. The United Company of Barber-Surgeons was set up in London in 1540 to give guidelines to people carrying out operations. However, most patients still died through infections due to lack of hygiene.

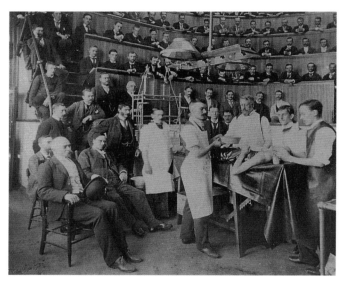

▶ SURGERY IN THE ROUND
This photograph, taken in 1898, shows surgery being performed at Bellevue Hospital, New York. Fellow surgeons and medical students look on, so that they can learn the latest surgical techniques.

EARLY SURGERY
Surgery was carried out in ancient Mesopotamia as long ago as 2000B.C., and in India in 100B.C. The Indian surgeons were especially skillful and left behind detailed descriptions of delicate operations to remove cataracts from the eye. In ancient China, however, any invasion of the body was discouraged, and surgery was seldom practiced. Advanced surgery was practiced by the ancient Greeks and the Romans, and spread into the Arab Empire, eventually returning to Europe much later.

▼ HUA TUO
Surgical treatment was discouraged in ancient China. Its only record is of Hua Tuo operating on the arm of General Kuan Yun. Hua Tuo was executed for treason when he offered to perform a trepanning operation on Prince Tsao Tsao. The prince suspected a plot to murder him.

◀ BLEEDING A PATIENT
Bloodletting was one of the earliest and most common forms of surgery. In later times it was carried out by barber-surgeons. Bloodletting was used to treat almost all diseases. Patients were usually already very ill. The loss of blood often weakened them so much that they died.

In 1547, the French surgeon Ambroise Paré abandoned the traditional, agonizing cauterization of wounds with a red-hot iron. He found that he could tie off the blood vessels to prevent blood loss, with far less shock and mortality in his patients. It was another two centuries before any further advances were made.

By the 1700s, improved knowledge of anatomy made the removal of tumors and bladder stones common operations. Amputations were carried out in less than five minutes to minimize pain and shock. Patients were sedated (quietened) with opium or alcohol and held down by attendants. However, many still died due to infection caused during surgery.

From the 1760s the British surgeon John Hunter turned surgery from amateur butchery into a scientific profession. He lectured, wrote widely, and collected huge numbers of medical specimens. Hunter was an expert dissector. As the number of hospitals had increased, so had the number of unclaimed dead bodies, which could be sent to the anatomy schools and used for training student surgeons.

Once pain and infection could be controlled, surgery became less risky. Operations became common for minor problems. Appendicitis had been recognized back in the 1500s, but surgery to remove the appendix was regarded as very dangerous. Then, in 1902, Frederic Treves drained an abscess on the appendix of the Prince of Wales, just before he was crowned Edward VIII of England. This won Treves a knighthood, and from then on, surgery to remove the appendix became highly fashionable.

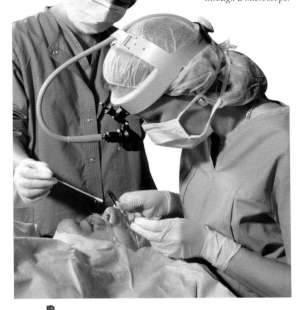

▼ EYE OPERATION
Modern surgery demands very precise instruments. This eye surgeon is using a scalpel that has a tiny blade made from diamond, which is extremely sharp. The doctor sees into the eye by means of a powerful magnifier. Some operations are so delicate that they are carried out looking through a microscope.

▲ LOSING A LEG
Amputations were a brutal business. They had to be carried out very swiftly so the patients would not die from bleeding and shock. In this picture, printed in 1618, the barber-surgeon already has cauterizing irons heating in the fire, ready to seal the wound.

▼ BLOOD STOPPER
The tourniquet was developed to stop blood loss after an amputation. The strap was fastened tightly around the limb above the place where the cut was to be made. Then the screw was tightened down to squeeze the arteries and cut off the blood flow.

▲ SURGICAL SAW
At first, ordinary carpenters' saws were used for amputations. Later, specialized surgical saws were produced.

Key Dates

- A.D.600s The Ayurvedic *Sushruta-Samhita* describes over 120 types of steel surgical instrument.

- 1728–1793 Life of John Hunter, who revolutionizes the teaching and practice of surgery.

- 1793 French army surgeon Dominique-Jean Larrey introduces the first ambulance service, *Ambulances Volantes*.

- 1809 American Ephraim McDowell pioneers gynecological surgery when he removes a tumor from a woman's ovary.

- 1902 Frederic Treves treats the Prince of Wales's appendicitis.

Germ-free and Pain-free

▲ KEEPING CLEAN
Washing the hands is still one of the most important ways to limit the spread of infection, both in hospitals and in the home. Modern surgical staff use antibacterial soap to prevent infection.

▶ IGNAZ SEMMELWEISS
Semmelweiss realized that lack of hygiene was causing many deaths among his patients, so he insisted on rigorous washing. His views were considered outrageous, and he was forced out of his hospital in Vienna.

SURGERY IN THE 1600s was a very dangerous business. There was no concept of hygiene. Surgeons worked in their normal clothes, which became splashed with blood. They used instruments in consecutive operations without any attempt at cleaning. Childbirth fever was a particular hazard, killing many women within a few days of giving birth. A Hungarian doctor, Ignaz Semmelweiss, realized that patients were more likely to suffer infection after being examined by medical students who had been carrying out dissections. He saw that when students had not visited the dissection rooms, infection did not occur. As a result, Semmelweiss insisted on high standards of hygiene in his hospital, and this cut the death rate dramatically. He

was violently opposed by many medical colleagues, however, and eventually had to leave his practice in Vienna.

At this time no one realized that microbes spread disease. It was not until the 1860s that Louis Pasteur discovered bacterial infection. The British surgeon Joseph Lister made the next major advance. He was alarmed at how many people died of severe bone fractures. Lister observed that if a bone was broken without penetrating the skin, infection seldom occurred. If a bone fragment punctured the skin, exposing it to the air, there was usually an infection, and this led to amputation or death.

When Lister found out about Pasteur's work, he realized that it was not air that caused the problem, but bacteria contaminating the wound. Lister had heard that carbolic acid could be used to kill bacteria in sewage, so he tried spraying a mist of diluted carbolic acid on wounds. His experiment had dramatic results. Out of his first 11 patients, only one died. This discovery was resisted at first, but as it became accepted it was possible to carry out

KILLING THE PAIN

Anesthesia has a long history. The ancient Greeks used drugs to provide pain relief. By the 1800s, opium was widely used as a soporific (to make the patient sleepy). Alcohol was also used in surgery to help the patient relax. Ether and nitrous oxide were the first modern anesthetics. They were introduced at about the same time and were both inhaled. Shortly afterward, chloroform was introduced. After initial resistance, all three of these anesthetics were enthusiastically accepted and became very widely used.

▼ WILLIAM MORTON
Morton was an American dentist who experimented with the effects of ether as an anesthetic. In 1846 he anesthetized a patient for the surgeon John Collins Warren.

▲ FIRST FAILURE
In 1848, Hannah Greener became the first person to die from the poisonous effects of chloroform. Greener had only had a minor operation to remove a toenail.

▼ CHLOROFORM MASK
Chloroform and ether were both applied by soaking a cloth mask. The mask's wire frame closely covered the nose and mouth so that the chloroform or ether fumes were breathed in by the patient.

routine operations with hardly any risk to the patient. Asepsis (keeping free from infection) was safer than allowing a bacterial infection to take hold and then trying to treat it with antiseptics. To achieve this, surgeons tried to keep bacteria away from wounds by sterilizing their instruments and wearing masks and gowns.

At about the same time that asepsis was discovered, several doctors discovered how pain could be relieved by the use of anesthetics. In 1846 the American dentist William Morton showed how ether could be used to eliminate pain during surgery, while John Warren also experimented with the use of nitrous oxide (laughing gas). Nitrous oxide had been used for a while as a party novelty. Breathing in the gas made people collapse in fits of giggles. Chloroform was another form of anesthetic. After John Snow gave it to Queen Victoria during the birth of Prince Leopold, its use became more widespread.

▲ STEAM SPRAY
Joseph Lister invented the carbolic steam spray. It produced a fine mist of mild carbolic acid in the operating room and killed bacteria. The death rate among Lister's patients fell from 50 percent to 5 percent.

◀ UNDER THE KNIFE
From the 1860s, operations were carried out in antiseptic conditions. A carbolic steam spray pumped an antibacterial mist into the room. Surgery was not only safer, it was more comfortable for the patient. Chloroform masks kept them unconscious during the operation.

▶ THE MODERN ANESTHETIST
Anesthesia is now usually carried out using a mixture of gases. Anesthesia depresses (slows down) all of the body's functions, so the patient's condition must be carefully monitored during surgery by the anesthetist, on the right.

Key Dates

- 1800 Humphrey Davy reports that nitrous oxide can produce unconsciousness.

- 1831 Chloroform is discovered.

- 1844 Horace Wells uses nitrous oxide to anesthetize a patient.

- 1846 William Morton uses ether to anesthetize a patient.

- 1847 Ignaz Semmelweiss makes his staff wash their hands.

- 1865 Joseph Lister uses his carbolic steam spray in surgery.

- 1884 Cocaine is used as a local anesthetic, painkilling drug.

- 1886 Aseptic surgery begins.

Quacks and Charlatans

▲ KOLA MARQUE
This French poster is advertising a stimulant containing the drug cocaine. Some quack cures were completely useless. Others, such as Kola Marque, contained dangerous and addictive ingredients.

I T IS EASY FOR US to dismiss doctors in the past as being quacks or charlatans (people who swindled their patients by selling them useless cures). This was certainly true of some of them, but their strange activities need to be put into the context of the level of scientific learning of the time. For instance, it would not have been possible to convince Hippocrates or Galen about the existence of bacteria, or that bacteria cause disease, because it was possible to see them only through a microscope.

▶ QUACK MEDICINES
Salespeople drew attention to their wares by any means at their disposal. Many wore outrageous and eye-catching outfits, and they all perfected their own style of patter (sales talk).

Although surgery could sometimes be effective, most medicine was not able to cure disease. Doctors were forced to desperate measures in order to find cures. Sometimes a patient recovered by natural means, but then the experimental method used by the doctor would be accepted as a miracle cure.

Prayer and the use of holy relics might be dismissed by some as quack medicine, but they are still widely used today, along with the laying on of hands (blessing the patient) and other forms of therapy based upon spiritual cure.

Quackery began to flourish in North America even before the Revolutionary War, and it enjoyed its heyday in the 1800s. Outlandish cures were sold and advertised in newspapers. People with no medical training displayed fake diplomas and even performed operations—sometimes with fatal results. At the same time, medical societies were set up in the various states. They worked to establish high standards of medical knowledge and treatment and to get laws passed that would prevent quacks

FALSE HOPES
As medicine becomes more advanced, cures that were once promoted by respectable doctors are rejected as quackery. For example, spa baths were a popular cure in Western Europe around 1900. They have now dropped out of favor, and many doctors would consider their use as quack medicine. However, they are still mainstream practice in parts of Eastern Europe.

▼ MUDBATHS
Baths in hot mud are widely used to treat diseases such as arthritis, especially in Eastern Europe. Elsewhere, mud treatments are considered harmless but ineffective.

◀ ELECTRICAL CORSETS
Electricity was considered a magical cure-all in the 1700s and 1800s. Electrical currents were applied to parts of the body to cure a whole range of conditions.

▲ FRANZ MESMER
The German physician Franz Mesmer developed techniques for what we now call hypnosis (putting someone into a trance). He called his discovery animal magnetism, and used it to treat patients who suffered from hysteria. His cures sometimes worked, even though they were scientific nonsense. Eventually, Mesmer was exposed as a fraud.

from practicing. Gradually, too, laws were passed to stop products from being sold with outrageous promises.

Lydia Pinkham's Vegetable Compound, introduced in 1873, was one of the most popular quack remedies —probably because it contained huge quantities of alcohol. This was sold first as a treatment for "female weaknesses" and later as a cure for just about anything.

In the United States, quacks advertised cancer cures at high prices. These were aimed at desperate cancer sufferers, willing to pay almost any price for life. Quacks had to pay heavy fines if they were caught, but the practice still exists. Since the 1970s many people dying from cancer have visited Mexico to buy a so-called cure called laetrile, which is, in fact, poisonous. The same happens with AIDS—unscrupulous dealers sell dubious pills and potions to those infected with HIV.

◀ FRANZ GALL
The German doctor Franz Gall developed the concept of phrenology. Phrenology is a form of diagnosis based on examining the skull. Gall claimed that skull shape revealed the functions of parts of the brain. He "read" the skull by feeling for bumps. Phrenology survived for many years, but it is no longer considered to have any use to medicine.

▼ PHRENOLOGY
This porcelain head is marked with the regions identified by Franz Gall. Each area was identified with an aspect of a person's personality or behavior, such as secretiveness or wit.

Key Dates

- 1700s Benjamin Franklin praises air bathing (sitting naked in front of an open window).

- 1775 Franz Mesmer develops his theory of animal magnetism.

- 1780 James Graham opens his Temple of Health in London.

- 1810s Franz Gall develops the concept of phrenology.

- 1970s Laetrile is promoted as a cure for cancer.

- 1991 The American Cancer Society declares laetrile to be poisonous, but it remains on sale, especially on the Internet.

Public Health

▲ CHOLERA
This image from the 1800s shows cholera in the form of a specter that descends on the Earth to claim its victims. More than 7,000 Londoners died in an outbreak in 1832.

PUBLIC HEALTH is not a new idea. The Romans understood the need for clean water supplies and built huge aqueducts to bring in water to the center of their cities, along with water pipes and public baths. They also constructed elaborate sewage systems to remove waste from their cities. The Romans were not even the first to build aqueducts. The Etruscans had started to build them in 312 B.C.

Ancient Chinese and Indian religious writings had recommended good diet and hygiene to protect health, but in medieval Europe, all of this was forgotten. The Church frowned on washing, as it seemed too much like a bodily pleasure. There was no concept of hygiene, and sewage and garbage were just thrown out into the street. It is no coincidence that during this period Europe was ravaged by plague, leprosy, tuberculosis (TB, also known as consumption),

typhoid, and cholera. People thought that these diseases were spread by miasma (unpleasant smells). This idea probably did encourage some disposal of waste. The miasmic theory of infection persisted into the 1800s, until the effects of bacteria were finally demonstrated.

The cholera epidemics had already brought matters to a head. For centuries the river Thames had been London's sewer and source of drinking water. It was black and stinking, and finally everyone had had enough. The government commissioned a report from a civil servant named John Chadwick, which turned out to be the most influential document ever prepared on the subject of public health. It was published in 1842. The report described the probable causes of disease in the poorer parts of London, and also suggested practical ways to solve the problem. These public health measures included supplying houses with clean running water and proper sewage drainage.

Not long after this came the first proof of the risks from contaminated water, during a terrible cholera outbreak in 1854. John Snow, a London doctor, realized that many cholera cases were clustered in a small area near Broad Street. Investigation showed that they all drew their water from a public pump. Snow removed the pump handle, and within a few days the epidemic stopped. Even so, it took several years for the medical profession to accept that cholera was not spread by foul air, but by drinking water contaminated by sewage.

CLEAN SOLUTIONS
Flushing toilets and clean running water in the home remained novelties into the 1800s. Before then, people had to visit public pumps and taps for their water. In the late 1800s local authorities began to demolish the worst slums and replace them with better housing. By the 1900s children's health was improving. Schools provided meals for the poorest, and medical inspections allowed disease to be detected early.

▶ FOUL WATERS
Dr. John Snow started as a surgeon in Newcastle-upon-Tyne, England, and moved to London in 1836. After halting the cholera epidemic, he recommended improvements in sewerage.

▶ WATER CLOSET
Flushing toilets, such as this one from the 1880s, were a great improvement in public health. The first toilets were often elaborately decorated and were almost works of art.

▲ AMERICAN SINK (1888)
The kitchen of the 1800s was not always very hygienic. Hot water on tap, as shown here, was a rare luxury. Cleanliness depended on having enough servants to scrub all the work surfaces and floors, which often harbored germs.

▶ LONDON LIVING CONDITIONS
During the 1800s, living conditions for the poor were atrocious. They lived in cramped housing without proper sanitation. These people are going through the rubbish on the river. Such conditions provided an ideal breeding ground for disease.

▼ BUILDING A SEWER
Repeated outbreaks of disease finally led to the building of sewers, such as this one being dug in London in 1862. These enormous mains sewers were connected to outfalls far down the Thames, where the tides could sweep the sewage away.

▲ ROYAL VICTORIA HOSPITAL, MONTREAL
Many hospitals were built in the 1800s, such as this one in Canada. These were often magnificent buildings, but as there were still few effective medical treatments, many patients came to hospitals to die.

Key Dates

- c.1700B.C King Minos of Crete has a flushing toilet in his palace.
- 312B.C. The Etruscans build the first aqueduct.
- A.D.300s Two-seater toilet, shaped like a temple, in use in Greece.
- c.1590 John Harrington invents a flushing toilet.
- 1770–1915 Development of the modern water closet, or toilet.
- 1854 John Snow shows dirty water is the cause of cholera.
- 1869 First effective state department of public health is established in Massachusetts.

Microbe Hunters

▲ BACTERIA
Researchers grow bacteria on agar jelly in petri dishes. They draw a contaminated glass rod across the surface of the jelly, and the colonies grow in a streak along this line.

BACK IN THE RENAISSANCE, people had speculated that contact with an infected person might spread disease, but no one knew why. Then, in the early 1700s, the Dutch scientist Antonie van Leeuwenhoek described tiny animals that he saw when looking at body fluids under a microscope. These might, it was thought, be associated with disease.

Two hundred years later, the French scientist Louis Pasteur finally proved that microbes (germs) cause disease. First, he proved that microbes made milk sour and wine ferment. He also found that heat treatment killed off these microbes. This process, known as pasteurization, is still used to help preserve milk today. Pasteur went on to show how bacteria caused disease in chickens, and also caused anthrax, a severe infection that affects cattle and humans.

Robert Koch was a German doctor who was also studying anthrax. Using some of Koch's bacteria, Pasteur made a vaccine to prevent the disease in livestock. Even more importantly he went on to produce a vaccine for the killer disease rabies. Pasteur was, however, unable to find the organism that caused rabies, because it is a virus, invisible except under a high-powered electron microscope.

Koch was a very painstaking scientist who was aware of the

◀ ROBERT KOCH
Koch became famous as the conqueror of diphtheria. Here, he is examining a patient with TB. Koch managed to reveal the bacterium responsible for causing TB, but he failed to produce an effective vaccine against it.

ON THE TRAIL

Colonization (settlement) of the warmer parts of the world introduced Europeans to a whole range of tropical diseases, to which they had no natural immunity. West Africa, in particular, was nicknamed "the white man's grave." Malaria, yellow fever, and many other tropical diseases spread by insect bites caused prolonged disease and death. It was not until 1897 that it was realized that a mosquito bite could spread malaria. Within a few years people discovered that bites from infected insects also caused sleeping sickness, plague, and yellow fever.

▶ THE FIRST MICROSCOPE
Van Leeuwenhoek was an expert at making lenses. He developed the first practical microscope in 1671. He jealously hid his technique for making lenses, but he did share his discoveries by describing what he saw.

▲ MAGGOTS
In 1699 Francesco Redi showed that maggots did not appear on meat that had been kept free of flies. Before then, people had thought that maggots just appeared on decaying materials. We now know that the flies laid their eggs in the meat.

▼ RUDOLF VIRCHOW
Virchow demonstrated that disease did not arise spontaneously from humors, but that "all cells come from cells." In other words, bacteria give rise to more bacteria, rather than appearing by themselves.

need to identify disease organisms accurately. He laid down rules for proving that a particular microbe is the cause of a disease that are still followed today. Koch said that a microbe must be present in every case of the disease. It must be grown experimentally and in laboratory animals, and it must also be found when the disease is transmitted to another animal. Following these rules, Koch was able to prove that tuberculosis (TB) was caused by a bacterium. Next he traveled to Egypt and India to study cholera. He proved that it, too, was caused by a bacterium. Koch discovered that it lived in the human gut and was spread by polluted water. By 1883 he had provided scientific evidence for John Snow's earlier findings on the causes of cholera. Koch went on to discover the organisms responsible for diphtheria, typhoid, leprosy, and many other infections.

◀ LOUIS PASTEUR
Pasteur's experiments proved that life did not arise from nowhere. He explained how microbes are responsible for making things spoil and also for diseases.

▼ GERM EXPERIMENT
Pasteur proved that microbes exist with this experiment. He heated a nutrient broth (a substance in which bacteria will grow) in a flask. This killed any microbes already there. He sealed the flask to stop new microbes from getting in. The broth did not spoil until he opened the flask and germs were allowed to enter it from the air.

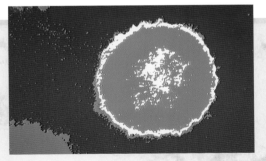

▼ MOSQUITO
In 1897, Ronald Ross made the discovery of malaria parasites in an *Anopheles* mosquito. This finally proved the link between these insects and the killer disease.

▲ HIV VIRUS
The discovery of the virus causing HIV in 1983 finally explained the mysterious appearance of AIDS. The HIV virus attacks and weakens the immune system. This allows the body to be attacked by other organisms and causes AIDS.

Key Dates

- 1673 Antonie van Leeuwenhoek describes the tiny life forms he has seen under a microscope.

- 1858 Rudolf Virchow states, "All cells come from cells."

- 1878 Louis Pasteur presents his germ theory of infection to the French Academy of Medicine.

- 1882 Robert Koch isolates the tubercle bacillus which causes TB.

- 1883 Robert Koch isolates the bacterium that causes cholera.

- 1897 Ronald Ross explains how mosquitoes carry malaria.

- 1983 The HIV virus is discovered.

Immunization

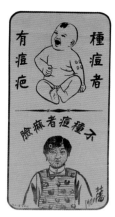

▲ THE END OF
SMALLPOX
*One of the reasons for the
success in wiping out
smallpox was widespread
advertising explaining the
need for vaccination. This
example comes from China.*

THE STORY OF VACCINATION is largely also the story of smallpox. This viral disease killed or disfigured people throughout Europe and the American colonies, where it wiped out the civilizations of the Incas and Aztecs.

In 1717, Lady Mary Wortley Montagu, wife of the British Ambassador in Constantinople, reported that the Turks had a traditional method to prevent smallpox. They took pus from infected smallpox sores and scratched it into the skin of another person. This caused a mild infection that did not produce scarring. Most importantly, it seemed to make the person immune from later infection. Lady Montagu was confident enough to try this on her own child. Soon the method was used widely across Europe.

The next development came when Edward Jenner, a British physician, heard that milkmaids who caught cowpox from their cattle did not seem to catch smallpox. Cowpox was a mild disease. In 1796, Jenner injected a local boy with the cowpox virus. Six weeks later Jenner tried to infect the boy with smallpox. This experiment would have landed him in prison today. Fortunately the boy survived, and the technique spread. Because smallpox does not infect any animals other than humans, it was possible to completely eradicate (wipe out) the disease by the 1970s. Smallpox was the first organism that we have deliberately made extinct.

Immunization works by using the body's own natural

◀ EDWARD JENNER
*This statue commemorates
Jenner's first experimental
vaccination of James
Phelps with cowpox. This
protected Phelps against
smallpox infection.*

PROTECTING PEOPLE

Viruses such as the influenza (flu) virus and HIV mutate, or change, very quickly, so the pattern of proteins on their surface also alters. This means that the body finds it difficult to produce strong immunity, because the disease is always changing. Other diseases such as polio and measles tend not to change, so vaccination provides powerful and permanent immunity.

▶ THE RABIES VACCINE
Louis Pasteur was able to produce rabies vaccines by growing the virus in rabbits' brains. Drying their brains and spinal cords for two weeks weakened the virus so much that it could be injected into people. This gave them immunity without their catching rabies.

▲ POLIO SUFFERER
In 1921, Franklin D. Roosevelt fell victim to polio. At the time, the disease was called "infantile paralysis," although it struck Roosevelt at the age of 40. The disease crippled Roosevelt's legs, but he eventually went on to become President.

▶ COWPOX
Once the value of Jenner's discovery became widely known, people rushed to be inoculated with cowpox in order to be protected from smallpox. This cartoon from the time shows what some people feared might happen when they were injected with cowpox—cows start growing out of their bodies!

defenses against an invading microbe. This works whether the microbe is a bacterium, virus, or animal parasite. In a way this reflects the views of the ancient Greeks, who believed that the body could heal itself.

The immune system uses white cells in the blood, which recognize our own body cells by the pattern of proteins on their surface. When they come across invading microbes, they attack them because they do not recognize them. They produce substances called antibodies which destroy the microbes, then other white cells eat up the microbes' remains. In this way the infection is cleared up. Next time that kind of microbe gets into the body, the white cells "remember" which antibodies they used to eliminate it last time.

They produce an army of antibodies so quickly that the infection cannot become established.

Vaccination creates immunity in the same way. The vaccine contains microbes that produce only a mild version of a disease. It usually contains dead microbes or even just parts of the microbes. This is enough for the body to mount an attack and produce antibodies. These give protection later if they are exposed to more dangerous forms of the microbe, so long as these are the same type of microbe used in the vaccine.

▶ SINGLE-DOSE SYRINGE
Modern syringes are disposable, to reduce the risk of infection. They come ready-filled with vaccine.

▶ FIRING A VACCINE
For mass vaccination programs, a gun was sometimes used. It fired the vaccine through the skin under very high pressure, without using a needle. These guns have now been replaced with single-dose disposable syringes.

▼ LINING UP FOR SHOTS
Vaccination is especially important in developing countries, where there is little access to health care. Charities and governments carry out vaccination programs against many killer diseases.

Key Dates

- 1717 Lady Wortley Montagu reports on the traditional Turkish practice of inoculation to prevent smallpox.

- 1796 Edward Jenner inoculates a boy with cowpox and demonstrates that he is then immune to smallpox.

- 1885 Pasteur tests his rabies vaccine.

- 1955 Jonas Salk's polio vaccine is introduced.

- 1974 Smallpox is eradicated (although a later single case followed a laboratory accident).

Germ Killers

Howard Florey

Ernst Chain

WHILE VACCINATION COULD PREVENT many diseases, very few infections were treatable. The first was malaria, which could be treated with quinine, extracted from the bark of the South American cinchona tree. Mercury was used to treat syphilis but proved very toxic (poisonous). A new and synthetic (manufactured) treatment called Salvarsan was introduced by Paul Ehrlich in 1910. Then in 1932 the German scientist Gerhard Domagk produced Prontosil, a red dye that attacked the streptococcus bacterium that caused many infections, such as meningitis.

A range of antibacterial drugs was developed from Prontosil. They are known as sulphonamides and prevent the multiplication of bacteria. This gives the body's immune defenses time to create antibodies to destroy the bacteria. Sulphonamides were not always effective, however, and sometimes caused unpleasant side effects. Also, they were completely inactive against some types of bacteria. The search for new drugs continued.

Alexander Fleming was a researcher studying the natural antibacterial substances that are produced by the body. He was particularly interested in lysozyme, a substance that is found in tears.

▼ ALEXANDER FLEMING
Fleming's discovery of penicillin was a lucky accident, but he did not realize the importance of his discovery. It was another ten years before Florey and Chain found a way to produce large quantities of penicillin.

LIFE SAVERS
Antibiotics have been used to treat all kinds of infections. They are also given to livestock and poultry to prevent disease and to make them grow quickly. As a result of being exposed to antibiotics over long periods, some bacteria have evolved methods of avoiding their effects. Nowadays, doctors try not to prescribe antibiotics for minor infections, such as sore throats, so that bacteria cannot get used to them.

◀ ANTIBIOTICS
Most antibiotics are given in the form of a powder, inside gelatine capsules, which are swallowed. However, some antibiotics are damaged by digestive juices, so these have to be injected.

▼ ANTIBIOTIC ATTACK
Antibiotics work by damaging the cell wall of a bacterium.

◀ WORLD WAR II
When war broke out, the U.S. and British governments realized that there would soon be many wounded soldiers at risk of infection. They invested lots of money in finding a way to produce enough penicillin.

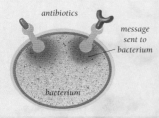

antibiotics

message sent to bacterium

bacterium

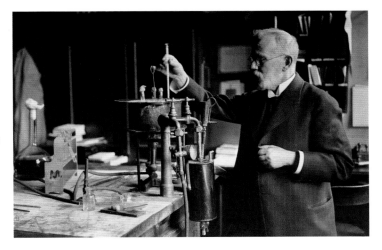

▶ PAUL EHRLICH
In the early 1900s Ehrlich produced and tested more than 600 new arsenic compounds, in an attempt for find a cure for syphilis. One of these substances, later named Salvarsan, proved very effective. It was the first drug to have a specific antibacterial effect.

Lysozyme protects the delicate surface of the eye from bacterial attack. Fleming had also been working with staphylococci, the bacteria that cause boils. He grew colonies of these bacteria on plates of agar jelly. Returning from a vacation in 1928, he noticed that a mold was growing on a discarded plate, and that the colonies of staphylococci that should have been growing around the mold had died off. Fleming identified the mold and discovered that it produced an antibiotic, called penicillin. He did not realize the importance of penicillin at the time, but ten years later, researchers in Oxford found Fleming's report. They carried out lots of tests and found penicillin to be amazingly effective against bacteria.

The new drug proved so successful that there was a huge and immediate demand. After a huge effort, two scientists named Howard Florey and Ernst Chain found a way to produce large quantities of the mold. The drug was used during World War II to treat battle wounds. The only problem with it was that it did not kill every type of bacterium.

The worldwide search for natural organisms that will produce new antibiotics continues to this day, with deep-sea missions and journeys into tropical rainforests. When researchers find a natural antibiotic, they work out what the active parts of it are, so they can recreate this ingredient synthetically.

Most antibiotics work by stopping the bacteria from being able to build proper cell walls when they divide. Without complete cell walls, the bacteria die. Antibiotics do not usually damage human cells, because they do not have a rigid cell wall.

▲ SELMAN WAKSMAN
This American scientist invented the word "antibiotic" in 1941. After the discovery of penicillin, Waksman looked for more antibiotics in soil microbes. In 1943 he found streptomycin, the first drug to treat TB. He received a Nobel Prize for his work.

▼ ANIMAL FEED AND ANTIBIOTICS
Antibiotics are often added to animal feed to make them grow bigger and stop them from catching disease. However, this practice has proved to be a medical disaster, because it encouraged the appearance of bacteria that could resist the effects of antibiotics. As a result, some antibiotics are now almost useless.

Key Dates

- 1910 Salvarsan is discovered by Paul Ehrlich.

- 1928 Alexander Fleming discovers penicillin by accident.

- 1935 Gerhard Domagk develops Prontosil.

- 1939 Howard Florey and Ernst Chain find a way to mass-produce penicillin.

- 1943 Selman Waksman discovers streptomycin, the first drug to successfully treat TB.

- 1945 Fleming, Florey, and Chain are jointly awarded the Nobel Prize for their discovery of penicillin.

Women Pioneers

WOMEN HAVE ALWAYS played a role in medicine, although right through history as late as the 1950s they were often dismissed by male doctors. Childbirth was an event from which men were usually excluded. Midwives looked after pregnant women and sometimes got rid of unwanted pregnancies. Midwives passed down their knowledge from mother to daughter, with the result that there is little written evidence of their work. Doctors rarely recognized the importance of midwives, although a few wrote about their techniques.

There were several famous women healers during the Middle Ages. One of these, called Trotula, practiced at Salerno in the 1000s. She wrote a book called *On the sufferings of women*, which was used as a medical text for the next 700 years. She gave detailed instructions on the technique of diagnosis, and also published works on the diseases of children and on skin diseases.

▲ FLORENCE NIGHTINGALE
Grateful soldiers in the Crimean War nicknamed Florence Nightingale the "Lady with the Lamp." In the 1850s Nightingale pioneered hygienic nursing techniques.

▶ SCUTARI HOSPITAL
Florence Nightingale and her team of nurses brought in strict nursing practices. Before their arrival the field hospital at Scutari (modern-day Usküdar, in Turkey) had a very high death rate. Nightingale used her experiences to improve nursing standards when she returned to England.

STRUGGLING TO SUCCEED

Women were not usually allowed to train as doctors. They were opposed by the Church, and by male doctors too. It was not until 1849 that a woman, Elizabeth Blackwell, became the first graduate doctor. In the early 1900s, suffragettes (women's rights activists) inspired many women. Margaret Sanger in the United States, and Marie Stopes, in Britain, championed birth control. This freed women from having very large families and improved the health of women and children.

▶ MARIE CURIE
Women were excluded from all areas of science, not just medicine. An exception was Polish-born Marie Curie. With her French husband, Pierre, she discovered radium in 1898. Thanks to their investigations into radioactive materials, a revolutionary treatment for cancer was discovered.

◀ DRESSING UP
Mary Walker was an assistant surgeon during the Civil War (1861–5). Her solution to men's distrust of female medics was to disguise herself as a man.

▲ ELIZABETH BLACKWELL
Many medical schools turned down Blackwell before she finally qualified as a doctor in the United States in 1849. The idea of a woman doctor scandalized the medical profession. It was many years before Blackwell was fully accepted.

▶ MILITARY NURSES
By World War II (1939–45), the armed forces had a well-developed system for providing nursing care to the wounded. Mobile field hospitals and ambulance services were established. These were staffed mainly by women, who were thought too delicate for combat duties.

Hildegard was a German healer living at about the same time as Trotula. She combined religious and medical writing, together with natural history. In particular she gave detailed descriptions of herbal remedies and other treatments, and was greatly respected by kings and popes.

In hospitals of the Middle Ages and the Renaissance, most nursing was carried out by nuns and other women attached to religious orders. When large hospitals were built in the 1800s, nuns played a less important role. Instead, working-class women were recruited, but they were not given any training, so the standard of nursing was poor.

The first non-religious school for nurses was set up in 1842 in Germany. Students took a three-year course, followed by exams. An English woman named Florence Nightingale briefly attended this school in 1851. She completed her training in Paris and then became head of the nurses at King's College Hospital, London.

In 1854 Florence Nightingale was sent out to nurse the troops during the Crimean War (1853–6). Conditions in the field hospital were very bad, but by improving the hygiene in the hospitals, Nightingale lowered the death rate from 40 percent to 2 percent. After the war, she opened a school of nursing at St. Thomas' Hospital, London.

It took a long time, and the hard work of many brave pioneers, to change attitudes towards women in the medical profession. One such pioneer was Dr. Elizabeth Blackwell. In 1869, Blackwell returned to England from the United States, where she had trained in New York, despite opposition from her fellow students. She helped to found the London School of Medicine for Women. Even so, medicine remained a male-dominated profession right up to the 1950s.

▲ MARGARET SANGER
A pioneer of birth control, Margaret Sanger was a nurse working mainly in slum areas. She was sent to prison for a month after opening the first birth-control clinic in the United States in 1916.

▼ MARIE STOPES
In 1921 Marie Stopes opened Britain's first birth-control clinic, offering free consultations and contraceptives. She recommended planned families. This meant that parents would be able to limit the number of children that they had.

Key Dates

- 1849 Elizabeth Blackwell qualifies as a doctor in the U.S.

- 1854 Florence Nightingale arrives at Scutari field hospital.

- 1857 Elizabeth Blackwell opens the New York Infirmary, staffed entirely by women.

- 1898 Marie Curie discovers the radioactive element radium.

- 1911 Marie Curie receives a second Nobel Prize for her work.

- 1916 Margaret Sanger opens the first birth-control clinic in the U.S.

- 1921 Marie Stopes opens the first birth-control clinic in Britain.

Rebuilding the Body

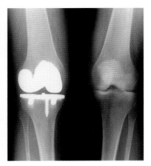

▲ ARTIFICIAL JOINTS
Many of the body's joints wear out in later life, often due to arthritis. This x-ray shows a replacement knee joint, made of metal and plastic. Many other joints can be replaced in the same way.

PROSTHESES ARE artificial body parts. False teeth are a type of prosthesis. They have been around for thousands of years, but thanks to modern plastics they are now hard to tell from the real thing.

Prostheses made huge advances during the 1900s. Artificial limbs became much lighter and looked more realistic. They can now be connected to the nervous system, so they can move like real body parts.

When limbs are broken, splints and plasters are applied

to hold them in position until the bone heals. If bones are badly shattered, metal plates are screwed onto the bone to give them extra support. Sometimes the bone is replaced with a material such as coral. New bone cells grow into the coral, replacing it with living bone.

Heart valves damaged by disease can be replaced with mechanical ones. If the heart's natural pacemaker (which produces the heart's regular beat) is faulty, a small artificial one can be fitted. This device produces regular tiny pulses of electricity that force the heart to beat.

Transplants are another way to rebuild the body. Skin grafts are one type of transplant, and blood

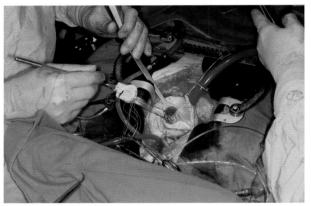

▶ HEART TRANSPLANT
Surgery to replace the heart is long and complicated. It depends on having a suitable transplant heart available. This has to be taken from a donor who has died in an accident, and must match the tissues of the recipient.

EARLY DAYS
The first example of a prosthesis was probably a tree branch. This would have been used as a simple crutch by a person with a broken leg. When surgery was developed, amputation of limbs was a common operation, though many patients died of infection. Survivors were fitted with wooden replacement limbs and hands. Sometimes simple metal hooks were used instead of hands.

◀ ROMAN FALSE TEETH
We know that false teeth were used as long ago as ancient Egyptian times. The Romans made complex gold bridges which held false teeth made from metal or ivory. Roman dentists also had various recipes for toothpastes to keep the teeth healthy.

▲ NOSE GRAFT
In the 1700s Western doctors were amazed to find that Indian surgeons were carrying out complex reconstructive surgery. This severed nose was rebuilt, and then skin was grafted on. Westerners soon copied these methods for themselves.

▼ WOODEN LEGS
This pirate was unlucky enough to lose a leg and an arm. With a wooden leg and a hook for a hand, he could get around for himself. However, modern artificial limbs are far more realistic and comfortable. They have working joints and are made of lightweight plastic.

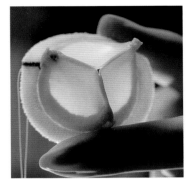

▲ ARTIFICIAL HEART VALVE
Leaking heart valves can cause ill health or death, so they are often replaced with artificial substitutes. These are simple one-way valves made from metal and plastic which will not be attacked by the immune system. Sometimes specially treated pig's heart valves are transplanted.

▶ PROSTHETIC ARM
Artificial arms can provide limited movement. Hooks or fingers are connected to the remaining arm muscles. New research is aimed at restoring more natural movement by making connections to the nerves in the arm.

transfusion is another. It was tried back in the 1600s, but became safe only with more knowledge of blood groups in the 1800s.

Transplants from another person are difficult, because the immune system immediately attacks any "foreign" organ. Very powerful drugs are needed to prevent rejection. This is why in blood transfusion the blood group of the donor (giver) has to match the recipient's (receiver's).

Another problem is finding available organs. Everyone has two kidneys and lungs, and so sometimes a donor will offer one of theirs to help a sick person. Other organs, such as the liver and heart, must be removed from a healthy person who has died in an accident, so there is always a shortage of them. The first human heart transplant took place in 1967. Since then, thousands of people have received donor hearts. Most survive for a long time, but they need to take anti-rejection drugs for the rest of their lives.

Current research is looking at ways to grow complete new organs from a patient's own tissues, so they would not be rejected. Another controversial possibility is xenotransplantation, using organs from animals such as pigs.

Washable, lifelike plastic sleeve covers the arm.

Beneath the plastic, a movable metal "frame" forms the hand.

▲ BLOOD GROUPS
Karl Landsteiner identified blood groups in 1901–2. He labeled the blood types O, A, B, and AB. This made it possible to give patients blood from donors who match their own group.

▶ KIDNEY MACHINE
The only treatments for kidney failure are a new kidney transplant or regular dialysis (purifying the blood) by a kidney machine. Dialysis was first used with dogs in 1914, and was used in humans 30 years later.

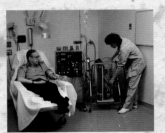

◀ TREATING DIABETES
In 1921, Charles Best and Frederick Banting saved the life of a diabetic dog with insulin, taken from another animal's pancreas. This led to the modern use of artifically-produced insulin to treat diabetes.

Charles Best   Frederick Banting

Key Dates

- 2500B.C. Egyptians use false teeth.

- 1901–2 Karl Landsteiner describes blood groups, making blood transfusion a practical possibility.

- 1921 Banting and Best use insulin to treat diabetes in dogs.

- 1950s Synthetic insulin is produced.

- 1954 First successful kidney transplant.

- 1960 First pacemaker is fitted.

- 1960s Artificial hips and other joints are introduced.

- 1963 First lung transplant.

- 1964 Christiaan Barnard performs the first heart transplant.

Healing the Mind

▲ STRAITJACKET
Before there were drugs to calm violent patients, straitjackets were used to restrain them.

▶ THE MADHOUSE
In its early years, the Bethlehem Hospital, known as Bedlam, was a place full of suffering. Patients were often kept chained up and even beaten.

AFTER THEY had been neglected for centuries, hospitals for the insane were eventually developed in the 1400s, mostly to keep the inmates away from the rest of society. The Bethlehem Royal Hospital in London was among the earliest of the asylums, taking live-in patients from 1403. The inmates were kept in terrible conditions. Most were chained up, and visitors were encouraged to come and view the patients as a form of entertainment. This was common throughout Europe.

The first real advance came around 1800. Philippe Pinel, a Parisian psychiatrist (doctor for the mentally ill), abolished the practice of chaining up the patients in the Bicêtre asylum for men and Salpêtrière asylum for women. Pinel's pupil, Esquirol, came up with the idea of a community where patients lived together with their

MODERN FORMS OF THERAPY

Psychotherapy marked a departure from traditional ideas about the cause and treatment of mental illness. Psychiatrists began to look closely at the emotional problems that seem to cause mental illness and to explore these with their patients in order to give them an insight into their condition.

▶ ECT
Electroconvulsive therapy (ECT) was widely used in the 1950s and 1960s to treat severe depression. Doctors pass a powerful current through the brain, causing a convulsion and, sometimes, relief of depression. It can also cause memory loss, however, so ECT is now used only as a last resort.

▲ ART THERAPY
Modern psychiatric clinics encourage patients to express themselves through painting. This is especially helpful to patients who bottle up their emotions because they are unable to speak freely about how they feel.

▼ PSYCHIATRIST'S CHAIR
It is very important, when a patient is being examined by a psychiatrist, that they be relaxed. This is why many psychiatrists will have comfortable chairs, like this one, or even couches, for their patients.

doctors in a group. Instead of being treated as crazed brutes, patients were seen as individuals who could be helped. This treatment sometimes improved their condition enough for them to be discharged (let out) into society.

Not all treatment became humane. Many famous psychiatrists still chained up their patients, beat them, or plunged them into cold baths in a form of shock treatment. However, living conditions in most asylums improved greatly.

In the mid-1800s Jean Charcot, another doctor at the Salpêtrière hospital, made a unique study of the patients in his care. He described their condition in great detail, and also studied hypnosis as a form of treatment. Then, at the end of the 1800s, the German doctor Emil Kraepelin began to classify the most serious mental illnesses. He was the first to accurately describe schizophrenia.

From the 1880s, Sigmund Freud developed psychoanalysis, which

▲ FREEING THE INSANE
Philippe Pinel was the first doctor to introduce humane treatment of the insane. He ordered the chains and restraints to be removed from patients in the French hospitals where he worked.

▶ SIGMUND FREUD
Freud's great innovation was to try to understand what caused mental illness. He encouraged his patients to talk about their past experiences. This is a very long-drawn-out process. It is not as practical as drugs for treating large numbers of people.

attempted to show how a patient's problems were the result of previous experiences. Carl Jung developed Freud's ideas further. Some Freudian and Jungian methods of exploring a patient's history are still used today.

The other big development during the 1900s was the use of drugs. Once it was known that there are chemical changes in the brains of the mentally ill, drugs were designed to help the brain chemistry become normal again. However, drugs brought a new set of problems, including addiction, and so the search for a perfect solution continues.

▲ WHAT MIGHT THIS BE?
The Swiss psychiatrist Hermann Rorschach came up with his inkblot test in 1918. He asked the patient what the spilled ink looked like. Their answers might give a clue as to what was worrying them.

▼ CHEMICAL TREATMENT
Prozac is one of a class of new drugs that are intended to restore the balance of brain chemicals. Scientists try to find drugs that restore normal mental health without causing serious side effects. Drugs are used to treat people suffering from depression, schizophrenia, and other psychiatric problems.

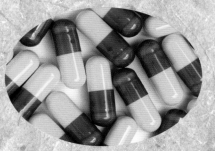

Key Dates

- 1377 Bethlehem Hospital begins to admit insane patients.

- 1793 Philippe Pinel frees the insane from their chains.

- 1856–1939 Life of Sigmund Freud, pioneer of psychoanalysis.

- 1943 The accidental discovery of LSD stimulates interest in the effect of drugs on the brain. This leads to the production of drugs to treat conditions such as anxiety and schizophrenia.

- 1950s–60s ECT is widely used to treat severe depression.

- 1990s Prozac and related drugs are used to treat depression.

Plants and Pills

ERBS HAVE BEEN used by people to treat disease since prehistoric times. They have been found in some of the most ancient tombs and burials. Some herbs were used because of their obvious benefits, while others were used for magical or spiritual reasons. The belief that the appearance of a plant revealed its possible use as a medicine was known as the doctrine of signatures.

It is said that 80 percent of the world's population still depends upon herbal medicine, though only a few herbal remedies form part of conventional Western medicine. Many of those used today are the same as those mentioned in ancient records of the Egyptians.

▲ DIGITALIS
Foxglove contains the drug digitalis, which is still used for the treatment of heart failure.

▶ APOTHECARY
The medieval apothecary diagnosed illness and carried out treatments, as well as making herbal remedies and other drugs.

ADMINISTERING DRUGS

Most drugs are given by mouth, in the form of tablets or medicine, but they come in many other forms. Lung diseases can be treated by breathing in a finely powdered drug, straight into the lungs. Injection is used to give large amounts of a drug very quickly, or to give a drug that would be damaged by the digestive system. Some drugs given by injection are in a form that is absorbed only very slowly into the tissues, so they have a prolonged effect.

▼ DRUG MANUFACTURING
Modern drugs companies use high-tech production lines to prepare medicines on a large scale. The process needs to be checked at every stage to ensure the quality of the drugs.

▲ SLOW-RELEASE CAPSULES
Some drugs disappear from the body very rapidly. People would have to take many doses throughout the day to keep enough of the drug in the bloodstream. Slow-release capsules let the drug out very gradually, so patients need to take only one or two capsules each day.

The herbal preparations described by Galen and other Greek doctors were preserved by Arab scribes. They continued to be used in the Middle Ages. Many monasteries and apothecaries grew herb gardens. Renaissance explorers brought back new herbs from freshly discovered lands. The herbal written by Nicholas Culpeper in 1649, titled *A Physicall Directory*, contains a wealth of detailed observation; it remains in print today.

Over the years, many of the plants listed in the old herbals fell out of fashion, but some of the most effective remedies are still used. Cinchona bark contains quinine and was introduced into Western medicine in the 1600s as a cure for malaria. Foxglove was used from 1785 to treat dropsy, and doctors slowly saw that this was a valuable treatment for certain types of heart disease.

Many herbs were extremely poisonous unless they were carefully prepared. For example, colchicine, extracted from the crocus flower, can be lethal, but is a good treatment for gout. The extraction of the active part of herbal remedies soon became a science after

alchemists discovered the technique of distillation. This involved boiling up a liquid so that the water evaporated (turned into steam), leaving behind a concentrated essence.

These techniques of purification led to the founding of the modern pharmaceutical (drugs) industry. Many modern drugs are synthetic, or artificially manufactured, versions of plant extracts. There are continuing worldwide searches to identify traditional remedies and to investigate their active ingredients.

◀ **THE GARDEN OF HEALTH**
The Hortus Sanitatis (Garden of Health) *is a typical herbal, written in Germany in the 1400s. It lists the drugs used by apothecaries and the properties the drugs were believed to have. Most of the information comes from the time of Hippocrates.*

◀ **WILLOW BARK**
Extracts of willow bark have traditionally been used as a painkiller, but it was not until 1852 that a version of the active drug was made synthetically. It was soon marketed as aspirin.

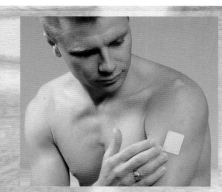

▲ NICOTINE PATCH
Some drugs can be absorbed through the skin. The nicotine patch allows small amounts of nicotine to flow into the bloodstream, helping smokers overcome their addiction to cigarettes.

▼ INHALER
Drugs for asthma are usually delivered straight into the lungs, by means of an inhaler. These drugs are sometimes in the form of a very fine powder. This puts the drug where it needs to be to work, and reduces any side effects elsewhere in the body.

Key Dates

- 1852 Aspirin is first synthesized.

- 1903 Barbiturate sedative (calming) drugs are introduced. They contain barbituric acid naturally found in the lichen *Usnea barbata*.

- 1930s Cortisone is isolated, leading to the development of modern steroid drugs.

- 1935 Sulphonamide antibacterial drugs are developed.

- 1961 The sedative thalidomide is withdrawn after causing terrible damage to unborn babies.

- 1980s AZT is developed as a treatment for AIDS sufferers.

Alternative Therapies

▲ CAMOMILE
Extracts of camomile are widely used for pain relief in homeopathic medicine. Homeopaths use tiny quantities of drugs that produce symptoms similar to those of the condition they wish to treat.

▶ MOXIBUSTION
One type of acupuncture is moxibustion, in which cones of herbs are burned on the skin at points on some of the meridians (channels) described by Chinese medicine.

Some people totally reject modern medicine. Christian Scientists, for example, believe that prayer and faith can cure all disease. Jehovah's Witnesses reject only some aspects of conventional medicine, such as transfusions.

Not all people reject traditional treatment for religious reasons. Some people find that their condition cannot be cured by orthodox (traditional) medicine, so look for an alternative. Also, while many people still respect a doctor's advice so much that they would never dream of questioning it, others may be sufficiently well-informed about their illness to wish to take treatment into their own hands.

In the 1990s there was increased interest in alternatives to traditional medicine. There is a difference between alternative therapies, in which a person rejects conventional medicine and seeks some other form of

MANIPULATION

The trend toward unconventional therapies is continuing in Western Europe, and is especially strong in Britain, France, and Germany. People who feel excluded from their treatment are now able to choose and to take control of their health care, knowing they can fall back on conventional medicine in an emergency. People who suffer conditions such as nagging back pain often prefer not to use strong painkilling drugs because they have inconvenient side effects, such as sleepiness. Osteopathy, chiropractic, and massage provide alternatives.

◀ WORKING ON THE SPINE
Both osteopathy and chiropractic involve manipulation (massage) of the body, especially of the spine. Although the methods vary, the outcome of this manipulation can often bring relief from back pain. Family doctors often recommend these practitioners to their patients.

▼ THE CHIROPRACTOR AT WORK
Chiropractors believe that parts of the spine may press against nerves, causing pain and illness. The founder of the method, David Palmer, is even said to have cured deafness. Chiropractors often use very strong manipulation to treat a whole range of disorders including pain.

therapy, and complementary medicine, in which patients take extra steps in addition to the treatment prescribed by their doctor. Many doctors accept that their patients may use complementary therapies and do not mind, so long as these do not interfere with conventional treatments. In Britain, 40 percent of family doctors routinely refer patients to complementary therapists. Alternative therapies, though, can cause a sick person to delay going to their doctor, and this can make their problem much more difficult to treat.

Some of these therapies are difficult to define. Herbal treatments, for example, can be a form of conventional medicine if they are known to contain medically active ingredients. Where their effectiveness is not proven, they are classed as alternative or complementary therapies.

Acupuncture is an ancient Chinese healing technique in which needles are inserted into the body. Science dismissed this technique as quackery until, in recent years, it was found that acupuncture at certain points has a powerful painkilling effect. Acupuncture is especially helpful for lingering pains that do not respond to drugs.

What is common to all forms of complementary and alternative medicine is that they have no scientific explanation. Some believe that they work because of the placebo (inactive drug) effect. Placebos given to patients in medical trials often work as well as the real drugs, probably because the patient believes that they will.

▶ AROMATHERAPY
Smells have a powerful effect on the body and on mood. Aromatherapy depends on massaging the body with scented oils, or on breathing in the fumes of heated oils. This helps the patient to relax and may have an effect on some illnesses.

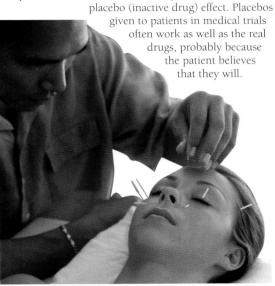

▲ ACUPUNCTURE
Scientific research has shown that acupuncture, the Chinese practice of inserting needles into the skin, really does kill pain. Serious operations have been performed in China with no form of painkiller except acupuncture.

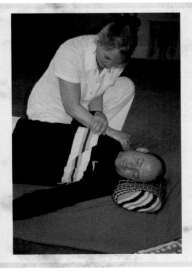

◀ SHIATSU
This is a technique to relieve pain which evolved in Japan during the 1900s. Practitioners of shiatsu use their fingers to press hard on acupuncture points, and also use massage and meditation to treat their patients.

▶ FEET FIRST
Reflexology is based on the idea that different areas on the feet represent different parts of the body. Massage and stimulation of these areas can help treat illness and generally improve health.

Key Dates

- 300 B.C. First descriptions of acupuncture in the *Nei Ching*.

- A.D. 1601 Acupuncture discussed in detail by Yang Chi-chou.

- 1796 Samuel Hahnemann says that "like cures like" and develops homeopathy in Germany.

- 1874 American doctor Andrew Still introduces osteopathy.

- 1895 Chiropractic is developed in the U.S. by David Palmer.

- 1900s Shiatsu is developed.

- 1930s Reflexology is introduced by Eunice Ingham.

Holistic Medicine

THE OLDEST FORMS of medicine are enjoying a comeback. Modern holistic medicine is an approach that treats the whole patient, not just the disease. It is a way to maintain good health rather than cure illness. The most important influences on today's holistic medicine are ancient Chinese medicine and Indian Ayurvedic medicine, both of which promoted whole body health.

Holistic medicine usually combines diet, physical exercise, and meditation, together with other alternative techniques such as aromatherapy, reflexology, and acupuncture. Herbal treatment is influenced by the writings of Nicholas Culpeper, as well as by Chinese and Ayurvedic medicine. Homeopathy is a form of holistic medicine that is widely practiced in the United States and Europe.

Homeopathy began in Germany in the early 1800s, when Samuel Hahnemann described how very tiny doses of a drug had an effect on his patients. According to Hahnemann, the more the drug was diluted, the stronger its effects. The substance selected would produce effects similar to the disease itself if given in large doses.

Meditation and contemplation have an important role in holistic therapy. They were brought to Europe by Indian teachers who combined Ayurvedic medicine with Western beliefs. Transcendental meditation is one

◄ HEALTHFUL FOOD
There is growing awareness of what a healthy diet must contain and how this improves health. Most people know that they should cut down on junk foods and also on sugar, salt, and fats if they want to reduce the risk of health problems later in life. Fresh fruit and vegetables are an important part of a healthy diet. They contain vitamins that supply the body with essential minerals.

DEALING WITH STRESS

Stress is an inescapable part of modern living. It can lead to illnesses such as high blood pressure and ulcers and to emotional problems such as panic attacks and depression. The conventional solution is to take drugs for these conditions. The holistic approach is to relieve stress by relaxation techniques such as yoga, t'ai chi, and meditation.

◄ EASTERN ART
T'ai chi is an ancient martial art which was developed in China in the 1700s. It uses the principles of *yin* and *yang* to balance body and mind in slow-motion exercises.

▼ INDIAN EXERCISE
Yoga is an ancient Indian discipline designed to exercise the body and the mind. The body is placed in various postures, some of which require a lot of training. Yoga helps to keep the body supple and the joints healthy.

▲ YOGIC MEDITATION
This yogi is meditating in a form of the lotus position, known as the half-lotus. Yogic meditation was made popular in the West by Indian mystics such as the Maharishi Mahesh Yogi and his movement for transcendental meditation.

◄ KEEPING FIT
Exercise is an important part of holistic therapy. It is used to burn up excess body fat and build up muscle. Another very important benefit is that exercise is fun. Feeling happy has been shown to have a good effect on people's health.

▼ LIFE ON THE STOCK EXCHANGE
Modern business life means constant stress and this can eventually produce changes in the body that cause illnesses such as anxiety, depression, and ulcers. Many holistic techniques try to work against this stress.

of the best known of these techniques. People repeat a mantra (chant) inside their head to reach a state of deep relaxation.

The holistic movement has made many conventional doctors look at the whole patient, not just the disease. Lifestyle, emotional problems, and diet are just some of the factors that can affect a person's health. Holistic therapy emphasizes good diet, exercise, and fresh air, all of which contribute to health. Some clinics now offer holistic therapy along with traditional treatments, so that their patients can choose a combination of therapies. One problem with holistic therapy is that it is difficult for people to be sure that a therapist is reputable. To solve this problem, many countries want alternative therapists to form professional bodies.

stretching

◄ MASSAGE AND GYMNASTICS
The benefits of healthy exercise and massage have been known for a long time. Breathing complaints, such as asthma, are helped by regular stretching exercises. Good posture (standing or sitting properly) is important, too.

massage

▲ BIOFEEDBACK
Electrical sensors attached to the scalp can measure brain activity during relaxation. Biofeedback is a technique in which a person uses information from these sensors to improve the level of relaxation they achieve.

good posture   *bad posture*

Key Dates

- 200 B.C. Zuang Zi describes the importance of maintaining balance of *ch'i* (vital energy or breath) in the body.

- 200 B.C. Yoga develops in India.

- A.D. 1700s T'ai chi develops in China.

- 1959 Maharishi Mahesh Yogi's first world tour brings transcendental meditation to the West.

- 1968 Aerobic exercise is developed by Kenneth Cooper.

- 1980s Biofeedback is developed as an aid to relaxation.

Modern Technology

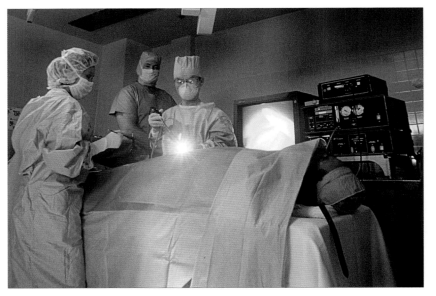

Since the 1960s medical technology has advanced faster than earlier doctors could ever have dreamed. For example, the laser, which produces a thin beam of intense light, was created. It can be used as a scalpel to cut through tissue painlessly. The laser beam can be moved very precisely, which means it can be used to remove tumors and to perform delicate surgery on the eye or even inside the brain, without any damage to healthy tissues.

▲ LASER SCALPEL
The intense beam of light produced by a laser can be used for very precise surgery. As it burns through tissue it seals the wound. Lasers are often used in skin surgery to remove birthmarks and tattoos.

▶ KEYHOLE SURGERY
Some modern operations are carried out through a tiny hole made in the patient's body. A small probe is fed through the hole. This sends a picture of the inside of the patient to a large screen, so that the surgeon can see what he or she is doing.

LATEST TECHNIQUES

Technological advances are constantly being made, along with more effective drugs. Sometimes simple devices can transform the life of a sick person; for example, a tiny tube can be inserted into a blocked blood vessel to keep it open. Some technology, however, is extremely complex, such as the computerized monitoring equipment used in life-support systems. Many modern techniques, such as keyhole surgery, have a quicker recovery time, and this cuts down how long a patient has to spend in the hospital.

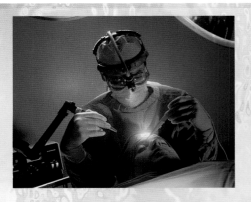

◀ THE CHANCE OF LIFE
Tiny premature babies would once have died. Today they survive in special-care baby units. They breathe filtered, warm air, and all their body functions are monitored. Sometimes they are given special drugs to improve their lung function.

▲ HI-TECH EYE SURGERY
Lasers can be used for surgery on the eye without the need to cut open this delicate organ. The laser can fire through the pupil, burning a series of tiny spots that can weld a displaced retina into place.

Pain relief is usually achieved with the use of drugs, but sometimes other technology is used to reduce the patient's dependence on these painkillers. The success of some types of acupuncture in controlling pain led to the experiment of applying tiny electrical currents to the nerves controlling pain. The experiment worked, and now TENS (transcutaneous [through the skin] electrical nerve stimulation) is a common method for the relief of chronic pain.

Patients suffering extreme pain—for example, in advanced cancer—need analgesic (pain-relieving) drugs continuously. This is achieved by implanting a needle in the affected area. The drug is drip-fed, using a tiny battery-powered pump worn at the waist on a belt.

Premature babies (babies born early) are always at risk because their lungs are not properly formed. The earliest technology to help these tiny babies was heated incubators that kept them warm. Today even a tiny infant weighing just two pounds can survive in a special-care baby unit. Computers monitor the amount of oxygen in the baby's blood, its body temperature, and its breathing. In the same way,

life-support systems keep people alive after devastating brain injuries that would once have killed them. People in a coma can be supported for many years, although after this time they rarely recover.

Electric shocks can kill, but the defibrillator is a device that delivers a powerful shock to the heart to restart it after a heart attack. It forms an essential part of the emergency equipment in a modern hospital.

Kidney dialysis is a method that removes wastes from the blood of people whose kidneys do not work. Normally the buildup of these wastes would quickly poison them, but with dialysis several times a week they can live a relatively normal life, although a kidney transplant is their only chance of complete recovery.

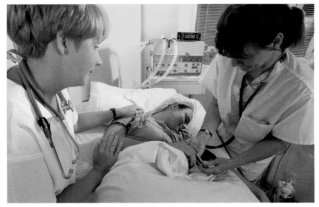

▶ LIFE-SUPPORT MACHINE
A life-support machine can carry out many of the vital functions of the body. People who have been severely injured in an accident can be looked after by the life-support machine. This allows time for their body to heal itself. Sometimes people with severe brain damage can be kept alive for many years on a life-support system.

▼ BRAIN SURGERY
The brain does not have any sensory organs on its surface, so brain surgery can be carried out on a fully conscious (awake) patient. A hole is drilled in the head under local anesthetic. This stereotactic frame allows the surgeon to position his or her instruments very precisely.

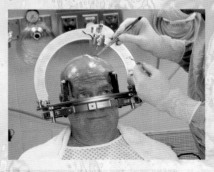

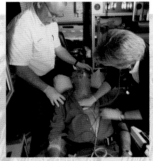

▲ TREATMENT ON THE ROAD
The original idea of an ambulance was to get a sick person to the hospital as fast as possible. Today, treatment is often begun during the journey. Paramedics trained in emergency medicine save the lives of people who may otherwise have died before reaching the hospital.

Key Dates

- 1917 Albert Einstein defines the scientific principles of the laser.

- 1928 The "iron lung" is invented to assist the breathing of people paralyzed by polio. It is widely used up to the 1950s.

- 1960 The laser scalpel is invented.

- 1978 The first "test-tube baby" is born after research by Patrick Steptoe and R.G. Edwards. This is opposed by many churches, but becomes widely used.

- 1985 Keyhole surgery becomes popular. Patients recover more quickly from this form of surgery.

Imaging the Body

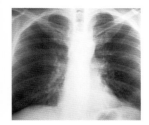

▲ CHEST X-RAY
X-rays pass more slowly through solid bone than through soft tissue. This means that bones show up in an x-ray image, but flesh does not. X-rays got their name because Wilhelm Röntgen, who discovered them, did not know exactly what they were. They are now also called Röntgen rays, and as well as in medicine, they are also used for looking for defects in solid objects.

THE ONLY WAY that early doctors could know what was going on inside their patients' bodies was to open them up, or to peer in through natural openings into the body. Stethoscopes helped to reveal the working of the heart, and soon ophthalmoscopes allowed doctors to look inside the eye. Endoscopes, developed in 1805, worked somewhat like a slim telescope. They were inserted down the gullet to view the stomach lining, up the anus to examine the rectum, or through the vagina to explore the condition of a woman's reproductive organs. Early endoscopes were rigid and extremely unpleasant for the patient, but in the 1930s flexible ones were introduced. These worked by fiber optics, in which a bundle of tiny flexible glass fibers was used

▼ AN EARLY X-RAY
Wilhelm Röntgen, who discovered x-rays, took the first x-ray photographs. This image shows his wife's hand. Her wedding ring is clearly visible, along with an old penny and a compass, because x-rays cannot pass through metal.

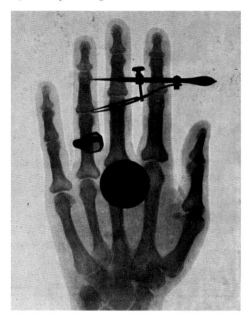

INSIDE VIEW
Accurate imaging of the internal parts of the body makes surgery safer and more accurate. Massive scanners are used for non-invasive investigations. The endoscope has now been refined so much that, in a procedure called a laparotomy, a tiny fiber-optic tube is inserted through a small hole in the abdomen. This allows the doctor to view the internal organs while the patient is under a local anesthetic. Sometimes a form of keyhole surgery can be carried out with tiny instruments fitted to the same device.

▲ ENDOSCOPE
The endoscope is a telescope-like device that is inserted into the body through a small cut. It can be moved around so that surgeon can identify a diseased area.

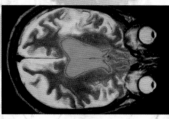

◄ SLICE OF LIFE
MRI produces a 3-D picture of the inside of the body. It uses powerful magnetic energy to photograph soft tissues that are not visible to x-rays.

▲ HOT SPOTS
Infection or inflammation can raise the temperature of the affected part of the body. Thermal imaging cameras detect these temperature changes and produce a thermogram (heat picture), to show the doctor where the hot spots are.

to conduct an image. Modern endoscopes have been refined so that they carry their own light source and tiny instruments such as scalpels and clasping devices, which retrieve samples of tissue. The bundle of light fibers can even take photographs inside the body.

The most important discovery to help doctors view the inside of the body was accidental. In 1895 the German scientist Wilhelm Röntgen discovered x-rays while investigating cathode rays. He received the Nobel Prize for his discovery six years later. Almost at once, people realized how useful x-rays could be for medical diagnosis. By the 1920s, x-ray clinics had become an important part of the war against tuberculosis.

A new method for imaging the inside of the body was developed in the 1950s, as a result of research during World War I. Sonar (sound navigation and ranging) used high-frequency sound waves which bounced off a submerged submarine and could be recorded at the surface. Using this technique, ultrasound could pick up echoes from soft tissues, such as tumors, that could not be readily seen on x-rays. The technique worked just as well on the fetus within the womb. Ultrasound scanning is now a routine procedure during pregnancy.

X-rays and ultrasound scans produce a simple image, but in 1967, Godfrey Hounsfield hit on the idea of producing sections through the body that could be put together by a computer to create a 3-D image. This resulted in the development of the CAT (computerized axial tomography) scanner, in which patients are placed in a huge machine while the x-ray device

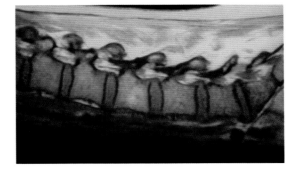

▲ CAT SCAN OF THE LOWER BACK
To produce a CAT scan, an x-ray machine is rotated around the patient's body, taking a series of pictures. Then a computer generates a scan picture which looks look a section through the complete body. CAT scans even show soft tissues that do not normally appear on x-rays.

revolves around them, photographing slices through their bodies. A similar method is to inject the patient with a radioactive dye which shows up in the photographs taken by the scanner.

The MRI (magnetic resonance imaging) scanner is one of the most recent innovations. It is safer than other imaging techniques, because it uses magnetic energy, not harmful radiation. It can even show changes in body chemistry as they take place. For example, it can show which parts of the brain become active as we think, talk, or move.

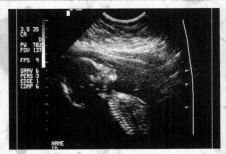

▲ UNBORN BABY
Ultrasound is used to check on the health of babies in the womb. They produce live images which even show the baby's heart beating.

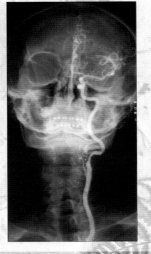

▶ ARTERIOGRAM
Damage to arterial (blood vessel) walls shows up when a dye is injected into the artery. X-rays cannot pass through this dye, and so the shape of the artery shows in the x-ray.

Key Dates

- 1805 A.J. Desormeaux develops the first endoscope in Paris.
- 1895 German physicist Wilhelm Röntgen discovers x-rays.
- 1916 Sonar is used to detect enemy submarines in World War I.
- 1950s Ultrasound scanning is developed by Ian Donald.
- 1953 Arteriography is perfected.
- 1967 Godfrey Hounsfield develops the CAT scanner.
- 1972 The first clinical test of CAT scanning is a success.
- 1980s MRI scans are introduced.

Looking to the Future

SCIENCE AND MEDICINE are still advancing at an ever-increasing rate. Modern innovations are usually the work of teams of people, each with his or her own special knowledge, rather than talented individuals.

One of the most important innovations has been techniques that allow us to read the genetic structure of the human cell. Before long, every one of the millions of genes in every human cell will have been mapped, and the function of many of them will be understood. This is significant because many devastating diseases are caused by genetic abnormalities (accidental changes that occur in the genes as cells reproduce). These affect the function of the body and cause disease. It will be possible to identify people carrying these defective genes so they can make a decision about whether or not to risk having children. Research is already taking place into gene therapy, in which corrected genes are inserted into an affected person's body. This is being tried in cystic fibrosis, an inherited lung disease. Modified genes are sprayed into the lungs of affected children to try to correct the condition.

▲ CODE OF LIFE
DNA holds the code for the structure of the whole human body inside each living cell. Research into DNA is revealing the causes of many diseases.

▶ VIRTUAL SURGERY
Virtual reality (VR) allows students and surgeons to practice surgery without endangering a real patient.

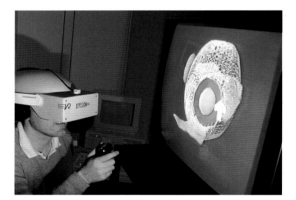

Drugs are providing treatments for more and more diseases. New drugs are designed on computers which produce images of the molecular structure of a whole range of similar drugs. This can show researchers how to modify the molecule to produce

WHAT NEXT?
Medical techniques are becoming more sophisticated and, at the same time, far more expensive. This has resulted in higher health insurance costs and, in turn, a rise in the number of uninsured people. Those without health coverage are less likely to receive adequate health care. In countries with public health care, such as Britain, there are long waiting lists for some operations.

◀ WORKING WITH THE IMMUNE SYSTEM
Immunology (studying the immune system) is a very important branch of medical science, because it makes sense to encourage the body to protect itself. At the same time, the wrong type of immune reactions can cause disease.

◀ GM FOODS
Bioengineers can already genetically modify (alter the genes of) our foods. For example, some crops now have built in resistance to insect pests. Maybe one day scientists will be able to give foods built-in medicines for good health. However, some people question the safety of GM crops.

▶ BUILT TO ATTACK
Bacteriophages are forms of virus that prey on bacteria like this. Genetic engineering may be used to design bacteriophages that fight specific diseases.

effects, even before a drug has been synthesized.

Modern technology is already helping many doctors. Sometimes, the patient's regular doctor may need to refer a patient to a specialist for a more detailed diagnosis. Modern teleconferencing enables the doctor, via his or her computer, to speak directly to a specialist, who could even be in another country. The specialist could then examine the patient by video link.

Technology concentrates mainly on medicine in developed countries, but throughout the world, millions of people do not have access to medical care at all or, if they do, cannot afford the treatment. It is a challenge for doctors and governments around the worlds to improve the standards of health for everyone. Agencies such as the World Health Organization have made huge efforts to set up global health programs. These are aimed at diseases that could be easily controlled by vaccination or the use of inexpensive drugs.

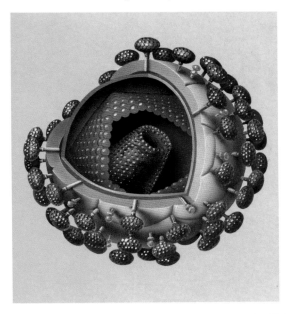

◀ HIV VIRUS

The HIV virus associated with AIDS has been studied more closely than any other virus, and its structure is well understood. What is less clear is how the virus constantly changes to avoid being attacked by the immune system. Frantic efforts are under way to find more effective treatments and vaccines to prevent the infection.

▶ SMART SEAT

A diagnostic toilet has been developed in Japan. Sensors check the weight of the user and measure the fat and sugar content of their wastes. The toilet sends its results direct to the doctor.

▼ ZERO GRAVITY

Research has already taken place in orbiting spacecraft to investigate new ways to purify drugs. The lack of gravity in space has profound effects on the body. It is possible that people with muscle-wasting diseases could survive longer under these conditions.

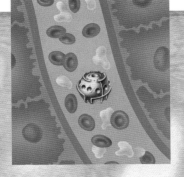

▲ NANO ROBOTS

There are plans to produce nano robots; robots small enough to travel around the body in the bloodstream. These robots could be programmed to monitor a person's health, attack tumors, or remove cholesterol (fatty buildups) from blocked arteries.

Key Dates

- 1869 DNA is discovered.

- 1943 Scientists discover that DNA passes on genetic information.

- 1953 James Watson and Francis Crick discover the double-helix structure of DNA.

- 1961 Yuri Gagarin is the first man to experience zero gravity—in space.

- 1970s Genetic engineering begins.

- 1980s Virtual reality is developed.

- 1994 First GM food in the US, a tomato, is put on the market.

ANCIENT WEAPONS

BY WILL FOWLER

Weapons have always been important to human beings, from prehistoric clubs to swords and gunpowder. This section examines how humans have attacked each other and defended themselves since earliest times.

Clashing Shields

THE USE OF WEAPONS is almost as ancient as humanity. Many early weapons came from hunting tools such as spears and bows, but probably the oldest and most useful weapon is the knife or dagger. A flint dagger from Scandinavia and dated around 1800 B.C. is one of the earliest examples found in Europe, but daggers have been made from stone, bone, wood, metal and plastic. Today, soldiers are armed with bayonets or combat knives, weapons whose origins can be traced back to the simple dagger.

The development of weaponry and warfare runs alongside the development of early civilizations. As Stone Age people moved out of caves and simple shelters they banded together to form tribes and clans and built villages. Bronze replaced stone and flint for tools, and then iron replaced bronze. People began to acquire valuable possessions such as food stocks and animals, agricultural equipment, clothing and cooking utensils, and finally precious and attractive adornments and decorations. For the first time, weapons were needed, not just for hunting, but for self-defense and attack against other humans. The horses which herdsmen used to move cattle also allowed armed warriors to travel further and faster than people on foot. Raids and ambushes by horsemen, as well as movements by nomadic mounted tribes, became part of daily life.

To reduce the chance of death or injury, men used shields and armor, made from toughened animal hide,

▲ ARMOR
This Japanese warrior wears armor made from bamboo wood. Today armor is made from plastic or nylon.

▼ KEY DATES
The panel charts the progress of weapons and warfare from the Stone Age to the 1600s.

▼ FORTIFICATIONS
Legionaries patrol Hadrian's Wall. Once territory had been won or taken, rulers needed to defend their lands or empires. Castles and walls guarded by troops were built all over Europe.

THE FIRST WEAPONS

10,000–5000 B.C. Cave paintings in Spain show men armed with bows in combat.

3500 B.C. The Royal Standard of Ur, Sumerian pictures made from shells and precious stones, shows men armed with clubs, axes and spears.

2500 B.C. First fortified city, Ur of the Chaldees in Modern Iraq.

1680 B.C. The Hyksos introduce horse-drawn chariots to Egypt.

Assyrian siege towers

1800 B.C. Flint daggers made in Sweden.

Hittite chariot

1600 B.C. Bronze weapons in Sweden and Greece.

1469 B.C. The first record of a battle, at Megiddo, between Egypt and the Canaanites.

1000 B.C. Assyrians make use of iron for weapons.

500 B.C. In China, Sun Tzu writes the first book on military theory.

GREEKS AND ROMANS

Mediterranean galley

490 B.C. The Battle of Marathon fought between the Greeks and the Persians. Both army and navy are used and the Greeks defeat an enemy once thought to be unbeatable.

401 B.C. Battle of Cunaxa between Greeks and Persians uses chariots with scythes near Babylon. The Persians won.

387 B.C. First siege of Rome by Gauls. The City is burnt but the government buildings remain.

327 B.C. Alexander the Great crosses the river Hydaspes and defeats the Indian king Porus.

216 B.C. Hannibal of Carthage uses elephants at the Battle of Cannae against the Romans. It was his greatest victory.

206 B.C.–AD220 Crossbows widely used in China.

A.D. 408–410 The Goths under Alaric besiege Rome and sack it on August 24, 410.

Roman legionary

wood or wood strengthened with metal. This ancient equipment forms a model for the plastic shields used by modern-day police to protect themselves from the oldest of weapons—the thrown stone. The breastplates worn by ancient cavalries are copied by the "flak jackets" worn by many soldiers and helicopter crews today.

Tribal raids to steal goods or settle territorial disputes led to the building of fortifications. The fences and ditches built to control wild or domesticated animals were just as effective against raiding parties. Wood was easy to get and to work with, but could be set on fire by attackers, and would rot in time. Stone or mud brick was tougher and more enduring. Today, fortifications may no longer be towering castles, but we still use sandbag parapets, trenches and bunkers.

Ancient weapons relied for their effectiveness on human or animal strength although heavy shields and armor made maneuvering awkward. Warfare stayed much the same until the late 1800s when the internal combustion engine was invented.

▲ ANIMALS

Before the invention of the combustion engine, animals—usually horses—were used to transport troops, weapons and supplies. In the Crusades in the Middle Ages, both European knights and Saracen warriors fought on horseback. A medieval knight wore such heavy armor that he had to be lifted onto his horse by crane.

▼ TECHNOLOGY

Gunpowder was probably invented in China in the 10th century. The Arabs made the first known guns in about 1300. From the 1400s, muskets were developed in Europe and were gradually improved to allow them to be carried into battle.

VIKINGS TO THE MIDDLE AGES

500 Saxon raids on Britain from north Germany.

778 Battle of Roncesvalles. The Franks under Charlemagne beaten by Basques and Gascons.

700s to 1000s Norse raids on Britain and Europe.

The Norman conquest

1066 The Battle of Hastings. William of Normandy invades Britain and seizes power.

1095–99 The First Crusade. European Christian armies fight for the Holy Land.

1120 Welsh archers use longbows for the first time at Powys.

1190 Mongols under Genghis Khan begin expansion south and west from the Gobi Desert.

1330 First steel produced by accident in the Middle East while making iron.

1326 First illustration of cannon appears in manuscripts in Europe.

1337 Hundred Years War between England and France begins.

Medieval cannon

GUNPOWDER AND AFTER

1400 Handguns first produced in Europe. *Hand cannon*

1400–1600 Rise of halberdiers and pikemen in Europe. Simple breech loading guns in use.

1411 Earliest illustration of a simple matchlock.

1415 Battle of Agincourt. The last great victory of the longbow.

1420s Jan Zizka and the Hussites pioneer the use of war wagons and shoulder-fired guns.

1453 Massed artillery used by Turks at the Siege of Constantinople.

1500 Metal shot gains widespread use.

1505 First battleworthy pistol developed in Germany.

1547 Flintlocks developed in Spain.

1595 English begin to use fire arms and cannon.

1635 Flintlocks perfected in France.

1620 Swedes first use light leather-bound cannon. First tactical use of artillery.

Clubs, Maces, Hammers, and Flails

THE EARLIEST KIND of weapons were clubs, maces and hammers. People could hold them in their hands. They could not break down and nothing could go wrong with them. The club is the oldest weapon. The earliest clubs were lumps of stone picked up from the ground. Prehistoric people used them as both tools and weapons. Clubs could be used to crush seeds for food. They could also be used as weapons to hunt animals or to fight with enemies. In South Africa, there are wall paintings made around 6000 B.C. showing two human figures with long heavy sticks that look like clubs. People made clubs from a variety of materials—long, heavy animal bones, or thick lengths of wood taken from trees, bushes or plants, for example.

When people learned how to make bronze, iron and steel, they used these metals to make stronger weapons. Using metal, the simple club was turned into a mace. A mace had a weighted, spiked

▲ CLUBS AND MACES AT HASTINGS
The Bayeux tapestry showing Norman cavalry, armed with maces and clubs, at the Battle of Hastings in 1066.

or pointed end. This could be used to batter through an enemy's shield or armor. It could be used in hand-to-hand fighting or by soldiers on horseback. Today in the United States, a ceremonial mace, made of ebony and silver, is used in the House of Representatives. In Britain, the scepter carried by the queen on special occasions is also a kind of mace.

The war hammer was like an ordinary carpenter's claw hammer, but had only one claw. This was a kind of spiked pick. The shaft, or handle, of a war hammer was up to a yard in length. A soldier using a hammer could reach out from his saddle to strike his enemy. Using the sharp claw of the hammer, the soldier could then puncture his enemy's metal helmet. This kind of blow to the head could be fatal, killing instantly.

The flail was first used by farmers to thresh corn. It was made into a weapon which is a mixture of mace and club. Between one and three lengths of chain were attached to one end of a thick metal stick. Weighted spikes were attached to the end of each length of chain. When the flail was used, the chains whipped through the air, and struck the enemy in several places at once.

▲ THE MACE
This elaborately crafted mace is a weapon of war but may also serve as a symbol of political or military status.

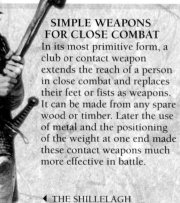

SIMPLE WEAPONS FOR CLOSE COMBAT
In its most primitive form, a club or contact weapon extends the reach of a person in close combat and replaces their feet or fists as weapons. It can be made from any spare wood or timber. Later the use of metal and the positioning of the weight at one end made these contact weapons much more effective in battle.

◀ THE SHILLELAGH
This Irish chieftain holds a shillelagh, a type of club made from hard wood like blackthorn or oak. Clubs are the simplest of contact weapons. In a more sophisticated version, they are still used today in the form of police night sticks.

African club

South Sea Island club

New Zealand club

▲ CLUBS FROM ACROSS THE WORLD
Clubs made from wood, bone and stone with both ritual and warlike functions can be found throughout the world. Some combine two materials, so a wooden haft may be weighted with stone. Another method is to pour molten lead into a hole made in the top of the club. Leather strips may be added to the handle to improve grip, or a loop for the user's wrist.

◀ THE ROUT OF SAN ROMANO
This detail from a painting by the Italian Renaissance artist Uccello shows armor-clad horsemen wielding maces, hammers and bows.

▲ HAMMER VERSUS MACE
Even though medieval knights wore complicated armor, they still fought with simple weapons. In this picture you can see how the hammer and mace were used, and how powerful they look.

16th-century war hammer

▲ WAR HAMMER
The spike on the war hammer was designed to penetrate armor. The flat end was used for smashing in helmets.

16th-century Polish mace

15th-century English mace

15th-century spiked mace

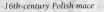

15th-century morning star mace

▶ DEATH STAR
This knight prepares to deliver a lethal blow with his morning star. The name came from the spiked metal ball on the end of the chain. It was said to look like the twinkling morning star as it sliced through the air.

◀ MACES AND MORNING STARS
The mace was in effect a metal club. The morning star was derived from the hinged agricultural flail, used to beat corn. Both came in a variety of styles. Some of them had deadly spikes or heavy blunt ends.

Key Dates

- 6000 B.C. Cave paintings of first clubs in Africa.

- A.D. 1066 Bishop Odo and William I carry maces at the Battle of Hastings.

- 1200–1600 Morning stars, maces, war hammers employed in battle.

- 1856 Truncheons used by police in Great Britain.

- 1914–1918 Clubs used in trench raids during World War I. They were used at night when silence and stealth were vital.

Axes and Throwing Weapons

T HE AX WAS FIRST USED as a woodsman's tool for felling trees. The first axes, like the first clubs, were made from sharp stones or flints. They were simply cutting tools. Later they were fixed to shafts or handles, which made them more powerful. They could be swung first to put more force behind the blow.

Axes were first made by tying sharp flints into forked or split branches. When people learned how to use bronze, iron and steel, they made stronger, sharper axes. By the time of the Iron Age, ax heads could be cast with a socket to fit the handle. Then the blade was hammered and ground to a sharp edge. Axes are still made in the same way today.

Axes have always been symbols used by powerful kings and rulers. The double-headed bronze ax was used as the symbol of the Minoan civilization in Crete. Pictures of the ax were used in wall paintings and as decoration on pottery.

The hand ax had a short handle. It could be used to hack the enemy in hand-to-hand combat. Soldiers could also throw the ax, although

▲ DECORATIVE AX HEADS
The simple wedge shape of an ax head has often been decorated for war or ritual throughout the world.

◀ KNIGHT WITH AX
Medieval knights often rode into battle armed with a heavy battle-ax. This had a sharp blade and a spike. The ax was attached to the knight's arm with a chain. These axes could cause terrible injuries to both men and horses.

this meant they might lose it. A good example of a fighting ax was the tomahawk used by Native North Americans. Tomahawks were first made of stone, then later of steel brought by traders. They were used for hunting and fighting. The tomahawk had a long handle which gave it a powerful swing. British soldiers fighting in North America in the 18th century adopted the tomahawk for their own use.

The last time an ax was used in combat in Europe was at the battle of Waterloo in 1815 between the

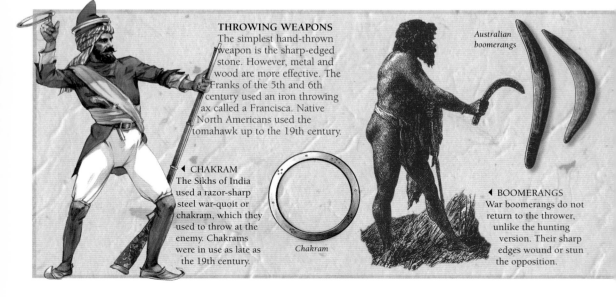

THROWING WEAPONS
The simplest hand-thrown weapon is the sharp-edged stone. However, metal and wood are more effective. The Franks of the 5th and 6th century used an iron throwing ax called a Francisca. Native North Americans used the tomahawk up to the 19th century.

Australian boomerangs

◀ CHAKRAM
The Sikhs of India used a razor-sharp steel war-quoit or chakram, which they used to throw at the enemy. Chakrams were in use as late as the 19th century.

Chakram

◀ BOOMERANGS
War boomerangs do not return to the thrower, unlike the hunting version. Their sharp edges wound or stun the opposition.

▼ NORSE RAIDERS
Norse raiders disembark from their longships and race into action armed with their single-headed war axes. These iron-bladed weapons were often elaborately decorated.

French and the British, together with the Prussians. During the battle, French troops used axes to break down the door of the farm at Hougoumont, which was being held by the British infantry.

The ax is still in use today. In some armies, it is the badge of the assault pioneers. These are soldiers who do engineering work. The badge shows crossed axes. Firefighters also use axes which look rather like ancient war axes. They have spikes and blades and are easy to hold and use in one hand.

▼ THROWING KNIFE
The leaf-shaped throwing knife was a war weapon used throughout Africa from Nigeria through the Congo to the Sudan. As it turned through the air in flight the blades of the throwing knife were intended to strike the victim in a sawing action. The disadvantage of a throwing weapon was that if it missed, it could be thrown back.

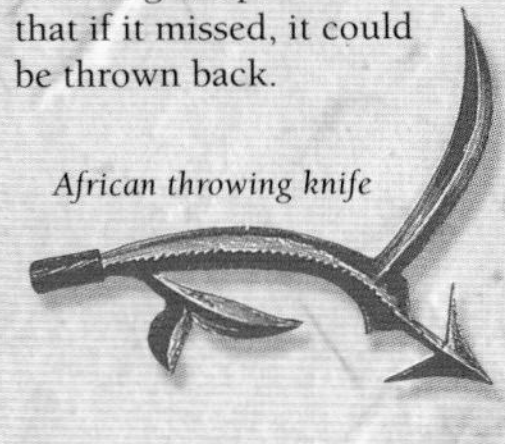

African throwing knife

◄ WAR BLADE
This African throwing knife had a steel, double-edged blade. The short handle was bound with grass or a leather thong to give the warrior a good grip. The knife was designed purely as a weapon, unlike an everyday knife, and could not be used off the battlefield for day-to-day tasks or hunting.

Key Dates

- 2000–1700 B.C. Double-headed ax used as symbol for the civilization of Minoan Crete.

- 700 B.C. Evidence that slings were used in Assyria.

- A.D. 400–500 Francisca throwing axes found in England.

- 700–1100 Single- and double-bladed axes used by Norse raiders.

- 900–1400 Heavy, long-handled battle-axes used by knights.

- 1700s Iron-bladed tomahawks manufactured for North America.

- 1800s Chakrams in use in India.

Slings, Bows, and Crossbows

THE SLING, LIKE the longbow and crossbow, is a "stand-off" weapon. This lets a soldier attack his enemy while remaining out of reach himself. Slings were used in early sea battles. Piles of sling stones were discovered at Maiden Castle, Dorset, England, where the Celtic defenders fought the Romans in A.D. 44.

▲ DAVID AND THE GIANT GOLIATH
The shepherd David defeated the Philistine warrior Goliath by stunning him with a sling stone.

Bows are among the most ancient weapons in the world. Ancient cave paintings, dating from 10,000 and 5000 B.C., from Castellon in Spain show figures of men using bows for fighting. Bows have been found in Denmark dating from 2000 to 1500 B.C. and in Egypt from around 1400 B.C.

The bow was also used for hunting. Many of the skills of the hunter were also those of the warrior. Experienced archers could fire accurately from horseback or chariot.

In the 16th century, Henry VIII of England ordered that young men should practice shooting their bows every Sunday after church. Most bows were made from yew wood.

The triumph of the English and Welsh longbow was in three battles against France: Crécy in August, 1346;

Poitiers in September, 1356; and Agincourt in October, 1415. English and Welsh archers were able to keep the French mounted nobles under a constant rain of arrows from 800 feet. As horses and riders crashed to the ground, others became entangled with them and they all became easy targets.

When muskets and rifles were first invented, the longbow, fired by a skilled archer, was still more accurate. It was not until the American Civil War that firearms became more effective. Muskets were adopted because it was easier to train soldiers to use them.

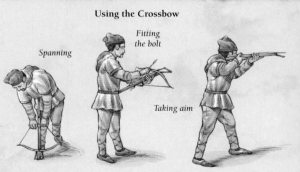

◀ TAKING AIM
A crossbowman takes aim. He operated the trigger, which held back the string with a hook called a nut, with his right hand. If the weapon was used to hunt game a stone was used in place of the bolt.

◀ TAKING COVER
A crossbowman takes cover with his weapon and equipment stowed in a shield carrier.

STAND OFF WEAPONS

The crossbow and longbow allowed ordinary foot soldiers to engage enemies at long range. This meant that mounted knights and foot soldiers could be killed before they could use their swords, lances or axes. Both longbows and crossbows could penetrate armor at short range, which meant that they could bring down a knight in full armor.

Longbow with six arrows

Longbow

Range of 245 yds

Crossbow with one bolt

Crossbow

Range of 390 yds

Using the Crossbow

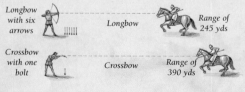

Spanning

Fitting the bolt

Taking aim

▲ SHOOTING RANGE
The expert longbowman could fire up to six aimed arrows in a minute to a range of about 245 yards, or twelve less accurately.

On the other hand, the skilled crossbowman had a longer range at 390 yards, but a far slower rate of fire. He could only shoot one bolt a minute.

▲ THREE STAGES
It took much longer to load a crossbow than to aim and fire an arrow. There were three stages to loading and firing a crossbow. Spanning was the first stage. It involved pulling

the bow string back and locking it. Then the bolt was fitted into the slot. Finally the bow was aimed and fired. With mechanical assistance as many as four bolts could be fired in a minute.

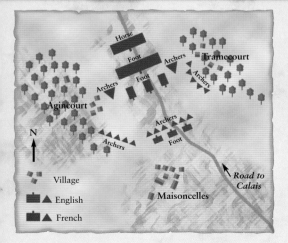

▼ LONGBOWS IN ACTION
English and Welsh longbowmen protected by a palisade of stakes fire at advancing French knights.

Some armies used men armed with crossbows. The crossbow is a short bow attached to a piece of wood or metal called a stock. The bowstring was pulled back by hand or mechanically and held in place by a hook and trigger mechanism. The short arrow, or bolt, was fitted into a slot and aligned with the string. The crossbowman had only to aim and operate the trigger.

The first description of a crossbow appears in a book called The Art of War by the Chinese military thinker Sun Tzu, writing in 500 B.C. In 1139 Pope Innocent II tried to ban the use of the crossbow against Christians because of the terrible injuries it caused. Richard I of England died in 1199 from gangrene caused by a crossbow bolt.

Forked steel tip

Barbed arrowhead

▲ ARROWHEADS
Archers used different shaped arrowheads. Barbs and forks were popular. Barbs ensured that the arrow stayed lodged in the target and made withdrawal difficult. The forked steel tip was used in the Far East.

◄ LONGBOWS SAVE THE DAY
The Battle of Agincourt was the last great victory of the longbow against mounted soldiers. Wet weather slowed down the French knights and the English and Welsh archers stopped two attacks before Henry V's forces attacked from the rear. The French were defeated and lost about 5000 of their men.

Key Dates

- 10,000–5000 B.C. Cave paintings in Spain show archers in battle.

- 500 B.C. Sun Tzu writing about military doctrine mentions crossbows.

- A.D.1100 Crossbows widely used in Europe.

- 1199 King Richard I of England killed by a crossbow at Chaluz.

- 1200s Longbow enters wide use in England and Wales.

- 1914–1918 Crossbows used for firing grenades in the trench warfare during World War I.

Map labels: Horse · Foot · Archers · Tramecourt · Archers · Foot · Archers · Agincourt · Archers · Archers · Archers · Foot · N · Village · English · French · Maisoncelles · Road to Calais

Daggers and Knives

SMALL, LIGHT AND EASY TO CARRY, daggers and knives are hand-held weapons. Daggers and knives make very good secret weapons as they can be used in complete silence. They were used on their own for hand-to-hand fighting, or for throwing.

Although the dagger design was based on the knife, there is an important difference between the two. The knife is a simple tool, sharp along one edge of the blade, it may have

a relatively blunt point. It can be used for everyday tasks like cutting up meat for example, as well as being used as a weapon. A dagger is double-edged and tapers along its length to a sharp point. It may have a guard between the blade and the handle to protect the user's hand. It is always classified as a weapon.

The earliest daggers were made from flint. Early daggers were also made from sharpened wood or bone. Daggers made from bronze, iron and steel lasted longer.

◄ SWORD AND DAGGER
A fully armored knight equipped with a sword and dagger. The sword was suitable for hacking and the dagger for thrusts to gaps in the armor.

► MURDER WEAPON
Lurking in the shadows, an assassin armed with a stiletto awaits his victim. This dagger was easy to conceal and deadly if it penetrated a vital organ.

Stiletto

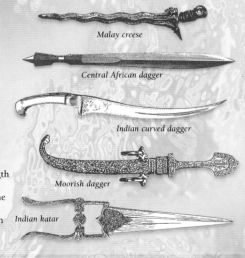

DAGGER DESIGN

As a weapon, a dagger or knife was inexpensive and very effective in even unskilled hands. It could be used for agricultural or domestic work if necessary. A dagger consists of the blade, the cross guard that protects the user's hand and knuckles, the grip or handle and the pommel. In a fight, the pommel at the base of the grip could be used in the same way as a hammer on an opponent's head. Dagger designs vary from country to country. The Indian katar or push dagger was designed to be used in a punching action.

Pommel

Grip or handle

Blade

◄ A BLADE FROM THE BRONZE AGE
This Swedish dagger dates from around 1350–1200 B.C. and shows all the basic design principles of a hand-held edged weapon. It has a separate riveted hilt, distinct pommel and double-edged blade with fullers or blood grooves. Later designs would have a full-length tang, an extension of the blade, built into the handle. This gave the dagger greater strength and better balance.

Malay creese

Central African dagger

Indian curved dagger

Moorish dagger

Indian katar

▶ A DUEL
Duels were considered an honorable way to settle an argument. The stiletto is used here to block the sword thrust.

In the 14th and 15th centuries sword fighters used daggers with their swords. A swordsman would hold the dagger in his left hand to block and deflect his enemy's sword. He would then make a thrust with the sword in his right hand.

Swordsmiths were the people who made swords and daggers. The daggers they made were almost works of art. They had beautiful inlays and precious and semi-precious metals and jewels set in the handles. The best known swordsmiths were the Saracens of Damascus in Syria. They used a method of hammering layers of steel together. This made blades of swords and daggers very hard and sharp and created a pattern rather like watered silk, known as Damascene.

In the 20th century the dagger and the knife are still used by soldiers in combat. In World War I the United States Army was issued with the Fighting Knife Mk 1 which protected the user's knuckles with a guard which could be used as "knuckle dusters" or "brass knuckles." Modern combat knives are more like multi-purpose tools, with a screwdriver, saw edge, and wire cutter as well as a sharp knife blade.

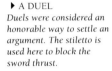

▲ TOLEDO, CITY OF STEEL
This Spanish city was a center for beautifully designed swords, daggers and armor which were manufactured for many centuries and exported through Europe.

▶ SWORDBREAKER
A 17th-century Italian swordbreaker was a dagger made for special use in a sword fight. It was designed to trap an opponent's sword thrust in its notched blade. The dagger would not be used just to parry a sword thrust. A vigorous twist of the wrist could either break the thin blade of the trapped sword, or wrench it from the user's hands.

Cross guard

Notched blade

Key Dates

- 2000 B.C. Bronze daggers were manufactured throughout Europe.

- 500 B.C. First Iron Age weapons produced and used widely.

- A.D. 1600s–1700s Stiletto manufactured in Italy. It was copied and used throughout Europe.

- 1700s–1900s Dress daggers worn as part of military or political uniforms.

- 1820s Bowie knife invented in the United States by Jim Bowie. Its classic design forms the model for most modern sheath knives.

- 1940s–1990s Combat knives issued to soldiers as multi-function tools.

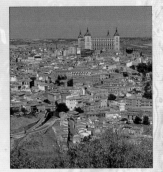

Swords, Sabers, and Scimitars

ONE OF THE MOST ANCIENT weapons in the world, the sword is now a symbol of rank for officers on ceremonial parades. Tools shaped like swords were used in farming work and to cut down trees. Like other working tools they were adapted to use in fighting. The kukri from Nepal is an ancient weapon that remains in service today with Gurkha regiments of the British army. Its broad, curved blade is ideal for chopping and even digging, but it is also a very good weapon for close combat.

Early swords were used to slice rather than to thrust. For many centuries European swords had a short, straight blade which tapered to a point. It was sharp on both edges. They were first made in bronze, later iron and finally steel. The short Roman steel

▲ VIKING WEAPON
A Viking sword from the 10th century. Its hilt is covered with silver leaf.

sword called a gladius was about 20 inches long. It was like a long, wide-bladed dagger. The gladiators who fought in the Roman circus or arena with these swords, got their name from the gladius.

Swords in the Middle Ages were longer. They were about 30 to 35 inches long with a cross-shaped handle and tapering blade. Long swords could be used to thrust at the enemy but most soldiers fought by hacking at each other. Swords could be used by soldiers on foot or horseback.

Very strong men used the two-handed sword, which was very long, with a broad blade. Swordsmen used both hands to fight with it. Scottish chieftains in the mid-16th century used a long, double-edged, two-handed sword called the claidheamh múr, or claymore.

◄ TWO-HANDED
Medieval knights in close combat. One of them is armed with a hand-and-a-half, or two-handed sword.

SWORDS
Swords today are made from steel and have been made from bronze, stone and even wood. Although not used in war, in many cultures, they remain the symbol of power and status within military organisations. Sword fighting techniques vary according to the design of the blade. The Japanese favor a chopping action, while the thin bladed rapier is best suited to a thrust.

▲ SWORD SKILLS
A Japanese samurai warrior from the 15th century. Samurai warriors usually wore two swords and a distinctive headdress.

▶ SAMURAI WEAPON
The Japanese traditionally used single-edged daggers and swords of different lengths. The traditional long-bladed sword is called a katana.

◄ EASTERN SWORD BLADES
Swords with curved blades came from the Middle East and India. They were lighter and easier to use with one hand than western swords. Soldiers from the west came across them when they fought in the crusades. Curved swords are called sabers or scimitars. This elegant saber was designed in Venice. The saber became popular with mounted troops who could use it against soldiers on foot or on horseback.

◀ DEATH AT DAWN
A Victorian print shows the victor of a duel armed with a rapier. His victim's weapon shows the guard or side rings designed to protect the hand.

▶ HEAVY BLADE
An Asian warrior armed with a bow and broad-bladed sword. The sword has the weight closer to the tip, which makes it ideal for a chopping action.

Knights and soldiers discovered the sword-making techniques of the Middle East during the crusades. This led to improved sword design in the west. Soldiers in the Middle East used a curved sword called a scimitar. These had long, narrow blades and very sharp edges.

The guard in front of the sword handle was made to protect the fighter's hand. Around 1600, Venetian sword makers produced a new guard design called the basket hilt. This was a curved, perforated guard that protected the whole hand. The basic design is still used today on many modern ceremonial swords.

The mounted soldiers of the cavalry charged towards their enemy with their swords pointing forward for a straight thrust. However, long swords became difficult to use once the soldiers were fighting close to each other. There was no room to make a good stroke. The saber was developed as a cavalry weapon. It had a short, curved blade and was used to slash and thrust. The blade cut as it went up and as it came down.

In Renaissance Europe, noblemen and courtiers wore weapons almost as fashion accessories. Rapiers were very popular. These were light, very narrow swords known with elaborate guards. The fashion lasted from about 1530 through to 1780.

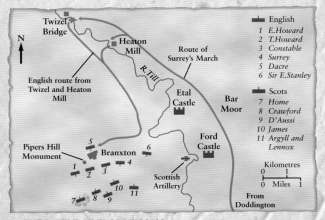

▲ THE BATTLE OF FLODDEN 1513
This battle between the English and the Scots, took place in Northern England. The Scots fought with the two-handed claymore sword.

English
1 E.Howard
2 T.Howard
3 Constable
4 Surrey
5 Dacre
6 Sir E.Stanley

Scots
7 Home
8 Crawford
9 D'Aussi
10 James
11 Argyll and Lennox

Key Dates

- 1300 B.C. Bronze swords used in war.

- 650–500 B.C. Iron swords in use.

- A.D. 900s Viking double-edged swords used in Viking raids all over Europe.

- 1300s Curved Turkish sabers in use as a cavalry weapon.

- 1500s Rapiers in use.

- 1500s Scottish two-edged swords in use.

- 1600s Venetian basket-hilt swords in use throughout Europe.

- 1850 Kukri in use with Nepalese soldiers.

Spears, Poles, Pikes, and Halberds

PREHISTORIC HUNTERS used spears to kill animals for food. They were more powerful and accurate than simple stones and could be thrown from safe distances. The earliest spears were simply straight saplings (very young trees) which were sharpened at one end. In the Far East, bamboo wood was used. It was light and strong and could be hardened in a fire to give a very sharp point. Flint, stone or metal points fixed onto a spear made it even more effective.

There were soldiers armed with spears in most ancient armies. Another name for the throwing spear is javelin. Throwing

▲ THE QUARTERSTAFF
This was the simplest weapon ever made. It could be cut from saplings. In Europe in the Middle Ages, the staff was used more in competitions and brawls than in war.

spears have one drawback. Once they have been thrown at the enemy, you cannot get them back. In fact, the enemy may use them to throw at you. The Romans solved this problem by inventing a spear called a pilum. This had a long, thin neck near the point. When the spear hit a target, it snapped at the neck. Then it could not be used by the enemy.

Longer, heavier stick weapons were used to fight with rather than to throw. In medieval times, country people used large sticks called staffs for walking. Various types of blades were attached to these to make weapons for both cavalry and

▶ PIKE WALL
Pikemen in the 17th century lined up to form a barrier for cavalry. This tactic gave musketeers time and space to reload their weapons behind the pike wall.

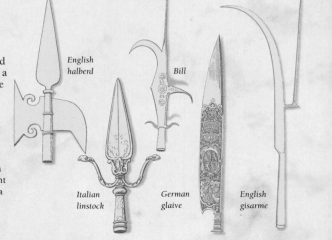

POLE ARMS

The advantage of pole arms like spears, pikes or halberds is that the user can stab, chop or even entangle his enemy at a safe distance. Peasants often fitted a pruning bill to the shaft of a quarterstaff to make a simple pole arm during revolts and insurrections.

◀ PIKEMAN
A pikeman in the splendid uniform of the 17th century. In addition to his helmet, he might also have a breastplate for extra protection. Some pikes were nearly 16.5 feet long, the same length as those used by the Macedonians around 350 B.C..

English halberd

Bill

Italian linstock

German glaive

English gisarme

infantry troops. A spear point would make a lance, used by cavalry. Knife blades and axes were also used as well as billhooks, which were tools for cutting hedges. A trident was made by attaching a sharp-pointed fork (like a pitchfork). Halberds were long poles with a spear point and an ax head mounted behind it. Pikes were long, heavy pole weapons with long blades of various designs.

In the 14th and 15th centuries, the Swiss developed specialized pike tactics. Using a pike that consisted of a twenty-foot shaft and a three-foot iron shank, Swiss soldiers marched in columns which had a front line of 30 men but could be 50 to 100 men deep. The massed pikes could stop a cavalry attack. Many rulers and generals hired Swiss pikemen to fight in their battles. Today, the Pope's Swiss Guard, armed with pikes, is all that is left of this force.

The bayonet fitted to the muzzle of modern army rifles is based on the pike. Bayonets were first used by soldiers with muskets. Although muskets were effective firearms, they took time to reload. By attaching long pointed blades, called bayonets, to their muskets and forming themselves into a hollow square with bayonets pointing outward, soldiers could break up a cavalry attack and protect each other while they reloaded.

◀ SWISS GUARD
The Swiss Guard at the Vatican still carry pikes and wear uniforms similar to those worn in the 15th and 16th centuries.

▶ CLOSE COMBAT
Two soldiers fighting with halberds. One tries to use the curved beak to trip his enemy while the other uses the spike as a spear.

▶ ON THE MOVE
An Etruscan warrior armed with a sword and throwing spear. The classic tactic for these lightly-armed men was to throw their spears, then to run forward as the spears were in flight. By the time the spears reached their target, the Etruscan soldier was within sword reach. The enemy was hit twice in one move.

▲ ISLAND WEAPONS
Spears have been used throughout history in many different cultures. This islander from New Caledonia in the Pacific Ocean is ready to throw one spear and holds two more in reserve.

Key Dates

- 600 B.C. GREEK hoplites use short throwing spears.
- 350 B.C. The sarissa (light spear) used in Macedonian phalanx formations.
- 200–100 B.C. Roman foot soldiers use the pilum, or heavy javelin.
- A.D. 900–1400 Lances used by knights for jousting and war in Europe.
- 1400s Pole ax enters service.
- 1400–1599 Halberd widely used.
- 1600s Pikes enter service.
- 1815 Cavalry lances adopted by Britain from France.

Ancient Firearms

IREARMS ARE WEAPONS that use gunpowder and shot. The earliest firearms in the west were made around the beginning of the 15th century. They worked like mini cannons and were small enough to be carried by a soldier on foot or on horseback. They looked a lot like the modern hand-held flare used to signal an emergency at sea. They had a short barrel attached to a handle.

By the late 15th and early 16th centuries, the standard firearm was about five feet long with a barrel, stock and butt. The stock supported the metal barrel and the butt rested in the crook of the firer's shoulder when the gun was being used.

The arquebus was a bigger weapon, often used mounted on a simple tripod. It usually needed two people to operate it. One aimed it and the second put a lit taper into the touch hole or vent. The soldiers who had to carry these heavy weapons were very eager for craftsmen to make them lighter and easier firearms. The matchlock was the first improvement. This weapon was fired using a fuse or length of cord which had been soaked in a chemical called saltpeter. This made it burn slowly. The cord was coiled into a curved lever called a serpent. A shallow pan filled with gunpowder had a thin tube leading into the barrel of the weapon. To operate the matchlock, the soldier lit the cord, opened the spring-loaded cover to the

▲ MATCHLOCK
The matchlock was used in Europe until the 18th century and in parts of India until as late as the 20th century.

▶ MOUNTED FIREPOWER
The wheellock was ideal for mounted soldiers who would need to keep one hand free.

HAND GUNS
Improved metal technology and designs made hand guns more reliable and easier to carry. Tactics for infantry and cavalry changed to suit these firearms. Weapons were still made by craftsmen. After the Napoleonic wars, muskets and guns began to be mass produced.

Mold

Inside a rifled gun barrel

Bullet spinning from the barrel

▲ POWDER HORN
Gunpowder was stored in a powder horn to keep it dry. Many of them were made from hollow animal horns. They had a spout through which an exact measure of powder was dispensed.

▶ HAND MADE
The lead ball fired by muskets was easily made using a simple mold. Once the molten lead had hardened, the handles of the mold were opened and the new ammunition was ready. Soldiers made their own ammunition as needed.

Shot

▲ RIFLING
Rifling was a system of grooves inside the barrel of a firearm which gave the bullet a spin as it left the barrel. This made the gun more accurate. Rifled weapons were still rare in the early 19th century. Now rifling is used in every modern gun.

◄ MUSKETEERS
*Musketeers armed with the heavy
Spanish style matchlock weapon that
required a fork rest for easy handling.
This weapon was used by armies
throughout Europe from about 1567 for
over 100 years and the musketeers were
an elite within the army.*

► WHEELLOCK
*This firearm used a spring-
loaded wheel and pieces of
iron pyrites to produce
sparks which ignited
the gunpowder at the
moment of firing.
But they were
expensive and not
in common use.*

pan and then
pulled the trigger. This
brought the burning cord, or
match, down into gunpowder,
which exploded.

The matchlock was not a practical weapon
for a soldier on horseback who needed to
have one hand on the reins. So the wheellock
was developed. It worked like an old-
fashioned cigarette lighter. When the
trigger was pulled the pan of
gunpowder was uncovered. A metal
wheel rubbed against a lump of iron
pyrites and produced a
stream of sparks. A mounted
soldier could carry two or three
short-barrelled wheellock pistols in
holsters on his saddle or tucked into
the tops of his riding boots.
The snaphaunce, miguelet and flintlock
were later firearms. They used flint and
steel to produce a spark. The flintlock was
in use until the mid-19th century. A shot
could be fired every 20 seconds from a
smoothbore flintlock musket, but the
weapon was inaccurate beyond 85 yards.

◄ AX MAN
An ingenious
combination of
wheellock pistol and
Ax head hatchet probably
produced in the 16th
century. Handguns of this
period were often
beautifully decorated with
inlay and engraving.

Ax head

▲ PISTOL BAYONET
A flintlock pistol made between
1788–90 which gave the firer
the back up support of a short,
bayonet-style blade.

Blade

Grill

Gun barrel

▲ SHIELD GUN
This shield has a
matchlock pistol in it. It
was probably made around
1544–47. The grill above
the barrel allows the user
to take aim while safely
under cover.

Key Dates

- A.D. 1411 Earliest illustration of simple matchlock.
- 1518 Wheellock banned within Holy Roman Empire.
- 1540 First pistols made.
- 1550 First examples of rifling developed .
- 1570 Spanish musket in widespread use.
- 1610 Flintlock developed.
- 1650 Flintlocks in widespread use.
- 1700 Matchlock no longer widely used in Europe.

Armor

SOLDIERS WORE ARMOR to protect the head, neck, eyes and chest. Early armor was made from bronze. Later iron and steel were used. Japanese warriors wore armor made from bamboo wood. There is a problem with armor. It must be thick or heavy enough to protect the soldier wearing it, but light enough for him to move around easily.

The ancient Greeks were the first to use bronze armor. They used it to protect their forearms, legs and chest. A Roman legionary wore armor which covered his chest, stomach, back and shoulders. This protected his lungs, heart and the important blood vessels in the neck. Although his arms and legs were not protected, he could still move and run quickly and easily.

A cheap way to make armor was to sew metal plates onto a heavily padded tunic. By the time of the Battle of Hastings in 1066, nobles and soldiers wore chain or link mail. It protected them from sword, arrow or spear thrusts. It could also move with their bodies. Mail was made by linking iron rings together to make a kind of metal fabric. Norman and Saxon soldiers both wore a tunic that covered the arms and body as far as the knees. A hood made from mail covered the head. Underneath ring mail, soldiers wore padded jackets. This stopped the mail being pushed into their skin by the force of a sword thrust.

Plate armor became very popular in medieval Europe. The whole body was covered with plates that were either strapped on to the wearer or hinged off one another. This was called a suit of armor. Each suit was made to fit exactly. Although the metal was heavy, its weight was so well balanced that a knight could walk about in reasonable comfort when wearing it. The parts of the armor that were most likely to be struck by a sword were specially angled so that

▲ ANCIENT ARMOR
A figure dressed in classical armor of Greece and Rome with a breastplate covering his torso and shinpads called greaves protecting his lower legs.

▲ JAPANESE WARRIOR
Japanese armor consisted of bamboo plates sewn to a padded jacket. Mythical motifs decorated the helmet.

PROTECTION
Chain mail was both light and sword-proof, but was never as strong as plate armor. The answer to this problem, for many centuries, was to use chain mail in areas such as the neck and limb joints and plate armor in slabs on the chest, back, legs and arms. The top of the head was protected by plate armor.

◄ NORMAN MAIL COAT
A Norman soldier wearing chain mail coat and helmet, light and flexible armor made from linked steel rings.

◄ INDIAN MAIL HELMET
This helmet uses a combination of plate and chain or ring mail to protect the head and neck. It is similar to the helmets worn by the Saracens.

▶ SHARK ARMOR
Shark's teeth stitched onto a simple tunic made strong armor for warriors of the Sandwich Islands in the Pacific.

▲ BRIGANDINE
The brigandine was a kind of 16th century flak jacket. It was a short, flexible coat with protective rivets on the inside and a rich fabric on the outside.

Simple rivets   Plates

◀ ROMAN BREASTPLATE
Roman armor was made of plates held together with bronze hinges. In later versions, these were replaced by simple rivets and strong hooks.

◀ MOUNTED ARMOR
Knights might be well protected, but their horses could easily get hurt in battle. To protect them, they wore their own armor.

The same care and attention that went into making armor for the knight was given to that for his horse. How much armor they both wore and how richly it was decorated, showed the owner's wealth.

Leather fasteners

Roman foot soldier

the sword blade would slide off without doing harm.

This kind of armor was very expensive. Both the knight who owned it and the armorer who made it wanted it to look beautiful as well as to work well. It was engraved and inlaid with metals such as brass and even gold. Enamel was used to color the metal plates so that knights appeared in black, green or even red armor.

Even though plate armor was worn in medieval times, soldiers still used chain mail to protect parts of the body that armor could not cover. Later, cavalry troopers, armed with sabers and ready to engage in hand-to-hand fighting, wore chain mail around their necks to prevent their throats being slashed open.

▶ A SUIT OF ARMOR
Knights had their armor specially made to fit. Armor was made up from lots of separate pieces. It was laced or strapped together and hung off a gorget. This was a metal collar that protected the neck and shoulders. A suit of armor from the 16th century was made up of at least 16 pieces and took a long time to put on. Knights needed a squire to help them get ready for battle. Armor was very heavy but, it was so cleverly made that the knights could still move around fairly easily. Most of the names of the pieces of armor are from the French language.

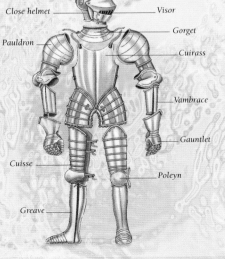

Close helmet — Visor
Gorget
Pauldron — Cuirass
Vambrace
Gauntlet
Cuisse
Poleyn
Greave

Key Dates
- 1500–1200 B.C. Bronze Mycenaean armor.
- 460 B.C. Corinthian armor.
- 102 B.C. Mail armor used by Romans.
- A.D. 75–100 Roman legionary interlocked plate armor widely used.
- 1100s Norman mail armor.
- 1300s Jointed plate armor.
- 1500s Horse armor widely used.
- 1600s Pikemen's armor.
- 1990s Body armor made from plastic or nylon is used today by police forces and armies.

Shields

BODY ARMOR was part of the wearer's "clothing". A shield was a piece of moveable armor. It was normally carried by or strapped to the left arm, while a weapon was held in the right hand. It could be used to push aside an opponent's sword or spear. Like all armor, a shield has to be strong enough to defend its user yet light enough for him to carry easily. It also has to be made in a shape that will give the user most protection.

The earliest shields were made from animal skin stretched over a wooden frame. They were something like the shields carried by African warriors in the 18th and 19th centuries.

The first metal shields were made of bronze. The ancient Greeks used large round shields. In ancient Britain, Celtic warriors used round bronze shields and figure-of-eight shaped shields. Circular shields were used by cavalry in both ancient Greece and Rome. Round

▲ RIOT PROTECTION
Modern German police with polycarbonate riot shields and helmets as protection against rocks in riots.

▼ GALLIC SHIELD
The Norman inverted tear-drop shaped shield covered the torso, but left the legs free.

shields were used later by the cavalry in the armies of the Middle and Far East. The Vikings also had round shields.

Roman legionaries used an oblong shield that was slightly curved. It was large enough to protect a man from his shoulders to his knees. The shields could fit together. A group of legionaries lined up in rows of four could fit their shields together and form a very strong barrier. Used in this way, the shields made a kind of temporary tank.

SHIELDS

Shields could be used to block a sword blow or protect the head and shoulders from arrows. The Greeks and Romans had finely crafted shields. In medieval times, shields were plainer but made from tougher materials.

◄ INSIGNIA
Knights wore insignia on their shields and armor to identify themselves on the battlefield. Here a simple bar and two dots are repeated, like a brand name, on the knight's shield, lance and the trappings of his horse.

▼ OUT OF AFRICA
The Zulu war shield is made from hardened animal skin on a wooden frame. It is light and tough. The warrior can use it to deflect blows.

▶ CELTIC CRAFT
The bronze Celtic shield is like a Roman design. The metal decoration on the front shows the wealth and position of the shield's owner.

Well protected, the whole unit moved forward to attack with their short swords.

The Romans developed a shield technique for attacking walls and castles. The soldiers fitted their shields together above their heads making what was called a testudo, or tortoise. Once the "tortoise" had reached the walls of the castle, the shields provided a platform for men to climb up to the fortifications.

By the time of the Norman invasion of Britain in 1066, shields had changed to a distinctive kite shape. The shield tapered downward, so the user could move his legs, but protected his upper body. Both cavalry and infantry used this type of shield.

The medieval shields were smaller. English and Welsh archers used a small round shield while knights had shields which were flat along the top edge and tapered to a point. This shape is now the accepted pattern for modern heraldry. It was in this period that shields were painted with the coats-of-arms of their users so they could be recognized by their followers on the battlefield.

▲ THE TOUGH TORTOISE
The Roman interlocked shield pattern called a tortoise allowed troops to approach the enemy fortifications under cover. Soldiers would then climb on their shields to attack the enemy walls.

▶ ANCIENT PERSIAN SHIELD
This shield from Persia has cut-outs at arm level. These allowed the soldier to attack with his spear while still protected by his shield.

▲ MOON POWER
The raised symbols of the sun and moon on this Persian shield were meant to give extra power to the user.

◀ BUCKLER SHIELD
This round German shield called a buckler has decorative studs called bosses set in an unusual random pattern.

Key Dates

- 1750-1600 B.C. Wood and hide shields used by Mycenaean soldiers.

- 480 B.C. Bronze and wood shields used by Athenian hoplites.

- 400 B.C. Celtic shield fittings found in England.

- 400 B.C. Hide shields replace bronze types for Athenian troops.

- 300 B.C. Roman soldiers equipped with hide and wicker shields.

- A.D. 1000–1200 Norman and Norse troops use tear-drop shields.

- 1400s Shields with coats-of-arms used by knights.

Helmets and War Hats

▲ SAXON HELMET
This helmet from the 7th century comes from the Saxon burial ground at Sutton Hoo. It is inlaid with silvered bronze.

SOLDIERS HAVE ALWAYS worn helmets of some kind to protect their heads and eyes in combat. They came in all shapes and sizes, to suit the kind of weapons soldiers were likely to come up against. Ancient helmets were designed to protect soldiers from attack by cutting weapons such as swords or thrusting weapons such as spears or arrows. Some helmets were simple round metal hats. Others were more like iron masks. The ancient Greeks invented the nosepiece. This was a strip of armor running from the brim of the helmet along the bridge of the nose. It was still in use in the 17th century. The Romans favored helmets with deep cheek pieces. These were hinged flaps that hung down the sides of the helmet, covering the ears and cheeks, but leaving the front unrestricted. This made it easier for the wearer to see clearly as he was fighting.

In the 11th century, the Normans wore conical helmets with nosepieces. They also wore a chain mail hood which completely covered the ears and back of the neck. This gave them added protection.

PROTECTING THE HEAD
Because the head incorporates the brain and face with important organs such as the eyes, ears, nose and mouth, it has always been protected in war. Helmets were made from bronze, iron or steel. Today they are made from modern plastics and polymers, which are light but very strong.

◀ THE GREAT HELM
By the mid-14th century the helm was the helmet most widely used by mounted knights. A visor pulled down to protect the face. Helms often sported elaborate crests at the top showing the owner's coat-of-arms. Today's motorcycle helmets resemble the helm.

Assyrian war hat

Hoplite helmet

Assyrian helmet

▲ ANCIENT HELMETS
Helmets began as simple metal hats. Later, hinged flaps were added to give protection to the cheeks, nose and neck without making it too difficult for the soldier to see or move. The flaps were often decorated.

◄ SPEED OR STRENGTH
During the crusades of the 11th and 12th centuries, European knights, who wore heavy armor and helmets, met Saracen warriors who wore lighter mail coats and small helmets that fitted close to their heads.

The most magnificent helmets were made during the medieval period in Europe. Ordinary foot soldiers had simple armor including a plain helmet but royalty and noblemen had splendid armor and helmets. The helmets were engraved and inlaid and were made with angles to deflect sword blows and a hinged visor that protected the wearer's eyes. A three-dimensional model of the family crest was often set on top. These elaborate helmets were like badges to show the nobility of the wearer.

By the time of the English Civil War (1642–1651), helmet design had changed. There was neck and earflap protection, a hinged peak and a face guard. The helmet was known as a "lobster-tail pot" because it looked like a lobster shell. When the helmet was revived in World War I, the British army adopted the style of the brimmed war hat worn by archers at the Battle of Agincourt (1415). It was called the "kettle."

▶ LOBSTER POT
The pot or lobster-tail pot helmet worn by Parliamentarian cavalry in the English Civil War gave them their nickname of "Roundheads."

▶ MEDIEVAL HELMETS
Armorers in the Middle Ages produced helmets and armor for wealthy and discriminating customers. Some designs were very fanciful. Others had carefully constructed angles and shapes which could deflect sword or mace blows.

English 13th century

French 15th century

French 12th century

French 13th century

German 15th century

Key Dates

- 1700–1100 B.C. Bronze helmets in use in Mycenae.

- 55 B.C.–A.D. 100 Roman cavalry and infantry helmets introduced.

- 1000–1100 Norman helmets with nosepiece.

- 1300s Basinet hinged helmet.

- 1350s Helms in use by European knights in battle and in tournaments.

- 1400s Kettle-hat or war hat.

- 1500s Nuremberg close helmets.

- 1600s Pot or lobster-tail pot helmet worn by Cromwell's Roundhead army in the English Civil War.

Animals at War

ELEPHANTS, HORSES, DONKEYS, bullocks and camels have all been used to fight wars. Most of them were used to carry soldiers or pull wagons. Elephants were used rather like modern tanks. An elephant could trample enemy soldiers, while archers riding in a large basket on its back could pick off targets with their arrows.

▼ HANNIBAL'S TANKS
The most famous elephants in war belonged to Hannibal the Carthaginian general. In 216 B.C. he brought them from Spain to fight against Rome at the battle of Cannae in southern Italy.

WAR BEASTS
Elephants are not aggressive by nature but could be used to frighten troops who had never seen them before. A panicking elephant could trample its own soldiers. In India, handlers called mahouts carried a spike. If their elephant went out of control, they killed it.

◄ ELEPHANT POWER
The elephant has three natural weapons: its great weight, its huge tusks and its powerful trunk.

▲ THE HEAVY BRIGADE
Elephants were used on the front line of battle to frighten the enemy infantry and to block cavalry charges. Like modern tanks, they were protected from close range attack by special groups of foot soldiers.

▼ ARMOR
The Indians put armor on their elephants as well as fighting towers on their backs.

One of the earliest battles to use war elephants was fought at Arbela, now modern Irbil, in 331 B.C. The Persian leader Darius led an army, including 15 war elephants, against Alexander the Great of Macedonia. Alexander's troops were frightened of the elephants at first, but so well-disciplined that they did not run away but fought and won the battle.

War elephants had been used in India by the Hindus from around 400 B.C. They were as important as chariots on the battlefield. At the battle of Hydaspes in India in 327 B.C., Porus, the Rajah of Lahore, led elephants against Alexander the Great. This time, Alexander's horses were frightened by the elephants. However, his foot soldiers attacked the elephants with battleaxes. The animals panicked and the Macedonians won.

The most famous war elephants belonged to Hannibal, the Carthaginian general. He fought against Rome in the Second Punic War (218–203 B.C.). The elephants were used in several battles but Hannibal was eventually beaten.

Elephants were first seen in England in A.D. 43 when the Romans used them to invade. War elephants were still in use in India during the 18th century. The elephants had iron plates fixed to their heads and were driven forward like four-legged battering rams to break down the gates of the town of Arcot in 1751. They panicked when they were fired at.

▲ CAMEL ARMY
The camel has been used for transport in battle in the Middle East. It has lots of stamina and can move fast. Camels can also travel a long way without much food or water. Here, camel-mounted soldiers use lances and swords in a lively battle.

◀ OVER THE ALPS
Hannibal marched with his elephants across the Pyrenees and the Alps to attack Imperial Rome. When he set out from Saguntum in 218 B.C., he had 50,000 infantry, 9000 cavalry and about 80 elephants. By the time he reached the Po valley in northern Italy six months later, only a few elephants were still alive. Hannibal had lost 30,000 infantry and 3000 cavalry.

Key Dates

- 327 B.C. Battle of Hydaspes. Alexander the Great meets Indian elephants.

- 275 B.C. Battle of Benevenetum, Italy. Carthage uses elephants for the first time against Rome.

- 218 B.C. Hannibal crosses the Alps.

- 202 B.C. Battle of Zama. Hannibal defeated and his elephants taken.

- 190 B.C. Battle of Magnesia. Syrian war elephants panic and confuse their own troops.

- A.D. 43 Roman Emperor Claudius uses elephants to invade Britain.

Horses in Battle

ORSES MADE IT POSSIBLE for armies to move around quickly. They could pull wagons and siege weapons or carry loot and possessions. On the battlefield, they could be ridden by scouts or messengers taking news to and from the generals planning the battle. Large horses, working together as heavy cavalry, were unstoppable on the battlefield.

The first people to use the horse in war were the Assyrians around 800 B.C. They used them as cavalry, to pull chariots and for hunting. The Romans bred from European, Middle Eastern and African stock to produce racehorses, hunters, chargers and harness-horses.

The saddle with stirrups, which were probably invented in China, reached Europe in the 2nd century AD and transformed mounted operations forever. They made it easier to ride a horse. A Roman soldier on foot could cover about 5 miles a day. When he was on a horse, he could travel twice as far as that.

The horse also made it possible for groups of people to move far away from their home lands. In the 13th century, the Mongols roamed from Central Asia as far as Vietnam, the Middle East and Europe.

There were two kinds of cavalry, the light and the heavy. The difference between them was based on the size of the horse. Most ancient armies had both light and heavy cavalry. About two-thirds of the Mongol riders

▲ PARTING SHOT
Horse archers from Parthia, an ancient country now part of Iran, used to pretend to retreat then turned and fired their arrows backward to take the enemy by surprise.

◀ A LIGHT SKIRMISH
Persian light cavalry troops, carrying round shields and armed with lances and maces, fight a running battle.

HORSES AT WAR
Horses have been used in war for centuries. They can pull wagons and guns as well as being ridden. They are strong and fast, but can be stopped by long-range weapons.

▶ BAREBACK WARRIOR
The fast, lightly-armed Numidian cavalry played an important part in the victories of Hannibal during the Punic Wars with Rome. They fought and rode bareback.

◀ HEAVY DUTY
German knights in the heavy armor worn in medieval battles. This protected both horse and rider.

▼ JOUSTING TOURNAMENT
Today, tournaments and battles are re-enacted by "knights" on horseback.

▶ AT THE CHARGE
The horse wears a piece of head armor called a chauffron. Its spike is almost as much of a weapon as the rider's lance. Both are pointed toward the enemy when the horse charges.

were light cavalry. They had small, fast horses, wore protective helmets and carried bows and arrows. The heavy cavalry had big, strong horses, wore mail armor or heavy leather clothing and were armed with lances.

Armies in medieval Europe had only foot soldiers and knights on horseback. To carry a knight in full armor the horse had to be big and strong. The knights were a kind of heavy cavalry. By the 16th century the armies of Europe had concentrated on heavy cavalry. The French called them gendarmerie and the Germans called them Schwarzreiter or "Black Riders." It was when they fought with Turkish armies in the 17th century that Europeans began to see how useful a light cavalry could be and to set up light brigades of their

own. The Hungarian light cavalry, called hussars, wore Turkish-style uniforms.

The heavy cavalry wore helmets and breastplates, rode large horses and carried a pistol and heavy saber. The light cavalry had no armor and rode horses chosen for their speed. The riders carried two or even three pistols and a light sword.

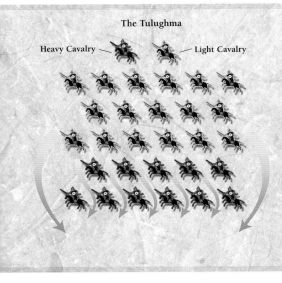

The Tulughma

Heavy Cavalry — Light Cavalry

◀ MONGOLIAN WAR TACTICS
The Mongolian army used light and heavy cavalry and many different tactics. This one is the tulughma. The heavy brigade led the charge and broke up enemy lines. At the same time they protected the ranks of light cavalry behind them. When the enemy ranks were broken, the lighter horses ran through or around their own heavy ranks.

Key Dates

- 500 B.C. Persians employ lancers and horse archers.
- 53 B.C. Parthian horse archers defeat Romans at Carrhae (modern Iraq).
- A.D. 100s Stirrups are introduced.
- 200–400 Horse archers and lancers used by Romans.
- 977–1030 Mahmud of Ghazni uses cavalry horse archers in north India.
- 1000–1200 Crusaders use Moslem mercenaries called Turcopoles.
- 1396–1457 French cavalry, gendarmes, in action.
- 1500–1600 German "Black Riders" in action in Europe.

Chariots and War Wagons

horses, the archer riding beside him was free to concentrate on fast and accurate firing at the enemy. Not all chariots were two-man vehicles. If there was only one rider, he would tie the reins around his waist to keep his hands free so he could use his weapons. Some chariots, pulled by three or four horses, could carry several men, armed with a variety of weapons. Used all together, chariots could break up ranks of enemy infantry. Some later chariots had the protection of armor. They may also have had blades or scythes fitted to the hubs of their wheels to prevent enemy infantry or cavalry approaching too close. The drawback with chariots, like many wheeled vehicles, was that they could bog down in mud and it was hard for them to cross rough ground.

Between 1420 and 1434 the Hussites, a group of people from Bohemia

CHARIOTS WERE A CLEVER WAY to combine speed and action. Most of them were pulled by horses. The driver was called a charioteer. For the armies of ancient Egypt, Assyria, Persia, India and China, chariots were the weapon of surprise, racing in and out of battle. Most chariots held two people, the driver and the bowman. With the driver to handle the horse or

▲ ROMAN CHARIOT
The chariot was not used a great deal in war. It was a popular sight at the public Games held in Rome and other major cities of the Empire.

▶ EGYPTIAN TACTICS
An Egyptian courtier on a hunting trip fires his bow and arrows from a moving chariot. The same skills would be used in war.

▲ WARRIOR QUEEN
Boudicca, chieftain of the British tribe called the Iceni, used war chariots in her battles against invading Romans.

WHEELS OF WAR
Chariots were first used in the Bronze Age in the 15th century B.C. in the Middle East. They could be pulled by two to four horses, but the larger number were harder to control. They could move easily on the flat deserts of Egypt and around the Euphrates, but they were not ideal transport in muddy, broken or rocky terrain. The war wagons used by the Hussites in Europe in the 15th century A.D. were almost like the first tanks. They were formed into circles like mobile forts. Soldiers fired cannons and muskets from the shelter of the wagons.

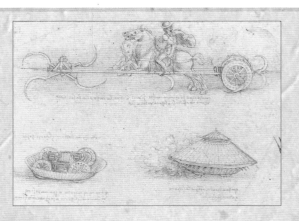

▲ LEONARDO'S TANKS
Leonardo da Vinci, the genius of the Renaissance, had many ideas that were ahead of his time. This sketch shows armored vehicles of various kinds. They look like early versions of modern tanks.

▼ GUN CARRIAGES
In 15th-century Europe, horses and carts were used to haul heavy cannons around the battlefield. This meant that the guns could be taken to positions where they could be most use. As artillery troops became more mobile, they could do more harm to the enemy.

German cavalry at bay. There were 350 wagons in a Wagenburg, linked together with chains and sometimes dug in. Within the circle of wagons were 700 cavalrymen and 7000 infantry. Gaps closed with chains, posts and spikes could be opened to allow the Hussite cavalry out to attack.

(now the Czech Republic), fought with the Germans. The Hussites were followers of the religious reformer John Huss. Their army, commanded by Jan Zizka, used armored carts. The wagons were formed into a circle of wagons called a Wagenburg, or wagon castle. Behind the wagons, crossbow archers and musketeers kept the When the Hussites brought in cannon mounted on special wagons, the German cavalry refused to attack them any more because they were too dangerous.

Some historians have suggested that the Hussite Wagenburg was the first tank in history as it combined fire power, protection and movement.

▲ CHARIOTS OF MARBLE
Many artists have made paintings and sculptures of chariots. This Roman sculpture of a chariot and a pair of frisky horses is in the Vatican Museum.

Key Dates

- 1400 B.C. Chariots used by Egyptians.

- 331 B.C. Persian chariots armed with scythes at Battle of Arbela.

- 327 B.C. Indian chariots used at Battle of Hydaspes.

- 225 B.C. Last use of chariots by Celts in Battle of Telamon, Italy.

- A.D. 60 Boudicca uses chariots against the Romans in Britain.

- 378 Romans use wagons to defeat Goths at Adrianople (modern Turkey).

- 1420-34 Fighting wagons used by Jan Zizka and the Hussites.

Cavalry Weapons

THE WEAPON USED BY A MOUNTED soldier reflected his skills as a rider. The Mongol cavalry riders of Genghis Khan could ride without reins, which meant they were able to use a bow while in the saddle. The lance or spear could be used in one hand. It was long enough for a rider to reach enemy foot soldiers. Cavalry normally rode straight at their enemy using the speed and impetus of the horse to add weight to the lance thrust. The cavalry lance became popular in medieval Europe and continued to be used in battle by horsemen in Poland and Hungary. Polish Lancers used it against the French during the Napoleonic Wars in 1800–1815. Medieval knights used the lance in battle, and practiced their skill in tournaments. The knight's horse also became a target, so craftsmen began to make armor for horses.

Horse armor was called bard. At its simplest it was made up of the chauffron, a plate covering the front of the horse's skull, and the peytral which covered the breast above the front legs. Full horse armor included the crupper and the flanchard. The crupper covered the horse's rump. The flanchard was an oblong plate fixed to the base of the saddle. It protected the horse's flanks and closed the gap between the crupper and peytral.

▲ SAMURAI BOWMAN
Japanese samurai warriors did not only use swords. Many were also masters of the longbow. A mounted archer on a trained horse had two advantages. He could move fast and he could fire his weapon from a distance, out of the range of his enemy's swords and lances.

▲ PERSIAN HORSEMAN
The light cavalry trooper of the Persian army carried a short spear. His horse was not protected by armor so was fast and nimble.

THE HORSE AT WAR

The horse changed combat forever. On horseback, soldiers could travel further and transport more equipment. They could also cover more ground on the battlefield. Stirrups gave the riders more control over their mounts, leaving their hands free for fighting in battle.

◀ MONGOLIAN PONY
Tough, fast little Asian ponies provided transportation and mare's milk for the Mongol warriors as they crossed Europe.

▲ HORSE ARMOR
Medieval horse armor protected the animal without slowing it down. The rider's legs covered its bare flanks in battle.

▲ A GREAT TEAM
Chain mail protects this horse's neck. The weight of horse, man and armor at the gallop swept them through the ranks of the enemy's foot soldiers.

Chauffron

Blunted lance

Knight's insignia

European cavalry troopers had been using straight swords from Roman times. When fighting in the Middle East, European soldiers came across the curved sword, which was used as a pattern for the curved cavalry saber. This was ideal for the slashing backstroke.

The wheellock pistol was developed in the 16th century. It was designed to be used with one hand so that the rider could shoot while keeping full control of his horse. Because of the noise, flashing and smoke, horses had to be trained to carry men through gunfire.

▶ GOING WEST
In 1190 the Mongol emperor Genghis Khan led his great army westward. It was divided into groups of 10,000 men called hordes. The hordes were named after different colors. By the 13th century they had swept deep into eastern Europe and reached almost as far as Austria. They could not have gotten so far or gone so fast if they had not had such swift horses.

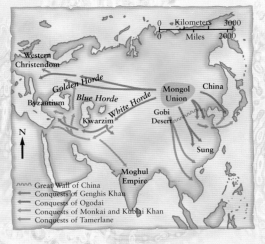

Key Dates

- 400s B.C. Persian mounted archers.

- 400 B.C. Spartan cavalry armed with short javelins.

- 330s B.C. Alexander the Great uses mounted lancers.

- 200s B.C. Hannibal uses Numidian mounted lancers.

- A.D. 1200s Mongol hordes, mounted on horseback, invade Europe.

- 1300s–1500s Jousting lances in use.

- 1400s Heavy horse armor introduced.

- 1600s Sabers introduced as cavalry weapons.

Castles and Fortifications

THERE ARE NUMEROUS EXAMPLES of prehistoric and ancient fortifications throughout the world. The people who built them often used natural features such as hills, cliffs and crags or rivers, lakes and swamps to enhance their strength. Where these features were not present, people created them, making ditches, mounds and later walls and towers. Sometimes castle builders used earlier sites. For example, at Porchester in Hampshire, England, in the 1120s, Henry I built a motte-and-bailey castle using the square fortifications of an earlier Roman Saxon fort.

The outlines of square Roman forts can be seen throughout Europe. These forts were called castra, which is where we get the word castle. Castra were built

▶ THE MEDIEVAL CASTLE
This typical castle has crennelated walls, which meant the defenders could shoot through the gaps.

Crenellation

Gatehouse

Drawbridge

Portcullis

◀ SCOTTISH CASTLE
Caerlavarock Castle, Scotland, is a classic moated castle. The pattern of stone bricks on the top of the round towers is known as machicolation. It is to protect soldiers inside the towers as they fight off an attack. The moat which surrounds the walls gives even more protection. The castle was hard to storm.

CASTLES FROM MUD TO STONE

The earliest fortifications were made from earth. Mud bricks and stone were used in the Middle East. The Romans were the first to build fortifications in Europe. In Britain after the Norman Conquest of 1066, the Normans built a large number of castles. These became the foundations for many of the great medieval castles. Crusader knights brought back many castle-building techniques from the Middle East.

▲ MOTTE-AND-BAILEY
These simple wooden forts were built by the Normans. The motte, on the raised mound, was where the family and servants lived. The bailey was the walled yard for animals and food stores.

▶ STONE CASTLES
Later castles were built of stone. The central keep is surrounded by curtain walls to defend it from attack.

◀ NORMAN TOWER
To replace the wooden forts, Normans built square stone keeps. The most famous example is the White Tower of the Tower of London.

Keep

Moat

Curtain wall

by legionary soldiers as a secure base at the end of a march in hostile territory. Sometimes these temporary bases became more permanent. They were called Castra Stativa. Rations, stores and baggage could be dumped there while lightly-armed legionaries patrolled enemy territory.

Norman motte-and-bailey castles in England were built as bases for the occupying power after the defeat of King Harold at Hastings in 1066.

The medieval castle was a base for a lord or baron. It was defended by a large garrison of soldiers. Towns grew up around the castles and, if the community was wealthy, they would build strong walls around the outside. Knights and nobles who had fought in the crusades against the Saracens brought back many new ideas about castle design. The curtain wall surrounding the castle was a Saracen idea. For the baron in his castle or the citizens of a town, the time and resources expended improving the defenses were like an insurance policy against bad times.

◀ WELSH CASTLES
In the 13th century, King Edward I of England built a large number of castles in Wales. This was to strengthen his grip on the country. The Welsh people did not care for English rule. Craftsmen were brought from all over England to help in the building work. Edward's wife and queen, Eleanor, gave birth to their first son, the future Edward II, at Caernarfon Castle. He became the Prince of Wales, the first English man to hold the title.

Key Dates

- 2500 B.C. Ur of the Chaldees, first fortified city, built (in modern Iraq).

- 701 B.C. Jerusalem fortified.

- 560 B.C. Athens fortified.

- A.D. 1058–1689 Edinburgh Castle.

- 1066–1399 Tower of London.

- 1181–89 Dover Castle.

- 1196–98 Chateau-Gaillard built by Richard I in France.

- 1200s Krak des Chevaliers, a Crusader castle, built in Syria.

- 1538–1540s Henry VIII builds forts along England's south coast.

Towers, Keeps, and Gates

To DEFEND THEIR CASTLES people built tall towers and keeps. Standing at the top, they could see enemy ships or army columns a long way off. This gave the people in the castle time to prepare for attack. When the enemy arrived at the castle walls, the lookouts on the tower could see down into their camps or siege weapons and fire missiles at them.

Towers can be square or round, but always have very thick walls.

Towers are safe places to hide when an enemy attacks. In the 9th and 10th centuries, Vikings raided England and Ireland. To defend themselves, Irish people built high towers in villages or near monasteries. These stone-built towers had no outer defenses. They had arrow slits or embrasures and a simple door built high up the wall that could only be reached using a ladder.

After the Norman Conquest of England, Norman barons built many castles. They were mostly of the motte-and-bailey kind. A curtain wall stood around the bailey. Towers were built at the corners of the wall and at intervals along the sides. Soldiers could use the towers as safe bases. The towers had a thicker belt of stone at the base. This was called a batter. It was there

◀ IRISH DEFENSES
The high towers of Ireland were built as refuges from invading Vikings. They were not intended to hold out against a long siege but were good look-outs and safe places to hide.

▶ BAMBURGH CASTLE
Bamburgh Castle Keep, in Northumberland, England, dates from 1200. The keep was the strongest part of a castle.

THE KEY TO THE CASTLE

The gate was the most vulnerable part of a castle because it was the point of entrance. When it was open, attackers could force their way in, and the castle could be captured very quickly. It was very important that the opening could be closed quickly. An iron gate called a portcullis could be dropped into place in seconds. The drawbridge only needed to be lifted a short way to prevent the enemy crossing the moat.

▶ DRAWBRIDGE
The drawbridge was made from very thick wood. It could be raised very quickly. It was operated by a system of weights which worked in the same way as a see-saw.

◀ PORTCULLIS
The portcullis was operated by a winch. The guards could release it quickly, and let it crash down under its own weight. Spikes on the bottom of the portcullis could trap attackers caught underneath it.

to strengthen the towers against battering rams and make it difficult to mine through the walls.

The gate was the weakest part of the castle. It was protected by a gatehouse and a portcullis. Some gatehouses had two portcullises. Attackers could be lured through the open gate only to find their way barred by an inner portcullis or gate hidden around a corner. Once the attackers were inside, the defenders would lower the outer portcullis and trap them. The passage between the gates became a stone tunnel. In the roof of the tunnel were slots known as "murder holes."

Defenders could shoot arrows, drop rocks or pour boiling oil or water through the holes onto their trapped enemies.

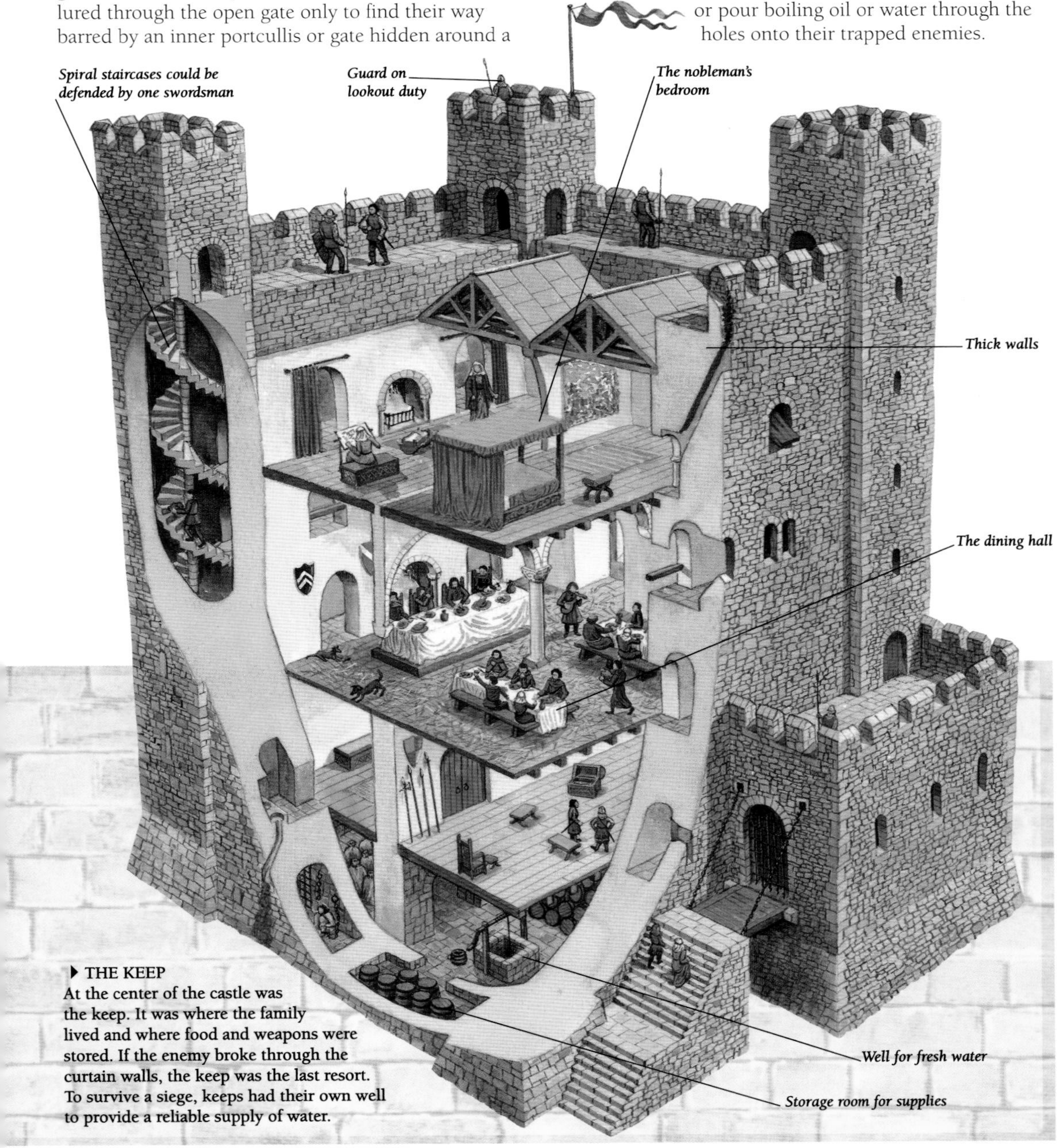

Spiral staircases could be defended by one swordsman

Guard on lookout duty

The nobleman's bedroom

Thick walls

The dining hall

Well for fresh water

Storage room for supplies

▶ THE KEEP
At the center of the castle was the keep. It was where the family lived and where food and weapons were stored. If the enemy broke through the curtain walls, the keep was the last resort. To survive a siege, keeps had their own well to provide a reliable supply of water.

Walls

CASTLE WALLS were built to a set pattern. Surrounding the castle was a curtain wall. This could be fifteen to twenty-five feet thick and wide enough for people to walk along. On top of the wall was the parapet. The parapet was a wall about one-and-a-half feet thick. In some castles they were built only at the top of the outer face of the wall. Others had them on both sides. They were about six feet high, so that they completely concealed and protected any soldier standing guard on the curtain wall.

Along the parapets were regular gaps which were low and wide enough for an archer to shoot at enemies. The gaps were called crenellations. The sections of raised wall between the gaps, which protected the archer, were called merlons.

At intervals in the wall and in towers of the castle, the builders cut narrow windows from which archers

▲ KEEPING THE NIGHT WATCH
Castles were defended day and night. Norman soldiers on the parapet check on the sentries manning the gatehouse and curtain wall defenses below.

could fire. These were called embrasures. When soldiers began to use cannon, the embrasures were made larger to fit the muzzles of the guns. Circular holes were cut at the base of arrow slits so that both the artillery men and the archers could fire from the same embrasure. This embrasure was known as a "cross-and-orb." Larger embrasures were covered by hinged shutters when they were not being used. From the outside, an embrasure looked like a narrow slit. On the inside, it opened up so that an archer could lean to one side and shoot at targets to the left or right. A variation on this design was the balistraria, a cross-shaped slit for crossbows.

If an enemy force reached the base of a wall the defenders had to lean out to attack them. This would leave them open to attack by enemy archers. The castle builders invented machicolation, which was made to

---

SLITS AND EMBRASURES
The walls and crenellations of castles were pierced with holes called embrasures. These were made so that the soldiers could fire arrows or crossbow bolts at their enemy below. Later, castle walls were pierced with loopholes for cannon and muskets. The hole was shaped to fit the kind of weapon being fired through it. On the inside face of the wall the sides of the embrasure were angled so that an archer or musketeer could shoot at targets to one side.

▼ ARCHER'S SLIT
The earliest kind of slit was made to fit arrows. Arrow slits also let light and air in to the inside of the castle and through the curtain walls.

▲ CROSSBOW EMBRASURE
This design was used by crossbow archers. It allowed them to aim at targets to the left or right of them, or even to track a moving target before firing their bolts.

▼ LOOPHOLE
When cannons began to be used, arrow holes were changed to fit them. A round hole was cut at the base of a narrow slit.

◄ CARCASSONNE
This walled city in southern France looks much the same today as it did in medieval times. With such strong defenses, the only way an enemy could capture the city would be to starve the citizens.

▲ WINDSOR CASTLE
The towers on each side of the gatehouse at Windsor have machicolations at the top.

protect the defenders. This was a battlement wall built out on stone supports. It had embrasures that faced downward so that defenders could drop rocks and stones on their attackers.

Henry VIII made many changes in the design of fortresses. To fight off the threat of French invasion in the mid-16th century he built a number of forts along the south coast of England. Their walls were not high, but low and massive. This was to provide a wide platform for cannons and large guns to stand on. As the power and range of cannons got better, the walls of fortifications became wider and lower.

◄ WALLS WITHIN WALLS
The Roman general Scipio, also known as Africanus, built a wall with seven forts around the Spanish city of Numantia. He then besieged the city for eight months in 133 B.C. Its 4000 citizens finally gave in after Scipio had blocked off the river access.

► CITY WALLS
In ancient times cities were often under threat of attack and invasion. It was common to build fortified walls around the city for protection. This imposing wall surrounds the Moroccan city of Essaouira.

Key Dates

- 1451 B.C. Walls of Jericho stormed.
- 598 B.C. Nebuchadnezzar destroys the walls of Jerusalem.
- 493 B.C. Piraeus, the port of Athens, made secure with fortifications.
- 478 B.C. Athenian city walls restored.
- 457 B.C. Athenian long wall built.
- 393 B.C. Conon rebuilds long walls at Athens following their destruction by the Persians.
- A.D. 93–211 Walls of Perge (southern Turkey) built by Septimus Severus.
- 447 Ramparts of Constantinople rebuilt after earthquake.

Defending Borders

Most fortifications in ancient history have normally protected families and their retainers in castles, or citizens behind curtain walls with fortified gates. When the movement of large numbers of people threatens a civilization, bigger walls have to be built. The Great Wall of China and Hadrian's Wall in England are two very famous examples of land barriers made to defend whole territories.

The Great Wall of China was built over four distinct periods. The building of earthworks in 476–221 B.C. was followed by the Great Wall of Qin Shi Huangdi (221–206 B.C.). The Great Wall of Wu Di (140–86 B.C.) and other emperors was finally finished as the Great Wall of the Mings (A.D. 1368–1644). The Great Wall of China was originally built to delay Mongol attacks along the north frontier long enough for the main force of the Chinese army to get to the threatened area and defeat the enemy.

The Roman Emperor Hadrian toured northern Britain in A.D. 122 and ordered the construction of a physical barrier against the lawless tribes in Caledonia (modern Scotland). At first, the barrier was made from

▲ THE GREAT WALL
Large enough to be seen from space, this famous earthwork in China took centuries to build.

▶ HADRIAN'S WALL
Named after the Roman Emperor Hadrian, the wall was originally a wooden palisade with a bank and ditch. It was later rebuilt as a stone-faced wall 16 feet high and 8 feet thick. Small emplacements, called mile castles , were placed at every mile along the wall.

Roman legionary

THE WORLD'S EDGE
The Romans and the Chinese had huge empires to guard. Just beyond their borders were people ready to invade. To mark and defend their borders, they built long walls or earthworks. A system of signaling allowed sentries to alert the garrisons if raiders tried to cross the wall. Then soldiers could quickly get to the site to drive them off.

◀ LEGIONARY FROM AFRICA
Roman soldiers were recruited from all parts of the enormous empire.They were often sent on duty far away from their home country. This was to make sure they did not desert.

▲ WALLS AROUND WALLS
The Romans used walls and ramparts as weapons in their siege tactics, closing off a city or fort from any outside assistance or supplies and starving it into surrender. This is the siege of Massilia laid by Julius Caesar in 49 B.C. Massilia is modern-day Marseilles.

◀ MILE CASTLES
Protected from the Picts (the painted people) from the north by Hadrian's Wall, small towns grew up around the mile castles along the wall. There were shops and markets, taverns and baths. Many of the Roman legionaries who manned the wall married and settled down in the towns.

timber and turf. In its final form, Hadrian's Wall was just a stone wall. It ran from Wallsend on the east coast to Bowness in the west, a distance of approximately 73 miles. The wall used natural features such as crags to give it extra height. It varied from 7 to 10 feet in width and was 15 feet high with a crenellated parapet 5 feet above that. There were mile castles along the wall at regular intervals of one Roman mile (4,856 feet) and two guard turrets between them. The mile castle was in a kind of gateway with a garrison of about 16 soldiers. The turrets may have been shelters for soldiers on guard or signal stations. Ten forts were built to house the garrison for the wall.

Hadrian's Wall was an effective military obstacle, and, like similar Roman barriers, it marked the limits of the Roman Empire. Beyond it were barbarians.

▶ JERUSALEM
The walls of the Holy City have been stormed and fought over ever since biblical times. Jerusalem is a city divided into the Jewish western area and the Arab territory in the east. The last battle took place in 1967 during the Six Day War between the Arabs and the Israelis.

◀ BUILDING THE GREAT WALL
During the Ming period, the wall was made from dressed ('finished') stone and brick. It was about 30 feet at its widest and varied in height from 25 to 40 feet. The parapet added an extra 5 feet. The top of the wall was wide enough for horses to gallop five abreast. Every 200 paces there were towers 12 feet high which straddled the wall. Crossbow archers could cover the gap between the towers north and south of the wall. Signal flags or beacons were used to pass messages between towers.

Key Dates

- 476–221 B.C. Various earth walls built in northern Chinese provinces.

- 221–206 B.C. Emperor Qin Shi Huangdi orders earth walls to be joined together to make the first Great Wall of China.

- A.D. 100 Romans build walls (called limes germanica) across Germany and Romania.

- 122 Emperor Hadrian orders wall to be built at northern edge of Roman Empire.

- 700s King Offa of Mercia, England, builds a dike to separate England from Wales.

Under Siege

A SIEGE IS WHAT happens when an enemy army surrounds a castle or a city planning to capture it. They can attack, or they can wait until the people inside get too hungry and surrender. A strong, well-stocked castle or fortified town could easily withstand a siege if their besiegers ran out of food. The defenders of a castle or even the wall around a town were higher up than the besiegers so they could see what the enemy was doing. They were also protected by a wooden palisade or a stone wall. From behind these walls, sniper archers could pick off the attackers as they came to the foot of the wall.

If the attackers reached the wall, they tried to make a hole in it so that they could get into the castle or city. Another way to get in was to climb the wall using ladders and grapnel hooks. This was dangerous, because the defenders waited until an attacker was half way up the ladder then pushed it away from the wall.

To attack the enemy camp the soldiers of the castle could use many of the weapons that the besiegers had been using. Each side lobbed rocks or cannon balls at one another. If a battering ram was used, the defenders might try to set fire to it. Another way to disarm it was to use huge tongs hanging from a crane to grab the ram and pull it up inside the castle or curtain walls.

Castles often had secret passages leading to a hidden exit called a "sally port". This could be further down a river or along the coast and from here the defenders might make their escape if the siege became too severe. Sally ports were also very strong doors from which the defenders could launch quick raids on their attackers. The plan was to destroy the enemy's siege weapons, generally by setting them alight. The defenders would also capture prisoners and steal food stocks.

▶ HOT RECEPTION
As storming ladders are raised against a castle, defenders fight back by pouring boiling water or oil on the shed protecting a battering ram crew.

HOLDING OUT
Siege was not always easy for the besiegers. If the castle was well defended and the people inside had lots of water and food supplies, they could sit out any number of attacks. If the siege went on for a long time, the besiegers could run out of food themselves, or die from disease and be forced to stop the siege.

◀ SIEGE SEE-SAW
The tenelon was a crane or see-saw with a basket on one arm. Troops inside the basket could be hoisted over the walls.

▲ WHO'S WINNING?
Every kind of siege weapon is used against the defenders in this castle keep. They are fighting back but seem to be outnumbered and may be running out of food. One of the soldiers is lowering a basket and water pot for supplies.

◀ A CASTLE FALLS
Battering rams, scaling ladders and towers can all be seen in action in this medieval siege. It is the end of the siege. The walls have been finally breached after heavy bombardment and the besiegers are within the walls.

◀ ROMAN SIEGE
The Roman army were very successful at sieges. They invented many techniques and siege engines. In this scene, the besiegers are attacking on three points. A ram batters at the tower. Soldiers advance under cover of their shields locked into the testudo, or tortoise, formation. Some have reached the wall and are scaling it. A tenelon hoists men on to the far tower. The defenders crowd the battlements, but they only have rocks to throw at the enemy.

Key Dates

- 415–413 B.C. Siege of Syracuse. Athenians fail to take city.

- A.D. 70 Siege of Jerusalem, part of the Jewish Wars of the Roman Empire.

- 1189–91 Siege of Acre (Israel), part of the Third Crusade.

- 1487 Siege of Malaga.

- 1544 Siege of Boulogne.

- 1565 Siege of Malta, part of the wars of Islam. Turkish army try to capture Malta from Christian forces. They fail.

- 1688-89 Siege of Londonderry.

Siege Attack

THE ROMANS HAD A VERY SUCCESSFUL method of siege attack. First, they would take a good look at the target fort or city to see if a siege would be practical. They would then surround their objective with an outer belt of defenses so that it could not be relieved by friendly forces and set about systematically destroying it. Several specialty weapons were needed to do this. The most important was the siege tower.

Historic pictures of siege towers often show something that looks like a mobile multi-story building. The height varied. The three iron-clad towers used by the Romans in the Siege of Jerusalem in A.D. 70 were 30 feet high with catapults on top. The towers were fitted with drawbridges that were lowered to span the gap to the castle wall. The military engineers Gaston de Bearn and William de Ricou, employed by the Crusaders

▶ ANCIENT ATTACKERS
Babylonian siege machines batter down the walls of an enemy fortress while archers fire on the walls.

in 1099 in another siege of Jerusalem, designed two towers of about the same height as the Roman towers.

The earliest descriptions we have of siege weapons come from around 400 to 200 B.C. Among them were those developed by the engineer Diades, who worked with Alexander the Great. Diades developed two unusual siege weapons, which do not seem to have been copied by future generations. The first one was a mural hook, also known as a crow. It was slung from a wooden gantry like a ram but it had a huge double

Siege tower

Animal skin covering

Battering ram

SIEGE TOWERS
In order to reach the top of the walls and take on the defenders, soldiers had to be at the same height and within range. Mobile siege towers could be pushed forward until the soldiers inside them could fire at the enemy and eventually cross simple drawbridges onto the walls.

Mantlet

▲ SIEGE GRIFFIN
A fantasy siege engine designed to be winched toward the enemy as it fires the cannon from its mouth. The ramp in the chest would be lowered for the assault.

◀ ALEXANDER
Alexander the Great was a fine general. He laid many sieges. The best known was the Siege of Tyre, a fortified town. It lasted for seven months.

▲ MOBILE SHIELD
The mantlet was either a row of set hurdles, or in this example a mobile shield which could be wheeled close to the enemy wall to give cover to archers.

clawed hook. This was used to pull down the battlements along the top of a city or fortress wall. The second was the telenon, a kind of crane. A large box or basket hung from it. Soldiers got into the basket and were swung onto the enemy's walls to attack.

Smaller items were also used. Scaling ladders were lightweight ladders, sometimes with hooks at the top. The besiegers used these to assault the walls. The soldiers would run forward, place the ladders in position and scramble up them.

Grapnels or grappling hooks were hooks attached to a length of rope. Soldiers would throw the grapnel so that it hooked over the parapet of the wall and then climb up the rope.

While the soldiers were climbing the walls, archers would keep shooting from behind their mantlets to keep the enemy occupied. Otherwise the defenders would just cut the ropes or push away the ladders.

Another way to get inside was by using a trick. In the Trojan War between the Greeks and the Trojans, the Greeks pretended to give up. They gave the city of Troy a large wooden horse as a parting gift. The Trojans took it inside the city, not realizing that there were Greek soldiers hiding inside the horse. Once inside the city walls, the Greeks jumped out and, after some fighting, they took the city and won the war.

▼ GOING IN
The drawbridge on an Assyrian siege tower crashes onto the enemy wall as the assault party storms in.

◀ ENGINEERS AT WAR
The Romans were masters of the planning and building work as well as the tactics of a siege. The siege of a large city was like a major engineering operation. Large numbers of timber structures had to be made very quickly and put into position. Sieges could go on for many years so any building had to be quite sturdy.

Key Dates

- 612 B.C. Nineveh (modern Iraq), capital of the Assyrian Empire, besieged and destroyed.

- A.D. 1346-47 Siege of Calais. Town officials prepare to die following surrender.

- 1429 Siege of Orleans relieved by Joan of Arc.

- 1453 Siege of Constantinople. Turks take the city ending the Holy Roman Empire.

- 1871 Siege of Paris. Citizens driven to eat zoo animals.

Bombardment

EFORE SOLDIERS had cannons, bombardment weapons were built based on natural forces.

Classical and medieval siege weapons worked on one of three principles: spring tension, torsion or counterweight. Spring tension weapons were like giant crossbows. They used springy wood that bent easily, such as ash or yew.

▲ GETTING YOUR OWN BACK
In this medieval picture, trebuchets are used to lob the severed heads of prisoners over the walls of a castle.

Torsion means twisting. Torsion weapons were powered by twisted rope. The tighter it was wound up, the more power there was when it was released. This method could be used to fire stones or javelins. The Romans of the 3rd century A.D. nicknamed one of their torsion weapons onager, meaning "wild ass." This was because of the violent kick of the machine's arm when the rope was released. They used a rope made from human hair for this weapon because it was very elastic.

The ballista was a little like a crossbow. The tension was produced by bending two lengths of wood held in coiled cord or braided hair.

The counterweight weapon or trebuchet reached Europe from China around A.D. 500. It was like a giant see-saw with a heavy weight at one end and a sling at the other. A stone or other missile was placed in the sling which was tied down so the heavy weight was in the air. When it was released, the weighted end would drop and lob the stone.

Stones were not the only thing that the trebuchet threw. Burning materials were hurled over the walls to try to start fires. Corpses of humans and animals were also thrown. This was to spread infection and to bring down the spirits of the defenders.

Looking at these weapons today, they seem crude and simple. However, in medieval Europe, with its poor roads and simple carpentry tools, building a weapon such as a trebuchet or a catapult and bringing it into action was a very impressive feat.

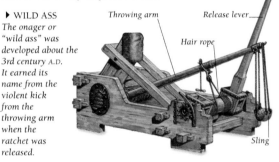

▶ WILD ASS
The onager or "wild ass" was developed about the 3rd century A.D. It earned its name from the violent kick from the throwing arm when the ratchet was released.

Throwing arm   Release lever
Hair rope
Sling

GUIDED MISSILES
Before gunpowder, muscle power was used to throw missiles at the enemy. Soldiers had to be very strong to stretch or twist the ropes and springs or lift the heavy counterweights that gave catapults and trebuchets their power.

◀ ARCHIMEDES
A Sicilian scientist, Archimedes designed weapons for the defenders of Syracuse during the siege of 213–212 B.C. His engines were very effective against the Roman fleet.

▶ GREEK FIRE
Siege machines could be adapted to throw "Greek fire," a mixture of chemicals, over the walls to burn the enemy.

◀ MASS ATTACK
This machine was designed to fire a barrage of arrows or javelins at one time. It was probably not very accurate.

◀ BALLISTA
The Romans developed the ballista, a weapon to launch missiles at the enemy. It worked rather like a crossbow and could be adapted to suit various kinds of ammunition. A light field ballista such as this could fire stones or javelins.

▼ CATAPULT
Protected by a mantlet, three soldiers tighten the tension on a catapult while a fourth prepares a stone for launching. The largest catapults could fire a 50 pound stone as far as 400 yards.

▶ ROMAN INVASION
In A.D. 43, the Romans invaded Britain in the south. They got as far north as the Plautian frontier, named after the Roman leader Plautus. Maiden Castle in Dorset was the site of a battle between the Britons and the Romans. At this battle, catapults and ballista were used by the Roman army. There had been a fort of some kind on this site since the Stone Age, but by the time the Romans came, it was well fortified by ramps, walls and dikes.

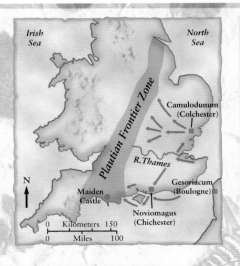

Irish Sea
North Sea
Plautian Frontier Zone
Camulodunum (Colchester)
R. Thames
Gesoriacum (Boulogne)
Maiden Castle
Noviomagus (Chichester)
N
0   Kilometers 150
0   Miles   100

Key Dates

- 400–200 B.C. Catapult introduced into Rome from Syria.

- 211 B.C. Mounted crossbow, possibly designed by Archimedes, in use to defend Syracuse.

- A.D. 100 Greeks build a catapult with an iron frame.

- 101–107 Ballista used by Romans in the Dacian wars (central Europe).

- 300 Onager in use with Romans. It was still used in medieval times.

- 1250s Trebuchet in extensive use.

- 1000–1400 Spring engines used in medieval Europe.

Ramps, Rams, and Mining

S O THAT THEY COULD BRING their weapons in closer to
the enemy, besieging troops built ramps outside
the walls of the city or castle. Ramps or causeways
were needed to cross ditches or moats filled with water.
Ideally more than one ramp would be built so that the
enemy would not
know where the
main assault was
going to fall.
The Romans
pioneered

the technique of building a ramp, known as an agger,
from hurdles, packed earth and stone.

Once the besieging forces had filled in the moat and
built a ramp up to the enemy's walls, the battering ram
was wheeled into position. The battering ram was one
of the oldest siege weapons. It was made from a heavy
tree trunk hung on chains from a timber frame. The
whole thing was covered by a wooden shelter called a
penthouse. The roof and walls of the penthouse were
often covered with animal hides that were kept wet as a
protection against fire.

The battering ram could have a metal knob,
sometimes in the shape of a ram's head, that was
mounted at the front end of the tree trunk. By swinging
the ram and driving it against the wall, the soldiers
operating it would, with time and effort, make a hole.

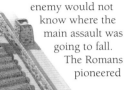

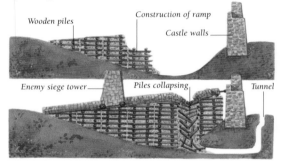

Wooden piles   Construction of ramp

Castle walls

Enemy siege tower   Piles collapsing   Tunnel

▲ ROMAN RAMP
*The agger or ramp is protected
by flanking towers. Soldiers
work on the ramp under long
protective sheds.*

▶ UNDERMINING
*Defenders could destroy a ramp
by digging a tunnel under its
wooden piles and setting fire to
them to make the ramp collapse.*

**BATTERING
TO VICTORY**
The battering ram was
the heavyweight siege
weapon used to smash
holes in the walls of a
castle or town. There
were many
different designs.
It was an accepted
rule in Roman siege
tactics that once the
ram had been
brought into action,
the defenders within
the fort or town could
expect no mercy when
the walls finally came
down. So a ram was a
frightening weapon in
more ways than one.

▲ GREEK BATTERING RAM
*This wheeled tower is a two-
in-one weapon. The ram
batters the wall while the
arm above it pulls down the
castle battlements.*

▶ RAM TOWER
Rams could be carried on the
shoulders or mounted on
wheels. This ram tower
was pushed forward on
wheels or rollers until it
was within range of the castle
wall. The gantry structure
allowed the crew to
develop a good, powerful
swing with the ram.

◀ DEMONSTRATION
This picture shows how
an 11th-century ram
worked. In a real battle,
the ramming crew would
be protected from fire and
missiles by a penthouse.

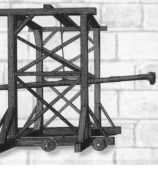

◄ HOOKING A RAM
A hook mounted on a crane grabbed the siege weapon, which could be lifted and dropped until it broke up.

Mining was another way to break through a city or castle wall. First, the attackers would build an easy-to-move shelter and put it against the wall. Protected under the shelter, the soldiers could begin to knock down the wall. They supported it with wooden beams so that it did not fall down too soon. When enough of the wall had been weakened in this way, a fire would be lit under the beams. When the beams had been weakened by the fire, the wall collapsed, and the besieging forces could then storm across the gap that had been created. The soldiers inside the castle could dig their own mine beneath the attackers' mine shaft. They could try to make the enemy's mine collapse, or fight underground.

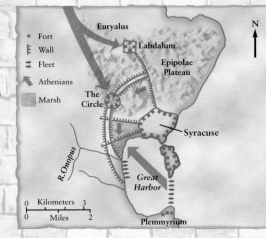

► SYRACUSE
The map shows the Siege of Syracuse in 415 B.C. by the Athenians. They built the square fort at Labdalum and a circular fort with surrounding siege walls. But Syracuse held out and inflicted Athens greatest defeat. The Athenians lost nearly 200 ships and 40-50,000 soldiers.

Map labels:
- Fort
- Wall
- Fleet
- Athenians
- Marsh
- Euryalus
- Labdalum
- Epipolae Plateau
- The Circle
- Syracuse
- R. Onoppus
- Great Harbor
- Plemmyrium
- N

Kilometers 0 3
Miles 0 2

Key Dates

- 429–427 B.C. Plataea, in Greece, besieged using ramps and defeated by Spartans.

- 415–413 B.C. Siege of Syracuse (Sicily). Archimedes, born in Syracuse, designs some of the defense machinery.

- 52 B.C. Siege of Alesia in Gaul. Vercingetorix the Gaulish leader finally surrenders to Romans.

- A.D. 72 Siege of Masada, Jerusalem. Romans build ramps to get over the huge walls of the fortress. Many defenders choose to kill themselves rather than be captured.

Gunpowder Arrives

▲ POWDER RECIPE
The formula for gunpowder—one part sulphur, six parts saltpeter and two parts charcoal—was first written down by the Englishman Roger Bacon around 1242.

SOLID GUNPOWDER turns quickly into gas when burnt. If it is loose, gunpowder produces a flash, a cloud of white smoke and not much noise. If it is enclosed, the noise and the explosive force increases. This produces energy which can be used to push a solid object along a tube, or to blow up a building. The first use of gunpowder

in battle in Europe was by the British at the Battle of Crécy (1346). King Edward is said to have had three to five guns which were called roundelades or pots de fer because of their bottle or pot shape. Early weapons fired stones or arrows similar to crossbow bolts.

Cannon design did not change much over three hundred years. Gunpowder was poured into the open end or muzzle, and then packed down with a rammer. The packed gunpowder was secured in place with batting, which was rammed home. A cannon ball was then loaded. Loose gunpowder was poured down the touch hole, a small hole at the closed end of the cannon. It was lit using a slow match, a length of rope soaked in saltpeter, which would burn slowly. The explosion that followed pushed the cannon ball out of the gun muzzle. It could reach ranges of between

▶ WHEELED CANNON
Protected by a penthouse, this cannon sits on a simple frame that allows the crew to move it around the castle to fire stones at the enemy battlements. The cannon is held in place with guy lines and pegs which absorb the recoil when it fires and ensure it is correctly aligned.

Penthouse

Cannon

Wooden frame

EXPLOSIVES
Gunpowder was first used in Europe for weapons in the 14th century. It had been used in China since the 11th century to fuel battlefield rockets. It was more powerful than ropes, counterweights or springs, but gave off big clouds of smoke.

Double cannon

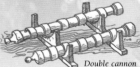

◀ DOUBLE SHOT
These cannons are on a static mount and would be fired in quick succession against a wall or gate—almost like a double-barreled weapon.

▶ HAND MORTAR
A 16th-century short-barreled weapon used for lobbing shot into enemy ranks.

Hand mortar

▲ HAND CANNON
The hand cannon was first used in 1364 and was the first step towards hand guns as we know them today. The gunner had to support his heavy firearm with a forked pike to keep it steady.

▶ SNAKE GUN
This drawing by the artist Dürer shows a cannon called a serpentine as it was thought to look like a snake or serpent. Many early cast cannon were shaped to look like serpents.

Serpentine

220 yards and 765 yards depending on the size of the cannon and the ball. By the 1860s, ranges for a 12 pound cannon ball fired using a 2.5 pound charge had increased to 1,640 yards.

The ninth Siege of Constantinople by the Turks from April to May 1453 is the first example of the power of cannon. Constantinople was then the capital of the Eastern Roman Empire. It was ruled by Constantine XI. The Turkish leader was Sultan Muhammed II. A Hungarian engineer called Urban made a very long bronze cannon for the Turks.

◀ ENGLISH GUNS
One gunner raises the mantlet as the other prepares to light the touch hole to fire the stone ball.

▲ CANNON WITH COVER
Early cannon were built in a similar way to beer barrels. Lengthwise cast iron strips were bound with iron hoops and mounted in a static wooden carriage.

It measured 26 feet and was capable of throwing a 1,455 pound stone a mile. Loading and firing took some time, so the weapon could only fire seven times a day. After 12 days of heavy bombardment, the Turks had broken through the walls of the city. Constantinople fell on May 29, 1453.

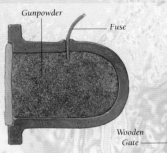

Gunpowder

Fuse

Wooden Gate

▲ PETARD
The petard was an explosive device designed especially to blast wooden gates. It was used by army engineers of the 15th and 16th centuries. It looked like a cut down cannon. It was about one foot long, 10 inches wide, weighed about 60 pounds and had a touch hole and open muzzle.

▼ USING THE PETARD
The petard was attached with its muzzle pressed up against the wooden gate and then the fuse was lit. It was a dangerous thing to do, particularly if the fuse was too short or burned too fast.

Petard

Key Dates

- 1242 Roger Bacon writes down the formula for gunpowder.
- 1324 Cannon believed to have been used at siege of Metz, in France.
- 1342 Reports of cannon at siege of Algeciras, Spain.
- 1346 Confirmed use of cannon at the battle of Crécy, France.
- 1450–1850 Most cannon were cast in bronze, iron or brass.
- 1500 Metal shot had replaced stone.
- 1571 At the battle of Lepanto, Greece heavily gunned galleys were used.

War at Sea

THE MEDITERRANEAN Sea was central to the ancient world. Its name means "in the middle of the earth." Many countries depended on it for food and trade. Whoever controlled the sea therefore, had power over all the countries which surrounded it. The Mediterranean has hardly any tides. Ships were not dependent on the tide coming in to launch and could not become stranded when the tide went out. The sea became part of the battlefield. Fighting methods and weapons were much the same as they were on land. The key to sea fighting was transportation. Fast boats with a reliable power source usually won the battle. The Greeks, Romans, Persians and Carthaginians all developed warships which could deliver troops quickly to the scene of the battle. As each would try to stop the other, they adapted land weapons for use at sea, such as grappling hooks, siege towers and catapults.

A good general used sea power to help his land battles. The tactics developed by the ancient sea

▲ OAR POWER
There were many kinds of warship design. This is a Greek galley with a single bank of oars.

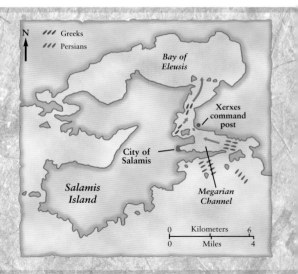

▼ OARS AT WORK
There were three layers of galley slaves in a trireme. To be effective they had to be able to row in time, so they probably used a drum to keep the time. Clearly the best position was on the top row.

SEA POWER
Most warships relied on banks of galley slaves to row them into action. Some ships had sails which could be used when the wind was favorable.

◀ XERXES
This Persian king came to power in 486 B.C. and launched a massive land and sea assault on Athens and her allies in 480 B.C. but he was defeated.

▶ THE BATTLE OF SALAMIS
This classic sea battle was fought in 480 B.C. between the Athenians led by Themistocles and the Persians under Xerxes.

N
/// Greeks
/// Persians

Bay of Eleusis

Xerxes command post

City of Salamis

Salamis Island

Megarian Channel

| 0 | Kilometers | 6 |
| 0 | Miles | 4 |

captains still work today. The Athenian plan for the Battle of Salamis was so successful that it is taught in military school. The sea battle at Lepanto in 1571 was fought between Austria and the Turks; it was the last time galleys were used in war. Austria captured 130 Turkish galleys and destroyed 80 more. The battle ended Turkish control of the Mediterranean.

Different kinds of ships and skills were needed to deal with larger seas, more extreme weather and tides. Countries with coastlines on the Atlantic or Pacific built boats that could land in shallow water if the tide was out. The Vikings who sailed the Atlantic owed their success to their long, flat-bottomed boats which could land almost anywhere.

Boats were used to deliver troops to a land battle or invasion. Vikings, Saxons, Danes and Normans invaded Great Britain by sea between 800 and 1066. During the Crusades in the Middle East, knights were brought from Europe by sea. Ships were also used to help in the sieges of coastal cities.

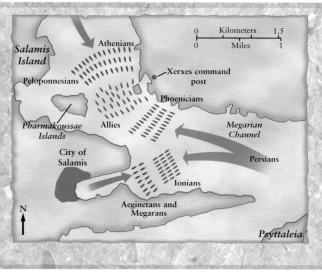

0 Kilometers 1.5
0 Miles 1

Salamis Island
Athenians
Peloponnesians
Xerxes command post
Phoenicians
Pharmakoussae Islands
Allies
Megarian Channel
City of Salamis
Persians
Ionians
Aeginetans and Megarans
Psyttaleia
N

◀ TACTICS
The Persian fleet of 1000 ships had trapped the 370 Greek triremes in the Megarian Channel. The Greeks retreated northward, luring the Persians into the narrow waters near Salamis. Once there, the Persian fleet could not maneuver. The Greeks turned and went on the attack. They sank 300 Persian galleys and lost only 40 ships of their own.

Key Dates

- 480 B.C. Battle of Salamis. Greeks beat Persians.

- 31 B.C. Battle of Actium. Caesar Octavian defeats Mark Antony in Roman Civil War.

- A.D. 1340 Battle of Sluys between French and English as part of 100 Years War. Warships become battlefields.

- 1571 Battle of Lepanto. Austrians beat Turks.

- 1588 England defeats Spanish Armada.

Sail or Oar?

I N THE ANCIENT WORLD, trading ships used sails and windpower to move around the seas. Captains of warships could not rely on winds and tide alone. They used manpower as well. Greek, Roman, Turkish and Spanish ships used massed oarsmen. Others, such as the Anglo-Saxons, Norsemen and Normans, used a combination of sail and oars. The French and British preferred sail-powered vessels and improved their design through the centuries.

The Greeks were first with the oar-driven warship. They used vessels called triremes which had three rows of oars and 150 rowers. Athenian sailors developed a way of fighting using their rowing skills. They would approach an enemy ship at full speed, come alongside and at the last minute pull in their oars. This smashed

◀ ARMED GALLEY
A Roman sculpture shows the banks of oars with armed soldiers at the ready on deck.

▲ THE MARY ROSE
Henry VIII's flag ship was armed with cannons low down which could fire broadsides.

A HARD LIFE
Few people wanted to row a galley. Criminals in countries such as Italy or Spain in the 15th and 16th centuries were often condemned to the galleys as a punishment. Prisoners of war were also made to row in their enemy's galleys.

▶ OARS AT WORK
There were three layers of galley slaves in a trireme. To be effective they had to be able to row in time, so a drum was used to beat out the rhythm.

▲ GALLEY SLAVES
Chained to their benches in the dark, hot smelly hull of their boat, galley slaves could be worked until they died. Their bodies would be thrown over the side.

◀ MEDITERRANEAN GALLEY
Fast, light, unarmed boats were used to transport troops. If the boat was sunk in battle, the soldiers and the rowers were picked up by their own side and the boat was abandoned.

▶ FLOATING BATTLES
Spanish and English ships engage in battle in 1372 as part of the 100 Years War. The warships sailed very close together and the soldiers fought across the decks as if on land.

all the oars on the enemy ship, which were still sticking out.

The oarsmen in the galleys were normally slaves. Some were convicted criminals, but many were prisoners of war. By the time of the Battle of Lepanto (1571) the Turks had smaller galleys called galiots with 18 to 24 oars, and the Venetians had developed a large vessel called a galleas. Galleys were equipped with sails so that with favorable winds they could operate without using the oarsmen.

The Scandinavian raiders who roamed as far away as the Mediterranean and Black Sea used both wind and manpower. Under Bjarni Herjolfsson, a Viking longboat reached North America in A.D. 985. The Vikings could row their long, narrow boats when there was no wind or they were close inshore. Because the vessels were light and almost flat on the bottom they could land on gently shelving coasts or even mud flats.

By the 14th and 15th century, all warships in northern Europe relied on wind power. The sailors working in the tidal, stormy waters of the English Channel and North Sea needed to be very skillful.

Under Henry VIII ship design began to change. By the time of the Armada, British warships were sleek and low. They were about 115 feet long and 33 feet wide and were called galleons. Like the galley, they were ships built specially for war. New designs in sails and rigging made the vessels even more seaworthy. The galleon was able to make long distance voyages and so it became the vessel used by navigators and explorers.

▲ FAST AND FURIOUS
Vikings used their fast boats to make lightning raids. They were able to sail as far as America. The chance of plunder and easy targets made the risky journey worthwhile.

Viking warrior

Key Dates

- 241 B.C. Lilybaeum. After a long siege, Rome defeats Carthage, and Carthaginians lose 120 ships.

- A.D. 655 Battle of the Masts. Moaviah governor of Syria attempts to capture Constantinople from the sea.

- 841 Vikings reach Dublin.

- 1027 Normans land near Naples and establish stronghold.

- 1281 Mongol invasion of Japan defeated by "divine wind" or "kamikaze."

- 1588 Spanish Armada in running battles with the English fleet along the south coast of England.

Ramming and Grappling

BEFORE GUNPOWDER ALLOWED SHIPS to stand off at a distance and bombard one another, warships used light siege weapons, archers and slingers. The siege weapons could kill and injure people and damage sails and rigging. The archers and slingers acted as snipers, finding targets on the enemy ships.

Ramming could cause major damage. From the Greeks in 600 B.C. to the Spanish Armada of 1588, galleys powered by oars were fitted with a long ramming beak. The trick was to drive this into the hull of the enemy ship.

▲ GREEK FIRE
Fire can be used as a weapon at sea. "Greek fire," an inflammable chemical, was used by Byzantine ships around the 4th century.

▲ SHIP RAM
This massive bronze-cased ram could easily pierce the hull of an enemy ship if it struck broadside.

The Romans introduced a new weapon in 260 B.C. at the Battle of Mylae in Sicily. The corvus or "crow" was a hinged gangplank with a weighted hook. It could be swung out over an enemy ship and dropped so that it was stuck in the deck. Then a boarding party raced across the corvus on to the enemy ship. The Romans won at Mylae and took control of the Mediterranean.

Grappling irons, hooks with heavy chains, were later used in sea battles to assist boarding. Once the ships were alongside and the boarding parties in action, the fight became a land battle at sea, with hand-to-hand combat. Medieval ships showed this in their design with crenellated wooden "castles" in the bow and stern.

WAR AT SEA
Before gunpowder changed war, ships could ram the enemy, or slice off their oars. Other weapons were the corvus and twin-hulled siege vessels which could carry fighting towers.

◄ DECORATIVE RAM
This finely worked prow with its ram shaped like a row of swords shows the quality of the work on classical warships.

▲ ROMAN SEA BATTLE
Some battles between the Romans and Carthaginians were on a huge scale, with ships locked together as boarding parties fought.

▲ FIRE SHIP
This ingenious little ship is designed to carry a tub of burning tar into the middle of an enemy fleet at anchor. It could damage rigging and sails and had the potential to sink ships much larger than itself. The English sent fire ships like this one against the Spanish Armada when it was at anchor.

CROWS AND TOWERS
The Romans developed a grappling weapon called a corvus, the Latin word for crow. It looked something like a crow's big beak. It was a hinged gangplank with a hook which sank into the enemy ship's deck. Special twin-hulled siege vessels could carry fighting towers to the enemy.

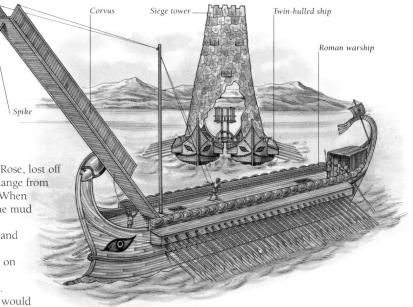

Corvus   Siege tower   Twin-hulled ship

Roman warship

Spike

This is why the front of a ship is known as the forecastle or fo'c'sle.

The English warship the Mary Rose, lost off Portsmouth in 1545, marks the change from ancient to modern warfare at sea. When she was recovered in 1982 from the mud into which she had settled, her weapons included both longbows and cannon. The ship was designed without castles but with gun ports on the lower decks. Heavy broadside cannons stood on these gun decks. When they opened fire, their shot would damage the hulls and masts of enemy ships.

In the running battle with the Spanish Armada in 1588, the English Royal Navy demonstrated that modern ship design, skilled sailors and good weather could shift the odds in favor of a smaller force. The Spanish had 20 great galleons, 44 armed merchant ships, 23 transports, 35 smaller vessels, four galleases (a double sized heavily armed galley) and four galleys.

The warships mounted a total of 2,431 guns. The English had 68 ships in Plymouth, a London squadron of 30 ships and an additional squadron of 23 in the eastern English Channel. Aside from seafaring skills and ship design, their strength lay in their 1,800 heavy cannons, mostly long-range cannons called culverins.

In running battles up the Channel the English finally prevented the Spanish from landing in England.

◀ ARMADA
Before dawn on July 28, 1588, the English sent fire ships into the Spanish fleet off Flanders as part of their running battle with the Armada. It forced the Spanish to cut their anchor cables. In the great sea battle that followed, only a storm prevented the English fleet from capturing or destroying 16 of the most damaged Spanish ships.

Key Dates

- 480 B.C. Battle of Salamis, Greece. Greeks defeat Persians.

- 262 B.C. Battle of Mylae, Sicily. Romans win and take control of the Mediterranean Sea.

- 241 B.C. Battle of Lilybaeum, Sicily. Romans defeat the Carthaginians.

- 31 B.C. Battle of Actium, Greece. Romans defeat Cleopatra and the Egyptians.

- A.D. 1571 Battle of Lepanto. Christian Allies defeat Turks.

- 1588 Defeat of the Spanish Armada by the English.

Sailing to War

CARRYING SOLDIERS AND THEIR WEAPONS, vehicles, horses and food by sea and landing them on an enemy shore is called an amphibious operation. Amphibious means able to work on land and in water. In ancient times, this was a simple operation. Coasts weren't always defended and boats were flat enough to land directly on sand or shingle shores.

As ships became bigger, they had to remain off shore and troops transferred to smaller boats before they could land. Horses could swim ashore on their own, but artillery and wagons posed an extra problem. In bad weather these operations could be dangerous and so sailors and soldiers looked for sheltered anchorages where they could land and unload in safety.

One of the earliest recorded amphibious operations were the Punic Wars of 264–241 B.C. between the Carthaginians, who lived in what is now Tunisia, and the Romans, in modern Italy. Both sides transported men and horses across the Mediterranean. The Carthaginian general Hannibal even took about 80 war elephants by ship from North Africa into Spain.

There were earlier operations. The most famous is described in Homer's Iliad, an epic poem that includes both myth and fact. To lay siege to Troy (a city located in what is now Turkey) the Greeks, under Agamemnon, had to sail across the Aegean Sea. Archeological evidence of both Troy and the Trojan Wars dates the sea crossing to around 1200 B.C.

BATTLES BY LAND AND SEA
Islands could not be attacked without the use of ships. Sometimes the landings were the beginning of a long campaign. They could be part of the siege of a fortified port, or the means of escape for a battle fought on the coast. Vikings used their boats like a modern "getaway car," raiding a settlement and escaping quickly.

▲ HELEN OF TROY
The wife of the king of Sparta was so beautiful that her face was said to have "launched a thousand ships." She was kidnapped by Paris of Troy, which began the Trojan Wars.

▲ NATURAL LIFT
A Sumerian warrior uses an inflated animal skin as a float to help him to cross a fast-flowing river.

◀ TROOP CARRIERS
Boats like this one were used to ferry troops across the Mediterranean to fight battles on land.

At Marathon in 490 B.C. a Persian invasion fleet landed a force of 20,000 on the Greek coast near Athens. They were defeated by the Athenians, who numbered only 11,000, but despite heavy losses they were able to reach their ships and escape.

In Europe there was usually no need for soldiers to travel by sea. The waves of raids by the sea-going Saxons between A.D. 205 and 577 and the Viking raids between 800–1016 reached eastern England and northern France. They were not so much amphibious operations as military "smash and grab raids," The Anglo-Saxons and the Vikings eventually settled in the territories they had been raiding.

For island countries, such as Britain, that might be threatened by enemy landings, it was a good idea to build watchtowers and fortifications at the harbors and likely landing sites.

▲ THE NEW WORLD
In the 16th century, Spanish and Portuguese explorers sailed west and invaded large areas of South America.

▼ INVASION
In 1066, William of Normandy transported 9000 men with all their horses and equipment for his invasion of England.

HIC EXEVNT:CABALLI DE NAVIBVS ET HIC:MILITES:FESTINA VERVNT:hESTINGA

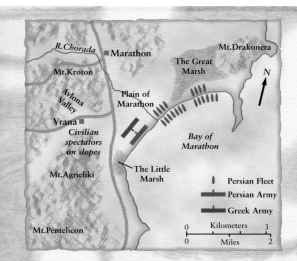

◀ THE BATTLE OF MARATHON
In 490 B.C. Persia invaded Greece. The Persian leader Darius worked his way down from modern day Turkey in the north, with a force of 150,000 men in ships. He landed an army 20,000 strong near Marathon. The Greeks met them on the coastal plain with about 11,000 soldiers and lost only 192 to the Persians' 6400.

Map labels: R.Chorada, Marathon, Mt.Drakonera, The Great Marsh, Mt.Kroton, Plain of Marathon, Avlona Valley, N, Vrana, Civilian spectators on slopes, Bay of Marathon, Mt.Agrieliki, The Little Marsh, Persian Fleet, Persian Army, Greek Army, Mt.Pentelicon, Kilometers 0 3, Miles 0 2

Key Dates

- 490 B.C. Battle of Marathon. The Greeks defeat the Persians.
- 415 B.C. Athenians land in Sicily and besiege Syracuse.
- 54 B.C. First Roman invasion of Britain.
- A.D. 43 Second Roman invasion of Britain.
- 400s Raids on England by Jutes, Angles and Saxons.
- 700s–800s Vikings raid Europe.
- 1027 Normans land in southern Italy.
- 1066 Normans invade England.

MODERN WEAPONS AND WARFARE

BY WILL FOWLER

*From hand-held rifles to stealth bombers,
advances in technology have armed human
beings with increasingly powerful killing
machines. This section charts the revolutions in
weaponry and warfare over the last 300 years.*

War Games

BETWEEN THE YEAR 1700 AND THE PRESENT DAY, the ways that wars are conducted has changed beyond all recognition. Flintlock muskets have been replaced by automatic machine guns, and horses have been replaced by armoured tanks and assault helicopters. Change has been most rapid in the last hundred years. World War I was fought mostly hand-to-hand, but the main battles of the Gulf War were fought by missiles and planes.

The introduction of steam power and petrol engines meant that soldiers did not have to rely on animals for transport, which could get tired or injured. The ships which relied on the wind for power, were replaced by vessels that moved at greater speeds against winds and currents when powered by steam.

Armor plating which protected knights in the Middle Ages, found new uses protecting ships, land vehicles, and even aircraft. New lighter, stronger, and even fire-resistant materials were developed. These new materials were initially used to provide clothing to protect crews, but were later also used for fire fighters and the emergency services.

Before World War I people were optimistic about science. They believed that technological advances would make life safer, healthier, and easier. In part this has been true, but science has also been used for war. Destruction on a huge scale has now become a reality. But though the two world wars led to the development of weapons of mass destruction (nuclear, chemical, and biological weapons), they were also the spur for life-saving medical techniques.

▲ RIFLES
Ever since they were invented in the 19th century, rifles have played a critical role in warfare.

▼ KEY DATES
The panel charts the development of modern weapons, from early developments in gun design, to the introduction of stealth technology in modern aircraft.

▼ FORTIFICATIONS
As the technology of warfare has developed, the means of defending against ever-changing weaponry have altered dramatically.

PISTOLS AND ARTILLERY

The Gatling gun

- **1784** Invention of the shrapnel shell
- **1807** Forsyth patents the percussion ignition.
- **1835** Lefaucheux patents the pin-fire cartridge.
- **1835** Colt patents his revolver design.
- **1883** Maxim patents fully automatic machine gun.

- **1901** British 10-pounder cannon introduced.
- **1914–1918** World War I: long-range artillery in use
- **1934** First general-purpose machine gun introduced
- **1939–1945** World War II: self-loading rifle developed. Recoilless guns, rocker artillery, and anti-tank guns in use
- **1947** Kalashnikov designs the AK47 assault rifle.
- **1957** Italian 105mm Model 56 pack howitzer appears.

Colt automatic pistol

FIGHTING ON THE LAND

- **1850** Morse Code invented
- **1858** First aerial photography
- **1865** First antiseptics used
- **1882** Armored steel developed
- **1914–1918** World War I: land and sea camouflage developed
- **1916** September: first tanks used in World War I
- **1925** French demonstrate the half-track vehicle
- **1939–1945** World War II: aerial photography and infrared technology developed
- **1943** Infrared night-vision viewer used

- **1944–1945** German missiles launched against Britain
- **1944** June 6: D-Day, the largest amphibious operation in history, takes place
- **1957** First space satellite launched
- **1991** Iraqi SCUD surface-to-surface missiles launched in the Gulf War

World War II Sherman tank

▼ **AVIATION**
The development of military air power has been one of the most important changes to modern warfare. Controlling the skies above any battlefield has become critical to modern tactics and critical to military success. Aircraft are now more deadly than ever. They can fly faster and for longer, and over greater distances, carrying more weaponry than ever before.

The 1940s saw the rapid development of the airplane as the jet turbine replaced the piston engine. New planes could fly further and with more weapons than ever before.

Radio communications began at the end of the 1800s as a laboratory experiment. One hundred years later it had become an essential part of the equipment of war. The world wars showed how important communication was, and scientists developed the technology to meet the demands of soldiers.

Helicopters had existed in a basic form before World War II, but by 1945, engineers in the United States and Britain were designing new, more powerful versions of these rotary wing craft. By the end of the 1900s the helicopter had become a life saver, lifting sailors from the sea or survivors from burning buildings.

The soldiers of the developed world are no longer troops sent to fight. They have become peacekeepers, attempting to prevent brutal wars. Fast communications allow them to keep their national leaders informed about developments on the ground on an hour-by-hour basis.

▲ **MOBILITY**
The ability to move large numbers of troops and equipment quickly and easily is an essential part of any successful campaign.

▼ **TECHNOLOGY**
Warfare has always pushed back technological boundaries, from the first tanks to stealth bombers like this B2 bomber.

FIGHTING ON THE SEAS

- **1805** Battle of Trafalgar
- **1863** The steam-driven submersible *David* attacks Federal ironclad ship
- **1904** *Aigret*, first diesel-powered boat
- **1906** Launch of H.M.S. *Dreadnought*
- **1914–1918** World War I
- **1916** May 31: Battle of Jutland
- **1939–1945** German U-boats use "wolf pack" tactics against Allied shipping
- **1941** May 27: sinking of the *Bismarck*
- **1942** June 4–7: Battle of Midway

- **1944** June 6: D-Day
- **1954** *U.S.S. Nautilus*, the first nuclear-powered submarine, is commissioned
- **1961** *U.S.S. Enterprise* is first nuclear-powered carrier
- **1966** Soviet Osa-class missile-armed craft enter service
- **1990-1991** Osa-class craft see action in the Gulf War

U.S. Knox-class frigate

REACHING FOR THE SKIES

F86 Sabre

- **1903** Wilbur and Orville Wright make the first powered flight
- **1907** September 29: helicopter first lifts a man off the ground into the air
- **1912** Machine gun fired from aircraft for first time
- **1914–1918** World War I
- **1914** October 5: first aircraft to be shot down
- **1939–1945** World War II: first strategic bombing
- **1945** August 6 and 9: atomic bombs dropped on Japan
- **1945** December 3: the first jet landing and takeoff from an aircraft carrier

- **1950** First jet-versus-jet victory in the Korean War
- **1951** Canberra bomber is the first jet to fly across the North Atlantic nonstop
- **1955** B-52 enters service with the United States Air Force
- **1977** December: first flight of Lockheed Martin F-117
- **1989** July 17: first flight of Northrop Grumman B-2A Spirit stealth aircraft
- **1991** February 24: 300 helicopters used in Gulf War in the largest aerial assault in the history of aviation

Pistols and Rifles

▲ RIFLEMAN
A 19th-century French soldier carries a bolt-action rifle.

Y OU CAN SEE PISTOLS every day in most countries because police officers carry them. In thrillers and westerns, the heroes and villains are usually armed with pistols. You have probably seen lots of pistols, but do you know how they work?

There are two sorts of pistols. A revolver has a cylindrical magazine with six rounds of bullets. Newer pistols are self-loading, with a detachable box magazine that fits into the handle and can hold up to 14 rounds of ammunition. Rifles are bolt-action, semi-automatic, or automatic weapons, and have a magazine that holds between 5 and 30 rounds. An automatic weapon automatically places the next round in the chamber for firing, so fires repeatedly when the trigger is pulled.

▶ RIFLES
British soldiers of the late 19th century use their massed firepower to compensate for the short range and inaccuracy of their flintlock muskets.

The most famous revolvers are the "Six Guns" used in the 1800s in the United States. These were famous as they enabled the user to fire six shots in quick succession. In World War I (1914–1918) and World War II (1939–1945), British troops used the .455inch Webley MarkVI revolver or the .38inch Enfield Number 2 Mark1.

The Germans used the Luger pistol as it was easy to reload. It was named after Georg Luger, a designer at the Ludwig Löwe arms factory in Berlin. It weighed 2lbs, had an eight-shot magazine and fired a .36inch round.

The U.S. Army carried the .45inch Colt 1911 self-loading pistol throughout both world wars, the Korean War, and the Vietnam War. It weighs 2¾ lbs. and has a seven-round magazine. The Belgian 9mm Browning High Power was first manufactured in 1935. It weighs 2½ lbs. when loaded and has an effective range of 55–80 yards. Its magazine holds 13 rounds in two staggered rows—a feature copied in later designs.

The British used the bolt-action .303inch Short Magazine Lee Enfield (SMLE) rifle during World War I

A SOLDIER'S TOOLS

The rifle and pistol have always been the tools of the infantryman. They are light and portable, and have become more accurate and faster firing. Cavalry, artillery, and support troops such as engineers also carry these weapons, primarily for self-protection rather than attack. The rifle and pistol cartridge have also allowed the weapons' mechanical feed to be improved.

▲ THE U.S. ARMY RIFLE
In the years before the Civil War, the U.S. Army used a .58inch rifle. Rifling made the bullet more accurate by spinning it, causing the bullet to fly straighter. The bayonet was used in close-quarter fighting.

▲ SHORT MAGAZINE LEE ENFIELD
(SMLE) BOLT-ACTION RIFLE
The compact bolt-action rifle was 45¼ inches long, weighed 10lbs. and had a ten-round magazine. It was used by the British Army from 1907 to 1943. More than three million were made in Britain, India, and Australia.

▲ BOLT ACTION
The Mauser action had five rounds. They could be loaded into the breech, the back part, by moving the bolt.

▲ THE AUTOMATIC
The U.S. Colt 1911A1 (right) and Browning 1903 are two classic self-loading pistols. Their ammunition is in a magazine in the pistol grip.

▲ THE M16
The M16 is now widely used throughout the world. It was first used by the US Army in Vietnam. At that time the M16 was revolutionary because it fired a .22inch round, was made from plastics and alloys and weighed only 8lbs.

and for much of World War II. The German .31inch Karabiner 98K was a very accurate weapon but only had only a five-round magazine. The U.S. Garand M1 rifle and M1 carbine were popular self-loading rifles during World War II as they were tough and reliable.

Two weapons have dominated armed conflicts since 1945; the U.S. .22 inch M16 Armalite rifle weighing 9lbs., and the Soviet-designed .3inch AK47 weighing 10¾ lbs. Both can fire on full automatic at 700 (M16) and 600 (AK47) rounds per minute (rpm).

▲ THE ENFIELD L85A1 RIFLE
This is the current rifle issued to British troops. It weighs 8¾lbs. and is 31½ inches long. On automatic it fires .22inch rounds at 700 rounds per minute (rpm). The Enfield L85A1 has been used in action in the Persian Gulf, in Kosovo, and in Northern Ireland.

▼ THE SNIPER'S HIDE
In World War II, snipers built camouflaged positions called hides in which they could observe and shoot at the enemy. They were often concealed for long periods in the hides, which needed to be well built and weatherproof. This hide is covered in turf.

▲ THE SNIPER
A soldier is camouflaged to blend into the woodland. He aims his Accuracy International L96A1 .30inch sniper's rifle. It is fitted with an optical sight.

A turf roof conceals the hide.

The hide is deep enough to allow the sniper to stand.

Key Dates

- 1807 Dr. Forsyth patents the percussion ignition.

- 1812 Pauly patents the first cartridge breech-loader.

- 1835 Lefaucheux patents the pin-fire cartridge.

- 1835 Colt patents his revolver design.

- 1849 The Minié rifle replaces smooth-bore rifles.

- 1886 French adopt the first small-bore smokeless-powder cartridge.

- 1888 Britain adopts Lee–Metford bolt-action repeater.

- 1939–1945 Self-loading rifle developed.

Automatic Weapons

▲ THE GARDNER
This early water-cooled, hand-cranked machine gun is mounted on an adjustable tripod. Its ammunition is fed into the chamber from the top.

THE FIRST MACHINE GUN dates back to 1718, when Puckle's gun was developed in Britain. It was a large hand-cranked revolver on a stand that fired seven rounds per minute (rpm). The Gatling gun was also hand-cranked. It fired at a rate of 100–200rpm. It was developed in the United States in 1862 and used in the Civil War.

The first successful automatic machine gun was the .32inch Maxim gun designed by the American Hiram Maxim. It used the energy of the exploding cartridges to operate the mechanism and fired at 500rpm. This rapid firing rate heated up the barrel, so it was cooled by a water-filled jacket. The British used the Maxim gun in action in 1895.

The French Hotchkiss machine gun used the gases of the exploding cartridges to operate its mechanism. It had a heavier barrel designed not to need a water jacket, but which

cooled in the air. Ammunition was fed in on a cloth belt, where other similar weapons used metal belts.

The belt-fed British Vickers .303inch machine gun was designed in 1891 and was not withdrawn from service with the British Army until 1963. The World War II German MG42 was a .32inch general-purpose machine gun (GPMG). Stamping and spot welding speeded its manufacturing process. It had a top range of 6,560 feet and fired 1,550rpm. Features of its design were copied in the postwar Belgian FN MAG and in the U.S. M60 machine guns.

The first submachine guns (SMGs) fired

◀ THE GATLING GUN
The hand-cranked Gatling gun, used here by British soldiers, was introduced in 1862. Designed by Dr. Richard Gatling, it had between six and ten barrels. It saw action in the Civil War and was later adopted by the U.S. Army during the Spanish-American War. Later models were mounted on a light artillery carriage.

SUBMACHINE GUNS (SMGS)

The first submachine gun to go into service was the Italian Villar Perosa, which was used in World War I. SMGs fire pistol-caliber ammunition such as .45inch at the same rate as a conventional machine gun. They are not accurate over long ranges but are ideal in situations where intense close-range firepower is required.

▶ THE STEN MK II SMG
This .36in SMG weighs 7½lbs empty and fires at 550rpm. More than two million were made in World War II.

◀ THE AK47
The AK47 assault rifle fires a .30inch round, which is halfway between a rifle round and a pistol round.

◀ THE TOMMY GUN
The Thompson M1 was the simplified World War II version of this SMG. It had a 30- round box magazine and weighed 12lbs. empty.

▶ THE UZI SMG
The Uzi is a .36inch SMG developed in Israel. It weighs 8¾lbs. empty and fires at a rate of 600r.p.m.

pistol-sized ammunition and could be carried by one person. They were developed at the end of World War I. The .45inch Thompson (Tommy) gun, designed in the 1920s in the United States, became notorious in the gang wars of the 1920s. It was widely used by British and American troops in World War II.

The World War II German MP38/40 was the first submachine gun to have a folding metal butt. This feature reduced its size from 33 inches down to 25¼ inches. It fired at 500rpm. and had a thirty-round magazine.

Modern SMGs are compact and lightweight weapons. They are a common weapon for bodyguards as they can be carried inside jackets or briefcases.

▲ HELICOPTER MOUNTED
Machine guns were first fitted to helicopters by the French in the 1960s. They are now used by helicopters to protect the aircraft when flying into "hot" landing zones or to attack enemy infantry.

▲ VEHICLE MOUNTED
A Belgian .30inch MAG machine gun is mounted on a vehicle in the desert. The MAG is in service in many countries and can be mounted on a tripod for long-range fire, or on a built- in bipod for shorter ranges.

▶ THE M60
The poor reliability of the U.S. .30inch M60 general-purpose machine gun in Vietnam earned it the nickname "the Pig." It has since been modified and improved and is widely used around the world.

▼ BEATEN ZONE
A machine gun fires long bursts over long ranges, spreading its bullets into a cone-shaped area called a "beaten zone." It is fatal or very risky for soldiers to enter this bullet-swept zone.

Machine guns are very effective defense weapons when used in pairs. Two machine guns can be positioned so that they fire from the side across the path of an aproaching enemy. This arrangement makes their fire overlap, creating two overlapping "beaten zones." This combined fire power creates a doubly dangerous area for the enemy.

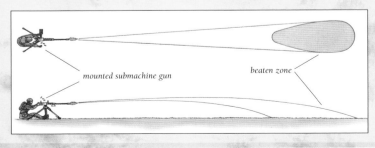

mounted submachine gun

beaten zone

Key Dates

- 1883 Maxim patents fully automatic machine gun.

- 1896 United States orders Browning-Colt gas-operated gun.

- 1926 Czech ZB/vz26 light machine gun designed.

- 1934 MG34 introduced, the first general-purpose machine gun .

- 1942 MG42 creates the basis for many postwar designs.

- 1947 Kalashnikov designs the AK47 assault rifle.

- 1961 U.S. Army evaluates Armalite rifle.

Artillery—Cannons and Mortars

BATTLES IN EUROPE and North America between the 1500s and 1800s were thundering smoke-filled affairs, as artillery soldiers manned their cannons and each side bombarded the other.

Cannons were loaded from the muzzle (front end) and fired round shot or cannonballs. The major development in artillery weapons came with the introduction of rifled barrels in 1858. A rifled barrel makes a shell spin in flight, and so it is more accurate. Breech loading—loading the gun from the back— was introduced in around 1870. Recoil mechanisms to absorb the "kick" of the firing followed in 1888.

▾ RAPID-FIRE CANNON
These cannons were mounted on warships or used for close-range coastal defense. They entered service in the late 19th century. Improved recoil mechanisms permitted the gun to remain stable while firing. The crew were protected by an armored shield, but in later years they would be enclosed in a turret.

▾ DESERT FIREPOWER
A howitzer is an artillery piece designed to fire at a steep angle, usually over fortifications. This is a U.S. M198 155mm howitzer in action during the Gulf War of 1990–1991. It entered service with the U.S. Army and U.S. Marine Corps in 1979. The howitzer weighs 7,163kg and has a crew of 11. It has a maximum range of 59,530feet with standard ammunition, but this increases to 98,400m with a rocket-assisted projectile (RAP).

BIG BOYS
Before aircraft that could drop large bomb loads had been developed, artillery was used to bombard fortifications or defend important locations such as ports and capital cities. The bigger the caliber (diameter of the barrel), the bigger the shell and so the greater the volume of explosives that could be enclosed in the gun. Big shells were therefore more destructive.

▸ U.S. ARMY BREECH-LOADING HOWITZER
This siege howitzer is mounted on a turntable and has a hoist for loading.

▲ RAILGUNS
Railroads have been used to carry heavy guns and mortars since the Civil War. The world's biggest guns were the German guns that were used in World War II.

▾ MODERN MORTAR
A soldier loads a British 3¼ inch mortar with a high-explosive (HE) bomb. On the left a second soldier kneels ready with another bomb to ensure a rapid rate of fire.

▲ SELF-PROPELLED GUNS
The U.S. 6¹/₂ inch M109 SP gun (above) and the U.S. 8 inch M110A SP howitzer (right: side and top-down views). The tracked chassis gives them greater mobility on the battlefield.

Mortars were muzzle-loading weapons, which fired their shells in a high-angled trajectory (curved path). The modern mortar can be traced back to the British Stokes mortar of World War I.

Modern artillery ranges from World War II weapons, such as the huge German railway siege guns—the 32inch K(E) Gustav bombarded Sevastopol and Leningrad—to the tiny Japanese 2³/₄ inch battalion gun Type 92. The K(E) Gustav fired a 12,000lb. shell to 29 miles. It had a crew of 1,500 men. The Japanese gun, with a crew of five, fired a 9¹/₄lb. shell to 4,500feet.

World War II mortars included the massive German 24 inch Karl, which was also used to bombard Sevastopol, as well as Warsaw. It fired a 3940lb. shell to a maximum range of 7,300 feet. It was mounted on a tracked chassis, but this gave it very limited mobility and it crawled along at only 6mph. Karl mortars had a crew of 18. There was also the little British 2inch mortar. It weighed 10¹/₄lb., fired a 2¹/₂lb. bomb to a maximum range of 1,496 feet and had crew of two.

Future artillery designs may include a 6¹/₄inch howitzer built with new materials that is as light as a 4¹/₄inch weapon. Shells will soon be guided and capable of changing their path during flight.

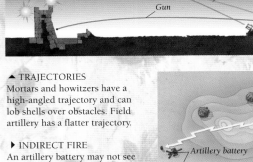

▲ TRAJECTORIES
Mortars and howitzers have a high-angled trajectory and can lob shells over obstacles. Field artillery has a flatter trajectory.

▶ INDIRECT FIRE
An artillery battery may not see its target when it fires. It can be instructed to adjust its fire by an observer who watches where the shells fall.

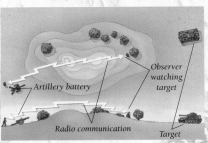

Key Dates

- 1784 Invention of the Shrapnel shell.

- 1858 French adopt rifled artillery.

- 1870 Breech loading widely used.

- 1884 French develop smokeless gunpowder.

- 1888 Konrad Hausser develops long-recoil cylinder.

- 1899 Maxim "Pom Pom" automatic cannon in use.

- 1914–1918 World War I: long-range artillery developed.

- 1939–1945 World War II: recoilless guns, rocker artillery, and anti-tank guns.

Artillery—Pack Guns

IN JULY 1999 the last Royal Tournament was held in London. It marked the end of the annual British Royal Navy field gun race between crews from Portsmouth and Plymouth. The crews dismantled a Victorian 10-pounder mountain gun and raced across a series of obstacles then re-assembled it and fired a blank shell. It was an exciting test of strength and coordination. Pack howitzers like the 10-pounder were designed to be dismantled and carried by men or five mules across mountainous or rough terrain. If the pack artillery could then be assembled on a mountain ridge, their fire could dominate the roads through the valleys below.

▲ FIELD PIECE
Horse-drawn artillery consisted of the gun, the limber that contained the ammunition and charges, and the team of horses.

The 10-pounder was used in India on the Northwest Frontier between 1901 and 1915.

▶ ITALIAN PACK GUNS
Alpine mountain troops move their guns to new positions in World War I. Pack guns could be broken down into about four sections for ease of transportation.

It fired a 11¼lb. shell out to 18,000 feet. The gun became famous as the "screw gun" because its barrel broke down into two sections that were screwed together when it was assembled for firing.

The 10-pounder was replaced by the 3.7inch pack howitzer which soldiered on during both world wars. The howitzer's maximum weight was 5,500lbs., and it fired a 22¾lb. shell out to 18,000 feet.

MOVING AROUND

Pack howitzers, or mountain artillery, and light anti-aircraft guns were designed to be dismantled so that they could be carried by troops or mules to remote mountaintop positions. Today's light guns can be carried by helicopter, which is faster and more reliable.

◀ MUSCLE POWER
Royal Navy sailors at the Royal Tournament in London, demonstrating how the British 10-pounder mountain gun can be dismantled and reassembled.

▲ ANTIAIRCRAFT GUN
A Soviet-made, Iraqi ZPU-4 1 inch antiaircraft gun in a coastal position. It was captured in 1991 in Kuwait at the end of the Gulf War.

▲ CIVIL WAR CANNON
The breech-loading cannon used in the 1860s in the United States were very similar to those used during the Napoleonic Wars.

During World War II, the U.S. 75mm M1A1 pack howitzer proved a very effective weapon for airborne forces. It was originally designed for carriage by six mules. The M1A1 fired a 6.24kg high-explosive shell out to 29,290 feet and weighed 588.3kg. The 105mm M3 howitzer was a bigger version of the M1A1 and weighed 1132.7kg. It could fire a 14.98kg shell out to 21,760 feet.

Postwar mountain artillery has been dominated by the Italian OTO Melara 105/14 Model 56 4.2inch howitzer. It was introduced in 1957, and since then more than 2,500 have been built. The Model 56 has been used by more than 17 countries. Its design is so good that it has been effectively copied in India with a 3 inch pack gun howitzer. The Model 56 can be broken down into 11 parts which can be transported by mules or even carried on soldiers' backs for short distances. It weighs 3225lbs. and can fire a 47½lb. high-explosive shell out to 34,770 feet.

The use of helicopters and the widespread need for air mobility make the requirement for light guns and pack howitzers almost universal. They can be transported slung beneath helicopters and brought into action very quickly.

The guns of the future will be constructed from new materials, many of which are currently used in modern aircraft design. These materials are strong but much lighter than steel and alloys.

▲ PACK HOWITZER
The Italian 4⅕inch Model 56 pack howitzer in action. The shield can be removed to save weight. The howitzer's hinged trail legs can be folded, which makes the gun easier to transport.

▼ ANTIAIRCRAFT FIRE
Antiaircraft gun crews developed the skill of aiming just in front of a moving aircraft. This meant that the shell, with its time fuse, exploded as the plane flew into the blast and fragments. Radar now makes the job faster and easier.

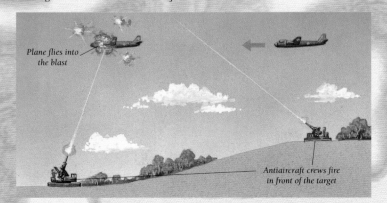

Plane flies into the blast

Antiaircraft crews fire in front of the target

Key Dates

- 1901 British 10-pounder introduced.

- 1901–1915 The 10-pounder used on Indian Northwest Frontier.

- 1914–1918 World War I: antiaircraft guns used.

- 1932 Swedish 1½ inch Bofors antiaircraft gun appears.

- 1936 German 3½ inch Flak 36 anti-aircraft gun developed.

- 1939–1945 World War II: U.S. 75mm M1A1 pack howitzer used.

- 1957 Italian 4½ inch Model 56 pack howitzer appears.

Bombs, Rockets, and Torpedoes

ROCKETS PROPELLED by gunpowder are a common sight in the United States on the Fourth of July and in Britain on November 5 (Guy Fawkes' Night). People watch as the rockets streak into the sky and burst into a shower of colored stars. Rockets were originally used by the ancient Chinese as a weapon. They called them "fire arrows."

Later, in the 1800s, the British employed rockets against the French during the Napoleonic Wars. They were used in 1815 by a Royal Artillery troop at the Battle of Waterloo. American and European armies experimented with them throughout the 1800s.

▲ TRENCH WARS
British troops on the Western Front in World War I, with a stock of mortars.

▶ STINGER SAM
The U.S. low-altitude surface-to-air missile (SAM) has a maximum range of about 13,120 feet and a maximum speed of Mach 2.2. It has a $6^1/2$lb. high-explosive warhead.

The self-propelled, or "fish," torpedo, developed in the late 1800s, revolutionized naval warfare. In World War I rockets were fitted to British fighter planes to attack German Zeppelin airships.

The first aerial bombs were used in World War I when pilots threw hand grenades at enemy troops. By the end of the war British bombers, such as the Handley Page 0/400, were carrying 1500lb. bombs to attack targets in Germany.

From World War II to the present day, bombs have been either high-explosive (HE) or incendiary devices. HE bombs are designed to explode on the surface or to penetrate reinforced concrete. Incendiary bombs burn at great heat and include napalm, a jellied fuel that splashes over a wide area. Cluster bombs are small HE bombs that are scattered from a larger container over a much wider area.

World War II rockets included the huge liquid-fuel German V-2, which was designed by Werner von Braun.

FLYING BOMBS
Aircraft and artillery use rockets and bombs to deliver high-explosive or incendiary payloads to target areas. Torpedoes launched from ships and submarines or dropped from the air proved very effective against ships of all sizes in World War II. Rockets have become a more effective weapon and are now launched from helicopters as well as from ships.

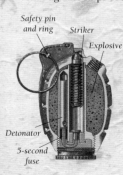

Safety pin and ring
Striker
Explosive
Detonator
5-second fuse

◀ HAND GRENADE
The British 36 grenade was introduced in 1915. It uses a mechanism with two safety features; a pin and also a handle.

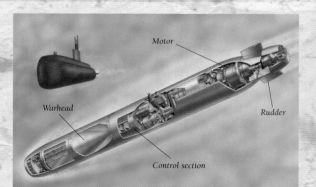

Motor
Warhead
Rudder
Control section

▲ TORPEDO
A torpedo consists of a warhead, fuel supply, motor, and rudder. Modern weapons also have wire guidance systems and warheads like those of an anti-tank weapon. When the warhead explodes it can penetrate deep into a ship's hull.

◀ MULTIPLE ROCKET LAUNCHER
The U.S. Multiple Rocket Launcher System (MRLS) was used in action during the Gulf War of 1990–1991. Its tracked chassis allows it to move rapidly around the battlefield, and it can reload in a few minutes.

Warhead

Computer Fuse

▲ SMART BOMB
The U.S. Paveway laser-guided bomb follows the reflected laser energy bounced back from its target. Laser- guided bombs were first used in the Vietnam War.

It weighed 13.3 tons and had a range of more than 185 miles. Another World War II rocket was the crude but effective solid-fuel 8inch rocket projectile (RP) fired from Allied aircraft.

Postwar rockets include intercontinental guided missiles with nuclear warheads, air-to-air missiles for combat aircraft, and anti-tank missiles with ranges of between 9,840 and 16,400 feet.

Robert Whitehead and Giovanni Lupis developed the first torpedo in 1866. It took its name from a Caribbean electric-ray fish. Torpedo boats were designed to carry the new weapon, and ships designed to destroy torpedoes, known as "destroyers," were in turn developed. The torpedo

made battleships vulnerable to attack by smaller vessels and submarines. In World War II torpedoes were also launched from airplanes. Modern torpedoes, with sophisticated guidance systems and warheads, are still carried by submarines. Torpedoes are also designed to seek and destroy submarines.

▶ ANTIAIRCRAFT MISSILE
The British Rapier surface-to-air missile was first used during the Falklands War in 1982. It has a maximum speed of 2,132 feet per second and a range of 22,960 feet.

▶ ALFRED NOBEL
Swedish scientist Alfred Nobel (1833–1896) developed a range of high explosives. These included dynamite (1863) and nitrocellulose (1888), from which smokeless propellant was developed. Nobel's explosives changed warfare in the 20th century.

▲ CLUSTER BOMB
The cluster bomb unit (CBU) dropped from aircraft contains smaller bombs, or submunitions, which are ejected to scatter across the ground. The CBU is used against soldiers in open or unarmored vehicles.

Key Dates

- 1860–1880 Hale rockets in use in the United States and Britain.

- 1890 Whitehead develops torpedo.

- 1903 Russian rocket engineer Konstantin Tsiolkovsky develops liquid-fuel rockets.

- 1944–1945 German V-1 and V-2 cruise missiles and ballistic missiles launched against Britain.

- 1981–1986 Air-launched cruise missiles enter service with U.S. Air Force .

- 1991 Iraqi SCUD surface-to-surface missiles launched in the Gulf War.

Mines and Fortifications

▲ ANTI-TANK MINE
An Italian plastic-bodied anti-tank mine which could destroy a truck and cripple a tank or armored vehicle.

SINCE THE US CIVIL WAR mines have been used as part of defensive fortifications to create obstacles and defend positions. But they are a major problem in the developing world today as they have been laid by warring parties in civil wars, causing injury to innocent civilians

The first mines were used as long ago as the Civil War (1861–1865), but these were crude devices. In the same war trenches were employed in field fortifications for the first time.

The design of forts had changed with the development of gunpowder. They were now no longer built upward but outward, with bombardment- proof barracks and gun batteries. From the late 17th century the French military engineer Sébastien Vauban was a major influence. He designed

huge star-shaped fortresses which allowed artillery to be used effectively. He also developed siege techniques for attacking fortresses.

Concrete was developed in the 20th century and was quickly adopted for fortifications. Barbed wire was first used extensively in the Boer War (1899–1902). In World War I the trenches of the Western Front were made of concrete, barbed wire, and corrugated iron. They stretched from Switzerland to the English Channel. At the end of the war the Germans produced

▶ WORLD WAR I TRENCHES
Trenches were dug deep enough so that men could walk along them below ground level. When the soldiers needed to shoot, they climbed up onto the firing step. To prevent the trenches from collapsing they were reinforced with material called a revetment.

Berm

Revetment

Parapet

Dugout

Firing step

PROTECTION

Trenches and bunkers were first dug in the Civil War, although earthworks had been built in the Napoleonic Wars. In Britain the Victorians built coastal forts to protect key harbors.

By World War I, improved artillery and the introduction of large numbers of machine guns forced the infantry underground. Materials such as steel girders and concrete make modern defenses very strong.

▶ ANTI-TANK OBSTACLES
American soldiers stand among concrete anti-tank obstacles called "dragon's teeth." They were built by the Germans in World War II to protect the western borders of the Third Reich.

▼ TUNNELS
In the Vietnam War the Vietcong (North Vietnamese) used tunnels like this one for concealment and as protection from bombs and shellfire.

Sentry   Concealed entrance

Accommodation / storage chamber

Escape route into water

◄ PORTABLE DEFENSES
British soldiers deploy barbed wire in the desert in the Gulf War of 1990–1991. Barbed wire was first made in 1874. It is a portable, economical, and rapid form of perimeter defense used by armies around the world.

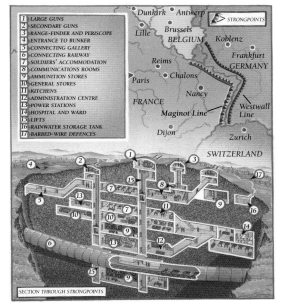

1 LARGE GUNS
2 SECONDARY GUNS
3 RANGE-FINDER AND PERISCOPE
4 ENTRANCE TO BUNKER
5 CONNECTING GALLERY
6 CONNECTING RAILWAY
7 SOLDIERS' ACCOMMODATION
8 COMMUNICATIONS ROOMS
9 AMMUNITION STORES
10 GENERAL STORES
11 KITCHENS
12 ADMINISTRATION CENTRE
13 POWER STATIONS
14 HOSPITAL AND WARD
15 LIFTS
16 RAINWATER STORAGE TANK
17 BARBED-WIRE DEFENCES

SECTION THROUGH STRONGPOINTS

▲ MAGINOT LINE
Built by the French before World War II, the Maginot Line was a series of fortifications 200 miles long, built to defend France's border with Germany. It took more than ten years to construct. It has been described as "a concrete battleship on land." Strongpoints in the Line had extra guns and equipment. They had underground tunnels and storage rooms, and air-conditioned barracks which protected against gas attacks. The fortifications included long-range artillery, mortars, and machine guns. When the Germans attacked, they outflanked the Maginot Line through neutral Belgium and Luxembourg.

the first anti-tank mines. They rigged standard artillery shells to explode when run over by a tank.

The two types of mine—anti-tank (AT) and anti-personnel (AP)—were developed in World War II. AT mines are designed to destroy trucks or to stop tanks by damaging their tracks or wheels. The German Teller AT mine contained 15lbs. of high explosive and has been the model for Russian and Israeli AT mines since 1945. AP mines kill or injure soldiers and civilians. Modern mines are made from plastic, which makes them almost impossible to detect. Techniques have been developed for detecting and clearing mines. Alternatively engineers may simply blast a path through a minefield.

In World War II lines of concrete fortifications were constructed, such as the coastal Atlantic Wall, built by the Germans, and the 200-mile-long Maginot Line, built by the French. However, the use of tanks and aircraft had made this kind of static defense outdated.

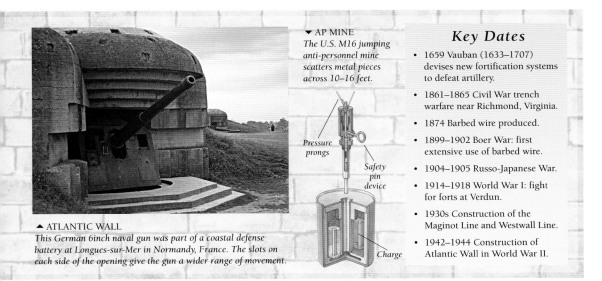

▼ AP MINE
The U.S. M16 jumping anti-personnel mine scatters metal pieces across 10–16 feet.

Pressure prongs

Safety pin device

Charge

▲ ATLANTIC WALL
This German 6inch naval gun was part of a coastal defense battery at Longues-sur-Mer in Normandy, France. The slots on each side of the opening give the gun a wider range of movement.

Key Dates

- 1659 Vauban (1633–1707) devises new fortification systems to defeat artillery.

- 1861–1865 Civil War trench warfare near Richmond, Virginia.

- 1874 Barbed wire produced.

- 1899–1902 Boer War: first extensive use of barbed wire.

- 1904–1905 Russo-Japanese War.

- 1914–1918 World War I: fight for forts at Verdun.

- 1930s Construction of the Maginot Line and Westwall Line.

- 1942–1944 Construction of Atlantic Wall in World War II.

Guerrilla Warfare and Terrorism

▲ CHE GUEVARA
The Argentinian-born Cuban guerrilla leader was executed in Bolivia in 1967. Guevara was an icon for the young revolutionary movement during the 1960s.

EVEN DURING PEACETIME, terrorism is a threat on the streets of many cities and towns. Political groups and campaigners who have decided to break the law to further their aims use terrorism. They hope to frighten governments and the public into accepting their views. Together with revolutionary and guerrilla warfare, terrorism is war waged by the weak against the strong.

Much of the fighting during the Revolutionary War (1775–1783) could be called guerilla warfare. Frontiersmen often launched sneak attacks on British forces, who were unprepared for such tactics.

▶ COUNTER-TERRORISM
Armed with Heckler and Koch MP5 sub-machine guns, a counter-terrorist team prepares to board a plane. They wear respirators with darkened eyepieces to protect against exploding stun grenades.

The word "guerrilla" was first applied to fighting during the Peninsular War of 1808–1814, when the Spanish attacked French troops in the mountains of Spain. Their operations were called *guerrilla, or* "a little war."

In 1871 in Paris, following the defeat of the French by the Prussians, the population rose in revolt against the French government. People felt that the government had betrayed them. They formed the Commune, which ruled Paris from March 19, 1871 until May 1871, when it was brutally suppressed by the French Army. The name that

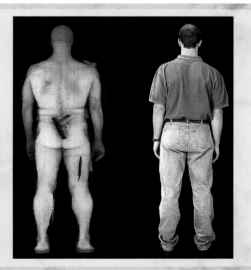

TERRORISM: THE WAR OF THE WEAK

The word "terrorism" dates back to the so-called Reign of Terror which followed the French Revolution in 1789. Between 1793 and 1794 more than 17,000 French citizens were executed, and many more perished in less formal circumstances.

Modern terrorism uses the shock value of an act, such as a random bombing, a hijack, a kidnap, or a shooting, to create a widespread sense of fear and insecurity in the community. The terrorists hope that this fear will eventually affect government policies. Terrorists who overthrow repressive governments can in turn sometimes fail to respect human rights.

The driving force behind a terrorist group may be politics, nationalism, or religion. Terrorist tactics have also been employed by criminal organizations for blackmail, extortion, or punishment.

▶ CONCEALED WEAPONS
Terrorists have devised various ways of carrying handguns, knives, and grenades in places where they will not be detected in quick body searches by police or security forces.

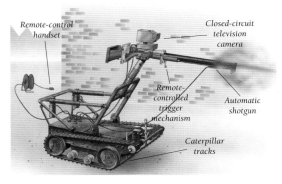

▲ ROBOT AID

Robot-tracked vehicles have been developed to approach, examine, and disrupt terrorist explosive devices. TV cameras mounted on the robot allow the operator to see the device on remotely located monitors, and shotguns or very high-pressure water blast the device apart before it can explode.

the members of the Paris Commune gave themselves — communards—lives on in "communist."

In Russia, from 1917 to 1921, the revolution against the csar (emperor) and his government turned into a civil war. The two opposing sides were the Bolshevik "Reds" and the pro-Western "Whites." The 20th century also saw the growth of guerrilla war, as those countries defeated and occupied by Nazi Germany continued to fight secretly and "resist" their occupiers. The French Resistance, for example, was assisted with weapons and equipment sent from Britain by parachute at night.

Mao Tse-tung led the Chinese Communists against the Japanese in World War II and against the Chinese Nationalists both before and after World War II. Along with Che Guevara, who fought for Castro in Cuba, Mao Tse Tung is one of the most famous writers on the subject of guerrilla warfare.

During the Cold War, the period of tension between the former Soviet Union and the West between the years 1945 and 1989, the Soviet Union supported wars of national liberation or decolonization. In most of these campaigns guerrilla, or terrorist tactics were used. Modern society is very vulnerable to such pinpoint attacks, which can throw ordinary life into chaos. The targets are usually public figures, policemen, or small groups of soldiers, who are ambushed. Public utilities, transportation, and communications can be attacked with explosives. The aim of terrorists is to make a country ungovernable so that the population force its government to strike a deal in order to achieve a peaceful life.

◀ CLIMBER
The rubber tracks on this explosive ordnance device (EOD) vehicle allow it to climb steps and enter buildings where a device may be hidden in a totally inaccessible location.

▼ THE TERRORIST CELL
The cell structure has evolved in terrorist organizations during the 20th century. If contact between large numbers is avoided, it is harder for the security forces to insert their own secret agents into the organizations. If the number of members in contact with each other is kept down to two or three, it is difficult to break up an organization even if some of its members have been arrested.

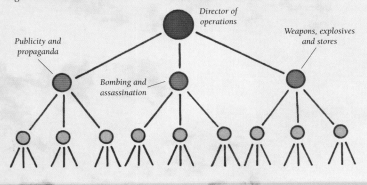

Director of operations

Publicity and propaganda

Bombing and assassination

Weapons, explosives and stores

Key Dates

- 1789 French Revolution begins.
- 1808–1814 Peninsular War.
- 1871 Paris Commune.
- 1917 Russian Revolution.
- 1923–1949 Chinese Revolution.
- 1934– Arab-Israeli conflict .
- 1939–1945 Resistance operations in Nazi-occupied Europe.
- 1945–1962 War in South-east Asia.
- 1949–1962 Algerian War.
- 1945–1975 Indo-China War.
- 1956–1960 Cuban Revolution.
- 1978–1982 Islamic revolution.

Tanks

▲ WORLD WAR I TANK
The Mark I tank could cross a 10-foot trench and had a range of 15 miles.

WHEN THE FIRST TANKS lumbered through the smoke and mud toward German trenches in World War I, the startled Germans thought that they had seen monsters from hell.

The first tank was the idea of Colonel Ernest Swinton in World War I. He took the tracked chassis of the gasoline-driven Holt tractor and combined it with armor plate protection and field-gun or machine-gun armament. These vehicles were called "land ships," but when they were shipped from Britain to France hidden under canvas sheets they were described as "tanks." Curious soldiers were told that they were large water tanks. The name "tank" stuck. Large numbers of these

▶ TIGER TANK
The German Tiger tank weighed 56 tons and was armed with a 3½ inch gun.

armored tracked vehicles went into action in France, at Cambrai in 1917 and at Amiens in 1918.

In the interwar years tank designs changed. New features included improved suspension and radio communications, and the main armament was mounted in a rotating turret. World War II saw the development of fighting tactics that used the protection, firepower and mobility of tanks to attack and advance quickly, outflanking or encircling a less mobile enemy. Tanks grew in weight and firepower throughout World War II, finishing with the Soviet IS-3 which weighed 44.2 tons and was armed with a 5inch gun.

In the postwar years, changes in tank design included improved engines, suspension, armor, fire control systems, and armament. The American M-60 and the British-designed Centurion saw action in Asia and the Middle East. The Soviet T-54/55 was used throughout the 1950s and 1960s by many countries.

New armor developed in the 1980s includes systems that explode outward if hit by an anti-tank missile and plates of very hard materials that can be bolted on as extra protection. Fire control systems consist of onboard computers which automatically give the correct elevation, the angle of the gun's barrel, and

CLASSIC TANKS

Since 1916 tanks have played a major part in all significant land actions. In World War II some tanks achieved fame because of the quality of their design—for example the Russian T-34 or German Panzer. Others, such as the Sherman, were mass produced, and it was their quantity that caused the greatest impact. However, tank designs since World War II have become increasingly like combat aircraft, with electronics and automation taking over many of the functions that used to be taken on by the crew.

◀ CHALLENGER II
Britain's Challenger tank of the 1980s and 1990s has four crew and weighs 62,000kg.

▶ AMERICAN 1940S SHERMAN
The Sherman weighs 74,400lbs., has a 100-mile range and carries a crew of five.

▲ SWEDISH CV90
This tank weighs 65,000lbs. and has three crew and eight soldiers.

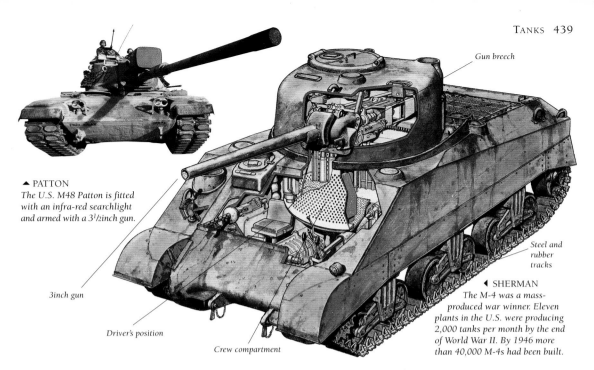

▲ PATTON
The U.S. M48 Patton is fitted with an infra-red searchlight and armed with a 3¹/₂inch gun.

Gun breech

3inch gun

Driver's position

Crew compartment

Steel and rubber tracks

◀ SHERMAN
The M-4 was a mass-produced war winner. Eleven plants in the U.S. were producing 2,000 tanks per month by the end of World War II. By 1946 more than 40,000 M-4s had been built.

ammunition type to the gun once a target has been identified. The fire control is linked with sights that allow the crew to see the heat patterns of enemy vehicles by day and night. The new armament includes guns that fire shells or guided missiles. The new shells are made from very hard materials and are designed to punch through the armor of enemy tanks. One of the most recent major tank actions was fought as part of the Gulf War, between the Coalition Forces and the Iraqis in 1991 following the invasion of Kuwait by Iraq. The new, state-of-the-art technology of the American Abrams and British Challenger tanks gave them the advantage over the older Russian- and Chinese-built T-72 and Type 59 tanks.

▼ TANK TACTICS
Using the terrain, an experienced crew locates the enemy. They can fire at the enemy without exposing themselves. If the main armament can be depressed low enough, the tank can fire from this position. If it drives forward, the gun can still be depressed to point at the enemy tank, but would be more exposed to attack.

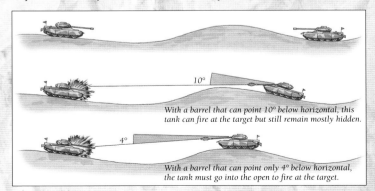

10°

With a barrel that can point 10° below horizontal, this tank can fire at the target but still remain mostly hidden.

4°

With a barrel that can point only 4° below horizontal, the tank must go into the open to fire at the target.

Key Dates

- 1916 September: first tanks used in World War I.

- 1943 July–September: Battle of Kursk—2,700 German tanks against 3,300 Soviet tanks.

- 1945 August: invasion of Manchuria—5,500 Soviet tanks attack 1,000 Japanese tanks.

- 1967 Middle East War—1,000 Israeli tanks vs. 2,050 Egyptian, Syrian, and Jordanian tanks.

- 1973 Middle East War—2,000 Israeli tanks vs. 4,800 Egyptian, Syrian, Jordanian, and Iraqi tanks.

- 1991 Gulf War—2,200 Coalition tanks vs. 4,000 Iraqi tanks.

Anti-tank Weapons

▲ EXPLOSION
A Swedish BILL anti-tank missile explodes above the turret of a target tank.

ANTI-TANK GUNNERS need to have the cool nerve of an old-style big-game hunter. As the enemy tank crashes toward them, perhaps firing its machine guns, the anti-tank crew must wait until their enemy is in range and then fire at its most vulnerable point.

As soon as tanks had appeared on the Western Front in World War I, all the combatants began to think of ways of stopping or destroying these machines by using anti-tank weapons.

The Imperial German Army developed a powerful bolt-action anti-tank rifle firing a .50in bullet. Most armies, however, relied on the crews of field guns to shoot it out with these early tanks. Anti-tank rifles were used by the British and Soviet armies in the opening years of World War II, but thicker armor and new weapons soon made them obsolete.

The true anti-tank gun, which was developed in the 1920s and 1930s, fired a very hard shell at high velocity. Early guns were between 1½inch and 2¼inch in caliber. As World War II progressed the guns grew bigger, and the Germans used the 3½inch antiaircraft gun as a very effective anti-tank gun. The Russians used a huge 4inch gun.

The major change in anti-tank weapons came with the development of the shaped charge and short-range rockets. The shaped charge penetrated all conventional armor, while there was no recoil with a rocket projectile. The weapon that combined rocket and shaped charge was the American 2⅓inch rocket launcher M1. It was nicknamed the "Bazooka" after the musical instrument played by the U.S. comedian Bob Burns.

▲ INFANTRY ANTI-TANK
Anti-tank weapons may have a crew, for example the M40 4¼inch recoilless rifle or the TOW or Milan missiles, or they may be single-shot one-man weapons such as the M72 or the RPG-7.

PENETRATION
Most infantry anti-tank weapons have a shaped charge warhead. This consists of explosives shaped around the outside of a copper cone. When the warhead explodes, the energy of the explosion is pushed inward and forward, creating a jet of molten metal and gas. A slug of metal at the front then melts its way through the armor of the tank.

◀ CARL GUSTAV
Canadian soldiers use the Swedish 3½inch recoilless anti-tank weapon called the Carl Gustav. It can fire a wide range of ammunition.

▲ BILL
The launcher of the revolutionary Swedish BILL missile is fitted with a thermal imaging (TI) sight. It can detect the heat generated by the engine of a tank or fighting vehicle and use it as a target. This technology can also be used just as a night-vision device by troops on reconnaissance missions during darkness.

▶ FAIRCHILD A-10
The Fairchild A-10A has the official title Thunderbolt II, but is known as "the Warthog" by its crews. It has a powerful multi-barrel 1¹/₅inch GAU-8 cannon in the nose and can also carry anti-tank missiles and bombs.

At the close of the war the Germans had looked at the concept of an anti-tank guided weapon (ATGW), which they designated the X-7. It had a range of 3,280 feet, weighed 25lbs. and would be guided to its target by signals passed along a light wire that was on a spool on the launching mount. The X-7 was reported to be capable of penetrating 8 inches of armor.

Most modern ATGWs are wire guided

because this is a reliable system that cannot be jammed by the enemy. Warhead design has changed as armor has improved, and now consists of two or even three shaped charges that detonate in succession. In 1979 Sweden produced a missile designated BILL, which explodes above the tank, sending its shaped charge jet through the thin top armor. These two designs, called "tandem warheads" and "top attack," indicate the direction that anti-tank weapon technology will take in the 21st century.

◀ TANK DESTROYER
A British Alvis Striker firing a wire-guided Swingfire anti-tank missile. The Swingfire has a maximum range of 13,120 feet.

▼ LAW
The M72 LAW is a telescopic rocket launcher that weighs 8¹/₂lbs. It has an effective range of 722 feet. It was first used in action in the Vietnam War, and later by the British in the Falklands in 1982.

▼ DESTRUCTION
An Iraqi tank destroyed by American A-10s during the Gulf War. The tank has almost blown apart, because the ammunition and fuel inside have exploded. Internal explosions are a constant worry for all armored vehicle crews.

Key Dates

- 1918 German .5 inch anti-tank rifles in use.

- 1927 First dedicated anti-tank guns developed.

- 1942 "Bazooka" rocket launcher developed in U.S.

- 1943 German PaK 43/41 anti-tank gun enters service.

- 1956 French introduce Nord SS10 wire-guided missile.

- 1972 Euromissile Milan produced.

- 1973 Egyptians use Sagger guided missiles in Sinai.

- 1979 Swedish BILL developed.

Transportation

▲ AIRBORNE
A rocket-armed Blackhawk helicopter carries a two-man reconnaissance vehicle as an underslung load.

WHEN ARMIES GO to war they use forms of transportation similar to those used by ordinary people—car, train, ship, and plane. For centuries they relied on human or animal power for transportation. Oxen, horses, and mules pulled wagons and guns; and troops carried heavy loads in packs.

Ships were vital for island nations such as Britain because they could transport troops overseas and, if necessary, evacuate them. In World War II amphibious operations became highly specialized, with landing craft designed to put troops and vehicles ashore on open beaches.

The steam locomotive made troop transportation faster and allowed large numbers of troops and equipment to be moved around. The Civil War (1861–1865) demonstrated the importance of a reliable railroad system. Railroad lines, and particularly, bridges became a key target for raids by troops and, later on, by aircraft.

At the beginning of World War I vehicles such as taxis and buses were used to move troops quickly. Later, trucks became more readily available. Huge numbers of trucks were used in World War II, increasing the need for fuel supplies. After D-Day, in June 1944, a fuel pipeline was laid from Britain to northern France across the Channel. It was codenamed PLUTO, which stands for Pipe Line Under The Ocean.

Among the wheeled vehicles produced in World War II the ¼-ton Jeep remains the

◄ MOTORBIKE
A German Afrika Korps BMW R75 motorcycle combination, armed with an MG34 machine gun, roars through the Libyan desert in 1942.

AMPHIBIOUS OPERATIONS
World War II saw the development of specialized landing craft to carry vehicles, troops, and stores for amphibious operations. Before 1942 soldiers went ashore from small boats, ships, or modified freighters. In the Pacific, the U.S. Marine Corps used tracked amphibious APCs to carry marines ashore.

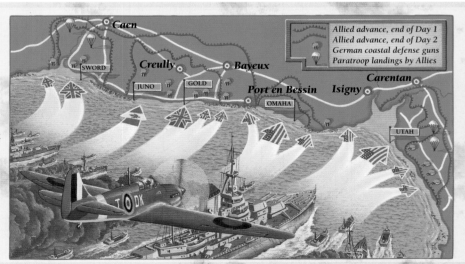

Allied advance, end of Day 1
Allied advance, end of Day 2
German coastal defense guns
Paratroop landings by Allies

Caen
SWORD
Creully
JUNO
GOLD
Bayeux
Port en Bessin
OMAHA
Isigny
Carentan
UTAH

◄ *EXTRA ARMOR*
An Israeli M113 APC, in desert camouflage, is fitted with extra armor and carries a .50in Browning machine gun. APCs have enough internal space to make them ideal weapons carriers for missiles, AA guns, or spare ammunition. They are also used as ambulances and for radio communications.

▼ *HUMVEE FIREPOWER*
A TOW anti-tank missile streaks away from its launcher, which is mounted on an HMMWV, a wheeled utility vehicle known to U.S. soldiers as a "HumVee." The rugged and reliable HumVee is popular with U.S. service personnel because it is easy to drive.

most enduring symbol. The U.S. produced 639,245 Jeeps before the war ended, and the Jeep continued to serve in many armies into the 1960s. In World War II the U.S.-designed DUKW, a six-wheeled amphibious truck, was used during amphibious operations to ferry stores from ships to the shore. Despite their age, DUKWs were still being used by the British Royal Marines in the late 1990s.

Most armies now use 4-ton trucks and light ³/₄-ton vehicles. However, some specialized Alpine regiments still use mules to carry heavy equipment such as mortars, pack howitzers, and ammunition up narrow mountain tracks.

◄ D-DAY LANDINGS
Landings at beaches in Normandy, codenamed Utah, Omaha, Gold, Juno, and Sword, began at 6.30 a.m. on June 6, 1944. By midnight 57,000 U.S. and 75,000 British and Canadian troops and their equipment were ashore.

▲ LANDING CRAFT
U.S. soldiers approach Omaha Beach in Normandy in June 1944. They are in a Higgins boat, a landing craft designed to carry soldiers.

◄ DUCK
The DUKW, a wartime amphibious truck, was nicknamed the "DUCK." It is still in service with the Royal Marines in Britain.

Key Dates

- 1885 Four-wheel motor carriage developed.

- 1914 French use 600 taxis to transport troops at the Marne.

- 1925 French demonstrate the half-track vehicle.

- 1927 British Army tests mechanized warfare tactics.

- 1940 Germans conduct trials for an amphibious invasion of Great Britain.

- 1943 U.S. DUKW used in combat.

- 1944 D-Day, the largest amphibious operation in history, takes place in northern France.

Reconnaissance

IMAGINE PLAYING CHESS or another tactical board game, but seeing the board only occasionally or being told about its layout by someone else. You would be "in the dark." A chess player wants to see how the game is developing, perhaps look at the opponent's expression, and make moves based on this information.

In war, reconnaissance is somewhat like watching the board and the player. It is the tactical method of learning about enemy positions, movements, or plans and finding out about the terrain or weather in which combat may take place.

For many centuries the job of reconnaissance was done by small patrols of light cavalry riding ahead of the main body of troops. The only special equipment available was a telescope or a pair of binoculars. If they

▲ SAS JEEP
A U.S.-made Jeep fitted with Vickers K machine guns in service with the SAS in North Africa.

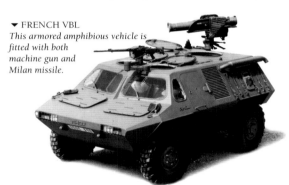

▼ FRENCH VBL
This armored amphibious vehicle is fitted with both machine gun and Milan missile.

saw the enemy, they would then ride as fast as possible to pass the information back.

The pedal bicycle was popular at the turn of the 19th century because cyclist troops were fast, silent, and very mobile. However, reconnaisance changed dramatically with the development of the internal combustion engine and of small, reliable radios.

Armored cars and motorcycles had been developed in World War I. Between 1939 and 1943 German soldiers used them most effectively and set the style for armored reconnaissance. Pushing ahead, they would find undefended bridges, gaps in minefields, and weak points

MODERN VISION
Reconnaissance by land, sea, and air uses a huge range of sensors to gather information about the enemy and its plans and forces. Once this information has been collected, the most important step is to put it all together and assess its value. This assessment must then be passed as quickly as possible to the commanders and units so that they can make best use of it.

▶ PHOTOGRAPHY
Photographs are useful because they can be processed quickly and are easy to handle. Extra information can be overprinted on them, combining the accuracy of a photo with the information found on a map.

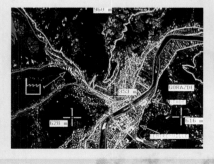

▲ DRONE LAUNCH
A remotely piloted vehicle (RPV) is also known as a drone. It is a small aircraft fitted with cameras and sensors. Drones are designed to be flown by remote control over enemy territory.

◄ AERIAL RECONNAISSANCE
Aerial reconnaissance began as long ago as the Franco-Prussian War, when a photograph was taken from a hot-air balloon. Even today manned flights are still used to gather photographic intelligence.

▼ SATELLITES
Modern cameras aboard satellites can produce remarkably clear images. They have made every part of the world accessible.

in defended positions. This valuable information would be quickly radioed back, and the main forces would follow up.

Reconnaissance could also be undertaken by foot patrols working away from their vehicles, and even by scuba divers and midget submarines. In the months before D-Day, in 1944, the beaches of northern France were visited by small groups of divers. They swam ashore to check the gradient of each beach and its defenses, and to discover whether it was sand, shingle, or mud, as this was important for the landing troops.

In the war in the Falklands in 1982, men of the Special Boat Service (SBS) and the Special Air Service (SAS) landed on the islands to observe Argentinian positions. They helped the planners to build up a picture of the strength and quality of the garrison. In the 1990–1991 Gulf War, the British SAS entered Iraq to report on the terrain. It was what they hoped for: a gravel desert which was better for the tanks and armored vehicles.

Reconnaissance intelligence is also gathered from aerial photographs and radar images taken by special reconnaissance aircraft. The most recent technique for gathering reconnaissance intelligence is by remotely piloted vehicles (RPVs). They are usually small aircraft fitted with cameras that transmit TV images of the terrain to the base from which the RPV is being operated. They give information about enemy movements and positions.

▼ DRONE FLIGHT
Modern drones send back "real-time" TV and sensor information as they fly a search pattern over a designated area. If the operator "sees" something of interest, the drone can fly lower or use more powerful sensors.

Drone flies a set route over the target area in order to ensure the best possible coverage

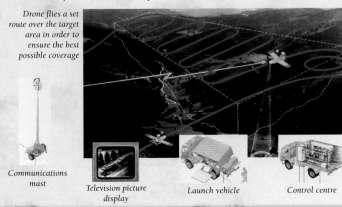

Communications mast

Television picture display

Launch vehicle

Control centre

Key Dates

- 1858 First aerial photography.
- 1866 Typewriter invented.
- 1888 First portable roll-film camera.
- 1923 Cathode-ray tube, used in televisions, invented.
- 1943 Infrared night-vision viewer used.
- 1957 First space satellite launched.
- 1960 U-2 reconnaissance aircraft flown by Gary Powers shot down over the former Soviet Union.
- 1982 SAS and SBS forces used for reconnaissance in the Falklands.

Communications

▲ CARRIER PIGEON
A homing pigeon carries simple messages in a capsule attached to its leg.

IN A FAST-MOVING GAME such as a football match, information can mean the difference between victory or defeat, communicating tactics and positions. In wartime, this kind of communication is even more critical—the lives of thousands of soldiers are at risk. Ships, aircraft, and many other military units report their positions, which allows a commander to build up a picture of the battle.

For centuries messages were sent either verbally or as a written dispatch and carried by foot or horseback. Beacons positioned on high hills were lit if there was a threat of enemy invasion or attack. Signal flags used at sea were a key to the British victory at Trafalgar on October 21, 1805. In 19th-century India and South Africa, where the air was clear and the sunshine constant, devices called heliographs used reflective mirrors to flash Morse code signals.

The Morse code could also be used with signal lamps; this method of communication was particularly effective at sea. The telegraph, which allowed Morse messages to be sent over long distances, was first used in the Civil War (1861–1865).

▲ FIELD RADIO
A modern field radio is light and reliable. It may even have a built-in security system which makes it impossible to decode a message without the correct equipment.

CODES AND SIGNALS

Signaling systems were initially visual ones, using flags, light, or even smoke. They allowed people to communicate beyond the range of the human voice. Telegraph, telephone, and radio increased the range. However, the danger of interception by the enemy made it essential that signals be in code.

◀ SEMAPHORE
The British Army and the Royal Navy used this signaling system before radio was developed. The advantage of semaphore is that flags don't operate from an electronic system, which can break down.

▲ MORSE CODE
Invented by Samuel Morse in 1850, this "dot and dash" code was the key to the telegraph system. It was first used operationally during the Crimean War.

◀ WARTIME RADIO
French troops with American uniforms and equipment operate a radio during fighting in Germany in 1945.

▶ CONCEALED
Men of the U.S. Army's 82nd Airborne Division during the invasion of Grenada in 1983. The soldier carries the radio in a medium pack to conceal it.

The telephone was in widespread use by 1880 and was used in the Boer War (1899–1902) and the Russo-Japanese War (1904–1905). In World War I, field telephones were developed, and telephone cables were laid quickly to connect headquarters with the artillery batteries.

The first radios were cumbersome and required a wagon and team of horses to transport them. In 1915, an observer used a radio in a hot-air balloon over the Dardanelles in Turkey. During the interwar years radios became small enough to fit in a backpack.

Most military radios operate in the very high frequency (VHF) range between 30 and 200megahertz (MHz) and in the high frequency (HF) range between 1 and 30MHz. Anyone with a radio receiver tuned to the right frequency could listen to a radio conversation, and so codes were introduced. However, even if a message

was encoded, the station could be jammed by a powerful signal. One technique for ensuring security and avoiding jamming was "burst transmission." A message would be prepared and then sent in a few seconds to another station which would display it on a screen. In the 1980s radios were designed that could change frequencies at random intervals. If the receiving station was correctly tuned it would follow the "hops," and so a conversation could take place without interruption.

The latest development in radio communications are satellites. They receive radio signals and rebroadcast them, allowing messages from remote locations to be transmitted reliably over huge distances.

▲ SUNLIGHT
A British soldier uses a signaling mirror to contact a circling helicopter. It is a silent but effective communications tool.

▶ THE ENIGMA CODE
During World War II the Germans used a variety of codes. Most of them used a machine to jumble up the letters of the message. The British, assisted by the French, Poles, and Americans, were able to break the German codes. This literally saved Britain from starvation because some of these codes were for the U-boats, which were sinking ships carrying food and fuel to Britain. The code machines were like very complex typewriters.

Key Dates

- 1850 Morse Code invented.
- 1858 Heliograph invented.
- 1876 Telephone invented.
- 1892 First detected radio signal.
- 1901 Transatlantic radio link established.
- 1921 Teleprinter developed.
- 1925 Shortwave, crystal-controlled radio invented.
- 1926 Enigma coding machine developed.
- 1949 Transistor invented.
- 1960 Microchip first used.

Protecting the Soldier

▲ THE HELMET
The helmet, such as this M1 steel helmet, is the oldest and most effective protection for a soldier.

ARMOR HAD PROTECTED soldiers when firearms were awkward and heavy and the sword was still used in warfare. However, armor was no longer worn once firearms improved and freedom of movement had become more important.

Like the "hard hats" worn by construction workers on building sites, the steel helmets introduced in World War I were intended to protect soldiers from objects falling on their heads. Such objects are normally shrapnel, the tiny fragments that fall from the sky when a shell explodes. During World War I armored protection was introduced for snipers—soldiers who use powerful rifles with telescopic sights to shoot at an unwary enemy or important targets such as officers. This protection was very unwieldy and heavy, and resembled the breastplates of medieval soldiers.

Following the use of poison gas by the Germans on the Western Front in World War I, gas masks or respirators were produced. The first masks were simply cotton pads worn with goggles, but by the end of the war respirators were not only more effective but also more comfortable to wear. Modern masks use charcoal filters. Charcoal is a very useful filter against impurities, hence its use in domestic water filters. It is also used in soldiers' protective jackets and trousers.

▲ REACTIVE ARMOR
Explosive reactive armor (ERA) comes in bolt-on slabs. It explodes outward when hit, counteracting the penetration of charges.

PROTECT AND SURVIVE

As weapons became more effective and more lethal, soldiers looked for ways of improving their protection. Soldiers who were fighting a defensive battle dug themselves in, and built log or sandbag defenses or, even better, reinforced concrete ones. The difficulties came when they were in the open. Thick steel plates gave protection, but their weight meant that soldiers could move only short distances at low speed.

In the 1980s and 1990s new materials have allowed soldiers to move freely with protection from shell fragments and bullets. Fireproof materials, used in tank and aircraft crew overalls, protect the wearer against flash burns from exploding fuel tanks. In bad weather troops now have the comfort of breathable raincoats.

British helmet, World War I

British paratrooper's helmet, 1944

British helmet no. 4, 1944

U.S. M1 steel helmet, World War II

Current British no. 6 helmet

Current U.S. PASGT Kevlar helmet

◀ EVACUATION OF
CASUALTIES
*U.S. soldiers carry a casualty
on a litter to a Blackhawk
helicopter. Helicopters were
first used for flying wounded
from the battlefield during the
Korean War and have become
a vital link in the casualty
evacuation chain. Nicknamed
"Dust Off" in the Vietnam War,
helicopters could literally take
an injured man from deep in
the jungle and fly him to a
modern hospital. He could be
admitted to a fully equipped
operating room in less than an
hour. Many troops who would
have died in earlier times
because of a lack of prompt
and thorough medical support
now survive terrible battlefield
injuries.*

In World War II protective jackets with overlapping
steel plates were produced to protect American bomber
crews from the shrapnel from German antiaircraft (flak)
guns. The jackets were called "flak jackets."

Today's body armor is made from materials such as
Kevlar, which is light and strong. Its woven form is
used for jackets and even boots; it can also be bonded
into a plastic for used in helmets. These new materials
can protect a soldier, even at close range, from shots
from handguns and even rifles.

In the confined spaces of aircraft, warships, and
armored vehicles, fire has always been a major threat.
In World War II, leather jackets and gloves, as well as
goggles, provided some protection. The crews on
warships wore steel helmets and anti-flash hoods made
from an asbestos-based fabric.

The development of artificial fire-resistant fabrics
such as Nomex has allowed gloves, flying overalls,
jackets, and trousers to be made from a material with a
high level of protection. Tanks and aircraft now have
fire detection systems that operate instantly, swamping
potential fires with a gas that cuts off the oxygen.

▶ ANGLE OF ARMOR
If the armor on an armored fighting
vehicle is sloped, this increases the
distance through which a projectile has
to pass before it breaks through to the
interior. If a projectile strikes the armor
at an oblique angle it may even ricochet
and fall away harmlessly.

*Armor that is 8mm
thick when vertical, is
11mm thick when tilted*

8

8

11

Key Dates

- 1856 Bessemer steel produced.

- 1865 First antiseptics used.

- 1882 Armored steel developed.

- 1914–1918 World War I: steel
  helmets introduced to protect
  soldiers from shrapnel.

- 1920s Gas masks and respirators
  introduced after the use of
  poison gas in World War I.

- 1939–1945 World War II:
  penicillin, plastic surgery, and
  blood transfusions introduced.

- 1970s Explosive reactive armor,
  ceramic armor, Kevlar, and
  Nomex developed.

▲ ARMORED TRAIN
A Soviet armored train captured by the Germans in World War II. Armor protected the
crew, but the train was vulnerable if the tracks were destroyed or damaged.

Armored Vehicles

▲ ARMORED CAR
The first armored car, the Charron Girardot et Voigt, was built in France in 1904.

A S FAR BACK AS 1482 the idea of an armored fighting vehicle (AFV) appeared in sketches drawn by Leonardo da Vinci. It was propelled by muscle power, with the crew operating geared hand cranks and firing muskets through slits. However, it was the British War Office that saw

the first true AFV in 1902 when the Simms "War Car" was demonstrated. It used a gasoline engine to drive a wheeled vehicle at a maximum speed of 11mph. It was protected by ¼ inch of armor and armed with two machine guns and a one-pounder gun.

The Belgians and British Royal Navy used armored cars with machine guns in 1914. However, the mud of the Western Front was unsuitable for wheeled vehicles. Armored cars were used in the Middle East by the British when fighting against the Turks.

The interwar period saw the development of six- and even eight-wheeled armored cars and the half-track. This vehicle had tracks at the rear of its chassis and wheels at the front. It had the cross-country performance of a tank but could be driven like a truck. The German Sdkfz 251 and American M3 half-track were widely used in World War II.

◀ ARMORED PERSONNEL CARRIER (APC)
This M113 APC is fitted with TOW anti-tank missile launchers. APCs are used in both wartime conflicts and civil disturbances.

PROTECTION AND MOBILITY
Armor protection is used for combat vehicles and also to protect VIP (Very Important Person) cars and vehicles used by the media in hostile locations. Protection may be quite basic, consisting of plates and panels, or it may be a system that is both bulletproof and mineproof.

◀ ARMORED INFERNO
A Swedish APC burns after being hit by an anti-tank weapon in a demonstration on an army range. APCs contain fuel, hydraulic fluid under pressure, and ammunition, so internal fire can be catastrophic. This vehicle had its rear doors closed, but the explosion has blasted one open. Fire suppression systems need to operate quickly for soldiers to survive a fire. Recently, if not under fire, troops have sat on the roof of their moving APC in case it hits an anti-tank mine, catches fire, and explodes.

▲ BRITISH SAXON APC
The 4 x 4 Saxon is effectively an armoured truck. It weighs 24,850lbs., can carry 10 soldiers and has a top speed on roads of 60mph. It has been used in Northern Ireland and Bosnia to transport troops under armor.

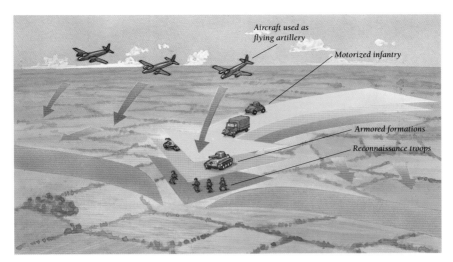

◀ ARMORED ATTACK
The armored tactics pioneered by the Germans in 1939–1942 used aircraft as flying artillery. At the front were reconnaissance troops, followed by armored formations and backed by motorized infantry in trucks. The tanks were massed to punch through enemy defenses. The infantry secured the flanks as the armored troops plunged deeper into enemy territory.

Aircraft used as flying artillery

Motorized infantry

Armored formations

Reconnaissance troops

After the war the M3 was used by the Israeli Army up to 1967. The half-track also allowed infantry to keep pace with fast-moving tanks. Artillery mounted on tracked chassis could bombard enemy positions before the infantry and tanks attacked.

Before D-Day, on June 6, 1944, the British developed several special tanks, nicknamed "Funnies." They included tanks that could clear paths through minefields, lay special matting roads across shingle beaches, or lay bridges over ditches. Another of these special tanks was the Armored Vehicle Royal Engineers (AVRE) which could fire a 45lb. demolition bomb

690 feet against German fortifications. The armored engineer vehicle that can lay bridges or bulldoze rubble is now a standard vehicle in most major armies.

Since the end of World War II, AFVs have been developed as armored ambulances, recovery vehicles, mobile workshops, headquarters, nuclear biological and chemical (NBC) detection vehicles, and troop carriers. They are wheeled like the French VAB or fully tracked like the American M113. The wheeled APCs are widely used in United Nation peacekeeping operations because they give protection against rifle and machine gun fire as well as from shell fragments.

▲ FRENCH PANHARD ERC
Armed with a 3½ inch gun, the French ERC Sagaie armored car has a top speed of 60mph on roads. Its six wheels give it a better cross-country performance than a normal four-wheeled vehicle. The ERC saw action during the Gulf War of 1990–1991 against Iraq.

Key Dates

- 1904 First armored car.

- 1914 Armored car shoots down German Taube aircraft.

- 1919–1922 Armored cars used in Ireland against the IRA.

- 1920 Rolls Royce armored car introduced; it serves until 1941.

- 1931 First cast turrets introduced by France for the D1.

- 1932 Japanese field the first diesel-powered armored vehicle.

- 1936 Torsion bar suspension introduced by the Germans.

- 1944 Tetrach light tanks land by glider in Normandy, France.

Camouflage

EXAMPLES OF CAMOUFLAGE exist all around us in nature. Birds, fish, and other animals have self-protection in the form of colors that help them blend into the background of vegetation, sky, water, or sand.

The earliest military camouflage consisted of the dark-green tunics and black buttons adopted by the British rifle regiments during the Peninsular War of 1808–1814. The British had learned camouflage and field craft from the experience of fighting the American Colonists and Native Americans in North America in the late 18th century. The red coats of the British stood out clearly in battle, making them easy targets.

In India in the 1800s, British troops dyed their white tropical uniforms with tea to produce a shade of brown that Indians called *khak*, or dust colored. These "khaki" uniforms helped the troops to blend into the dry terrain as they fought against tribes on the Northwest Frontier.

In World War I camouflage, a word taken from the French *camouflet* meaning "smoke puff," became a serious technique. The French Army used conscripted artists to devise color schemes to conceal artillery and vehicles. Some were in fantastic shapes and colors, and also included nets with strips of colored cloth that were draped over buildings, guns, and vehicles.

▲ GREEN AND BROWN
A British soldier in the black, green, brown, and buff camouflage that was introduced in the early 1970s. It is designed to mimic the shadows and highlights of natural vegetation. It is effective in tropical and temperate terrain and has been adopted by the Dutch and Indonesian armies.

▲ DESERT
A soldier in the desert with his helmet garnished with nylon "scrim" to break up its outline. His equipment and clothing have softened with use and do not present hard, unnatural lines and shapes.

MEN AND MACHINES
Camouflage conceals soldiers, vehicles, and buildings. It may consist of paint patterns, netting, painted screens, planted vegetation, or even fake buildings and vehicles. Good camouflage fools the naked eye, but special photographic film and night-vision equipment will penetrate ordinary camouflage. Special nets and paints have, in turn, been developed to counter this technology.

▶ FACE PAINT
A soldier with some of the elaborate patterns that can be painted to break up the shape and color of the human face. Grass has been added to his helmet.

▲ HELMET COVERS
U.S. military helmets with cotton drill desert camouflage covers. This spotted pattern is known to U.S. service personnel as "chocolate chip cookie" camouflage. The elastic band around the helmet is used to secure vegetation for camouflage.

▲ SNOW
In the course of an exercise in the 1980s in northern Canada, Canadian Army Special Forces slog through the snow in white camouflaged uniforms and backpack covers. They have fixed white tape to their weapons to break up the outline.

▼ SLOGGING
U.S. soldiers armed with M16 rifles and carrying knapsacks slog through the dust. They are wearing camouflaged uniforms. Their Kevlar helmets have cloth covers made from the same material.

The development of aircraft and aerial photography during the two world wars made camouflage essential. Elaborate deception schemes included building fake vehicles and constructing huts with lighting that operated by itself at night.

By the end of the 20th century new methods of detection had taken camouflage out of the simple visual detection range. These methods included night-vision equipment and thermal imaging, enabling the viewer to see the heat generated by humans or equipment. Modern camouflage can conceal the shape, color, heat, and radar picture of aircraft, ships, and tanks.

◄ FOOLING THE EYE
A USAF Rockwell B-1A bomber in "viscam," the visual camouflage designed to make the bomber blend into the background over which it is flying. Although electronic aids such as radar and thermal imaging can be very accurate, pilots and soldiers also rely on their eyes to double-check.

▼ JETS OVER THE DESERT
Two F-15 Eagles are in flight with a chase plane over the desert. The Eagles are painted in pale "air superiority" camouflage which is designed to blend into the sky.

Key Dates

- 1775–1783 American Revolution: use of field craft by Colonists.

- 1808–1814 Peninsular War: the British riflemen wear dark-green camouflaged tunics.

- 1857–1858 Indian Mutiny: white uniforms dyed "khaki".

- 1914–1918 World War I: land, sea and air camouflage developed.

- 1939–1945 World War II: aerial photography and infrared technology developed.

- 1970s Black, green, brown, and buff camouflage introduced.

Battleships

▲ NELSON
Nelson was one of the greatest naval commanders. One of the secrets of his victories was an efficient flag signaling system.

A CAPITAL SHIP IS A major naval warship. Today's capital ship is probably a submerged submarine with nuclear missiles aboard, or an aircraft carrier. Yet for centuries the capital ship was a battleship such as H.M.S. *Victory,* which was powered by sail and armed with cannons along its hull.

Sea war in the 18th and 19th centuries was a test of sailing skills, stamina, and courage. The gunners learned to load and "run out" the cannons and fire them as quickly as possible to ensure that there was a steady barrage against enemy warships. The wooden-hulled ships were very strong, and when soaked with salty seawater they did not burn easily.

The change came in the mid-19th century with the development of steam propulsion, armor plating, and breech-loading guns. In 1859 the French launched the first steam-powered ironclad battleship, *La Gloire.* It was armed with 36 6½inch guns. Within two years the British had launched the *Warrior,* an ironclad ship with superior protection and armaments.

During the Civil War the indecisive battle between the ironclad battleships *Merrimack* (renamed *Virginia*)

and *Monitor* in 1862 gave some clue about the likely outcome of future naval battles.

The battle of Tsu Shima (Toshima) on May 27and 28, 1905, pitted Russian battleships against Japanese ones. The battle ended with a decisive victory for the Japanese naval forces. The Russian defeat at Tsu Shima led ultimately to defeat for the Russian forces in the Russo-Japanese War.

◀ ABOARD THE *MONITOR*
The battle of Hampton Roads, Virginia, on March 8–9, 1862, saw the Confederate armored steam frigate *Merrimack* fight an inconclusive battle with the U.S.S. *Monitor.* The *Monitor* had 11inch guns in a revolving turret.

Muzzle

▶ U.S. CANNON
This 19th-century muzzle-loading ship's cannon has simple gearing on its wooden carriage, which allows the muzzle to be lowered or raised.

FROM WOOD TO IRON
Steam power and armor plate made the new ironclad warships "wolves among a flock of sheep" when they first appeared in a world dominated by wooden sailing ships. An "arms race" developed, with new and more sophisticated ironclad ships being built throughout Europe in the 19th century.

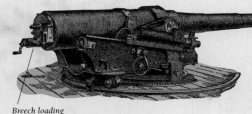

Breech loading

Muzzle

◀ A U.S. 8IN GUN
This gun could be used aboard capital ships or for coastal defense. It is breech loading and is mounted on a turntable trackway to allow it to rotate fully through 360 degrees.

▼ BATTLE OF TRAFALGAR

The Battle of Trafalgar was fought on October 21, 1805, off the Spanish coast. It involved 27 British and 33 French and Spanish ships. The battle was a victory for the British under Nelson.

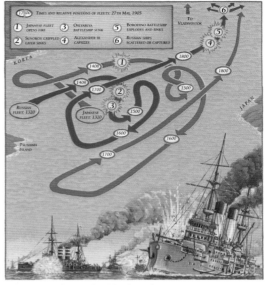

▲ BATTLE OF TSU SHIMA

This battle between the Imperial Russian Baltic fleet and the Imperial Japanese fleet took place off Korea between May 27 and 28, 1905.

At the beginning of the 20th century the launch of H.M.S. *Dreadnought* in 1906 marked another change in the design of capital ships. It was armed with 10 12inch guns and 27 12-pounder guns. By this time battleships had a speed of 18 knots and weighed 15,000 tonnes.

▲ SEA BATTLE

In a sea battle in 1862, during the Civil War, the *Merrimack* (*Virginia*)(*right*) fights it out with the U.S.S. *Monitor*. This battle, which lasted more than four hours, saw the first operational use of armored steam-powered craft in war.

Key Dates

- 1805 October 21: Battle of Trafalgar.

- 1859: French launch the first steam-powered, ironclad battleship, *La Gloire*.

- 1862 March 8–9: Battle of Hampton Roads.

- 1864 August 5: Battle of Mobile Bay.

- 1866 July 20: Battle of Lissa.

- 1898 May 1: Battle of Manila Bay.

- 1905 May 27–28: Battle of Tsu Shima.

- 1906: Launch of HMS *Dreadnought*.

20th-century Battleships

▲ NIGHT SALVO
A U.S. battleship fires a battery salvo at night.

THE BATTLE OF JUTLAND (1916), in World War I was fought between the capital ships of the British Royal Navy and the Imperial German Navy. The outcome was indecisive.

In the interwar years several countries attempted to reduce the weight of capital ships and the size of their fleets. However, both the Japanese and the Germans were building warships in secret, and they entered World War II with powerful modern ships. The Germans saw their ships as a powerful weapon to attack Allied merchant shipping. As a result, German warships, such as the 49,360-ton battleship *Bismarck,* became a priority target for the Royal Navy. The *Bismarck* was sunk on May 27, 1941, after being pounded by the guns of the battleships H.M.S. *King George V* and H.M.S. *Rodney.*

The development of aircraft carriers and submarines made capital ships very vulnerable. The Japanese battleships *Yamato* and *Mushashi*, the largest and most heavily protected ships of their class in the world, displaced 64,170 tons each. They were armed with nine 18inch guns and twelve 6inch guns. They

had crews of 2,500 men and carried six spotter aircraft. The *Yamato* and the *Mushashi* were sunk by torpedo and dive-bomber aircraft from U.S. carriers on April 7, 1945 and October 24, 1945 respectively. Earlier, H.M.S. *Prince of Wales*, which had fought against the *Bismarck*, was sunk by Japanese aircraft on December 10, 1941.

Battleships fired huge shells, which were very effective in the bombardment of coastal defenses before an amphibious landing. During World War II battleships were used on D-Day and to support the U.S. Marine Corps landings throughout the Pacific.

Today the title of "capital ships" has passed to aircraft carriers and nuclear submarines armed with

▶ CLOSE IN SUPPORT
This U.S. Navy 20mm Phalanx system is radar controlled. The gun fires at 1,000–3,000rpm. Its very hard depleted-uranium rounds are designed to destroy surface-skimming anti-ship missiles such as the Exocet. The Phalanx has a maximum range of 19,680 feet. It can rotate through 100 degrees in one second, and elevate up to 68 degrees in one second. The gun has a 989-round ammunition drum which can be reloaded in 10–30 minutes.

CAPITAL SHIPS

Capital ships, the big warships around which naval fleets are formed, were originally big-gun battleships. Today's surface fleets and task forces are based around the aircraft carrier. Carriers and submarines are nuclear powered, which gives them the ability to stay at sea almost indefinitely and to travel huge distances.

▶ PRESTIGE
Capital ships were the centerpieces of the great navies of the 20th century. In peacetime these great ships would travel the world "showing the flag," visiting the ports of other nations whom their government wished to impress. In wartime, capital ships were the flagships for the admirals in command of battle fleets.

▲ DRESSED OVERALL ▼
These armored, steam-powered warships are "dressed overall" with signal flags displayed as decoration. Modern warships have a more streamlined appearance.

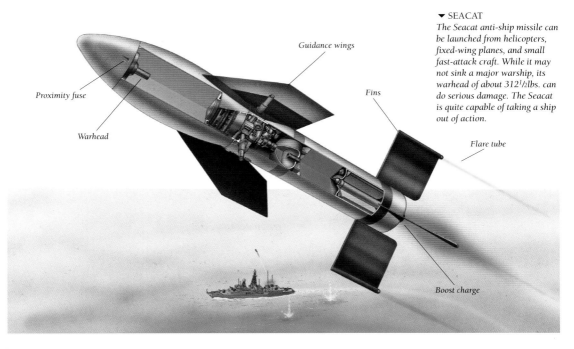

▼ SEACAT
The Seacat anti-ship missile can be launched from helicopters, fixed-wing planes, and small fast-attack craft. While it may not sink a major warship, its warhead of about 312½lbs. can do serious damage. The Seacat is quite capable of taking a ship out of action.

Guidance wings

Proximity fuse

Warhead

Fins

Flare tube

Boost charge

ballistic missiles (SSBNs). The United States Navy has the largest number of SSBNs in the world.

In March 1992 the U.S. Navy decommissioned the last operational battleship in the world, the U.S.S. *Missouri*. The 45,000-ton *Missouri* was launched in 1944 and served in the Pacific during World War II and later in the Korean War. The *Missouri* was armed with nine 16inch guns. These were last used in action as recently as 1991, when the battleship bombarded Iraqi positions in Kuwait during the Gulf War.

▼ BROADSIDE
A *Missouri*-class battleship lets rip a broadside with her 16inch guns. The guns have a maximum range of 136,450 feet and fire an 2125lb. shell. The U.S. Navy was the last force to use battleships in action.

Key Dates

- 1914–1918 World War I.

- 1914, November 1: Battle of the Coronel.

- 1914, December 8: Battle of the Falklands.

- 1916, May 31: Battle of Jutland.

- 1939, December 13: Battle of the River Plate.

- 1941, May 27: Sinking of the *Bismarck*.

- 1944, June 6: D-Day.

- 1945, April 7: Sinking of the battleship *Yamato*.

Smaller Fighting Ships

▲ PATROL
A warship fires one of its Harpoon missiles.

THERE WAS SHOCK and surprise among senior naval officers in both North America and Europe when the first torpedo boat was launched in 1878. It was the 19-knot British-built *Lightning,* with a torpedo tube in its bow. This compact torpedo boat had the speed and fire power to race after larger ships and to sink or damage them.

Japanese torpedo boats proved very effective against the Russians in the Russo-Japanese War during nighttime action at Wei-Hai-Wei in 1895 and again at Port Arthur on February 8, 1904.

In World War I the British Royal Navy deployed coastal motor boats (CMBs) and motor launches (MLs) in the narrows of the English Channel.

▶ PATROL
U.S. warships patrol, their masts cluttered with radar and radio antennae.

During World War II the German motor torpedo boats were designated *S-Boot,* or *Schnellboot,* meaning "fast boat." They were known by their crews as *Eilboot (E-Boot)* meaning "boat in a hurry." Several classes of *S-Boot* were built. Most were powered by three-shaft Daimler–Benz or MAN diesel engines and had a maximum speed of 39–42 knots with a range of 220 miles.

World War II armament was varied, but for most of the war it consisted of two .8inch antiaircraft (AA) guns and two 21inch torpedo tubes. From 1944, defensive armament was upgraded and became one 1½inch and three .8inch AA guns, or one 1½inch and five .8inch AA guns. Larger types of ship could also carry six or eight mines in place of reloading torpedoes.

During World War II, John F. Kennedy, the future President of the United States, commanded a U.S. Navy patrol torpedo

INDIVIDUAL SHIPS

The anti-ship missile and torpedo have given smaller craft a powerful punch, making them a dangerous enemy for larger, slow-moving naval vessels. Modern materials and improved engine design give these craft a performance similar to racing speedboats. They are able to dart toward larger, slower ships, launch their missiles, and retreat very quickly.

▼ SAETTIA
An Italian Saettia-class small-missile craft has a crew of 33 and a maximum speed of 40 knots and weighs 400 tons fully loaded.

▼ PATRA
A French Patra-class craft has a crew of 18 and a maximum speed of 26 knots and weighs 147.5 tons fully loaded.

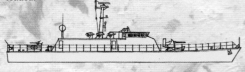

▼ SPICA
A Swedish Spica II-class torpedo attack craft has a crew of 27 and a maximum speed of 40.5 knots and weighs 230 tons fully loaded.

◀ PATROL BOAT
Small nations with coastlines to protect make extensive use of patrol craft such as this one. These boats are used to police maritime borders and for anti-piracy and anti-smuggling operations.

(PT) boat in the Pacific. The boat was powered by three gasoline engines which gave it a maximum speed of 40 knots.

The surface-to-surface missile was developed after World War II and gave small craft new hitting power. The postwar Soviet Osa ships were capable of speeds up to 38 knots and were armed with four SS-N-2A "Styx" missiles. Nearly 300 Osas were built and were used to equip 20 navies throughout the world. Osas saw action in the Middle East in the 1973 Yom Kippur War between Israel and her Arab neighbors, and also in the Gulf War in 1990–1991.

Patrol boats are ideal for landing small groups of special forces. These kinds of attack are usually undercover, amphibious attacks. Patrol boats are also widely used in peacetime for search and rescue missions, fishery patrols, and anti-piracy operations.

◀ KNOX
A U.S. Knox-class frigate has a crew of 300, and a maximum speed of 27 knots and weighs 4,260 tons fully loaded. It is armed with guns, torpedoes, and missiles. Knox-class frigates are no longer in service with the U.S. navy, but are still used by smaller nations.

▼ TESTS
Verifier, a British Aerospace trials craft, launches a Sea Skua anti-ship missile during evaluation trials. Missiles such as the 362lb. Sea Skua with its 22½lb. warhead, although originally designed as an airborne anti-ship missile, give even the smallest craft a considerable punch.

Key Dates

- 1878 *Lightning* 19-knot torpedo boat launched.

- 1914–1918 World War I: British Royal Navy coastal motor boats and launches reach 35 knots.

- 1939–1945 World War II: German E-boats reach 42 knots.

- 1958 Soviet Komar class missile-armed craft enter service.

- 1966 Soviet Osa-class missile-armed craft enter service.

- 1973 Soviet Osa-class craft see action in the Middle East.

- 1990–1991 Osa class craft see action in the Gulf War.

Submarines

THE FIRST SUBMARINE attack was carried out during the Civil War by a semi-submersible steam-propelled Confederate craft called *David*. It damaged a Federal ironclad ship with a spar torpedo. No one would have guessed that this crude underwater craft would be the forerunner of the most sophisticated and powerful weapons that the world has ever known.

Electric and oil fuel motors made fully submersible boats practical. In 1886 Lt. Isaac Peral of Spain built an electrically powered boat. The following year the Russians built a boat armed with four torpedoes. In 1895 the streamlined *Plunger* was built in the United States by John Holland. On the surface it used a steam engine to charge the batteries that powered it when moving underwater.

The German U-boats in World War I showed how submarine warfare could be a strategic weapon in attacking commercial shipping as well as launching tactical attacks on enemy warships.

▲ THE *TURTLE*
This hand-propelled craft was devised by the American David Bushnell in the early 19th century.

On August 8, 1914, the U-15 fired a torpedo at the battleship H.M.S. *Monarch*. Although the torpedo missed, it was the first time that an automotive torpedo had been fired against an enemy from a submarine.

In World War II the Germans capitalized on this experience by concentrating U-boats into "wolf packs" to attack British convoys in the North Atlantic. The Allies were able to defeat the U-boats by breaking the coded signals transmitted to them and by using improved detection systems and weapons. In the Pacific, the U.S. Navy waged a highly effective submarine campaign against Japanese commercial and naval ships.

In the postwar years nuclear power changed submarines forever. Now they could, in theory, stay submerged for indefinite periods of time. The first

Navigation instrument panel

Forward battery

Speed control

Control box

Control stick

Breathing mouthpiece

Propulsion motor

Aft battery

Explosive charges

◀ TWO-MAN SUBMARINE
Pioneered by the Italians in World War II, these vessels could be steered by two divers. They would position the detachable warhead beneath an enemy warship.

HUNTER KILLER

Modern submarines are divided into two classes: the nuclear-powered submarines armed with nuclear missiles (SSBNs) and the hunter killers (SSNs). The latter may attack enemy surface ships, but they are also very effective at hunting SSBNs. In World War II Allied submarines made torpedo attacks on surfaced enemy U-boats. However, modern SSNs can hunt and kill underwater, using sonar to locate the enemy and firing sophisticated guided torpedoes.

▼ DIESEL POWER
A diesel-powered hunter-killer submarine. Diesel power is a very quiet form of propulsion.

Periscope

Hydroplanes

Control fins

Control room

Crew's quarters

Sonar

Propeller

Two turbo-charged "Hedomora" diesel engines

Electrical control room

Torpedoes

nuclear submarine was the U.S.S. *Nautilus*. It was commissioned in 1954 and could dive to more than 650 feet. In 1959 the launch of the U.S.S. *George Washington* marked the arrival of the world's most formidable weapon. This nuclear-powered submarine was armed with Polaris nuclear missiles which could be launched while the boat was submerged.

On May 2, 1982, off the Falklands, the submarine H.M.S. *Conquerer* torpedoed and sank the Argentinian heavy cruiser *General Belgrano*. Despite the use of very efficient anti-submarine tracking systems and weapons, submarines remain a powerful weapon because of the secret nature of their operations.

▶ BOMBER
An SSBN is known in the British Royal Navy as a "bomber." Its missiles are housed in launch tubes astern of the fin, or conning tower.

Type A3 Polaris missile

Periscopes and radar mast

Bridge (for surface use)

Machine control room containing nuclear reactor control panels

Communications room

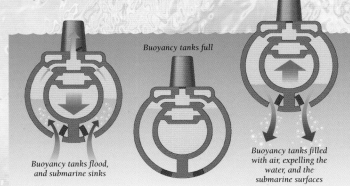

Electrical generating plant

Nuclear reactor (top-secret)

Missile compartment

Navigation center

Torpedo tubes

▲ ATOMIC SUBMARINE
First developed by the U.S., the nuclear-powered submarine is the most powerful warship in history. It is armed with intercontinental nuclear missiles which can be fired from underwater.

▼ NEGATIVE BUOYANCY
A submarine dives by letting water into its buoyancy tanks, and this makes it heavy enough to sink. To surface it "blows" its tanks, pushing air into them so that the water is forced out.

Buoyancy tanks full

Buoyancy tanks flood, and submarine sinks

Buoyancy tanks filled with air, expelling the water, and the submarine surfaces

Key Dates

- 1863 October 5: steam-driven submersible *David* attacks Federal ironclad ship.

- 1895 U.S.S. *Plunger,* the first battery-powered boat.

- 1904 *Aigret,* first diesel-powered boat.

- 1914–1918 World War I German U-boats wage war against Allied commercial shipping.

- 1939–1945 World War II German U-boats use "wolf pack" tactics against Allied shipping.

- 1954 U.S.S. *Nautilus,* the first nuclear-powered submarine, is commissioned.

Aircraft Carriers

EARLY AIRPLANES WERE FRAGILE and underpowered. They were still a dangerous and risky form of transportation when U.S. airman Eugene Ely made the first successful flight from a platform rigged on the deck of a U.S. Navy cruiser in 1911. Two months later the intrepid Ely also made a landing on board a ship. He had effectively become the first carrier pilot, although at that time aircraft carriers did not yet exist.

▲ VERTICAL
A Royal Navy Harrier takes off in the Falklands in 1982.

In 1913 H.M.S. *Hermes* pioneered aircraft carrier design with its short flying-off deck and three airplanes. A U-boat sank her in 1914, but her successor, completed in 1919, was a true aircraft carrier. During World War I the British used seaplane carriers from which aircraft were lowered into the sea.

The interwar years saw a rapid development in carrier design and capability. H.M.S. *Ark Royal*, which was commissioned in 1938, incorporated all the latest features: arrester wire to halt incoming aircraft, net crash barrier, batsmen to guide pilots, and catapults to launch aircraft. In 1939 Britain had ten carriers. In 1941 Japan had eleven, and the U.S. had three. By the end of the war the U.S. Navy had over 100 in action.

At Taranto, Italy, in 1940, 21 Swordfish aircraft from the British Royal Navy carrier H.M.S. *Illustrious* attacked ships of the Italian Navy, severely damaging three battleships. The Japanese are believed to have modeled their attack at Pearl Harbor on December 7, 1941, on Taranto. They committed 360 aircraft armed with torpedoes and bombs, and sank or immobilized eight battleships, three cruisers, and other craft. The U.S. Navy carrier fleet, which was at sea at the time of the attack, formed the nucleus of a new Pacific fleet.

In May 1942, the U.S. Navy fought the Battle of the Coral Sea against the Japanese. It was the first sea battle fought entirely by aircraft attacking ships. In June 1942,

▲ TAKE-OFF
A British RNAS Sopwith Pup fighter planes takes off during trials in World War I.

LARGE AND SMALL
In the 20th century aircraft carriers have grown from simple "flat tops" to virtual cities at sea. The U.S.S. *Nimitz,* for example, has a crew of more than 6,000 with 50 planes as well as helicopters. In World War I H.M.S. *Hermes* was the first planes carrier and had only three planes. *Hermes* was sunk by a U-boat; even today aircraft carriers are vulnerable to submarine attack.

▲ LAUNCHING
This McDonnell Douglas Hornet is preparing to take off.

◀ SIZE
A huge U.S. carrier is maneuvered into harbour by small tugboats.

▲ ARRESTING
A McDonnell Douglas Hornet hits an arrester net.

▲ FIGHTER POWER
McDonnell Hornet fighters aboard a US carrier. The Hornet's six
Phalanx missiles can be used against six targets simultaneously.

the Battle of Midway was another complex air and sea action. These two battles cost the Japanese six of their ten carriers, and the U.S. Navy four of the original eight.

After 1945, more enhancements were incorporated into carrier design. The addition of helicopters allowed carriers to launch operations against enemy submarines and also to land marines to secure coastal positions. The angled flight deck allowed aircraft to take off while others were landing. In 1961 the U.S.S. *Enterprise* was completed—at 75,700 tons it was the largest aircraft carrier ever built. It could carry 100 aircraft and, being nuclear-powered, had a cruising range the equivalent of 20 times around the world.

In 1967 the British decided that they would phase out fixed-wing aircraft in favor of the Vertical Short Take-Off and Landing (VSTOL) BAe Sea Harrier. The upward-angled ski-slope deck made takeoffs easier for Harriers, and subsequently both Italy and Spain have adopted this less expensive option of a carrier equipped with Harriers. In the mid-1970s the Soviet Union began building carriers equipped with VSTOL Yakovlev Yak-36MP "Forger" aircraft and helicopters.

Carriers were involved in the Korean War, at Suez in 1956, in Vietnam, in the Falklands, and in the Gulf War of 1990–1991.

▼ CARRIER POWER
This U.S. Navy Kitty Hawk-class
conventionally powered carrier
has a crew of nearly 6,000. It
can carry up to 50 planes,
including F-14 Tomcats
and F-18 Hornets, as
well as
helicopters.

▼ BATTLE GROUP
A modern naval battle group is built up around a carrier, with supporting vessels to provide cover against enemy aircraft, surface vessels, and submarines. The carrier's combat aircraft can attack ships and installations at a safe range from the group.

Key Dates

- 1911 Eugene Ely flies off a ship.
- 1913 H.M.S. *Hermes* is commissioned.
- 1940 November 11: British Fleet Air Arm air attack on Italian fleet at Taranto.
- 1941 December 7: Japanese carrier aircraft attack U.S. Navy in Pearl Harbor.
- 1942 May: Major carrier action in Battle of the Coral Sea.
- 1942 June 4–7: Battle of Midway.
- 1961 U.S.S. *Enterprise* is first nuclear-powered carrier.

Early Fighter Planes

▲ RED BARON
The German fighter ace Baron Manfred von Richthofen was killed in 1918. He commanded a squadron called the "flying circus."

THE EARLY PILOTS were often wealthy and enterprising sportsmen, so the idea of shooting at each other in war was considered to be ungentlemanly. However, it was not long before pilots carried rifles and pistols when flying, and took pot shots at each other. The first true fighter action took place during World War I on October 5, 1914, when a French Voisin V89 brought down a German Aviatik aircraft with its machine-gun fire.

The interrupter gear invented by the Dutchman Anthony Fokker allowed German aircraft to fire forward through the arc of their propeller. This meant that fighter pilots could aim their aircraft at enemy planes.

▶ FOKKER TRIPLANE
The German World War I Fokker Dr-1 fighter had a maximum speed of 24mph and was armed with two .31 inch Spandau machine guns.

Between 1914 and 1918 aircraft speeds increased from 105mph to 168mph. The first fighters flew at a height of 13,000 feet, but by the end of the war they were up to 19,700 feet.

One of the most successful British fighters was the SE-5a. It had a maximum speed of 41mph and was armed with a single synchronized Vickers or Lewis machine gun. The German D1 Albatross had a maximum speed of 34mph and was armed with twin .31inch Spandau machine guns.

The interwar period saw the development of the all-metal aircraft with wing-mounted machine guns and also cannon that fired explosive rounds. By 1939 the Messerschmitt Bf-109E had a top speed of 355mph, and by 1945 the 109G with a 1,900hp inline engine had a top speed of 428mph. Armament was a 1¼ inch cannon and two .31 inch machine guns.

The World War II Allied fighters, the British Supermarine Spitfire, and the North American P-51 Mustang were classic types. The Mustang, fitted with

FIGHTERS OF THE WORLD WARS
Early fighters were slow scout planes with simple armament. By the beginning of World War II they were all-metal monoplanes with cannon as well as machine guns. By the close of the war the first jet fighters were in action, and many aircraft were equipped with radar.

◀ BATTLE OF BRITAIN
A Spitfire with a postwar Merlin-engined Messerschmitt Me-109 photographed during the film *The Battle of Britain*. Spain used the Messerschmitt 109 after the war but put in new engines to improve its performance.

▲ P-38 LIGHTNING
With a top speed of 414mph the Lockheed Lightning, introduced in 1941, was armed with four machine guns and a .8 inch cannon. It could carry 4500lbs. of bombs.

Aerial

Armor plate

◀ HAWKER HURRICANE
*Armed with eight .303inch
machine guns, the Hurricane
was older and slower than the
Spitfire. However, it shot down
more German planes during
the Battle of Britain than the
Spitfire did. Hurricane pilots
concentrated on attacking the
slower, more vulnerable
bombers, while Spitfires fought
with the escorting
Messerschmitt 109 fighters.*

Cine camera

Radio

Battery

Reserve gasoline tank (armored)

Gasoline tank

Merlin II engine

Ammunition boxes

Four Browning 0.303inch
machine guns

Landing light

▼ "THE FEW"
*RAF Spitfire pilots wait on an airstrip in the
long summer air battle of 1940 that was
called the Battle of Britain. The small
number of pilots were nicknamed "The Few"
following a speech by Winston Churchill.*

extra fuel tanks, had a top speed of
437mph and sufficient range to allow
pilots to escort bombers to Berlin and back. The Spitfire
went through 21 different marks between 1936 and
1945, becoming a more powerful and more heavily
armed fighter with each version. The Spitfire MIX,
powered by a Rolls-Royce 1,660hp Merlin engine, had
a top speed of 657kph and was armed with .303inch
machine guns and .8 inch cannon.

Some of the fighters continued in service into the
1950s and 1960s as ground-attack aircraft. Those
fighter aircraft that are still flying today are in the hands
of aviation enthusiasts.

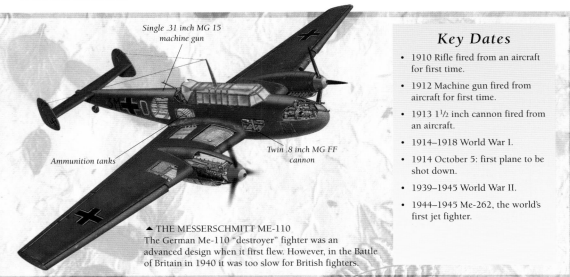

Single .31 inch MG 15
machine gun

Key Dates

- 1910 Rifle fired from an aircraft
  for first time.

- 1912 Machine gun fired from
  aircraft for first time.

- 1913 1½ inch cannon fired from
  an aircraft.

- 1914–1918 World War I.

- 1914 October 5: first plane to be
  shot down.

- 1939–1945 World War II.

- 1944–1945 Me-262, the world's
  first jet fighter.

Twin .8 inch MG FF
cannon

Ammunition tanks

▲ THE MESSERSCHMITT ME-110
The German Me-110 "destroyer" fighter was an
advanced design when it first flew. However, in the Battle
of Britain in 1940 it was too slow for British fighters.

Jet Fighters

URING THE 1930s aircraft powered by jet propulsion featured in science fiction comics, along with men from Mars and moon rockets. However, both the British and the Germans were conducting research in this field before World War II. The first jet to fly was the German He-178 in 1939, followed by the British Gloster Meteor, which flew fitted with jet engines in 1941. The two planes never met in combat, but science fiction became reality in 1944 when RAF Meteors took to the air to chase and shoot down German V-1 flying bombs.

Deliveries of the world's first operational jet-powered fighter, the German Messerschmitt Me-262 *Schwalbe* (Swallow), began in May 1944. However, these aircraft were initially configured as bombers, and the fighter did not enter service until later that year. It had a maximum speed of 540mph and was armed with four 1¼inch cannons, and 24 2inch R4M rockets. Me-262s took a heavy toll of U.S. Army Air Force (USAAF) bombers during 1945. On the Allied side, the Gloster Meteor had a maximum speed of 410mph and was armed with four 8inch cannons.

The Korean War saw the first jet-versus-jet action when U.S. Air Force F-86 Sabres, F-80 Shooting Stars and U.S. Marine Corps F9F Panthers fought with Chinese MiG-15s. The first victory went to a U.S. Air Force (USAF) F-80 Shooting Star on November 8, 1950 against a Chinese MiG-15 over the Yalu River.

Jet fighters have been in action, either in air combat or attacking ground targets, in most parts of the world since the 1950s. Over North Vietnam, in the conflicts between India and Pakistan, in the Arab–Israeli wars, in the Gulf Wars between Iran and Iraq, and between the Coalition Forces and Iraq, U.S.-designed aircraft have fought with Soviet aircraft. In the Falklands in 1982 British Harriers were pitted against U.S. and French-designed aircraft. Soviet jet aircraft were used in ground attack operations during the Afghan War.

Among the most versatile jet fighter aircraft are the Russian MiG-21 and the American McDonnell Douglas F-4 Phantom, which

◀ FIGHTING FALCON
The American F-16 Fighting Falcon multi-role fighter is made by General Dynamics, and is in service in more than 14 countries worldwide. Painted in striking livery, it is flown by the USAF Thunderbirds display team.

A NEW BREED OF WAR PLANE

Immediately after World War II there was a move to design and build jet fighters. U.S. and Chinese jets clashed in the Korean War in 1950–1953. Although missiles such as the Sidewinder have been widely used in combat, the 1¼ inch cannon is still a very effective weapon and can be used against ground targets.

◀ MIRAGE 5
The French Dassault fighter has a top speed of 1,188mph. Operating in a ground-attack role, the Mirage can carry bombs, rockets, or missiles.

▼ PHANTOM
The F-4 Phantom has been built in larger numbers than any Western combat aircraft since World War II.

▲ F86 SABRE
The first woman to fly faster than sound, Jacqueline Cochran, achieved the record in a Sabre on May 18, 1953.

▲ HAWK
The British BAe Hawk is a versatile combat plane which can also be used as a trainer.

▼ FORGER
The Russian Yak-38, or "Forger," was a vertical take-off combat plane that first flew in 1971.

Weapons system
ranging radar

IFF aerials
(identification
friend or foe)

Koliesov lift
engines

GSh-23L
cannon pack

▼ HARRIER
The BAe Harrier has proved an effective fighter and ground-attack aircraft in the Falklands and in the Gulf War.

have fought in Vietnam and the Middle East.

In many of these combats the AIM-9 Sidewinder heat-seeking air-to-air missile has been the key weapon. The AIM-9 heat-seeking missile takes its inspiration from nature. The sidewinder snake locates its prey by detecting their body heat with special sensors in its head. The AIM-9 Sidewinder missile detects the heat from the engine exhausts of its target.

▲ EAGLE
A missile-armed USAF McDonnell Douglas F-15 Eagle multi-role fighter maneuvers into position during in-flight refueling.

▼ EUROFIGHTER
Built by a consortium of Spain, Germany, Italy, and Britain, the Eurofighter Typhoon first flew on March 29, 1994. The project has been hampered by political problems because Germany has reduced its requirement and has argued for a less expensive aircraft now that the Cold War has ended.

Key Dates

- 1939 German Heinkel He-178 jet fighter flies

- 1944 German Me-262 enters service

- 1944 British Gloster Meteor in action against V-1 flying bombs

- 1944 Lockheed Shooting Star enters service with USAAF/USAF

- 1945 December 3: De Havilland Vampire makes first jet landing and takeoff from a carrier

- 1950 First jet-versus-jet victory in Korean War

- 1966 August 31: Hawker Harrier makes first hovering flight

Early Bombers

▲ LANCASTER
The British bomber was used in the "Dam Buster" raids against Germany.

THE POTENTIAL FOR AIRCRAFT to operate as a platform for delivering bombs to enemy targets was realized as early as 1911. In that year the first bombs were dropped from an aircraft during the Italo-Turkish war.

In World War I bombers started as scout planes, in which the crew had taken a few grenades to lob at the enemy lines. Bombers grew from these small single-engined two-seater aircraft to types such as the British Handley Page 0/400. Around 550 of these twin-engined bombers were built. When they attacked German military and industrial targets, they flew in formations of 30–40 aircraft.

The German Gotha GIV and GV bombers attacked targets in London and southern England in World War I. They carried between 750lbs. and 1250lbs. of bombs, had a crew of three, and were capable of 109mph with a range of 373 miles.

In the interwar period there was considerable fear that bombers carrying bombs loaded with poison gas would attack large cities, causing huge casualties. The German Air Force was re-formed secretly after World War I, and the sleek Heinkel He-111 and Dornier Do 17, both described as airliners, were re-engineered as bombers for World War II. The He-111 carried 6250lbs. of bombs and the Do 17 2500lbs. The Junkers Ju 87 became notorious as the Stuka dive bomber, and the Ju 88 made the transition from bomber to heavily armed fighter.

◀ HANDLEY PAGE 0/400
With a crew of three the RAF Handley Page 0/400 could carry up to 2,250lbs. of bombs. It was armed with up to five .303inch Lewis machine guns.

BOMBERS OF THE WORLD WARS

In the two World Wars the payload and range of bombers increased dramatically. At the beginning of World War II the German He-111 was carrying 6250lbs. of bombs at 261mph. By the close of World War II the four-engined Avro Lancaster was carrying 15,875lbs. of bombs at 287mph for 1,600 miles.

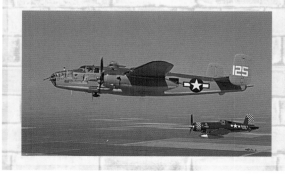

◀ B-25 MITCHELL
A U.S. Mitchell medium bomber escorted by a Vought F-4U Corsair carrier-based fighter. The Mitchell could carry 3500lbs. of bombs. Several examples of Mitchells have been restored in the U.S.

▲ LANCASTER
The RAF Avro Lancaster entered service in March 1942 and became the mainstay of the bombing campaign against Germany. By 1944 there were 40 Lancaster squadrons in action.

▶ B-17 FLYING FORTRESS
The B-17 could carry 6,750lbs. of bombs
at 312mph. By the end of the war over
4,700 were in front line service with the USAAF.

On the Allied side, bombers grew in size, range, and bomb load. In 1939, the Vickers Wellington could carry 7500lbs. of bombs. By 1945 the Avro Lancaster could carry 15,875lbs. of bombs to 1,658 miles. The USAAF Boeing B-17 had a maximum bomb load of 14,500lbs. and a range of 3,298 miles. The Consolidated B-24 Liberator carried up to 9,000lbs. of bombs at 300mph.

Supporters of strategic bombing say that it made a major contribution to the Allied victory in World War II. However, despite the importance of bombing, history has shown that victory is guaranteed only when ground forces enter enemy territory and occupy it.

▼ DRESDEN 1945
German authorities sort through bodies in the ghastly aftermath of the attack on Dresden. Attacked by 773 RAF bombers by night and by the USAAF during the day, nearly 8 square miles were destroyed by fire. In the overcrowded city more than 100,000 died in the firestorm.

Key Dates

- 1911 Bombs first dropped in the Italo-Turkish War.

- 1914–1918 World War I: tactical and rudimentary strategic bombing established.

- 1936–1939 Spanish Civil War: tactical bombing perfected.

- 1939–1945 World War II: first strategic bombing.

- 1942 Pressurized B-29 Superfortress flies.

- 1944–1945 German Arado 234 jet bomber in action.

- 1945 Atomic bombs dropped on Japan by B-29s.

Modern Jets and Stealth

THE CLOAK OF INVISIBILITY is a feature of many ancient myths. Although it may not be a reality, new techniques in aircraft design have made planes very hard to detect by systems such as radar. These features are known as "stealth," and all modern combat aircraft now have some stealth features. Stealth in aircraft design is the attempt to minimize the ways in which aircraft can be detected by ground or airborne air defense systems.

In its earliest form, camouflage paint was a stealth feature, but the echo from radar would show the location of the most ingeniously camouflaged plane. One technique for defeating early radars was to fly very low and so hide the aircraft among the clutter of radar echoes. Modern radars can now discriminate between clutter and moving targets, so the next move was to design a plane that gave very little or no radar return. This was achieved by giving the plane as few surfaces as possible

▶ STEALTH
The Lockheed/Boeing F-22A Rapier, the new fighter for the USAF, has "stealth" features within its design.

from which a radar beam could bounce off and so give an echo. Besides having a profile designed to avoid radar, the plane was coated with a radar-absorbent material which would further reduce or limit the echo. If there is no discernible radar echo, the heat from

▲ NIGHTHAWK
The Lockheed F-117A Nighthawk first saw action in 1989 in Panama and later in 1991 in the Gulf. An F-117 was shot down over the former Yugoslavia in 1999.

MODERN DEVELOPMENTS

Radar and thermal detection systems have made combat aircraft vulnerable, even if they are flying low and at night. Since radar reflects off flat hard surfaces, any plane with a less angular shape and a "radar-absorbent" coating is less likely to be detected. The engines produce hot gases which can be picked up by radar. However, these gases can be cooled or screened before they pass into the air.

F-107 WR-400 turbofan jet engine

Folding wings

Nuclear warhead

Tercom guidance system

▶ SCALE MODEL
A wind-tunnel model of an American experimental combat aircraft. Computer modeling is used to evaluate new designs.

▲ CRUISE MISSILE
The German V-1, the earliest cruise missile, was slow and fairly inaccurate. In the late 1970s the United States produced a cruise missile that could be launched from land, sea, or air. It has a guidance system that is very accurate and can fly a circuitous route to its target. Cruise missiles have been used in the Middle East and Serbia.

▼ FIGHTER
The Boeing Joint Strike Fighter will replace several types of combat aircraft from 2004.

▶ BOEING B-52
The veteran USAF B-52 strategic bomber has been used since 1955. It can carry up to 22,680kg of air - launched cruise missiles or 51 1,135lb. conventional bombs.

▶ SPIRIT
The Northrop Grumman B-2A looks back to the German Gotha flying design which was developed at the close of World War II. The B-2A can carry 57,700lbs. of ordnance at 475mph and has a range of 11,500 miles with one refuelling.

the engines of a modern aircraft can still be detected. The solution to this problem is to position the engines so that the hot gases from them flow over the top of the wings. The gases are cooled as they pass over special ceramic plates.

The classic stealth aircraft are the U.S. Lockheed F-117 fighter, which was used in action in 1989 as a bomber in the invasion of Panama and later in attacks on Iraq in 1991. An F-117 was shot down during the air attacks on Serbia in 1999.

The Northrop B-2 Advanced Technology Bomber is a dedicated stealth bomber. It is capable of carrying 42,300lbs. of ordnance over a maximum range of 6,096 miles.

The USAF Advanced Tactical Fighter program took place in the 1990s. It was a competition between the Lockheed/General Dynamics YF-22 and the McDonnell Douglas YF-23, two fighters with stealth features. The Lockheed aircraft, now designated the F-22 Rapier, has been accepted and will enter service by 2011.

▼ STEALTH TECHNOLOGY
Although stealth is associated with aircraft, it has also been employed in the design of modern combat ships and even in tanks. Ships and tanks can be detected on radar and thermal imaging, so their exhausts need to be screened and any radar-reflective surfaces have to be softened.

Engines are either side of the cockpit. The exhaust flows are set well forward. This allows the exhaust to cool as much as possible as it passes over the wings, minimizing the heat trail.

Two-person crew compartment

Sawtooth trailing edge minimizes radar visibility by breaking up the normal straight edge of a wing.

Key Dates

- 1951 Canberra bomber is the first jet to fly across the North Atlantic nonstop.

- 1955 B-52 enters service with the USAF.

- 1977 December: first flight of Lockheed Martin F-117.

- 1983–1984 U.S. stealth research ship *Sea Shadow* built.

- 1989 July 17: first flight of Northrop Grumman B-2A Spirit.

- 1991 March 14: Smyge Swedish stealth patrol craft launched.

- 1991 April: F-22 Rapier selected by USAF.

Airborne Troops

▲ PARACHUTE
The light fabric of a parachute traps air, slowing down the descent of the soldier or paratrooper.

IT IS HARD FOR US to realize how unusual paratroops seemed when they first appeared, in World War II. Most soldiers had never traveled in an airplane, so men who arrived by parachute from planes seemed almost as fantastic as spacemen. The Soviet Union pioneered airborne forces in the interwar years. However, it was Nazi Germany that made first use of them in World War II.

Airborne troops could be delivered to the battlefield either by parachute or in gliders. Troop-carrying gliders carried between 10 and 29 troops and could also be used to transport vehicles and light artillery. They were particularly effective when an operation called for a formed group of men to attack a target such as a bridge or coastal artillery battery. The problem with paratroops was that they could be scattered over a large area if they jumped from too high a position.

The German attack on the island of Crete in May 1941 involved 22,500 paratroops and 80 gliders. The airborne forces suffered very heavy losses: 4,000 were killed, 2,000 wounded, and 220 aircraft were destroyed. Hitler declared that "the day of the

paratrooper is over." The Americans and British were quick to learn from the Germans' mistakes, and airborne forces were used on D-Day in Normandy in June 1944. Airborne forces were also in Sicily in 1943, and at the Rhine crossings in 1945. In Burma in 1943, British and Commonwealth troops known as Chindits were landed by glider deep inside Japanese lines. In this way they drew Japanese forces away from the front lines in India.

After World War II, the French made extensive use of paratroops in Indochina (Vietnam) between 1948 and 1954. However, in May 1954 at

▶ PARATROOPER
A British paratrooper in World War II. The buckle in the middle of his chest operates as a quick release for the parachute harness.

▲ JUMPING FOR FUN
A sports parachutist exits from an aircraft in the "spread stable position." Before he pulls the release on his parachute he will enjoy a period of "free fall."

AIRBORNE OPERATIONS
Attacks by paratroops and glider-borne soldiers in World War II were sometimes a gamble, because these lightly equipped soldiers could be defeated by ground troops with tanks and artillery. If friendly ground forces could link up with them, airborne troops could sieze and hold key positions such as bridges, fortifications, and causeways. They could help to keep up the momentum of an attack.

▶ TRANSPORTATION
Transport planes can carry trucks and vehicles which can be unloaded if a suitable airfield has been captured and secured.

▲ DROP ZONE
Parachutes float down and collapse in a mass military drop. The flat area allocated for such an operation is called a drop zone, or DZ. Helicopters put down soldiers on a landing zone, or LZ.

Dien Bien Phu they were defeated when they set up an airborne base deep inside Viet Minh lines. They lost 11 complete parachute battalions in the fighting.

On November 5, 1956 French and British paratroops landed at Port Said to recapture the Suez Canal, which had been nationalized by the Egyptians.

Today, helicopters mean troops no longer need to parachute from aircraft. However, airborne forces are still considered an elite group within all national armies.

▲ SEALS
These Seals, U.S. Navy Special Forces troops, are wearing harnesses that clip onto a ladder. They are being lifted by a Chinook helicopter.

▶ HOW A PARACHUTE WORKS
The umbrella shape of the parachute, called a canopy, was first made from silk; later, nylon. It traps air and so slows the descent of the parachutist or cargo. A small hole in the center canopy allows air to escape and prevents the parachute from swinging from side to side.

Modern square parachutes are called "ram air." They can be steered, allowing the parachutist to land with very great accuracy. The latest development is a remotely controlled steerable canopy which can be used by special forces in remote locations to take delivery of cargo. The load is dropped at a great height.

Key Dates

- 1797 Parachute invented.

- 1927 Italians are first to drop a "stick" of paratroops.

- 1930s Soviet forces develop paratroops.

- 1939–1945 Airborne operations in Europe and Far East.

- 1941 German airborne attack on island of Crete.

- 1944 British and Polish landings at Arnhem.

- 1953–1954 Battle of Dien Bien Phu in Vietnam.

- 1956 French and British paratroops capture Suez Canal.

Helicopters

A S THEY CLATTER IN AND OUT of heliports, helicopters are an everyday sight. Most people think that they are a postwar invention. However, the first free flight by a tandem-rotor device was by Paul Cornu on November 13, 1907. Igor Sikorsky built two helicopters in Russia in 1909–1910.

Helicopters were used at the close of World War II, and in Korea and Indo-China the Americans and French used them to evacuate wounded soldiers from the battlefield. The most widely used helicopters in this period were the Sikorsky H-19 and the Bell H-13 Sioux.

▲ SEA KNIGHT
A U.S. Marine Corps Sea Knight with an underslung load lifts off.

On November 5, 1956, at the Suez Canal, British Royal Marines were landed by helicopter in the first airborne assault. In the Algerian war of 1954–1962 the French used helicopters to carry troops. The helicopters were fitted with anti-tank missiles and machine guns.

The American involvement in Vietnam, from 1962 to 1975, saw the use of helicopters in assault, casualty evacuation, and transportation and liaison missions. In airborne assaults 16 troop-carrying helicopters nicknamed "Slicks" were supported by 9 attack

▲ APACHE
The U.S. Army's Apache attack helicopter has a crew of two and a maximum speed of 227mph.

Warhead   Autopilot electronics   Fuse   Laser seeker   Propulsion section

▶ HELLFIRE
This laser-guided anti-tank missile was used in action in the Gulf by U.S. Army Apache helicopters.

VERTICAL FLIGHT

Helicopters are used in wartime to transport troops, casualties, and supplies. They can rescue shot-down pilots and attack ships, submarines, and ground targets. Some are even equipped for air-to-air combat.

▼ OSPREY
The American Bell Boeing Osprey tilt-rotor aircraft can carry up to 24 combat-equipped troops or 22,675lbs. of cargo. The U.S. Marine Corps was an enthusiastic advocate of the Osprey, which can transport troops quickly from offshore to secure beachheads.

▲ TRANSPORT
The Boeing Vertol CH-47 Chinook has a crew of two and can carry up to 44 troops.

▲ RESCUE
A British Royal Navy GKN Westland Sea King has airborne early-warning radar to warn surface ships about enemy missiles or warships. The Sea King can also winch people from the sea.

▶ BLACKHAWK
The Sikorsky UH-60 Blackhawk has a crew of two and can carry 12 soldiers.

Hellfire missiles

Rotor head

Rotor mast

Blade pitch control rods

Electronics bay

Solar T-62T-40-1 auxiliary power unit

Nose glazing

▲ TROOP MOBILITY
The big doors of a Blackhawk allow infantry to dismount quickly.

Main undercarriage

M-23D .3 inch machine gun

Engine intake

General Electric T700-GE-700 turboshaft engine

Gear box

Titanium and glass-fiber rotor blades

helicopters nicknamed "gunships." The gunships were armed with 48 rockets and machine guns. The Bell H-1 Iroquois, which is universally known as the Huey, became the helicopter of the Vietnam War. Since 1958, some 9,440 Hueys have been built. The Bell AH-1 Cobra was the first dedicated attack helicopter and became the first helicopter to destroy tanks with anti-tank missiles from the air. The Boeing Vertol CH-47 Chinook twin-rotor helicopter was widely used to carry between 22 and 50 troops. By the end of the Vietnam War, the United States had lost nearly 5,000 helicopters.

The Soviet Union looked to the Cobra and developed the Mi-24 attack helicopter, which is known by NATO as the Hind. It saw action in Afghanistan between 1979

and 1989. Among the helicopters produced by the Soviet Union was the Mi-26 "Halo." It could carry 20 tonnes and was used to dump lead and concrete on the nuclear reactor at Chernobyl following its dramatic explosion in 1986.

The American Sikorsky H-60 Blackhawk troop-carrying helicopter and the McDonnell-Douglas H-64 Apache attack helicopter were used by the U.S. Army in the Gulf War in 1991.

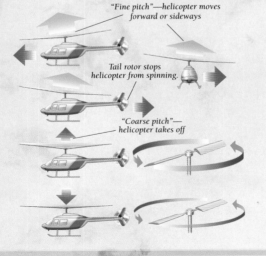

▶ HOW IT WORKS
A helicopter is sometimes known as a "rotary wing aircraft" because its main rotor can be tilted. This creates the current of air that flows over the wings to lift the aircraft into the sky. The angle of tilt of the rotor blades is called pitch, and "coarse pitch" is the sharp angle needed to lift the helicopter off the ground. The smaller tail rotor pushes against the rotation of the main rotor and so keeps the helicopter flying straight and level.

"Fine pitch"—helicopter moves forward or sideways

Tail rotor stops helicopter from spinning.

"Coarse pitch"— helicopter takes off

Key Dates

- 1500 Leonardo da Vinci sketches helicopter idea.

- 1907 September 29: first helicopter lifts a man off the ground into the air.

- 1914–1918 Austrians fly helicopters in World War I.

- 1942 American Sikorsky R-4 becomes first military helicopter.

- 1963 First true attack helicopter, the American Model 207 Sioux Scout.

- 1991 February 24: 300 helicopters used in Gulf War in the largest aerial assault in the history of aviation.

Doomsday Weapons

▲ GAS DRILL
British soldiers wear anti-gas uniforms during a gas drill in 1939.

FOR CENTURIES WARS HAVE caused destruction on a large scale. However, it was not until the 20th century that the term "weapons of mass destruction" (WMD) came into use to describe chemical, biological, and nuclear weapons. Yet biological and chemical weapons are some of the oldest in existence.

In ancient times armies poisoned wells with dead animals or used disease-bearing rats to spread infection around besieged cities.

The first modern use of chemical weapons was in World War I. On April 22, 1915, the Germans released chlorine in support of an attack against the British and French at Ypres. In World War I most of the types of war gases that now exist were developed; these caused temporary choking and blistering on the skin or poisoned the blood. The blistering agent was called mustard gas because of its mustard-like smell.

By the end of World War I these gases had been contained in artillery shells. The shells were fired as part of a conventional high-explosive barrage when soldiers attacked.

▶ RESPIRATOR
These U.S. troops are equipped with the ABC-M17 respirator, which is a hood that fits over the head.

WEAPONS OF MASS DESTRUCTION

Nuclear, biological, and chemical weapons are particularly horrible because the damage they cause can be vast and almost open-ended. Viruses and germs used in biological weapons reproduce themselves and radiation after a nuclear explosion remains a hazard for centuries. These facts distinguish these weapons from conventional explosives, whose effect lasts for just one detonation.

None of the weapons of mass destruction has a localized effect like that of explosives. Wind and weather can spread the damage.

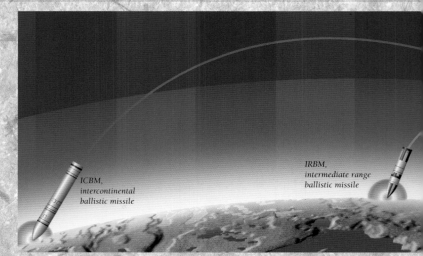

ICBM, intercontinental ballistic missile

IRBM, intermediate range ballistic missile

▼ FIRST ATOMIC BOMB
This bomb, codenamed "Little Boy," was dropped on Hiroshima on August 6, 1945. It had the power of 20,000 tonnes of TNT. It killed 78,150 people and destroyed 4 square miles of the city.

▲ BALLISTIC MISSILE
A U.S. ballistic missile lifts off during a test launch. With improved guidance, missiles are very accurate and capable of hitting small targets such as enemy missile silos.

The chemists of Nazi Germany produced the most effective chemical agent when they discovered nerve gas poisons. Called Tabun, Sarin, and Soman, they affected the human nervous system and killed within a few minutes. The Nazis never used this weapon, because they feared that the Allies also possessed it and would retaliate; in fact, the Allies did not have the weapon.

Iraq used mustard and nerve gases in 1984 during the Iran–Iraq war (1980–1988). They caused 40,000 deaths and injuries to the unprotected Iranian troops.

Atomic weapons were developed in the U.S. during World War II by a team of Europeans and Americans led by Robert Oppenheimer. They worked by releasing the energy from splitting the atom of uranium ore. The drive for this program had been the fear that German physicists might be developing a similar bomb. The first atomic bomb test took place in New Mexico on July 16, 1945. On August 6, an atomic bomb codenamed "Little Boy" was dropped on the Japanese city of Hiroshima. Three days later a device codenamed "Fat Man" was dropped on the city of Nagasaki. The explosions were the equivalent of the detonation of 20,000 tonnes of high explosives. In Hiroshima more than 70,000 people died or disappeared: in Nagasaki the figure was 40,000.

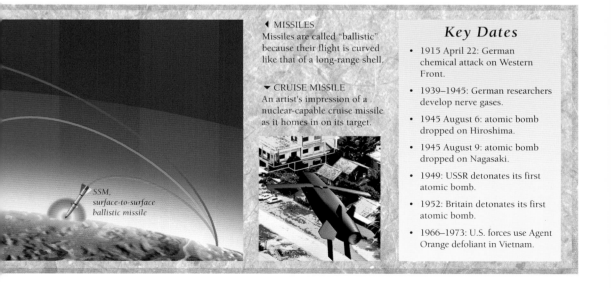

◀ MISSILES
Missiles are called "ballistic" because their flight is curved like that of a long-range shell.

▼ CRUISE MISSILE
An artist's impression of a nuclear-capable cruise missile as it homes in on its target.

SSM, surface-to-surface ballistic missile

Key Dates

- 1915 April 22: German chemical attack on Western Front.

- 1939–1945: German researchers develop nerve gases.

- 1945 August 6: atomic bomb dropped on Hiroshima.

- 1945 August 9: atomic bomb dropped on Nagasaki.

- 1949: USSR detonates its first atomic bomb.

- 1952: Britain detonates its first atomic bomb.

- 1966–1973: U.S. forces use Agent Orange defoliant in Vietnam.

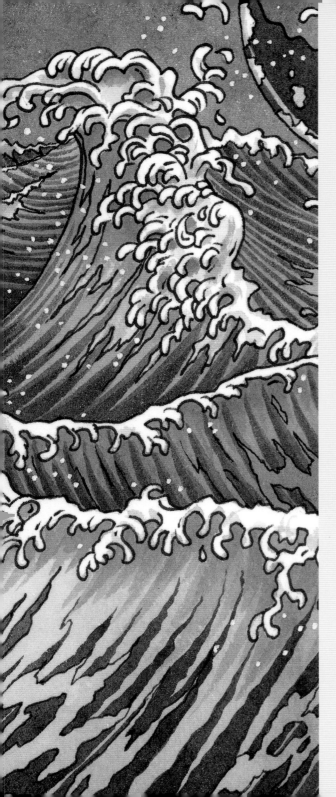

REFERENCE

Ancient Civilizations

The first civilizations tended to develop in areas with fertile land, a good water supply and an even climate. This was because people had to develop efficient farming methods and ways of storing and trading food before they could build large cities. The type of soil, the distance from water sources, whether the ground was high or low, and the climate, all affected the nature of the civilization that emerged in any given area. In North Africa and the Middle East, great rivers such as the Nile in Egypt and the Tigris and Euphrates in Mesopotamia (in present-day Iraq) allowed the development of increasingly complex civilizations. Natural barriers, such as mountains or deserts, limited the growth of some civilizations, such as the Greek city-states. By contrast, the landscapes of Central and South America were important in creating and defining the unique cultures that developed there.

HELLENISTIC AGE
Alexander the Great (356–323 B.C.) was a brilliant general who built up a huge empire, including Macedonia, Greece, Egypt and Persia.

THE ETRUSCANS
From 800–100 B.C., the Etruscans built a series of cities between the Arno and Tiber rivers in western Italy.

NORTH AMERICAN PEOPLE
The Hopewell civilization in North America began in around 200 B.C.

EARLY MEXICANS
The Olmecs ruled north-central Mexico between 1200–900 B.C.

CENTRAL AMERICAN SUCCESS
The Maya civilization lasted between 300 B.C.–A.D. 900. Maya cities were built in southern Mexico, Guatemala, Honduras and Belize.

AFRICAN CIVILIZATIONS
Many civilizations and kingdoms developed on the huge continent of Africa. That of Benin flourished from A.D. 1100–1897.

PEOPLE OF THE ANDES
The civilization of Chavin de Huantar in the high Andes mountains reached its peak from 850–200 B.C.

ANCIENT ROME
The mighty Roman Empire developed from the city of Rome in central Italy. It was at its largest extent in A.D. 117.

ANCIENT EGYPT
On the fertile Nile Delta in northern Africa, the ancient Egyptian civilization flourished between 3100 B.C. and 333 B.C.

THE MYCENAEANS

In 1600 B.C., this warlike group came to power in mainland Greece.

CLASSICAL GREECE

Greek city-states developed around 700 B.C. The Greeks did not have a huge empire but their learning had a great influence on the Western civilizations that followed.

MINOAN CRETE

The Greek island of Crete was home to the Minoan civilization, which flourished around 2000–1700 B.C.

THE HITTITES

This warlike people from central Anatolia (modern Turkey) were at the height of their power between 1600 and 1200 B.C.

THE ASSYRIANS

Between 744 and 727 B.C. Assyria (modern-day Iraq) reached its greatest power. The Assyrians were the most feared people of the ancient world.

EARLY JAPAN

Japan is a chain of islands between China and the Pacific Ocean. In A.D. 350 the Yamato emperor ruled the whole of Japan.

ANCIENT CHINA

Civilization in China grew up separately from the rest of the world. One of the earliest ruling families was the Shang dynasty, begun in 1650 B.C.

INDUS VALLEY

Two great cities, Mohenjo-Daro and Harappa, grew up on the plain of the Indus river (in present-day Pakistan) around 2500 B.C.

PARTHIANS AND SASSANIANS

The Parthian dynasty ruled the Persian lands (modern-day Iran) from 240 B.C.–A.D. 226. They were followed by the even more successful Sassanians (A.D. 226–646).

PERSIAN EMPIRE

The Persians were a small nation from the region near Babylon. By 549 B.C., their empire stretched from modern Turkey to India.

ANCIENT BABYLON

Babylon on the Euphrates river was the chief city of the Amorites from around 1900 B.C.

THE SUMERIANS

The Sumerians were a farming people from southern Mesopotamia (in present-day Iraq). They established a city at Ur in 2100 B.C.

THE KHMERS

Deep in the jungles of Cambodia in Southeast Asia, the Khmer civilization flourished. It was founded in A.D. 802. The civilization lasted for 500 years.

World Exploration

The desire to know the world in which we live has led many brave people to explore wild regions, risking their lives in the pursuit of discovery. Throughout history, trade has been the main driving force of exploration. It was the search for a new trade route to China and India that sent Vasco da Gama into the Indian Ocean, and Christopher Columbus across the Atlantic. Many European explorers set out seeking fame and fortune. Others were motivated by religious conviction, feeling it was their duty to convert other races to Christianity. Today, there are few places on Earth that have not been fully explored, except for the high mountains of Tibet and the ocean floor.

AROUND THE WORLD

In trying to find a westerly route to the Spice Islands in Indonesia, the Portuguese sailor Ferdinand Magellan and his crew became the first people to circumnavigate the Earth.

EXPLORING CANADA

In May 1497, the Italian adventurer John Cabot set sail from Bristol, England. A month later he landed in Newfoundland off the coast of Canada.

THE NEW WORLD

Early explorers returned from Central and South America with stories of vast temples and huge amounts of gold. In 1521, a Spanish lawyer named Hernán Cortés made his fortune by seizing the Aztec capital city of Tenochtitlán and capturing its ruler.

HEYERDAHL'S VOYAGE

The Norwegian explorer Thor Heyerdahl set out to prove that the Polynesians could have come originally from South America. He built a raft, like those used by early settlers, and sailed from Peru to the South Pacific.

THE VOYAGE OF COLUMBUS

An Italian named Christopher Columbus devoted his life to finding a sea route to Asia by sailing west across the Atlantic Ocean. Financially supported by Queen Isabella of Spain, he set out in 1492, and after 36 days at sea, he found what we now call the Bahamas.

VIKING EXPEDITIONS

In A.D. 992, Leif Eriksson set out from the Viking colony of Greenland, traveling due west. He sailed via Baffin Island to a place in eastern Canada he called Vinland.

THE NORTHEAST PASSAGE

In 1878, Nils Nordenskjold tried to find a route northeast from Europe to the Pacific Ocean. He set out from southern Sweden on board his ship the Vega. In 1879 he finally sailed into the Pacific Ocean.

DEVOTED TO TRAVEL

Ibn Battuta was born in 1304. He spent a total of 28 years traveling around the Islamic Empire, as well as much of Europe, Southeast Asia and China.

MARCO POLO

The explorer Marco Polo was born in Venice. He claimed to have stayed in China for 20 years, from 1271.

THE SILK ROAD

Merchants from Europe, the Middle East, central Asia and China traveled along the Silk Road to buy and sell goods.

DR LIVINGSTONE

The missionary and doctor, David Livingstone, went to Africa to convert the local people to Christianity. Once there, however, he traveled extensively and helped to transform European knowledge about Africa.

ROUTE TO INDIA

The Portuguese navigator Vasco da Gama was the first European to reach India by sea. Between 1497 and 1498 he traveled around the coast of Africa, eventually arriving in India.

INTO AFRICA

From the 1760s Europeans explored northern and central Africa, mapping the Nile and Niger rivers and the Sahara Desert. The south, however, remained largely unexplored by Europeans until the late 1800s.

COOK

Between 1768 and 1779, James Cook of the British Royal Navy explored much of the Pacific Ocean, including Eastern Australia, which he called New South Wales.

Timeline 2 million–1 B.C.

	2 million–12,000 B.C.	12,000–10,000 B.C.	10,000–3000 B.C.
EUROPE	**1 million years ago–400,000 B.C.** First known settlement of *Homo erectus* in Europe. **400,000–30,000 B.C.** Neanderthals and "modern" human beings are living side by side in Mesopotamia. **30,000–12,000 B.C.** Europe freezes in the Ice Age. Artists make great cave paintings in France and Spain.	**12,000–900 B.C.** The great ice sheets begin to thaw as temperatures increase. Sea levels rise.	**10,000–5000 B.C.** Cave paintings in Spain show men armed with bows in combat. **6000–4000 B.C.** Farming spreads to eastern Europe, probably from Turkey. **4000–2000 B.C.** Stone circles and other megalithic monuments become common in western Europe.
AFRICA	**2–1 million years ago** Early hominids, the first human-apes, are alive in Eastern Africa. **1 million years ago–400,000 B.C.** *Homo erectus*, a type of early human, use stone hand axes as a multipurpose tool. **400,000–30,000 B.C.** *Homo sapiens*, human beings, appear in various places south of the Sahara.		**6000–4000 B.C.** The climate of what is now the Sahara Desert is very wet. Cattle herding is common in many parts of the region. **3100 B.C.** The kingdom of Egypt is founded. King Narmer unifies the Upper and Lower Kingdoms of Egypt and becomes the first pharaoh. The ancient Egyptians worship many gods.
ASIA	**2–1 million years ago** *Homo erectus* is established in both Java and China and has probably mastered the use of fire. **400,000–30,000 B.C.** Neanderthals and "modern" humans are living side by side in Mesopotamia.	**12,000–9000 B.C.** The dog is domesticated in the Middle East. The first pottery is produced by the Jomon civilization in Japan.	**9000–6000 B.C.** Farming is established in the Fertile Crescent in the Middle East. **6000–4000 B.C.** Trading towns such as Çatal Hüyük, Turkey, begin to develop. **5000 B.C.** The Sumerians, a farming people, settle in southern Mesopotamia. **2900 B.C.** Earliest known writing, cuneiform, is developed in Mesopotamia.
AUSTRALASIA	**30,000 B.C.** Human settlement of Australia probably begins. **29,000 B.C.** People are living in Tasmania, which is linked to the Australian mainland by a land bridge. **25,000 B.C.** Puritjarra Rock Shelter near the Cleland Hills, Northern Territory, is occupied. **24,000 B.C.** Signs of human occupation near Lake Mungo, New South Wales.	**10,000 B.C.** The population of native Australians is about 300,000 people.	
AMERICA	**30,000–12,000 B.C.** The first settlement of North America begins as men and women cross the Bering land bridge from Siberia.	**12,000–9000 B.C.** People in Chile build houses from wood and skins—the first evidence of shelters in the Americas.	**9000 B.C.** The Clovis culture: on the Great Plains people hunt using stone-pointed spears. **4000–2000 B.C.** The farmers of Mexico domesticate the corn plant. Other crops spread to North America.

2500–2000 b.c.	2000–1500 b.c.	1500–1000 b.c.	1000–500 b.c.	500–1 b.c.

2000 b.c. First iron working transforms tools and weapons.

2000 b.c. The Minoans of Crete build a palace at Knossos.

2000 b.c. Celtic tribes practice local religion with their own groups of gods.

2000–1700 b.c. The Minoan Civilization in Crete is at the height of its success.

1900 b.c. Cretans use potter's wheel.

1800 b.c. Flint daggers made in Sweden.

1600 b.c. Bronze weapons used in Sweden and Greece.

1400 b.c. Phoenician sailors explore the Mediterranean.

1450 b.c. The Mycenaean civilization on the Greek mainland invades and conquers the Minoans of Crete.

1200 b.c. Decline of the Mycenaean civilization.

900 b.c. Greeks begin to trade in the Mediterranean.

753 b.c. According to legend, Rome is founded by Romulus and Remus.

700 b.c. Greek city-states develop.

509 bc Rome made a republic.

490 b.c. The Battle of Marathon fought between the Greeks and the Persians. The Greeks defeat an enemy once thought to be unbeatable.

146 b.c. Greece comes under Roman rule. Many Greek gods are renamed by the Romans.

27 b.c. Augustus becomes the first of the Roman emperors.

2686–2181 b.c. Old Kingdom in Egypt. The pharaohs build up their power and are buried in pyramids.

2040–1786 b.c. Middle Kingdom of Egypt.

1786–1567 b.c. Invading forces sent to Egypt from Syria and Palestine.

1570–1085 b.c. New Kingdom. Egyptian pharaohs rule once more and the civilization flourishes.

1490 b.c. Egyptians sail to Punt on the East African coast.

1083–333 b.c. The Egyptian empire collapses. Egypt divides into separate states.

500 b.c. Hanno, from Carthage, in modern Tunisia, explores the coast of Africa.

333–323 b.c. Egypt becomes part of Alexander the Great's empire.

2500 bc Ur in Mesopotamia becomes a major city.

2500 b.c. The first cities are built on the plains of the Indus River in Pakistan.

2500 b.c. First fortified city, Ur of the Chaldees, in modern Iraq.

2166 b.c. Birth of Abraham, founder of the Jewish nation.

1700 b.c. Ur declines, and Babylon gains in strength.

1680 b.c. The Hyksos, a group of Asian settlers, introduce horse-drawn chariots to Egypt.

1500 b.c. Hindu beliefs spread throughout northern India.

1469 b.c. The first record of a battle, at Megiddo, between Egypt and the Canaanites.

c.1200 b.c. Zoroaster lives in Persia.

900 b.c. Hindu beliefs are written down in the four *Vedas*.

605–562 b.c. Reign of King Nebuchadnezzar. He builds the fabulous hanging gardens in Babylon, the most sophisticated city in the Near East.

660 b.c. Legendary date of the unification of Japan and the start of Shintoism.

500 b.c. In China, Sun Tzu writes the first book on military theory.

500 b.c. Silk Road opens.

500 b.c. Mahavira founds Jainism.

c.500s b.c. Life of Lao-Tzu, legendary founder of Taoism.

551–479 b.c. Life of Confucius.

485–405 b.c. Life of Buddha.

2000 b.c. Islands of the South Pacific are uninhabited.

1000 b.c. Polynesians settle in Tonga and Samoa. Over the next 2000 years the Polynesians slowly spread out across the South Pacific Ocean.

The Polynesians sail north to Hawaii, east to Easter Island and finally south to New Zealand.

2300 b.c. Farming leads to permanent settlement in villages in Mexico.

2300 b.c. Use of pottery in Mexico and Guatemala.

2000 b.c. First evidence of metal working in Peru.

2000–1500 b.c. Pottery spreads among farmers in Peru.

2000–1000 b.c. The beginning of Mayan culture in Mesoamerica (Central America). Farmers begin to settle in villages.

1800–900 b.c. The Initial Period in Peru. People settle in permanent villages, and there is evidence of social and religious organization. Pottery spreads.

1500 b.c. Agriculture reaches the southeast and later, the midwest of North America.

1200–900 b.c. The Olmec people of Mexico build the region's first large cities.

850–200 b.c. The Chavin de Huantar civilization in the high Andes mountains reaches the peak of its success.

200 b.c. Beginnings of Hopewell civilization in North America.

200 b.c. Many small, independent cultures develop in the valleys of the Andes.

300 b.c.–a.d. 200 Maya cities established in Mexico, Honduras and Guatemala.

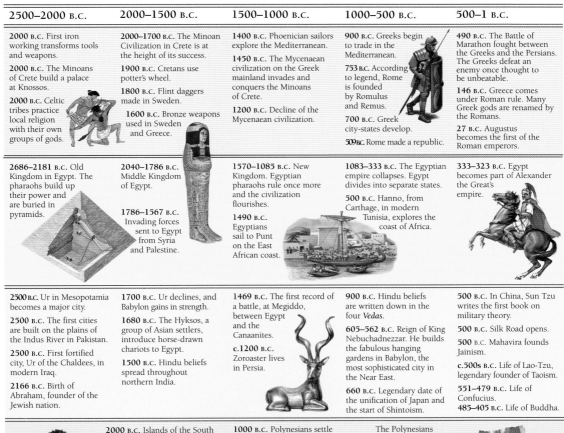

Timeline A.D. 1–A.D. 1000

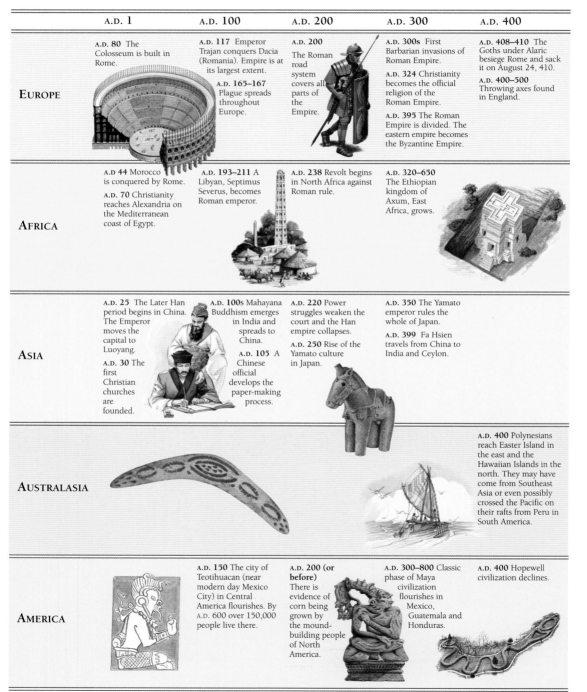

	A.D. 1	A.D. 100	A.D. 200	A.D. 300	A.D. 400
EUROPE	A.D. 80 The Colosseum is built in Rome.	A.D. 117 Emperor Trajan conquers Dacia (Romania). Empire is at its largest extent. A.D. 165–167 Plague spreads throughout Europe.	A.D. 200 The Roman road system covers all parts of the Empire.	A.D. 300s First Barbarian invasions of Roman Empire. A.D. 324 Christianity becomes the official religion of the Roman Empire. A.D. 395 The Roman Empire is divided. The eastern empire becomes the Byzantine Empire.	A.D. 408–410 The Goths under Alaric besiege Rome and sack it on August 24, 410. A.D. 400–500 Throwing axes found in England.
AFRICA	A.D 44 Morocco is conquered by Rome. A.D. 70 Christianity reaches Alexandria on the Mediterranean coast of Egypt.	A.D. 193–211 A Libyan, Septimus Severus, becomes Roman emperor.	A.D. 238 Revolt begins in North Africa against Roman rule.	A.D. 320–650 The Ethiopian kingdom of Axum, East Africa, grows.	
ASIA	A.D. 25 The Later Han period begins in China. The Emperor moves the capital to Luoyang. A.D. 30 The first Christian churches are founded.	A.D. 100s Mahayana Buddhism emerges in India and spreads to China. A.D. 105 A Chinese official develops the paper-making process.	A.D. 220 Power struggles weaken the court and the Han empire collapses. A.D. 250 Rise of the Yamato culture in Japan.	A.D. 350 The Yamato emperor rules the whole of Japan. A.D. 399 Fa Hsien travels from China to India and Ceylon.	
AUSTRALASIA					A.D. 400 Polynesians reach Easter Island in the east and the Hawaiian Islands in the north. They may have come from Southeast Asia or even possibly crossed the Pacific on their rafts from Peru in South America.
AMERICA		A.D. 150 The city of Teotihuacan (near modern day Mexico City) in Central America flourishes. By A.D. 600 over 150,000 people live there.	A.D. 200 (or before) There is evidence of corn being grown by the mound-building people of North America.	A.D. 300–800 Classic phase of Maya civilization flourishes in Mexico, Guatemala and Honduras.	A.D. 400 Hopewell civilization declines.

| A.D. 500 | A.D. 600 | A.D. 700 | A.D. 800 | A.D. 900 | A.D. 1000 |

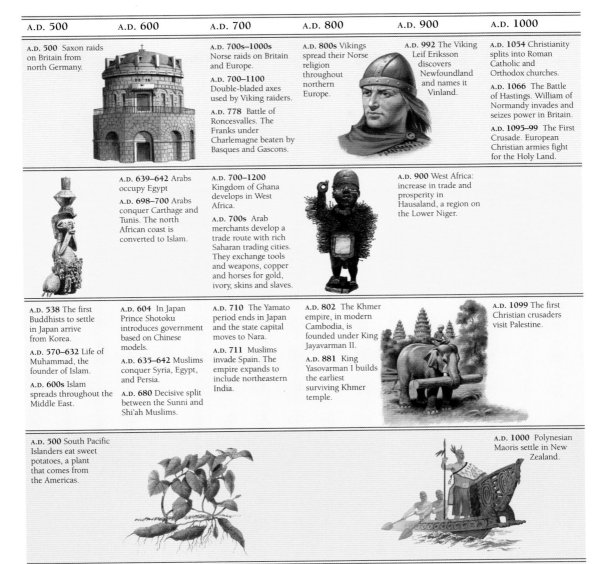

A.D. 500 Saxon raids on Britain from north Germany.

A.D. 700s–1000s Norse raids on Britain and Europe.

A.D. 700–1100 Double-bladed axes used by Viking raiders.

A.D. 778 Battle of Roncesvalles. The Franks under Charlemagne beaten by Basques and Gascons.

A.D. 800s Vikings spread their Norse religion throughout northern Europe.

A.D. 992 The Viking Leif Eriksson discovers Newfoundland and names it Vinland.

A.D. 1054 Christianity splits into Roman Catholic and Orthodox churches.

A.D. 1066 The Battle of Hastings. William of Normandy invades and seizes power in Britain.

A.D. 1095–99 The First Crusade. European Christian armies fight for the Holy Land.

A.D. 639–642 Arabs occupy Egypt

A.D. 698–700 Arabs conquer Carthage and Tunis. The north African coast is converted to Islam.

A.D. 700–1200 Kingdom of Ghana develops in West Africa.

A.D. 700s Arab merchants develop a trade route with rich Saharan trading cities. They exchange tools and weapons, copper and horses for gold, ivory, skins and slaves.

A.D. 900 West Africa: increase in trade and prosperity in Hausaland, a region on the Lower Niger.

A.D. 538 The first Buddhists to settle in Japan arrive from Korea.

A.D. 570–632 Life of Muhammad, the founder of Islam.

A.D. 600s Islam spreads throughout the Middle East.

A.D. 604 In Japan Prince Shotoku introduces government based on Chinese models.

A.D. 635–642 Muslims conquer Syria, Egypt, and Persia.

A.D. 680 Decisive split between the Sunni and Shi'ah Muslims.

A.D. 710 The Yamato period ends in Japan and the state capital moves to Nara.

A.D. 711 Muslims invade Spain. The empire expands to include northeastern India.

A.D. 802 The Khmer empire, in modern Cambodia, is founded under King Jayavarman II.

A.D. 881 King Yasovarman I builds the earliest surviving Khmer temple.

A.D. 1099 The first Christian crusaders visit Palestine.

A.D. 500 South Pacific Islanders eat sweet potatoes, a plant that comes from the Americas.

A.D. 1000 Polynesian Maoris settle in New Zealand.

A.D. 500–1000 Civilizations of Huari and Tiahuanco in Mexico.

A.D. 615 The great Maya leader Lord Pacal rules in the city of Palenque in Mexico.

A.D. 650 The city of Teotihuacan begins to decline. It is looted and burned by unknown invaders around A.D. 700.

A.D. 850 The Toltecs of northern Mexico begin to create the city-state of Tula.

A.D. 900 Most Maya cities in Central America are in decline.

A.D. 900–1200 Cities in the northern Yucatan (in Mexico) flourish under the warlike Toltecs from Tula.

A.D. 980–90s Vikings settle in Greenland and explore parts of North America.

A.D. 1011–1063 The Mixtecs are ruled by the leader Eight Deer, in the area of Oaxaca, central Mexico. The Mixtecs are master goldsmiths.

A.D. 1050–1250 Cahokia is a major centre of civilization near the Mississippi in North America.

Timeline A.D. 1100–2001

	1100	1200	1300	1400	1500
EUROPE	**1100–1300** Medical schools are founded throughout Europe. **1199** King Richard I of England killed by a crossbow at Chaluz in France.	**1215** The Pope decrees that all doctors need church approval. **1200s** Longbow enters wide use in England and Wales. **1258** Medical texts preserved by the Arabs flow back to the West.		**1419** Henry "the Navigator" establishes a school of navigation in Portugal. **1492** Christopher Columbus crosses the Atlantic.	**1517** Roman Catholic Church splits as the Reformation gives rise to Protestant churches. **1543** Copernicus shows that the Earth circles the Sun. **1543** Vesalius accurately illustrates human anatomy.
AFRICA	**1100–1897** Kingdom of Benin, West Africa.	**1200–1500** Kingdom of Mali, West Africa. **1270–1450** Great Zimbabwe is capital of Shona kingdom.	**1350–1600** Kingdom of Songhai, West Africa. **1300s** The city of Timbuktu becomes a prosperous center for trade across the Sahara Desert.	**1480s** Portuguese cross the equator and sail around the Cape of Good Hope. **1482** The Portuguese open a trading post for exporting slaves to the New World.	
ASIA	**1100s** Islamic invaders bring new medical practices to India. **1187** Muslim leader Saladin retakes Jerusalem and overruns most of the crusader kingdoms. **1189–92** Third Crusade recaptures Acre from Saladin.	**1211** Ghengis Khan begins invasion of China. **1234** Mongols overrun northern China. **1271–95** Marco Polo visits China. **1291** Acre, the last Crusader stronghold in Palestine, is lost.	**1368** Mongols thrown out of China by the Ming dynasty.	**1405–33** Zheng He, from China, leads expeditions to Southeast Asia. **1444** Final crusade. **1498** Vasco da Gama, from Lisbon, Portugal, sails to India.	**1500s** European settlers bring European medical ideas to India. **1549** Xavier, a Spanish Jesuit, goes to Japan as a missionary. **1594–97** Barents, a Dutch mariner, explores the Arctic Ocean.
AUSTRALASIA	**1000–1600** Statues on Easter Island.				**1520–21** Magellan crosses the Pacific on his around-the-world voyage.
AMERICA	**1100s** Incas start to dominate central Peru.		**1325** Aztecs found the city of Tenochtitlán on the spot now occupied by modern-day Mexico City.	**1450s** Incas build Machu Picchu. **1492** Columbus finds the West Indies. **1497** Cabot finds Newfoundland.	**1502** Amerigo Vespucci finds the Americas. **1513** Balboa sights the Pacific Ocean. **1519–33** Spanish conquer the Aztecs of Mexico. **1535–36** Cartier journeys up the St. Lawrence River.

1600	1700	1800	1850	1900	1950

1610 Galileo spies Jupiter's moons through a telescope.

1628 Harvey shows how the heart circulates blood.

1661 Boyle describes the chemical elements.

1668 Newton establishes 3 laws of motion.

1752 Franklin shows lightning is electricity.

1783 The Montgolfier brothers' balloon carries two men aloft.

1789 Lavoisier writes the first list of elements.

1789 French Revolution.

1804 Trevithick builds the first steam locomotive.

1830 Faraday and Henry find that electricity can be generated by magnetism.

1850 Morse code invented.

1871 Paris Commune.

1876 First detected radio signal.

1914–18 World War I.

1917 Russian Revolution.

1926 Enigma coding machine developed.

1939–45 World War II.

1945 Cold War begins.

1947 Kalashnikov designs the AK47 assault rifle.

1960 Microchip first used.

1989 End of the Cold War.

1710–1810 More than seven million Africans sent to the Americas as slaves.

1795–1806 Park, from Scotland, explores the River Niger.

1841–73 Livingstone, from Scotland, explores southern and central Africa.

1844–45 Barth, from Germany, explores the Sahara Desert region.

1874–77 Stanley, a reporter from Wales, sails down the Congo river.

1601 Yang Chi-chou writes his ten-volume Ch'en/Chiu Ta-Ch'eng, describing acupuncture.

1600s The first medical descriptions of Chinese medical practice reach the West.

1699 Guru Gobind Singh forms the Khalsa (Sikh community).

1725–29 Bering, from Denmark, crosses Siberia.

1734–42 Teams of explorers map Siberian coasts and rivers.

1878 Nordenskjold, from Finland, discovers the Northeast Passage.

1945 Atomic bomb dropped on Hiroshima, in Japan.

1945–62 Chinese Revolution.

1945–75 Indochina War.

1945–62 War in South-east Asia.

1966–73 Vietnamese War between Communist Vietcong and United States.

1978–82 Islamic Revolution.

1991 Helicopters are used in the Gulf War between the forces of NATO and Iraq.

1605 Jansz explores Queensland.

1642–1643 Tasman discovers New Zealand.

1770 Cook lands in Australia.

1802–1803 The Australian coast is surveyed by English navigator, Mathew Flinders.

1828–62 Australian interior explored.

1911 Amundsen reaches South Pole.

1947 Thor Heyerdahl makes his Kon-Tiki expedition from Peru to the South Pacific.

1967 Discovery of Lystrosaurus fossils in Antarctica.

1603–15 Champlain explores Canada and founds Quebec.

1610–11 Englishman Henry Hudson searches for the Northwest Passage.

1680–82 La Salle, from France, sails down the Mississippi River.

1700s Iron-bladed tomahawks manufactured for North America.

1800s Several scientific expeditions explore the Amazon.

1830 Joseph Smith translates the Book of Mormon.

1835 Colt patents his first revolver design.

1861–65 American Civil War.

1908 Ford's Model T is the first mass-produced car.

1908 Peary, from the United States, reaches the North Pole.

1956–60 Cuban Revolution led by Fidel Castro.

1961 Cuban Missile crisis.

1961 USS Enterprise is the first nuclear-powered aircraft carrier.

1963 John F. Kennedy is assassinated.

People and Places

A

Abbasids, dynasty of Muslim caliphs (rulers), who ruled the Arab world from A.D. 749 until 1258.

Abu Bakr, the first caliph (ruler) of the Muslim empire, who succeeded Muhammad in A.D. 632.

Agincourt, site of the battle in France in 1415, at which English and Welsh longbowmen defeated the French.

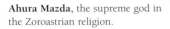

Ahura Mazda, the supreme god in the Zoroastrian religion.

Alexander the Great, king of Macedonia from 336 to 323 B.C., who created a huge empire that included the Middle East, Near East and northwestern India.

Allah, the Islamic name for God.

Altamira, site in Spain known for its prehistoric cave paintings.

Amritsar, Sikh holy city in northwestern India founded by Guru Ram Das, where the sacred Golden Temple was built between 1574 and 1581.

Amundsen, Roald, Norwegian explorer, who was the first to successfully travel along the Northwest Passage in 1903–06; the first person to reach the South Pole in 1911.

Angkor Wat, site of the temple city in Cambodia that was built from 1113 as the capital of the Khmer empire.

Appian Way, the first of the major Roman roads, constructed, in Italy, in 312 B.C.

Arbela, site of the battle in the Middle East at which Alexander the Great's army defeated the Persians in 331 B.C.

Archimedes, Greek citizen of Syracuse (c.285–212 B.C.), the world's first true scientist, who used mathematics and practical experiments to prove his theories.

Armstrong, Neil, American astronaut who became the first human to set foot on the Moon in 1969.

Asgard, the realm of the gods in Norse mythology.

Asoka, ruler of the Mauryan Empire from 269 until 232 B.C., who established Buddhism as the state religion.

Athens, the most important of the ancient Greek city-states, at the height of its power in the 5th century B.C.

Auenbrugger, Leopold, Austrian doctor who, in 1761, proved that sounding the chest reveals information about the state of the lungs.

Augustus, the first emperor of Rome (27 B.C.–A.D. 14), who founded the Roman Empire to replace the Roman republic.

B

Babylon, city on the Euphrates river in Lower Mesopotamia (modern Iraq) that was the capital of the Babylonian Empire from about 1700 B.C.

Baekeland, Leo, inventor, in 1909, of Bakelite, the world's first entirely synthetic plastic.

Baird, John Logie, Scottish pioneer who demonstrated practical television in 1926.

Balboa, Vasco da, Spanish explorer and soldier who was the first European to see the Pacific Ocean, after crossing Central America in 1513.

Barents, Willem, Dutch explorer who tried to find the Northeast passage around the north of Russia to the Pacific Ocean in several voyages (1594–7).

Becquerel, Antoine, French scientist who discovered radioactivity in 1897.

Benz, Karl, German engineer who offered the first gasoline-powered car for sale in 1888.

Bering, Vitus, Danish explorer who crossed Siberia and voyaged around the northern Pacific Ocean along the coasts of Siberia and Alaska between 1725 and 1741.

Bougainville, Louis, French navigator who led the first French voyage around the world (1766–79), and after whom the Papua New Guinean island of Bougainville was named.

Boyle, Robert, Irish scientist (1627–91) who said that everything in the material world is made of elements and compounds.

Brahman, the supreme Hindu god.

Bruce, James, British explorer who, in 1770, discovered Lake Tana, source of the Blue Nile (a tributary of the Nile).

Burke, Robert O'Hara, Australian explorer who, with William Wills, was the first to cross Australia from south to north in 1860–61. Both men died on the return journey.

Burton, Richard, British explorer who, in 1857, set out to find the source of the Nile with John Speke and explored the lakes of East Africa.

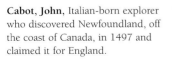

C

Cabot, John, Italian-born explorer who discovered Newfoundland, off the coast of Canada, in 1497 and claimed it for England.

Canaan, the land promised to the Jews by God (modern Israel).

Carthage, an ancient town in modern-day Tunisia, which was the most important Phoenician and, later, Roman colony in North Africa.

Cartier, Jacques, French explorer who, in 1534, explored the St. Lawrence estuary in Canada and then sailed upriver to Montreal.

Catholic, at first, the universal Christian Church which, in 1054, split into Western and Eastern (or Orthodox) branches; today, it usually refers to the Roman Catholic Church headed by the Pope in Rome.

Celts, people who lived in central and western Europe during the Iron Age, just before these areas were occupied by the Romans.

Champlain, Samuel de, French explorer who founded Quebec in 1608–9.

Chandragupta, founder of the Mauryan Empire in 322 B.C., which extended over much of modern India and Pakistan.

Charlemagne, Frankish king who, during the A.D. 770s, took control of most of western Europe and was crowned first emperor of the Holy Roman Empire in A.D. 800.

Clark, William, American soldier and explorer who, with Meriwether Lewis, led the first expedition (1804–6) across the North American continent to reach the Pacific Ocean.

Columbus, Christopher, Italian-born Spanish explorer who, in 1492, became the first modern European to sail across the Atlantic Ocean and reached the West Indies in the Caribbean.

Confucius, Chinese philosopher who lived from 551 to 479 B.C. and whose peaceful teachings formed the basis of Confucianism.

Constantine the Great, Roman emperor who, in A.D. 312, granted tolerance of Christianity, which soon became the official religion of the Roman Empire.

Constantinople, capital of the Byzantine Empire until its capture by the Turks in 1453 (modern Istanbul).

Cook, James, British naval officer and explorer, who sailed around New Zealand and mapped the eastern coast of Australia, explored Antarctica and discovered Hawaii.

Copernicus, Nicolas Polish astronomer who, in 1453, showed that the Earth revolves around the Sun and not the Sun around the Earth.

Coral Sea, an arm of
the Pacific Ocean, off
northern Australia,
where an American
aircraft-carrier force
inflicted the first naval
blow to the Japanese
in World War II.

Cortés, Hernán, Spanish soldier who conquered the Aztec
empire in Mexico at Tenochtitlán, the Aztec capital,
in 1521.

Crécy, site of the battle in France in 1346, at which
English and Welsh longbowmen defeated the French.

Crete, Greek island that was home to the Minoan
civilization in around 2000 B.C. and was ruled at various
times by Greeks, Romans, Turks and Arabs; it was the site
of a major airborne German assault
and victory in May 1941.

Crick, Francis, British scientist who, along with James
Watson, discovered the double-helix structure of DNA in
1953 and helped to pave the way for modern genetics.

Culpeper, Nicholas, English herbalist who wrote the first
modern herbal in 1649.

D

Damascus, major Muslim city in Syria, where high-grade
steel weapons were made in the Middle Ages.

Dardanelles, strait in northwest Turkey that links the
Mediterranean and Black Seas, and where Allied Forces
suffered a grim defeat in 1915.

Darius I, king of Persia (522–486 B.C.),
who extended his kingdom to include
parts of Egypt and India, but who
failed to conquer Greece and was
defeated at Marathon in 490 B.C.

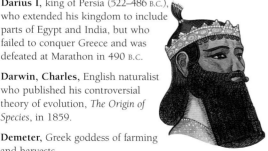

Darwin, Charles, English naturalist
who published his controversial
theory of evolution, *The Origin of
Species,* in 1859.

Demeter, Greek goddess of farming
and harvests.

Dezhnev, Semyon, Russian explorer who sailed around the
eastern tip of Siberia in 1648.

Dias, Bartolemeu, Portuguese explorer who rounded the
Cape of Good Hope and reached the Indian Ocean in
1488, thus finding a sea route to the East.

Dien Bien Phu, village in Indochina (modern Vietnam)
gained by Communist forces in 1954, thus signaling the
end of French colonial rule.

Dionysus, Greek god of wine.

Domagk, Gerhard, German scientist who developed
Prontasil, one of the first antibacterial drugs, in 1932.

Dordogne, region in southwest France where important
Cro-Magnon finds have been made.

Drake, Francis, English explorer who led the second
voyage round the world between 1577 and 1580.

Duat, the underworld in ancient Egyptian religion.

E

Einstein, Albert, revolutionary
physicist, who published his
theories of special relativity and
general relativity in 1905 and
1915 respectively.

Ely, Eugene, American aviator
who made the world's first
successful take-off from and
landing on a ship in 1911.

Empedocles, Greek
philosopher who, in
the 400s B.C., described
the four humors
(elements) that make up
the body.

Eric the Red, Viking explorer who sailed from Norway in
A.D. 982 and reached Greenland via Iceland.

Euclid, Greek mathematician who taught at Alexandria
and wrote his *Elements of Geometry* in about 300 B.C.

Eyre, Edward, Australian explorer who walked along the
south coast of Australia from Adelaide to Albany in
1840–41.

F

Fa Hsien, Chinese monk who visited India and Sri Lanka
in A.D. 339 to study Buddhism.

Falkland Islands, British colony in the south Atlantic
Ocean and the scene of a short war in 1982, when British
troops expelled the Argentine forces that had occupied
the islands.

Faraday, Michael, English chemist and physicist
(1791–1867) and pioneer in the field of electricity.

Fleming, Alexander, Scottish bacteriologist who discovered penicillin in 1928, paving the way for modern treatment of infectious diseases.

Franklin, John, English explorer and the first to try to find the Northwest Passage around northern Canada, starting in 1845 but dying in the ice during 1847.

Frobisher, Martin, English explorer who reached Baffin Island off the northwestern coast of Canada in 1576, while seeking the entrance to a northwest passage to the Pacific Ocean.

G

Gagarin, Yuri, Soviet cosmonaut who, in 1961, was the first man in space.

Galilei, Galileo, Italian scientist (1564–1642) who was the first to use a telescope to examine the night sky and whose astronomical achievements included the discovery of four of Jupiter's moons.

Gama, Vasco da, Portuguese explorer who was the first modern European to reach India by sea in 1497–98.

Gautama, Siddhartha, generally known as the Buddha (enlightened one), the founder of the Buddhist system of belief around 500 B.C.

Ghengis Khan, ruler of the Mongols, who conquered northern China in 1234.

Great Zimbabwe, site of the city in Zimbabwe that was the capital of one of the first civilizations of southern Africa.

Guru Nanak, the Indian founder of the Sikh religion, who lived from 1469 until 1539.

H

Hall, Charles, American explorer who made three attempts to reach the North Pole on foot, and died on the last in 1871.

Halstaat, the first stage of the Iron Age in Europe, from the 600s to the 500s B.C., named after an Iron Age archaeological site in Austria.

Hammurabi, king of Babylon (1792–1750 B.C.), who conquered Mesopotamia and is best known for his Code of Laws, which included the first code of practice for doctors.

Han Wu Di, emperor of China (140–87 B.C.), who extended the Han empire to its greatest extent after defeating the northern nomads.

Hanno, Phoenician explorer who sailed around the coast of West Africa in 500 B.C.

Hartog, Dirk, Dutch explorer who, on a journey to the East Indies, sailed too far south and discovered Western Australia in 1615.

Harvey, William, English physician who described how the heart pumps blood around the body in 1628.

Hausser, Konrad, the designer of the first effective long-recoil mechanism for artillery in 1888.

Henry the Navigator, prince of Portugal and founder of a school of scientific navigation, who financed voyages of discovery along the coast of West Africa during the 1400s.

Hillary, Edmund, New Zealand explorer and mountaineer who, along with Tenzing Norgay, became the first to scale Mount Everest in 1953.

Hipparchus, a Greek who compiled a catalogue of the stars and became the first truly great astronomer, though much of his work was based on records left behind by the ancient Babylonians.

Hippocrates, Greek citizen of the island of Kos who lived from 460 to 377 B.C. and who is known as the "father of medicine" for his works and writings on the accurate diagnosis and treatment of disease.

Hiroshima, Japanese city on which the first atomic bomb was dropped in August 1945.

Holland, John, American engineer who developed the world's first practical submarines in the 1890s.

Homer, supposed writer of the *Iliad* and *Odyssey*, Greek epic poems about the Trojan War and its aftermath.

Hubble, Edwin, American astronomer whose discoveries in the 1920s led to the "big bang" theory of the universe.

Hudson, Henry, English explorer who, in 1610, sailed into the bay in northern Canada that is now named after him; his crew later mutinied and returned home without him.

Hunter, John, Scottish surgeon of the 1700s, who transformed surgery into a science.

I

Ibn Battuta, Islamic traveler who explored the limits of the Islamic world (1325–53), as far west as Mali in West Africa and as far east as Xiamen in China.

J

Jansz, Willem, Dutch explorer who sailed south from the East Indies in 1605 and discovered what is now known as Queensland, in northeastern Australia.

Jayavarman II, founder of the Khmer empire in Southeast Asia, who ruled from A.D. 802–850.

Jenner, Edward, English physician who revolutionized the prevention of disease in 1796 when he successfully inoculated a boy against smallpox.

Jericho, the earliest-known town, where the first domesticated cereals were grown; also the scene of a famous siege during the Israelite conquest of Canaan.

Jerusalem, holy city for Jews, Christians and Muslims and the site of the Jewish Great Temple built by King Solomon.

Jesus of Nazareth, a Jew born around 7 or 6 B.C., who Christians believe was the son of God and whose life, death and teachings are the foundations of the Christian Church.

Jolliet, Louis, French explorer who, along with Jacques Marquette, charted the upper parts of the Mississippi River in 1672.

Julius Caesar, the last leader of the Roman republic, a great soldier, who conquered Gaul, launched raids into Germany and Britain, and was killed in 44 B.C.

Jutland, site of the greatest naval battle of World War I, fought in May 1916 off the west coast of Denmark.

K

Knossos, city in Crete that was the center of the Minoan civilization until about 1450 B.C.

Korea, country in Asia, and site of a conflict between 1951 until 1954, in which jet-powered fighter planes were first used against each other.

L

Lao-tzu, the Chinese founder of Taoism, a philosophy based on following a natural path through life.

Lascaux, cave in the Dordogne region of France known for its prehistoric cave paintings and engravings of animals.

Lavoisier, Antoine French chemist who helped to prove that all materials are made up of basic elements.

Leeuwenhoek, Antonie van, Dutch scientist who made the first practical microscope in 1671, through which he identified microbes which he called "animalcules."

Leif Eriksson, son of Eric the Red, Viking explorer, who sailed from Greenland in A.D. 992 to establish a small settlement at Vinland in eastern North America.

Leonardo da Vinci, Italian engineer, inventor, architect and artist, who was a true master of many fields.

Lepanto, site of a naval battle off the coast of Greece, at which, in 1571, the Austrians defeated the fleet of the Turks.

Lewis, Meriwether, American administrator and explorer who, with William Clark, led the first expedition (1804–06) across North America to reach the Pacific.

Lindbergh, Charles, American aviator, who made the first non-stop solo transatlantic flight (from New York to Paris) in 1927.

Livingstone, David, Scottish doctor and missionary who explored southern and eastern Africa and discovered Victoria Falls (1852–6); after disappearing in the region of the Great Lakes, he was found by Henry Stanley.

Luger, Georg, Austrian who, in 1899, designed an automatic pistol, used by the Germans in the two World Wars.

Luther, Martin, German religious reformer whose condemnation of the Roman Catholic Church in 1517 led to the Reformation and the establishment of Protestantism.

M

Magellan, Ferdinand, Portuguese-born navigator who captained the first around-the-world voyage in 1519; on the way he discovered what is now called the Magellan Strait and named the Pacific Ocean. When he died in 1521 Juan de Elcano completed the voyage.

Mahavira, Indian founder of the Jain religion in the 500s B.C.

Makkah, also spelt Mecca, holy Islamic city in modern-day Saudi Arabia that was the birthplace of the prophet Muhammad.

Malpighi, Marcello, Italian physician of the 1600s who contributed to the understanding of blood circulation by his discovery of the capillaries that link arteries and veins.

Marathon, site in eastern Greece of a battle at which the Greeks successfully defended themselves from Persian invasion in 490 B.C.

Marconi, Guglielmo, Italian-born scientist who sent the world's first radio message in 1895.

Marquette, Jacques, French explorer and missionary who, along with Louis Jolliet, charted the upper parts of the Mississippi River in 1672.

Maxim, Hiram, American-born British magnate who invented the first fully automatic machine gun in 1883.

Meadowcroft Rock Shelter, site in Pennsylvania of the first known settlement in North America.

Mercator, Gerhardus, Dutch mapmaker who, in 1552, created a projection of the world that accurately represented the surface of a sphere (the Earth) on a flat plane (map).

Mesopotamia, the fertile area of land between the Tigris and Euphrates rivers in the Middle East, where the world's first civilizations emerged.

Midgard, the middle world in Norse mythology, where humans live.

Midway, Pacific islands, off which American aircraft-carriers defeated the Japanese navy in June 1942.

Moses, prophet who brought the Jews out of Egyptian captivity in about 1466 B.C., and to whom God revealed the Ten Commandments.

Muhammad, also spelt Mohammed, prophet born in Makkah in A.D. 570 and founder of the Islamic religion.

N

Nagasaki, Japanese city on which the second atomic bomb was dropped in August 1945.

Nebuchadnezzar II, king of Babylon from 605 to 562 B.C., best known for creating the Hanging Gardens of Babylon, one of the Seven Wonders of the ancient world.

Nelson, Horatio, British naval hero and commander who defeated the French and Spanish navies at the Battle of Trafalgar in October 1805, but died during the battle.

Newton, Isaac, English scientist and mathematician who came up with his famous theory about gravity in 1666, and who also made important scientific discoveries about motion and the nature of light.

Nightingale, Florence, British nurse who pioneered modern nursing methods during the Crimean War (1853–56) on the Black Sea coast of Ukraine.

Nineveh, city near the River Tigris in Mesopotamia that was the capital of the Assyrian Empire from the 880s B.C. until its destruction in 612 B.C.

Nordenskjöld, Nils, Finnish explorer, first journeyed around the Northeast Passage into the Pacific Ocean (1878–79).

Norgay, Tenzing, Nepalese mountaineer who, along with Edmund Hillary, became the first to scale Mount Everest in 1953.

Normandy, part of northern France and site of the D-Day campaign that began in June 1944, when Allied troops landed on the Normandy coast, marking the start of the liberation of German-occupied territory.

O

Odin, also known as Wotan, the primary god of Norse mythology.

Offa, king of Mercia in northwestern England in the A.D. 700s, who built Offa's Dyke to protect his kingdom from Welsh raids.

Olduvai Gorge, site in northern Tanzania at which great prehistoric finds have been made, including remains of *Australopithecus*, *Homo habilis* and *Homo erectus*.

Oppenheimer, Robert, American nuclear physicist who led the development of the atomic bomb during World War II.

P

Park, Mungo, Scottish explorer who drowned while exploring the River Niger in West Africa (1795–1806).

Pasteur, Louis, French scientist who, in the 1860s, established how bacteria cause infection and who developed pasteurization, a technique for destroying microbes with heat.

Peary, Robert, American admiral and explorer who led the first expedition to the North Pole in 1909.

Pericles, Athenian statesman (443–429 B.C.), who lifted the city-state to a peak of political and economic power, and began the construction of the Parthenon and other buildings on the Acropolis in 447 B.C.

Persepolis, city in southwest Iran, founded by Darius I and the capital of the Persian Empire from about 835 B.C.

Pilate, Pontius, Roman governor of Judea who condemned Jesus of Nazareth to crucifixion in about A.D. 30.

Pizarro, Francisco, Spanish soldier, who conquered the Inca Empire of Peru in 1532.

Planck, Max, German physicist who published his quantum theory in 1900, revolutionizing scientific understanding of atomic processes.

Plate, River, also known as the Río de la Plata, river in Argentina in whose estuary the German pocket battleship *Graf Spee* was trapped by British forces in 1939 and deliberately sunk by her captain.

Polo, Marco, Italian explorer who claimed to have traveled to China and the Mongol Empire in the 1200s.

Priestley, Joseph, English chemist who identified oxygen in the 1700s.

Ptolemy, Egyptian astronomer who lived in Alexandria (A.D. 90–170) and whose Earth-centered picture of the universe went unchallenged until the 1500s.

Puritjarra Rock Shelter, early site of habitation in the Northern Territory of Australia.

Pythagoras, Greek philosopher and mathematician, born in Samos in 560 B.C.

Pytheas, Greek mariner of Massilia (Marseilles) who, in 330 B.C., sailed around the coast of Spain, Gaul and through the English Channel, to reach "Thule" (either southern Norway or Iceland).

R

Re, ancient Egyptian sun god.

Rome, city in the western part of central Italy that was the capital of the Roman Empire.

Ross, James, Scottish explorer who discovered the magnetic north pole in 1831 and charted much of the coast of Antarctica in 1841.

S

Saladin, Muslim leader in the Middle East, who recaptured Jerusalem from the Christian Crusaders in 1187.

Sargon, king of Assyria at the peak of the Empire's power in the late 700s B.C., who founded the capital city of Khorsabad (in modern Iraq).

Scott, Robert, English polar explorer, who led the second expedition to reach the South Pole in 1912, but died on the way back to the coast.

Shiva, one of the three main gods of the Hindu religion, responsible for both the preservation and the destruction of life.

Snow, John, British doctor who traced the cause of the London cholera outbreak of 1842 to contaminated water supplies.

Solomon, Jewish king known for his wisdom, who completed the construction of the Great Temple in Jerusalem in about 960 B.C., which had been begun by his father, King David.

Stonehenge, site in southern England of a large prehistoric stone circle.

T

Thule, name of what the ancients regarded as the northernmost land of the world, probably Norway or Iceland.

Torres, Luis, Spanish explorer who, in 1607, proved that Australia was an island by finding the strait that separated it from New Guinea.

Troy, a city in eastern Turkey that the Greeks besieged in the Trojan War (1200 B.C.).

V

Valhalla, the heaven of the brave in Norse mythology.

Vishnu, one of the three main Hindu gods, responsible for preserving the universe.

W

Waterloo, site of the battle in Belgium at which, in 1815, Napoleon was finally defeated by the British and Prussians.

Watson, James, American scientist who, along with Francis Crick, discovered the double-helix structure of DNA in 1953 and helped to pave the way for modern genetics.

Wegener, Alfred, German scientist who, in 1923, first put forward the theory of continental drift and who also suggested that there was once one giant supercontinent.

Whitehead, Robert, British engineer based in Italy who developed the first effective locomotive torpedoes from the 1860s.

William I, Duke of Normandy, who became King of England after defeating the Anglo-Saxon King Harold at the Battle of Hastings in 1066.

Willoughby, Hugh, English explorer who reached Novaya Zemlya off the northern coast of Russia in 1554.

Wills, William, Australian explorer who, along with Robert O'Hara Burke, was the first to cross Australia from south to north in 1860–61, but both men died on the return journey.

Wright, Wilbur and Orville, American brothers and aviation pioneers who achieved the world's first powered and sustained flight in a controllable heavier-than-air craft in December 1903.

X Y Z

Xavier, Francis, Spanish missionary who traveled to India and then on to Japan, which he reached in 1549.

Yamato, ruling clan of Japan in about A.D. 350, who organized the first unified control of the Japanese islands.

Yangtze Delta, region at the mouth of the Yangtze river in China, where rice was first cultivated around 5000 B.C.

Zeus, supreme god in Greek religion.

Zheng, king of Qin (246–210 B.C.) and, later, Emperor Qin Shi Huangdi of China (221–210 B.C.), who created the first great Chinese empire and started building on the first Great Wall of China.

Zheng He, Chinese explorer who led seven voyages of discovery into Southeast Asia and the Indian Ocean between 1405 and 1433.

Zoroaster, Persian priest who lived around 1200 B.C. and whose teachings form the basis of the Zoroastrian religion.

Glossary

A

alchemy
An early form of chemistry, which looked for a way to change base metals into precious ones, and for the secret of eternal life.

alignment
Term used to describe objects that are lined up neatly. A stone alignment is a long row of standing stones, often lined up to correspond with the movements of the Sun, Moon or stars.

alloy
Material made by mixing two or more metals. The most common alloy in prehistoric times was bronze, made from copper and tin.

amphitheater
A circular or oval open-air theatre, with seats arranged around a central area.

anatomy
The study of the structure of the body—where everything is and how it fits together.

anesthetic
Substance that prevents feeling in all or part of the body.

antibiotic
A drug, typically based on a natural substance, that attacks germs.

aqueduct
A manmade channel to supply water.

archaeologist
A person who studies the buildings, tools, pots and other remains of past societies.

armada
A fleet of battleships.

artillery
Large weapons that need transport to move them around the battlefield and a crew to operate them.

astrolabe
Navigational instrument once used to measure the height of the Sun at noon, thus giving a ship's latitude.

Australopithecine
A hominid of the genus *Australopithecus*, alive more than a million years ago.

Ayurveda
A series of Indian religious texts dating back to about 2000 B.C.

B

bacterium
Member of a group of microbes (bacteria) that cause many common infections.

bayonet
A blade fitted on to the end of a musket, named after the French town of Bayonne.

Bronze Age
Period in which the use of bronze for making tools and weapons became well established (3000–1000 B.C.).

burial mound
Artificial earth mound containing human graves.

C

city-state
A city that is also an independent state or country.

civilization
A settled society that has developed writing, organized religion, trade, grand buildings and government.

clone
A perfect genetic replica of a living thing.

constellation
One of the patterns of stars that astronomers use to find their way around the night sky. The pattern is visual and there is no real connection between the stars in a constellation.

crusade
A military expedition launched from Christian Europe to attempt to recover the Holy Land from Muslim rule.

cuirass
Armor for the front and back of the upper body, originally made from leather.

cuneiform
A type of writing that uses wedge-shaped figures, carved with a special tool. It developed in Mesopotamia from about 3000 B.C.

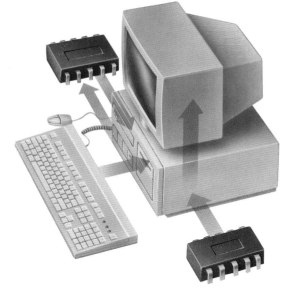

D

decimal system
A numerical system based around the number 10, first developed by Hindu mathematicians in A.D. 662.

diagnosis
Identification of a disease from its symptoms.

E

earthwork
A bank or rampart of earth, often built for defense.

emplacement
The position of an artillery gun on the battlefield or outside a besieged castle.

epidemic
A widespread outbreak of an infectious disease.

evolution
The gradual change of living species over time.

F

fossils
Part of an animal or plant that is preserved in stone.

G

genus
A group of animals or plants that have characteristics in common. A genus normally has more than one species.

glacier
A slow-moving river of ice.

glaze
Layer of material spread onto a pot before firing to create a hard, waterproof finish.

H

hieroglyphics
Ancient Egyptian picture writing.

hominid
Member of the family Hominidae, which includes humans and australopithecines.

Homo erectus
Upright-walking member of the
human genus *Homo*, which lived over
500,000 years ago.

Homo habilis
Early member of the human genus
Homo, alive in Africa about
1.7 million years ago.

Homo sapiens
The modern human
species, which
developed around
100,000 years
ago, and
to which
we belong.

hoplite
A heavily armed infantry
soldier from ancient Greece.

hunter-gatherers
People who live on meat that they hunt and plants that
they gather.

I

Ice Age
Period when the temperature was much lower than today,
and large parts of the Earth's surface were covered in ice.

infantry
Foot soldiers with hand-held weapons.

Iron Age
Period during which iron became the main metal
used for tools and weapons, from about 2000 B.C.

irrigation
The use of manmade channels to
water farmland.

J

jousting
Sporting combat between two
knights on horseback.

L

land bridge
Area of land connecting two landmasses that are
now separate.

latitude
Imaginary horizontal lines that circle the Earth and are
measured in degrees north or south of the Equator.

La Tène
Style of abstract art produced by the Celts, dated around
450–50 B.C.

legion
The main unit of the Roman army,
made up of Roman citizens.

longitude
Imaginary vertical lines that circle
the Earth and are measured in
degrees east or west of a line
called the prime meridian,
which runs through
Greenwich in England.

M

medieval
Term describing
people, events and
objects from the
Middle Ages.

megalith
Large stone, standing alone or used as part of a tomb,
stone circle or other monument.

Mei Ching
Chinese book about the pulse by Wang Shu-ho, published in A.D. 280.

Mesolithic
The Middle Stone Age. The period during the Stone Age when people improved their hunting techniques and began to make smaller stone tools.

Middle Ages
Period in history that lasted from around A.D. 800 to 1400.

mummy
A preserved dead body, like those of ancient Egypt.

myths
Stories told by ancient peoples. Myths often describe the activities of gods and goddesses and were frequently used to explain natural events such as thunder.

N

Neanderthal

Early hominid, shorter and stockier than humans, who lived in Europe and the Middle East and died out around 35,000 B.C.

Neolithic
The New Stone Age. The period when people began to farm but were still using stone tools.

nirvana
Name of the perfect state of existence that Buddhists seek to reach.

nomads
People who move around as a group in search of food, water and land for grazing animals.

Northern Hemisphere
The half of the Earth that lies north of the Equator.

O

obelisk
A tall, four-sided tapering pillar with a pyramid-shaped top.

obsidian
Naturally occurring glass-like substance formed in volcanoes. Used in prehistoric times in the same way as flint for making tools.

oracle
A means by which ancient peoples could contact the gods to ask for advice or find out about the future.

ore
Rock containing deposits of metal.

P

pack ice
Ice floating on a sea or ocean that has become packed together in huge sheets.

Paleolithic
The Old Stone Age. The period when human life first emerged. This time was typified by a hunter-gatherer way of life and by the use of simple stone tools.

paleontologist
A person who studies fossils.

papyrus
A kind of paper made from layers of papyrus reeds.

pharaoh
A title for the later kings of ancient Egypt. The word pharaoh means "great house."

philosophy
A set of beliefs and values held by an individual or group.

pommel
The weighted end of the handle of a broad sword, used to deliver a hammer blow in battle.

prehistory
The period before there were any written records.

prophet
Someone through whom God speaks.

Q

quadrant
Navigational instrument, consisting of a quarter-circle marked in degrees. It was used by sailors to calculate the angle of the Sun and thus to work out the ship's latitude.

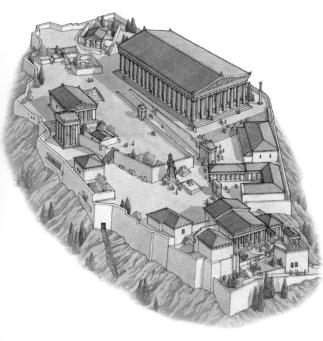

quantum theory
The idea that, on a subatomic level, energy is always broken into tiny chunks or quanta.

Qur'an
The holy book of Islam as spoken by Muhammad, also known as the Koran.

R

radiation
The spread of energy as particles or waves, for example X-rays, light or gamma rays.

Ragnarok
The final battle foretold in the Norse religion.

rampart
Wide earth mound built to fortify a castle or town.

Rastafarianism
Religion of the West Indies ordaining a belief in the Old Testament but worshipping Haile Selassie, emperor of Ethiopia from 1930 until 1974.

reincarnation
The belief that when a person dies, he or she will be reborn in another body.

relief
A carving that stands out or is raised from the surface.

republic
A country or state, such as ancient Rome, ruled by elected representatives of its people.

ritual
A ceremony in which the order of events, and the words used, rarely change over the years.

S

saltpeter
A name for the mineral potassium nitrate. It is used to make gunpowder, explosives, matches and fertilizers.

samurai
A word first used to describe the imperial guard of ancient Japan. Later it was used to describe a high-born warrior class in general.

Sanskrit
The language of the earliest Hindu writings.

seal
An engraved disk used to leave an impression on soft wax. Official government documents are often sealed.

Seven Wonders
A list of seven magnificent structures found in the ancient world. They include the Hanging Gardens of Babylon and the Great Pyramid at Giza in Egypt.

Shi'ah and Sunni
The two primary branches of the Islamic religion which developed from A.D. 680.

Shinto
The major religion established in Japan during the 6th century A.D.

shrine
A sacred place or container where religious objects or images may be kept.

Silk Road
The ancient overland trading route between China and Europe.

South Pole
The southernmost point of the Earth's axis of rotation, which lies in Antarctica

Southern Hemisphere
The half of the Earth that lies south of the Equator.

Spanish Armada
An armada is a fleet of battleships. The Spanish Armada was sent, unsuccessfully, by Philip of Spain to invade England in 1588.

Stone Age
Term describing any period when people made their tools out of stone.

superpower
A country possessing immense economic and military power, such as the United States or the former Soviet Union.

Swiss Guard
Group of Swiss soldiers chosen to guard the Pope. The tradition was begun by Pope Julius II in the early 1500s. Today, a Papal Swiss Guard is still used to guard the Pope.

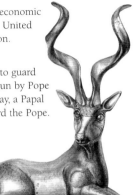

T

Torah
Hebrew name for the first five books of the Bible.

tournament
Armed contest between knights, fought for honor and ceremony.

trade
The process of buying and selling goods.

transfusion
Passing a liquid, often someone else's blood, into the bloodstream.

transplant
An organ or piece of tissue put into a patient's body that has been taken from another living thing.

tribe
A group of people descended from the same family or sharing the same language and culture.

trident
large fork with three prongs used as a weapon

Trireme
Warship used by ancient Greeks. Its name comes from the Greek words for "three" and "oars," because it was powered by men rowing in three banks.

tsar
The title of the hereditary emperor and ruler of Russia. Also sometimes written as czar.

Z

Ziggurat
A pyramid-shaped temple built by the ancient Babylonians.

Index

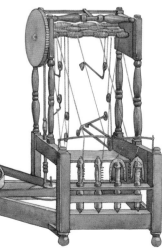

H

This edition is published by Lorenz Books

Lorenz Books is an imprint of Anness Publishing Ltd
Hermes House, 88–89 Blackfriars Road, London SE1 8HA
tel. 020 7401 2077; fax 020 7633 9499
www.lorenzbooks.com; info@anness.com

UK agent: The Manning Partnership Ltd,
6 The Old Dairy, Melcombe Road, Bath BA2 3LR;
tel. 01225 478444; fax 01225 478440;
sales@manning-partnership.co.uk

UK distributor: Grantham Book Services Ltd, Isaac Newton
Way, Alma Park Industrial Estate, Grantham,
Lincs NG31 9SD; tel. 01476 541080;
fax 01476 541061; orders@gbs.tbs-ltd.co.uk

North American agent/distributor: National Book Network,
4501 Forbes Boulevard, Suite 200, Lanham, MD 20706;
tel. 301 459 3366; fax 301 429 5746; www.nbnbooks.com

Australian agent/distributor: Pan Macmillan Australia, Level 18,
St Martins Tower, 31 Market St, Sydney, NSW 2000; tel. 1300 135 113;
fax 1300 135 103; customer.service@macmillan.com.au

New Zealand agent/distributor: David Bateman Ltd, 30 Tarndale Grove,
Off Bush Road, Albany, Auckland; tel. (09) 415 7664; fax (09) 415 8892

Publisher: Joanna Lorenz
Managing Editor, Children's Books: Gilly Cameron Cooper
Senior Editor: Nicole Pearson
Designers: Joyce Mason, Ann Samuel

Previously published as *Chilldrens Illustrated Encyclopedia:
Exploring History*

The Publishers would like to thank the following artists who contributed
to this book:

Julian Baker; Andy Beckett (Illustration Ltd); Mark Beesley; Mark Bergin;
Richard Berridge, (Spec Art); Vanessa Card; Rob Chapman (Linden
Artists); James Field (SGA); Wayne Ford; Chris Forsey; Mike Foster; Terry
Gabbey (AFA); Roger Gorringe (Illustration Ltd); Jeremy Gower; Peter
Gregory; Ron Hayward; Sally Holmes; Richard Hook (Linden Artists); Rob
Jakeway; John James (Temple Rogers); Kuo Chen Kang; Aziz Khan; Stuart
Lafford (Temple Rogers); Ch'en Ling; Steve Lings (Linden Artists); Kevin
Maddison; Janos Marrfy; Shane Marsh (Linden Artists); Rob McCraig;
Chris Odgers; Alex Pang (SGA); Helen Parsley (JM & A Associates); Terry
Riley; Andrew Robinson; Chris Rothero (Linden Artists); Eric Rowe
(Linden Artists); Martin Sanders; Peter Sarson; Mike Saunders; Rob
Sheffield; Don Simpson (Spec Art); Sue Sitt; Guy Smith (Mainline Design);
Nick Spender; Clive Spong (Linden Artists); Stuart Squires; Roger Stewart;
Ken Stott; Steve Sweet; Mike Taylor (SGA); Catherine Ward; Ross Watton
(SGA); Mike White (Temple Rogers); Alison Winfield; John Woodcock.

PHOTOGRAPHIC ACKNOWLEDGEMENTS

PREHISTORIC PEOPLES: AKG Photo 18bl/ Erich Lessing 19b, 48tr; Ancient Art
and Architecture Collection 51b; English Heritage Photo Library 54tr, 62c, 65t,
68tr; E.T Archive 28br, 38br, 26br; Hutchison Library/ Mary Jellife 45b, 21b/
Southwell 71bl; The Stock Market 38br.

ANCIENT CIVILIZATIONS: AKG London 121tl/ Paul Almasy 87tl/ Erich Lessing
81bl/ Jean-Louis AKG Berlin Nou 90br; Mary Evans Picture Library 108tr.

WORLD RELIGIONS: The Bridgeman Art Library 153tr, 179bc/ Donodia Picture
Agency, Bombay 160cr/ The National Museum of India 150br/ Victoria and
Albert Museum 147tr; Corbis 185tl/ Dave Bartruff 173cr/ Bennett Dean: Eye
Ubiquitous/ Bettmann 182tr, 186tl/ Kevin Fleming 177bc/ 159tr/ Lindsay
Hebberd 149tl/ Earl & Nazima Kowall 160br/ Lake County Museum 186cr/
Charles & Josette Lenars 160bc/ Daniel Laine 168br/ Denis O'Regan: 187br/
David H. Wells 172br; Sonia Halliday Photographs 181bc, 183tr; Robert Lesley
184bl; Judy McAskey 139bc; Clare Oliver 166c, 167tr, 167bc; Panos Pictures/
Piers Benatar 180br/ Alain le Garsmeur 155bl/ Kaveh Kazemi 142bc.

EXPLORATION AND DISCOVERY: Corbis: 252bl; Hutchison Library: 226br,
228cr/A. Zvoznikov 222cr/ R. Francis 224br/ N. Haslam 226tr/ E. Parker 226bl/
C. Pastini 232c/ A. Singer 230bl/ N. Smith 243bl; Popperfoto: 239b, 240br,
242bl/ Reuter 242tr; The Stockmarket: 230tl.

SCIENCE AND TECHNOLOGY: American Institute of Physics 271tr, 292bl;
Apple Computer U.K Limited 293c Corbis: 259cr, 260c, 266br, 267bl, 279c,
281tr, 282tr, 282bl, 282tl, 286c, 286bc, 303bl; Image Select: 253bl, 263cr/
Allsport 301tc Mary Evans Picture Library: 262tr, 271bl, 275tr, 287tr; Frank
Spooner Pictures: 299bc, Naoto Hosaka 298tr/ R. Benali/ S. Ferry 302bc; NASA:
263bl, 265cl, 295bl/ Ford Motor Company: 277cr; Ann Ronan: 252cr, 261tr,
261bl, 266tr, 268bl, 268br, 272br; Science Photo Library: 301bl, 280tr,
Firefly Productions: 292cr/ Richard Morrell 283tr/ Adam G. Sylvester 298br/ Tek
Image 291bl/ Geoff Tompkinson 287bl, Sony Computer Entertainment UK
293cr/ Virgin Atlantic Airways Limited 278br.

THE STORY OF MEDICINE: Bridgeman Art Library: 321tr; British School of
Shiatsu-Do (London) 347bl; Corbis 325cl, 332c, 334tl, 352bl /AFP 349cr/
Nathan Benn 341tl; Bettmann 319tr, 321cl, 324cr, 336cr, 337tr, 339bl, 339bc,
342bl, 343tr/ Hulton-Deutch Collection 331bl, 334bl/ Buddy Mays 305bc; Lisa
M McGeady 347cr; Roger Ressmeyer 351bl; Mary Evans Picture Library: 359tl,
360br, 316bc, 317tl, 328bl, 330tl, 345tr; Ann Ronan Picture Library 318cr,
340bc, 352tr; Science Photo Library/ Hank Morgan 354c.

ANCIENT WEAPONS: AKG London 382tr/ Erich Lessing 367tl; E.T Archive:
382tr, 392tl, 411tr, 417bl/ British Museum: 390br; Mary Evans Picture Library:
405bl, 415tr, 415bl, 419tr.

MODERN WEAPONS AND WARFARE: Imperial War Museum: 447bc; Popper-
Hanke Collection: 433bc; Popperfoto: 462cr, 469bc; Solo Syndication Ltd: 430bl;
Science Photo Library: 436br.
With special thanks to Will Fowler for supplying the following images:
423cl, 425tr, 425c, 426br, 428bc, 428br, 429tl, 430br, 431cr, 432c, 433tl, 433cr,
433bl, 434tl, 434br, 436c, 437cr, 438cr, 440tl, 440cr, 444bl, 444br, 441cl,
441bl, 441bc, 442c, 443tl, 443bl, 444cl, 444bl, 444br, 445cr, 445bl, 446tr,
447tl, 447bl, 448cr, 449bl, 450bl, 450br, 451bl, 452tl, 453tl, 459bl,
462cr, 462bc, 462tl, 462br, 466br, 467cl, 467bl, 470c, 470br, 470bl, 472br,
474bc, 474tl, 474br, 466br, 467cl, 467bl, 470c, 470br, 470bl, 472br, 474br,
477tl, 477bc.